SEEING BEYOND:
Movies, Visions, and Values

26 Essays by
William R. Robinson and Friends

Annie Dillard • R. H. W. Dillard • George Garrett

Armando José Prats • A. Carl Bredahl, Jr. • Steve Snyder

Vincent B. Leitch • David Lavery • Elaine Marshall

J. P. Telotte • Walter C. Foreman, Jr. • Susan Lynn Drake

INTRODUCTION AND ESSAY BY
Frank Burke

EDITED WITH AN ESSAY BY
Richard P. Sugg

GOLDEN STRING PRESS
New York & Miami
GoldenStringPress.com

I give you the end of a golden string,
Only wind it into a ball:
It will lead you in at Heaven's gate,
Built in Jerusalem's wall.
– William Blake

SEEING BEYOND:
MOVIES, VISIONS, AND VALUES
*26 ESSAYS BY WILLIAM R. ROBINSON
AND FRIENDS*

Annie Dillard, R. H. W. Dillard, George Garrett,
Armando José Prats, A. Carl Bredahl, Jr., Steve Snyder,
Vincent B. Leitch, David Lavery, Elaine Marshall,
J. P. Telotte, Walter C. Foreman, Jr., Susan Lynn Drake.

Introduction and Essay by
Frank Burke

Edited with an Essay by
Richard P. Sugg

Studies in the Film Series

Published by:
Golden String Press
Cathedral Station
P. O. Box 28
New York, NY 10025

www.GoldenStringPress.com • GoldenStringBook@cs.com

Book design by Barbara A. Shaw

Cataloging-in-Publication Data

Sugg, Richard P.
   Seeing beyond : Movies, visions and values : 26 essays by William R. Robinson and Friends
/ edited by Richard P. Sugg.
   p. cm.
   Includes bibliographical references and index.
   ISBN 0-970678-1-6 (pbk.)
   1. Film criticism. 2. Motion pictures. 3. Motion pictures – History and criticism.
   I. Title.
PN1995 .S84 2001
791'.83   00-093296

International Standard Book Number (ISBN)
paper: 0-9706768-1-6

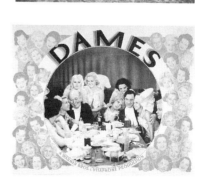

1. *Last Tango In Paris*, Marlon Brando and Maria Schneider, dir. Bertolucci; pp. 92-113: Stripping The Eye: Some Observations On The Movies As Strip Tease.

2. *Stagecoach*, John Wayne, dir. John Ford; pp.281-302: After Words: The Western Movies of John Ford and Sam Peckinpah.

3. *Bonnie and Clyde*, Faye Dunaway and Warren Beatty, dir. Arthur Penn; pp. 20-39: Making Sense of the Movies.

4 and 11. Giulietta Masina, Fellini's wife and the Juliet of *Juliet of the Spirits*, as Gelsomina in *La Strada*, dir. Fellini; pp. 135-152: If You Don't See, You're Dead, Part II.

5. *The Searchers*, John Wayne and Natalie Wood, dir. John Ford; pp. 281-302: After Words: The Western Movies of John Ford and Sam Peckinpah.

6. Giulietta Masina and Suzy in *Juliet of the Spirits*, dir. Fellini; pp. 135-152: If You Don't See, You're Dead, Part II.

7. *Carnal Knowledge*, Candace Bergen, dir. Mike Nichols; pp. 92-113: Stripping the Eye: Some Observations on the Movies as Strip Tease.

8, 9 and 10. *2001: A Space Odyssey*. Part III, an image of the starchild emerging from the eye of the astronaut; Part II, spaceship and pod on deep space journey; Part I, ape inventing a tool; dir. Stanley Kubrick; pp. 47-59: The Movies As a Revolutionary Moral Force, Part I; pp. 77-91: *2001* and the Literary Sensibility; pp. 161-187: The Birth of Imaginative Man in Part II of *2001: A Space Odyssey*; pp. 364-370: Preparing to See "The Birth of Imaginative Man…"

12. Director Federico Fellini instructs actors in *Fellini-Satyricon*; pp. 153-160: *Fellini-Satyricon*'s Moral Process; and pp. 225-244: "If We Were All Devils": *Fellini-Satyricon* as Horror Film.

13. *Dames*, Ruby Keeler, choreographed by Busby Berkeley; pp. 319-330: Busby Berkeley and the Tradition of Emersonian Vision.

14. *The Usual Suspects*, Kevin Spacey, et al; pp. 371-383: Rounding Up *The Usual Suspects*: The Comforts of Character and Neo-Noir.

15. *Last Tango In Paris*, Marlon Brando and Maria Schneider, dir. Bertolucci; pp. 92-113: Stripping the Eye: Some Observations on the Movies as Strip Tease.

16. *Shane*, Alan Ladd and Brandon de Wilde, dir. George Stevens; pp. 248-280: A New Geography of Paradise: George Stevens's *Shane* as Trans-Edenic Vision—A Meditation in the Spirit of and Dedicated to W. R. Robinson.

Contents

ACKNOWLEDGMENTS

THANKS TO ALL who helped in the production of this book, especially the contributing authors, who were uniformly generous with permissions and encouragement. Bill Robinson supported the book throughout; Frank Burke was a co-founder of the project, and though other things demanded his time as the book evolved, he continues to give strong support, as is evidenced by his Introduction. Barbara Shaw, whose production experience, design skills, and patience were just as valuable as her recommenders from the Bethesda Writers' Center had promised they would be, deserves a great deal of credit. Bob Johnson helped with the scanning, Beverly Shinn produced the Web site, and various people at the Small Press Center shared useful advice on current publishing practices.

Thanks to William R. Robinson, the author, for permission to print the following:
"The Movies, Too, Will Make You Free"(which originally appeared in *Man and the Movies*, Louisiana State University Press);
"The Movies As a Revolutionary Moral Force, Parts I and II" (which originally appeared in the journal *Contempora*);
"If You Don't See, You're Dead: The Immediate Encounter With The Image in *Hiroshima Mon Amour* And *Juliet of the Spirits*, Parts I and II" (which originally appeared in *Contempora*);
"*Fellini-Satyricon's* Moral Process," first published in this book.
"The Birth of Imaginative Man in Part III of *2001: A Space Odyssey*" first published in this book.
"Making Sense of the Movies" originally appeared in *The Georgia Review*, Volume XXIII, No. 2 (Summer 1969), ©1969 by the University of Georgia. Reprinted by permission of *The Georgia Review* and the author.
"'2001' and the Literary Sensibility" originally appeared in *The Georgia Review*, Volume XXVI, No. 1 (Spring 1972), ©1972 by the University of Georgia. Reprinted by permission of *The Georgia Review* and the author.
"'Damn Your A Priori Principles—Look!' W. R. Robinson Discusses the Movies As Narrative Art," by John Graham, originally appeared in *The Film Journal*, Summer, 1971, 49-53. Reprinted by permission of *The Film Journal*, Thomas R. Atkins, Editor-Publisher, and the author.

"Stripping the Eye: Some Observations On The Movies As Strip Tease"a revision of "The Imagination of Skin," originally appeared in *The Film Journal*, vol. 2, no. 1(1972), 44-53. Reprinted by permission of *The Film Journal*, Thomas R. Atkins, Editor-Publisher, and the author.

Thanks to the following authors and publishers for permission to print:
"Total Eclipse" and "An Expedition To The Pole," by Annie Dillard, originally appeared in *Teaching A Stone To Talk*, HarperCollins Publishers, 1982. Reprinted by permission of the publisher and the author.
"Fellini: Changing the Subject," by Frank Burke, originally appeared in *Film Quarterly*, vol. 43, no.1(Fall 1989), 36-48; © 1989 by The Regents of the University of California. Reprinted by permission of the publisher and the author.
"Rounding Up *The Usual Suspects*," by J. P. Telotte, originally appeared in *Film Quarterly*, vol. 51, no.4(Summer, 1998), 12-20; © 1998 by the Regents of the University of California. Reprinted by permission of the publisher and the author.
"Personal Retrospective on Theory: Changing Paradigms From The 1960s Through The 1990s," by Vincent B. Leitch, originally appeared in *The Massachusetts Review*, vol. 40, no.1 (Spring 1999); reprinted by permission of the publsiher and the author.
"Federico Fellini: Bifocal Views," by R. H. W. Dillard, is © 1971 and 1994 by R. H. W. Dillard. Reprinted here by permission of the author.
"After Words: The Western Movies Of John Ford and Sam Peckinpah," by A. Carl Bredahl, Jr., was originally published in *New Ground: Western American Narrative and the Literary Canon*, by A. Carl Bredahl, Jr. © 1989 by the University of North Carolina Press. Used by permission of the publisher and the author.
Helix and Scimitar: Hemingway's "Green Hills of Africa" As Evolutionary Narrative, pp. 24-26 & 97-118, by Susan Lynn Drake and A. Carl Bredahl, Jr., With the Assistance of William R. Robinson, was originally published by The Edwin Mellen Press, © 1990. Reprinted here by permission of the publisher and the authors.

Preface

THIS BOOK OF TWENTY-SIX ESSAYS by fifteen authors on movie theory and criticism is focused around the approach to movies of one person, William R. Robinson, a member of what one might call the Discoverer generation in America of university-based theorists and critics of the movies. This was the first group of university professors to make a career commitment to study, teach, and defend movies as art, and therefore worthy of intellectual consideration. Through the 1950's and 60's these critics contributed importantly to, and in return were fed by, the increasing enthusiasm of an expanding American audience for the new phenomenon of "art movie" theaters offering a mix of contemporary foreign films (by Bergman, Fellini, Antonioni, Bertolucci, Resnais, Truffaut, Godard, Tony Richardson, Richard Lester— just to name directors Robinson's essays discuss) and new movies by American masters and newcomers (Ford and Hawks, as well as Kubrick, Altman, Penn, Peckinpah, and others—again, all discussed in this book). The reviews of Robinson's seminal book *Man and the Movies*, published in 1967, reveal that general enthusiasm: "A 21-gun salute for this editor and his splendid book!...The mood is highly contemporary"—*TV-Radio Mirror*; *The New York Times*: "assertive, knowledgeable, very articulate"; *The Los Angeles Times*: "One of the best books ever about motion pictures."

This Discoverer generation of university movie theorists and critics typically was self-taught, since there wasn't a university film major until 1948 (N.Y.U). Of course most had Ph.D.'s, generally in a humanities discipline, but they were the generation that had to discover, invent, and defend an intellectual approach which matched only their experience of seeing movies, rather than rules they had been taught by others. They were free to discover movies as a source of new vision and novel possibilities.

The passion of the Discoverers for the movies shone through their writings, as is readily seen in a few of Robinson's essay titles: "The Movies, Too, Will Make You Free"; "The Movies As a Revolutionary Moral Force, Parts I & II"; "If You Don't See, You're Dead: The Immediate Encounter With the Image in *Hiroshima Mon Amour* and *Juliet of the Spirits*"; and "The Birth of Imaginative Man in Part III of *2001: A Space Odyssey*." Robinson's background in philosophy has disposed him to approach movies as moral phenomena that offer us new visions of life as a continually recurring process of seeing creatively—of seeing in, through, and beyond what the the physical and conventional eye allows that it sees. This process, he explains, generates new values by which we live our lives. The first essay title above alludes to the famous dictum to "Know the Truth and the Truth Shall Make You Free," and it is in the same spirit of moral passion that Robinson declares the movie maker "a moral educator." Reading through his eleven essays, one can follow Robinson's intellectual movement towards developing a complete moral view of the movies, a project on which he continues to work.

The fifteen essays in the second half of the book are presented by Robinson's colleagues and former students to honor him both as an intellectual influence and a friend. All of the authors are university professors—their biographical profiles, often with photos, are included in the book. Each addresses in one way or another some aspect of Robinson's intellectual vision, so that their essays constitute an elaboration of Robinsonian ideas, as well as a source of new thinking on their chosen topics. Frank Burke and R.H.W. Dillard write on a number of Fellini's films, while George Garrett, Armando José Prats, and A. Carl Bredahl, Jr. discuss the Western movie genre (*Shane*, and the Westerns of John Ford and Sam Peckinpah), and J. P. Telotte analyzes the *film noir* genre and neo-*noir* in *The Usual Suspects*. Vincent B. Leitch surveys theory of the last forty years, and David Lavery recounts his experience as a student with Robinson's theory. Steve Snyder traces the Emersonian vision in Busby Berkeley movies, and Richard P. Sugg calls on Robinson's ideas to analyze elements of Robert Altman's *The Player* and *Short Cuts*. Elaine Marshall writes on Robinson's approach to *2001*, Walter C. Foreman Jr. on Meriwether Lewis's vision in his Journals, and Susan Drake and A. Carl Bredahl Jr., assisted by Robinson himself, discuss the evolutionary narrative in Hemingway's *Green Hills of Africa*. Annie Dillard opens and closes this second half of the book with two eloquent essays about vision and exploration and the human moral passion to keep seeing and moving beyond, "Total Eclipse" and "An Expedition to the Pole."

Near the end of Fellini's movie *Roma* there is a "Festival of Ourselves." After the camera has surveyed this ancient city of famous ruins, invoking its gods and heroes and storied grandeur, we suddenly turn a corner to discover the living inhabitants of the here-and-now city sitting down at tables uniting families and strangers outdoors in the street for a feast to honor themselves. So let this Preface conclude on a similar note: this book is a cooperative effort that honors not only Bill Robinson but also all of the contributors, as well as all the readers who still care enough about movies to believe that they may discover the secret of life by opening their eyes in the dark.

Introduction

THE CONTRIBUTORS to this celebration of W.R. (Bill) Robinson fall into roughly five groups in terms of the nature of their association with Bill: his doctoral students at the University of Florida (Dick Sugg, myself, Armando Prats, David Lavery, Elaine Marshall, Susan Drake), doctoral students at Florida but not writing for Bill (Steve Snyder, Jay Telotte, Vincent Leitch), colleagues of Bill's at Florida (Carl Bredahl), colleagues of Bill's from Virginia (Annie Dillard, R.H.W. Dillard, George Garrett), and colleagues of former doctoral students of Bill (Walt Foreman). This comprises quite a spectrum of attraction and influence, and I must emphasize that I can only write from one part of the spectrum: as someone whose ideas and career were strongly shaped by Bill at an early moment in his intellectual formation. However, what I say will also be partly based on the contributors' offerings, so I hope my words will in some way reflect the full spectrum.

I think the most compelling thing about Bill's pedagogy and writing is its emancipatory promise, which coincided for me with the revolutionary energy and sense of imminent transformation rampant everywhere in the late 1960s. For students in their early twenties, it was not only a matter of the '60s, but of casting off the chains of one's upbringing, of becoming an independent adult. For students both in their twenties and living in the '60s (like Dick Sugg and me), it was also a matter of casting off the stifling conformity of the 1950s. When Armando Prats writes "Shane comes not to issues conagrarian vision of the father but to liberate the son from it," closures both vincingly of Shane's role in breaking down fences constraints of the past. personal and historical, I think immediately in the importance of the ing his young students to think them at follow (Annie Dillard's first The liberationist strain in Bill' American West to so m piece, Prats, Bredahl, Foreman), as well as the theme of expedition or odyssey that runs through the volume (Foreman, Marshall, Annie Dillard's second piece, etc.).

One of the principal imperatives within Bill's emancipatory vision, mirrored in the writings that follow, is a fierce rejection of abstraction. George Garrett's poem "Little Movie Without a Middle" says it most humorously, with its big bad abstractions in battle with generalizations in full dress uniforms, to be followed by the oompah-oompah, chinka-chink scholars who can only operate at several removes from anything resembling concrete reality. But a predilection for the work of Federico Fellini on my part and on the part of R.H.W. Dillard and David Lavery also is linked to a rejection of the abstract, which for Fellini appeared in many monstrous guises, from the Church to arid intellectualism to left wing ideologues (as opposed to vital left-wing politics). Abstraction for Bill is, of course, the old, the dead, and the traditionally literary in the face of movies—the new and revolutionary art of concrete movement, image, and vision. And the eye actively engaged with the world is the great instrument of liberation from a past trapped in texts and language. This image/word, concrete/abstract distinction is, of course, consistent with certain strains of modernism, and has been overshadowed by the "ideology-is-everywhere," "there-is-nothing-outside-language," precepts of various postmodern theorizing. But it was heady stuff in the 1960s, particularly when articulated in terms of the genius/character, imagination/intellect, distinctions so persuasively employed by Bill. It had enormous explanatory power for the cultural production (including theory) of the time. It still does, as Dick Sugg's and J.P. Telotte's essays, on quite recent films, make clear. Moreover, the emphasis on the visual, temporarily eclipsed by the so-called "language paradigm" of poststructuralist theory, itself continues to have explanatory power, "locally" in Steve Snyder's essay on Busby Berkeley, and globally in the recent emergence of an entire area of academic work dubbed "visual culture" that, while not entirely renouncing the language paradigm, at least restores the visual to a more appropriate place in theoretical ~d critical discourse.

to rage against abstraction was to rage against dogma (Fellini again comes
engagement more than that, to reject false consciousness through direct
piece on Bill). he world (something clearly implied in Elaine Marshall's
counters with the world
in "Total Eclipse": "og of the mind and imagination through close en-
blinding you. But durisely what Annie Dillard's narrator experiences
it of a trick to keep your knowledge from
easy. What you see is much more

convincing that any wild-eyed theory you may know." And in a Robinsonian universe, cleansing was not far from religious epiphany, or "the Via Negativa, the lightless edge where the slopes of knowledge dwindle, and love for its own sake…begins" (Annie Dillard again, this time from "An Expedition to the Pole").

In fact, as a rapidly lapsing Catholic in search of spiritual methadone, I found the religious strains within Robinsonian method quite appealing. The work of the imagination, as he taught it, had much in common with the Renaissance "poetry of meditation," based on the Ignatian exercises and embodying a process through which one gradually sloughed off the "slopes of knowledge" and opened oneself to insight and grace.

There was also something both Ignatian and epiphanic in the New Critical close readings that are so much a part of Bill's method. They required a concentration and discipline, a vertiginous exactitude, that became thoroughly exhilarating—liberating one, as Foreman puts it, from passivity. They were both an end in themselves as intellectual-spiritual experience and seeming justification for what otherwise would be only the indulgent solitude of the academic. And the making pleasurable of academic solitude is one of the things I remember most fondly of working with Bill. There was, of course, a moral imperative to close reading, to "getting it right." For we were involved in a most intense and serious process of problem solving. And if art, the movies, and the imagination represented the highest form of reality, then unlocking the mysteries of narrative art meant successfully tackling the challenge of living—the consummate task for an intellectual and, equally so, for a teacher bent on educating, in the most meaningful sense, his or her students. Wright Morris (as quoted by Annie Dillard) claims "each time the writer creates and solves the problems of fiction, he makes it possible for men and women to live in this world." One need only adapt this to the context of the scholar/teacher to turn Morris's words into Robinsonian ethics.

The relationship between close reading and living in the world led, of course, to the analysis not just of film and literature, but of an expanding range of objects. With his ever-active eye, trained through film viewing, Bill could read a street sign or a football game and make it open onto an immense world of meaning. This "seeing of signs" everywhere again, to me, had something of the religious in it. But, in retrospect, it had far more of the "semiotic," putting Bill fully in synch with emerging branches of literary, cinematic, and ultimately cultural theory with which he would want absolutely nothing to do. (His is a theory of value, not of meaning, hence anything that hinted of semiotics or semiology is anathema.) It also aligns him with theorists of the everyday, such as Michel de Certeau, and analysts of alternative cultural production, such as the "Birmingham School," who have contributed to the enormously vibrant field of inquiry we know as "Cultural Studies" today. The notion of the practical imagination engaged productively with the everyday makes its way into several of the selections below and is central to Foreman's appreciation of Meriwether Lewis's Journals and Drake and Bredahl's reading of *Green Hills of Africa.*

The ability to see significance everywhere made life enormously rich. It also had important professional consequences. In exposing Dick and me and those who followed us at Florida to the study of popular culture and film, Bill helped make us employable at a moment (marked by the Denver 1969 Modern Language Association Annual Meeting) in which the job market for traditional English PhDs imploded. And of course Bill's inclusion of film within literature courses, leading to the development of upper level and graduate courses solely in film, placed him in the vanguard of a movement in which the teaching of film throughout North American came to evolve principally from English departments.

The expansive range of Bill's analyses is equalled by his love for "the big picture." Despite his eye for the particular, he never gets lost in it. He is always a theorist and an historian of theory, of civilization, of Western and American thought, of narrative tradition, of value, and, perhaps most important, of "the story of the eye." He is a relentless synthesizer, able to join the most diverse events and issues into breathtaking unities that repeatedly make you rethink your assumptions and the very foundations upon which you make them. His models in this were other brilliant thinkers and synthesizers such as Marx, Darwin, Freud, Fraser, Mumford and, most important, that consummate harmonizer of theology, philosophy, science, and culture, Alfred North Whitehead. Working with Bill one learned, or at least aspired, to see the world in a grain of sand, transforming unique specificity into global relevance.

Bill's encyclopedic bent is reflected in Vincent Leitch's essay below but is even better seen in Leitch's career, which has produced several penetrating surveys of the history of literary and cultural theory from the 1930s to today, leading to his current position as general editor of the forthcoming *Norton Anthology of Theory and Criticism.* Similarly, Drake and Bredahl wed their intensely close analysis of Hemingway's *Green Hills of Africa* to far broader developments in the history of Western narrative tradition and in the Hemingway corpus. And of course the fictional worlds of Annie Dillard, as reflected in this volume, are global (at times galactic!) and encyclopedic, not necessarily through any influence on Bill's part but through a kinship of mind that brings her to this compilation.

I have already suggested ways in which Bill work was ahead of its time in the 1960s and linked to major theoretical developments of more recent years. I would like to point to a particularly strong kinship between Bill's writings and those of two major postmodern thinkers: Gilles Deleuze and Felix Guattari (1972/1980, 1980/1983, 1976/1983). Critics of essentialism and of conventional notions of stasis, order, and harmony,—whether philosophical, psychoanalytical, or political—Deleuze and Guattari speak of flows and intensities, dynamic fields of random (though not meaningless) interrelations, a world in constant flux and motion. In contrast to Freudian psychoanalytical emphases on lack and prohibition, they affirm the positive, productive, nature of desire, in its relentless flights from oppression.

Much as Bill distinguishes between "character" (conventional notions of fixed identity and role) and "genius" (the ability to "morph" in a world that itself is constantly in transformation), Deleuze and Guattari renounce humanist notions of a unified and stable subject or center of consciousness in favor of "nomadic subjects" and "bodies without organs":

> The nomadic subject is a point of pure intensity traversing the grid of the body without organs, a mobile locus of becoming commingling identities as it migrates.... The nomadic subject traces a process of becoming other ...becoming all the names of history as it moves across the natural, social and historical body without organs of the world. At every point of intensity, the nomadic subject effects a conjunctive synthesis. (Bogue, 95)

Consistent with Bill's renunciation of surface-depth relations (see his essay on "skin flicks") and critique of hierarchy and dialectical opposition (i.e., the "binary") Deleuze and Guattari seize on the "rhizome" as an exemplary model of dynamic organization:

> A rhizome...is the antithesis of a root-tree structure, or "arborescence," the structural model which has dominated Western thought from Porphyrian trees, to Linnaean taxonomies, to Chomskyan sentence diagrams. Arborescences are hierarchical, stratified totalities which impose limited and regulated connections between their components. Rhizomes, by contrast, are non-hierarchical, horizontal multiplicities which cannot be subsumed within a unified structure, whose components form random, unregulated networks in which any element may be connected with any other element. (Bogue 107)

Ultimately, Bill's work and that of Deleuze and Guattari, despite various divergences, can both be described as: "a politics of creativity, a theory of revolution that is based neither on beginnings (the conquest of the old system) or on ends (the implementation of a new system)but on middles—interregnums, intermezzos, the space in between, the unpredictable interstices of process, movement, and invention" (Bogue, 105).

Politics may initially seem to be somewhat distant from Bill's work, focused as intensely as it has been on aesthetics, philosophy, and, issues that, in general, have been peripheral in our current (though also receding) moment of political correctness. I say this as someone who has welcomed post-1968 politicized theory and would describe himself today as an ideological critic concerned with the way in which art and culture participate in the reproduction of power relations. Nothing could be further from Bill's writing and theorizing. However, one of the things I value most about Bill is a sensitivity to equality that has been fundamental to his writing, his pedagogy, and his very way of being.

This reflected itself in his attitude towards the classic doctoral student dilemma: what do we call Him? For one thing, he never referred to himself formally as Dr. Robinson, always Mr. Robinson, and he linked this to Southern academic tradition encountered during his days at the University of Virginia. What he didn't say was that while Southern tradition avoided the "Dr." to reinforce hierarchy (the Southern gentleman did not want to identify himself as a quotidian professional), he chose it to eliminate distinctions between himself and others. And when we came in fear and trembling (but without chastisement) to call him Bill, and then asked why he had never invited us to do so, he said simply that it was our choice and that he had left it up to us to decide when and if.

In the broader context of Bill's work, one of the most striking things I remember about "The Movies Too Will Make You Free" is his observation: "the movies evoke an emotional rather than an intellectual response—the thing directly perceived is directly felt... Consequently, they tend to be egalitarian, and literature elitist—only those who know how to read and think are admitted to its domain, while anyone with eyes qualifies as a citizen of the movie world." In fact all his writing on movies ("the democratic art" as it was so often called in the 1960s), though often couched in aesthetic and moral terms, was fundamentally political and egalitarian in motivation. And his discussion of individual film texts inevitably entailed a strong awareness of class and ideology, linked to his profound understanding of history, culture, and politics. I felt this deeply as a student in the 1960s, and it has been instrumental (perhaps somewhat ironically) in my ending up as an ideological more than a Robinsonian critic.

(By the way, I got a Christmas card from Bill yesterday, in the wake of the 2000 federal election mess, declaring Florida a "banana republic" and lamenting: "politically the place stinks to high heaven." Clearly his political conscousness has not eroded.)

I would like to conclude with some thoughts on humor and good humor. First of all, it was fun to work with Bill. For people like Dick and me it was, of course, the euphoric and apocalyptic Sixties, and Robinsonianism just made it all the more euphoric and apocalyptic. It was the ultimate head trip. Then, as David suggests, it was fun seeing ourselves, the Robinsonians, as part of a small (and thoroughly undiscovered) group of "Geniuses" at odds with all the "Characters" (largely of 18th-century persuasion) all around us.

Secondly, Bill gifted us with his own good humor. Lavery describes so accurately his "Olympian laugh." It is something that resounds to this day. He has always had a wry and often self-effacing way of describing himself. When I, in backsliding Catholic mode, asked him if he believed in God, he announced playfully that he was a polytheist. And as Lavery recalls, he liked to comment, tongue in cheek, that he would have been the Aristotle of the 20th Century had the heat and humidity of Florida not sapped his strength.

This comment captures for me two crucial poles of "the Robinson experience." On the one hand, he approached his writing and his teaching as a vocation, with utmost seriousness and with a sense of the highest possible stakes involved. On the other hand, he did so with a sense of the absurd born of the humility of an endlessly curious imagination that can never be self-satisfied because, as Teilhard de Chardin affirms, "there is always something more to be seen." Tempering a seriousness of purpose, a moral imperative to "get it right," was always the "desire to escape from heaviness" that Bill speaks of in "The Movies Too Will Make You Free": a desire to escape the weight not only of deadening abstraction and an unilluminated material world, but of the killing gravitational pull of ego and self-importance.

This coupling of serious intent and humility is reflected in words of Annie Dillard that, for me, capture the condition of being an academic: "Wherever we go, there seems to be only one business at hand—that of finding workable compromises between the sublimity of our ideas and the absurdity of the fact of us." Growing into academia within Bill's ambience meant maintaining a healthy awareness of the smallness of the self, but in a way that only served to enhance the sublime sense of the possible.

For this and for so much else, thank you Bill.

WORKS CITED

Bogue, Roland. *Deleuze and Guattari*. London: Routledge, 1989.

Deleuze, Gilles and Felix Guattari. *Capitalisme et schizophrénie 1:L'Anti-Oedipe*. Paris: Editions de Minuit, 1972. *Anti-Oedipus: Capitalism and Schizophrenia*. Trans.Robert Hurley, et al. Minneapolis: U of Minnesota P, 1983.

——. *Capitalisme et Schizophrénie 2: Milles plateaux*. Editions de Minuet, 1980. *A Thousand Plateaus*. Trans. Brian Massumi. Minneapolis: U of Minnesota P, 1987.

——. *Rhizome* Paris: Editions de Minuit, 1976, "Rhizome." Trans. John Johnston. In *On the Line*. Gilles Deleuze and Felix Guattari. New York: Semiotext(e), 1983.

The Movies, Too, Will Make You Free

WILLIAM R. ROBINSON

NOT TOO LONG AGO there was no film theory. Today—as exemplified by the recent flood of paperbacks on the subject—it has reached the saturation point. Yet most of what passes for film theory is not, strictly speaking, theory at all; or, rather, it is applied, not pure, theory, for in it the theorizing faculty is made to defend personal causes or taste. When employed for special pleading, such theory contributes little toward identifying the necessary and sufficient properties of the movies as art.

In an argument waged at one time on the nature of cinema, for example, Sergei Eisenstein insisted that montage is the essence of film. And it may be the essence of an Eisenstein film—certainly, without his total dedication to it the intellectual cinema would have missed some of its supreme achievements. His purpose, he rightly sensed, made this device absolutely necessary to his art. But from a truly theoretical perspective, montage is, as Eisenstein himself eventually admitted, just one device in the film-maker's repertoire, useful for some purposes, not for others. What his films and theory actually prove is that montage can be used for certain effects—sensations of speed, power, hostility, alienation, disorder, violence (impressions that the world threatens to overwhelm the perceiver).

In the same vein is Alfred Hitchcock's insistence on using a shot of a glass of champagne gone flat as a metaphor for a finished love affair. Though more simple-minded than Eisenstein's theorizing, Hitchcock's attempt at defining something essential to films is actually an assertion of taste—a preference for wit, an intellectual delight in clever analogy instead of the thing itself directly seen. (This literary quality in Hitchcock's work is one reason why, despite the slightness of his films, he is a favorite among intellectuals.) The same holds true for the purist, realist, surrealist, and other sectarian definitions of the movies; these, like those of Eisenstein and Hitchcock, are rhetorical supports for a value espoused independently of the movies as an aesthetic phenomenon. In every case one aspect of the movies is singled out as definitive and assigned ontological dominance.

At work in film theory and responsible for much of the confusion that reigns in it, as the above instances illustrate, is a careless mental habit, a variation on what philosophers call the naturalistic fallacy. For a quality in art or life to be truly valuable, film theorists almost invariably assume (and they differ from no one else, including philosophers, in this respect) that it must be supported by a theory which attributes reality to it—indeed, proclaims it to be the "realest." In other words, their theorizing stems from a hunger for substance or weightiness, and their theory serves to anchor an airy moral entity to solid intellectual earth. Deeper yet, underlying this hunger, is man's most adamant presupposition: that only what endures can be really valuable—only if our souls are immortal does life have meaning and therefore value; only if love is forever is it true and good. Disguised as ontological definition but actually support for a value, the normal adaptations of theory for determining the nature of film attempt to put intellectual muscle into the ethereal in the hope of justifying it on the intellect's terms, thereby capturing intelligence for moral ends. A difference in taste is mistaken for a difference in reality, and, whether or not overtly, "reality" performs a service decidedly normative, functioning as the ultimate honorific epithet.

The principle, "the more transitory the less valuable," probably is responsible for much of the resistance against recognition of the movies as serious art, since they reek of temporality. They come and go at the theaters with great frequency and in great haste, never to return, and they are not possessable like books or paintings or records. We cannot live and grow in their immediate company or display them as status symbols. Above all, they take the transient—from Plato on, the lowliest aspect of life—as their subject. Western culture has been predominantly intellective, and so its art and criticism, following the natural propensity of the intellect, have been heavily biased toward permanence. They have always proclaimed plenitude and imperishability the *summum bonum*. Thus it comes as no surprise that early movie directors, especially European ones, sought a cinematic means to give body to the universal truths underlying the appearance of things or to evolve a style by which to elevate human consciousness out of time. Today that object is not so strenuously pursued, although its absence, nostalgically lamented, is still profoundly felt in the latest European films—particularly in the solemn movies of Antonioni, Visconti, Truffaut, and Resnais, but also in the more joyous ones of Bergman and Fellini.

From this traditional distaste for the ephemeral emerges the most persistent theme in Western art—the problem of appearance and reality—and the artist's most enduring challenge—to counterbalance transitoriness by formal strategies capable of articulating the truths behind the mask, a realm beyond change. Now every art or work of art with any pretensions to seriousness at least tacitly solves these problems and is to be judged by the intelligence with which it does so. Yet the movies appear to be attached to the physical and particular much more than any other art and so seem to resist cooperating quietly with the old values and the old aesthetic. For this reason they ought to be more at ease in the hands of Americans, for whom traditionally process is reality. But the American director, when he isn't a European, looks to the Old World for guidance. As American literature did, the American movie will probably come of age when it looks to other sources, native and abroad, for its inspiration and guiding principles. Its major indigenous form to date has been the western, and probably its greatest achievement is also to be found there, not because the cowboy is a mythic hero but because the western, to a large extent a drama of the solitary figure against the wilderness, combines the two main traditions in American visual art.

A bad mental habit and an aesthetic bias issuing from it, then, vitiate the art, criticism, and theory of the film. The immense quantity of "theory," contradictory and confined to a movie's obvious or accidental features, is more an obstacle to accurately understanding the movies as art than anything else. Consequently, to arrive at a true theory it is necessary to begin at the beginning, with the aesthetic phenomenon itself. What can be said in the way of theory without making a value commitment and turning theory into propaganda is decidedly limited: something like, the movies are an art of light produced by mechanical means. Beyond that you're in trouble. But you're already in trouble anyway—for the definition provokes the question: Yes, but what is art? That's obviously a moot matter. In fact, the confusion in film theory results largely from confusions in the theory of art, which in turn result from deeply imbedded fallacies in moral reasoning. So it is necessary at this juncture to enter into questions of aesthetics in order to free film theory from its many false entanglements.

As art a movie is a complex phenomenon, a multifaceted diamond whose glitter can be muted or magnified depending upon the intensity and angle of the light. This is because, as the end result of a deliberate human act, it is imbued with all the intangible emotional, intellectual, and moral attitudes man necessarily expresses in everything he does. Its material base is different from man's—one inorganic, the other organic; but, allowing for that, a movie as art is almost an incarnation of man, standing in relation to him as he has been conceived of standing in relation to his Maker. As such, it invites nearly every question that can be asked of life and even seems to promise an answer to most.

Since a movie reflects human nature, the key to its aesthetic being must be found there. Indeed, as soon as one asks any other than a technical question of it, the inquiry is about man. But man is a complex phenomenon, too. Traditionally, he has conceived of himself as a tripartite creature, with the parts variously designated as reason, passion, and desire in Plato's view; the religious, the moral, and the aesthetic in Kierkegaard's; the id, ego, and superego in Freud's, etc. And each of these three facets has its corresponding ideal, formulated by classical thought as the True, the Beautiful, and the Good. The product of human will, a movie is inevitably a composite of all three facets and so can be said to reflect the organization of man's being—the degree of his wholeness or fragmentation, his balance or madness. Moreover, the movie is expected to incorporate all three ideals simultaneously. To pass critical judgment with a perfect score it must be simultaneously Beautiful, Truthful, and Good. That is, it has to excite the senses with striking forms, satisfy what William James called "the sentiment of rationality," and confirm the imagination's intuitive sense of what is right for man.

Perfection will always elude the moviemaker. His work cannot be fully realized in every respect simply because, though all three facets are inescapably present in his art, he must emphasize one at the expense of another. His work will necessarily favor Truth over Beauty and the Good, or Beauty over the Good and Truth, and so on. None of the three ideals has a determinable priority; each opens out upon a unique vista; all, from a theoretical standpoint, are equally real and valuable. A work will always be just a view, never *the* view; it will always be an art of Truth or of Beauty or of the Good, never of all to the same degree. Similarly, a film "theory," and movie criticism as well, will inescapably lean toward either an aesthetic of Truth, an aesthetic of Beauty, or an aesthetic of Value, as has happened historically, with the classical era favoring an aesthetic of Beauty and the modern era an aesthetic of Truth.

A movie, it follows, is a pluralistic phenomenon of such a complexity it is undefinable. For this reason there is no such thing as "the movies," no one essential quality common to all movies; there are only movies. All essentialists—whether moviemakers, theorists, or critics—are necessarily moralists. The numerous schools and styles already on the books demonstrate beyond a doubt that as a medium the movies are alive with possibilities. Some things, to be sure, come more easily to them than others—action, comedy, and spectacle more easily than analysis, tragedy, and verbal theme. Nevertheless, the argument that good cinema can be produced by doing only what comes naturally with the camera makes a neat deduction but a poor observation. As the Modern novel illustrates—in its case a descriptive, temporal genre gets sharply wrenched in order to render an essential, atemporal reality—the most exciting artistic achievements may be generated from a tension between the medium and a view of things unnatural for it.

Movies are certainly recognizable as a distinct phenomenon, but their identity lies not in what they are but in what they do—or, more accurately, in what one chooses to do with them. Film per se is just celluloid strips, as useful for decorating posters, starting fires, or recording information as for making visual narratives. It becomes art when a choice is made to employ it for aesthetic ends. When those ends, not rhetoric, profit, or propaganda, are regarded as worth trying for, a movie becomes an end in itself, a vehicle by which the human spirit becomes free. Indeed, to choose to use the movies for the purposes of art is to make freedom the supreme value.

The most persistent and unjust criticism leveled at the movies has been that they are *sui generis* "escapist." But this critical term, the nastiest epithet conceivable within a very narrow-minded aesthetic of truth which sprung up alongside realism, absurdly distorts our sense of what art is or should be. It implies that only an art as grim and dour as the realist thought life to be under the aegis of materialism can qualify as serious aesthetic achievement. It is easy to understand why the realist would think this; inhabiting a cold, indifferent, inhospitable universe, nothing remained for him except to endure stoically the ruthless pushing about to which man seemed subjected. Yet even in the dourest realistic view truth is a human triumph; through it man transcends suffering and determinism. Nikolai Berdyaev saw this clearly when he argued that all art is a victory over heaviness. It is always escape. When a movie is called "escapist," therefore, all that can legitimately be meant is that it wins its battle too easily. Take, for instance, the simple examples of *From Russia with Love* and *Thunderball.* Every sophisticated Bond fan unquestionably preferred the former because, while still a hero, Bond fought as a human being reliant upon his human wits and strength against a formidable but vulnerable enemy. In *Thunderball,* on the other hand, he is a superhuman creature beyond being ruffled by normally overwhelming adversaries and extreme circumstances. A good movie, like a good athletic contest, offers a true test against a worthy opponent. It wins its victory after genuine struggle, with honor and dignity. And this applies to the movie itself, not just to the characters in it; the movie as art, as the result of a battle between imagination and reality, persuades us that its escape, the victory of the human spirit over the material medium, has been duly earned. If the triumph for the protagonist or the artist comes too easily, if little wit or courage is expended by them, then the human spirit has not been tried to its depths and so is not profoundly entertained and refreshed. Winning is inevitable—the existence of the work bears witness to that— but what is defeated and how the victory is won is the heart of the aesthetic matter.

The desire to escape from heaviness is so fundamental and universal a passion that it pervades everything man does and may even be the major moving force behind his culture and history. Certainly, he has cultivated the various intellectual disciplines in order to transcend his necessity, in the hope that he could "choose himself." Religion has always been devoted to making man free through liberating the soul from spiritual ignorance or guilt, while science has been employed to equip man with a powerful knowledge capable of freeing him from nature. The arts in general, the movies included, are a part of man's intellectual armament in this war to liberate himself from heaviness, but they serve in a distinctive capacity. Like religion and science, art frees man's consciousness from the pragmatic pressures of living for a moment's respite to meditate upon isolated qualities before he plunges again into the stream of life. But whereas religious dogma focuses upon the conceptual truths of the spirit and science upon those of nature, art, a conjunction of spirit and nature, takes moral truth as its province. In effect, it discovers or creates values; by incarnating the Good, a spiritual entity, in a concrete form, art frees it to be.

The primordial truth about a movie as art, then, is that it confronts its viewer with moral fact and engages him in a moral dialogue. Though ignored by theorists, the moral power of art is so evident as to have made it the center of a vociferous, protracted quarrel from Classical Greece to the present. The movies simply stepped into the middle of a centuries-old row when, as soon as they appeared on the scene, censors and critics attacked them for distracting people from their proper moral development by stirring up their lower depths. The record clearly testifies that moral reaction to the movies— and to art in general over the ages—has seldom, if ever, been free of specific moral biases, so that the true moral character of the movies has remained obscured by parochial passions. This impasse can be skirted with the observation that the most likely remarks made or heard after a movie are: "I liked it. Did you?" "That was a good movie, don't you think so?" "It was awful; it wasn't any good at all; it's worthless." Although they use more formal language, the reviewer and critic concern themselves with the same matters. In short, everyone instinctively recognizes that a movie—all art, in fact—invites him to exercise his taste in making a value judgment. He senses that a value assertion has been made and that a reply is demanded of him. And, except for the most diffident, everybody also senses that he is qualified to reply, for, despite the scholar's defense of his hard-earned learning, no special knowledge is required and no greater moral authority exists than the individual's own conscience—which must be defended at all costs, since his identity is inseparable from it.

What transpires in the moral dialogue becomes clear when the movies are contrasted with science, a companion empirical discipline. Science—pure science, that is, not applied science—clarifies phenomena. It opens our eyes to the facts of nature by concentrating our attention on objects, events, and relations not immediately obvious. What was hidden before, presto, we now behold. Its terminology literally discriminates what has been beyond our power to see. To record what he has seen for public and perhaps personal benefit, a scientist molds language (whether mathematical or verbal) into a proposition which accurately represents the state of affairs he has observed. Or, if working with models, he makes a visual metaphor to perform that task. But he has seen something—call it a fact—which acts as a criterion in molding his proposition or model. The moviemaker, a storyteller, has to have a similar principle of selection to tell him when he has got his tale right, when what he is making accurately embodies what he has perceived. That principle is not a fact, however, but a quality, for his subject is man, not nature. This moral fact, even if vague initially and clear only when his story receives its final touches, has precedence over and determines the devices he selects from the cinematic bag of tricks or creates on the spot to serve his unique purposes. The finished product is imbued in every part by the quality which it is constructed to embody, and as the scientist invites his reader to view the reality he has seen, so the moviemaker invites his audience to behold the moral fact he has discovered. A "pure" movie, like pure science, enhances awareness by bringing a hidden or vague quality out into the open.

We cannot overlook the power of a movie to strike and pierce the senses and thereby arouse passion and emotion and even awaken the soul. With its vigorously impersonal method science cools us off emotionally and morally to receive a dispassionate truth about objective matters. Its icy illuminations may be a great delight for the intellect, but they are not intended to bring joy to the heart or conscience. Perhaps the most evident thing about a movie is its power to excite; but like a church service it does so of necessity, for we can receive its insight, actually a state of being, only if it elevates us into exalted consciousness. Similarly, the demand that a movie be exciting, engaging, alive, that its moral truth be felt and feelable, springs from the intuition that a value is a vital existence, something worth living for and caring about. For a value is a sensation, or a feeling, as Susanne Langer calls it, given an objective state before consciousness. Art fixes sensations in form and thereby allows them to become objects of knowledge and desiderata, states of being to be achieved and returned to as a vital creature's good.

When properly employing his craft, the moviemaker does not imitate, refer to, or symbolically represent a value but gives body to it there in the movie. All he therefore has to do to become a serious artist is to dedicate himself to making "objects of value"—not of meaning or for communication, nor of social or historical or psychological import, nor as vehicles for avoiding greater moral clarity. A movie which depends primarily upon a topical subject, a fashion in taste, or rhetoric for its appeal, although considerable artistry may be expended for these purposes, has a short life span. When these lose their interest the movie is dead. If, however, it primarily, accurately, and vividly embodies a quality which, despite changes in taste, is an eternal good, the movie has what used to be called universality: it is always alive and relevant; it remains a living option.

To carry out his serious intentions the moviemaker ideally has to have complete control over his medium, which means that as a storyteller he must master not only the narrative denotations but also the moral connotations of the images with which he works. All the implications of character, plot, pace, lighting, camera angle, cutting, and such highlighting elements as dialogue and music have to be within his control. These are determined by traditional usage and are public for the most part, although in a young art like the movies many of the connotations are not yet clearly fixed. Thus the preview. Because most defects in craftsmanship are immediately apparent, nobody gets damned simply for being a poor craftsman; he is just ignored. A certain level of seriousness and craftsmanship has to be self-evident for a movie to attract attention in the first place. No one gets excited over the worthless; and craftsmanship, except in someone like Hitchcock, where it is all there is, receives only a passing comment. Our central concern is values. Confronted with a certain pretension to seriousness, as in a Jules Dassin film, we test for authenticity by looking for intellectual blindness and for moral crudity owing to viciousness or insensitivity. We mean by sensitivity, in fact, the capacity for subtle moral discriminations. Correspondingly, the sensitive moviemaker, if truly an artist, via his imagination-conscience feels and thinks his way in and through his medium, making an ironic, romantic, realistic, or surrealistic movie, not one which abstractedly asserts the desirability of those qualities. He creates these values; he gives them flesh; he brings them to life.

The moviemaker as artist, it should now be clear, is a moral educator. Like every artist, he forges, in James Joyce's phrase, the conscience of his race. Take as an example Richard Brooke's recent movie *The Professionals,* not likely to be a classic but still a good film. This is an especially handy movie to illustrate the moral role of art because its title specifies the quality the movie is constructed to define. Professionalism as a value comes naturally to an era dominated by technology and technicians and prone to a taste for craft, camp, and the cool. But the movie is not a sociological tract, nor is it a treatise on the virtues of professionalism. Instead, it is a professional work, or at least it aspires to be. Not only are the major characters professionals in skill and temperament but the movie itself exemplifies complete knowledge and know-how. In effect, defining its value structurally, stylistically, and tonally as well as narratively, it not only identifies the good of professionalism but in doing so establishes a criterion by which the movie itself is to be judged. The movie insists that its viewers clearly perceive what professionalism is, then turn it back upon the movie, asking, "Does it measure up to the criterion it affirms? Has the director met and mastered every problem that came up in his professional bailiwick, moviemaking? Has he been cool and calm, always on top of the situation?" If art is creative, if it does add something to matter which wasn't there previously, it is this moral illumination inherent in form. Moreover, since the movie brings new qualities into existence, established criteria are irrelevant for judging it. Movie criticism and theory, always waiting upon art to educate them, stand disarmed before moral truth while the movies dig out within and bring to light in objective form new dimensions of moral reality.

The normative logic inherent in the sort of persuasion the movie attempts forces the viewer to ask whether the movie fulfills itself on its own terms. Intuitively sensed from man's first encounter with art, this has always been the question art poses—does it pass the test of unity and coherence? In deciding if a movie is coherent or unified, we ask first whether it is being true to itself as art—does it embody value?—and then whether the quality has been so treated as to include everything necessary to its embodiment and nothing extraneous. In other words, we ask if it does what art is supposed to do in the way art must do it. The movie succeeds as art, it successfully embodies a value, when both conditions are fulfilled.

This role the movies play in our moral education is tacitly recognized by our educational practices. In the sciences students are not asked to read the original authors but a textbook or one authoritative work stating a commonly acknowledged public truth. And the same is true for religion, although it is not formally taught in the school system—unless students are old enough to become comparativists, they study the one true doctrine. But in the arts the original artists, and many of them, are studied, since the human-moral reality they serve as texts for is too complex to be exhaustively treated by one man. Even in school systems where one literary figure, such as Dante or Goethe, is looked upon as a national institution, that writer is not taught exclusively. Every writer is limited to construing the truth available within the purview of one moral perspective. Although within some schematic approaches the possible perspectives on moral reality may be reduced to a few categories, the wide variety of conservative and liberal, romantic and classical, middle-class and working-class perspectives, for example, is so great that an accurate sense of man's moral predicament can be arrived at only through reading widely. The fact that just a small part of the moral spectrum can be relevant to any individual's purpose is no argument against extensive reading, for to be able to choose what our own temperaments, equally committed to a specific value, need to clarify and strengthen their impulses, we have to weigh the pros and cons of the whole moral truth.

We study the value spectrum so that we may become more precise about our specific good, with tolerance, it is hoped, as a side effect. Because the arts are habitually used to teach history, it is customary to emphasize their temporal aspect, whereas science, a body of constantly verifiable knowledge about nature, is taught independently of history. Yet the movies no less than science are devoted to the discovery and establishment of timeless truth. The movies, like the other art works created in the past and accumulated as our heritage, pass on moral knowledge from one generation to another; they thereby allow us to possess now the possibilities of good discovered by our forebears. As a body of work on the books, they, like the sciences, constitute an encyclopedia of knowledge. That heritage is not sufficient, however. Movies must be constantly in the making; old stories must be forever told anew; to remain living options, values must be continually validated within ever-changing reality—every moment requiring a new synthesis of Beauty, Truth, and the Good. Thus the movies, when art, explore on the frontiers of knowledge, refurbishing old values, refining discrimination in areas already charted, and producing new insight in areas of the moral spectrum previously ignored.

Because the movies play such a crucial role in our education, they must be free to follow moral truth wherever it may lead. This means they have to be as free from censorship as political thought and the other intellectual disciplines are. Censorship, long a bugaboo for the movies, defends the moral status quo, prohibiting search and discovery where they are most needed. Freedom of taste clearly is as important as freedom of speech. For the quality of our private and public lives depends upon their being nourished by living values, and only constant reassessment and refinement of the values we live by, through aesthetic meditation, can assure that. The complexity, nuances, and consequences of a value must be aired if the naive and pretentious ones are to be unmasked, the invidious exposed, and the confused clarified. Satirical movies, for example, quite overtly seek to demonstrate that a value cherished by some individual or the public is phony, a sham supported by nothing better than fear, ignorance, or malice. The genuine, of course, bear up under scrutiny and survive.

The moral dialogue a movie invites us to participate in, ideally a free field without favor, can, if it leads to the conclusion that taste is not disputable, beget disabling doubt about the profitableness of discussion or the trustworthiness of our own values. Cynicism arises from diffidence or from a failure to impress our reality cogently upon others—if we cannot intellectually establish what we value, then nothing is valuable; all is meaningless. Because our consciences cannot ultimately tolerate one another, critical dialogues quickly turn into ego contests leading nowhere but to ever louder shouting. The aim of the dialogue is not, and should not be, conversion, however, but clarification. Even if a moviemaker wanted to, he could not force his viewers to believe or act as he wished. As art a movie persuades by its power to illuminate. Most often, as with education in general, it facilitates rational defense of what otherwise would be called prejudice. Instead of converting, it brings into lucid focus a good that has been wrongly understood or obscured, correcting an error in reason or awareness. The dialogue initiated by the movie, whether directly or indirectly and regardless at what remove from the work itself, leads in its most aesthetically profitable instances to an understanding of what one's good truly is and wherein it truly lies. It does not incite to action; it clarifies for action, should the individual be so inclined.

Thus a movie as art objectively and vividly displays man's good. It brings moral truth into the world. Psychologically, by being out there, it confirms us, assuring us that our good is real. We go to a movie, certainly in our most serious moods, but probably on all occasions, in search of our moral truth; and when we find it, for the moment we dwell spiritually or meditatively in it, it is our fulfillment, our fullness of being. And if we don't like the movie, still, through the friction of an imperfect meeting of consciences, we become clearer about moral alternatives.

Taste may not be disputable in the sense that differences can be arbitrated by logic, but nevertheless disputing it is our means to personal and public wisdom. When the logical positivists and their disciples legislated that what cannot be empirically verified is meaningless, their logic was sound but their common sense was asleep. From a scientific perspective all cinematic or aesthetic utterances are nonsense, and all but descriptive propositions about a movie are sales pitches designed to persuade others to buy our way of packaging life. The trouble here is that movies are not utterances; they make no claim—nor does any art, as architecture and music illustrate glaringly—to propositional truth or falsity. Their province is taste; and taste, not truth, at least not truth independent of taste, is our preeminent concern as living creatures. To live is to act, and efficient action requires clear goals. By contributing to the enhancement of moral awareness, the movies as art help free man to know and pursue his true good. Whereas our scientific education equips us to use the world more effectively, the movies, assisting in our moral education, help prepare us to act more wisely.

And not just movies themselves but their criticism and theory, part of the moral dialogue they stimulate, contribute to the clarification of ends. In the final analysis, despite some impurities that creep in, applied theory magnifies and thereby facilitates examination of the values which particular schools, movements, directors, and critics have espoused. Their commitment and its resultant distortions, perhaps misleading to the unsuspecting mind, function as a necessary agency in our moral illumination. Thus that mental atavism of justifying taste with ontological argument, for all its logical absurdity, turns out to be the heart of the aesthetic matter. It is an instrument, as the movie itself is, to confirm man's being by giving substance and permanence to his supreme good. Although his commitment keeps him from being cool and therefore a reliable pure theorist, the applied theorist's intellectual power issues from his belief in himself, in what he has seen, and in his pressing need to justify himself and make living room for his moral kind.

The movies, via the moral dialogue they initiate and participate in, open our eyes to values. At their best they excite and refresh not simply the ordinary emotions but the profoundest feeling in our deepest moral reaches as well. To reiterate, they are one means by which man, through the powers of his imagination, perceives for himself possibilities without precedent in nature. Incarnations of the Good, providing opportunities to contemplate imaginatively concrete moral truth, they enhance and enrich consciousness. They are instruments helpful in lifting man up literally by his own bootstraps to contemplate the ideal and perhaps eventually to direct his effort towards its realization. When properly charged, their images empower men to behold and enjoy their finest life. No art does any more, and on the contemporary scene none surpasses them in scope and power, none more "realistically" confirms man's truth, none liberates or is liberated more completely.

That the movies possess the depth and breadth necessary for articulating contemporary moral reality, or the aesthetic means to bring it into vivid relief, is borne out by the difference between them and literature. Both are predominantly narrative arts employing images—one directly, the other indirectly—as vehicles for storytelling. Because of that slight difference, however, they are worlds apart. Literature and the literary imagination are metaphorical; they seek to make explicit a reality hidden to the senses. From one point of view literature, an art of words, duplicates the acts of creation by the Greek Logos or the Christian God: through it the Word, the primordial ontological power in Greek and Christian metaphysics, brings order into the world by imposing itself upon chaos. Since words are not natural or material entities, literature is inherently deductive— words issuing from the Word— both alienated from the physical and constituting a self-enclosed system which locates the source of the Good outside the physical world, within the Word, an *a priori* realm which validates particular words. But from another, a human, point of view, literature, originating within a worldly predicament, arises either from the longing of words to be themselves or from man's hunger to dwell in the realm of ideas or reason. Not inherently inclined to be denotative, words much prefer to consort among their own kind and, indeed, ardently long to return to their source. In any case, the literary imagination works from a fallen state and, nostalgically lamenting its paradise lost, aspires to regain verbal heaven.

Drama nicely illustrates the bias of literature and one of the ways in which it functions. In drama, at least when it is authentic art, words turn characters inside out, manifesting their inner being with language. For this reason the dialogue, in, say, *Who's Afraid of Virginia Woolf?* can be heard from a recording and still be aesthetically effective. With neither the theatrical nor cinematic spectacle distracting attention from the words, they intensively activate the hearer's imagination and turn him, too, inside out. Characters serve as the metaphorical vehicles by which the Word is made manifest. In a verbal medium such as drama the visual element complements the words and is eventually dispensable. Poetry—lyric poetry in particular—reigns supreme among the literary arts because the words are relatively unencumbered by the sensory, although in poetry, too, imagery is indispensable as metaphorical agency. Its object is, of course, to let the human spirit sing out. Verbal narrative on the other hand relies more heavily on the referential dimension of language, and words as a consequence tend to function analytically, pointing to underlying patterns, causes, or essences. Not by accident fiction favors temporal and historical explanations. Read in solitude, it cultivates the mind, and whatever the circumstances it proffers the intellectual satisfaction attained through comprehending the abstractions governing life. Nevertheless, despite being more abstract than drama or poetry, verbal narrative is also governed by the principle that literature be concrete and specific or "make sense"; and with drama and poetry it paradoxically employs words as the instrument by which man can penetrate through the mask of phenomena to the Word beyond it and transcend his finite condition. Literature and the literary imagination are bound by the laws of language, which is always metaphorical; through postulating likenesses, they put the mind in contact with intangible intellectual essences not directly perceptible.

In contrast to literature, the movies and the cinematic imagination are literal. A visual medium in which the word is complementary and dispensable, the movies illuminate sensory reality or outer form. They are empirical revelations lighting the thing itself and revealing change as nothing more than it appears to be. In their world there is no becoming, only being, or pointless change, no innate potential to be realized in time, no essence to be released from original darkness, no law to be learned and obeyed. For this reason analysis is rarely successful in the movies, *Citizen Kane* being the most famous of the very few exceptions. Even the Russian intellectual cinema, which on first impression seems analytical, at its best is hortatory—it inspires the viewer to be. Or, more specifically, in individual frames, by composition and photographic style, it endows the lowly and exploited with splendid being. Whatever a movie illuminates it has already celebrated, saying, in effect, "So be it." Its atomic constituents seem to have a greater life than the enclosing forms, while order, causality, and pattern appear arbitrarily imposed. And, with the atomistic quality so pronounced in them, the movies evoke an emotional rather than an intellectual response—the thing directly perceived is directly felt, and intellectual reflection follows upon the emotion, whereas in literature the emotion follows upon the word after the mind has made the initial encounter. Understandably, movies more perfectly satisfy Tolstoy's requirement that art appeal to the universal innate feelings in man. Consequently, they tend to be egalitarian, and literature elitist—only those who know how to read and think are admitted to its domain, while anyone with eyes qualifies as a citizen of the movie world. From these differences it is clear that literature testifies, while the movies witness. As a verbal medium, literature gives voice to the mind's lust for meaning. In seeking to commit the mind to what is not at once evident to the senses, literature demands belief; it insists that its report, always an interpretation, be trusted. The movies, on the other hand, a visual art, are immersed in the sensory, physical world, viewing it from within as a passing parade ceaselessly coming and going. They have no way, except for words, to gain a vantage point outside it. In this respect they are the archetype for the contemporary intellectual predicament characterized by the twilight of absolutes—they have no revealed word or *a priori* ideas, nor any criterion within experience itself, by which to ascertain reality or value; they are face to face with what is in its full multiplicity and glory. They dwell in the present, in a world all surface. Lacking a second level of reality, they are without complexity—without irony, meaning, or necessity. On the face of things appear process, activity, energy, and behind this mask is nothingness. Whereas the word is mysterious, the image is evident; everything it has is showing. Thus for movies the created world is good, not fallen; they offer no salvation through belief, as Christianity and rationalism do, but instead regard the given world as redeemed. They are existentialist, valuing the concrete, existence, or what is.

Little wonder, then, that the literary sensibility is not at home in the cinematic world and suspects movies of being superficial—without soul, intellectually impotent, and morally frivolous. One devoted to ideas, the other to particulars, one committed to transcendent truth, the other to ever-present reality, the verbal and visual modes are fated to eternal hostility. Yet despite this inherent hostility, the movies have their inevitable literary aspect—in their title and dialogue, and in the property or scenario from which they are derived. (Perhaps this literary origin raises major obstacles to successful filmmaking, since the film is in effect a translation and the viewer is invited— or does so out of habit—to translate it back into its original, and truer, literary prototype. The film functions, in this case, as literature did in classical theory, as a decorative illustration for a truth known through a prior and more authoritative faculty.)

There are those who lament the fact that movies must have a literary aspect; purists of a sort, they long for a return to the era of the silent film, when movies were movies and that's all there was to them. That nostalgia is understandable, for the pure movie demands a less complex response and poses less complex critical problems. The fact is, however, that the movies, allowing for the proper dominance, are an image-word medium, as is litera-ture, and all for the better. For, despite the invidious criticism which can arise from a bias favoring either the intellect or the senses, the presence of the antagonistic elements reflects the human predicament. The tension gener-ated between images and words in an impure movie and our ambivalent response to their interaction beget a truth that would otherwise be lost. As literature is enriched by the tension between word and image, so are the movies. The beneficent effects of this tension can be readily observed in many movies, but it has become consciously explicit in such recent ones as *Alfie,* in which a narrator terrified of death tries unsuccessfully, through directly ad-dressing the audience or from a verbal point of view, to determine what his life comes to within a cinematic context; and *Fahrenheit 451,* in which a French director flatly and ludicrously repudiates his own art in lamenting the demise of book man.

The tension in these movies also appears, reversed, in recent literature, perhaps most notably in the work of Alain Robbe-Grillet. Words are being adapted to cinematic reality, with the result that they no longer mean any-thing. Readers trained in the traditional ways of words, predictably, are deeply frustrated by the literature of nothingness. Paradoxically, the impurity of the movies makes them a more perfect art, capable of more extensively exploring its own possibilities and limitations, and thereby of more profoundly and more precisely giving body to man's truth.

Once the movies are acknowledged to be art and what they unveil is taken seriously, we have to face the fact, extensively argued by Existentialists, that the word has been superseded by sensation. The movies define better than any other art what we feel today to be the relation between the intellect and the senses. Among other things they make it quite clear, to the verbalist's distress, that the word is an adjunct of the image. In their version of the play between the eye's truth and the mind's, the ancient theme of appearance versus reality is reversed. In contrast to, say, Elizabethan poetry, in which images decorate a rational framework, in the movies reason rides on the tiger back of images in motion.

This new relation between the senses and the mind is the contemporary form assumed by an ancient and enduring antagonism. For at stake ulti-mately in the difference between literature and the movies are the preroga-tives of two moral universes, two cultures, and two ideas of creation. Both art forms, just by existing, pay tribute to their source, the power which makes them possible—literature to the Word, the movies to the Light. But beyond that, by implication when not directly, literature celebrates a God transcendent, the movies a god immanent; one affirms creation by fiat, the other creation by emanation. These inevitably hostile alternatives, if Joseph Campbell's account in *The Masks of God* is correct, led to the division of East from West some eight thousand years ago—the East following the way of the Light and the West the way of the Word—and has been the source of their mutual suspicion ever since. But the Light and the Word have also vied with one another for supremacy within Christendom. The Old and New Testament offer conflicting accounts of the instrument responsible for creation, and St. John indiscriminately mixes creation by the Word with creation by the Light. St. John's confusion, a careless mixture of Judaic and Greek attitudes, may well be the source of the traditional friction in Western culture between the Light and the Word. At any rate Judaism's existential, worldly faith has persistently contended with Greek rationalistic idealism for dominance in Western culture. The Word has been clearly dominant until recently, but as a result of science's corrosive effect upon Christianity, the Light is now in the ascendant. So the difference between the movies and literature is rooted in a fundamental antithesis in man's being, and the rise of the movies as an art is one sign of a profound change taking place in Western culture—a transformation begetting what pundits have been variously calling a post-Christian, post-rationalistic, post-typographical, or post-literary period.

The movies derive their aesthetic stature, obviously, from being a closer analogue to reality than is literature. For the alert film-maker and his audience today a movie can and should be a microcosm of life. All the world's a movie screen. Thus the director's medium is inherently closer than any other to life, and he is the most advantageously equipped artist for adventuring in moral reality.

The movies at their best have always performed the task of art, even when film-makers, critics, and theorists claimed that, paradoxically, the movies could be art only if the imagination was weighed down by materiality. Accepting this condition in *Greed,* Erich Von Stroheim created serious art in spite of the inherent bias against the medium. Nonetheless this assumption hurt the movies in the pressure it exerted on moviemakers to honor piously the dominion of the mechanical, material, and causal over their art. And theorists, including such sophisticated ones as Erwin Panofsky and Susanne Langer, in their turn were impaled on a dichotomy which forced them to choose between conceptions of the movie as dream or as bound to physical reality.

The movie of the last decade, along with developments elsewhere in thought and the arts, has put this realistic assumption to rest. It was a period's taste, time has made evident—a corruption of reality. Today the movie is explicitly and confidently committed to freedom as the supreme value and truth, and the moral dialogue it is now participating in is probing the career of man's good in that direction—whether in great, good, bad or indifferent films, in parts of films or in their entirety; in the character of the emancipated female: Mrs. Waters in *Tom Jones,* Jeanne Moreau or Brigette Bardot in *Viva Maria,* Jean Seberg in *Breathless,* or the various roles played by Natalie Wood; or the cool, resilient male: Belmondo in *Breathless* and elsewhere, Anthony Quinn in *Zorba the Greek,* or Vittorio Gassman in *The Easy Life;* or as a theme in the work of Bergman and Fellini.

The free camera, moreover, supports the free character. It has always been understood that the camera used with skill is a projection of an individual's sensibility, not a mechanical eye; foreign films especially, coming out of visual traditions different from our own, have been constant reminders of this fact. Today there is not even a shadow of a doubt that the movies, instead of being by nature or moral precept enslaved to physical reality, are a technological vehicle by which the human spirit can escape material limitations once thought to be narrowly restrictive. Not too long ago regarded as man's nemesis, technology, in the movies as well as in the airplane, enlarges his power of flight. The movies, consequently, need no longer be an illusion of the "real" but are at liberty to be artifice and even to call attention to their fictional character, as Tony Richardson does in *Tom Jones* and as Richard Lester does in *A Hard Day's Night.* A still more striking example is Mario Monicelli's *The Organizer,* in which, although the movie is ostensibly a realistic treatment of capitalistic inhumanity, the artistry draws attention to itself, contradictorily and ironically proclaiming the dominion of the imagination over substance.

But the movies' greatest contribution to today's moral dialogue over freedom does not lie in characters or camera technique. It lies, rather, in the emancipation of the image. Not long ago it was excitedly argued that the camera gave painting a new life by freeing it from photographic representation, but the camera has done even more than that: it has freed itself, too, at least from all debilitating forms of representation. This child of empiricism, repudiating its parent, has liberated form from the physical world. Marilyn Monroe, never a physical actuality for moviegoers, lives on every time the camera projects her image on the screen, and so, although physically dead, she has gained immortality. She has been released, as has the moviemaker and the viewer, and, indeed, man's mind everywhere, to dance in the imagination's heaven. Actually physics is mainly responsible for destroying the idea of substance, but the movies have done more to set the imagination free to dream upon human moral possibilities within a substanceless universe. By conclusively demonstrating that an image does not necessarily signify substance, they have destroyed the last vestige of our materialistic mental habits. Unburdening us of the hunger for and anxiety about meaning, the free movie teaches us that to be is enough; existence needs no justification. Ironically, in the new intimacy between the senses and the mind which the movie achieves, Plato's realm of forms is realized through physical vision.

Once regarded as a puerile, cowardly escape from life because they begot and simulated dreaming, the movies are now recognizable as an extension of the supreme power inherent in a universe of energy, chance, evolution, explosiveness, and creativity. In such a youthful, exuberant universe the movies' kind of dreaming gives concrete probability and direction to the ongoing drive of energy, and as a consequence what at one time was thought to be a vitiating defect is now their greatest virtue. The new freedom they reflect and extend is freedom within the world, contingent and not absolute, a heightened vision of existence through concrete form beyond abstraction. In a world of light and a light world—unanalyzable, uninterpretable, without substance or essence, meaning or direction—being and non-being magically breed existence. Out of the darkness and chaos of the theater beams a light; out of nothingness is generated brilliant form, existence suspended somewhere between the extremes of total darkness and total light. Performing its rhythmic dance to energy's tune, the movie of the imagination proves, should there be any doubt, that cinema, an art of light, contributes more than any other art today to fleshing out the possibilities for good within an imaginative universe.

aking Sense of the Movies

WILLLIAM R. ROBINSON

To Generalize is to be an Idiot.
To Particularize is the Alone Distinction of Merit.
                                                    –William Blake

And yet none of his certainties was worth one strand
of a woman's hair.   – *The Stranger*

THE OCCASION FOR THIS ESSAY is four books released by Doubleday in its Cinema World series, published in association with *Sight and Sound* and the Education Department of the British Film Institute: *How It Happened Here,* by Kevin Brownlow; *The New Wave,* edited by Peter Graham; *Alain Resnais: or the Theme of Time,* by John Ward; and *Howard Hawks,* by Robin Wood. As aids to seeing movies, these books are quite unsatisfactory; out of more than 700 pages perhaps ten to fifteen of consequential material beyond names, titles, and dates can be culled, a low yield by any standards. Yet they are typical of the rapidly proliferating literature on the movies, no worse, certainly, than anything else now in print on the films, and their deficiencies do not single them out for special condemnation. In fact, they are probably not too far off par for art criticism in general, including literary criticism, where close scrutiny of the art work qua art is an exception rather than the rule. It just happens that the movies, a "hot" item being written and read about extensively, have captured the attention of a large sophisticated audience, and these books are at hand when the time is ripe for clarifying the direction and method of talk about the movies. For until this talk becomes systematic, that talk will continue to be, though it increase voluminously, a babble of nonsensical voices and serious inquiry into the movies will remain ineffectual. So, with apologies to the authors and publisher for exploiting these four books as scapegoats, I want to consider the means for attending to what is there and going on in the movies aesthetically.

By consequential I mean what is directly effective in opening one's eyes to look with greater alertness and accuracy at a movie as narrative art. Now that, admittedly, is no mean task, since art is excruciatingly complex and, despite its concrete guise, a habitation of the intangible. It is not surprising that those without the gift of metaphor, indispensable to the best criticism, gain relief from the exacting demands of art by taking refuge in periphery distractions that allow them to talk around rather than to the aesthetic point, and, moreover, in the process go to considerable trouble to justify their *raison d'être* as specialists in cataloging and dismembering the corpse or its physical environment rather than beholding the spirit. Which is what John Ward, a philosopher by trade, does in his discussion of Resnais' films. He goes in search of philosophy—disguised as theme—and discovers, as is inevitable, that Resnais is not nearly as good a thinker as Bergson or John Ward—or more trenchantly that he is "not an original thinker." But the obvious presence of memory and mental associations in Resnais' films suggests Bergson, and that leads, illogically, to the notions that "an excursion into philosophy is an unavoidable prelude to an analysis of Resnais' themes" and that "None of Resnais' feature films is entirely self-explanatory. We have to refer to a theoretical tradition to understand them fully." Besides implying that Resnais' films are deficient art, which contradicts his claims that they are "a perfect congruity of the elements out of which they are constructed" and so self-reliant, they are amusingly refuted by Ward's failure to "understand" at all what is going on in a Resnais film. Obviously, a knowledge of Bergson may alert one to the presence of something otherwise undetectable (and in general the more one knows about anything and everything the greater his powers of perception are likely to be); but however useful, such knowledge is neither indispensable nor sufficient.

Actually, Ward instinctively senses where the aesthetic matter is. *Hiroshima Mon Amour,* he recognizes, "is a success because it makes inspired connections, not because it makes a correct statement." And he even allows Resnais to tell him what to look for in his film when he quotes him as remarking, "Pessimist I most certainly am, but I am not prepared to be satisfied with this. There must surely be a way out. In any case, if I were nothing more than a pessimist, I wouldn't make films." But he has other things on his mind—philosophic truth, what Resnais thinks, "Resnais' view of memory"—and he can't be bothered with looking at the films, at the inspired connections or the something more than pessimism inherent in making a film. Hence he over-looks the readily apparent—that *Hiroshima Mon Amour* and *Last Year at Marienbad,* for instance, are not case-study analyses of the psyche either of the characters or of man. They are affirmations, quite simply, of themselves, of the specific sort of thing or kind of art they are. They enact the process whereby they themselves came to be, tracing, defining, creating their own reality. Had Ward attended to such matters in *Hiroshima Mon Amour* as the moment focused upon—the post-climactic phase of erotic passion rather than its awakening and intensification, the relation of the movie to the movie being made within it, or the recurrent cat, to mention but three of its ele-ments, he could have easily seen that it is the aesthetic memory, and not merely that of the characters, that is crucial. Seeing this he could have readily followed the transformation of pain and death and horror into art and new existence. But since in his view ideas are more valuable than images, he ig-nores what the film shows him and searches for a truth rather than a process. He plays the critical one-upsmanship game of ravaging the art to be able to cry out triumphantly, "This is what he really means or really means to say."

The error lies in giving overweening importance to what is said or meant rather than to what is done or happens. Approached with the latter in mind, there could be no mistaking, as Sartre put it, that "there is not a single one of our acts which does not at the same time create an image of man as we think he ought to be. To choose to be thus or that is to affirm at the same time the value of what we choose, because we can never choose evil." Art is a choice, and a specific work is the end result of a choice acted upon and brought to fulfillment— it is a value realized. Ward knows that, I think, since he allows that Resnais' films have something to do with "creative memory," that their value resides in their inspired connections, and that Resnais is not, finally, a pessimist. He knows what counts in a movie as an aesthetic phenomenon, but he doesn't know how to get at it. All his praise of Resnais as "the finest film maker since the war" and of his achievement in effecting "a personal style," "a kind of formal necessity," "profound psychological studies," "a genu-ine liaison between literature and cinema," and "a consistent philosophic attitude" comes to nothing; it may be valid but he cannot demonstrate it. While he comes by it through a leap of the imagination, his language under-cuts that leap: it measures by the criteria of thought—and whatever persua-siveness it has rests entirely upon his reader's faith in his sensibility.

An axiom more than two thousand years old claims that fine art, as op-posed to practical art, is an end in itself. Yet Ward's discussion perversely derives from a persistent false assumption about art that denies that axiom. His statements about an incursion into philosophy and reference to a theoretical tradition being necessary to understand Resnais' films sound sensible because they have been repeated so often by authorities of stature that they possess an aura of self-evidence. Art does not, however, and cannot make propositional assertions; it cannot be false or true in any logical sense; thus it cannot "say" or "mean" anything in the normal sense of these words. As an end in itself it absorbs all attention in itself, at least when aesthetically beheld. It is its own subject, inviting its beholder to know it for what it is. And what it is when a narrative, if a subject must be attributed to it, is a study or measure or rendering of change, of creative change or transformation, to be exact. That is to say, it is a "myth" of creation which identifies and pays tribute to its source, the power that makes it possible. If it can be true or false, it is only in the sense of being true to itself. It can be more or less alive, thus more or less dynamically coherent and vitally realized. Ward's approach to Resnais' art, representative of the rationalistic or intellective notion that art refers beyond itself—imitates or represents—seeks to reduce it to static concepts or principles. His emphasis upon theme, or ideas, amounts to a raid upon the films to pursue an interest of his own. That interest is legitimate in its own province, but turned upon Resnais' films it keeps his attention outside the art, with the result that he views it extensively rather than intensively, and so he cannot see, or aid others in seeing, what they have to show as narrative art.

His raid on Resnais' films is, however, a minor skirmish compared to the theologian's raid upon modern literature. Historically, revelation gave way to *a priori* knowledge, first in reason then in conscience; and now art has succeeded the latter as the primitive evidence of existence, including the divine or the life of the spirit. The theologians blatantly and consistently select those writers or works or passages from works that nicely support their doctrinal commitments arrived at prior to their encounter with art. But Ward and the theologians really prove only that anything or nothing can be proven with art if one has a talent for spotting what seem like confirming texts or the patience to search long enough for likely looking data. The result, however, over and above their negation of the creative event, is that their own arguments, built upon false evidence, collapse under rigorous examination.

Until they see what actually faces them in a work of art their generalizations about it, even should they be eventually possible, can amount to nothing more finally than self-expression, the vice they traditionally delight in attributing to the artist. Inevitably, as happens in John Ward's essay, nothing is clarified or finally satisfactory and only odds and ends of diverse information manage to be helpful in perceiving the film aesthetically. The ideas extracted cannot survive on their own; nor can the dissected movies, which like Humpty-Dumpty lie fragmented at the bottom of the wall.

The fundamental error responsible for this devastation and underlying the denial of art as an end in itself, is a confusion regarding the cause of art. For the thinker art results, in Aristotle's distinction, from material, efficient, or formal causes (the first being the medium, the second the psychological and social circumstances, and the third genres or ideas). The thinker's method subsumes the aesthetic under the intellectual, and obliges him to claim that the artist transcends man's involvement in the physical or in necessity as the thinker does—by truth, by acquiring, or by dimly suggesting a reflective knowledge and stoic superiority to (or Faustian power over) the material conditions from which thought has allowed him to dissociate himself. Left out of his considerations, indeed, out of his view of the world, is the final cause, the vital center and distinctive soul of art. His method forbids him to talk logically about ends; so when he does, as in Ward's case, he risks absurdity; and to avoid that rationalistic horror, he either stirs up clouds of obfuscation or blindly deduces a value judgment from the material part, the ought from the is, in philosophers' parlance. When up to the intellectual mark, he admits the foolishness of reasoning about ends in his conceptions of the naturalistic and the "intentional fallacy." And with these, especially the latter, he completely disarms himself for talking to the point about art. But that merely compounds error with error, for art, the artist, or the imagination have *their* intention and are truly comprehensible only in relation to it. The added error in the "intentional fallacy" is the assumption that intention resides in the material, efficient, or formal cause—the psychology, social motives, ideas, etc., of the artist. Given the error of the thinker's concept of the causes responsible for change, the second error follows automatically and even appears to make sense.

The heart of the matter is that the way of the artist is at odds with the way of the thinker, for the way of the imagination differs radically from the way of the intellect. Ward and Alain Resnais "study" change from two wholly different points of view, in other words. Where the philosopher explains change, the artist participates in it. He renders it from the inside. He escapes man's necessity by a creative act, that is, by bringing into the world what had previously not existed in time and space. He introduces a novel, unnatural form into nature. His eye is not on the material conditions but on the possibility; he is a prophet looking into the future. He lives in and through value, not the ideal— value occurs only in the concrete and as a particular, whereas the ideal is an abstraction, an idea of the good generalized from a value. "What ethics and art have in common," Sartre detected, "is creation and invention." Which makes them one and the same. A movie is an ethical phenomenon, or, more accurately—and I think the translator is probably more at fault here than Sartre—a value phenomenon. Art is value. The imagination dwells in a universe of qualities. Ward's book, then, for all its placid surface turns out to be an arena in which the two rival modes of intellect and imagination engage in a power struggle weighted to favor the thinker. In that warfare the conservative force in life attempts to enchain the liberal force. But Ward was doomed to failure, because, as L. L. Whyte recognized, "The community can always, through its informed specialists, attempt to weigh the truth in any interpretation of the past, but it has no technique for a rational estimate of anticipations of the future." Neither Ward nor Whyte, despite this statement, nor the thinker in general, possesses such a technique, and so "rational estimates" of values which anticipate the future lie beyond his powers.

Ward's error is not confined to intellectuals of the exalted speculative variety, I must hasten to add. The moviemaker himself, when he reverts to critic, theorist, or commentator on his work or that of others, becomes a thinker prone to stumbling into the pitfalls Ward encounters. Certainly that is true of the representative New Wave spokesman and adversaries collected in Peter Graham's book. Being more closely associated with movie art, they possess a more intimate feeling than Ward for the movies as narrative art. They recognize that its province is "relationships," that "every style has its moral attitude," and that "the moral attitude of the director toward his subject justifies his role." On a rare occasion they can make a useful descriptive distinction, though not in descriptive language, and always morally weighted according to the bias of their cause, like the one between "directors who believe in the image and those who believe in reality." And they can even talk at times directly about a film, as André Bazin does in discussing a scene from William Wyler's *The Best Years of Our Lives* to illustrate "composition in depth," which I would like to quote at length:

> The characters grouped on the right, in the middle ground, seem to form the main dramatic point of interest, as everyone has gathered in this room to attend the wedding of the disabled sergeant. In fact, since this action is a foregone conclusion and, in a sense, already over, the spectator's interest is focused on Teresa Wright (in white in the background) and Dana Andrews (on the left in the foreground), who are meeting for the first time

since they broke off their engagement. Throughout the whole sequence of the wedding, Wyler manipulates his actors with consummate skill so as gradually to bring to the fore the two protagonists, who, the spectator is sure, are continually thinking of each other. The reproduced still shows an intermediate stage. At this point, the two centres of interest, Dana Andrews and Teresa Wright, have not yet come together, but the natural though carefully calculated movements of the two actors throw their relationship into clear relief. Teresa Wright's white dress, standing out almost in the centre of the frame, makes a kind of dramatic fissure, so that if one were to cut the image in half at the point where the walls meet the action would also be bisected into its two elements. The two lovers are visually and logically thrust into the left part of the frame.

The importance of the direction in which people look should also be noticed in this still. The look always forms the skeleton of Wyler's *mis-en-scene*. As well as the actual look of the characters, Wyler also excels at getting across to us the virtual look of the camera, with which our own eyes identify themselves. Jean Mitry has drawn attention to the low angle shot in *Jezebel* which places the lens right in line with Bette Davis's gaze as she sees the walkingstick that Henry Fonda has in his hands and intends to use. In this way we can follow the gaze of the characters better than if the camera, as in a ordinary shooting script, showed us the stick from above as if through Bette Davis's own eyes.

There is a variant of the same principles in *The Little Foxes:* in order to make us understand the thoughts of the character who notices the small steel box which used to contain some stolen shares (their absence is going to reveal his theft), Wyler puts the object in the foreground, this time with the camera at the same height as the man, but still symmetrically placed in relation to the actor and to what he is looking at. Our gaze does not meet that of the actor directly through the regarded object, but, as through the interplay of a mirror, the angle of incidence of our own gaze on the box is somehow equivalent to the angle of reflection which leads us to the eyes of the actor. In every case, Wyler guides our mental outlook by means of the strict laws of an invisible dramatic perspective.

The spectator has only to follow the gaze of the characters like a pointing finger and he will have an exact understanding of all the intentions of the director. If these could be made tangible on the image by a pencil line, we would see, as clearly as we see the ghost of a magnet in iron filings, the dramatic forces which are crossing the screen. All Wyler's preparatory work consists of simplifying the mechanics of *mis-en-scene* as far as possible by making it as sufficient and as clear as he can. In the film *The Best Years of Our Lives,* he attains an almost abstract purity. Every point of dramatic articulation is so sensitive that a shift of a few degrees in the angle of somebody's gaze is not only quite obvious to the most obtuse spectator, but is also capable, through a kind of leverage, of turning a whole scene upside-down.

The movie viewer's object, Bazin admits, is to understand "all the intentions of the director," but in discussing these intentions he restricts himself to dramatic and rhetorical considerations. That restriction is nicely ironic, since the rest of his essay and the anthology as a whole is, as criticism should be, a heated dialogue. These New Wave spokesmen apparently cannot link the values so much on their minds with the images they are making and viewing.

Bazin can discuss the artistry but not the art, and that inability to carry through on what he begins and the implications of his own language afflicts all the New Wave writers. They are collectively on to something, probably pretty accurately identified by the title attached to the movement, "New Wave," with the commitment to the new and to all that a wave implies regarding energy, movement, and forward thrust. But again, like Ward, they can't say straightforwardly how that commitment gets realized in their films or guide their readers and viewers to seeing such values on the screen. That commitment, for instance, seems to entail moderation, not iconoclasm or revolution:

Bazin favors the stable image because it can "bring out the deeper structure of reality," Robert Benayoun attacks the *Cahiers du Cinema* faction for pursuits divorced from social problems, and François Truffaut emphasizes pleasing the ordinary viewer and, like Bazin, working within the trade's established institutions. Their vagueness offends even more than Ward's, in the end, because they engender an expectation— they appear to be on to something crucial. But they can't clarify it in their statements, and they haven't succeeded in clarifying it to any great degree in their films either. Their vagueness carries over to their pictures, undoubtedly because their approach is basically intellectual. Other than Resnais, and maybe Godard in a movie or two, they thought up a doctrine then tried to make movies in conformity to it. Moreover, the doctrine is bad doctrine, a lot of nonsense about the director being the author, the film a form of writing, and a movie a vehicle for ideas and philosophy. Truffaut has probably been the most guilty in this respect; after *400 Blows,* a fair movie of innocence by an innocent director, he became heavy-handed in *Jules and Jim* and has degenerated into the most run-of-the-mill kind of thesis movies, an inevitable price of thinking out ideas outside of rather than in and through the medium. The film becomes a rhetorical tool to be manipulated for effects; the gimmick takes precedence over art. Unavoidably, once leaning in that direction, he ends up without an appropriate method for either art or criticism, which has been the flaw of the New Wave as a whole.

The difference between what an artist says his intention is and what he actually does, or between the value that guides him as artist and his ability to explain it, gets displayed in blown-up proportions in Kevin Brownlow's story of the making of *How It Happened Here* (1968), a film he began at the age of sixteen in May, 1956 and finished eight years later in May, 1964. He claims to have "learned about the incredible waste of the professional industry" and "the historical background of our subject," the Nazis, while making the film, which had its origins in an incident:

> Walking toward the laboratories, I was jolted by a black Citroën screeching to a halt. The driver leaped out and ran to a delicatessen. He paused at the door and shouted to his companion in German. The scene was straight out of a war film; only the surroundings were unusual. The incident triggered a train of thought. What *might* have happened if the Germans had invaded England?
>
> From this premise, I worked out the basis for an extravagant piece of historical fiction. The single page outline was entitled, emphatically, *It DID Happen Here!*
>
> 'While studying the national characteristics of the English and German, the film will try to demonstrate the inevitability of war, by showing from one side its utter futility, and from the other its invaluable stimulus to the development of the human race.'

Subsequently his movie, he says, shifted in emphasis from a "conventional war film" to the "psychological effects of occupation." Some kind of human and probably aesthetic growth undoubtedly took place here, but though his account is highly readable, he never explains aesthetically what he does or finally achieves. As a consequence his narrative leaves the impression that he produced a thesis film, a piece of anti-Nazi propaganda that succeeded briefly and locally as a political *cause celebré*. But who needs to know that the Nazis were bad guys? If the film uses them as vehicles for novel moral insight, then it could be significant as art. But Brownlow does not address himself to that matter: he instructs his readers in the mechanics of movie production, not in its aesthetics. I trust that his impression misleads and that he made a film rather than an argument. An artist doesn't have to explain himself; his talent lies elsewhere, and he supposedly has his say in his art. But also evident in Brownlow's narrative, as in the New Wave film makers, critics, and theorists, is the absence of a method by which the artist can make intellectual sense of what he has done or has made. He has his feelings or intuitions and nothing more to rely upon. The conclusion that has inevitably to be drawn is that

Western thought has never formulated such a method, and so within the very being of the artist and his art, the reflective intelligence remains dissociated from the imagination. The intellect cannot make contact with art or value; its language is alien to the aesthetic.

It is refreshing by comparison to turn from the vagueness and irrelevancies of thinkers to Robin Wood's book on Howard Hawks. He obviously likes to look at films and wants to aid others in seeing them. And aware that values are the heart of the aesthetic, he primarily and directly attends to them. The result is an admirable clarification— not of Hawks' films, but of English taste. All four books, incidentally, were written by Englishmen, and what they have in common, despite different subjects and varying degrees of moral obliqueness in their approach to the movies, is a commitment to what Wood characterizes in praising Hawks' films with such phrases as "the individual need for integrity and self-respect within a naturalistic framework," "a man who exists exclusively from his own centre," "the aliveness of so many of his people," a "defense of civilized order and civilized values," "never rejects his past," "most completely personal and individual when his work is most firmly traditional." The latter is quite a feat for a boy from Goshen, Indiana, and a clear tipoff that an Englishman has gone a long way off to discover his own image. Yet that's not nearly as remarkable a feat as Peter Graham's putting together an anthology of statements by Frenchmen who almost without exception appreciate what Englishmen do. The four books, that is to say, unconsciously participate in a moral polemic that has as its real intention the clarification of the English idea of what movies morally should affirm. Read within that framework, unmasked for the moralists they are (and Englishmen cannot help being moralists), their books are both instructive and entertaining. Their collective case is argued not upon the evidence of the movies, however, but against it; they don't look closely at movies because they distrust them, for the world of the movies, they correctly sense, is incompatible with their values. (*Alfie, Darling, The Yellow Submarine, The Charge of the Light Brigade,* the predominant tendency in recent British films, will bear this out. Each rejects its own cinematic "nature." Films made by Americans like Richard Lester or Stanley Kubrick or Europeans like Karel Reisz—for example, *A Hard Day's Night, 2001, Morgan—convert* English technical skill in movie making into the release of that nature.) And that is as true of Robin Wood ultimately as of the others. One no more sees a Hawks film through his eyes than one reads Dickens through the criticism of F. R. Leavis, Wood's acknowledged mentor and the moralist *par excellence* of twentieth-century

British literary criticism. His method, even more narrowly than Bazin's, focuses upon dramatic features—upon characters and their relationships—and as useful as that can be at times in following a movie narrative he could just as well be talking about plays. Character is what he values and drama celebrates character more fully than any other narrative medium, but because he engages exclusively in dramatic analysis, his judgments about Hawks' films and his explanations of their unevenness are curiously askew of cinematic values.

Nevertheless Wood does attend directly to moral fact and comes close, much closer than Ward, to meeting the movies as art on their own ground. But typical for moralists, who are, after all, a breed of thinkers, he approaches them knowing what he likes or what is right and so his discussion is an exercise in applying or confirming what he knows to be good before seeing the movies. One of the most flattering things he can say about a Hawks film is that we "never have the feeling that a 'message' is being 'put across'." A message there is nonetheless, or at least Wood has a message and Hawks provides him with the texts. A moralist has made his kind of raid upon art. His method aims beyond the art, too, and, accordingly, though it lingers a while, does so while always remaining mindful of its proper mission. Though a benevolent instance of it, one in which the moralist has discovered something he can embrace rather than something that provokes him to a rage of moral indignation, Wood still represents the most familiar of critical methods, what has been dubbed "ethical criticism," meaning a criticism that makes deductive value judgments about art employing a dogmatic moral premise derived from some institutional or intellectual authority such as Christianity, Marxism, Freud, or humanism, to cite but four well-known sources of moral absolutes in recent criticism.

Movie reviewers, watchguards of public taste, licensed to perform as the public conscience, invariably practice this method. Most of them are hacks and unworthy of notice except as ad men, but some acquire reputations and eventually publish their collective reviews, like James Agee, Pauline Kael, Stanley Kaufman, and Susan Sontag, writers of some reputation in movie criticism today. Yet even then they are rarely instructive about films or reliable as guides to quality, much less to looking into a film. Agee writes well and has his particular interest—character, whether in the form of the personages in the narrative, or of the actors, or of the directors. He's wonderfully humane and superbly sensitive to people, but, as with Wood, that commitment predisposes him to favor dramatic factors and ignore cinematic ones.

Humanism prevails and the value phenomenon in itself doesn't exist for his consciousness. Consequently, he doesn't reveal much about the art of movies beyond character or, what amounts to the same thing, the technique of such figures as comedians and directors, of whom D. W. Griffith and John Huston are his special favorites. The others are flagrant moralists, though sometimes they slightly disguise that fact under the analysis of theme. Pauline Kael is a Billy Graham in cinematic skirts who hates movies and prefers hell, fire, and damnationing their audience to writing about them; Susan Sontag defends "reflective" values; and Stanley Kaufman, an emissary from Parnassus, polices against aesthetic thievery and vulgarity. In fact, all these "sophisticated" reviewers are essentially doctors of society; using the movie as a symptom, their passion is to diagnose moral sickness in man, the culture, the times, a class, the artist. Whatever they attack they do so doctrinairely, praising or condemning in the name of a faction or ideal. Their criticism, correspondingly, is elitist and conservative; it discriminates against the present, viewed as "fallen," and against the movies, the living art of the present, as a medium. But, more importantly, the moralist's method is absurd. It rests upon moral absolutes that, unjustifiable, are simply false. His criticism, postulated upon moral obtuseness and ignorance is, to put it bluntly, immoral.

Movie reviewers write under a deadline and other conditions that bring out the worst in a critic. Robin Wood doesn't have that excuse, since he had plenty of time for deliberation and was under no burden to produce timely journalistic copy. Nor do movie critics writing now in the quarterlies, and as a consequence some very solid material on the movies has begun to appear in them. I have in mind particularly an essay on Antonioni by Charles Thomas Samuels (*The American Scholar*, Winter, 1967-68), and though most of his essay gets bogged down in the infighting among New York literati, a fair portion of it settles down to describing the particulars of what Antonioni is doing with the images of *Blow-Up* and other films. He makes some outlandish claims, such as "Antonioni stands alone in making the visual image his fundamental mode," betraying his cinematic innocence but also establishing that his eye is on the ball. And with his eye where it ought to be he goes on to describe astutely the visual content of some selected images and scenes. The trouble arises from his selecting the images that suit his moral bias and even limiting what he notices in them to what will support his thesis. For despite his allowing the visual image to be fundamental, he cannot resist examining society's health, and instead of looking with care at *Blow-Up,* he presses hard against its inherent tendencies to make it reveal "the era's sickness," the "lovelessness," "paralysis of will," and "loss of faith" in the modern world, those tired old moralistic preachments of T. S. Eliot. In the first place, like the anti-Nazi theme in Brownlow's film, those moral revelations are so commonplace that only the dull could take them seriously. Surely, Antonioni has more to show than that. But such moralizing, besides being trite, obscures and falsifies what is morally there in the film. It distorts the moral fact and in doing that promulgates a vicious morality.

Another piece of moralistic criticism in a quarterly, far more attentive to the facts of a film than Samuels', is William J. Free's essay "Aesthetic and Moral Values in *Bonnie and Clyde*" (*The Quarterly Journal of Speech*, October, 1968). Pointing out that "the movie is essentially moral," a tautology betraying aesthetic innocence comparable to Samuels', Free further notes a moral contradiction in the film, or a double moral perspective. The first of them, dominant in the early part of the movie, complements the protagonists: "they are alive and the other world is essentially dead, we accept their values." The second emerges toward the end of the movie: there occurs a "reversal of moral norms as they succeed . . . and become subject to the world's morality," "our normal moral judgments." Now Free, whose essay is an exceptionally fine description of many facets of *Bonnie and Clyde,* avoids the traps of doctrinal self-righteousness such social diagnosticians as Samuels fall into, but he does not elude the root error of the moralistic method. When he reverts to "normal moral judgments," going outside the movie for a moral criterion with which to judge the characters in it, who are not actual people, he falls back upon an untenable habit of mind limited to confirming what is already known, the moral status quo. The sheriff is after all not morally defined by a criterion imported from the outside, but by a criterion which an image in the context of a world of images generates out of its own aesthetic being. The movie, like any other work of art, creates the only criterion by which it can be legitimately judged. The moral insight it is, is posited as its standard—and man's. No ground endows "our normal moral judgments" with absolute authority, nor do they rise logically from moral reality. They reduce the complex living moral fact to a simplified segregated condition. Free correctly sees the double perspective or moral irony within *Bonnie and Clyde,* but apparently unable to tolerate its complexity, he resolves the irony, as his title signifies, by categorically separating the aesthetic and moral. An abstraction is given hegemony over the living moral truth, and though a moral judgment is made, nothing new morally is gained. Also, his abstraction of his conscience from personal involvement in the movie dichotomizes; it morally dissociates, which the movie itself does not do—it holds antitheses in a living suspension. More-over, in addition to negating innovation in morality or moral growth, he has denied art's creative capacity, its power to expand consciousness, to initiate new modes or directions of awareness. Having segregated the two, he elects morality over art. That means he has violated art, repudiating what *Bonnie and Clyde* is, the truth and values that it has staked out as its distinctive province.

Either art matters or it doesn't; either it contributes something unique to life or it is merely decorative; either it is a form of knowledge that a man of passionate and serious curiosity can inquire into or it is an irrelevancy. All the instincts of the writers considered above, including Free's, and our own, in-sist that the movies are a moral phenomenon, that, indeed, they are a means to knowledge of values. The aesthetic and the moral are indivisible, that is self-evident; it is a pristine fact of human experience. Qualities are the life blood of the aesthetic object and the aesthetic response. Yet none of the writ-ers, we have seen, could directly and therefore adequately or accurately dis-cuss value. They talk around movies and thereby suggest their values, but their eyes are not open to nor can they open the eyes of others to see the qualities there and delineate the significance of their relationships. (And only qualities, the power within purposive life, it might be said here, can generate the action a narrative relates as well as the narration itself; equally applicable here is L. L. Whyte's principle, "There can be no materialistic interpretation of history… Permanence cannot account for novelty or development.") Their predicament issues from a mental bias, like the one Renata Adler, a New York *Times* critic, exhibits in her remark that "the medium is somehow un-suited to moral lessons … movies glamorize… They cannot effectively con-demn." She speaks for them with her old-fashioned notion that morality consists of "lessons" against violence or acts and the distortion she indulges in by stating that notion they commonly share. What she actually detected in the movies, but can't allow, is a new morality. She couches her statement in negative tones, implying, in typical essentialist logic, that the medium is amoral, if not immoral, because its morality differs from her conventional one.

The indelible fact, despite the resistance and confusion of these writers, is that the movies, along with the other art, in James Joyce's image, forge the conscience of mankind. Thus what is there to be known is not the crux of the aesthetic question in movie criticism; that much is obvious: quality is the "substance" of its art. Rather, it is the perceiving and making of accurate statements about quality that perplexes. The way out of the impasse movie criticism is stuck in at present, the way to moral knowledge through movie art, consequently, is a method that concentrates upon describing qualities and their relationships. Everything a movie has to show exists out in the open, so no special concept or intellectual scheme or analytical tool is privy to what it is. As the camera, setting the example, points toward and beholds what light illuminates, so movie criticism must follow its lead by opening the mind through opening the eyes, and that can happen only via specifying, or pointing to, what is there in fact. The movie provides the model of how to study it and, indeed, study "reality," for as a moral phenomenon, as art, it exemplifies the true and the good. It persuades by the power of its being, not by precept; by attraction, not compulsion—as all art does. Its superior vividness, in comparison to thought and other art media, relocates the frontier of man's exploration into self-knowledge, or the knowledge of good and evil. The living morality gets daily and progressively clarified in the movies; that is where for consciousness the moral action is; and every innovation in technique or novel combination in movie art constitutes a revelation, not just a variation in technique. Through such innovation in the movies, novel human possibilities are illuminated, and the central task of movie criticism, then, is to behold and advertise them.

Take, as an example of the descriptive approach and its yield, the end of *Bonnie and Clyde,* the scene in which the ambushed white car, reliefed against a green natural setting, is sadistically riddled in a massive overkill, the "law" voraciously spilling the blood of Bonnie and Clyde and thereby brutally triumphing over their youthful restlessness to escape the confines of themselves and their world. What one sees is inseparable from the total context of the movie; every particular, of course, defines and is defined by every other particular as well as by its own inherent qualities. Thus description of the example must perforce be restricted here because of space limitations to a selected feature of the scene. A good base for a succinct description of the context is provided by Free's observation that "they are alive and the other world is essentially dead." Postulating as a premise the notion that the movie affirms life, and assuming that the movie s intention is to flesh out that value (which, incidentally, originates in the Romantic passion to exist; but in a descriptive approach mention must be focused on how that passion is qualified, not on influence, though identifying it can be a useful if not sufficient notation), the essential quality of the images, pervading the narrative and so present from the first frame on, is high-spirited action. To be alive is to be set free in exuberant self-assertion—thus the repeated pattern of enclosing space and the break out, beginning with Bonnie in her room looking out a window and ending in the inescapable ring of death around the mortal creature. Far and away the dominant action of the final scene, overwhelming in vividness everything else surrounding it, is the convulsive slow-motion jouncing of the limp puppet-like bodies of Bonnie and Clyde. The alive, who evoke great fear of their fierce energy, are no longer propelled by their own vital powers but by mechanical forces impacting upon them. The action of evil cancels out the self-generated action of life, denying life's will to be. The definition does not depend solely upon the savage burst of gunfire and its effects. Behind the gun is the sheriff, the villain of the peace, who provides a continuous bad action in counter-point to the good living action. Everything Bonnie and Clyde did was done in youthful zest without intention of hurting another human being until the sheriff insulted them. What harm they did happened accidentally. In every respect they are open, honest, overt. The sheriff, on the other hand, sneaks up on, plots, tricks, persistently seeks personal vengeance, broods, scowls, is vicious, sly, a man of oaths. When the gunfire erupts, he is in hiding behind nature's greenery, so that, generalizing to the ultimate qualities of the image, one can say that the element of reason and necessity cuts down the spontaneous and the growing. A further inherent moral quality, more explicit in a film like *The Stalking Moon,* where the villain, an Indian who wantonly murders without ever being seen or heard, is that evil in the world of color, as for Existentialism, is negation, abstraction, vagueness, indefiniteness, non-being, etc. The opposite to it, the good inherent in colored light, is the concrete, distinct, specific, vivid, etc.

Free would have it that the violence of the final action in *Bonnie and Clyde* thrusts the audience into the moral recognition that "these beautiful people and their beautiful world are essentially false." But if that were so, then the movie itself is false; it negates its own moral commitment as established by its form. Many movies do repudiate themselves—for instance, *Fahrenheit 451, Darling, The Emperor Worm,* all posit the moral superiority of the word; and *Elvira Madigan,* in which the lovers also die, in one-shot mercy killings, ends with a frozen image of Elvira smiling happily after releasing a butterfly, signifying her joyous release from the nauseating earth. *Bonnie and Clyde* is not rhetorical or essentialist; on the contrary, it celebrates "the beautiful world," but via tragedy, its value being poignantly affirmed by its painful, sorrowful loss. It displays a sort of Bergsonian catastrophe in which the *élan vital* is battered into rigidity. And in contrast to a Shakespearian tragedy such as *Hamlet,* which ends with a restoration of harmonious order when evil is purged, in *Bonnie and Clyde* the rottenness of the establishment persists, and cannot be cured, since it is doomed forever by its commitment to static order to seek to entomb life. Whereas the establishment is hateful, Bonnie and Clyde are pitiful because their death issues inexorably, not from the law, but from themselves, from the blood within that runs upon the white. Their tragedy as the living and therefore growing is that they have developed beyond return; their youth has been spent. But the final dimension of the film's tragic vision is an eternal irreconcilability between "self" and "society," an inexpungeable ironic ambivalence in man's existence.

Or, as an another example, consider the final images of *Blow-Up,* the figure of the photographer dissolving into the green grass of the park. Samuels says that here, and in all of Antonioni's movies, nothing happens or is achieved, and cryptically links the photographer's disappearance with his namelessness and impotence. But something does happen in the movie: for instance, cinematically the narrative moves from a mill to a park, from night to day, from black and white, in effect, to green, from a character disguised and studying as an observer to one involved in a game of nothing tennis. Samuels notes but prefers to discount these changes because he came to the movie with the traditional idea of human change being a metamorphosis, a radical transformation such as Christianity imagined taking place when fallen, sinful man was elevated by salvation into spiritual grace. *Blow-Up* is ineluctably a "study" of change, and as such, with the photographer, a maker of images, appropriately as its protagonist, it defines the nature of human change and man's good in the universe of light. That change, Antonioni's final image reveals, is not a change of substance but of mind. It does not beget a transcendence of the world but an enlightened entry or diffusion into it. (The archetypal movie in this respect is *Tom Jones,* an eighteenth-century, rationalistic story in which evil results from errors of judgment originating in social conventions and good comes from a change of mind, a clear recognition of what is actually so.) And it can only happen that way in the depthless universe of color; there is no other realm to escape to. Inevitably for his human condition, like Meursault in Camus' *The Stranger,* the photographer's educated consciousness finds its home in the green world, where names or words are inconsequential, at least for the artist, whose consciousness sets in at the undifferentiated level of existence. That fecund color is the vital detail. It is the power, the source, like Whitman's leaves of grass, for creative ventures; the movie grows from it. And it makes possible the "transcendence" of life by art, or, rather, the extension of life in art and a living art. That possibility inheres in color and Antonioni in turning to color, and a certain kind of color, in *Blow-Up* (quite different from the color of *Red Desert)* employed its qualities with consummate skill to realize the values his imagination chose to commit itself to on that occasion. In inquiring into the moral knowledge the movies make available, the qualities of the framing elements, so to speak, are as important as a specific color or image; for, after all, not only should everything in a work of art be functional, it is inescapably so, either for good or bad. An accurate description must encompass everything of which a movie consists.

Contrasting actions in *Bonnie and Clyde* and contrasting colors in *Blow-Up* are vehicles for moral discovery and articulation, and these elements unavoidably operate in every film, since they are indispensable facets of the medium. But color, that is, technicolor as opposed to black and white, is the major aesthetic and moral factor in recent movies. A medium, by its inherent character, emphasizes one or a few sensations in the spectrum of human experience, and in "selecting" those qualities for the focus of attention establishes a norm or center with which to assess value and measure truth. The color movie occupies our consciousness with color: we distinguish things—things are characterized—by their color, and the worth of anything resides in its color, both in reference, of course, to the basic qualities inherent in color *per se.* Looking more closely at these two color films, while keeping in mind that the evidence lies in what is done with or done by light, it becomes apparent that the good white and green radiate. From that cornucopian radiation emanate more specific qualities, defining by realization the good inherent in radiating. The most general quality is the process itself, its "commitment" to release of potential or fulfillment of possibility. It aims toward concreteness and individuation. To those ends, it acts upon the principle exploited by an insurance company giving tips on economy to sell its product—that "light-colored cars are six times brighter than dark cars or six times easier to see." And by means of that principle it opts for the sensory world or existence, identical with the exalted individual, the separate entity raised to the supreme vividness of which life is capable. And, as other films have more fully shown, that leads to affirmation of the "human form divine"—when not of the body, of the face—as cultivated in recent "adults only" films; closeness, contact, and touch (this latter is beautifully looked into in Zefferelli's *Romeo and Juliet* but all of them are more familiarly present in the classic embrace, kiss, and sex scenes): the pleasures of eating, the machine as an extension of man's creative urge, the socially and sexually emancipated woman, the incorrigible hero—in short, the ethics of joy.

It has been said that "beneath the surface of the responses and struggles of all of us, there lies a new ethical metaphor waiting to be born." The author of this statement claims that the new metaphor to replace "good and evil" will be "responsibility," which pairs off against "irresponsibility." Without a doubt he is right about a new ethic being in the making, but he writes, like a proper moralist, from the conservative view. The new ethical metaphor has already been born—it is involvement, of which responsibility is but a facet. Had he paid attention to the movies, where the new morality is being created through the moving colorful image rather than through the word, he would not have been so narrow-minded. He could have seen, and at great length, since any number of recent movies have been devoted to examining the contrasting moral qualities of the word and the image by playing them off against one another, that by its complexity the image is involvement incarnate. Whereas it is, and presents, its complex self, the word abstracts and reduces to one aspect. It is for this reason that it appears that only the movies possess the depth and breadth required for clarifying contemporary moral reality. And it is for this reason that they are so disconcerting morally. When the protagonist in *Mickey One* imploringly asked the question he got from Jeremiah, "What is the word?" he saw, and the screen was flooded, by a white light. The Alfies and Darlings and Book-men cannot let themselves be, but when *Mickey One* asks for an explanation and for answer is shown the power made manifest, his walls tumble down and he makes music against the open skyline of lit-up downtown Detroit. He is a free creator who learns that morality is not a matter of simplemindedly imposing inhibiting or repressive principles on the living passions but a matter of the living conscience complexly being and doing good, not just thinking it.

Of necessity, inquiry into man has become inseparable from inquiry into, as opposed to about, the moving image, which is what twentieth-century narrative art has presupposed since Joseph Conrad's preface to *The Nigger of the Narcissus*. Accordingly, significant progress in the humanities depends upon close scrutiny of changing images and images of change. It is now commonly recognized that art is a closer analogue to reality than logic, the imagination's methods a closer imitation of nature than reason's. And among the arts, obviously, the movies, an art of light, emanate from greater depths within the living center than any other art in a universe of light. The essence of words, the mass of sculpture, the harmonies of tones—these modes, for example, are aesthetic epigones in such a universe. The advantage of the movies places them on the frontier of moral history, and so to them we must go if we are to know ourselves and exist in our time. In the metaphysics, epistemology, and morality of the moving image lies the possibilities for man in the emerging affluent, leisure culture of the imagination and the further realization of what William Blake espoused; and what has been the *summum bonum* of Western civilization since the beginning of the Renaissance—the individual and concrete. The movies arise from that moral impulse and carry it forward at this point. Its progress depends not only upon ever greater sophistication in the making of movies but also upon greater sophistication in talking about them. For the revelations of the moving image, despite its overtness, will continue to elude us until we see the qualities of that specific action or that specific color, until our eyes are opened by an appropriate method to see what is there and going on morally in the movies as narrative art.

 amn Your *A Priori* Principles—Look!"

W. R. Robinson Discusses the Movies as Narrative Art

INTERVIEW BY JOHN GRAHAM

The following interview was conducted by JOHN GRAHAM, Professor of Speech and Drama at the University of Virginia, for his weekly radio program, "The Scholar's Bookshelf," and published in THE FILM JOURNAL.

W. R. Robinson describes his course, 'The Movies as Narrative Art," as follows:

> The aim of this course is to learn the conditions and possibilities of movement in human existence. To this end, the course is devoted to examining feature-length movies, predominantly though not exclusively of the last 15 years, as studies of change. It is postulated for the purposes of the course that the movies have an inherent story to tell and that a movie maker is under unrelenting pressure to tell that story when he engages in making a movie. To determine whether the movie maker got his story right, the action narrated in a movie is carefully considered, of course, but so is the movie as a created entity or at least an attempt at creation. In fact, once it is established that the movies are an art of light, the course is given over to assessing the degree of coherence and consistency with which a movie renders "the myth of creation" that becomes inevitable when light becomes the ultimate source. More specifically, they are analyzed and weighed according to their insight into the possibilities of human change or growth with light as the primal energy and the medium in and through which man lives out his life. The total composition is taken into consideration in assessing a movie's insight but special attention is

given to lighting and cutting, the first because it is the key in movie art to where and what man is and the second because it is the key in movie art to how his life happens and he can move. That is to say, the medium and the devices for working it are studied not simply as material or technical elements but above all as aesthetic instruments by which man reflects upon himself and becomes free through organic, creative action.

Q. *How do you relate your interest in literature and philosophy to the study of film?*

A. Film is one of those subjects that can be approached from numerous perspectives. One that has been favored in the past, especially in magazine articles, has been that of the inside professional craftsman who has worked in the Hollywood industry and who knows the movies chiefly as technology. Then, of course, there is the perspective of the scholar who is interested in the theoretical and historical points of view. I come to film from a literary background. I carry through my philosophical interests by applying certain epistomological questions to art: What do you know through art, when do you know what you know through art, how do you know what you know through art? Instinct led me to the movies as the most fertile ground to pursue this line of inquiry. My course is titled "The Movies as Narrative Art," which means that I'm interested in film primarily as an aesthetic phenomenon. The course is concerned with movies as a form of storytelling.

Q. *Isn't this a carry-over from literature?*

A. All literary art, and I mean fictional literary art, is narrative; there is a dramatic situation, there is an agent or voice, and there is something acted out. So in my course movies are studied as an extension of the epic and the novel.

Q. *Yet the epic and the novel communicate verbally...*

A. While the movies communicate visually...with images. But all of these art forms are concerned with change and movement. Inherently, film is about movement—it moves and it attempts to study and determine the nature of movement.

Q. *Both physical and psychological movement?*

A. Yes. In teaching my course I begin with the assumption that since narrative is a study of change, it is in itself a rendering of something or somebody starting at one point and going to another. It entails intention. The only way you can talk specifically and sensibly about art is to approach it from the point of view of its final cause. You remember the old Aristotelean set of causes. One problem with students is that they are analytically oriented and tend to focus on the characters or director as personality; they try to analyze motives, causes of behavior. This analysis can go into matters psychological, sociological, historical or philosophical; but the purpose is to find a source outside of the art for its cause.

Q. *In other words, we try to bring to the art our own interpretation of cause and effect—whether it be Freudian or Pavlovian or Jungian—and attempt to superimpose this interpretation on the experience of the art.*

A. When we bring our own already established notions of causality to a movie, then we are not prepared to accept the movie on its own terms; we are not open to learn from the movie its particular revelations about the cause of change and the nature of change.

Q. *Some people have difficulty relating to a movie like Alain Resnais'* Last Year at Marienbad, *for instance, because it radically challenges their sense of chronology and time.*

A. The next step in my film course, after establishing film as a narrative art governed by its final cause, is to establish that in the realm of the film art, time and space are plastic. In Western culture we have a long tradition, connected with science and philosophy, of believing that the material world is not plastic but hard and adamant. It's just there, and one has to accept its there-ness. In order to understand movies, however, the student has to be liberated from his fear, his reverence for the "thereness" of the so-called objective world.

Q. *Do you see the dialogue and the image as mutually important and reinforcing in the film art?*

A. I am a creature of both mind and sense, word and image, and the art that is going to fully articulate my being has to be a composite of both. People who argue that film ought to be free of words are speaking nonsense; they're denying the richness of their faculties and the richness of their own existence.

Many directors today don't sufficiently explore the properties and potencies of the image. They get trapped in dialogue or theme. Often they are technically trained in photography and are more interested in design and abstraction— as photographers naturally are—than in the image as a living and moving phenomenon. But the image is the film director's medium, and he should be a kind of adventurer or explorer, a front line scientist in the realm of the image. A large number of recent movies are concerned with the confrontation of the word with the image.

Q. *Would you give an example of a film dealing with this confrontation?*

A. Ingmar Bergman makes a heavy film in the moral and intellectual sense, and it teases the mind to puzzle out his work. He has been a favorite of literary and philosophical types for this reason. In order to understand a film such as Bergman's THE HOUR OF THE WOLF, for example, you have to see what happens on the screen. You have to ask not "What is the film saying?" or "What does it mean?" but "What is it doing?"

THE HOUR OF THE WOLF opens with a black screen and a single voice. That voice gives way to a chorus of voices and then the first image appears: the camera pans by a tree in late autumn or early winter, past a picnic table with apples on it to the door of a cottage. A woman comes out of the door, and the camera follows her until, moving a little faster than the camera, she arrives at the table. She sits down at the table, facing the audience, and begins to tell the story of her husband who was a painter and who died recently.

In this opening sequence the basic conflict of the movie and the whole bias of the story are established. The conflict is between the woman of words who narrates and the man of images who paints. In THE HOUR OF THE WOLF the word dominates over the image. When the wife appears on the screen and directly addresses the audience, she establishes a human or social connection between herself as a woman of words and you as a listener to her words. The story she tells about her husband concerns a man who goes seeking for the ultimate image, a man who seeks in excess and, in effect, freaks out. The man who lives for images in Bergman's movie cuts his bond with human society and destroys his own humanity.

Q. *Is there any special conflict or type of narrative that characterizes American movies?*

A. The American sensibility has always been in the vanguard of movie art because Americans like to move; they're committed to movement. Unlike European directors who try to intellectualize time and slow events down to a meditative or contemplative speed, American directors are usually on the inside of change and are trying to articulate and direct it from the inside out. All of Western culture and technology—and movies are technological—is an attempt to take the powers inherent in the earth and to release them, to explode them under control: automobiles, airplanes, rocket ships and even movies.

Three American directors who have excelled in this release of explosive energy in man and his world are Arthur Penn, Richard Lester and Stanley Kubrick. The basic story for American movies—and it's the basic event in American history, in the formation of the American character—is the story of breakout: the breakout of Europe, the breakout of the old order into the new world.

In Penn's BONNIE AND CLYDE, for instance, you have the story of a gangster who, along with his moll, is hemmed in socially and who seeks to break out. But the more Clyde tries to break out, the more things close in on him. The crucial image is the first one in the movie where you see Bonnie suffering physical discomfort from being penned in her room. She's looking out a window, and she's got this tension or malaise that has built up inside her. She has a longing to break out, and her escape vehicle appears before her eyes in the form of Clyde.

Q. *Unless I'm mistaken, this opening image of Bonnie works without any words—except perhaps she may be singing or listening to the radio. You know from this image that something has to happen.*

A. Richard Lester's A HARD DAY'S NIGHT could have been just another commercial gimmick to put a popular rock-and-roll group before their howling teenage fans and to make a fortune. But Lester sensed that his real subject was those individual, beautifully distinguished and articulated human beings being put under the pressure of the establishment and the industry to produce, to perform. The whole movie is about the effort of the Beatles to explode and to escape. The most memorable scene is when the Beatles sneak out of the studio away from the control of the TV director. They go to an open lot and, with the camera recording in fast motion, they do all those hijinks—dancing and playing hopscotch. It's a beautiful release.

Q. *A beautiful breakout.*

A. The camera is also breaking out. You can see this in the scene which begins realistically with the camera shooting the Beatles with an older man in the train compartment. Then suddenly the camera is outside of the train, and so is Paul McCartney, just floating along in the air, as it were, beside the train. McCartney looks in, making faces and jeering at the old man. The camera is not tied to its physical, temporal condition. The camera is free.

The major development in the movies after the post-World War II period and Italian Neorealism is the freeing of the camera from the pressures of time and space, which is the freeing of the human eye, the freeing of the human soul to look and to explore and to create. Penn, Lester and Kubrick are masters of this new kind of movie.

One of the first images in Kubrick's 2001: A SPACE ODYSSEY is of a leopard With a gleaming eye—"Tiger, tiger, burning bright…" The most beautiful and impressive achievement in recent film is the end of the movie when the astronaut's spaceship is out of control and begins to approach the speed of light and then breaks out into another dimension of speed. You have an extensive series of images, beginning with galaxies in the form of eyes. The camera eye establishes its own condition and presence through the motif of the eye.

Q. *Why is it often difficult to get students to respond to images instead of searching for an outside theme or meaning?*

A. We live in a word culture. Our school system is verbally oriented. It rewards and promotes those who are verbally talented, and it discriminates against those who are visually talented. English courses, for instance, are required from the first grade through high school; but drawing courses are usually regarded as play. After kindergarten and the first or second grade, drawing courses are optional. Even in college where English courses are still required, drawing or image courses are voluntary.

We're surrounded by sensory images all the time and yet we don't care to look because we're conditioned by a culture that says images don't matter. You recall it was Plato who said that the particular is of little consequence, it is the idea that matters.

Q. *I was trained as an Aristotelean, but perhaps I am a born Platonist. This may be my innate problem when it comes to dealing with movies.*

A. We're immersed in a world of images but we pay little attention except on special occasions—and only when we are forced to pay attention. We don't know how to pay attention because our consciousness, led by a bias against visual images, has trained our minds to attend to other things. What we need to do is to think about the image. What is an image? What are the properties of an image? How does it work?

One of the first things to be perceived about the visual image is that it doesn't denote or signify. It doesn't mean, it just is. The primary and definitive characteristic of the image is that it radiates. The word connotes, directs one line to one object. But the image has multiple facets and radiates in multiple directions.

Q. *In reading poetry we deal with images but these are images conveyed through verbal symbol rather than through direct, sensory contact. In order to appreciate movie images, perhaps we need to consider Shelley's advice in his* Defense of Poetry *and learn to "strip the veil of familiarity" from what we're experiencing as sensory beings.*

A. Yes, and if I may speak in grandiose terms, this is what Western civilization has been trying to do. With the emergence of scientific empiricism, man began to get interested in his vision alone. He has been developing his power of sight ever since Galileo said to the church fathers: "Damn your *a priori* principles—look!" The difficulty of looking is illustrated by the fact that it has taken us three or four centuries to reach the point where we can see what we do.

You frequently hear the phrase, "The movies are the art of our time." What this usually means is that movies have a bigger audience or that more people see movies than read books because movies are more exciting. But those are superficial explanations of what movies are to our time. The movies are not an accident of technology. They are an instrument created by a culture that is under pressure to see clearly and to see accurately. The movies are actually an extension of Western, scientific, empirical man's passion to know the visual world.

The Movies as a Revolutionary Moral Force
Part 1

WILLIAM R. ROBINSON

WE ARE IN THE THROES of a revolution. All the social and political signs agree that this is so. The general tenor of this change asserts that what has been and is, is not good enough. The insistence that the corrupt and exhausted yield to the innocent and fresh is no novelty, however. Ezra Pound sounded the rallying cry of this cause not only for modern poets and poetry but modern life as well early in this century with the slogan "MAKE IT NEW."

Nevertheless, the prevailing assumption among today's youth is that the urge to make it new sprang full blown from their divine heads. And that illusion is lent support— if not exploited—by a steady stream of pronouncements on the meaning of contemporary affairs issuing from professional commentators and self-appointed pundits who invariably talk off the top of events as well as the top of their heads. As always, the sensational newsworthy aspects of contemporary affairs are advertised in the bustling market place as startlingly new historical departures. But the simple fact of the matter is that we live in a society whose dominant tradition is devoted to revolution—or, to be less fashionable and more accurate, to progressive evolution. This dominant tradition was officially granted the status of an Establishment when its sanctified origins were located in that quartet of capitalized heroic events of the late 18th century, the American, French, Industrial, and Romantic Revolutions. But youth is not altogether wrong in its claim that the revolution began with them, nor is the media when it suggests that the present is unique. It is quite true that we are in a distinctly new phase in the revolution of Western civilization that has been underway for at least 200 years now, the phase already familiarly known as the electronic or technological revolution.

What is distinctly new about this latest phase can be readily seen in the difference between industrialism and electronic technology. The former put wheels upon man's hands in order to increase his work efficiency, the latter puts wheels upon his intelligence to increase his intellectual efficiency. The most glorified of the tools designed as extensions of man's intelligence to speed up thought has been, of course, the computer, which is a whiz-bang at data-storing and processing. But the movies, too—"the art of our time," as they have frequently been called, whose career has been co-extensive with the history of the 20th century—they, too, are creations of the technological revolution and vehicles for bearing forward modern man's revolutionary intellectual energy. Their most illustrious ancestor in this respect is the telescope, the instrument with which Galileo challenged the authority of the Catholic Church and thereby fired the first intellectual shot in the revolution, long before its social manifestations in the 18th century. The movies continue this tradition of enhancing man's visual power by putting wheels upon his eyes.

Visually mobilized via movies, modern man has been able to gather great quantities of data about motion and contribute immensely to his knowledge of it. The movies are a complement to the computer in their usefulness for storing and processing information. But in addition to being a technological aid to intelligence, they are also an art form—that is, a tool of the human imagination. As a tool of the human imagination, their province is the creative act and creative possibility: it is, in a word, value. The stories told through them are not merely reflections of the human condition in our time but change in the making, the creative thrust and break-through of the present that is shaping our future. Thus the movies not only enable man to examine more closely the mechanisms of motion and growth but also equip him to peer more profoundly than hitherto into the springs and processes of human action. By putting wheels upon the imagination, the image-making power, they mechanize man's potential for envisaging the act and its ends. In that capacity they become a force for revolution at the same time that they are a product of revolution.

The movies, accordingly, are instruments of greater moral as well as greater intellectual efficiency. That puts them right at the center of the 20th century's intellectual revolution spotted by Nicolai Berdyaev around the turn of the century and described in 1911 in the comment, "The world-crisis of culture, so much talked about, is also a moral crisis, a revolution of moral consciousness…the world will come to a new creative morality of youth."

He made these remarks at the time the movies were becoming an art form. That was not accidental nor is the fact that they have subsequently assumed the burden of carrying out this subtlest dimension of revolution. For the movies are the most powerful visionary instrument at man's disposal today. More than any other gadget of the Electronic Technological Revolution they are helping to overthrow the old morality and replace it with the new.

The revolutionary impact of the movies is readily evident in what is happening to the word-image relationship in them. Take, for example, Ingmar Bergman's *The Hour of the Wolf*, a movie of conservative bent that has this relationship as its primary subject. (It is, incidentally, one of the numerous instances of the sophisticated self-consciousness of today's mature movie art. An art of an era of self-centeredness, movies have always had a penchant for employing themselves as their subject; only earlier, instead of scrutinizing the image, they focused upon the star, their self-image being projected as the story of a rising young actor on the make or some grand old personality whose success embodied the glories of the industry.) *The Hour of the Wolf* is the story of a painter named Johann who is driven to destruction by the powers of darkness. But the actual protagonist of the narrative is his wife, Alma. She directly addresses the audience at the beginning and end of the movie, appealing for sympathetic attention while announcing and carrying out her purpose of relating the truth about her life with her husband. As the film's narrator, she mediates between her audience and her husband, cushioning the force of his images, which came close to overwhelming her, and the images of the story she tells by swathing them in her words. In that way she makes herself the center of visual attention and forces everything in the movie to function as a projection of her consciousness.

She allows that her consciousness provides the scene for the movie's events when she questions, at the end of her story, whether it is possible in love to become the other person. Her ability to see her husband's hallucinations during the course of the film leaves no doubt that the question is rhetorical: she did in fact assume Johann's visioning power. Her husband's passion for images is clearly a dimension of her existence and her story is an attempt to explain the restless, difficult marriage of words and images within her own being.

To explain that relationship, Alma retells the story of man's fall, clearly alluded to by the shots of the tree of knowledge of good and evil and its fruit with which the movie visually opens. This device, intended to serve the same purposes as Alma's words, casts the movie into an established mold and thereby counteracts and restrains Johann's explosive visual energies. But in addition to the forbidden fruit motif of the Biblical version of the fall Bergman also expropriates for his story the primordial Biblical principle that "In the beginning was the Word." This principle governs the overall structure of the film. In its actual beginning a single indistinct voice issues from a black screen, then is followed, behind the credits, by a babel of voices (that seem to be "creating" the sets for the action that follows). Immediately after the voices the opening sequence of images leads up to an individual woman, in a full face close-up, directly addressing the audience while explaining her intentions in relating the narrative. The movie ends on a final close-up, full face shot of Alma completing her explanation, though she asks questions instead of asserting conclusions indicating that she cannot reduce her life to an intellectual certainty. In part Bergman invokes the metaphysical principle enunciated by St. John as the formal law of his creation, which includes Alma. But he also invokes the much older, moral principle, the assumption that what is good for man was prescribed by the Word—by aboriginal ideas in Greek thought or commandments in Judaism.

The word functions as *The Hour of the Wolf*'s source and provides both its truth and its form. (It is so thoroughly the foundation of Alma's life that she has to read Johann's diary—she has to know what he is thinking—in order to be able to understand what is happening to him). But the most important virtue of words for Bergman in *The Hour of the Wolf* is their power to communicate in the sense of "to make common to all what one presently possesses." Alma's words are her means of sharing with her audience what it is possible for human beings to hold in common. Her words can do that because, abstractions, they ignore the unique characteristics of the individual to emphasize the properties shared by the species. For that reason they can serve as a basis for social life. That is to say, her words mediate between men and bind them together in a curable, dependable relationship of rational responsibility. Thus it is within the power of words to forge a community and that community provides a defense against the terrors of the fall into existence and individuality.

But words cannot and do not save Johann from his fall. His original sin was that as a painter he abandoned words for images. Without the straining power of words at his command, he was prey to the demonic energies lurking in the dark recesses of his imagination. But to be an artist and create he had to turn inward—which he even employs words to do in the secret, self-searching he records in his diary—and tap his potent inner sources. Part of this sin is his gratuitous destruction of his innocence in murdering a youth who fishes with him off a large rock. (Within the context of Bergman's extensive Biblical allusions in *The Hour of the Wolf,* that murder is the rock upon which Johann builds his ego-centered church.) The destruction of his innocence only emphasizes the degree to which he is on his own, however. For his original sin radically alienated him from public words and placed him irrevocably beyond being saved by them from his imagistic doom.

His personal sin and fall, on the other hand, results from the loss of his imaginative powers. Through Veronica Vogler, a model whom he had fiercely loved and who had inspired his imagination to attain the supreme aesthetic heights, he had tasted visual honey. But he has lost that love and the image of Beauty it inspired is forever beyond his grasp. His imprudent, excessive efforts in his desperation to regain his creative powers turn loose the dark demons in his head. Those demons people his world with nightmarish grotesques that haunt him into extreme isolation, bitter self-knowledge, and death. All of which come to a climax in his frantic resurrection of Veronica from the dead. That feat turns out to be a hideous mockery of the creative powers. Immediately thereafter, while mad with the futility and horror of his egotistical predicament, Johann's head is picked apart by black birds of prey in a primeval forest where naked power wreaks its effects uninhibitedly.

Within the moral framework of *The Hour of the Wolf* the individuating power of the image is patently evil. The image releasing in Johann an exorbitant and insatiable passion set him out on a course of selfish imaginative indulgence that induced discontent, conflict, and disruption. In submitting to the rule of his monomania, he unhesitatingly abandoned normal social ties—the movie, accordingly, is set on a remote island— and repudiated the marriage bond between Alma and himself. The image can produce these results simply because its properties equip it to mark off formally the solitary and autonomous. It is the device by which things are singled out in perception from one another and from their environment. In contrast to the word, which possesses the virtues of restraint and self-sacrifice, and exemplifies acceptance of limits and place, and therefore is humane and humanizing, the image's encouragement and facilitation of unbridled individuality is baldly vicious.

Bergman openly acknowledged the devastating power of images in an interview where he spoke of what he had learned about man from his work in the movies. "I experience art," he said unflinchingly there, "as being meaningless…art is free, shameless, irresponsible. Man has made himself free, terribly and dizzyingly free. A boundless, insatiable, perpetual regeneration, an unbearable curiosity drives me on, never lets me rest, completely replaces that past hunger for community. Everything is unreal, fantastic, frightening or ridiculous. But it has one great advantage: the artist coexists with every living creature that lives only for its own sake." These statements issue obviously from the point of view of the artist, of Johann, not Alma, of the image rather than the word. In them Bergman candidly confesses that the verbal morality of *The Hour of the Wolf* is an impotent intellectual atavism. He frankly allows that wholly new impulsions and values are abroad today and that a new kind of community is in the making, one in which art and the artist are decisive forces.

Yet in *The Hour of the Wolf* he strenuously reins in with words the revolutionary impact of the medium to which he has chosen to devote his life's work. As an artist, he knows that he is a revolutionary; by vocation he chose to dedicate himself to morally challenging and destroying his given created world in order to transform it into a new creation. And he knows that words can't stop his fall as a creator into existence and individuality. They are powerless except as a drag upon the energy of images. Within the movie that omnipotence is evident in the fact that the man of images and his images provide the generative force that not only begets Alma's pregnancy but also impregnates her mind. Structurally the vital center within the verbal shell of the movie, Johann's imagistic existence and adventures stir up her vital depths, thereby enriching her experience, making her humanly interesting, and giving her a story to tell. He is the source of everything of any consequence that happens, and can happen, to her and in the movie.

The result of Bergman's moral timidity is that Alma's explanation of the marriage of words and images in her life doesn't make sense, nor does their relationship in Bergman's film. His resorting to words as a defense against what he has called "the necessary fears of creation" suspends him absurdly between an acknowledged metaphysical truth and an obsolete morality. While he feels directly the vigorous thrust of images, the old demands of reason for self-sacrifice and social order weigh down his imagination. His pointless resistance amounts to reneging on his artistic responsibility. It amounts to a failure of imagination, an admission of his inability to manage the values inherent in images and of his unwillingness to give himself wholly to the task of forging the new community. The guilt readily evident in his choice of the story of man's fall as his narrative vehicle blocks not only Johann's but, more importantly, his own imaginative freedom.

A less inhibited treatment of the word-image relation can be found in *Alfie*, a British film that indicates by its title a closer focus upon the individual. It allows no bumper of abstraction between the individual and reality, and therefore stacks the cinematic deck less severely against the image.

A playboy of the cool urban world who has enough intellectual sophistication to be bothered by sickness and death, Alfie asks, "What's it all about?" He tries to explain himself directly to the movie audience because, as a man of words, he is anxious to discover—and communicate a rational meaning to life that will secure him against pain and dying. But he fails; his words yield nothing. Quite the contrary, in fact. He gets the shock of his life visually. It occurs when a late middle-aged woman, a sly old adept at living, blithely rejects him for the wilder kicks of a younger, less conventional man. The hard truth he has to behold in this eye opener is that life is cooler than he is and always in charge, and that he is expendable. Unwilling to grow, he is stuck with his debilitating anxiety and his vulnerability in a world of images. He knows no more than that things come and go, that he may win a few but he'll also lose many, and that—as imaged in the final shot of the movie—his is a dog's life. Despite his intelligence, he is a vagabond of the street, without depth, ties, superiority, or safety. He's foot loose but not fancy free.

Security serves as the standard for assessing the relative merits of image and word in *Alfie*. Judged by that standard, images obviously do no good. Cheap, flimsy, and ephemeral, they defeat the heart's desire for dominance and immortality. Nevertheless they are real, and words, though good, are fictions, a nostalgic crutch upon which a frightened man attempts to rest his sentimental dreams. The best they can do is passively try to fend off the attack of images. But the most important point to be made about *Alfie* in comparison to *The Hour of the Wolf* is that the word cannot keep the image in its place. The image unabashedly claims its place in the sun, and its due. Above all, it refuses reconciliation with the word on the word's terms.

His loyalty vied for uncompromisingly by the word and the image, Alfie serves unwittingly as a battleground of forces opposed in eternal enmity. His existence splits into the polarization of head and heart, intellect and imagination. Words are less reliable for him than they are for Alma because he is more existentially exposed. He shares with her the compulsion to intellectualize life, but he has been swept further than she has from the verbal havens by the radical forces of images. The price of her safety is immobilization. She must sit, unable to release outwardly the vital motions astir within her, while Alfie, despite his mental blocks, is on the move in the world. Words are less of a burden on him and less inhibit the movie, which appropriately, is in color. Both the man and the art carry a lighter load of verbal illusions than Alma and Bergman. As a result defenseless Alfie is caught in no-man's land on the revolutionary frontier. He is not free, however, to move with affirmative exuberance.

Both *The Hour of the Wolf* and *Alfie* attempt to curb the revolutionary impact of the image by countering it with words and end up as negating and self-abnegating movies and thereby exemplify the old morality. They would take the movement out of movies. Fearful of the image's potency, they will allow it to be only if it submits to being filtered through the word. *2001: A Space Odyssey*, a cosmic comedy and creation story, confidently lets the revolution of the image happen and is therefore able to surpass both of them as an agent of the moral revolution.

In this movie's three-part structure Parts I and II consist of images totally free of words, while the second section, from the trip to Clavius to HAL's disconnection, is a talkie. There, people and even machines are singled out by names and are in competition with each other. Contrasts abound in such pairings as man against machine, rough woolen clothes against a streamlined metallic and plastic background. Man solves problems by discussion and exercises control over his environment through knowledge of cause and effect. Change occurs by inference and will. That is, instead of binding together in a stable community, talk polarizes into opposites and serves as an instrument of aggression. Thus, while they facilitate cooperation, words also segregate, and that segregation begets friction. That friction comes to its fruition when the apparently flawless computer HAL, endowed not only with man's intelligence but also the lust for power inherent in it, jealously demands absolute control of the space ship and becomes adamantly intolerant and coldly murderous. A creature of pure reason whose existence lies totally in words and thought processes degenerates into irrationality. And in doing so he makes manifest the evil potential of words.

So despite their contribution to man's emergence from the anthropoid condition of Part I, words result eventually in more harm than good. But their evil effects are short-circuited. The images of Part I and III that suspend them in a visual ambience see to it that the words contribute to purposes larger than their own. After HAL's mind has been blown, and abetted by the cobalt slab, an inexplicable image from nowhere and vibrantly active within itself, the astronaut is abruptly launched into a journey beyond words and through a creative transformation in which he dies out of his old self and is born into a greater new life. That process occurs via a montage of surrealistic images in which, beginning with galaxies, the cosmos begets in appropriate stages a super-human embryo. From the movie's opening scenes, where the fiery eye of the leopard gleams in predatory fury, the eye, the source of images and the appreciator of their delights, turns out to be potent vessel of good. That eye purifies itself in two stages, first of bestiality, then in Part III, of rationality—the eye of reason yielding hegemony to the creative eye—and then triumphantly recreates its life in the embryo whose sparkling eye looks afresh upon a vast, open new world. No foreign obstacle prohibits its expansion; it grows healthfully in accordance with its inner potential.

The eye's purification consists of a progress through three kinds of motion. Random motion excited by fear, a pressure from without, within space of fixed boundaries is followed by deliberate, controlled motion from left to right (it's going someplace in a consistent specific direction), with everything being in motion and all relations exteriorized and relativized, and eventuates in inner organic motions, transformative energy that exfoliates from the vital center. As these motions supercede one another, their speed accelerates, and as the acceleration increases, the living creature undergoes a change in which, first, he acquires a name and personality, then his ego is annihilated, and finally the creature bolts through a series of instantaneous metamorphoses. In other words, the pre-personal, aroused, aspired to the personal; the personal worked toward self-transcendence or death, then the impersonal elected to become particularized. In the life spiral enacted in the movie, the image approaches and reaches the speed of light, then the light reverses the process and suffers its energy to be incarnated in an individual form.

What began rather simply as an image culminates in the most intricate - and sophisticated of dynamic interrelationships. This transformation into greater life occurs, as already noted, through the agency of a charged black cobalt slab, a kind of casket that evokes greater effort, including murder, as if in response to the challenge of death. Simple physical motion is excited by the slab to a pitch where it shifts into intellectual motion, which in turn the slab excites to an even higher pitch where the imagination is ignited. And when the imagination has accelerated to its optimum speed, when the three stage rocket of human consciousness has realized its full potential for movement, all possible motions inside as well as outside the embryonic sac are harmoniously coordinated. A distillation of the cosmic essence, the living organism in the end moves confidently and gracefully in a moving universe, combining in its motion internal and external activity, the personal and the impersonal powers, in a mutually complementary enhancement.

It is this refined, free, organic mobility that sets *2001* apart morally from *The Hour of the Wolf* and *Alfie*. All three movies acknowledge that the image is not an "impression," a static chunk of matter that registers its grey mass upon the retina as the sensational philosophers and the behaviorists claimed, but a charged particle, electric and electrifying. In short, all agree on the given condition of human existence. They differ in how they morally confront that condition and what benefit, as a consequence of their moral attitude, they derive from it. In the moving medium, their success depends not upon doctrinal correctness, a verbal value, but results—upon what they get done. Completeness of story, if you will, or completeness of act is the inherent test they perforce measure themselves by and that we are forced to bring to them and apply to ourselves.

Specifically, the moral question each faces is whether to negate or affirm the image's potency. Bergman's version of the image-word relationship, emphasizing verbal restraint over the urge of the image to move—it comes to you, presenting itself unabashedly—and the movie medium's commitment to motion, favors stop-action. Alma, by sitting herself down to explain in words Johann's sin of succumbing to the temptations of the image to rival God as a creator, Alma keeps Johann's imagination grounded. Her thick, plain, dull, "physical" appearance and Bergman's shooting in black and white—an abstraction of the intellect since we see the living world in color—imposes heaviness and darkness upon the image's electric potential. In these ways, among others, *The Hour of the Wolf* prohibits the image from releasing its charge. Its negation grants dominance to substance, shadow and understanding; and allows it to give preference to guilt, identity, and resignation—to the world, oneself, and the community as they are—over the completion of the act. Like confused Alfie, who would put a stop to change so that he might frustrate aging and death, Bergman prefers not to assume the existential moral burden of a commitment to action. The result is that both movies check growth and as a consequence their protagonists do not grow and they get nowhere.

The creation denied Johann and the impotent anxiousness of Alfie are eluded in *2001* by the turn of the moral tables previously noted. It boldly lets the light shine through. As an aesthetically serious science-fiction in which the knowing faculty serves the fictional one—the reverse of popular science-fiction—it lends itself unreservedly to a transubstantial change for the better. Vertical transcendence—the old ascension into heaven or ideas—is not allowed as a possibility even in *The Hour of the Wolf* and *Alfie*, but only *2001*, while accepting, like them, the condition of being world bound, envisages horizontal grace and salvation. Its affirmative acceptance of vital aspiration and activity as good allows the individual to become one with the light and puts all the lights, inner and outer, together in a unity of free action. That generosity permits the camera eye to generalize itself confidently and exuberantly. Through animal eyes, space ships shaped like eyes, a computer eye, and eye-like cosmic forms, it celebrates a round, circular, concentric, cyclic universe that emerges from a vital center and expands radiantly outward like a blossom. By thus letting the eye and image have their way, *2001*, its fancy free, discharges the potential of images and gets the good out of them.

Which of the three movies is right morally? As art the movies cannot be either true or false. Their role consists not of making our decisions for us but of illuminating the possibility of good. They vivify and clarify, and if they persuade, it is by example, not precept. Nevertheless, the course of modern Western History has witnessed the switch from the values of the word to those of the image traced through these three films. Historically, the eye has in fact supplanted the voice as the arbiter of truth, beauty, and goodness. Modern history has undergone a revolution in which what Bergman placed in a subordinate position and judged adversely or left implicit has been put down by what Stanley Kubrick in *2001* allowed to be explicit and dominant. But collectively, despite superficial moral differences, these three movies reveal the potency of the image to be the first fact of life in our time, the reality, or rather the power, with which every man, like the director, must come to terms morally. Beginning with Giotto and Galileo the image has irrepressibly and persistently been a subversive force undermining the foundations of doctrinal orthodoxies and the intellectual culture dependent upon them. The three movies testify, in other words, to the vigor and vitality of the image as a medium, and as movies they cannot help but release the forces stored up in their medium.

In releasing that force they all exemplify, regardless of Bergman's conservative strategies, what Kubrick claimed for *2001* and so masterfully rendered in it when he said of this movie that it is "basically a visual, nonverbal experience. It avoids intellectual verbalization and reaches the viewer's subconscious in a way that is essentially poetic and philosophic. The film thus becomes a subjective experience which hits the viewer at an inner level of consciousness…without the traditional reliance on words. It succeeds in short-circuiting the rigid cultural blocks that shackle our consciousness to narrowly limited areas of emotional comprehension." Though somewhat cautiously phrased, Kubrick sees quite clearly that *2001* in particular, and movies in general, entail a whole new way of knowing and being. (Which, incidentally, Bergman concurred with in his remark, one of numerous to the same effect, that a movie "plays directly on our feelings without touching our minds"; thus "by using film we can bring in previously unknown worlds, realities beyond reality.")

What Kubrick has seen, less timidly stated, is that because of their properties, the movies, in the Elizabethan sense, "move" their viewers toward a certain kind of virtue as man's good. Specifically, they move us to a knowledge of life—the Europeans call it existence—as individuated, contingent, pluralistic, equalitarian, relativistic, emmanentistic, dynamic, creative, pragmatic, unitive, and comic—among other things. This cryptic list is a shorthand method for identifying the values that inevitably emerge from the kind of creation a movie is. An even more succinct manner of making that identification is to note that by its form—only the concrete, for instance, can be photographed—a movie necessarily favors the exalted individual, the separate entity raised to the supreme vividness of which life is capable. At their best the movies celebrate the divine during its moment of manifestation, loving Christ in and for his finite human particularity, not his transcendent origins and promises. And the vocation of the movies is precisely that—to flesh out to the fullest extent in art the at present dimly sensed possibilities inherent in the image. Like the three discussed here, every movie unavoidably displays the image in its newness and assertiveness, its presentness and vitality. It affirms by existing the truth that

> At worst, one is in motion; and at best,
> Reaching no absolute in which to rest,
> One is always nearer by not keeping still.
> (Thom Gunn, "On the Move")

But even beyond that truth each movie is bound as a narrative to tell, not a true thought, but a true action. Its burden is to show in its action where the action is. And when it does that, it not only directs the eye to behold what is happening but encourages us to value action. It displays, regardless of the director's intentions, the power of a self-contained form for growth, creativity, and realization.

As a moral educator, the movies do not teach us that we live in the age of the image—any number of sociological and philosophical studies will make that evident if everyday affairs don't—but what the moral possibilities of imagistic man are. They charge and direct our action, thereby showing us how to act and what to act for. Products of the age of the image, their special assignment as art is to urge us to espouse as man's good the will to go on going on, to remain eternally young and continually grow, to expand, create, and realize, to open up and move out in adventure and joy on the frontier of life. There is no more truly revolutionary force abroad today than their call to action, their urging that we abandon the exhausted morality of the word and allow ourselves, as the movies are doing, to be moved by the moral potencies of the image. Actually, we have always known the list of values previously cited to be the properties of life and our culture long ago was moved to embrace these values as a good. The difference the movies make is that they equip our consciences with the models we needed in order to accept openly and fully temporal earthly growth, conversion and creation as the inciting and guiding light of our lives. With the image's revolutionary force unharnessed in them, they are morally preparing us and our culture to let our lives be, free of arbitrarily and falsely imposed conditions. Accordingly, it is to them we must go with our intelligences alert and our imaginations active if we are to direct sanely the magnificent energies exploding in and about us today.

The Movies as a Revolutionary Moral Force
Part II

WILLIAM R. ROBINSON

Like it or not, the image, not the word, sets the moral pace today. There is no way to deny its value. Its indelible presence in the foreground of our public affairs forces us to measure our lives by its virtues And when that is the case the moral impact of the movies obviously far exceeds the moral impact attributed to them by authorized and would-be censors. Stirring up dangerous unconventional erotic passions and abetting to crime via images of violence, even should the movies be guilty of them, rank at best as superficial moral effects. Movie censorship aimed at curbing pornography and violence is simply misformed and futile. The only possible way censorship can hold the moral status quo against movies is to ban them entirely.

But, then, it would have to ban TV and TV commercials, too. For there as well as in the movies the image has infiltrated middle-class morality, which traditionally has rested upon account book, contract, and law, all verbal instruments for insuring a regulated order. For example, not long ago the pictorial aspect of advertisement, in both practice and theory, was considered to be no more than an eye-catching adjunct to the verbal pitch that did, supposedly, the hard selling. The image attracted attention then the words persuaded the mind, which, in turn, compelled the will to buy. Today, on the other hand, the visual prevails over the verbal in advertising. It not only catches the eye but, by-passing the intellect, directly influences the will, to the extent that the intellect now tags along behind, docilely lending its talents to promoting the virtues of the image. The degree to which the verbal component has surrendered to the visual aspect stands out blatantly in such sales pitches as Pepsi's "generation" and its accompanying refrain, "You've got a lot to live"; Schlitz's "You only go round once. You've got to grab for all the gusto you can"; Dodge's "rebellion," "fever," and "future"; and Equitable Insurance's "There's nobody else like you." Too irrepressibly active to submit passively to Madison Avenue exploitation, the image has softly sold itself— its virtues of generation, youth, action, excitement, vividness. intensity, possibility, and uniqueness—to the solid citizens, proving its irresistible moral power beyond doubt in this most practical of ways.

Of course, nobody is about to ban TV and TV commercials. Even that would do no good, however. As the above cited commercials suggest, the image has so pervasively and subtly infiltrated our lives that its revolution cannot possibly be stopped now. The extent to which its revolution has advanced in undermining our cherished values can be readily seen in the movies in what is happening there to character. Although the somewhat esoteric image-word relation serves as an overt subject in a surprising number of the better movies of the last two decades, that subject can be "relevant" only for those viewers whose intellectual inner sanctum has been penetrated morally by the moving image. For most viewers the movies remain a dramatic encounter, that is, a confrontation of character with character. This is because they live amid and for social appearances. They draw their life's blood in movies, as they do in everyday affairs, from the interaction between themselves and others as conventional public personalities. Such a perception and response to movies carries inherent within it a resistance to change in the outer form of man or in the external relations between men. When that resistance receives sufficient provocation to blossom into anxiety, any hint of human evolution in the movies gets virulently attacked in the name of character for departing from the moral status quo. Critics as well as ordinary movie goers indulge liberally in such a venting of their moral indignation. The latter, in fact, tend to be the more virulent of the two, not only because of their greater articulateness, but because they are more highly developed characters and so have more at stake in the preservation of character.

Now "character" specifies exactly what the term means etymologically, "an engraved mark or brand." It designates the rigid properties that a man bears indelibly, like the mark of Cain, throughout his existence. That means that character is that part of him that has an enduring indentifiability, a reliable stability, and predictability. For this reason character is that part of him that can be named. And since it can be named, it dwells in names—in titles or functions and roles—and thrives on words—in beliefs and ideologies, or intellectual stances and philosophical positions. For this reason it achieves its finest flowering in the intellectual, the sort of thinking man who has been the hero of the modern European novel and the rational ideal of modern Western civilization. This three-dimensional man of perspective, depth, substance, and contrary forces uses his intelligence, like a navigator uses geometrical coordinates, to locate himself at a fixed point in existence. He intends to know at all times who he is and where he is. That knowledge allows him to feel that he is rational master over the forces of change. Character, as the intellectual exemplifies, provides just such an absolute in man.

In sum, character is an abstraction, an inorganic fixation resulting from the conceptualizing powers of man's intelligence; it is a man's idea of himself. As such it is his base of intellectually comforting certainty in the flux of all that changes in and between man. The abstractness of character makes it a comfort to the community as well as the individual, it might be further noted. For on the social level the continuous recognizability and perpetual dependability of character provides an external standard by which others can know whether anything a man does is "in character" or consistent with his permanently restrictive personality limitations. By so imposing its limits upon individual growth character is ideally equipped to serve as the pillar of social order. Society depends upon its regularity to such an extent, in fact, that character readily becomes a sacred cow. It is as such a conservative bastion that it is defended by social artists and critics. Using it as a moral citadel, they seek to exert pressure upon art and the artist to shore up the social order rather than promote such values as novelty, freshness, expansion, adventure, and possibility.

Now character is quite obviously a possibility in human experience. It is one of the infinite values made available to man in the universe's moral cornucopia. It was selected for preferred attention by the ancient Greeks and raised to the status of an honorable social institution in Western civilization beginning in the Italian Renaissance. English civilization has specialized in its cultivation. At one time character was a historical innovation in human culture, a genuine breakthrough in human individualism, and so a fresh creative force endowing life with vision and zest. It enabled man to lift himself out of the slough of unself-consciousness, release his rational powers, and shape himself into a uniquely intellectual creature capable of standing above nature in his towers of thought and his self-created civilizations.

But by the time of the first movies, character was a hallowed moral preserve, enthroned and jealously guarded over several centuries by humanism—or, to be exact, we must say today, the old humanism. Its defense in movie criticism stems, therefore, from habit. Its being an atavism does not, however, invalidate the intuitive sense underlying the defense of character, that

the movies are radically altering the outer form of man and the external relations between men. Indeed, they are—and they inevitably will, since the
attritional forces they exert on character inhere in the medium—and they are
bringing about this phase of their revolution through their "image of man."
This phenomenon, so frequently and innocuously remarked upon in psychological, sociological, and philosophical literature that it seems a harmless
enough replacement for "soul," "human nature," and "self," in actuality marks
a thoroughly new departure in man's sense of himself.

The decline and fall of character can be readily seen in the three movies
discussed in Part I. Alma, of Bergman's *The Hour of the Wolf*, generously
inserting her voice between her audience and the image of man, protects the
viewer from being directly challenged by the image of man. Her stable, comforting, martyr-prone character standing between the viewer and Johann allows the viewer to observe Johann's horrifying adventures in the dark from
behind the safe walls of his conventional character. The protagonist of *Alfie*
lets the viewer off the hook by having such a weak character and being so
pathetically half-hearted an image of man that he can take comfort in the
smug conviction that Alfie deserves his fate because of his personal weaknesses. *2001*, on the other hand, undoubtedly leaves most viewers humanly
untouched because it offers no continuous character in whom the viewer can
get sympathetically interested or with whom he can identify. Sympathy or
empathy are decidedly discouraged by *2001* in favor of what appears to be an
abstract, impersonalized fantasy space adventure. The movie's principal action does not lie, however, in its account of the evolution of *homo sapien* or of
scientific technological prospects. It lies, instead, in its faithful rendering of
an individual's life. This individual, and the hero of the movie, happens to be
an eye; it is this eye that adventures forth to undergo metamorphoses and
reincarnations. *2001*, as a consequence, confronts its viewers with the most
serious of challenges to their idea of themselves by quietly annihilating character or the ego and replacing it with the image of man—with, indeed, man
the imager, a creature who is an eye, whose essential feature is his visual and
envisioning power.

What appears at first to be a narrative shortcoming in *2001* is a stroke of
genius. Character is simply irrelevant in *2001*, the heroic venture in its modern form. For in it, via the vehicle of the eye, the imagination goes forth
beyond the walls of reason to confront the great darkness, there in a personal
interaction with the impersonal to win the new light. The eye can perform
that feat only if it is mobile enough to leave behind restrictive old modes and
go it all the way on its own. And that is decidedly what is imaged in the very

form of Kubrick's movie, a purely visual space adventure in which the moving eye organically abstracts itself from normal earthly circumstances. That abstraction disemburdens its action and human consciousness of the debilitating weight of character and expands them to where the possibilities for regeneration and greater life latent in man can be embraced.

The man of character undoubtedly misses Kubrick's deft stroke of character assassination because without a character with which to identify himself he is at a loss regarding what humanly to make of the events in *2001*. What transpires in *2001* passes him by as fanciful speculation. Michelangelo Antonioni's broader stroke of character assassination in *L'Avventura* cannot be readily missed. And it hasn't been missed. Ever since the film's premiere ten years ago a controversy has continued to boil over whether the protagonists of the movie, Claudia and Sandro, are real people —that is, characters—or "abstractions."

At first *L'Avventura* brought joy to literary hearts. It was applauded, for instance, as "the best new novel of the past few years." Dwight Macdonald, following suit, saw fit to praise Antonioni because "he can explore character with novelistic subtlety. His people are related to each other in scenes which are not determined by the necessities of advancing the story—the Hollywood plot line—but rather by the author's search for cinematic expression of their human essence." But when Antonioni's "relentless character study," as another critic phrased it, was closely scrutinized, lo and behold, no character lurked behind Antontoni's cinematic masks. On second thought, Macdonald, applying one of the five "guidelines" he judges movies by— "Are the characters consistent, and in fact are there characters at all?"—to the performance of Monica Vitti in *L'Eclipse* and also *L'Avventura* found that she is "inexpressive—clumsy in motion and blank in repose. Everything is vague about her." He concluded that Antonioni was guilty "of a defect of sensibility or craft." He should have said, in the light of Antonioni's enthusiastic assertion that "Monica Vitti is extraordinarily expressive…[she] has an extremely expressive face," that Antonioni is a complete visual dolt. But the sophisticated artistry of *L'Avventura* and its haunting cinematic emanations immediately belie that kind of nonsense.

Monica Vitti and her face obviously "express" what matters for Antonioni. He knows what he is doing. Macdonald's complaint, made under the disguise of knocking an actress' professional ability, is simply a red-herring. He compulsively introduces a criterion indigenous to the dramatic theatre to judge cinematic art. In movie making actors are cattle, Hitchcock let it be known in his pungent way some time back. The director obviously bears full responsibility for managing them along with every other detail of his *mise-en-scene*. Macdonald and Antonioni actually differ over what is "expressed" in the latter's movies, that is, over what Antonioni reveals to be the "human essence."

Characters in the sense of dramatic personae are unquestionably present in *L'Avventura*. The human forms in the movie have names, though the major characters have only first names—which is a matter of no little consequence, since this kind of name sets them apart from the historical and social restrictions a family imposes. And they remain continuously identifiable as "physical" forms throughout the movie. The one possible exception is Anna's disappearance: but her physical disappearance presents no problem at all when viewed one step back from the characters; from the perspective of the stream of events in which the characters participate, she simply dissolves into Claudia and Sandro, possessing their spirits and driving them to reenact what she has gone through on an intellectual level on the next higher moral plane. On the other hand, it is equally true that the movie is abstract or unrealistic and that Claudia and Sandro—well, they're not abstract or abstractions, because they are literally concrete images, but they undergo a kind of abstraction. They along with everyone and everything else become increasingly abstracted away from being realistic human beings or characters as the movie progresses. A major event of the film is, in fact, the abstractive process working itself out. In effect, Anna, intellectually awakened, thinks herself out of existence, and Claudia and Sandro, under Anna's influence, forgetting their loyalties and their grief, proceed via such abstractive agencies as machines, a primeval island, and an abandoned town to a final mind-blowing illumination.

That illumination appears for them in the image of Gloria Perkins, an American whose name suggests vitality and joy, who writes in trances—mental excitement beyond character—and who, most significantly of all, is interested in a movie career. This interest in the movies identifies Gloria as the cinematic center of Antonioni's art; it equates what she is and does with Antonioni's urge to make it in the movies. The human image of his art, through her he examines and assesses the intentions of his own creative power. That power unabashedly evinces itself when early in the movie Gloria performs the wondrous feat of inducing chaos in a large city. By unashamedly exploiting her skin for personal acclaim and fortune, she produces panic in the streets by "turning on" the male population of an entire community. Gloria's powers for stirring up the vital passions of others parallel those of Anna, but Gloria doesn't suffer, like Anna does, from being of two minds, one that wants to be alone for metaphysical pursuits and another that wants to be bound in affection to another human being. She does things and she wants things to happen to her. She looks to her future possibilities, not to already established social bonds, and her self-promotional venture issues solely from herself. As well as an inciting force, she is a self-caused phenomenon; she overflows with vital exuberance. Out of her own bountiful energy, she acts to invent her image, inviting the world to behold and admire her splendid existence at the same time that the world thereby participates in its invention and benefits from her image. And it is crucial that the excitement she induces is sexual, both in the town and in Sandro, for sexual energy, the primal urge of life to perpetuate and celebrate itself, springs from an aboriginal source antecedent to character, identities, social bonds, fidelity, etc.

Just before they behold the image of Gloria, Claudia and Sandro are charged with life in just the way Gloria is, which they reveal in mocking and laughing at the automatous behavior of a bell boy. Claudia beholds in Gloria, then, the image of her own vital powers, the current of life running strong in her and sweeping aside the conventional obstacles in its way to going on going on. She sees that life's revolutionary power to transform itself continuously constitutes the "essence" of her existence. The price of that new insight into herself is the loss of her character. It is this loss that she and Sandro weep for as the movie slowly closes without a word. Reduced to images and touch, they grieve for the demise of the last basis in principle for a reliable social bond between humans. Each having lived only for themselves and therefore having only themselves, they participate in the death of an institution within themselves and for their world. Thereby Gloria's image initiates them into the new community Bergman spoke of in which "the artist coexists with every living creature that lives only for its own sake."

The image of Gloria Perkins shocks Claudia and Sandro into visual self-recognition. But it also very explicitly establishes that *L'Avventura* is a movie about the birth of the image of man. With Gloria's image clearly in focus, the viewer cannot miss the obvious aesthetic fact that Antonioni's movie shows him "characterless" man taking shape before his eyes. For Antonioni's movie creates the new man at the same time that it narrates his creation. Antonioni claimed as much himself when he commented in reply to a question about what is happening in *L'Avventura*, that "today a new man is being born, fraught with all the fears and terrors and stammerings that are associated with a period of gestation…this new man…burdened with a heavy baggage of emotional traits which cannot exactly be called old and outmoded but rather unsuited and inadequate…reacts, he loves, he hates, he suffers under they sway of moral forces and myths, which today, when we have reached the moon, should not be the same as those that prevailed at the time of Homer, but nevertheless are. The present moral standards we live by…are old and obsolete. And we all know they are, yet we honor them. Why?"

Antonioni's statement commits him to assist in the birth of the new man, and his choice of the movies as a medium testifies to his further admission that it must be achieved by means of the image. That is, in fact, how Claudia grows in *L'Avventura*. Her move out of the doldrums of her character starts in the art gallery she visits near the beginning of the movie where her indifference to the paintings and such remarks on them by surrounding spectators, as "Very derivative"; "Too much canvas and nothing happens. Nothing at all"; and "He's got a long way to go" define her state. Not long after that she watches a magazine, that is, words, being swept overboard into the perpetually active sea.

Claudia's visual awakening gets overtly underway when Anna's disappearance forces her visually to search the primeval island. Images further demonstrate their exciting effect when the nude paintings of Goffredo sexually arouse Guilia and she exclaims to Claudia, "Tell him [her husband] my heart is beating very fast, and that is all that matters to me now." And that is all that matters later to Claudia in the field outside the abandoned town and afterwards until the discovery of Gloria Perkins. Goffredo himself injects an acute observation about what is at stake in Claudia having her eyes opened—and the predominance of women in the movie—with his comment, "It is strange how women enjoy displaying themselves. It seems to come quite naturally to them." He might have added, "It is strange how men are excited by and appreciate—as Sandro does—their display of their image." After that scene, in which she remains an aloof observer, Claudia discovers her image in mirrors, dances and clowns joyously before them, and enjoys their exhilarating release of the protean alterability of her form that a donned wig exemplifies. Correspondingly, as she more and more attends to the image, and especially her own, emotions run freer in her, her body increases in agility, and her social mobility expands. When, finally, the image of Gloria Perkins rises from the well of the dark couch to confront her with the full and naked imagistic truth about what has been growing and emerging from within herself, her desire to have clear ideas is consummated, but ironically: the image of her existence, not an idea, stares her brazenly in the face.

Claudia sees the image of man, and when she beholds it, she is the image of man. When she and Sandro see the new creatures that they have become, they are horrified. Their unsponsored individuality, the inevitable condition of their being images, is morally intolerable. Turning their eyes away from their image in panic, they flee, and in tearful blindness, after the ancient model of Oedipus, they give themselves over to the spiritual agony they then suffer. Their reaction makes no sense, however, It can arise only from the old self, the character they have obviously outgrown. Maybe they can be excused for the confusion George Bernard Shaw speaks of in the line, "You have learnt something. That always feels at first as if you had lost something." But very decidedly their reaction is an emotional atavism, and since it is out of "character" for Claudia and Sandro, that emotional atavism has to be in Antonioni.

Antonioni's statement about the birth of the new man and what is blocking that birth turns out to be a personal confession. He was describing a tension within his own imagination that he could not resolve. He has admitted further to that failure in subsequent remarks about changes he would make toward the end of *L'Avventura* were he making the movie now. But the hard evidence of his failure, and no other need be called upon, exists in the last shot of the movie, a wide screen divided equally in half between a misty Mt. Etna standing lofty and white in the distant left background and a grey stone wall, a human edifice and barrier, in the right foreground. Claudia and Sandro face this scene at middle-distance from the camera, their existence, as imaged by the scene, bifurcated and immobilized, Antonioni pulls back from Claudia and Sandro, refusing to look them in the eye, as it were. Instead, he looks away at the scene. As a result, the new man is not born; Antonioni fails to imagine him into existence. Instead, he lapsed into sentimentality: he let emotion prevail over passion.

Claudia's abhorrence at the image of herself reflects Antonioni's inability to look unflinchingly at the image of man, He flinches because, finally, he distrusts the image. That distrust blatantly obtrudes itself in the emotional necessity of his imagination to blacken Gloria Perkins. She is a disruptive and destructive force, to be sure, but by putting the pall of death over her, his imagination rejects its own creative thrust. Divided against itself, his imagination cannot carry through on its own commitment. It ends, consequently, as the last shot reveals, stopped dead. Neither his people nor his art have opened up or are on the move. They have arrived at an end, not a beginning

If all Claudia and Sandro had experienced or Antonioni was able to imagine in *L'Avventura* was the death of character, there would be plenty for them, and us, to weep for. But up to the point where Claudia beholds the image of herself in Gloria, no matter how sharply Antonioni shies away from it after that, he did see the new man and did faithfully create the image of man. As a consequence, *L'Avventura* does not simply record the loss of the old man.

With the demise of character, another human option arises. Sandro tells us what it is when he says, "When I was a boy…I saw myself living in a rented room somewhere…a genius. As for being a genius. I never got into the habit. What do you think?" The desire to be a genius—in the root meaning of the word, a "spirit of generation and birth"—had been Sandro's guiding aspiration from early in his life, before he sold out for a comfortable position. Do what he might to betray it, it would not be denied. Claudia's refusal to assent to Sandro's self-deprecation acknowledges Sandro's genius in making a new woman of her as well as a new man of himself. After all, it was his genius that overcame her resistance to his advances and freed her for their rapturous love-making in the field outside the abandoned town and the subsequent joy. True, his genius depended upon Anna to activate it, but once aroused, it is life's chosen vehicle for bearing forward life's urge to create. And that is precisely the virtue of the genius. His essential feat is to act, not to think, and he acts creatively. An artist by vocation, Sandro had so acted in creating Claudia but he could not recognize and allow that he had. Those old habits of emotion and conscience Antonioni spoke of divorced his intellect from his imagination. Still, Sandro awakened Claudia's genius and both exercised their geniuses to liberate themselves from their given human condition and their roles within it.

Their liberation was made possible by the abstractive process that the image activated in them. Genius' talent for abstraction asserts itself, among other ways, in Claudia's breaking the chains of the past. Her character puts her under pressure to refuse birth to the new life welling up in her by insisting that she remember her loyalty to Anna, who, in effect, was dead and gone. To grow, she had to learn to forget. She observes the effects of her genius in this respect when she notes, "Everything's becoming so simple— I'm even depriving myself of pain." When Patrizia retorts, "There's no need to be melodramatic," Claudia concludes, "You're right. Why should I cry? I'm tired of being like this." Hand in hand with her gathering excitement and mobility go this simplification she speaks of here.

In simplifying her existence Claudia performs the genius' feat of sloughing off the intellectual and moral baggage that would keep anything from happening in her. When she lightens her psychic load, she sloughs off the entire onus of traditional culture, not just pain. For in depriving herself of pain and refusing to cry she repudiates the old humanistic claim that her humanity resides in suffering. Implicit in that repudiation is the further implication that she rejects the tragic sense of life and, beyond that, the notion that a valid human identity must be rooted in sin or guilt—that is, moral memory. By means of these jettisonings, she throws out as obsolete and dead, also, all the attendant moral claims that order and family and patriarch or God the father are necessary to save life from its inherent evil, and that there is no compassion, negotiation, compromise, communication, or liberty unless individual lives and society are founded upon man's indelible depravity, upon his limitations, rather than his possibilities. Thereby Claudia illustrates the capacity of genius to abstract vital energy from its encumbering circumstances, enabling it to let go and go on. Casting off all but one last remnant of the past, the fragment from which she weeps and pities at the end, she has by and large abstracted herself from her conventional entanglements.

But while Claudia and Sandro are undergoing abstraction from themselves leading up to their final knowledge, the culminating intellectual abstraction which allows them stand outside the husks of their old selves and look back, they paradoxically become more highly individuated persons. Indeed. in the primary action narrated in *L'Avventura* they quite explicitly are singled out as individuals from their environment and the group until they stand radically alone. Though he backed off eventually from the consequences of his own ingeniously imagined structure, Antonioni did keep the abstractive process contained within the individuating one up to the reaction of Claudia and Sandro in the moment of illumination. To that point he did direct his camera and action undistractedly toward the individual and the abstractive and individuating processes in a vitally enhancing relationship within the one concrete consciousness and person of Sattdro.

The abstractive process, as exemplified by Anna's dualistic penchant, equips man to grow by envisioning more than what he is at any given moment. But in envisaging and then desiring something better than she at present is, Anna induces a dissociation within herself and between herself and her world. This predicament created for herself by Anna opposes opposites in such a way that one pole has to be renounced in order for her to embrace the other one. Finally, she must abandon the world entirely for an impossible abstraction. By containing the abstractive power within the individuating one, Antonioni was able to imagine a man who, besides being the consummate abstractor, is also the supreme individual, the most empowered of solitary agencies dedicated to begetting the best of possible individuals. His impulsions are integrative, to fuse together in himself and between himself and his world what Anna had set apart. He seeks to grow continuously, to ever expand and enhance life, and he coordinates all his faculties. including his intelligence, toward performing life's quintessential task of creating greater life. A man of life, he takes on the challenge of putting all the vital powers together in an organically coherent, workable individual, and succeeds.

Such a man is Sandro, creator, in effect, of Claudia, an exuberantly awakened human individual free of family, roles, and past. Underneath his coldness, expressionlessness. and indifference—indeed because of them, that is because he acts out of passion not emotion—for all his remoteness and unlovability, Antonioni's genius is a creator and thereby man's savior, his pilot on the treacherous frontiers of consciousness and human realization. And such a man, too, is Antontoni. For in *L'Avventura* up to the illumination scene he coolly, expressionlessly, and indifferently gave himself over to his creative passion and rendered ingenuously its revolutionary thrust in an adroitly accomplished work of art that saves man from the old morality. Antonioni brings off his remarkable creation because, until after the illumination scene, he never lets the image of man escape from his sight. Like Claudia, he gives his attention to images and allows his story and man to grow by means of them. As a consequence. Antonioni's "world" is simply the image universalized. And his new concrete man is the image humanly incarnated: his genius extends, magnifies, and realizes the potentialities of the image.

Because of his fidelity to the image Antonioni was able to see, before he looked away from Claudia and Sandro, that genius combines in one consciousness that abstractive process and exalted individuality. As the most specific of agents with the largest of perspectives, his abnormal scope equips him, as it does Sandro and Claudia, to burst his character and range outside the normal boundaries of life's conventionally fenced in regions at both ends. For genius, he saw, is neither a mystic nor a sensualist, a passivist or an activist, cool or hot, empty or full. He does not discriminate against anything in life by taking a doctrinaire intellectual stand favoring one facet of it. That would be to fix himself to a dead abstraction and stop his growth. Nor does he splay himself out helplessly upon the rack of human existence, as Anna does, when expanded to encompass its full reach. He nimbly spans its furthest extremes. Though he excels at moments of crisis when adventuresomeness is called for, he always keeps in touch with both poles of his existence. With this distinctive reach, he can operate anywhere, at any phase, in the living process. Nothing in life is alien to him, so he can perform all the living acts, and, above all, the complete living act. Accordingly, Sandro and his creation, Claudia, inheritors but also refiners of Anna's penchant for abstraction while serving as bearers of the individuating power, embody the total living process as a dynamic unity. Impelled by life's inherent drive to manifest itself in individuals, they are the key individuals in a chain of individuation. They exemplify life's particularizing powers and tendency and so are one within themselves and within their world.

Like the new universe of relativity, the new man, ranging in consciousness to the 10th power in both directions from himself, is the broadest, most complex and subtle, most empowered, active, and dedicated of men. But, above all, he is the most moral of men. What Antonioni's atavistic emotions and conscience would not permit him to see in *L'Avventura* is that the genius' greatest virtue is his awareness that, in Iris Murdock's words, "nothing matters except loving what is good. Not to look at evil but to look at good. Only this contemplation breaks the tyranny of the past, breaks the adherence of evil to the personality, breaks, in the end, the personality itself. In the light of good, evil can be seen in its place, not owned, just existing in its place." Without Antonioni recognizing and allowing that they had, Sandro and Claudia had lived for the good. The good they lived for is not an ideal, principle, or other worldly realm; it is not an intellectual abstraction. Their geniuses, contrary to their intellects, knew that evil is a place and that to do good they must elude being placed. Life is bad from the genius' point of view when it is at a standstill, when it has nothing going for it.

Genius knows that it must take care not to ignore or mete out pain callously, so it instinctively takes suffering into itself and instead of ghoulishly lingering upon it makes good things happen from it. Suffering is its raw material, not its end. Now it is true that, as the age-old notion of inspiration maintains, genius submits to seizure by a power greater than ego or character that momentarily depersonalizes. Sandro and Claudia are just so seized by life. But previously, when espoused, that experience in a pure and isolated, eternal form was uncompromisingly insisted upon. The new man in Antonioni's movie lives toward, in, and out of that moment. He does not, like religious men of old did, seek to end his life in it. Not a man of God in the conventional sense of the phrase, genius gives himself to the condition, way, and ultimate value of life. That is to say, this new man willingly labors in the world for the good of life and man by collecting the rays of possibility and focuses them into new supremely alive individuals. He is an artist of life.

And that means he is a man of action, the kind of man that is naturally favored by the movies, a medium, obviously, of movement. Claudia and Sandro perpetuate and improve upon this inherent tendency of the movies to favor action by being on the move within themselves. They are subtler, more complex men of action than the two-fisted man of action is. Antonioni's attempt to hide their action under a blanket of incongruous black and white photography cannot obscure the fact that they are fuller realizations of the man of action. Via the liberation and growth they undergo, both extend and complement the active principle in their world: they are the offspring who issue as specific embodiments from its living processes. It is these currents that take them on their adventure, their explorations beyond the pales of ordinary human experience, which the movie's title identifies as the crucial event of its narration. As they did not choose to exist, so they do not choose their adventure. Rather, it chooses them, and it chooses them for an ostensibly intellectual quest that culminates in the image of Gloria Perkins.

Their adventure can occur, of course, because they possess the talent for it, the scope, complexity, and subtlety of life that allows them to be singled out for the very special events they participate in and the expansion of their vital power that result from those events. That is why they are chosen. Since their adventure does entail an intellectual quest—Anna's aroused mind begets the mystery of what happened to Anna and the movie then becomes a who-done-it or a what-caused-it, an intellectual inquiry devoted to determining the truth about events—they act out the traditional European intellectual passion of a rational observer intent upon determining the truth regarding cause and effect in external relations. But in acting out the European story, they adventure intellectually beyond the intellectually certain and thereby examine the foundations of reason and rational culture. That is to say, their adventure takes them outside realistic or external relations into the treacherous currents of life. The fact that the mystery of Anna's disappearance is not only not solved but quietly abandoned reveals that Claudia and Sandro—and Antonioni's movie, too— give themselves up to a passion more vigorous than the rational one. Their eventual abandonment of the hunt for Anna frees them to find a new truth, a truth beyond reason and the order of cause and effect in external relations, an imaginative truth about man in motion. That profound human change from the man of reason to the man of action, an elementary change in Western morality, is finally what they are caught up in, behold starkly and ineluctably in Gloria, and act out for us.

Because of his fidelity to the image, Antonioni was also able to see, despite his moral refusal to condone it, that the powers of genius reside in his image. Again, it is Gloria who demonstrates the equation of image and energy. When she splits the husk of her dress, she reveals her skin to be where the action is and her "human essence." It is this fact that Macdonald's conscience could not tolerate and therefore his eyes behold. But there can be no question in the age of relativity when energy—or light, energy in its supreme activity—is the ultimate source that there is nothing but skin. Light can play upon and illuminate no more. Peel away layer after layer, still all is skin, the empirically witnessed exterior that happens to be charged with energy. Actually like the electrons in an atom, the outer rings are energy charges and all human interactions—everything that happens in *L'Avventura*—result from discharging them. And as images of man themselves Claudia and Sandro reveal their charge of life through their "skins," or through their appearance, to fall back upon traditional parlance. Indeed, they have no existence in the world of the movie, as we have no existence in the world of movement, apart from appearances.

Genius thrives on images. Certainly, in investing his imaginative energy in making a movie Antonioni testified to the power of the image to release his genius. And as a very concrete, highly individualized creation made of images by Antonioni's genius, *L'Avventura* in its entirety images Antonioni's humanity and so man's. That is to say, the director as well as his protagonists uses images to peel away his character and let his genius live. Their final emotional tantrum to the contrary notwithstanding, both prove that it is through his image and images that man, instead of losing his soul by peering at his reflected visage as Narcissus did or by the sinful indulgence of the sense the Christians were warned against, breaks free of the mass that would weigh him down and the labels that would fence him in. The image of man, they prove, is his genius made manifest.

It is understandable, therefore, that from the point of view of character, genius is intolerable. Like the image, genius is superficial, shallow, changeable, ephemeral. Without a name genius antecedes and perpetually eludes the bondage of family, society, and culture, and without a past—no father and no institutional and ideological connections—he travels light. So he is just what he presents to be seen, no more, no less. Yet however unnamed or unnameable he may be, genius is not inhuman or a freak. For rather than being a weakness, his depthlessness is, instead, his strength. It is the condition of his radiance. versatility, plasticity, resiliency, and mobility and makes it possible for him, since he doesn't have to keep looking back while dragging his historical tale behind him, to expend his energy in thrusting forward. Owing to it, he can live for enjoyment and joy, those transitory, unsustainable peaks exemplified by Claudia and Sandro's erotic ecstasy. That means that the "character" of joy, as Sandro illustrates, is unpredictable; he's always threatening to metamorphose into a strange new creature, to succumb to the temptation of any novel possibility that excites new dimensions of his existence. That makes him upsetting to the personal security of others and social order because he can't be stood in his niche and made to stay there. All that is what Antonioni laments in the name of the old morality.

With all of the inherent qualities of the image inherent in the image of man, the genius is prepared to move out now; he is ready for and inclined toward growth, expansion, evolution, and revolution. Of course, genius has always been a revolutionary. What we now can allow through the agency of the movies is that he does more than Iris Murdock ascribes to him—merely contemplate the good, as though it existed prior to his appearance, and define evil. The new man specializes in creating good. To do that he must be anything but frivolous, for he performs the most difficult of all human feats requiring the greatest possible human dedication and discipline. He bears the thrust of the individual against all externally imposed systems, against the order of all words, roles, and institutions. The radical of radicals, he follows the root of life to its deepest source in order to carry out its most compelling task. From that matrix he expresses the "human essence" with a profundity and relevance never dreamed of in character and equips himself to forge the new community free of Bergman's terror. What Antonioni saw most astutely but his conscience could not face, then, is that not character but genius is man's concrete living spirit and that only through the greater adeptness of genius at living can man authentically exist. No more profound or subtle rendering of the image's assassination of character is to be found in either literature or the movies. Nevertheless Antonioni's atavistic emotions kept him from seeing that in living for his own sake the genius lives for the sake of all other individuals. Decreation, to be sure, figures in the genius' creative act, for he must feed upon and break down old structures. But decreation is only one phase in his creative act, and an early phase at that. Whereas those who hold tight to the familiar out of fear of destruction or out of guilt merely encumber the feet of creative change, and their counterpart, the rebels who repudiate in hate, would explode the world vainly and to no purpose, the genius cannot get off so easily. He has to win his way through what was, and destruction, to the new living possibility.

Though the image and the image of man may appear analytically superficial, much obviously happens in them and because of them. They make possible the feat Sandro performs and the growth Claudia undergoes, neither of which are within the power of a program or an ideology. Actually, all programs and ideologies adamantly prohibit both the feat and the growth. For only by means of the intricate, dynamic interweaving of the abstractive within the individuating power exemplified in the free image and the image of man can the new man and the new community be forged. And then only if the supremely stringent economy, functional efficiency, and genuine moral intention also exemplified by them is emulated. The weak at heart will invariably take refuge in dreams of utopia, nihilism, or authoritarianism. They will seek to destroy wantonly or to impose hard and fast order rather than submit to the ordeal of creation. The new revolutionary accepts the risks entailed in wresting from his existence the form inherent in its living impulses. Free of debilitating fear and trembling, he lets the image have its way with him. And because he does, whereas old revolutionary types learned the necessity of organization from politics, he more profoundly and relevantly learns from the image the necessity and discipline of concrete form.

All the image media are vehicles for insinuating a new mode of valuing throughout our lives and culture. Or perhaps it would be more accurate to say that they were created to aid in the realization of the values that beckon us when the image becomes the source and the means of our moral life. Whatever the reason may be, the visual phenomenon they directly confront us with demands a radically different manner of perception, awareness, and judgment than we have customarily employed. But among the image media the movies most profoundly and sophisticatedly challenge us to become the new kind of human being who abjures rational man's dependence upon the authority of reason over the will or belief over action, and replaces it with immediate visual response to the thereness of his world as value and valuable. They do so simply by being a medium of images but also by clarifying and disseminating the image's potential. In this way they radically alter our moral priorities, and in doing that they radically alter our sense of who we are and what our lives must be. The image of the human emerging as their central figure operates in accordance with the inherent laws of the image, which are the laws of generation and birth, and as a consequence is a much truer revolutionary than the ideologue. It is this different kind of facet of the human, a freer, more mobile, more individualized human being, that *L'Avventura* and the movies in general are moving us to value. That is what is meant when the movies are called the art of our time.

001 and the Literary Sensibility

W. R. Robinson and Mary McDermott

Surely no one could have sat through the long visual sequences at the beginning and end of Stanley Kubrick's *2001: A Space Odyssey* without sensing that the movie had taken them on a visual "trip." But should anyone have missed that fact, or been confounded by it, Kubrick has taken the trouble on repeated occasions to explain that in making *2001* he was "dealing in a purely visual experience, and telling a story through the eyes," and he makes it clear that he is not simply succumbing to the temptations of fashionable cinematic gimmickery in doing "the visual thing" by further noting that dealing with purely visual experience and telling a story through the eyes is his way of "showing the viewer something he can't see in any other way." He knew beyond the shadow of a doubt, these remarks forcefully establish, that he had a story to tell that could be rendered, perceived, followed and completed only through moving images. In other words, though he did not directly make such a claim himself, he committed himself to telling the story of the active eye.

A story that so slights words as the source, be-all, and end-all of life was inevitably bound to offend the literary sensibility—and that means almost all movie critics. And it did. Ray Bradbury, a science-fiction writer in direct competition with Kubrick as a story-teller, bluntly voiced the common complaint of the literary sensibility with his caustic dismissal of Kubrick's work with the remark, "Unfortunately, there are no well-directed scenes, and the dialogue is banal to the point of extinction.... I just think he's a bad writer who got in the way of Arthur C. Clarke, who is a wonderful writer." (Whatever the merits of Clarke as a writer on other occasions, certainly his book based on *2001* is a pale imitation of the movie.) Kubrick has sought to head off the irrelevancies of literary criticism by simply pointing out that he "tried to work things out so that nothing important was said in the dialogue, and that anything important in the film be translated in terms of action." But his efforts to that effect have been of no avail. That failure should not have come to him as a surprise, however. For he is well aware that the problem not only with movie critics but also "with the movies is that since the talkies the film industry has historically been conservative and word-oriented.... Too many people over thirty are still word-oriented rather than picture-oriented."

Kubrick has proven that he is not word-oriented, and that his commitment to his visual story was a conscious and consistent choice from the inception of *2001*, by eschewing all invitations to append a point or meaning to *2001* in dialogue not only in it but also about it. As he did in his *Playboy* interview, where he refused to let anything said during that dialogue say anything important about what is happening in his movie. There, for example, when asked, "What was the metaphysical message of *2001*?" he turned away from the question with his much reiterated explanation: "It's not a message that I ever intend to convey in words. *2001* is a nonverbal experience...I tried to create a visual experience, one that bypasses verbalized pigeonholing and directly penetrate the subconscious with an emotional and philosophic content. To convolute McLuhan, in *2001* the message is the medium." The interviewer, apparently assuming that Kubrick's reply meant the movie soared off into romantic fantasy and so was trivial, turned the dialogue from that point into a "serious" discussion of man's future with technology and in space, matters which Kubrick is no better qualified to discuss than is any reasonably well-educated man on the street.

In denying a "metaphysical message" for *2001* Kubrick was not removing his movie from serious consideration, nor did he intend to so remove it. The degree of seriousness he brought to the making of his movie and to his discussions of it emerge brilliantly in his convolution of McLuhan, which amounts to a great deal more than a mere play on words. McLuhan's notion that "the medium is the message" implies that all media seek to emulate words; they aim at becoming messages. Since words by nature refer, they direct attention to something other than themselves, acting as messengers bearing news of other events in other realms. An outsider to all media except words (he was trained in literary history), McLuhan cannot allow that a medium other than words has its own inherently unique aims. As a consequence, his comments on *2001* are particularly wrongheaded: "A movie like *2001* belongs to 1901, or even to the world of Jules Verne. It is filled with nineteenth-century hardware and Newtonian imagery. It has few, if any, twentieth-century qualities." As an outsider McLuhan can see only the content and not the form of the movie—ironically in violation of his own much repeated dictum that the latter is the "message." Since he cannot see the movie, he can see nothing good in what may be the most affirmative work of art in Western visual culture. Demanding that *2001* conform to an uncinematic, verbal ideal, he can perceive only the discrepancy between his ideal and the fact of the movie. He disguises his alien standard and blindness with his typical historical mumbo-jumbo.

On the other hand, Kubrick's vocation as a movie-maker places him inside the medium. He brings to *2001* the same serious involvement in seeing that Pierre Teilhard de Chardin does to *The Phenomenon of Man*, where Teilhard lays down this fundamental principle:

> *Seeing*. We might say that the whole of life lies in that verb—if not in the end, at least essentially…. Union can only increase through an increase in consciousness, that is to say, in vision. And that, doubtless, is why the history of the living world can be summarized as the elaboration of ever more perfect eyes within a cosmos in which there is always something more to be seen. After all, do we not judge the perfection of an animal, or the supremacy of a thinking being, by the synthetic power of their gaze? To try to see more and better is not a matter of whim or curiosity or self-indulgence. *To see or perish* is the very condition laid upon everything that makes up the universe, by reason of the mysterious gift of existence. And this, in superior measure is man's condition.

Kubrick's insistence in *2001* on visual experience is his way of informing us that his movie—and, it might be added, any movie and also our lives, properly seen—requires that we bring this more serious use of our eye to the viewing of it. He places that requirement explicitly upon us when in his own way he echoes Teilhard's statement by suggesting that *2001* succeeds "if it stimulates, however inchoately, [the viewer's] mythological and religious yearnings and impulses." The prerequisite of the visual "trip," Kubrick insists, is that we do take our eyes with Teilhard's kind of seriousness—with philosophic seriousness—for his odyssey is, finally, a metaphysical adventure.

Our rational tradition disposes us to hold a very narrow and, in fact, erroneous notion of the metaphysical enterprise. We customarily think of it as reason's attempt to formulate a cosmology, a systematic account of the order of things such as Plato offers in the *Timaeus*. Even in our subtler reflections we allow it at best to be no more than exercises in ontology, attempts to define being conceptually or, actually, reason's relation to being. William Gilmore Simms, a second-rate nineteenth-century Southern writer, had a profounder perception than the one our rational tradition is based on when he saw that "the mouth, and not the eyes, had been endowed with the faculty of eating. Had the eye and not the mouth been employed for this purpose," he went on to observe, "there would soon be a famine in the land, for of all gluttons, the eyes are the greatest." This observation appears rather innocently in the context of explaining how an Indian brave happened to fall and break his leg while walking through the forest. Though given to moments of imaginative genius that his intelligence could not make much use of, Simms nevertheless had an astute vision of how the hunger of the eyes, greatly exceeding that of the mouth, makes them the authentic metaphysical faculty. Their voracity, he saw, would devour all and would settle for no less. Now it may appear as rank nonsense in our rational tradition to claim that the eyes, a physical sense, could be the instrument for transcending the physical. To "meta" the physical, we have been conditioned to assume, we need and must rely upon a faculty that is not physical—and reason with its penchant for and delight in abstraction fits that requirement nicely.

Correspondingly, the metaphysical enterprise traditionally demanded, and got, a vigorous restraint placed upon the voracity of the eyes. It has severely censored what we have been allowed to look into or directly behold. Christian apologetics besides assigning Satan domain over the visual world has for centuries compulsively sought to deny the "untutored" eye an uncensored look at the glories of creation. Thus the half-hearted metaphysics of reason could sit securely on its slightly raised throne above the physical. That restraint is readily evident in Simms' way of stating his perception—and, incidentally, the cause of his never becoming an artist of any great consequence. He openly denounces the eyes morally—as gluttons, to begin with— but he also attributes to them the harm of a broken leg or even the power to make a wasteland of life. (Not by chance that image recalls the more recent stricture of the eyes among such diverse modern literary sensibilities as T. S. Eliot and Yvor Winters.) Whether or not a danger to life and limb, the eyes by now in Western civilization have proven themselves to be the stronger, more persistent, and more demanding metaphysical faculty. In the war between mathematics and empiricism in modern science since Galileo, they have quite clearly survived as the dominant determiner of "reality." What puzzles us—and it is the metaphysical issue of our time—is how the physical senses can transcend themselves, how the "physical" can metamorphose into another life beyond the "physical." That is the mysterious creative problem Kubrick addresses himself to and works out in *2001*.

The condition of Kubrick's having carried out his metaphysical adventure and of our making it with him is that anything of importance in his film be translated into the terms of action. That means specifically in his movie, into images—or, precisely, into moving images. It follows that his success as a cinematic story-teller depends upon his willingness to take the traditional restraints off the eyes and his ability to let them satisfy their metaphysical hunger. It also follows that the key to his metaphysical vision lies exclusively in what his images are and what they are doing. Once we bring a more serious kind of seeing to *2001* than we customarily employ and look carefully at its images and what they are doing, *2001* can immediately be seen for what it is, an elaboration of Teilhard's idea of the perceptive eye in a cosmos in which there is always something more to be seen. This appears as the main visual event in the movie through the increase in size and power of the yellow eye that first appears in the predatory leopard among the apes, enlarges into the ubiquitous, objective, rational yellow, red and blue eye of the computer HAL during the astronauts' space travel, and finally during the light trip in Part III expands to fill the entire screen and blink through a series of psychedelic colors in a very "elaborate" performance of self-perception, self-cleansing, and self-reincarnation.

The potential for the growth in size and power of the eye that is reincarnated in the open-eyed embryo at the end of the movie is present in the forms of the universe with which the camera eye is initially occupied at the beginning of the movie. The opening shot of the conjunction of the three spheres, earth, moon, and sun (significantly a visual title that precedes the verbal one), posits, first, the primacy of the circle (the sphere, orb, globe), as the originating form and guiding force. Second, it posits a process of development through three stages that progresses from the earth (the senses, i.e., the physical and bestial) to an intermediate and mediating plateau, the moon (reason), a specious end which is not really a source of light but only a partially lit up reflection of the source, to, finally, the sun (the imagination), a self-generating body and the true source of light. The opening three strains of *Thus Spake Zarathustra*, recurring with increasing intensity, announces these three stages of perception that man will undergo in the movie. The music constitutes the intangible vibrations, the cosmic and inner strivings, from which materialize the visual creation, which in turn issues into the title and later dialogue. The rising motion of the camera vertically ascending over the earth, then the moon, and finally centrally focusing upon the distant sun, integrated with and further qualifying the musical motif, completes the clarification of the source and intention of the motion that will contribute and regulate what can and will happen in the movie thereafter. By means of and within this trinal structural pattern (three is magically the number of infinity, religiously the number of the trinity and wholeness, and scientifically the number of realization, three being the first real number), *2001* will enact man's release and expenditure of his living powers to transcend two barriers and become a purified, lightened, self-generating embryo eye gliding silently through space, simultaneously on the move and going somewhere.

The most obvious recurrence of the opening pattern appears, of course, in the division of the movie's overall action into three parts: The Dawn of Man, Jupiter Mission, and To Infinity and Beyond. This appearance is, however, but the largest of numerous exfoliations from that pattern, which develops like a seed, by expansively elaborating the compact potential life within it. The images of the first part show that "The Dawn of Man" is the dawning of man's rational faculty in his discovery of the tool. The images of Part II show man having reached a crisis in his rational development, a point at which he encounters an unsolvable problem that sends him on a journey to discover, in effect, the source of his intelligence. Here reason's quasi-metaphysical hunger, appropriately represented by an angular, predominantly vertical visual image in the form of the cobalt slab, which is sharply at odds with the dominant circular forms of the movie, seeks to find the cause of the slab on the assumption, derived from reason's sense of its insufficiency, of a cause that lies outside of and antecedes the slab. The hypothesis he acts upon postulates a rational source older than his own on earth and requires a causal explanation for its solution. The images of Part III show the expansion of his perceptive faculty into immediate and spontaneous union with its universe beyond the problems of self, history, causality, calendar time, etc. Over the course of three parts, then, a lethargic physical creature is sensuously aroused; that awakening begets the aspiration to stand up and to fly, but his flight, ironically, turns upon his inspiration to trace the slab back to its origins; then, in the end, his vital energy gets turned loose from the center of himself for creative transcendence—but, again ironically, that creative transcendence is a return to the "physical" condition of finite existence. In short, a motion arises that goes backward so that it may finally move forward in creative joy.

As man evolves through these three phases of growth, the images of the three parts show him moving from the periphery of the circle (the first close-up shots of the earth emphasize its round horizon and the apes living on its skin, outside it) to inside the circle (where, as with the stewardesses and astronauts, man walks on the inside of the skin of various circular forms without any orientation regarding such matters as up and down, or top and bottom), and finally in Part III, during the light trip, to the center of the circle.

In each of these phases man transcends a limitation by releasing a potential within himself for growth toward the next higher level in his development. But the major limitation he must surmount is that of words, the foremost obstacle to his progress at this point in his history. Besides beginning with a "dawn" and ending "beyond" by means of the progress through three parts, *2001* suffers from a visual-verbal dichotomy. The first half of Part I and all of Part III are totally free of words; only the images of the second half of Part I and those of Part II are accompanied by a dialogue: only that portion of the movie is a talkie. From this perspective the three parts of the movie are counterpointed and complemented by three phases that subtly interweave themselves throughout the surface plot structure, thereby introducing an asymmetrical, organic motion into the orderly rational one on the movie's surface. (This tension also exists between the square frame of the film and the curvature of the cineramic screen; both the three phases and the relation of frame to screen obviously are further instances of the principle of the angular being encompassed by the circular.) The presence of this subtle underplot, as it were, means that the crucial new thing in Kubrick's story turns upon the relation of the visual and verbal elements within it. It is this relationship that is at issue between him and his literary critics, and so it is in how he connects words with images, thought with seeing, that his answer to them and his achievement as an artist in telling the new story and creating the new man resides.

The first phase begins the movement in the evolution of the creative eye by taking the eye through the first stage of purification, the progression from bestiality to rationality. The repeated eating scenes, supported by such other organic events as the numerous deaths (two apes, one zebra, many tapirs, HAL, Frank, and Dave) and birthdays (Man, Dr. Floyd's daughter, Frank, and Dave), provide the most explicit visual evidence that what is happening throughout the three phases is organic in nature; they also testify to the importance of ingestion in the birth of imaginative man. This new man cannot come into being without taking his world into himself, for his only source of organic nourishment is his world. Should he turn his eyes in disgust away from it or spit it out in distaste and refuse to assimilate it once the eyes have taken it in, he will suffer from organic starvation and have, at best, a living death.

The eye's organic capacity for growth manifests itself in the ferocious yellow eye of the leopard, a compact microcosm of the sun, guarding his dead prey as he sits on a precipice above the apes. His elevated and unbound position indicate that at this stage of growth the wild eye is able to dominate its carnal sources and thrive upon them. The frightened apes who peer from the restricted dark cave below and venture only to the boundaries of a small, muddy waterhole hemmed in by barren rocks, are in direct contrast to the eye of the lofty, free ferocious, and victorious leopard. In order to rise above their ignorant, fearful, dependent state, the eyes of the ape must emerge from the cave and perceive a means of assuming the leopard's dominance over the physical, animal condition. Their stereoscopic vision equips them for that triumph, and for considerably more than is attainable by the wild-eyed leopard. The last shot of the ape shows that he has effected that change. Breaking out of the confining naturalistic space that had previously imprisoned him in a walled-in, fixed environmental cage, except for a slight opening high in the rear that lets in a dim light, he rises from a crouching position on a limitless plain, and his eye is no longer shifting from left to right, top to bottom, in a random search for food or in watchfulness for enemies. His gaze is fierce and wild and directly focused. Random ambling about in a confined location to pick burrs out of fellow apes' hair is channeled into the specific motion of directing the bone so that a kill may be made. Most importantly, the master ape turns his head from side to side to put his eyes in a new relation to his environment and thus to evolve into a new form. Appropriately, the camera has traveled from the opening shot of celestial bodies in a dark heaven to the full daylight of rationality as the first phase ends with the shot of the bone thrown by the ape rising into the sunlit sky. The eye has emerged from primeval darkness. Stirred by the sun at the apex of the vertical-oriented cobalt slab that uplifted them, the newly charged sun-drunk eyes leap free of their locked-in condition and limited range, escape the exhaustion of ceaseless caring for basic animal needs and of being a fearful prey to darkness, and aspire to a new image of man.

The technological leap from the bone to the moon-bound Pan-American spacecraft, imaged against the black background of infinite and unknown space, emphasizes that the next stage of man's evolutionary rise continues the initial development begun by the ape. Nevertheless, the blackness of the setting contrasts sharply with the daylight world in which the ape was last seen at the zenith of his achievement, and man is now in the initial stage of his next perceptual advancement. The cut from bone to spacecraft, focusing not upon ape and man but upon tool and tool, underlines the meaning of the tool in man's growth. But the most important tool man possesses during the second stage of his development, the basis for the development of all his tools beyond the rudimentary bone, is language. For this reason the central event of man's existence during this phase is that the polarizing dialogue which began at the waterhole, where competing bands of apes screeched to ward each other off, reaches its full development in the H.A.L. 9,000 computer, the ultimate tool that extends to perfection in speed and accuracy man's power of verbal thought. During this development, the eye of reason assumes hegemony over the wild eye; man, now a rational creature with depth perception, lives by and for words. His motives, relationships, values, his opportunities and fate, take their shape from that medium.

From the trip to Clavius until the disconnection of HAL, the verbal abounds. Hotels, restaurants, instruments have identifying names; procedures for carrying out simple bodily functions entail lengthy verbal explanations; people are acknowledged by "Voice identification" machines; and nationalities are separated by labeling people according to their country of origin. Moreover, a telephone call is Heywood Floyd's first act at the Orbiter Hilton. And, when asked what she wants for her birthday, his little girl's response is "a telephone." The very message of the call is that "Daddy phoned and will phone again tomorrow."

The effect of this everpresence of words, the instrument of stereoscopic depth perception, is separation. They make it possible for man to escape the huddled, dependent, tribal condition of the apes by putting space, or a third dimension, between men. That space allows them the heightened self-identity that a name makes possible at the same time that it endows them with the room to stretch out and be mobile. This new individuality comes, however, at the price of division and polarization both without and within man. That polarization appears, for example, in the black and white decor of the Orbiter Hilton, in the contrast between the black dress of the Russian woman and the stewardesses' white uniform, and in the opposing textures of Dr. Floyd's rough woolen clothes and the space station's sleek metallic and plastic surfaces. More importantly, it also appears in the relation of words and images. A pen floats front and center inside the Pan American aircraft while Dr. Floyd sleeps in his seat in front of a television image; that is, a tool for working with words occupies the foreground of dramatic events. Furthermore, Dr. Floyd is not only oblivious to the image before him on the screen but equally to the fantastic world of the mechanical inventions about him. The visual-verbal relationship in this scene tells all. The speech occurs mediately between the television image and the camera image, consistent with the position that words have throughout 2001. The double perspective of man has dissociated man's mind from its concrete world. Dr. Floyd's eyes are closed; abstraction is his value and fate; his imagination cannot be stirred. He has to be awakened by a stewardess—by a force from outside him! When he uses his eyes deliberately, it is to recognize or to read. And that is true of the pilots of the space crafts and of HAL, whose most astounding feat is to read, not the faces, but the lips, of the astronauts.

Thus the eye escapes the prison of the physical body only to find itself imprisoned in reason. During the second phase of its growth the eye, as a consequence, is filtered through thought. Its relation to its world mediated by words, it ignores images (even when they appear on television screens as a fruit of technology: neither Dr. Floyd nor Frank look at the members of their family with any interest or comment on their visual qualities) in order to designate names and dates, classify, understand—in short, to carry out rational purposes. The growth of the eye during the second phase entails its objectifying itself so that it becomes dependent upon its environment, like the men in space, in order to sustain its life and to carry our its development. Thus the eye seems to abandon itself to its opposite and endures the humiliation of serving in an inferior capacity. Like man during this phase of the movie, the eye is outwardly passive; it has been tamed, domesticated—it is always indoors; its movement is not generated by its own energy. Locked within the "I" of reason, man appears irredeemably at odds with his world and within himself. He is "spaced"—suspended in mind between his origins and his destiny.

The most evident effect of tools (including language) in the second phase of man's growth is that, while they extend his faculties, they also extend the distance between men. And that begets the problem of communication. Dr. Floyd's phone call is an attempt to bridge the divide between himself and his wife. But his conversation with his daughter is a miserable failure of communication. His words are sterile for this purpose; they cannot unite what they set asunder. Accordingly, the dialogue is repetitive ("Did you have a pleasant flight") and banal ("Yes, very nice, thanks"). The jargon of classification reaches the point of absurdity: "Z-Ray-Delta-One, this is Mission Control, acknowledging your 2-1-0-3. We are reviewing telemetric information on our mission simulator and will advise. Roger your plan to EVA and replace Alpha-Echo 3-5 unit prior to possible failure." Emphasis is on such words (and concomitant actions) as "control," "review," "numerical classifications," "simulator," and "echo." Words control and restrict rather than liberate. Floyd says, "I'm really not at liberty to discuss it," in speaking with the Russians about his trip to Clavius. Words separate not only nations but, even more destructively, individuals. Speeches become a series of "cover stories" as shown by Floyd's "great speech," which tells nothing but the euphemistically glorified need for "absolute secrecy" beyond the walls of the lunar briefing room.

Words, literally, are dividing walls.

Much more decisive than the failure of words to bridge the gap they create is their obstruction of growth. For with reason dissociated from the vital source in the concrete world, it can only relentlessly pursue its doomed course to death. Which is precisely the case with the H.A.L. 9,000 computer, the most interesting character, everyone readily acknowledges, in 2001. Known as "HAL" among friends, the huge electronic brain and nervous system of the ship expresses more human concern for his own performance, the mission, and his fellow astronauts than either of the emotionless *tabula rasa* faces of Frank and Dave, who admit that HAL "acts like he has genuine emotions." HAL's birthday greeting to the indifferent Frank, whose condition is almost that of the cold, sleeping hibernauts upon which the camera focuses, is indeed far more "personable" than the passive astronaut.

But for a machine to be the most human of the *dramatis personae*, and, above all, to have feelings—that has to be a parody or a stupidity on the director's part. It is at this point and on this matter that the literary sensibility begins to be annoyed, as Ray Bradbury was. His criticism of *2001* comes down finally to this issue: "The test of the film is whether or not we care when one of the astronauts dies. We do not.… The freezing touch of Antonioni, whose ghost haunts Kubrick, has turned everything to ice." With no character except a machine that we can sympathize and identify with (and who can feel for a machine even if it feels?), the movie, from Bradbury's point of view, is worthless. Not just the literary sensibility, however, but old-school humanists in general find HAL unpalatable. Even "icy" Antonioni balked at the sacrilege of a machine being human. "I don't like *2001* completely," he commented. "It's very beautiful visually and technically as a film. But I don't agree with Kubrick. I don't understand exactly what he's saying about technology. I think he's confused." (One would expect better of Antonioni since he is a movie maker—unless they have seen his films: he has been stopped by the technology obstacle and has been unable, therefore, to work the movie story through in his own art.) The literary sensibility and the old-school humanist *should* be disturbed by HAL, for he bears their traditional motive, virtues, and concerns. Their values and, indeed, their lives stand or fall on his performance.

He is not the main character of the movie, it hardly need be noted. It should already be clearly apparent that the eye is. The eye is what endures the entire adventure and undergoes development. But HAL is the main character of the second phase, and appropriately so. He is reason perfected, the aspirations and potentiality of rational men taken to their ultimate development. Given the separation imposed by words, feelings or sentiments become necessary as a means of bridging the gap between men. But once feelings become a part of a relation in a rational context, then the profoundest feelings of a rational creature, vanity and the urge for perfection (and for a rational creature that means absolute knowledge) and dominance, eventually push out all others. Thus, despite his initial amiability, HAL is totally dependent upon the infallibility of his words for his existence. When the possibility of error arises, HAL's human nature manifests itself as a will to survival, an implacable urge to kill the human astronauts in order to preserve the integrity of his honor, of his own "good word." Nothing more vividly embodies the destructive tendency inherent in the word and therefore HAL's character than the three dying hibernauts imaged by focusing, not on the human figures, but on the diminished activity of linear graphs and pulsating neon signs that replace pulsating breasts and finally read "Life Functions Terminated."

The profoundest rational feeling and his murderous impulses are HAL's hallmarks. Nevertheless his deepest feeling—his abiding passion—is reason's obsession with getting to its source, which it assumes exists prior to and outside itself. Thus its existence is devoted, as the name of the space ship that bears HAL indicates, to discovery—that is, to determining the truth about something that has already happened or already exists. This means that rational man is searching for the cause of an observed effect (the appearance of the cobalt slab), and ultimately for the first cause, which means the first cause of reason's existence. That is the significance of rational man's postulate that the slab was produced by a greater, older, and more distant intelligence— an ancestor, in effect. HAL presides over the journey into the past. Only he knows the purpose of the Jupiter mission and in the end he wants it, like a good rationalist bent on formulating a systematic monism, all for himself. HAL wants to be Faustian master of his universe, a creature who possesses ultimate knowledge and omnisciently rules its domain. Through him, reason seeks to extend the range of its power—actually to make its power absolute—by determining the first cause of its existence.

That uncompromising hunger drives HAL to the ultimate polarization— a confrontation in which it is either his life or the astronauts'. The two cannot tolerate one another. But he must commit suicide as well. Reason's quest for its origin is inherently futile simply because reason, severed from the concrete world and so without vital energy or the vital principle active within it, contains no self-sustaining or ultimate ground within itself. The discovery mission, inevitably, cannot be successfully completed and must be aborted.

There is no alternative to the consummation of rational hunger other than the disconnection of HAL's mind. For, were reason's mission successful, it would put a stop to motion. By getting back to its beginning, reason would reach the still point before time and history began. But its curiosity to know what is behind and moving events is frustrated, and reason ends up metaphysically baffled. Unable to transcend the physical world in motion, reason arrives at no absolutes, no infallible verbal truths, no incontrovertible facts concerning the precise nature of man's origin or destiny. Man's only certainty is the life he feels immediately within him, pendant with vital possibilities and throwing itself forward. Growth, which is of no interest to reason, prevails over what would negate it.

Words have their final heyday as Dave demands that HAL open the space pod door: Dave—"Do you read [not see] me?" HAL himself utters the death knell of the word—"This conversation can serve no purpose anymore." After vainly calling, "HAL…HAL" (reinforcing the egotism of the computer), Dave lobotomizes the machine. "I'm afraid," repeated three times, and "I can feel it," repeated five times, gradually wind down to the sluggish murmurings of an ego that can only proclaim, "I am a H.A.L. 9,000 computer." He is stuck with and on his solitary identity. The rhythmless tune which HAL sings as he dies is "Daisey," essentially a marriage proposal which seeks an answer: "Give me your answer, do." But he can never be married or fulfill organic functions. By stripping away HAL's emotional entanglements, identity compulsion, and his kind of marriage, Dave disencumbers the eye of the limitations reason places upon its growth. His disconnection of the computer prepares for another kind of connection. The second phase appropriately ends as Dave listens to the prerecorded story of the mysterious monolith found on the moon, the last words of which are—and they are the movie's last words—"Its origin and purpose are still a total mystery." The announcement admits the failure of reason. And, in admitting that, it also implicitly reinstates the primordiacy of the moving image and allows that the organic eye and its images, again exclusively occupying the screen, are the true vehicles of the odyssey.

The second phase, obviously, is an advance beyond the bestiality of the first, yet the phase of reason and complex mechanical tools is only an intermediary stage in the movement of the eye towards its final purification. Just as man tossed away the bone for more advanced tools, he eventually throws away, in a sense, his spacecraft and his pen or words as he perceives that they are no longer tools for progression but limitations upon the eye's capacity for growth toward a more perfect life. It is at this point that Kubrick, besides offending it, leaves behind the literary sensibility. Again Ray Bradbury's retort to the question, "Were you thrown any by the wildly abstract ending?" typifies the literary reaction: "I wasn't thrown off. I just didn't understand it." What Bradbury cannot follow is the triumph of the creative eye over the egotistic "I," or of the image over the word, or the eye over reason. But it is precisely because Kubrick works in seeing or images in *2001*, and treats them with ultimate seriousness, that he can tell the new story of the further evolution of the rational "I" into the freely creative imaginative eye. His genius is never more evident than it is in his rendering of this transformation in the "wildly abstract" light show during the trip to infinity and beyond that expands man's insight to dimensions incomprehensible and intolerable for the literary sensibility.

It is this final achievement that the title of the movie signifies: *2001* marks the inception of the third stage in human development, the new age of man's oneness, of unitive man, the birth of the new millennium. For this latest evolution to occur, man first had to evolve out of bestiality into rationality, which he does in the movie when the birth of reason incited by the cobalt slab transforms the foraging ape into *homo faber*, a tool-maker who develops a bone into a weapon and then that bone, the most rudimentary form of technology (the skeleton machinery of the body used by the living spirit to carry out its acts of life) into space environments and space vehicles. But this story of the birth and career of rational man is an old story. The new story, and the difficult one, in *2001* is the further evolution of man beyond rationality. Reason plays only a small part in the overall movement toward the evolution of imaginative man, who sees and thereby synthesizes the world that words could only analytically polarize. For the bitter rational truth is that reason is merely a tool used to its limits by the eye and then, as with all tools, when its job is done it is disposed of.

The pressure of life within the wild eye seized the "I" of reason, which it drove to its ultimate polarization and annihilation, unfeelingly using reason to go on going on and cruelly discarding it when there was no more good left in it. HAL looms as a sufficiently difficult obstacle for those who persist in demanding that *2001* satisfy the expectations and criteria of the literary sensibility. But when Dave Bowman appears in the space "pod" (itself shaped like a giant eye and the carrier of the seed of new growth) at the beginning of the third phase in the purification of the eye—its transcendence of rationality as well as bestiality—the literary sensibility is nonplused. Kubrick notes that "there's a basic problem with people who are not paying attention with their eyes. They're listening…and those who won't believe their eyes won't be able to appreciate this film." It is precisely at this point where the eye sets forth to transcend rationality as well as bestiality that the literary sensibility, which is phonetic or sound oriented, should it have stayed with the trip this far, bears out Kubrick's observation regarding the inevitable failure of listeners to appreciate *2001*.

For his new story looks beyond exhausted verbal sources and values. It takes as its province visual relations, connections too subtle for verbal articulation. Thus, rightly, Kubrick does not revert to the sentimentality of *Paths of Glory* or the doctrinaire satire of *Dr. Strangelove*, both highly regarded by the literary sensibility, to resolve his story in *2001*. Nor is he apologetic about it. Instead of defending or explaining it, he puts his case confidently in the affirmative. His movie thereby retains its purely visual coherence.

All statements quoted from Kubrick and his critics can be found in *The Director as Superstar*, edited by Joseph Gelmis, pp. 293-316, or *The Making of 2001*, edited by Jerome Agel.

Stripping the Eye:
Some Observations on the Movies as Strip Tease

WILLIAM R. ROBINSON

And God saw everything that he had made:
and behold, it was very good.
                                        –Genesis

THE MOVIES ARE A MEDIUM of the senses and therefore invite sensual indulgence. That is true of all the arts. Initial contact with a work of art, always
an empirical object, is made with the senses. The vigor of their activity or-
dains the degree to which the other human facilities can become involved in
the aesthetic phenomenon, and thus the intensity, completeness, and benefi-
cence of the aesthetic experience. The invitation of the movies to indulge the
senses differs from that of the other arts only in being more boldly extended.
Their scale (with rare exceptions, second only to architecture in magnitude)
and their immateriality (equivalent to that of music) combine to offer a flagrant, dream-like, fantasy indulgence in extravagant, sheer appearances over
and apart from the more ponderously realistic concerns attendant to the appeals of other art media. Any consideration of the movies as art has to begin
with the fact of their sensuality and face up to their sensual challenge. To
indulge or not to indulge, that is the question movie makers, critic or reviewer, and audience confront.

The preponderant choice at present, as usual, is not to indulge. It was the
choice, for instance, of Richard Schickel, when he was film critic for *Life* in a
statement he made in *Family Weekly* on Antonioni's *Blow Up* as the best film
of the '60's. His praise of *Blow Up* for its "pointed asides on such matters as
the idle eroticism with which many of us attempt to compensate for the

emptiness of our lives" was not intended to castigate merely a little band of wanton revellers loose in the land but the movies themselves. That becomes clear when he further remarks that we are "caught up in the grip of a dangerous delusion about the media," "one of the great fallacies of our time," the belief that "the lens has the power to reveal the most profound mysteries." This urge to restrain man's eye and the medium of the movies, an extension of the visual sense, perpetuates the traditional moral insistence that a lid be kept on the passions and the flesh. *Family Weekly* is an appropriate place to defend this traditional morality. More than any other publication, it provides a large audience sympathetic to Mr. Schickel's suspicions about the movies being a threat to old values.

But the trouble with Mr. Schickel's repressive morality is not just that it begets bad movie criticism—an abysmal misviewing of Antonioni, though, admittedly, Antonioni's visual prudery invites such misgivings—but, more importantly, bad movies. Take, for example, skin flicks. There's nothing special about them. All movies are skin flicks. That's because skin is all the camera can shoot. Should skin become translucent, as it tends to do in electron microscopy of biological forms, then color has to be added to bring the skin out. Without skin to intercept, reflect, and interact with light nothing is visible and a movie is impossible. Ideas and ideologies, concepts and theories, thought processes, even social and cosmic order cannot be photographic subjects. These abstractions, and all others, neither born of the light, inhabitants of it, nor needing light to sustain them, are denizens of the dark. If they enter the visible creation, it is only in specific incarnations like the words on placards in *Hiroshima Mon Amour* and those stamped out on a sheet of paper by a typewriter at the beginning of *Slaughter-House Five*. Or, more familiarly, in characters such as the defender of the old regime in *Gates of Hell* or the cleric who ecstatically destroys his own flesh for religious reasons in *The Diary of a Country Priest*. What both of these men live for cannot be photographed; only their individual activity lies within the camera's purview. The only possible "frame of reference," the only possible "order," in movies is the concrete particular individual related to all other individuals through his individuality. And since this individual is distinguished from all other individuals by his skin, that skin is the "ultimate truth" of his world. It is the source of his existence, his powers of action, his values, and his possibilities. Thus abstractions can be present and operative in the visible creation, and therefore the movies, only within the individual, or more accurately, within his skin.

For this reason great movies are inevitably skin flicks. Sergei Eisenstein's last movie *Ivan the Terrible* certainly is in its way. At the end of *Ten Days That Shook the World*, an early propaganda film of Eisenstein's, an official of the Communist Party armed with words and a document stems the tide of revolutionary fervor aroused in the repressed proletariat by laying his authoritative abstractions upon them. Just when the energies of the lowest order of human beings—the skin and flesh of society—whipped up in the name of the revolution threaten to demolish thoroughly not only the old but all order, they are smothered under the cloak of a rational cause. Ivan, in contrast, emerges from his initial predicament of being buried under the trappings of office and the symbols of state as a self-assertive personal wielder of power. Though he isn't down to his skin at the end of Part II, he has thrown off several layers of inhibiting garments, and the attitudes that go along with them. Most importantly, he and his world burst forth out of black-and-white into a new skin of vivid, dynamic color. Not class interests or general principles but an individual center of active energy whose skin (a loose, flowing robe in this case) is co-equal with and releases his vital power emerges triumphant—in Eisenstein's career as a movie maker, it should be noted, as well as in this movie.

And great movies, more and more, are explicitly skin flicks. *2001* is. It is a movie about removal of first fur then clothes from man in preparation for the freely nude and streamlined skin of the star child. So are Fellini's *La Dolce Vita*, *8 1/2*, *Juliet of the Spirits*, *Fellini-Satyricon*, and *Roma*. Taken together they constitute a progressive disrobing. Beginning with Sylvia's (Anita Ekberg's) full-length formal dress in the first, through Claudia's simple informal attire in *8 1/2*, Suzy's revealing bathing suit and costumes in *Juliet*, Encolpio's mini-tunic in *Fellini-Satyricon*, and ending, for the moment, on the gross flesh of the whores in *Roma*, more and more skin, while increasingly more potently active, is unveiled by Fellini as his cinematic imagination matures.

Even Antonioni's movies are. He somewhat deceptively displaces his fascination with skin by focusing his eye on the skin of the earth, where his attention centers upon such denuded terrain as the rocky island in *L'Avventura* and the primeval gullies of *Zabriskie Point*. But, at the same time that the earth is being reduced to its elemental features, so is man. Man's reduction can be readily traced in a recurrent scene in Antonioni's movies. Originally this scene is taken up with the fully-clothed love making by Claudia and Sandro in a grassy field outside the abandoned town in *L'Avventura*. There the primal erotic excitement is an affair of faces. Subsequently, the fully clothed love making evolves into the half-stripped love combat in a bedroom of nature's hues in *Red Desert* and the fully-stripped but fruitless love play between the photographer and two teenage nymphs in the turquoise paper surf of *Blow Up*. The appearance of human skin in the primeval gullies of *Zabriskie Point* and the primitive struggle of bodies there in rising up out of the aboriginal dust climaxes in both the amount of skin and the erotic potency displayed the shedding of burdensome coverings that begins in *L'Avventura* and develops through *Red Desert* and *Blow Up*. This shedding of burdensome coverings is not a vicious discarding of social responsibilities but the means of reaching the source of generative energy. Like the cinematic art of Kubrick and Fellini, Antonioni's is devoted to stripping the body beyond where Eisenstein could strip it, beyond the emergence of the individual from his office down to the creative potency of man.

This stripping away of false or dead skins in order to make contact with the living skin is not, however, the special province of great movies. It is an inherent feature of the medium's essential story, explicitly present, like it or not, in all movies. For the movies are part of the story of the revolution in Western civilization signalled by Jean Jacques Rousseau's call for man to cast off his cultural chains and resume the natural life of the noble savage. The movies directly contribute to this shedding of the deadening veneer of civilized conventions by bursting the chains of verbal abstraction with the concreteness of their images, and especially their color images. (In other words, within the history of the movies themselves there has been development toward greater concreteness and activity from the silent through the black-and-white to the color movie.) But while Rousseau was limited to an abstract call for action, the major contribution of the movies to the longstanding enterprise of empiricism, the science it has begotten, and the painting that has flourished alongside it in stripping away the arbitrarily imposed artifices of reason has been to locate and tap the springs of action. It is true that movies are no more than skin deep, but their focus upon skin assigns priority to change. Through them, the eye is no longer limited to its classical function of observing the transient parade of phenomena; it dwells upon the volatile aspect of things, leading consciousness to participate in the dynamic flux that sweeps along within as well as about it. Their being only skin deep, instead of a handicap, is the genius of the movies.

For skin is the key to the kingdom of motion. As an art of motion, the movies make available a fund of energy for the human imagination to work with and in doing that direct attention to the problems of action. By its very nature the medium takes it off. To make a movie is inexorably to choose to work in close to the primal sensory skin of experience and that means to reckon with its primitive powers.

It should not come as a surprise to anyone, as a consequence, that the strip recurs infinitely and in infinite variation in all kinds and quality of movies—as doffed hats in *Closely Watched Trains*, buckskins in *Man and the Wilderness*, and the killing of the head in *8½* and *Easy Rider* as well as in the more familiar instances of discarded body clothing, nudity, and anti-establishment rebelliousness. Sometimes the strip occurs even very overtly. As it does in *The Night They Raided Minsky's*, an exuberant comedy based upon the invention of the striptease.

In this movie a young woman named Rachel runs away from her severely puritanical father and his black Bible to go on the stage and start a new life for herself. Via the striptease with which Rachel successfully breaks her father's religious repression of her passion to exhibit herself, the director, William Freidkin, is able to see that skin is where the action is in movies. Rachel doesn't take it all off. But a split in the cocoon of her black sheath dress is enough to generate a pandemonium of excitement. Taking it off before and for her audience at Minsky's, she activates their vital energy. Their enthusiastic affirmation of her flesh induces, in turn, a radiantly ecstatic glow of excited life in her that cannot be dampened even by the uniformed police who arrest her for indecency. Rachel senses that her personal growth as a human being depends upon her exhibiting herself to others. What at first glance looks like vanity is the profound recognition that all exchanges of stimulating energy initiates in skin-to-skin contact and that whatever excitement occurs "inwardly" starts with the skin.

William Friedkin even more aptly renders what happens when the skin is seen to be where the action is in a simple repeated device, the instant metamorphoses of black-and-white shots of cars that burst into brilliant color, people who break out into radiantly colorful life, and dilapidated, desolate New York streets that miraculously erupt into fresh, vibrant street markets full of ripe fruits and vegetables and robust people. Whereas the young woman's irrepressible vitality merely cracks the life-denying restraints of authority, her world's burgeoning vital energy breaks clearly and cleanly on through out of the black. In this event even old skin demonstrates that skin is alive; that it is the concrete existence of the world and the means of its continuing existence, a fountainhead continuously erupting into greater life, either on its own or for a spectator when it is properly beheld. Rachel's enhanced individuality excites the visual powers of her audience, which in turn excite the individuality of the individual perceiver, challenging him to respond with his excited individuality to her exciting individuality. In that way, her skin is not only the source of her individuality but holds the potential for the further individuality of both her and her audience. Rachel's skin is her limitation, defining her as a separate individual. Yet it is also her means of mobility, including the expansion of her life. The removal of the pressure of the external forces of her father and his book upon her beget not a reduction of the higher spirit to the vulgar and profane but the liberation of her vital energy to expand in accordance with its natural inclinations. Though Rachel cannot fully emulate the example set by her world, nevertheless both together illustrate the tendency of skin, and so of the movies, to release the energy of life through sloughing off restrictive artifices draped over it like mantles of death.

Not afraid to let skin do its thing, Friedkin could see that as in atoms, where the excitable electric charges whirl about in the outer rings and fire off from there in energy transactions, so in perception the active powers reside in and discharge themselves from the surface. It is there, he sensed, that living bonds are forged and the transfer of vital energy takes place. *The Night They Raided Minsky's* is structured, and rather successfully as cinematic art, upon this perception that instead of being nothing more than an inert shell, skin is charged with life and vitally explosive. Among its properties are its powers upon the contact of one sense with another, specifically the skin with the eye, to energize and activate.

Pauline Kael noted this virtue and aptly identified it in her book title *Kiss-Kiss, Bang-Bang*, but, unfortunately, she meant her title to be a condemnation of the movies for their triviality. Her genius knew better than her elitist intellectual principles, however: it recognized, as Friedkin's did, that the supreme event in the world of skin consists of a sensory caress followed by an immediate explosion of exaltant life. That is precisely what happens in visual perception: light kisses the eye and explodes on the retina, igniting a series of firings in the synapses along the optic nerve that eventuate in an explosion of activity in the brain. What happens before and within the eye when artificially imposed and old skins fall away is not the discovery of nothingness but the discharge of radiant vitality in resplendently new skin. And that new skin is always coming on through.

Taking it off, then, is unquestionably what movies are about. For this reason the movies inherently tend toward the skin flick. Or, conversely, the skin flick only does what comes natural for the movies. Yet skin flicks without exception are bad movies. Indeed, the phrase "skin flick" is intended to be derogatory, and it very decidedly succeeds in being just that through combining two of the most morally abhorrent qualities in Western culture, mere surface with ephemerality. The phrase in itself stipulates that the movies it designates lack any redeeming virtues, so beg to be banned or censured, and can interest serious thinkers only as symptoms of vice, of something morally dead in degenerate individuals or the body social.

Certainly clothes are more or less completely removed from the body in skin flicks. It is not the absence of natural skin that makes them bad movies. Just the reverse, in fact. A surplus of skin to the exclusion of everything else necessary to art would seem to be to blame. But that is not the case either. Though the clothes are absent, something else, some artifice, unnatural and invisible, overlays the skin, acting as a transparent protective shield that prohibits the naked eye from negotiating a direct exchange with the natural skin, and the imagination, as a consequence, from contacting its creative source.

I Am Curious, Yellow provides a case in point. It is the story of an energetic young woman full of life, full of the urge to grow. She first attempts to grow through exercising her intelligence as a TV interviewer, confining her attention to people's heads and their opinions. The aggressive intellectual energy she expends, stirs up, and brings out into the open in the form of political animosities culminates, however, in destructive political action, specifically young revolutionaries murdering their opposition. When the intelligence proves a bust as an agency for her growth, her instincts lead her to abandon as the means of her growth the exertion of external force upon the outside of another body. From a spectator who pries into public matters, she turns to personal relations, to love and sex, but only to find herself strapped to the wheel of desire. Involvement in life is a torment for her. To elude that torment, she seeks to extricate herself by variously abusing her body, which proves to be a comically awkward, tyrannical, and burdensome master. She doesn't manage to escape her erotic predicament, entered by travelling up a vaguely vaginal-like elevator shaft, until the end of the movie, needless to say. Then she utters in relief during her descent in the same elevator, "I'm glad that's over."

What is over at the movie's end is the passion of life. With her arousal at the beginning of the movie, she is automatically caught up in the throes of the living process, and that entails her entering the world of skin and enduring, as a victim, the playing out of the creative ordeal. Appropriately, the last phase of her adventure in skin is taken up with the sublimated aesthetic considerations of her relation as a sense object to the imaginative intentions of the director. When the creative ordeal is in its final stage, she appears formally dressed up and defiantly argues back as an autonomous person within her role with the director. The passion that enslaved her ironically brings her to her independence, but instead of rejoicing in her freedom she is glad to be done with existence.

At first curious about other people's opinions, she later suffers the compulsions of her flesh without the slightest curiosity about her skin or the visible creation. Regarding it, both she and the director are indeed yellow, and especially the director. Though she finds her adventure in skin and creation an agony, he won't even get involved in it. He shoots her skin in the abstraction of unnatural black-and-white and studiously keeps himself aloof from any physical contact or sexual arousal by her. While she undergoes the ordeal of creation, his perspective upon her and his art never wavers from the intellectual detachment that she begins from. He remains an outsider to the passion of life and never undergoes any organic growth.

As a result, *I Am Curious, Yellow*, like all skin flicks, turns out to be an anti-skin movie. In it, an intellectual bias favoring control over mutability, though never explicitly injected as a theme into the movie, discriminates against skin. The indelible presence of that bias makes it appear that judging by its skin, life is hell bent on self-destruction (though no animal demonstrates such a tendency) and so a disgusting prison man must escape in mind and spirit. His leading lady embodies the creative energy of the director (who, it will be remembered, plays an unnamed role in his own movie) and in remaining detached from her, he exploits her skin with the consequence that her excessive, pudgy flesh and his dissociated intelligence remain sterilely divorced. She falls into life from her initial intellectual command post, while he keeps his intelligence securely on top of life in its intellectual Eden. From his dissociated view of it, her skin is a machine of pain. To avoid her skin's threatening pain, he manipulates his images so that her skin, though it emerges in the movie dramatically as the instrument of the passion of life, and therefore is the very heart of her existence, is cinematically not allowed to live.

But in avoiding her skin's pain he also voids its creative potential. For the immediate and real effect of the director's intellectual discrimination in keeping skin from discharging its energy is to prohibit direct, uncensored contact of the senses and a vital explosion. In the course of his movie he does replace politics with art, a daring enough exchange perhaps, since it entails a substitution of the imagination for the intellect, the creative for the dissective, destructive power, but because his protective shield of intellectualism nevertheless continues to alienate his imagination from the living skin, his movie is blocked from becoming charged with life. A stunted creation is the result.

A significant variation on this intellectual discrimination appears in *Trash*, a product of Andy Warhol's studio. In this movie of a heroin addict who can't get it up and his mate whose mouth is alternately employed in the blow jobs of haranguing and oral sex, skin is disgustingly unclean. The urge to live and grow appears in the movie when the protagonist and his mate get their heads straightened out in an effort to put their lives together by giving up dope, begetting a child, and improving their social lot by going on welfare. Supposedly they succeed in the first two, which suggests that perhaps the director sensed that an image is being gotten up, the creative potency of the universe manifested in an upright individual, but he cannot show directly either the protagonist gotten up or his mate's pregnancy. The aspiration by the protagonist and his mate to beget new life and improve their own suggests that the exchange and creation of new life is the director's aim. Certainly it is what the world of color in motion that he is shooting with his camera naturally does. So staring him directly in the face is a phenomenon that challenges him to emulate it.

He sees the phenomenon all right—the urge and power of life even at the lowest level to stand tall—but he ducks the challenge and pursues intellectual ends. His intellectualism stands out prominently in his "critical statements"—his rudely staged scenes to force the eye to see evil, such as one in a middle-class apartment where the protagonist is toyed with by a young married couple that callously throw him out while he is in a paroxysm and viciously quarrel among themselves. It stands out more prominently, however, in the director keeping his camera at a very conventional distance from his characters' skin and viewing their lives through flat, dull photography. This detachment parallels the detachment of the director in *I Am Curious, Yellow* and, indeed, issues from their common moral bias that grants hegemony to the intelligence over skin. The distance he keeps back from his images sufficiently diverts his eye from their skin so that he cannot look closely or honestly enough at them to find life in it. And his inability to allow his images enough vitality to support themselves disqualifies them for begetting new life. Too insensitive to be aroused by the skin of his images, the director's treatment of the skin of his movie is as imaginatively dull as the nude women in the movie are sexually unstimulating for his protagonist.

In short, the director's head is as out of it as his protagonist's is. The sensory world is lost to him. But at the same time he also shares their intellectual plight. Stoned by dope and spent in wasteful mouthing, their heads cannot be lifted above the living process. Like theirs, and unlike the director's in *I Am Curious, Yellow*, the director's intelligence has been reduced to its rudimentary sensations and defensive assertiveness. It has fallen into existence. And inextricably caught up in the passion of love, there is nothing left for it but skin.

In *Minsky's* and other movies such as *8 1/2*, skin saves man from the head's death. Here skin cannot save the head. And without any intellectual haven to take refuge in, the head cannot ever save itself from skin. Within the movies' intellectual perspective, all that remains for the head is a grimy complaint against the ugliness of life. All life under the impact of that complaint disintegrates into trash and is doomed forever to remain trash. Out of touch with skin, the director's head is as vicious, as self-absorbed and exploitative, as the heads of his characters are. His discrimination against skin adds up to no more than a cover up for his cynicism, his inability to find a regenerative source or anything to value within his head. To protect itself against the senses, unlike in *I Am Curious, Yellow*, where skin's rambunctiousness is not diminished but kept locked up at a safe distance, his intellect morally saps the energy of skin by dragging skin down with itself. And in dragging down skin under the weight of its own cynicism, his intellect lies down in the trash of its own making. Its discrimination backfires on itself. In seeking to control skin, it loses control of itself.

The presence and effect of the intellectual bias in *I Am Curious, Yellow* and *Trash* are fairly subtle. But they quite overtly obtrude in *Soldier Blue*, a movie that wouldn't normally be classified as a skin flick but surely is since it is predominantly taken up with a strip tease by Candice Bergen. Before the action of the movie begins, she has spent two years having her mind stripped of its civilized ornaments by living among the Indians as the wife of the brave who abducted her on the verge of her marriage to a white army officer. Thus the peeling off of artifice is well advanced when the movie begins even though she is completely hidden under the cover of a borrowed gingham dress and bonnet. Thereafter, in the course of completing her escape from the Indians, and beginning with her face, more and more of her skin is unveiled as her clothes are literally torn off her by nature in her effort to hike across 100 miles of wilderness and survive until she is down to her last stitch. And as she is disrobed she attempts to strip emotionally and morally the polite reserve of her companion, a young Southern soldier, the lone survivor along with her of an Indian massacre. During the course of their trek on foot across the 100 miles of wilderness, she works upon him with her foul mouth, an uncompromising will to live, and, of course, her luminous skin, and with enough success that eventually they lie comfortably as lovers beside one another—with their skin decently covered! For the last stitch never comes off. In the nick of time a trader appears, equipped to outfit Candice in a Pocohantas-style mini-shift.

With the donning of that new dress, the movie takes a turn for the worse.

Until then it was devoted to stripping the veneer of romanticism off life. From that point, the romantic, or more exactly, the sentimental, is draped over it. Specifically the skin that was almost gloriously liberated is covered over by a topical issue, the brutal maliciousness of Americans, rendered in an incident reminiscent of Mai Lai. In that way the director hides skin under a heavy blanket of a morally redeeming and socially uplifting comment on the state of things. Actually, he hides it under a very confused reactionary moral sentimentality that is only slightly less absurd than the kind of overt moral read by the narrator at the end of Russ Meyers' *Beyond the Valley of the Dolls*.

For when his intelligence asserts its control over the movie, his story doesn't simply let the blue of the soldier—his restraint and decorum, his self-denial and penchant for suffering—win out over Candice's rude and rough enjoyments. Completely unaware of its own implications in the brutality, his intelligence contradictorily allows itself to be preoccupied with the story of revenge, an old intellectual narrative form that embodies the notion of an eye for an eye or justice, and the conventional climactic violence of that story. Instead of the third world of blissful pacifism, ironically imaged in the Indians who perpetrated the initial massacre, to take refuge in from both the savage and civilized, the movie is finally mired in the complex, treacherous, ambiguous moral currents of the intellect's destructive aggressiveness.

The director, to be honest, had announced the presence of the intelligence in his opening sequence by having his camera pull back from the human scene and focus upon a rattlesnake crawling among rocks. He was telling his viewers that if they would look below the surface of human behavior, and his movie decidedly would, they would find the evil reptile in the heart of man. The real viper in his movie, however, is his intellectual "analysis." His lens showed him that the Indians, an intelligence of life, and skin were his leads to living movie art. But he couldn't keep his eyes on what was openly before them; easily distracted by seemingly more important concerns, he had to overlook them to concentrate on "real" matters. And "reality" required that he substitute abstract satire for concrete anti-romance, distort images, put clothes back on the human form, and plaster a sort of *deus ex machina* upon his plot. A story that first looks to be sharply focused upon life degenerates into the banally artificial, a social message, and a commercial product designed to cash in on a topical intellectual issue. That artificiality squeezes the life out of the movie. Reductively simplifying the living truth in order to produce a schmalzy version of the relation between violence and gentleness, it lies about life.

Soldier Blue only suffers more flagrantly from what the other two movies and skin flicks in general suffer from when an intellectual filter is inserted between light rays reflected from skin and the lens of the eye to insure that the supposedly dangerous frequencies in the spectrum of life's light don't reach the center of consciousness. Skin flicks are inevitably bad movies, and *Soldier Blue* is an especially bad one, not because of too much skin, but because skin is perversely viewed through a filter of polarizing rational values rather than the naked lenses of the camera and eye. Their affliction is not idle eroticism—which, if anything, is an effect rather than a cause—but idle intellectualism.

In a movie of little merit like *Soldier Blue* the abuse of skin by idle intellectualism can be passed over as a matter of no consequence. And in skin flicks in general it is easy enough to dismiss skin with nonchalance. Why bother about skin when the movies exploiting it are not worth bothering about? If they are so bad, then their subject must be equally awful. But with a movie of considerable promise such as *Last Tango in Paris* the debilitating effects of idle intellectualism are so pernicious that the sacrifice paid in skin cannot be lightly disregarded.

As in *The Night They Raided Minsky's* and *I Am Curious, Yellow*, the subject of Bertolucci's story is the growth of a young woman, who is on the move at the beginning of the movie for no reason. Out in the streets of a teeming metropolis where mobility abounds, she looks for a place of her own where she can get it all together for herself in her own way outside her subordinate position as the child of her mother. She is involved in a rite of passage from adolescence to maturity; that is, she is in transit between a lesser and a greater individuation. As a female, her blind urge is to begin her transformation to mature individuality by establishing her territory and building a nest.

The promising possibilities for her successfully maturing are borne by the love triangle of the dramatic situation consisting of herself, Jeanne, a bourgeois French girl, Paul, an animal American, and Tom, a frivolous visual imagination; by the parallel and interlocking love triangles of Paul with Jeanne and his wife, Rosa, and of Rosa's with Paul and her lover; by these three triangles together; and by repeated shots of three levels—an overhead railroad, a walkway over the street, and a street or water course below. But the threefold interaction of these situations and images have the doors shut on their intriguing possibilities by the opening and closing split-screen shots of the movie. These shots smother the subtler life of the triangles in a dualistic scheme, limiting what can happen in the movie to at best a reversal of its two halves. Which is all that does happen—namely, the prevailing red and blue tones of the opening split-screen shot switch sides in the last shot.

Jeanne finds herself afoot in the world of the imagination. That is clear from the movie opening with paintings, the implied sculpture in the apartment, most of the events occurring in the Rue Jules Verne, the title's reference to and the performance of the tango, and Tom, who repeatedly materializes out of nowhere, being an imaginary figure of Jeanne's own creation. Her life is in every respect an aesthetic phenomenon. The opportunity to participate in the creative venture lies at her feet; she only has to open herself to it and join in. But her double vision gets her in the fix of having to choose between the two extremes of Paul and Tom. She ends up verbally committed to Tom, now her non-existent and defunct imagination, but cinematically committed with neither, standing aloof and isolated, an unrelated "I." Her interpositioning of herself between Paul's skin and the powers of the visual imagination blocks anything from happening between them or for her. The promising imaginative context for the meeting of two values—the natural and the civilized; of two cultures—French and American; of two stages of culture—the agrarian and urban; of two modes of life—the itinerant (a hotel on the street) and the homestead (a second floor apartment); of two social classes, as well as of two opposed human types, bears no fruit. Jeanne's move down to Paul's level, as imaged in the agony with which she submits to his brutalizing sexual assaults, and admitted in words by her, amounts to enslavement, and his ascent to her level, as imaged in the last tango, is doomed to robotism. Only these two contrary moves and these two opposite, extreme climaxes are open to them. There is no middle ground where they can pool their resources. Accordingly, though Jean and Paul make out in private, they get nothing going in public, or in French society; the natural and the civilized, etc., remains categorically disjoined.

The vital energy that moves Jeanne and Paul simultaneously to the apartment retreat of their encounter and the urge of Paul as well as Jeanne to grow by getting his head clear of the pain and confusion induced by the noise of the passing train in his first appearance in the movie get squandered. Now Paul, under the inspiration of Jeanne, is aroused out of his animal sleep and undergoes development from a sensory to an intellectual man. But the mutual repulsion of the lovers prevails over their mutual attraction when Jeanne, at the end of the movie, while inside a dark enclosed space and standing up and still, denies any connection with Paul lying outside in a horizontal circular, still-born fetal position. Jeanne's exclusive emphasis on the differences that separate them in refusing to admit Paul as an equal into her intellectual domain aborts their mutual passion for union. Necessary complements of one another if either is to grow, they must penetrate each other's space. Jeanne's inability to tolerate Paul's love perpetuates the hegemony of place and its attendant hierarchy of vertical space—the basic conditions of her life and the movie—over their effort to get their lives together in one fully alive individual skin. A patent sign of Jeanne's futility is her allowing herself and her relation with Paul completely to upstage Tom, who, after he reacts with abhorrence to the stripped-down room, both too rudimentary for his taste and a bourgeois, rational, female trap to domesticate his creative energies, is relegated not only to the minor role on the periphery he has had throughout the movie, but to oblivion.

Jeanne's stripping down to the raw life of her skin in the stripped-down apartment of her love-making with Paul, in effect the stripping away of the veneer of French civilization by an American savage, culminates literally in an explosion—a gunshot in the chest with which her head kills Paul's body—that spells dissociation and death. In this explosion the energy that sets her going toward mature individuality gets discharged wantonly in self-defense. The consequence of that destructive use of energy is that she ends back before where she began, perhaps conscious of and insistent upon her divorce from the physical, masculine realm but still her mother's little girl closed up in her mother's place. Whatever happened to her beyond hunting for a place was initiated by Paul and when he is repudiated and dead, there is no power of life in her; she is simply the power of negation. From her opening movement she has arrived at a standstill, and is capable then only of killing. Perhaps she has ironically fallen from innocence, or risen into the first stage of maturity, intellectual selfhood or self-consciousness; nevertheless her "guilt" leaves her nothing with which to go on toward her stated marriage with Tom and the creative uses of energy available in his powers of imagination. The sacrifice exacted from her by the idle intellectualism that rules the movie is nothing less than her life.

Once again in *Last Tango* the creative potency of man is obstructed by an intellectualism that refuses to face up to the primitive energies of skin. As in all the other movies, the sacrifice of life to idle intellectualism results from the deflection of vision from sex, life's passion to indulge in its perpetuation and proliferation independent of social sanction, to the taboo, from the thing in itself to the idea of the thing, from existence to the essence, from the mythic to reason, from the individual to the class and categories. But *Last Tango* more profoundly than any of the other movies portrays the moral illusions that follow from the deflected vision of idle intellectualism. More intimately associated with Jeanne, the bearer of the movie's essential moral attitudes, than the other directors are with their protagonists, Bertolucci is in a position to see that the deflection employs the concept of matter to break skin down into a kernel and chaff, a living and a dying part, and arrange them in an order of dominance that assigns exclusive supcriority to the higher and finer element, the spiritual leavening, over the leaden material part. The upshot of identifying the abstractable, essential element as the true life and putting down the body as a dead weight is a moral perversion which dislocates the source of creative potency. Consequently, the disembodied and nonexisting pass for the real, while the actual locus of life gets treated with contempt. That is, death is made to look good and creative energy evil.

Jeanne lives for the abstracted element, as revealed by her passion for names and personal history, for identities and the past. But in living by and for the abstracted element she cuts herself off from the source of her vital energy. For her intellect has no powers of its own. Its distinctive virtue is that it is fascinated by and dwells among the eternal and immutable. Since it does not house the powers of motion, it cannot change, and without the powers of motion working in her, Jeanne cannot grow into mature individuality. There is no way she can develop or expand starting from abstraction; it is impossible for her to conceive her life then will it. When she deprives herself of Paul's explosive vital energy by killing him, she perversely shuts herself off from the source of growth. Thereby she dooms herself to ending cooped up in her mother's middle-class apartment, a pale reflection of life devoid even of the powers that were astir in her at the beginning of the movie.

The other side of the dislocation of the source of creative potency by Jeanne's double vision is that the alive looks dead. To begin with, her own skin lacks any special lustre or grace. Appropriately for her stage in life she has the undifferentiated body of an adolescent and her body does not change in this respect by the end of the movie. As her dark body resists mature definition, so Paul appears in her eyes to be a dense physical weight dragging her down into a slough of inertia. For her, skin can be no more than an indulgence. To yield to and gratify the erotic desires that become active in her as a vehicle of her growth is to have her mind raped. And that is precisely what Paul does to her when first he denies her hunger for the identities of names and personal history and then buries her under his enervated mind and saturnine body, violating her biologically and treating her as an object of his will to dominance in an unreproductive act of sodomy.

Owing to the dislocation of the creative source, Jeanne can see skin only as dead. But it never appears more deadly to her than when it moves on its own, which it does when Paul, self-propelled, begins his positive approach to her and himself becomes interested in names and personal history. Whereas the energy of the train that at first wracks Paul's head with pain does eventually set his head in motion, the agony of sexual penetration for Jeanne is nothing compared to the repugnance of having her head penetrated by Paul's autonomous motion. Neither has any enthusiasm for motion. They never enter machines at all, much less with the purpose of accelerating their activity, and this aversion includes their own bodies, the elementary machinery of their lives. Intolerant of the transformation and intensification of energy accomplished in the work of machines, Jeanne fights off the imaginative energy of Tom in the subway station, as Paul had held his ears against the noise of the train, and both scorn the tango dancers. But when Paul's mass, paralleled by the disappearance of the sculpture covered by the white cloth from the apartment, transforms into self-motivated energy, Jeanne is sent scurrying for the shelter of her familiar home. Paul's coming to life puts her intellectual control over life in jeopardy. Because of her moral illusion, she dare not let the energy of skin about her into her mind anymore than she dare let the energy of her own life work its way through it. By killing Paul and thereby granting exclusive authority to abstraction over skin and the living individual, she paranoidly closes out all spontaneous vitality, securing her mind in its aloof tower of disjunctive powers by reducing that kind of energy to the condition of her own static state. Her desperate killing of the supposed death without kills her chances for mature individuality. The crowning irony of her life is that she not only sees skin as dead; abiding by the illusions fostered by the moral perversions of idle intellectualism, she lives for death.

Seeing the dead as alive and the living as dead, Jeanne is totally blind to seeing the possibility of dynamic sensuality. Her blindness keeps skin from inspiring her, her senses from fueling her mind. In accordance with her illusion that skin is out to kill her, she resists playing in her own movie. Her imaginative powers create Tom, who would, in turn, recreate her as a free image by liberating her skin in the movie he is making. But Jeanne imagines Tom as a fixed quantity: he shrinks from the challenge of the stripped-down apartment, does nothing in particular, is vulgarly ignored by children, and fails to make his movie. Moreover, Jeanne conjures him up beside a train then fights him off in a subway station, shutting off the flow of energy between them as she does that between Paul and her. She can no more enter the machinery or tolerate the activity in her mind of the visual imagination than she can that of the body. She does in fact, as noted earlier, inhabit the world of the imagination. Because of the bias that alienates her from the source of vital energy within her, a thorough bourgeois, middle-class all the way, she cannot avail herself of the opportunity immediately before her to exercise and benefit fully from her own creative potency.

The opening abstract expressionist paintings of Francis Bacon, the implied sculpture, the locale of Rue Jules Verne, and Tome's movie making not only declare that Jeanne inhabits the world of the imagination; they also establish that *Last Tango* is patently art about art, and as such a self-image, a view of its own skin. As a movie about itself, about the life of the imagination, it sets out to be as fully alive as it can in its own unique, particular way. But it no more enters into the world of itself than Jeanne does. The story it tells from the first to the last shot of the movie is a transition from art to reality or death, from the image to the word (Jeanne's spoken renunciation of any connection with Paul), from the priority of the imagination to the dominion of the intellect, which is the old story of the emergence of intellectual man from his animal origins. The potential in the story's beginning is not worked out: Bertolucci fails to imagine the art in art, to perpetuate the life of the imagination from a work of the imagination, to derive a living individual from a living individual. His failure and Jeanne's results inevitability from a refusal to look directly at the individual. Unable to see the individual in his living wholeness, neither Jeanne nor *Last Tango* can be alive individuals themselves. The final sacrifice they pay to idle intellectualism is not just that of skin but of everything that goes with it—the life of art and the imagination, or mature living individuality.

As in *I Am Curious, Yellow*, *Trash*, and *Soldier Blue*, the intellectualism in *Last Tango* is certainly idle: it does nothing positive and contributes nothing in support of the active powers. All the intelligence can do in all these movies is proscriptively command, "Thou shalt not." Which is precisely what Richard Schickel's statement amounts to: beyond the ridiculous implication that he knows what the profound mysteries are and how they should properly be approached, his strictures of the lens simply mean don't pry, inquire, seek, move out, grow, or create. It has always been an offense to orthodoxy to look upon the face of God, and idle intellectualism, whether in skin flicks or movie criticism, would put blinders upon the eyes to keep vision within the narrow track of the moral status quo. Its purpose is to prohibit the eye from getting down to the raw creative potential in man, to interrupt the creative process short of genuine creative achievement lest its authority be undermined. Whether perched outside, cynically floundering about inside, a gross irrelevancy, or committed to death, idle intellectualism introduces its superficialities in the hopes of stemming the expansive organic and creative energies of life.

I Am Curious, Yellow, *Trash*, *Soldier Blue*, and *Last Tango In Paris* have the merit of starting from interesting possibilities within the medium but they shy away from seeing those possibilities through. And in shying away from them, they prove not the wantonness of the lens and skin, but the barrenness of their intellectual prohibitions against indulgence, which happens to be a prerequisite to vigorous exploration. Because they won't permit indulgence in skin, they are unable to involve consciousness in the passion of life. And shut out from the living process, they are doomed to be failures of imagination. Their incoherence, superficiality, offensiveness, and futility as individual movies would be of no consequence except that the failure to make a good skin flick is a failure to imagine life, love, and the individual, supposedly the enduring values of Western civilization. Thus everybody loses from bad skin flicks. As failures of the imagination they conspire to deprive us as living creatures of our birthright, our right to the realization of our individual lives.

To be sure, skin flicks merely reflect the deeply entrenched taboos of the West's intellectual culture against indulgence in the vital and erotic. These taboos have largely restricted our imaginations to the first phase in the act of love, the courtship period, when lovers discover and turn on one another. The freedom of our imaginations here is readily evident in the degree to which, especially in the movies, we have refined the surprise of recognition, the tensions, dynamisms, and strategems of courtship, and the exchange of vitalizing affection down to precise details of gesture—mostly in the face and hands but also in the general demeanor of the clothed body.

As for imagining the third phase of the act of love, the consummation or sex, we have at this point accomplished nothing, absolutely nothing. Sex is totally beyond our positive imagining. Mostly we still "leave it to the imagination," that is, suggest it. And when suggested, only those who have gone through the complete act in fact can really know what follows: the innocent or inexperienced are left ignorant. But the price even the experienced pay in "leaving it to the imagination" is the loss of a vision of what it might be. Without such visionings we remain stuck in the perspective William Faulkner spoke from when he wrote that if man was born double and could watch himself fornicate, the human race would disappear from the face of the earth in one generation. We are limited to negatively imagining sex, to seeing it as morally intolerable brutishness or as absurdly comic. In hard pornography movies, where it is devoid of passion, sex is restricted to inert physicality. When explicitly shown in movies with some pretensions to artistic merit such as *Camille 2000*, it is ludicrously phony. The usual close-ups of the contorted or enraptured female face or the clawing hands and the groaning of women under sexual assault and climax on the sound track are glaring imaginative cop outs. Sex as an exhilarating, triumphant liberation can be found only in comedies like *Rally Round the Flag, Boys*, which ends with the monumental surrogate orgasm of a giant phallic rocket spuming off its launching pad, permissible and unnoticed because it is rendered metaphorically. Our imaginations can handle sex as long as it does so with that kind of displacement. We dare not yet get up close enough to sex to begin to imagine it in a directly affirmative manner without blushing.

But we have, though only recently—for the last 80 years at the most—begun to break the taboos against skin and to image the second phase in the act of love, the strip during which the object of affection is intimately encountered and caressed. Those taboos are sufficiently relaxed now so that the major aesthetic enterprise of not only movies but our culture as a whole has become the imagining of the body of man and of his world. Extensive displays of flesh in the mini fashions and bikinis; encouragements to touch in encounter groups and sensitivity training; books on the sensuous man and woman, love's body, and the revolt of the body; and college courses on the philosophy of the body—all testify that our imaginations are active in the encounter of alive senses and the exploration of the mysteries of the body. All the great movies of the sixties have demonstrated that to be so.

Bela Belazs pointed out decades ago that the new visual culture of the 20th century, borne primarily by the movies, requires the development of a highly sophisticated body "language," an elaborate and precise articulation through physical details. And at the same time he was writing, Ernest Hemingway, while scorning his New England literary forebears for having nice clean minds but no bodies, repeatedly proclaimed the desirability of a body that fittingly houses the human spirit. The imagination of skin is still in a rudimentary stage, however. For instance, there is considerably less art to the strip in the movies at this point than developed for the stage by Gypsy Rose Lee. Unclothed actors are embarrassingly stiff and the director looks on at them with a frozen eye. The naked body in movies instead of experiencing the sense of liberation that comes with "skinny-dipping" remains stiffly encased. As Rachel in *The Night They Raided Minsky's* continues to be after repudiating her father's repressive morality and also the inhibitions of the verbal comic played by Jason Robards. And as Jill St. John is in *Diamonds Are Forever*, where despite being scantily attired most of the time her body remains a discomforting static object. Like Rachel, we have just reached the threshold of the liberation of the body and are still ill at ease, like adolescents, in our skin.

Ingmar Bergman exemplifies our inability still to imagine how to take it off gracefully. His advance from the intellectual writhing of Antonious Block in *The Seventh Seal* to the physical writhing of the two sisters in *The Silence* amounts to a considerable progress toward skin, human love, and earthly life through his involvement in the movies as a medium. Nevertheless he continues to imagine skin as a torment, and that is as true in his exceptionally fine skin flick *The Rite* and his latest color movies *The Passion of Anna* and *The Touch* as it is in *The Silence*. His inability to get over his bias that skin is what dies and both imprisons and betrays the self inhabiting it reveals his but also our limitations as a culture in imagining skin. His accomplishment has been to help bring the issue to a head. For guidance beyond where he has gotten to in seeing the living individual we must rely upon the great moments of skin in movies that appear casually when people of other cultures who live close to and comfortably in their skins pass unnoticed before our eyes. The native marriage dance at the beginning and the later charges en masse by the largely nude warriors in *Zulu* is such a moment. The nude and close-up skin shots in the Japanese movie *Woman in the Dunes* is another.

If we really care about life, love, and the individual, we will have to imagine skin. Skin can't be left to the imagination in the pejorative sense. Life, love, and individuality aren't laid full-blown in man's hands; he can clarify his potential for life and love only by disciplining his imagination upon progressively more fully realized embodiments of life and love as values in art, which will then act as a model for the actualization of them as values in everyday affairs. Without the imagination of skin, the adventure in life and love of modern Western man is at an end. The natural world, the individual, the good life on earth, all these inciting values of Western culture since the Renaissance, die on the vine if we fail to imagine skin as the boundary that locates an entity in the visible creation, distinguishes it from all other entities, and articulates its single existence.

Movie makers have no alternative to indulgence in skin. The quality of movies is inseparable from it. Distrust of the visible creation—of its "laws," its values, its kind of freedom—results in lifeless and false art. As it does in the movies of Mike Nichols, especially his *Carnal Knowledge*. His imagination hasn't been able to digest the terrors of death from aging as well as war or the perpetual alteration in human relations exemplified by sexual promiscuity. All outsiders to the mysteries of skin, Benjamin of *The Graduate*, Yosarrian of *Catch 22*, and the characters of *Carnal Knowledge* die a thousand deaths without ever living one life. Coming to the visible creation with a fearful eye, in protest, and defensively, they cannot muster the courage to let the life within them go and so they can't get into the life about them. This failure of nerve derives in part from the obsolete Arnoldian dream of seeing life steadily and seeing it whole. Contrary to this dream the eye jumps around continually in the thick of things. To see life, love, and the individual, it will be necessary for the movie maker to concentrate unfalteringly on the living individual, to get as close in and as close up as a lover. He will have to fall in love with the camera and make love with it. The authenticity of his loving will be immediately evident. His images will be as intensely and excitingly alive as lovers are in the presence of one another.

But the movie maker's indulgence in skin is also the golden bough for our entrance into the mysteries of life, love, and individuality. A medium of skin that has emerged in the time of Western man's growth when he can entertain with equanimity the likelihood of there being nothing more necessary to him than dwelling with enlightenment upon the face of the earth, the movies are our most direct means of exploring these mysteries. More importantly, the revelations achieved through the movies will be the measure of our lives and loves. We have always allowed that the medium of human existence, whether it be God, reason, nature, or whatever, sets the norm and judges man, not man it, and that to live a good life man must get right with that medium. The movies in fact are a moral phenomenon that shows us how to evaluate ourselves in relation to and get right with the visible creation. However, to reveal fully the normal or proper, the movies have to enter wholly into the profound mysteries of the visible creation through the lens. For the lens has the power, when approached with reverence, to reveal its own mysteries—not by force of will, that's an intellectual strategy—but by acting confidently upon and rigorously developing its own virtues—by going with its strength instead of negating it. In revealing the profound mysteries of the lens through so indulging it, the movie maker will automatically unveil the mysteries of the visible creation.

Eventually we will have to take off the protective shields over the eye. The good of our lives depend upon it—upon, that is, great skin flicks. However, it has to be imagined, not ripped, off. Maybe the latter is what is happening in skin flicks today. Maybe they are instruments for tearing our prurience and prudery out of our systems. On the other hand, it may be necessary to turn the revelations of the mysteries of the visible creation over to other cultures that are more at ease with skin than we are. Whatever course is followed, there can be no substitute for getting on with the imagining of skin and thereby liberating our lives from the superficialities of idle intellectualism.

Any doubts about the wisdom of taking it all off should be dispelled by a moment's consideration of which comes first and is the more subtle, resource-ful, and resilient, man's life or his idea of life. Obviously, the latter is shaped by men, whereas the former is a gift; the one an historical fabrication, the other Being. And that difference is further borne out by the fact that life loves moderation, reason extremes. A functional arrangement of numerous elements in a complex pattern, life can exist only through maintaining a delicate balance, immediately exemplified by the respiration cycle and the circulation system. Reason, on the contrary, enforces ideological polariza-tions upon life and either–or alternatives. Man's intellect, in other words, is his own making, his life the divine's doing. The mysteries of skin are nothing less, finally, than the mysteries of creation. Indulgence of the eye in the vis-ible creation acts as a corrective to dogma; it leads to conforming the mind to life rather than life to the mind. In a time when man senses that he inhabits a creative universe and that it comes as naturally to him to explode vitally intact the radiant and electrifying charges of life in himself as exploding the energies of nature with his technology does, it is inevitable that he should give priority to his creative potency. It is also only proper that his imagina-tion be fascinated with skin.

f You Don't See, You're Dead:
The Immediate Encounter With the Image in *Hiroshima Mon Amour* and *Juliet of the Spirits*
Part I

WILLIAM R. ROBINSON

A STUDENT IN A MOVIE COURSE felt impelled to write to the professor when it was over, "I understand why the intellectual and moral leaders of my denomination have shunned movies in general, and I agree with them. Maybe the film-makers of some such films as *Jules and Jim* have something to say, but is it worth saying?" This is not a frivolous comment. The student rightly sensed that when judged by the criterion of "something to say" the movies are a waste of good human time. They decidedly don't say it as words do, and can't; and if saying is all that matters for human beings, then there is no possible serious justification for bothering with them. But an even more astute observation results from the student's instinctive defensiveness. Alarmed, she recognized quite clearly that the movies pose a fundamental threat to the orthodoxy and authority of the church—or rather, just to orthodoxy and authority; that they are, from the perspective of rational values, an eminent danger. She speaks most astutely for entrenched attitudes, however, when she implies that the movies attack denominationalism, or "the tendency to separate into sects." Her denominational commitment sensitized her to the erosive effects of movies on dogma, the doctrinal base of all sects. And she was thereby enabled to recognize, quite accurately, that defense of her sectarian commitment required her to condemn the movies.

The complicated inclusiveness of this student's protest, all unconscious to be sure—but therein lies the significance of her attitudes: they represent a deeply entrenched idea of life and man—evidences a deep intellectual outrage at the image's audacity in tilting with the established moral order. Her mind revolted at the thought that a medium commonly denounced as an exciter of man's base passions, an opiate of the masses, and an escapist fantasy land for wish fulfillment should be admitted into the solemn rational and spiritual counsels of responsible leaders.

Many, of course, will resoundedly acclaim "Amen" to that sentiment. But most of us, I think, will be tempted to dismiss her reaction to movies nonchalantly as the grumblings of the uneducated and anti-intellectual. That is not the case, however. If anything, she is too well-educated—or maybe the right word is indoctrinated. Her reaction to the movies does not differ substantially from that of the learned sociologist Daniel Boorstein. Boorstein apocalyptically warns his reader toward the end of his book *The Image*, "Now, in the height of our power in this age of the Graphic Revolution, we are threatened by a new and peculiarly American menace. It is the menace of unreality. The threat of nothingness is the danger of replacing ideals by the image." Elaborating, he went on to explain further the nature of the menace with the comment, "Now we replace the dogmas by which men live elsewhere, by the images among which we live" and "have come to believe in our own images, till we have projected ourselves out of this world." But "men need not live in a world of images…our life of images is a strangely modern, New World life." What Mr. Boorstein means by an image suffers from vagueness, ambiguity, and blatant contradiction, but he leaves no doubt of his intention in these warnings when he drives his point home with the conclusion that "We have lost our grip on reality when we have let ourselves believe that the movies can ever give us the nub of the matter." The movies and images, in his view—and it is the student's view dressed up in a more sophisticated rhetoric—are trivial and distracting, unreal and irrational; they sap our moral vigor by seducing our minds into being satisfied with the shadow when we should demand the substance.

Though implicit in the student's remark, Mr. Boorstein's bitter complaint makes it very explicit that what images above all threaten is dogma, or reason, the faculty that specializes in formulating dogmas and thrives upon them. Both Boorstein and the student speak from the bias of Western intellectualism that, since Plato relegated the particular to insignificance and banished the artist from the Republic, has proclaimed the image enemy of the True, the Beautiful, and the Good.

One of the ways to justify images in order to accommodate them to the demands of reason is to claim that, in the end, they do exactly the same job words do. Rudolph Arnheim justifies images in precisely this way in his essay "Art as Thinking." Sympathetic and conciliatory, he writes in the image's defense, "We are the victims of an inveterate tradition, according to which thinking takes place remote from perceptual experience." In this tradition, "since the senses are believed to be concerned with individual, concrete events, they are limited to collecting the raw material of experience." With these remarks Arnheim bares the epistemological assumptions of the student's and Boorstein's categorical pronouncements. He goes on to bare the underlying moral bias of their objections when he observes that in this tradition it was "not enough for the senses to be considered inferior in their cognitive function, all enjoyment based on perceptual experience came to be reputed as carnal. Indulgence in the arts was thought of as sinful." But he cannot stop there. He compulsively goes on to say, "which indeed it is when the function of visual images is restricted to the mere entertainment and distraction of the senses." That is, the senses and art qualify as worthy only if they humbly serve the traditional standards of thought. Though Arnheim would stop short, as the student and Boorstein might not, of flatly banishing images, his formulations are also intended to keep them under the control of reason. Even he allows that the visual can be treacherous and therefore has to be kept in its place.

Undoubtedly the most famous alarmist regarding the danger of images is Marshall McLuhan. McLuhan has set going the cry of "media" to alert us to a terrifying predator that has stealthily infiltrated into the flock with the intention of devouring us all one by one. "The present book," he said of *Understanding Media*, "in seeking to understand many media, the conflicts from which they spring, and the even greater conflicts to which they give rise, holds out the promise of reducing these conflicts by an increase of human autonomy." This apparently ordinary, innocuous statement rests upon the assumption that media are compulsively given to inciting and intensifying conflict and therefore are insidious, malicious, and disruptive. That happens to be the same assumption that the student's remarks as well as Boorstein's issued from. From this moral base it follows inevitably for McLuhan that "any medium has the power of imposing its conditions upon the unwary." And by a media, it must be remembered, he means the technological extensions of one of the senses, so that all the evils he attributes to media originate in the senses. With the eyes, their images, and the movies, it follows for McLuhan, one can either enslave or be enslaved, be a servomechanism or a master mind.

The instrument for avoiding enslavement by the senses and the means for increasing human autonomy, their opposite and enemy, for McLuhan, is man's abstracting tool, analytical intellect. That intellectual power, properly employed, will enable him to find what McLuhan claims "we seek today, either a means of controlling the sense-ratios of the psychic and social outlook, or a means of avoiding them altogether." In the rude power struggle among the human faculties inevitable from his intellectual point of view, man can be free only if he dissociates his mind from his senses—and, by extension, his body, the primeval technology that has served as the mechanical vehicle of his life. Under the guise of prophet of the new, McLuhan performs the old trick of trying to sell us an ancient panacea. But he offers us nothing more than the old Baconian, Faustian use of "hot" knowledge to gain power over our world. As he sees it, the rule of reason is all that can save us from the living hell of media.

In pawning off on us an ancient panacea, McLuhan does manage to help alert us, should we have been suffering from the somnabulism he accuses us of, to the fact that all the objections to images and the movies enumerated above are rooted in a traditional rationalistic dualism—a view of things that he himself claims we have passed beyond in the present post-literary stage of our culture, at the same time that his work perpetuates and intensifies that dualism. The ironic upshot of that unintentional contradiction is that it is not the senses but reason that insidiously, maliciously, and disruptively induces conflict in and among men. Yet at the same time McLuhan also helps to remind us that media—images and the movies for present purposes—are dangerous revolutionary force. Of course, that is precisely what the student, Boorstein, and Arnheim intended too, but McLuhan reminds us by means of an apocalyptic flair that makes his pronouncements seem like startling news. In fact, however, his pronouncements are no more than the Christian sermon applied to one of today's topical subjects. Like the sermon, they seek to direct our eyes away from the world and force them upon the heaven of abstraction.

Can there be any question, indeed, has there ever been any question, that the senses and their extensions are, well, not necessarily dangerous but powerful? Hardly. The moot point instead, from Plato on, has always been whether their power is vicious or beneficial, for evil or good, and therefore is to be suppressed or liberated. Today that moot point takes the form of a very practical consideration because we have reached the stage in the development of our culture where the eyes and images are in a position to overthrow the rule of reason. Specifically, that very practical consideration is, does the emerging hegemony of images over the word forebode a colossal disaster for man or the dawning of a glorious new age? So extremely polarized, the alternatives, common sense impatiently proclaims, are false. As usual in real affairs, the answer lies somewhere in between. But it is in the movies, the discipline where today colors in motion can be studied, that the moral questions highlighted by the exaggerated alternatives are being worked out. It is not accidental as a consequence that in recent years the movies have extensively and at their best been explicitly given over to adjusting the ratio between images and words. The movies are our moral frontier today. Nor should it come as a surprise that as they have explored the juncture where images challenge words for moral hegemony, so the probing of the camera eye has evolved a solution to their relationship that puts the lie to McLuhan, Arnheim, Boorstein, and the student—to the position that images and the movies are inherently illusory, sinful, destroyers of autonomy, inducers of conflict, etc. That, in short, they are evil.

The threshold of the door to the new morality open within the movies can be stepped across in a wide variety of recent movies (actually through recent development in the medium itself, such as the replacement of black-and-white with color film), but none can serve that purpose better than do Alain Renais' *Hiroshima Mon Amour* (1959) and Federico Fellini's *Juliet of the Spirits* (1965). The first, the greatest of French movies in the post World War II period, marks a momentous cinematic breakthrough, and the latter brings to the first full fruition the new cinematic possibilities that begin to emerge in *Hiroshima Mon Amour*.

In these two movies two mature women go abroad in the world of images, to Hiroshima, Japan, in one case, to a summer home at the shore in the other. These places challenge the two women to achieve a viable relation with them. They are tempted to avoid such a relation by taking refuge from their human situations in the memory of an earlier love affair in *Hiroshima Mon Amour* and in the role of wife in *Juliet of the Spirits*. The challenge is extended when Hiroshima and the shore, acting like a psychedelic drug, blow the minds of the two women. That is what happens literally to the French woman during her sexual orgasm, a counterpart to the atomic explosion, that climaxes her "impossible love" with her Japanese lover, and to Juliet when she faints at the seance after being told, "Who do you think you are? You're no one to anybody. You don't count, you wretched thing." Their respective places open up for the two women a totally new human possibility, and their stories consist of what they do in response to that expansion of consciousness.

To follow what happens in the movies and thereby see this revolutionary new human possibility that opens up not only for them but for us, it is necessary to recognize that *Hiroshima Mon Amour* is not an anti-war and certainly not an anti-American film—"the personal story," Marguerite Duras noted in her script, "always dominates the necessarily demonstrative Hiroshima story"—and that *Juliet of the Spirits* is not a movie about a marriage which has lost its savor—her husband figures considerably less than many another person or spectre in her spiritual life. Rather, the first is a love story in which the primordial event is the "life that goes on," and the second renders the gestation and birth of a new individual, indeed, a new kind of individual. In both movies it is life carrying out its purposes that provides the motive power, direction, and coherence of what happens.

That is quite evident in the opening sequences of both movies, the template patterns for what can, and does, happen thereafter in them. *Hiroshima Mon Amour* opens with skin show, close-ups of the darkened shoulders and arms of nude bodies indistinguishably entangled with each other. At first the skin is sprinkled with ashes, then with beads of water; finally, it appears oiled and glows afresh. Each alteration occurs by means of a slow lap dissolve, so that in effect the sequence renders the cracking and sloughing off of the old skin as the new skin behind it pushes out into the light. Each alteration is also accompanied by a larger perspective and increased movement, especially in the hands. The total sequence, in sum, constitutes a metamorphosis, a resurrection of life from death: from ashes via water arises a renewed creature with an enlarging scope and power of action. *Juliet of the Spirits* opens with a searching camera, intent upon carrying out the eyes' inherent purposes, emerging from a woods and darkness, jumping a willow tree, entering Juliet's house, and there, after some delay among Juliet's things and servants, discovering her face. Eventually, when it sees through her eyes and witnesses her hallucinations, the camera even moves behind Juliet's face and uses her visual powers as the vehicle of its seeing and its inherent purposes. That face and its visual powers are the camera's subject, and in them resides all the talents that will guide the camera's movement and Juliet through the reconstruction of her new life after her mind is blown and the old worthless self is discarded at the seance. Out of nature and darkness and a social edifice emerges a potent human face and eyes about to embark upon an adventure in autoregeneration.

Hiroshima Mon Amour

A complicating factor present in the opening sequence of *Hiroshima Mon Amour* has been ignored. It is the introduction of words on the sound tracks.

Though words eventually appear on the sound track of *Juliet of the Spirits* also, the way they are introduced in *Hiroshima Mon Amour* makes all the difference between the two movies.

The complicating factor emerges in *Hiroshima Mon Amour* during the resurrection of the bodies when the Japanese lover protests, in the first line of the movie, "You saw nothing in Hiroshima. Nothing." (Quotations from Evergreen Press film script.) His remark obviously presumes an antecedent remark to which it is a reply. Hence he injects words into the action under provocation, to ward off an assertion that by implication is made by the French woman about the same time the new life is being born. Her incantatorily intoned recitation right after the first line of the movie leaves no doubt of the import of her words and what the Japanese is objecting to: the lofty stylization whereby her words enwrap themselves in themselves indicate she uses them to turn her back upon concrete sensory perception. Now in accusing the French woman of seeing nothing, the Japanese, while implying his own commitment to seeing, posits sight as the cardinal instrument for accurately apprehending the world man inhabits. And the French woman also grants sight that status with her immediate rejoinder, "I saw *everything. Everything.*" But the pressure of her insistent words upon his mind forces him also to do as she does, to counter her implied intellectual rejection of what she saw with his rejection of what she says. Moreover, his remark emphasizes the negative, both grammatically, by denying that she has seen, and conceptually, by asserting that she has seen the ultimate negation, "Nothing." Thereby his verbal defense of seeing ironically admits into the movie, in form as well as substance, an intellectual counteraction to the organic action of the initial images.

The Japanese introduces saying as the opposite and enemy of seeing, but it is the energy of the French woman's mind that makes its way into the movie via his words. In her love making, she had experienced the threat of nothingness Boorstein spoke of as occurring when images replace ideals, and in a violent reaction she ignites a war of words on images. She does so under the implicit claim that the images, not her words, are deadly. But the movie reveals the contrary. Her words inject a hostile quarrelsomeness between disembodied minds (the speakers are not visible as heads and so as sources of the words until well into the movie) into the living process already underway in the opening metamorphosis of bodies. And that quarrelsomeness extends beyond itself to polarize the movie's sound track and the images on the screen. On occasion images capture words and turn them to their purposes, as when the French woman exclaims about her lover's beautiful skin; at other times, as in the Nevers flashbacks, words dominate and exploit images. These complexities of their war are never lost sight of. They infuse everything in the movie, including the protagonists and their behavior. But the basic relationship between free images and words or images under the control of words is uncompromising incompatibility.

That uncompromising incompatibility is no more evident, as the Japanese rightly notes, than in the French woman's failure to see Hiroshima. For Hiroshima enacts on a macro-scale the regeneration of the opening skin show. It, too, exemplifies new life in the making. In the story told by the larger features of the movie's images—by the encompassing settings within which the protagonists move—space and activity, just like in the opening montage, tend to increase until the last sequence back in the hotel. More specifically, in the background the over-all action moves from the initial close-ups of the lovers absorbed in one another in a hotel room out into the open air and public affairs of the city. And while that expansion occurs the quick cutting of the opening montage gives way to longer held shots of explicitly identified places; the new world that rises from the city's ruins consolidates itself as man's environment in the Post-World War II period. Just recently built, this new world is literally new, but it is also new in kind: technological, electrical, and plastic, it is a wholly invented, unnatural environment that, appropriately, never sleeps. In this self-regeneration Hiroshima complements and extends the fertile bodies of the two protagonists.

So when the Japanese asserts that the French woman saw nothing, he accuses her, in effect, of not seeing what is happening in the images on the screen, for what is happening there has happened and is happening in Hiroshima. Beginning with the animals that arose again from depths of the earth and the ashes and the flowers that blanketed the city after the atomic holocaust and present in the rebuilt city bustling with activity in the day and lit up at night and continuing in Hiroshima's noisy, active streets, its lively residents (such as the smiling tour guide on the bus and its irrepressible children), the various cats, Western clothing and an American style bar, a hotel named New Hiroshima, water in a variety of forms, and the neon phallus dominating the night scene, the details of the background testify to the miracle of life's infinite capacity for as well as the actual accomplishment of its rebirth. The fact before the French woman's eyes is that a scorched human desert, emulating nature's capacity to be reborn seasonally, has resurrected itself out of an atomic graveyard. That miracle had happened to the French woman earlier at Nevers as well, in the regrowth of her hair, ascension from her tomb in the cellar of her father's house, and her marrying and having children. Indeed, hardly a scene occurs either Hiroshima or Nevers that life resurgent isn't present in one form another.

The French woman would have be literally blind not to see what is happening so extensively and repeatedly before her eyes. It isn't a matter of her being physically capable of seeing life resurgent as it perpetually happens in and about her, of course. She simply refuses to see it. Her willful blindness becomes immediately apparent when her Japanese lover asks her, not too far into the movie,"Why did you want to see everything at Hiroshima?" The French woman replies, "Because it interested me. I have my own ideas about it. For instance, I believe looking closely at things is something that has to be learned." The form of that statement blatantly exposes everything about her manner of approaching life. In a word, it is high intellectual. She can't express her motive as a passion; that motive has to have its source in an idea; and she has to give preference to "I believe" even in talking about looking.

Marguerite Duras' script instructions are, appropriately, "We never see her looking." And the camera follows them faithfully, except on one occasion when she stares at her lover's hand as he lies asleep. What happens when she does look at that hand reveals why she dares not look. The hand moves as though independently alive (when the Japanese lover awakens, she tries to attribute its movement to a dream, to a cause beyond it, but he denies that). In a mood of relaxed erotic fulfillment, she is off her guard and open. Then suddenly she has her first recall of her German lover and that mood is horribly shattered. A flick of life's wrist, so to speak, like a villain springing menacingly from the darkness, causes her to flinch, and during that flinch she suppresses the urge set astir in her by her love making, and exemplified by the hand's mysterious twitch, to break out of her asleep state into the present.

There is one occasion on which she sees though we do not see her seeing. That is when, at the end of her opening extended "operatic" incantation, she suddenly breaks off her self-obsession to remark, "It's extraordinary how beautiful your skin is." This amazing turn about in attention gives way to her Japanese lover laughing ecstatically and serves as a prelude to their mutual relaxation and laughter in the shower shortly afterwards. Looking is good for her; skin releases her into the present moment to enjoy innocently what is immediately before her senses. But even then her mind will not "let it be." Right after her eyes have beheld the wonder of her lover's beautiful skin she compulsively asks, "Are you completely Japanese…?" She can only deal with him by categorizing him. And when he tells her during the shower that she is a beautiful woman, gazing closely, adoringly, at her as he is wont to do, naturally, without having to learn it, she notes, "You speak French very well." Less dramatically than with the hand but no less compulsively, she translates the visual into the verbal. Her habitual attachment to the verbal gets further confirmed visually when she turns from her Japanese lover at his house to examine the books on his bookshelves and is shot standing with her back to them just before they make love. To win her love here and throughout the movie he must seduce her away from this rival—from the books and the words they house.

The French woman clearly had a deeply engrained habit of turning her eyes away from the things of the world before she looks at the hand. Events trick her into actually looking. Quite to her surprise, beautiful skin, directly and quietly presenting itself, offers her release from her verbal "hang-up" through aesthetic meditation. She lets down her guard, unaware that a formidable power inhabits that skin, and as her guard comes down her eyes further dilate. When her eyes are sufficiently open so that she can see what is really happening before them, the life force inside her, making contact with the life force outside her, explodes in her face and jolts her into recalling the terrible agony life had once afflicted her with. Her compulsive stratagem is to take refuge in her mind, supposedly a safe promontory above the treacherous currents of life. From that aloof vantage point, she can then avoid looking closely and see only what she wants to see.

Very definitely, she does see only what she wants to see. The things that normally call her back to this world, like the punctual cough of the old man outside her hotel window, invariably support her expectations. And when they don't, to prove her expectations right, she automatically transmutes life, joy, and love into dying, pain, and death, as she does in her reaction to the reconstructions of bombed Hiroshima in the museum, where she ignores in her verbal comment the people moving among the exhibits.

On the one occasion she claims to see she doesn't see at all visually. In reliving her time in the cellar she reaches the point where she remembers the breakthrough in her convalescence and comments, "I am beginning to see. I remember having already seen before—before—when we were in love, when we were happy." Seeing she associates with being joyously alive and coming alive (in a parallel incident her Japanese lover literally awakens her by staring at her while she sleeps). But she buries that crucial moral fact under a comparison (which is an exercise of analytical intelligence) to another kind of seeing, that of the mind's eye. Her words once again block her vision, and instead of actually seeing life's visible potentialities for love and happiness, she understands that on the visible plane her existence is prey to the cruelty of life. Her understanding, constituting the traditional enlightenment of intellectual man, is rendered in the subsequent lines, "I see my life. Your death. My life goes on. Your death goes on." In form—opposites paired—as well as content, these lines embody the French woman's ultimate intellectual truth. In them she goes as far as her verbal powers can take her in insight into life, to the final division that the first words of the movie instigate, the unfathomable juncture where life and death stand diametrically opposed. From that perspective she can see only the rending disjunctive effects of the living process and overlooks the resurgent unitive effects accompanying them.

Obviously, the French woman fails to see Hiroshima because her words, contrary to the forward-thrusting story in the background, impel her back in time, inward psychologically, and upward spatially toward abstraction from the generative current of life. This impulsion to become detached from concrete, empirical events, borne by the two protagonists, creatures of words and the specific foreground images within the environment of Hiroshima, reaches its climactic point dramatically and visually when all sounds and all but the minimal sights of a solitary face are erased from the screen during the French woman's recall of Nevers just before the Japanese lover slaps her. At that moment, the moment of the most intense concentration of her mental powers, she withdraws completely from the expanding environment into her head. That contraction of her mind into itself is what the camera focuses upon in its search for the force that governs her existence and begets her antipathy to the resurgent life in Hiroshima. (This visual identification of the French woman with her head is in sharp contrast to the visual identification of such supremely cinematic characters as Charlie Chaplin, who almost always is shot in full figure and whose genius resides in the means of his elusive mobility, his feet.)

A similar contraction occurs when the nude skin of the opening montage gets clothed. While the Japanese, after first appearing in a shirt, dons a dark Western suit, the French woman proceeds from nudity to a Japanese kimono bearing a flower design to a borrowed bathrobe to the nurse's uniform of her role in the peace movie to her all-white, colorless Occidental clothes. With these changes of apparel, she returns from a free, then exotic, to a role-playing, and finally normal identity state, and in doing so shrinks from direct existential engagement into the old familiar cell of herself. That shrinking back into the old familiar cell of herself, incidentally, is not interrupted by the second time they make love: the lovers are not seen then disrobing or disrobed. And as they don their clothes, the protagonists come to rest. Their diminishing activity is especially noticeable in the French woman, who had been vigorously active in seeking out her lover in Nevers, where she got around nimbly and indefatigably, while she moves reluctantly and lethargically in Hiroshima.

The contraction is even more evident on the sound track. There the protagonists indulge in more and more talk about the French woman's past while being less and less active physically. Called up by and embalmed in words—which embody experience over and done with, institutionalized in concepts—their talk is like an exoskeleton hardening into an adamant shell about the original soft center of flesh. The dead words, and the images they evoke, consummate their intention of obstructing the living process at the end of the movie, when the French woman names her lover "Hiroshima" and he names her "Nevers." This denominating kills the action begun in the opening images.

Marguerite Duras establishes quite clearly the import of this naming with her script notations: "She has succeeded in drowning him in universal oblivion…they look at each other without seeing each other. Forever." Owing to the nature of images, the movie proper prohibits such a decisive ending. When the French woman speaks the name "Hiroshima," the Japanese, while standing dominantly over her, places his hand on her mouth to stop the words and smiles benignly. Though his gesture overrules her demand for verbal absolutes, he doesn't put a stop to the effects of words. Instead, ambiguity then reigns, and Marguerite Duras herself disclaims any knowledge of whether the French woman stays in or leaves Hiroshima. But this much is certain. The French woman sits totally immobilized upon her bed and has abstracted her lover back into the place, the background, from which he had emerged. Thus in the story told on the sound track and by the specific foreground images, the individual human beings cover up their naked vital energy with clothes, burden themselves with their acquired customs and roles, and bury their uniqueness under place names.

In sum, against the background of an accelerating world, the protagonists wind down. Their words do them in, estranging them from the burgeoning fecundity of the body of the world as well as from their bodies, an estrangement readily apparent in their being fertile while stripped but barren when clothed. Despite having entered *in media res* as a secondary power after the movie's action had commenced, the French woman's words not only object to what her eyes behold; they progressively gather strength over the course of the movie until they adamantly resist the forward thrust of images. There is no question as to where her loyalties lie. Nor is there any question as to the effects of her words: their animosity toward images, by prohibiting a viable relation between Hiroshima and herself, exclude her mind from the new life in the making and so from a rebirth for itself. And never able to enter into the immediate present with her mind, the French woman compulsively seals herself off from the living process.

To appreciate fully what follows from the French woman's refusal to see, it must be kept in mind that *Hiroshima Mon Amour* is a love story. It is an odd love story, to be sure. Normally a love story relates development toward a union forged by passion and consummated in a marriage of some kind, unless it happens to be a tragic love story, and then adverse circumstances or a character flaw abort the potent union. *Hiroshima Mon Amour* is version of the tragic love story. Instead of focusing upon the meeting, incitement, growth, and culmination of erotic passion among young lovers, it begins at the moment of ecstatic sexual union and concerns itself with the return of experienced lovers to their separate selves after self-transcendence in a moment of intense erotic excitement. In short, it is a story of disunion. Against the background glow of the erotic fusion achieved in the sexual entanglement of the bodies at the beginning of the movie, an antibody invades the love of the French woman and Japanese, then proceeds to eat away its cohesive center. That antibody does not arise from circumstances; it has its origin in a flaw in the French woman's character.

In the love story a chance encounter erotically excites the French woman to venture for the second time in her life into the realm of "impossible" love. On one plane she is a happy wife and mother and successful actress—though this career suggests an inclination on her part to assume Protean forms rather than settle for a fixed role. In Hiroshima, where she is nameless and outside the conventions of French and Western mores, she wanders unawares into a no-man's land beyond normal consciousness. (She came expecting to play a part in a movie devoted to promoting peace and to take in the horrors of Hiroshima as a tourist, both routine, superficial enterprises; everything that happens to her beyond those intentions involves her more deeply than she came prepared to be involved.) Transcending all prescribed codes of human relations, her affair with the Japanese isolates her on the frontier of human existence. There, all is unconventional and intellectually incomprehensible; no rational ground supports her. She is thrown radically back upon herself and so challenged to engage herself erotically without the aid of anything in addition to her will to love.

But as her mind panics at its vision of nothing, so her heart takes refuge from such demanding love in her intellect. It is true that in the treacherous currents beyond normal consciousness she can tell the story of her German love to another for the first time, linking her two impossible loves together as common events, and she has the satisfaction of feeling "how nice it is to be with someone sometime." A union of sorts does occur. But at the same time the former love inserts itself interferingly into the new impossible love. It defines a class, and in doing so provides a prototype by which she restricts the new impossible love to being no more than the old one was. Legislating against novelty, her compulsive mind has its way again. The result is that she can't love, and never can say that she loves, whereas the Japanese does. She prefers to shut her heart to love as she prefers to shut her eyes to Hiroshima.

That willful erotic blindness reduces her to a cause and effect mechanism, most apparent in her plea, "You destroy me. You're so good for me...Take me. Deform me, make me ugly." Having shut itself off from her erotic center, her mind gets inextricably bound up in external relations, the logical conclusion to its inherent penchant for detaching itself from the concrete world via abstraction. Indeed, it so decisively abstracts the French woman's consciousness from awareness of the active powers within her that, as signified by the necessity of the Japanese slapping her to call her back to the things of this world, she can return to life from abstraction only through a hard knock like her impossible love. Otherwise she resides contentedly, without awareness of any greater possibility, in an intellectual limbo. Her inability to break the barrier of abstraction on her own is a sure sign not only of her failure to open herself to Hiroshima but of a deficiency of self-love. When her mind intercedes between her eyes and the resurgent life astir in Hiroshima, it simultaneously interposes itself between the energy set astir in her by the excitement of her eyes and her consciousness. In that position it keeps the circuit of vital energy from being joined and forces her to reject the resurgent life in herself. And rearing her own vital energies, she becomes dependent upon forces acting upon her from the outside for her positive action. Incapable of opening herself to her own vital energies, she cannot love on her own initiative. Her self-rejection gets blatantly spelled out when, oblivious to her lover's protest, "No, you don't have a memory," she compulsively intones, "I have a memory. I know what it is to forget. I have tried with all my might not to forget. I wanted to have an inconsolable memory...I struggled with all my might, every day, against the horror of no longer understanding at all the reason for remembering. Why deny the obvious necessity for memory?" What she remembers most, ironically, is her forgetting. That is her angst: she suffers from the shame of not being sufficiently ashamed to be able to keep intact the poignant agony of a lost romantic spiritual consummation, the ideal of her existence. For her, loving is remembering, fidelity to what once was. More precisely, she is in love with suffering, with the self-denial and self-sacrifice that automatically attends devotion to the dead past. And owing to this "ancestor worship," she cannot assimilate and thereby transcend the pain of her first impossible love, a prerequisite of her letting her second impossible love thrive.

The greatest horror of all for the French woman, plainly, is not the atomic devastation of Hiroshima but to be guiltless. She visits Hiroshima on a pilgrimage of sorts to pay homage to a shrine of suffering and death at which as a repentant sinner she can validate her existence as sufferer. Her devotions at that shrine pronounce suffering to be the hard core fact in her life. It above all else is what lasts for her, and certainly by her dedication to suffering she helps to perpetuate its duration. But instead of blaming her, as she hoped it would, Hiroshima offers to wash her sins away. However, without sin, that is, the painful moral memory that she betrayed her God and that He lies in wait to avenge that betrayal with His punishment if she does not punish herself, she will lose her identity. That already happened when she entered the nameless condition. She had forgotten; her impossible love with the Japanese eclipsed momentarily the horrors of Hiroshima. Most of all, she forgot herself. But she can't stand being nameless and not knowing who she is.

The love the French woman experiences in Hiroshima challenges her to recreate herself beyond the "possible," to grow into a radically new kind of human being who moves about easily in the realm of the impossible. But lacking the courage to forget her identity, let go of her past, and go on joyously, she shrinks from erotic entanglement, preferring to martyr herself to her suffering. The assault of the image of her German lover's death and her agonizing loss of that love had shocked the life out of her. As a defense mechanism against that shock, she eagerly embraces mental suffering. Her ploy is intended to one-up the rude, vicious suffering inflicted by life through replacing it with the more refined suffering of the mind. That stratagem obviously does not put an end to her suffering. Rather, it establishes suffering as the reason for her existence. In denying the suffering of life, she ironically exalts suffering to the status of lord of her existence. The stratagem does allow her the vain comfort of feeling morally superior in her mental suffering to life's aggressive energy, since she bears rather than causes suffering. But like her words with images, her suffering negates erotic passion and the motive of regeneration inherent within it.

Though the French woman decidedly maintains her identity, she does so at the price of permitting the demands of her mind to prevail over the excitement of her heart. Her erotic passion yields to her frenzy for the unconsolable, which turns out to be a predisposition to submit to the fixed point at the back of her mind. Very simply, she values her name more than her love. As a consequence, whereas her Japanese lover sees in her a thousand women and pushes her into recalling Nevers in order to know her before she had fallen into the identity she clings to in her mind, so that he could love her as pure possibility, she descends from their ecstatic union set upon reviving the conventional labels that will indelibly separate them as human beings from one another. Accordingly, when the impossible love is over, she has left only an abstraction, a memory labeled and filed away in her mind, the corpse of her impossible love. That conclusion terminates the love affair and leaves her crushed under the massive burden of suffering she so devoutly longed for. The French woman had come with the express purpose of looking closely and had looked closely enough to erotically single out a remarkable individual from the scene. But she could not give him the undivided attention necessary for sustaining his beautiful existence in her consciousness. And because her attention span for the living present was too brief, she not only never sees Hiroshima, she also never sees him. In fact, to see Hiroshima, which exists only in the specific entities that constitute it, she must rely upon the ability of her senses, noted by Arnheim, for perceiving the concrete individual to look lovingly at him, the central image for her in the field of images that is Hiroshima. But she never does—except for when she looks at his skin and at his twitching hand on the bed. Those brief fuelings of her imagination can only momentarily distract her from the dark pall that normally shades her eyes, and so she steadily sinks, as she inevitably must, into grief as well as immobility.

Though he does in his desire to know her abet the French woman's retreat into words and memory, the Japanese lover is not to blame for her failure to love. In the last shot of the movie he places his hand over her mouth and the camera focuses on his face looming over her while he solemnly assigns her the name "Nevers," acknowledging her abstraction from him. But otherwise he is a visual type. He has no mental images that compete with his present; he likes what he sees and wants to see it again (while her concern is, "Don't you want to talk to me anymore?"); he is quite ready to submit to self-obliteration in perceiving another, as he does in becoming identical with the French woman's German lover; and he does not hesitate to declare his fascination with her image, though her manner corrupts the form of his statement because in loving her he is uniting his consciousness with hers when he says, "I think I love you." He quietly exemplifies for her the virtue of images and the benefits to be gained by looking, but he is forced into the background by her, and quite literally so when she turns away from him and leaves him walking behind her out of her field of vision in scenes toward the end of the movie.

The fault lies decidedly with her. It is she who persists in driving the wedge of words ever deeper between the two lovers. Her negativism emerging ever more explicitly in the course of the movie until she very simply specializes in reiterating "No," she closes herself off from a living relationship with other human beings, not just her environment. Forbidden to look at the Japanese by erotic fixation, remembrance of things past, and conditioned anticipation of future terrors, her love humanly comes to nothing. It is just an affair, a repetition of an old experience that gets nowhere, an abstraction of the mind imperceptible by the senses, a classified memory. With that name she completes the closing of her eyes, totally negates the life resurgent in her, and slips back into the old rational mode.

The French woman's refusal to see Hiroshima and her failure to love the Japanese, it should now be evident, together add up to a rejection of the love of life. Admittedly, despite her surrender to an obsolete moral habit, the French woman has a talent for life, as her two "impossible" loves indicate, loves that took her soaring above artificial human antitheses such as Germany and France, East and West. Moreover, she is tormented by the sacrifice she must make in refusing to participate in the living process that surges invitingly about her. Were she simply a one-dimensional creature, the everpresence and expansiveness of life resurgent would not hound her into ever greater grief throughout the course of the movie. Nor would she plead as she does on two occasions to have her mind and identity once and for all destroyed by her Japanese lover, knowing that it will be good for her. She is chosen as a possible agent for the heroic venture of carrying forward life's urges for reforming itself beyond the pales of existing forms. But her mind and words succeed in bringing the life active in her to an impasse where "it is as impossible to stay as to go."

The impasse to which her mind and words bring her block off forever the opportunity extended to her by Hiroshima to become a human being commensurate with its potencies and potential. Her failure to see is finally a failure to come alive with Hiroshima. Certainly, the Japanese lover's accusation that she has not seen Hiroshima, in addition to accusing her of not using her eyes to see images, more profoundly accuses her of not being alive. He tells her, in effect, that to come alive she has to become a visual creature, that her visual powers—as they momentarily do with his beautiful skin—can carry her on an adventure beyond words into the impossible on the frontier of images if she will let them. But to see everything that her eyes can show her, he implies, she will have to love her eyes, their images, and, above all, the life inherent in images. For it isn't that she doesn't see; she very clearly experiences the active powers of life. Nevertheless she doesn't see everything. Her mind instantly intercedes in her perceptions to prohibit a favorable response to the exciting stimuli transmitted through her senses. What her mind won't let her see is the virtue of the powers of life active in her body and images. Her perversity is moral.

Hiroshima and her impossible love offer her the chance to act with or react against the powers of life. To come alive, she must become visually affirmative, which means visually active, not only by seeing the virtue of images but also by getting into motion with the world her eyes behold. This is the crux of the moral quarrel that sets the lovers at odds with one another: they disagree not over the fact but the value of life. The Japanese finds the active powers of life, despite what he has been through owing to the war and the atomic bomb, to be worthy of affirmation. On the other hand, to her mind the active powers of life are inescapably evil. She sees nothing because she is morally blind, because she cannot admit the capacity of the visible world for doing good. Her conscience imposes a myopia upon her eyes that confines their transmissions to the destruction the active powers of life leave strewn upon their creative path and the death they eventually entail.

Above all else, then, Hiroshima and her impossible love offer her a new moral awareness. She has only to embrace the full range of the living phenomenon with her conscience to receive the blessings of such an expanded consciousness. Then she will enter into the act of life and act creatively herself. Her body and her eyes will have saved her life. But when her eyes had been assaulted by the image of her German lover's death, she had learned in that traumatic moment that life is out to kill her and sooner or later will. Her spontaneous renunciation on this occasion of the image of death deactivates her eyes. Thereafter, rather than risk the terrors of being a creator beholden to demolish old forms of existence to clear the way for new ones, she always answers the question of whether to look or not to look by averting her attention to verbal matters. That discrimination by her conscience, ultimately against her own flesh and the body of the world, severs the vital link that unites her active powers with those of Hiroshima and her lover. As a result, she cannot metamorphose; her consciousness excluded from the vital matrix, she cannot enter into the living process and participate in life's profoundest activity: she cannot be born anew. The thought of carrying out life's necessary tasks intolerable to her conscience, she settles for the routine security and safety of a stable, or "possible," middle-class life on the social level and uncompromisingly commits herself to the eternal, the dead that cannot alter or grow, on the moral level. Her reaction to the image of death is to kill the life within her.

Therein lies her tragic flaw: she lacks the scope and depth to assimilate the pain of living into herself and then transmute it into new life. She lacks imagination. And lacking imagination, she is limited to reacting in passive negative condemnation. Merely a reflection of life and so unable to do as life does, she cannot vitally act and therefore pass over the threshold into the living world. And the inevitable fate that follows from her compulsive passivity is that she is stuck with a vision of death rather than freed by a vision of life. The triumph of her mind on this occasion makes of her existence a living death. Thereafter her mind insists that she see death in everything she looks at. Cutting decisively to the quick of her life as it does later to the lover's erotic passion, it pervades her existence with a sense of the end. While in the images on the screen, and according to the effect of images upon her, every moment is a beginning, she can see only the end in every beginning. Of necessity for her, every moment no sooner starts than it is over and done with. Her mind thereby strips her of her undeveloped possibilities. This is another dimension of the nothing she sees—her life without a future, her existence, swathed in death, a blank.

Though the French woman goes abroad in a world of images with the intention of learning to see (significantly, she had "learned to read in Nevers"), her persistent verbal negation blocks the transformative potential in herself. Yet despite her success in squelching life resurgent in herself, she can't accomplish the same feat with Hiroshima. Its resurgent life does not begin and end with her. Quite the contrary. She finds herself immersed in a creative environment on the move. Such is the way of the world in which she appears and her story occurs. Her province covers no more than her personal choice between the alternatives of to be alive or not to be alive, to see or to say, to get with the active powers and let them flow through and out of her or to set herself against them.

Now her personal story, in accordance with Marguerite Duras' instructions, remains in the foreground throughout the movie. Nevertheless it occurs within a larger story. That larger story, the over-all action of the movie reveals, entails the French woman leaving rural Nevers—her love there is seen in flashbacks to be an affair of fields—for, first, an urban life in Paris, and later a cosmopolitan life Hiroshima. Her story figures in this transition from an agrarian to an urban mode of life; it recapitulates upstage Europe's implied development from a provincial through a nationalistic to an international culture in the background. Without seeing or knowing it, her horizons expand with the development of European culture from the simple sensory life and attendant parochial morality in Nevers through the sophisticated rational life of Paris to the supra-national and supra-rational adventure in Hiroshima. In this context her entrance into the Orient, a visual culture, as an actress in a visual art, amounts to an opportunity to regain her innocence, to put herself back together again, after her "fall" from the Paradise of her childhood in Nevers owing to disruption of her rural bliss there by the evil nationalistic fervor of World War II that tempted her heart with forbidden love.

Personally, her adventure offers her a chance to be healed, to have her head and heart joyously reunited in regained innocence. Her opportunity is but one thread, however, in a tapestry occupied with the grand enterprise of the passage of Western man into the atomic age. The encounter of her French consciousness with the place Hiroshima, where atomic energy was displayed for the first time, not just as a theory, but as a condition of existence for mankind at large, is an evolutionary phenomenon. The blowing of her mind results from no less than the blowing of the intellectual foundations of European civilization. Moreover, as a result of the blowing of those intellectual foundations, the grand enterprise includes the healing of the division in man that goes back, so the archaeologists say, some 10,000 years (to when European and Asian man went their separate ways in the Tigris-Euphrates valley), through the meeting of East and West. Which, of course, occurs in the love affair between the Japanese and the French woman, and is especially evident in his Westernization—his facility with French, his interest in the French Revolution, and his Western clothes. He stimulates her eyes, she his mind. They are drawn to one another, ready to love, as specific agents in a monumental historical drama, and within that drama their impossible love moves them toward a common center where they can effect a viable fusion of Oriental and Occidental ways of life.

All these currents of change flow inexorably about the French woman. Her instantaneous retreat into the old rational morality at the beginning of the movie and her injection of its divisive negative force into the unified, generative life of images through the Japanese lover's opening utterance cut her off from nothing less than the "spiritual" adventure of our time, the uniting of man within and with himself and with his world. Her exclusion from the currents of change marks the extent of the triumph and tragedy of the words that issue from her mind. They unconditionally win the war. The war had the purpose of preserving the hegemony of words over images, and in retaining their dominion, words impale every facet of the French woman's existence upon a dualism that originates in the bifurcation between her sensory and her intellectual powers. This is where she begins, and this is where she ends: at the crossroads where words confront images in a standoff. Despite her having come to Hiroshima to look closely, the French woman had no disposition to do so, never learned to see while she was there, and did, indeed, as her love claimed, see nothing. She violates the criterion of seeing that she herself admits to be the key to truth and value by never looking into what is going on about her; but, in addition, since the image provides her with the means of perceiving the single, organically integrated, whole individual active within the living process, her mind prohibits her from reconciling her consciousness with its environment, her past with her present, and her conscience with her life. The way of the image lies open before her. But deprived of the image's beneficial effects by her mind's suppression of the image's active powers both outside and inside her, she cannot in the time of her life live. Instead, her mind estranged from her eyes, she remains forever alienated from her world, humanity, and herself.

This is the first part of a two-part essay.

f You Don't See, You're Dead: The Immediate Encounter with the Image in *Hiroshima Mon Amour* and *Juliet of the Spirits*
Part II

WILLIAM R. ROBINSON

JULIET OF THE SPIRITS

FOR ALL THE FRENCH WOMAN'S PERVERSITY, *Hiroshima Mon Amour* implicitly reveals the image to be the crucial agency in the human individual becoming vitally whole and active within the living process. It is true that the French woman fails to draw strength from the image and carry through on the image's potential life. But her failure does not totally eclipse the virtues of images. In fact, she herself pays tribute to those virtues with her disavowal that her Japanese lover is made to the measure of her body and the city of Hiroshima to the measure of her love. Though not acted upon, these assertions allow that her deepest hungers can he fulfilled in the world of images. What *Hiroshima Mon Amour* leaves implicit and incomplete, *Juliet of the Spirits* brings out into the open. Fellini's movie takes the adventure begun in Resnais' movie, but aborted at the threshold, on across into the new human possibility. As is glaringly evident in its opulent primary colors, *Juliet of the Spirits* directly encounters the image; and by doing so it permits the image to radiantly burst forth in the full splendor of its pristine glory and work its way out through the movie. Thereby it comically affirms the virtues obscured by tragedy and negation in *Hiroshima Mon Amour*.

For that to be possible Juliet has to be exactly opposite of the French woman in moral predisposition. She has to be a woman of images rather than a woman of words. And, indeed. that is the case. One indication of Juliet being a woman of vision is that she contains within herself the powers that the environment possessed in *Hiroshima Mon Amour*. Genius pronounces that to be so when he remarks, after testing for the presence of genius in Juliet, "There is a strong magnetic force…the reaction of the pendulum is positive" (quotations from Ballantine Books film script). The spirits confirm his assessment at the seance when, speaking through him, during his trance, they identify her as "A girl, naturally…very gifted… Oh, yes, this girl is gifted. Very, very gifted." As does Jose when he notices that the plants in her yard have received much love and comments, "If you can give so much love every-day, your heart must be filled with love." (For Juliet, this remark implies, the French woman's impossible love is natural and normal, not a rarity.) But it is her grandfather who incisively and succinctly designated what everybody else immediately responds to in Juliet when he tells her, "…you are full of life."

Coming very late in her story, her grandfather's testimony to her powers could be taken to signify that Juliet only comes to her fullness of life at the end of her adventure. But what is then thematically and narratively out in the open manifests itself immediately in the movie when her husband Giorgio shows up at home with a band of raucous revelers, having completely forgot-ten the day was their fifteenth anniversary. After all that she has planned, prepared, and looked forward to, Juliet, if an ordinary woman, should have been crushed. Instead, looking at her image in a mirror, and drawing strength from it, she says to herself, "don't be stupid. Don't start crying now." Not suffering, remembrance of it, grief, or regret, or any of the things the French woman gives her life to, but getting over it and getting on with the present possibility occupies Juliet. In this way, her fullness of life enables her, as it did Hiroshima, to see through adversity and take advantage of the possibility before her. That tiny episode shows she is disposed, not to remember, but to do as life does, to let go and go on, to be open and ready for growth, expan-sion, life now, the new.

Juliet's reliance upon her visual powers gets extensively displayed narra-tively in her avoiding the French woman's habit of defensively talking back to the images that impinge upon her vision throughout *Hiroshima Mon Amour*. Juliet prefers to look on noncommitally while from all about her spirits con-tinually subject her to a verbal barrage. That difference is more specifically evident in the French woman hostilely reacting with words to images on her own initiative, while Juliet has to be prodded into a verbal response. So little of a verbal initiator is she that, except for rare occasions and toward the end of the movie when she takes charge of words, the first words in a scene are always spoken by someone else. The same is true of the episodes in her story: she is led into them by verbal agents and guides such as Valentina in the Bhisma scene, her sister Adele in her first visit to Lynx Eyes' (a name used in the film script, though not in the movie, to designate the spirit played by Alberto Plebani) office, and Lynx Eyes' phone call on her second visit there. But most decisively of all in this regard, Juliet's marriage troubles, the personal crisis of her story, are initiated by Giorgio's utterance of the name "Gabriella" in his sleep. Nor does Juliet ever reply to the spirits in kind. To be sure, she rejects their verbal appeals. As, for instance, when she replies to Bhisma's advice, offered as a stratagem for not losing her husband by keeping him sexually aroused, that she ply her trade of wife with black stockings. "The prostitute's trade, eh? Good advice!" then exclaims, "I want to go out." But, as here, she never commits herself verbally in her response to the words of the spirits. She nightly senses that the spirits are abstractions begotten by words at the same time that they are temptations luring her into becoming an abstraction herself. Her refusal to respond in kind to them is her way of nimbly avoiding all their attempts to reduce her life to a single facet abstractable from its organic complexity.

Eventually, in exasperation Juliet cries out in reaction to the voices soliciting her allegiance, "My life is full of people who talk, talk, talk, Get out! All of you! Go away." Here she limits her use of words to rejecting words. She doesn't just refuse to enlist in a particular intellectual cause; with this exclamation she banishes all words from her presence. She had implicitly turned her back upon the polarizing effect of words when she fled from Bhisma's advice to yield herself in submission to her husband. In banishing the talkers, she goes one step further and overtly repudiates the spirit of abstraction, the force that begets polarization.

Like the French woman, then, Juliet, too, has a tendency to negate, to say No," and that tendency also increases in strength and frequency until it reaches a peak in a series of outbursts during the concluding montages of the movie, beginning with her exclamation directed at a huge breast, "Enough. Leave me in peace!" and ending with repudiation of her mother's authority over her with the assertion, "You don't frighten me any more." But her final rejection of words is too complete and subtle for words. Rather than directly confronting them on their own terms, she quietly leaves them behind. Which is what she literally does at the end of the movie when the spirits haunt her for the final time, as nothing more concrete than a voice, and all of them fused into a single voice, the aboriginal voice from which they splintered off, to beg her, "Listen to us. Listen closely." Her grandfather shows her how to regard the spirits with his remark to little Juliet, "Let's say goodbye to those boors." And she heeds his advice when, first, the spirits fade back into the walls of her "country" house (whose decor consists predominantly of foliage designs and colors) and the green of the bushes in her yard. But Juliet doesn't say goodbye to the boring boors. She simply walks away from them as she moves autonomously off to the right at the end of the movie. And in doing that she dissociates herself from the entire agrarian ethos, succinctly embodied in her husband, Giorgio, whose name means "farmer" or "tiller of the soil," whose extramarital love is a reactionary affair of fields, and who has the apartment of Gabriella done in the rustic style of a country gentleman.

Now words did once exercise supreme authority over Juliet's life. Otherwise she wouldn't be in the predicament she's in at the beginning of the movie nor have to go through the ordeal of growth she does in her adventure. They held their dominion over her, however, only during a phase of her life, the middle period between her childhood and the new phase she launches upon at the end of the movie. It is clear at the outset of Juliet's story that words are an atavism of this middle period in her life. Even then only a vestige of their authority over Juliet's vision remains. That is evident immediately from the way words enter into the action of the movie. In contrast to their entrance in *Hiroshima Mon Amour* as a negative counterforce intent upon blocking the flow of images, in *Juliet of the Spirits* words immediately disqualify themselves as moral forces of any final consequence. When Elisabetta, one of Juliet's maids, speaks the opening line, "Should I light the candles, signora?" and Teresina, her other maid, interposes, "No. She said she'd light them," words introduce a spirit of contention that threatens to divide the movie's action in the manner they succeeded in doing in *Hiroshima Mon Amour* in their first appearance there. But instead of opposing the flow of images, or more accurately for *Juliet of the Spirits*, the camera's movement and quest, the words quarrel among themselves. Teresina's negation cancels Elisabetta's words.

To begin with, Elisabetta's opening line, a question, does not seek to place another mind under the dominion of its truth such as the Japanese lover's assertion does. It invites a response, a reaction to a very specific possibility it poses for consideration; thus, instead of attempting to stop the action of another mind by aggressively attacking it, her question activates another mind by drawing it out. Then when Teresina negates Elisabetta's question, the first two lines together totally eliminate the possibility of Elisabetta acting for Juliet until Juliet acts first. With the alternatives of lighting or not lighting the candles herself laid before her, Juliet must act; the verbal circumstances leave her no choice in that. And act she does. She chooses. But she does not choose to enter the argument, to get caught up in the contentiousness of words. Her first word in the movie is an affirmative "Yes." Juliet's first word immediately eludes the self-centered verbal system of words. For whereas the French woman's first word, "I," founds her verbal cosmos upon the conceptual identity of a detached or abstracted, immobilized, self-centered consciousness, Juliet's "Yes," which is followed up with the statement, "I'll light them," diverts her attention away from words and focuses it upon light, and on a light to be lit in the future. This light pointed to by her words literally lies ahead of the words. The energy of her "Yes," an active verb, thrusts toward the object at the end of her statement and then beyond the statement to the object referred to by its final word.

It is true that words spur Juliet to action (as they do when Giorgio utters "Gabriella" in his sleep and on countless other occasions) and that the first thing to be directly perceived of Juliet is her voice, her verbal power. Nevertheless her use of words occurs within the action of the camera and serves as a prelude to action. Issuing from an action in progress, her words are an act performed by her, so are themselves on the move within a larger field of action. Accordingly, the negative inclination of words never cuts any deeper into the living process than the level of language; words cannot stop the action, only negate their own attempts to do so. Juliet's opening line, then, not only rejects Elisabetta's offer to act for her and Teresina's "No," but affirms a third alternative, an intention to act. And the act her choice commits her to perform continues the course of action already begun by the camera.

Moth-like, the camera had been attracted to and flew into the light of Juliet's house from the dark foliage of its opening shot. Juliet's line declares her willingness to carry on the camera's quest for the light. In linking into the camera's course of action, Juliet qualifies as well as extends that action by more specifically defining its intention. Since what she is specifically going to light are deep red candles, in effect, the potential for light within her own blood, the quest is shown to be aimed at discovering the light of life. And since the passions of life have to be sufficiently astir to assert themselves in her choice, her first line not only clarifies the camera's quest, it is also a step further toward reaching it. The camera found her by following the light; and it found her within the light; and when it has found her at the center of the light of her house, she announces her devotion to the light in such a way as to denote the presence of the light within her. There can be no mistaking this significance of Juliet's first line when it is viewed in the context of what happens to the light over the course of her story. The light the camera seeks out and Juliet adds to with her first line steadily increases in illumination over the course of the movie until, at the end, a new day dawns from the opening darkness, a "bright, warm" morning light floods her world.

When Juliet leaves her house behind, she moves in the light of the visible world guided solely by her visual powers. But before then her story abounds with verbal references and visual clues to the presence of those powers, including such unobtrusive details as shots of a band of light across Juliet's eyes, a comment on the "terrible yellow eyes" of Suzy's (for convenience this name is used for all the manifestations of the voluptuous woman played by Sandro Milo) cat, Lynx Eyes' insistence that Juliet remove her sunglasses, Valentina's casual remark to Juliet, "I'll see you at five," and Juliet's simple request when the red apple is being passed around at Bhisma's, "Let me see it." Juliet's visual curiosity here is a rudimentary form of her passion to see. She quite readily indulges that intention of seeing in giving attention repeatedly to mirrors, telescopes, eye pieces, movie and slide projectors, and TV's, instruments for extending the effectiveness of the visual powers. All the verbal references and visual clues to the visual powers, the unobtrusive as well as the blatant, reveal Juliet to he so fascinated by vision that her story is unquestionably the story of the eye.

Juliet's eyes assert themselves as the agents of her vital powers when she looks into the mirror and draws strength from her image to put a stop to her impulse to cry. Her doctor adds further testimony to this key function of Juliet's visual powers in her life by noting, on the beach, that "Our lovely Juliet always sees obscure, magical things everywhere." What he testifies to—her ability to see more profoundly than the normal person, into the subtler dimension of images where magical transformations occur—Juliet displays during the apple test at Bhisma's. To Valentina's pretentious notion that "one must see beyond appearance" (which is what the French woman employs her mind to do), Juliet candidly queries, "isn't that an apple?" and Bhisma's voice confirms her spiritual perceptiveness by remarking in support of Juliet, "It is an apple...only a little apple, red..." Here Juliet uses her eyes to see, not as an excuse for conceiving; to look at and into, not beyond. That kind of attention, she insists by her behavior among a band of intellectuals on this occasion, is the prerequisite to beholding the magical powers and feats of images.

Juliet identifies her passion to see, and establishes it as the passion of her life, of, indeed, life, when she recounts her talent as a child for closing her eyes and seeing visions. Indeed her visions are visual creatures, for her visions were mainly occupied by "tiny faces [that] would stare at me with huge. shining eyes." When she immediately thereafter demonstrates the revival of her visual powers by beholding, with her eyes closed, an image of Suzy, she not only confirms her passion to see but reveals that seeing images, and especially imaginative images, delights her more profoundly than anything else does. But her capacity to see visions as a child, it must be noted, was simply a talent then, not a developed skill. And because of the obstacles built into the rational bias of the second period of her life, Juliet, like the French woman, has to learn to see.

The education of Juliet's visual powers begins overtly early in her story while she watches TV with her maids. A TV instructress, while demonstrating eye exercises, remarks, "…more and more rapidly. These exercises will give back to your eyes the splendor…" and Juliet corrects the failure of Teresina, her romantic maid, to do the exercises right by commenting, "You shouldn't move your head. Only your eyes." The increase in the activity of Juliet's eyes and the refurbishing of their splendor proceeds through such events as Juliet's perception of the red apple, her grandfather's winking, Giorgio's focusing of the telescope for her after she says, "I can't see anything," Suzy's mirror, her repeated weeping, and TV. But the major means by which Juliet's eyes are prepared to be the explicit vehicle of her creative energy is Lynx Eyes.

By confessing his own obsolescence in noting that he is old and that movement is her concern and passing the tow rope to Juliet in the nightmare, thereby giving her a man's burden to shoulder, Lynx Eyes is the first to set her in action. Then, having gotten her in motion, he equips her during her two visits to his Eagle Detective Agency with the means for getting the firm footing for impelling herself forward that she lacks in the sand at the beach but has in the field outside her house. In opposition to Suzy's capacity for indulgence, Lynx Eyes objectifies the dynamic visual powers. His insistence over the phone that what he has to reveal to her can't be told but has to be seen and his requiring her to remove her glasses at his office and produce a picture of Giorgio establish that her visual powers offer her the way out of the death of the nightmare and her marital difficulties resulting from the word "Gabriella." For him the eyes are not passive recorders but a tool for solving problems. Juliet always turns to them in time of crises and they always see her through them, but Lynx Eyes incarnates the spirit of her empirical pragmatic capacities. Thus he is the right spirit for her to turn to in the hour of her supreme crisis. Other spirits such as Valentina and Adele encourage Juliet to know the truth (and to know the truth is, of course, the ultimate passion of the rational powers) but only Lynx Eyes directs her toward a useful form of knowledge. He does that by making her use her eyes and matter-of-factly guiding her toward worldly wisdom, toward an orientation of her intelligence that allows her consciousness to receive unimpaired what her eyes see .

Even Lynx Eyes' office is an eye-opener for Juliet. It literally lets light flow through its walls; its seni-opaque glass allows form to be murkily distinguished through it. Furthermore, it is an oasis of light inexplicably at the center of a desert of dark hallways, while inside it instruments for magnifying the intensity of light enhance the powers of vision. But it is Lynx Eyes himself who turns her reluctant eyes toward the light. In his priestly garb, while suggesting that Juliet "stop and reflect," he offers her the traditional otherwordly alternative, security against the terrors of being alive and free, by assuring her that there is an invisible spiritual world that will take care of her and make everything all right if she will just believe. But as he holds out this alternative, stated specifically as a renunciation of change and growth in this world in favor of reconciliation with her husband and holding "tight to the sweetness of a marriage maintained until old age," he removes his glasses and strips off his clerical garb. Underneath his disguise, Lynx Eyes turns out to be a priest of the magical powers.

Lynx Eyes' most astounding feat as a quick-change artist is to cite St. Augustine as a church authority for the notion that "the only way for two people to love each other truly is by knowing each other thoroughly," while inciting Juliet to commit the cardinal sin of Catholicism, the sin of intellectual pride, which she is guilty of when she blurts out, "Yes, I want to know. It's my right…I want to know everything, everthing, everything!" But throughout the movie, not only during Juliet's first visit, he metamorphoses more than any other male and as readily as Suzy does. And, of even greater importance, whereas Suzy is imagined as appearing in the two visual realms of remembered and present images, Lynx Eyes spans the two visual realms of present and purely imaginary images. He incarnates for Juliet's vision the bridge between imagination and reality and so exemplifies the capacities of the visual powers in league with the imagination of looking into the transformational possibilities of life now.

What Lynx Eyes illustrates with his clothing and the effects of his words, Valli, his assistant dressed in a white suit (and so the embodiment of integrated light), demonstrates by reading Giorgio's character from just a picture with an insight startlingly more perceptive than Juliet is capable of after fifteen years of marriage. Peering through a jeweler's eye piece at the photographic image, he comments, "a nervous temperament, docile only on the surface... One must watch him because he is capable of sudden irresponsible actions. Repressed fears and a great need for his mother." Valli doesn't merely read Giorgio's character here. Except for the last phrase, his words apply, for instance, equally to Juliet. She is of a nervous temperament and docile only on the surface, too, and also suffers from repressed fears and is capable of sudden irresponsible actions. In fact, Valli describes Juliet's behavior throughout her story. But, more importantly, she is illustrating the capacity of the eye to behold immediately the active, magical, creative center of things. Valli, that is to say, represents for Juliet's vision the phenomenon of its self-perception. He shows her how the eye can be used to behold its own image and face up to itself. Lynx Eyes clownishly hears out Valli's demonstration when later, on the second visit, he comments over the image of his own face which emphasizes his eyes moving toward the camera in a close-up shot, in a film supposedlvy devoted to a factual investigation of Giorgio, "I took these myself."

Lynx Eyes warns Juliet of what she will behold when she puts her visual powers to active use by stipulating that his investigation will present you with an image of your husband you've never known about ...you'll penetrate those shadowy portions of his life which you could otherwise never enter." In an immediately preceding remark he posits that "intimicy and secrecy [are] outdated concepts." While his remark sounds like it promises a callous invasion of privacy, he informs her that for the fully active visual powers nothing is hidden, as it isn't from Valli's eye; everything is out in the open if her intelligence is subtle enough to allow what the eyes see to pass through it uncensored. He subtilizes her intellect by explaining to her how his vision "penetrates" the image and therefore what she must emulate and surpass in order to enter into those portions of her life in pointing out that "Ours is an objective point of view, and therefore limited...the interpretation of this is up to you. We're just showing it to you." Interpretation, his remark implies, is irrelevant to seeing, and Juliet wisely doesn't interpret what he shows her—she existentially reacts to it. But in just showing his visual evidence to her, he speaks for the ability of her pragmatic intelligence to recognize that seeing entails abandoning the demand for universal truth—the grand, cosmic overview—and accepting the limited view that focuses on the finite, concrete object. He further directs her intelligence away from its tendency to divert its attention from images into rational abstractions toward the specific by letting it know that in visual perception, "Everything is important, exen the smallest detail. We can't neglect anything." Vision will occur, he is instructing Juliet's intelligence, only if it follows the eye's tendency to look into rather than away from things. Yet looking into things will not produce absolutes or certainty, conclusions or ends, he further reveals, in his remarks that "the photography is not always perfectly clear." No matter how assiduously the intelligence examines even the smallest detail it will not exhaust what is to he seen. Thus her intelligence must allow that "nothing is definite." But when nothing is definite, Lynx Eyes adds, "nothing is irreparable"; then "reality" appears "quite different, more innocent." Properly oriented and sufficiently subtlized, Juliet's intelligence will not stand in the way of her eyes moving "faster and faster" nor block their view of the creative energy inhabiting everything.

And it doesn't when she walks into the open field outside her house; her intelligence, following Lynx Eyes' instruction, admits directly into her consciousness what her eyes perceive. It lets the immediate encounter of her eyes with the image happen. And when that happens, her eyes pass the creative potency of images unhampered on to her consciousness, which, responding in kind to like kind, joins the circuit of creative energy. At that moment, a creature and a creator is born. She translates the external metamorphoses displayed for her by Lynx Eyes, and that Valli had located the source and means of, into an internal metamorphosis: change in appearance and of mind she subtilizes into a spiritual transformation. Then, and only then, do her eyes regain their splendor. In the aura of that splendor Juliet realizes in fact what Lynx Eyes had opened her intelligence to earlier and further clarifies in his final appearance when, eating from a bowl, he says while looking directly at her, "Very good! Very tasty! The very best!" She recognizes the spiritual world that she can see, and she recognizes that it is a world of value perpetually and everywhere charged with creative potency, with the good of the creation and creativity.

That is to say, with her eyes wide open, Juliet realizes what Bhisma had referred to when she said of the red apple, "it is the Buddha, the unique spirit. Things return to things. And the enlightened spirit sees the One and the Many at the same time, sees appearance and substance." But whereas Bhisma, owing to her intellectual bias, can only make a theoretical statement about what will be seen in living perception, Juliet achieves it in actuality and with a subtlety far beyond Bhisma's words. For after she rejoins the circle of her life by submerging the spirits into the walls of her house and the shrubbery, it is clear that all images exist equally as images within the visible world—and always have throughout the movie. (That fact is perhaps most strikingly apparent earlier when Juliet visits Gabriella's apartment. Though absolutely essential in Juliet's breaking away from Giorgio and emphasizing that break in its details in contrast to Juliet's house [the apartment is dimly lit, heavily shadowed, presided over by an old crone, done in dull reds and browns, and is a sedately home repository for a still photograph of Giorgio smiling happily ever after] nevertheless it is purely "imaginary." It totally lacks any "realistic" relationship in chronology or context to other episodes in Giorgio's love affair.) Valentina had noticed at the seance, "God, how many spirits. They're all around." And so they are at the end as well as at the beginning, as evidenced by their voices. The difference at the end is that Juliet successfully practices Iris' enticing prescription of "Love for everybody." And that means that she has attained a new kind of love, a love that radiates liberally from her. She no longer depends upon others loving her but out of the love of her existence loves all that exists. Thus she doesn't banish the spirits. Juliet rejects nothing and incorporates everything, every power necessary to life. And with nothing of her life alien to her, and so her visions no longer in conflict with her vital desires or passions, Juliet realizes the oneness of all that is in the unity of her visible world and the single, alive individual she exemplifies when she walks out of her house.

Her oneness with the oneness of all that is makes it unmistakable that all along Juliet lives in and by her imagination. The plain fact about Juliet is that as a woman of images and vision she is also a woman of imagination. The imagination incarnate, if you will. The child in her, owing to the influence of the summer shore setting, has been revived when the movie opens. Juliet's story renders the resurrection and development of her natural talent for seeing visions into a mature human instrument. That development ultimately entails her releasing the spirit child from its bed of flames, and in doing that she replaces the imagination of evil and death she suffers from throughout most of the movie with her mature imagination of life and good.

In the over-all act performed by Juliet's imagination, her visual powers emerge as the explicit vehicle of her creative energy. The vehicle of her visual powers, in turn, are the spirits, all the people in her life, who are, as Bhisma's assistant claims, "kind, generous, and useful even though at times they give the impression of being mischievous." And certainly that is true of Giorgio. As an image or spirit, he is as much her benefactor as anyone is. Of all the males, he is the closest to her and it is her attachment to him that she must, above all, break. But as the closest to her, he is also in the best position to be her "teacher," or her educator in the strict sense of the word, the one to lead her out of herself. Which he definitely does. That might seem most unlikely, since he blinds his senses and is apparently a man of words, talking in his sleep, conversing by phone, and turning to books under stress. But when he shuts his senses off by donning eye shades and plugging his ears and picks up books, he doesn't repudiate the sensory; he escapes Juliet and her house. All that is known about him, until Lynx Eyes' photography, is known through Juliet's conventionalized eyes. He is the captive one, the black bull penned by her.

An essential fact about Giorgio is his absence: he's gone. And when Juliet gets a glimpse of his life beyond her house in Lynx Eyes' photography, Giorgio moves facilely and indefatigably. So he exemplifies for her restless energy both the desire and the ability to escape. He demonstrates these virtues when he escapes the net of their marriage initially by forgetting their fifteenth anniversary and shattering Juliet's plans for a ritualistic commemoration of her social triumph, her control over her private little kingdom, by bringing home with him a motley assortment of very social revellers which keep Juliet from sitting him down at a table and having him all to herself. He reinforces that original demonstration by repeatedly departing in his car to hasten off to a vague public relations job and make contacts where the action is. He goes while she stays. He demonstrates his powers of mobility quite ostensibly when he and Cesarino "lengthen their legs" by practising giant steps outside in the yard while Juliet sits intellectually immobilized at the seance. And he is so elusive that Juliet cannot imagine his departures: Giorgio always slips away, gets out the door, without her being aware of or able to watch his leaving. His mobility and range extends unimaginably beyond hers.

Juliet's sister Sylva is right when she remarks to Giorgio, "You're much better than I thought you'd be. Very good!" He was a good catch, the exactly right kind of man for Juliet in the second period of her life: a man of the world without a specifiable role, an undefinable variety and versatility of interests, while mixing among exotic and active people. She could have chosen no better surrogate as the vehicle of her visual powers, for the life of her imagination during the rational dissociation of her vital powers. But he is a good man for her also during the break up of the second stage of her life. For instance, he is not much of a man of words. He spouts no philosophy, ignores ideologies, and doesn't lecture her or justify himself. In short, he is no intellectual. Indeed, unlike José, he is anything but that. He has so little respect for words that he casually admits "That it is much better to lie"—that his life is a lie. That characteristic, as Cesarino notes, makes him a hero. For he thereby illustrates for Juliet, who places a naive trust in words, the possibility of escaping her verbal confinement. And furthermore Giorgio gives her the lying word, "Gabriella," that initiates her distrust of words. At the same time that he manifests the capacity for not taking words all that seriously, Giorgio teaches Juliet to see women, first by his general erotic response to them, but decisively when he ogles the eye-exercise instructress on TV, using his eye while Juliet only exercises hers; shows Juliet how to get Suzy in focus in José's telescope while telling her, "You haven't got it set for your eyes"; then romantically dotes upon Gabriella in Lynx Eyes' photography. His lust, the passion of his eye, directs her attention to her own feminine center.

Giorgio not only contributes incisively to Juliet's freedom from words, he equips her with the means for valuing the visual. But like all the other spirits, Giorgio is expendable when he has done his job. And Juliet expends him after she has absorbed the go of his image into her. And as she waxes in absorbing his "vital juices," he wanes, until eventually he droops from fatigue and departs for a rest. He signals Juliet's rise and his decline when at the lawn party he calls her out by saying, "Come on. Everybody's waiting on you." She had waited for him at home and the revellers brought life to her house, but now, quite toned down in comparison to their initial appearance, the revellers and Giorgio wait on her to impart her life to them. But she doesn't, of course: they continue to diminish until they are nonexistent. She has drawn the life they stole from her back into herself. In other words, Giorgio not only embodies one of Juliet's beneficent powers of life; in their relationship over the course of the movie she reabsorbs that power. The condition of its dissociation from her imposed by her rational powers is overcome by that power being transferred back to her through a switch in the position of male-female dominance signaled by the manner of his disappearance. He isn't seen leaving: there is nothing left of him to leave—he fades into the dark, then is just a shadow and finally only the sound of a door closing.

That switch in dominance is played out, though somewhat more subtly, by the female spirits as well. Led by Suzy, they enact the reconnection of her imagination directly to its source. Reminding Juliet of her organic birthright, they signal the reawakening of her generative energy by reconcentrating her imagination within the circle of her concrete, earthly existence. This resurrection of her generative powers, appropriate and necessary at a time when she is ready to undergo a radical alteration in the form of her life, occurs most obviously through her getting Suzy sharply into focus. Suzy, who asks a friar, "Am I good" and is told in reply, "You're an angel," functions, like all the spirits, to further draw out Juliet's powers of life and promote her growth toward a true spiritual life.

Visually, Suzy is a model of generative potency. She not only variously manifests herself, however. Generation and regeneration go on all about her: the mirror above her bed multiplies lovers and thereby magnifies love; two minnows spontaneously generate in a glass of rainwater; transformational rites are performed at her party, and her house, open and circular, is undergoing transformation—amid, its "disorder," she is remodeling, "planning some big changes…to make it more colorful." In her house, as in her appearance, nature and artifice blend. A concrete imagination enhances the flesh and sexual energy by interfusing them in vital intimacy. Verbally. she articulates the attitudes appropriate to accepting the metamorphic potency she contains and is surrounded by, and she thereby educates Juliet to embrace rather than despise her female nature. That is the import of Suzy's professing that she accepts everything, denies herself nothing, wants to embrace everybody, and loves to fight—conflict being interest, as Bhisma points out, in zestful sex and living—and Juliet does fight, even against Suzy, when she finally asserts her own will to live.

One illustration of Suzy's powers is her constant activity: she is not only perpetually excited but constantly active: while Juliet lies on her bed and stares, for instance, she goes sliding off, down a vaginal-like chute, and swims luxuriously in the womb-like pool at its end. Suzy speaks for Juliet's generative powers in enunciating these attitudes, but she also demonstrates that inherent within those powers, in addition to active vitality, is an infinite tolerance for indulging, for laughing over and forgetting— as she does Alyosha's fetishism and Arlette's love sickness—and a readiness to allow that the world, instead of being a field of alien corn and a vale of tears, is a natural habitat where everything is "delicate and joyful" and man dwells under "a personal sun" within whose light things "don't project any shadows."

Suzy not only is good; she exemplifies Juliet's essential goodness, the goodness of herself as woman and womb or as a vessel of the generative powers of life. But for all her generative potency, Suzy has no go in her. She's boss in her house and she's constantly active, but her activity has no direction. Her metamorphoses are never completed; they don't get anywhere: the minnows are a biological regression, her remodeling is in transition, and she herself is biologically barren and, despite her many manifestations, never significantly changes, that is, never metamorphoses morally, as her confinement in the black pod of the basket that moves her in her final appearance in the movie underscores. That deficiency stands out graphically in the limousine that sits unused, gathering dust, in her yard. Suzy does have strength, and it is her strength that above all attracts Juliet. But while she learns from Suzy to embrace the generative powers of life at her own center, she ignores the advice that she "Be more feminine" and Suzy's example of that.

Just the contrary, actually. Juliet becomes more masculine. Not outwardly or in appearance, but in her eyes and imagination. Juliet doesn't imitate the male powers; she internalizes them. As her imagination emerges toward its final liberation, her eyes turn away from the frilly femininity of her sister Sylva and Valentine and are more and more occupied with the strong masculine figures of Dolores, the sculptress who wields mastery over large masses of physical material on the sensory plane, and Dr. Miller, the American psychiatrist that presides as the dominant intellectual force at Juliet's lawn party. And while her eye is so occupied, Juliet's strength vis-a-vis women increases, with the result that at Suzy's party everybody downstairs, including Suzy, who is more clothed, and more formally clothed, than at any other time, has diminished in power into listlessness and is caught up in a death cult. Suzy still possesses enough power at the beginning of Juliet's lawn party to figure prominently toward the beginning of the series of imaginative events that erupt there. She does not, however, initiate the series, as she does at the beach and Bhisma's, and she is soon eclipsed by Dr. Miller; and Juliet disputes with her, calling her a liar and screaming at her to go away. (Eventually, Juliet's masculinized imagination will be strong enough to drop Dr. Miller and disobey her mother, the ultimate feminist authority for it.) By the end of the series Suzy has been reduced to just another spirit in the crowd and a passenger on her grandfather's plane.

The female spirits, then, remind Juliet of her generative capabilities but their revival is tempered by her reassimilation of the male's inventive energy. With the reassimilation of the male's inventive energy, Juliet adds go to her generative powers: she harnesses them to the male's forward thrusting, linear energy and his structural powers. Thereby she checks their tendency to erupt startlingly and randomly on her, to beget sporadically and haphazardly while she supplements their strength and accelerates their activity. Thus the two sexes together play out a psychodrama in which Juliet's imagination rejoins the circle of her visual powers around the rational energy that broke the circle at the circus. Over the course of her story, in other words, her imagination makes her life whole again by fusing her generative and inventive powers into the creative potency that enables her to surpass Lynx Eyes' example of external transformation with a metamorphosis in consciousness.

In contrast to this broad accomplishment by her imagination, Juliet's supremely incisive feat of imagination occurs during her lawn party, which is what its initial images and words—Juliet's nieces in their confirmation dresses and Valentina similarly dressed and eliciting from Elena the comment, "Where are you going—to be confirmed?"—proclaim it to be: a confirmation rite. Obviously the lawn party is an ironic confirmation. Instead of admitting Juliet to full membership in the church and its otherworldly, abstract realm, it admits her fully into the creative universe. Her imagination uses the rite to replace José's intellect-confirming "reality" with life now and thereby opens up a new territory commensurate with its spiritual dimensions. In its new territory, all things are present in one another, joined by a direct immediate relationship center to center, and that includes a living connection and exchange between the images of her visual powers and her imagination. Her life has undergone the complete spiritualization she sought at the seance. She is a perfectly spiritual creature in a perfectly spiritual world. In this truest of marriages, Juliet no longer fears being happy. She eagerly substitutes a new morality of joy for the old one of sacrifice when she leaves her house behind. Unlike the French woman, who shuns Hiroshima's regenerative energy, Juliet enters the flow of the moving universe and flows continuously with it.

And that profoundly differentiates her morally from the French woman. Juliet does not find her eyes, their images, and the living process inherent in them morally offensive. So she does not reject the opportunity offered her by her environment to come alive, as the French woman does in Hiroshima. She participates in the life of the scene. That means literally in the images playing about her on the screen. And it is only because she does look at those images and assimilates what she sees that she is able to metamorphose into the living oneness she attains. For all she becomes is present as a possibility in those images—in their brilliant, luxuriant colors and their burgeoning forms; their luminous, highly defined individuality; an individuality that extends into the composition of the events in which they figure into prominently demarcated autonomous scenes (for example, the previously mentioned lawn party); and their fecund vitality that not only radiates benevolently from individual to indivdual but leaps across the autonomous scenes in a flow too relentlessly exuberant to need the support of realistic chronological or logical connections.

The French woman over the course of her story moves from an ecstatic erotic union to a separation from her lover and Hiroshima in immobilizing grief. Juliet, on the other hand, starts shut in and ends, not alienated, like the French woman does, but actively integrated within herself and with the open world of images from which her life derives. From the beginning she senses the virtue of images. Some time ago, John Crowe Ransom observed that images possess "a primordial freshness, which idea can never claim. An idea is derivative and tame…the image with its character beaten out of it…The image, on the other hand, which is not remarkable in any particular property, is marvelous in its assemblage of many properties, a manifold of properties, like a mine or field…in its original state of freedom, in their panoply of circumstances and with their morning freshness upon them," images are "a plenum of qualities," "sharp of edges," "given and nonnegotiable," "pure exhibit," "so whole and clean that they resist the catalyses of thought." Never anything but an image, and so always a direct extension of the properties of images, Juliet exemplifies these qualities singled out by Ransom. But in her willing espousal of these qualities, she further allows what Ransom could not because of his verbal bias as a poet—that the image is alive, active, plastic, and one, that the image, in sum, passes the creation, including its creative potency, through it intact. It is with this realization that she steps across the threshold of the new human possibility into the new world and the spiritual adventure of our time. Living by her eyes, she becomes the image of man, a new kind of individual that fearlessly opens herself to the image, ingests the creation it embodies, and then, after the example of the image, transmits the creative thrust of the creative universe on through her enhanced into a new creation. Necessarily a creation herself and creatively intact to operate in that capacity, in performing as a vehicle of creative energy she is free, pure potential in a universe of possibility.

Obviously Juliet's story is not, like the French woman's, a matter of putting her clothes back on and retreating into the abstraction of a name. Following the model of images, it is, rather, a stripping down of her spirit to its primordial freshness and a sharp delineation of a new given and non negotiable individuality. As a result, where the French woman comes through her adventure in the world of images fractured, abstracted, and immobilized, Juliet comes through hers turned on. The strength imparted to her by clean and whole images heal the breach in her existence, so that while the French woman makes a career out of her image as an actress and thinks that looking closely has to be learned but sees nothing, Juliet, with a passion for seeing, seeks out spiritual contact and succeeds in releasing her spirit to act creatively in the world.

It is true that Juliet does not increase her human autonomy by controlling the sense ratios or avoiding the conditions the medium would impose upon her. Contrary to McLuhan's prescriptions, she lets the medium of light and life have its way with her. And because she does, she successfully obviates the insidious, malicious, and disruptive conflict his ideas aggravate rather than allay. Actually all McLuhan has seen is that media are "moving" in the Elizabethan sense. Obviously, through the stimuli they amplify, media excite, as the created world and art has always done and always will do. In letting images have their way with her, Juliet is moved, with the result that her imagination is empowered to authentically increase her human autonomy. It is also true that she disobeys the strictures of Arnheim by sinfully refusing to regard as mere entertainment and distraction the lush parade of richly colorful images that swarm about her. But in so indulging herself, she comes to perceive herself and her world with a subtlety and precision far beyond the range of Arnheim's respectable thought. And it is also true that neither Juliet nor Fellini's movie gives us, as Boorstein demands they should, the nub of the matter—that is, that atomic lump of material at the rock bottom of things, the densest, heaviest of substances. Boorstein was right about moving images: they couldn't give Juliet the nub of the matter even if they wanted to. What they have to give, and do give her, instead, is the spirit of life. And that gift does not loosen either Juliet's or our grip on reality—unless you take the metaphor literally—but opens wide the opportunity for creative endeavor. That means that, as the student sensed, Juliet and the images of Fellini's movie do in fact threaten denominating and denominationalists. Their intention is decidedly not to denominate but to unseat authority and make room for the angelic particular. So their impact ultimately adds up to a religious revolution that revives the classical and mythic modes of worship described by C. Kerenyi in *The Religion of the Greeks and Romans* when he wrote, "for the Greeks the divine was a self-evident fact of the given world, in respect to which one raised not the question of existence . . . but the question of behavior worthy of a human being." Like the divine for the Greeks, images, in Juliet's final view of them, challenge her not to believe but to behave. And her response to their self-evident virtue is worthy of a human being. It is that self-evident virtue that begins to flow in *Hiroshima Mon Amour* and reaches fullness in *Juliet of the Spirits*, a movie, like its protagonist, full of life, full of the life of images.

ellini-Satyricon's
Moral Process

WILLIAM R. ROBINSON

IT WILL BE HELPFUL in considering the "cinematic cosmology" of Federico Fellini's movies to look at the narrative advance that occurs in *Fellini-Satyricon*. This narrative advance gets worked out in some way and to some degree in every movie Fellini has made, but its quintessential features are most explicitly evident in this particular movie.

The preparation for this advance was provided by aestheticism. As used here, this term refers to the period extending from 1750 to 1900, or to the beginnings of Modernism, not to any specific movement or doctrine. The initiative belonged to the aesthetic during this period. From its emergence through its development to its conclusion it provided the new value for artists, critics, and thinkers. It could be favored, adapted to, or resisted, but it could not be denied. Over the course of its career the emphasis shifted from its subjective to its objective side, or from the study of perception to the perceptual view of the world, that is, to philosophical assertions such as Nietzsche's that "the world is an aesthetic phenomenon."

This period during which aestheticism flourished constitutes the last phase of the intellectual era. Though its roots go back to Homer, the intellectual era's official reign began when the Greek philosophers analyzed change into space and time and simultaneously assigned space priority in the scheme of things. This spatializing led to Diogenes' atomic theory and to the recognition that the point was the basic component of geometrical figures and so of spatial structures. It also led in the other direction to systematic theorizing about human affairs, nature, and the cosmos based upon the hierarchical order of categories and classes.

If the term "cosmology" can be limited here to its common dictionary definition as "the branch of philosophy that studies the origins and structure of the universe," it can be said that the intellectual era's cosmology assigned exclusive dominance to structure or the spatial aspect, and set origins, or the originating, active, moral powers, outside its domain, limiting their activity to that of a first cause and an external impact from outside. In this cosmos— of order, plot, causality, frames, grids, etc.—structure incorporated the moral into its framework, from where it served to enforce the rule of structure over origins. And poetry—or art and the aesthetic—was either banished or required to prove its usefulness for attaining intellectual ends.

As the last phase of the intellectual era, aestheticism is appropriately a mental event, the aesthetic experience happening, of course, in the mind, not in the art object or in nature. It perpetuates, as a consequence, the spatial bias of the intellectual era's cosmology. This sense of the aesthetic as a mental event and as occurring within a spatial locus can be seen in this passage from one of Coleridge's essays on criticism:

> An old coach wheel lies in the coachmaker's yard, disfigured with tar and dirt (I purposely take the most trivial instances)—if I turn away my attention from these, and regard the figure abstractly, "still," I might say to my companion, "there is beauty in that wheel, and you yourself would not only admit, but would feel it, had you never seen the wheel before. See how the rays proceed from the center to the circumferences, and how many different images are distinctly comprehended at one glance, as forming one whole, and each part in some harmonious relation to each and to all." But imagine the polished golden wheel of the chariot of the sun, as the poets have described it: then the figure, and the real thing so figured, exactly coincide. There is nothing heterogeneous, nothing to abstract from: by its perfect smoothness and circularity in width, each part is (if I may borrow a metaphor from a sister sense) as perfect a melody; as the whole is a complete harmony. This, we should say, is beautiful throughout. Of all "the many" which I actually see, each and all are really reconciled into unity: while the effulgence from the whole coincides with, and seems to represent, the effluence of delight from my own mind in the intuition of it.

It is also apparent from this passage that aestheticism collapsed the intellectual cosmos' structure into the aesthetic, superseding the order that structure thrived upon with form, and at the same time it transformed that structure's elemental constituents, the atom and the point, into a locus of organic unity. Freed from the rule of structure over aesthetic form, aestheticism, since it unquestionably accepted the intellectual era's identification of the moral and narrative with the externally imposed connections of structure, discarded them. Aestheticism thereby abandoned cosmology and replaced it with originless, internally composed ecstatic moments or autonomous worlds complete within themselves and externally unrelated and unrelatable, just there. Socrates' fears that imitative poetry, or the aesthetic, would introduce disorder into the rational state turned out to be well-founded. Aestheticism did just that to the intellectual era's cosmology: it dissolved away both its foundation of atoms and points and its theoretical superstructure, leaving it in total disarray.

Fellini doesn't start from aestheticism, either in his career or in any given movie. Aesthetes appear in his movies, especially his early ones, but the aesthetic does not serve them well. Wanda of *The White Sheik*, Gelsomina of *La Strada*, Cabiria and Juliet of their respective movies become ecstatic over a male idol associated with art. Their fascination proves to be, however, a passing episode that either brings them grief or comes to nothing. Most notably, the cultivated aestheticism of Steiner, in *La Dolce Vita*, ends, after he kills his children, with his suicide. Since he manages in death to maintain a pose reminiscent of Rodin's *Thinker*, he perhaps images the death of aestheticism, of its attitude toward art, as well as of intellectualism for Fellini's imagination.

Fellini starts, instead, as the modernists in general did, from one of aestheticism's legacies, the autonomy of art. The assimilation of structure into form by aestheticism left artists free to turn to art itself, to draw upon its inherent resources, to act out of its potentialities. Fellini makes the most of that opportunity by almost invariably either starting his movies from art—sometimes the popular arts, sometimes serious art, even on occasion his own art—or having the dramatic action in them turn upon it. But he never makes more or better use of art than he does in *Fellini-Satyricon*, a movie consisting of nothing but the forms of art—beginning with Petronius' narrative and from there including such others as tragic and mythic drama, the farce theatre, sculptures, murals, poetry and tales. In addition to starting from the forms of art in *Fellini-Satyricon* and having the dramatic action turning repeatedly upon them, he works directly from and with the creative powers active in the center of art.

He penetrates to the center of the aesthetic immediately in the first shot of *Fellini-Satyricon*. There, while the fixed-in-place camera eye holds on a wall, Encolpio rises into and then disappears from its field of vision several times, protesting as he does so the loss of Giton, his youthful sexual companion. Whereas the painter's image is three-times removed from intellectual reality for Socrates, Encolpio, from the outset, and repeatedly thereafter, is three-times involved in art in the opening shot: he is an image in Fellini's movie, a character in the *Satyricon*, and a solitary player on a stage of sorts uttering a Hamlet-like soliloquy. Moreover, in lamenting the loss of Giton, Encolpio's attention is turned inward into himself, thus extending the camera eye's centering action this further step. At the same time, Encolpio's words, asserting passionately his intention of getting his life right again, point toward a course of action. His verbal activity complements his image's activity by adding its vectoral, or linear, assertiveness to his image's energetic movement.

Not from aestheticism's spatial loci and certainly not from the intellectual era's atoms and points, but from the moving center he looks into, Fellini's narrating begins. From this moving center come the inspiring energies that charge his vision and imagination with creative potency. The narrative advance he accomplishes in *Fellini-Satyricon* originates from this wholly new, specific source. It begins from the life rather than the forms of art, from the creative powers active within those forms, not the forms themselves.

The moment Fellini's eyes engage the moving center, his narrating is involved in the moral process. This process provides the method whereby progressive increases in its own powers of action, or its capacity for moral performance, can be enacted. The urge within the process to improve its powers of action can be seen in the three motives that ignite and direct Encolpio's quest: his misdirected desire to restore his life to what it was by regaining Giton, his seeking out a cure for his impotency, and his heading out to sea toward a new life beyond Rome. The moral process's inherent drive to increase its powers of action can also be seen at work in the thrust of Encolpio's image and his words out of the moving center in the first shot; in the quick transformation Encolpio's image undergoes from a silhouette to full color in the opening sequence; in the development occurring through the three phases of the movie's overall action; the physical phase that occurs in the Insula Felices, the intellectual phase that begins at Trimolcio's banquet and ends with Lica's beheading, and the imaginative, or mythic, phase in which Encolpio dies and is reborn sexually; and in the moral evolution of Encolpio in the movie's overall action. In other words, the moral process is the genius of the movie's action, permeating its every action.

As the movie's genius, the moral process, from the opening shot through the movie's overall action, spontaneously generates its activity from within itself. From that beginning it works out of units of action through units of action to beget units of action. Within those units of action, vision assumes priority: the moral initiative belongs to it rather than to the voice, or to words. Vision takes the lead, to begin with, from the fact that *Fellini-Satyricon* is a cinematic, or visual, narration. But its priority can also be seen in the moving center of the first shot. There it quickly becomes apparent through the growth of Encolpio's image from a flat black abstraction to full-bodied color that it moves out of abundance, whereas his voice bespeaks a deficiency that needs correction. Encolpio's words would return his life to, and define it by, a previous condition; his image, however, is rich with possibilities. And when vision prevails morally, the moral supercedes the intellectual perspective, and the originating powers supercede form and structure. Moreover, this turnabout in priority grants precedence to the temporal aspect over the spatial aspect of events; it "temporalizes" form and structure. In restoring primacy to activity, the moral process eliminates the last vestige of the intellectual cosmology's spatial bias.

Free to act upon its own inclinations in its own way, the moral process concentrates on actualizing the possibilities inherent in the moving center of the first shot, the movie's first unit of action, or the moral process's own beginning on this particular occasion. It avoids spending itself on becoming ecstatically aroused by an aesthetic experience as much as on coming to rest in the truth of structure. It seeks not the true or the beautiful, but the potent; that is to say, it is intent upon not a structural or formal unity, but moral coherence and continuity. The moral process obviously cannot be an exclusively mental event; it doesn't happen in the mind as the aesthetic experience does, but instead on the leading edge of the action where vision, bringing the mind out of itself, implicates it in an active exchange with the active images the eyes perceive. And as part of its activity out on the leading edge of the action, the moral process centers the moral. That feat completes the evolution of the moral from a factor in structure through its abandonment by aestheticism to the primary active force creatively projecting itself out of the center.

Beginning from the moving center, the moral process thereafter relates actions center-to-center while evolving out of those centered actions their moral prospects. Centered, it relates everything else, every other factor within action, to its center in a center-to-center relation. It overlooks nothing, leaves nothing out; it includes all that's integral to moral and creative affairs. Whereas structure excluded the originating powers and form dismissed the moral powers, the moral process encompasses both, carrying over form's body, its spatial organization, while reviving the linear, or vectoral, factor from structure that aestheticism had abandoned, to link actions temporally in progressive sequences. And so with art. It doesn't view art as a dangerous enemy to be suppressed or requiring justification, nor does it exalt it into an absolute end in itself. Working as well as originating from within art and so inseparable from it, the moral process sees art to be a source, means, and value. But it also seeks from existing art a more complete art.

For it, art, like everything else, becomes an action in its origins as well as ultimately before it can be anything else for perception, thought, or creative endeavor. Creative action in relation to the moral process is not, as aestheticism would have it, a momentary, rapturous incandescence, but a vigorous event issuing from a fertile event into a potent event. Encompassing art along with form's space and the linear, vectoral aspect of structure, the moral process specializes in begetting complex, subtle, potent space-time units of action temporally as well as spatially integrated. The centering that the moral process conducts comes to fruition in the full-face close-up shot of Encolpio on the beach as he reacts to the terms of Eumolpus's will. In this shot, Encolpio's image, which, it will be remembered, began in the movie three times involved in the forms of art, emerges from the forms that had enclosed him. Now beyond all structures, his image brings forward with its emergence the moving center and at the same time frees the originating powers within that center. Though he has recovered his potency, Encolpio doesn't think about going back to reenact the community's renewal ritual that he had been unable to perform earlier. His vision, clear of all obstacles, looks ahead confidently to the prospects before him. Not just Encolpio but everything benefits from the originating powers having come out into the open. The words spoken by a narrator subsequently in the scene on the beach, now enclosed with the image's fullness, no longer looking back or at things as they are, the reality of the moment, nor lamenting lost love nor pleading to be spared, have been cured of the deficiency they suffered from in the movie's beginning. Benefitting from the originating powers available to all, they speak of prospective events yet to happen in Encolpio's new life. Fellini's, or the camera's, eye similarly benefits. In looking through and beyond the group portraits painted on the remaining wall fragments to the moving sea beyond them, he focuses his attention on the space between the murals, not directly at them. Fellini's eye as well looks ahead, specifically beyond aestheticism to the moral action out front as it has been doing, though less overtly, from the beginning of *Fellini-Satyricon*. Under the full head of creative steam that the readily available originating powers enable him to get up, Fellini's eye completes the derivation of his own creation from the central energies or the spirit of creation, that the various forms of art have passed on through themselves to inspire and fuel its creating. Never letting itself become distracted by the aesthetic features of art or pausing to reflect intellectually on the truth it might yield, but concentrating on moral interaction with it, his eye completes its creation, namely, the movie itself. Fellini's eye derives out of the forms of existing art the new visual narrative, in effect enacting the birth of the movies. And in doing that, in deriving art from art, in turning into and absorbing itself in its own narrating, his eye evolves a new moral possibility, a creative morality. That feat doesn't end an era, as aestheticism did; it begins a new one.

Such is the narrative advance that occurs in *Fellini-Satyricon*. Technically, that advance just completes what aestheticism began, a 180 degree revolution from the exclusive dominance of structure to the inclusive priority of origins in the moral process. But that little difference in detail is so crucial that it makes all the difference cosmologically. Out on the leading edge of action where the originating powers operate, there can be no spatial points or immutable atoms, so no connections, and, without those as a basis, no structure. And with the obsolescence of structure everything that derives from or depends upon it goes, too.

No structure means nothing less than: no reference (there being nothing to refer to, no reality, since the "world" is in the making; and not to self either, since it will have moved on, changed, by the time the feed-back loop has been traversed); no metaphysics, epistemology, ontology, or ethics; no plots, no Zeus (i.e., no fateful designs, no first causes, no text, no signs or symbols, no meaning, no points of view, no dialogue or dialectic, no analysis, no theorizing, no character, no psyche, no spirit, spirits, or soul; and above all else no cosmology to connect these aspects of structure. Strictly speaking, cosmology, "the saying of order," gives way to the visible creation.

Having evolved beyond structure's cosmos, the visible creation, as it appears in *Fellini-Satyricon*, (and within the medium of his art since Fellini goes with his medium's requirement that the action be kept going, be moved on, keep proceeding ahead, and he devotes himself to imagining its inherent possibilities)—the visible creation, to repeat, begins already in motion and continues in motion (a la Encolpio), allowing only modifications within its on-going activity, for once it stops there's no starting it again. It appears as a process of origins, and nothing but origins, nothing but beginnings. Never is it still; always in transition, always attending to the transitional moment, that action wherein inspiration, exchanges of creative energy, occur; forever transforming, or more accurately, evolving, bringing into view, literally imagining images, even imagining the past as it does so, and at the same time looking ahead to the prospects before it.

In accordance with the primacy of origins, its business is visualizing, evolving into visibility, making appearances appear, "actualizing" prospects. And it works through units of action, not via flux or motion, always from within them, there being no inside and outside or points of view. And it proceeds by alignment (e.g., Encolpio's skin changing color to correspond to that of the surrounding circumstance), by correlating (moral interaction with comparably active partners), and by convergence (the coming together of discrete units of action to beget a mutual action).

It values the concrete, not the abstract, the individual creature, not the general or the universal. It moves out of moral passion, the urge to improve upon what has been achieved, seeing that movement is good, not evil, that it is the source of unity and unifies, and it is what endures in genius's and the imagination's passing on of the spirit of action from one creature to another, and that the Good surpasses in value the True and the Beautiful, that its source lies in the force exerted by the whole creation at any given moment equally within all its creatures, and that it thrives upon the complete unity attainable only through the coherence and continuity possible in the center-to-center relatings of discrete moral events. And just so the ship sailed on.

> Genius dies with its possessor
> and comes not again till another
> is born with it.
> —William Blake

The Birth of Imaginative Man in Part III of *2001: A Space Odyssey*

WILLIAM R. ROBINSON

The odyssey of *2001* appears on the verge of coming to a complete stand-still in Part II during the crisis between the computer HAL and the astronauts Frank Poole and Dave Bowman. Though known to be traveling at a tremendous speed in relation to the earth, the Discovery space ship only inches forward on the screen and nothing is being done on board to advance the mission. Quite literally, the only thing moving is thought, and following the tendency of words from their first appearance in the movie to introduce a divisive force into the flow of images, that thought engages in an intramural struggle for dominance. This verbal contentiousness has pretty well dissipated the forward thrusting energy of the mission in polarized quarreling well before the end of Part II. The astronauts sit still to discuss the crisis, and HAL, a stationary eye, reads their lips and formulates a counterplan for their death. When Dave frustrates HAL's intention by lobotomizing the computer—especially since Dave performs the lobotomy in self-defense (as a reaction to an external pressure exerted upon him, not as a self-initiated action of his own)—the last moving force has apparently been immobilized. The odyssey, and the movie, would seem to be at an end.

And that impression is reinforced by Heywood Floyd's explanation of the mission's objective and his admission of its failure. His remark that the aim of the mission is to locate the intelligence inferred from the cobalt slab found buried on the moon to exist outside the earth and to be millions of years older than human intelligence testifies that the mission is motivated by the assumption that the power of the slab originates from outside it and that therefore the slab is the effect of a cause anteceding it in time. Conceived from a rational response to the slab, the overt purpose of the mission is to seek out this first cause. But since the mission is an extension of the bias of the thinking powers of rational man, it is intended, actually, to allow reason to know itself by returning to its aboriginal rational source and the ultimate authority. Were this journey into the past successfully completed, the mission would arrive at the still point before time and thereby put an absolute stop to motion. But the mission aborts. It cannot push its research back beyond history. The thinking power unable to transcend the condition of continuous change, the analysis it expends in digging up the cobalt slab and formulating speculative deductions regarding the cause and significance of the slab come to nothing. That failure is admitted by Heywood Floyd—his words disqualifying words as a vehicle of metaphysical inquiry as he does so—in the last spoken words of the movie, which are the last activity of the thinking powers: it "has remained completely inert, its origin and purpose still a mystery." This admission cannot refer to the slab, however, only to the human intelligence. For the slab reappears, more active than ever before, shortly into Part III. It is human reason that has lost contact with its power source. And the further the mission abstracts itself from the image of the cobalt slab into theories about the slab, the more its movement diminishes. After Heywood Floyd's confession, even the thinking powers are inert.

For most viewers of the movie—if the comments of reviewers and critics are typical—something of the same sort happens to them. Even should they have followed the events of *2001* to the point where Dave lobotomizes HAL, their minds, blown along with HAL's, also become inert. Part III makes no sense to them. They can't recognize what is there before their eyes, and,what's more, allow that something really is there. For them the third phase of the odyssey amounts to no more than a mind-boggling light show embellished with some random surrealistic imagery. Their intellectual frustration perhaps parallels the neurosis that builds up when the forward thrusting energy of the odyssey gets suppressed by HAL's vanity. Certainly, when Dave explodes beyond the negations of HAL into Part III, an event not rationally explainable, they can no more continue on the odyssey than HAL can.

Yet the odyssey goes on; the movie continues. Something carries over, a power subtler than those previously evident and the exciting force of the odyssey from its inception. The lobotomizing of HAL, rather than being a misfortune, is necessary for the completion of the odyssey. It opens a gate through which the subtler power bores forward across the darkness of the cut between Part II and Part III and the latter's title to be excited anew, and for a third time, by the cobalt slab. What carries over issues, at the end of the movie, into a birth of sorts. That much is certain. Not immediately clear is what is born. The entire movie, of course, prepares for and therefore explains what is born at its end. But since Part III consists of the climactic events in the delivery of the embryo born in *2001*, it more than any earlier portion of the movie manifests the powers that initiate, govern the gestation of, and are realized in the birth—not only of the embryo, it should be added, but of *2001* itself.

The pod containing Dave Bowman is the most obvious thing to carry over from Part II to Part III. But the pod cannot complete the mission. It lacks the power resources—the communication and navigation instruments, the fuel, and the life maintenance supplies—to relay information back or return to earth. The trip beyond infinity is a one-way, not a round, trip. But Dave is not only out of communication with the earth; he has also severed his emotional link with ordinary mortals. An extraordinarily cool, expressionless man to begin with, Dave becomes ice-cold when HAL, while being lobotomized, cries out in panic, "My mind is going. I can feel it." Totally devoid of sympathy, Dave mercilessly continues the lobotomy, disconnecting HAL's feeling as well as his intelligence. When Dave disconnects feeling, he simultaneously jettisons rational change, or time, both its strict chronology and its chain of cause and effect. Rational connections no longer govern his movement when he appears at the beginning of Part III. While traveling through the star gate in Part III, Dave remains within rational or perspective space, but when he accelerates to the speed of light and attains infinity at the end of the star gate, not only has he sloughed off the chronology and causality of rational time but the boxes and perspective of rational space as well. That Dave completely eludes even these most basic categories of conceptual thought in the third phase of the odyssey is clear from subsequent images, but it is also indicated by the title of Part III, "Jupiter and Beyond Infinity." Since nothing beyond infinity can be rationally conceived, the title of Part III, a verbal paradox, itself signifies that Dave has embarked upon a venture too subtle for reason to comprehend. The pod, then, is an atavism of Part II. As such it is more of an indication of what is shed in the transition to Part III than of what carries the odyssey forward.

Since Dave Bowman eventually emerges from the pod and the birth issues specifically from him, he, not the pod, carries across into part III the powers that govern the gestation of the embryo and that come to the fore with its birth. Dave's name obviously enough signifies his role in the odyssey. He is the *bou* man of the ship, the mariner at the foremost part of the boat looking out ahead of the action as the boat surges forward into unknown seas, at the same time that he is a wielder of the golden bough, key to the realm of the mythic gods, and a *bo* man like Ulysses, one of extraordinary ability capable of pulling the bow that Penelope's suitors could not. And he is a David, the ingenious slayer of Goliath, singer and psalm writer, and the leader of his people from a tribal to a national political organization. Typically for words, Dave's name refers back to the past, linking him with Greek, Roman, and Judaic antecedents. But along with all words, his name is absent from Part III. Instead of being bound or explained by his name, he leaps free of his past there. Or his "mythic" past, for he lacks the usual kind of past to begin with. Unlike Heywood Floyd, he doesn't connect himself with a country or culture or even the human species and he has no family or marriage ties, personal relations outside his professional function, or age—that is, a birthday. The absence of these conventional relationships frees Dave of biological and institutional limitations and allow him to bypass ordinary growth of body or change of mind and undergo the startling metamorphosis he does at the end of the movie. When his name no longer applies, although its multiple associations indicate a complexity and subtlety of life far beyond that of any other person in the movie, the weight of historical relationships have been removed from Dave. So completely relieved of the various rational connections, Dave can avoid merely repeating the odysseys of others before him and carry the odyssey of life into new domains.

Only the images of Dave reveal his special aptitude for serving as a vessel of the energies that spend themselves in his adventure beyond the rational. That means all the images of Dave Bowman, not just those in Part III. For Dave's qualifications as the sole vessel of the powers directing the odyssey are well established before Part III. Whereas Frank Poole had been introduced jogging on the periphery of the circular space ship interior, and shadow boxing, in his first appearance in the movie, Dave emerges from a circle of light at the center of a circular passageway of the circular space ship and moves toward a yellowish pupil in the center of the screen. Thereafter, in Part III, he speeds toward the center of the colored lights that rain upon him, passes through a circle of white light at the point of infinity, and transforms finally, into a ball of glowing light on the bed where the embryo first appears. In short, Dave is a creature of the light and a central man; he moves out of, into, and through the eye of a circle of white light that always appears in the center of the screen. Born of light and himself a womb of light from which the new creature will be born at the end of the odyssey, he receives and embodies the light and passes it on through himself in a clarified form.

This distinction of his being a central man is further born out by the ways in which Dave differs from others associated with the Jupiter Mission, such as Heywood Floyd, the man in charge of carrying out orders to investigate the cobalt slab discovered on the moon and, as the last words of the movie indicate, in ultimate command of the Jupiter mission. The difference between them is blatantly designated by the name "hay-wood," which identifies its bearer as agrarian man, a form of life that, like vegetation, lacks the capacity of self-generated motion and obeys laws that harness change, such as the seasons, into prescribed channels. In contrast, Dave, who wears simple functional clothes instead of Heywood's seedy conventional suit and speaks a simple functional language instead of Heywood's socially formalized diplomatic language, is a technological man, a form of life based upon man's inventive ability to transform nature into artifact. Whereas the one is conservative or early rational man, the other is radical or late rational man. But Dave also differs as remarkably from Frank Poole, whose name indicates that he is, to begin with, a pool, a gathering of waters from an outside source, thus a repository of the evolutionary achievements of man up through the rational era of technology, and, in addition, he is frank—he has nothing in reserve. An end result, he is without vital subtlety, as lifeless as the hibernauts, a fact revealed by his lying in a roughly similar position as they, and head to head with them, while indifferently receiving a birthday greeting from his family. Both Heywood and Frank, in short, are no more than the forces acting externally upon them.

Dave's greater complexity and his subtlety are even more evident in the way he differs from HAL. Whereas HAL, because Frank is nothing more than his uncomplicated exterior, can know him completely and therefore outwit him at chess and destroy him at will, Dave, on the other hand, puzzles HAL. That's because HAL has very limited visual power. His numerous eyes all stationary, his vision is restricted by a point of view, a fixed intellectual stance, as it were. Thus he either perceives only mouths, as he does in reading the astronauts' lips—that is, he is only sensitive to the conceptual aspect of things—or when he perceives the individual, as on the occasions the camera looks through his eye, he sees in distortion or is blind to the image before him, as he is when he focuses upon Dave's drawings. Those drawings of the hibernauts establish that Dave lives through his eye, nourishing himself upon images. HAL notes that Dave's drawing is improving. He can see that Dave is getting better at it, that he's increasing his accuracy in catching the likeness and in refinement of detail. But HAL cannot see that Dave's line drawings, evolving a single figure from a white paper background, issue from a passion to see the individual, to assimilate the whole picture by perceiving the hibernauts as coherent singular entities rather than as the fragmentary statistical data of the life functions fed to HAL. Nor can HAL see that Dave's unfinished sketches as well as his improvement indicate that Dave is growing, that his consciousness is increasing its powers of vision. HAL's blindness keeps him from seeing that the abstractness of the line drawings that catch his eye, instead of being the conclusion it is for him, has a function in the growth process.

When he draws them, Dave, in effect, robs the hibernauts of their life by ingesting their concrete sensory image and then recreating it in the invented intellectual images of his drawings. When he progressively lessens the heavy black outline around the figures, he disinters their buried life. The hibernauts, who look like mummies to start with, are sealed initially into their tomb by a thick encasing of death. Dave's aesthetic touch releases their life from its mechanical, dormant state to fuel his life. Significantly, after Dave draws the hibernauts, nothing comes of them; they are reduced to the instruments recording their life functions and their termination. They die when there is nothing left of them but the analytical data of their mechanical body functions. But, most importantly, in contrast to the hibernauts' "inner life," Dave's benumbed, characterless face masks uncommon vital energies. He drops a clue to the authenticity of his vital powers when he casts doubt on HAL's humanity with the comment, "Whether he has real feelings is something I don't think anyone can really answer." Dave takes the measure of HAL in this remark, for it implies that HAL, the rational characters Heywood Floyd and Frank Poole, and reason in general aren't truly alive but merely reflect life, that HAL may be capable of emotion (which is evident in his desire to control events and maintain the status quo) but not passion. Dave has to speak from an awareness greater than HAL's to make such a judgment, an awareness of "real feeling." It is this larger awareness that allows Dave not only to make his judgment about HAL but to act of his own initiative out of the subtler currents of real feeling that elude HAL in his perception of Dave and makes Dave unfathomable for him.

In missing the signs of life in Dave, HAL also fails to detect the fact that Dave's drawing and his interest in the image and individual signify that he is a man of imagination. Dave's efforts as an incipient artist, rudimentary as they may be, amount to absorbing a lower form of individuality into his own greater individuality in preparation for giving birth to a yet greater individuality, first in his art, then in the embryo at the end of the movie. Dave's imaginative powers get further demonstrated, and practically applied, when, abandoning the old procedure based on words, he quietly improvises with the explosive bolts of the pod to outwit HAL's attempt to lock him out of the Discovery. Though he can easily and soundly beat Frank at the rational game of chess, HAL is no match for Dave's imaginativeness in a fight for life. A machine bound by mechanical principle, HAL is not, despite his technological complexity and his advantages over the apes, truly alive. He cannot, for instance, sleep or die, only be turned on or off. His internal mechanisms, those of reason brought to their highest development, confine him to manipulating under the compulsion of electronic forces the materials with which he has been programmed. His role in the odyssey can be no more than to bring the rational phase of it to a culmination and then turn the remainder of the odyssey over to a man capable of the kind of expanded field of perception Dave demonstrates when his eye springs fully open in Part III, shed not only of HAL's fixed positions and encased state but also of the black outlines and abstractness of his own drawing style.

When HAL's mind is blown, so are the restrictions on Dave's eye. Its limits removed and its urge to move liberated (the eyes are the most sensitive to motion and the most mobile of the senses), it surges free of rational confinement. Then HAL is decidedly obsolete, as is Frank Poole, the unimaginative repository of old knowledge whose inert body Dave dropped of necessity to take action against HAL in order to bring forth the potential life in him. Dave's employing a tool designed for one purpose in a new way tips the balance in his favor in his fight for life with HAL, but Dave's victory is complete when on two occasions during the lobotomy HAL's eye is full of Dave's reflected image. Already at that moment HAL's powers of perception have been superceded by Dave's powers, the rational powers by the powers of the image and man of imagination. But HAL's most glaring deficiency for the odyssey turns out to be, finally, the inability of his immovable eye to blink. Unable to blink, as Dave's eye, or just the eye, does in Part III when it occupies the entire screen, HAL cannot clarify his vision. And because he can't, HAL cannot know the truth of William Blake's observation that "If the doors of Perception were cleansed, everything would appear as it is, infinite." That failure of perception bars HAL from entering into the third phase in *2001*, the trip to infinity and beyond.

As a central man, then, Dave is distinguished from everyone else associated with the mission, including HAL, by his being an individual who really feels, a visual and imaginative man of passion who acts out of indeterminate resources at his center. His unique vitality is not just too complex and subtle for the rational minds of Heywood Floyd, Frank Poole, and HAL; it makes him a wholly different kind of creature than they are. That is evident in the fact that whereas they dote on deception, restrictions, limitations, ends, and defects, as HAL does in his diagnosis of the supposed failure of the AE 35 unit in the Discovery's outside antenna, Dave specializes in beginnings. Neither death nor grief over the loss of a fellow astronaut, being utterly alone, mechanical failure, or personal crises deter him from carrying on the forward thrusting energies of the odyssey. The eye of life, not the "I," Dave all along is the vital center of the odyssey during the Jupiter Mission and of man's evolution beyond the second stage of his development.

Despite first impressions, a great deal more than thought is in motion during the quarreling of HAL and the astronauts in Part II. Should there be any doubt of that or of the kind of powers governing and directing the odyssey from its beginning, they are dispelled by the identification of the vehicle Dave proceeds from the Discovery in as a "pod" and the appearance of the space suit he wears while in the pod. The accordion-like construction of the space suit, its red color, and the red and green colors of his helmets (the colors of blood and chlorophyll) plus the shape of the helmets with the two black eyes on top of them, prominently visible when Dave removes the AE 35 unit for examination, graphically reveal that what moves in and through the darkness of the cut and the title between Part II and Part III is nascent life. The pod contains a larva: vegetative life houses animate life. That elementary animate life, in turn, embodies a human face that identifies a rationally named human individual capable of consciousness, and that face is a blank facade containing two eyes, traditionally the windows of the spirit, leading the human consciousness into a new era of expanded awareness. In the sequence of events that progresses from the first to the last of these forms of life, the ontology of life's evolution recapitulates its phylogeny.

As those and other images and that process show, Dave's intelligence does not direct Part III of the odyssey. His mind blown along with HAL's, in Part III he sits catatonically spaced before the magnetic pull of the cobalt slab and the hail of colored light that rains upon his face. Unquestionably, the odyssey has passed out of the control of the thinking powers and the aborted Discovery mission has metamorphosed into a wholly different kind of affair than overtly governed by the rational phase of the odyssey. As Dave's eye is wide open, so is he to receive directly the exciting energy of the light that plays upon his face. His receptiveness is the equivalent of total disinterestedness, or negative capability, defined by Keats as "capable of being in uncertainties, mysteries, doubts, without any irritable reaching after fact and reason." But in addition to expunging the latter anxieties, Dave's openness is an acceptance of his predicament in the on-flowing stream of life, which has motives his intelligence cannot comprehend. He submits to and is inspired by the light, becoming an agent of its super-personal motions. That submission allows the light to have its way with him rather than his controlling it toward ends of his own choosing. When he reaches infinity, literally the center from which the colored light streams upon his face, and has shed the last remnant of rational form, perspective space, whereby things are related externally and in depth, Dave's non-teleological visual and imaginative powers, beginning with a spiral galaxy, concentrate upon the "inner" space of single, depthless, circular fields of force at the center of his visual field. Previously the camera had cut back and forth between Dave's face and the objects of his perception. Beyond infinity subject and object fuse into a common objective image. Then he operates outside point of view in an aperspective, immediate, total encounter with the light.

Moreover, when he passes beyond purpose, including purposelessness, Dave doesn't move things with the lever of his reason, nor is he moved by the weight of things pressing against his will. He moves without a preconceived design of where he should get to. Like the hibernauts, his emotions and intelligence are asleep. But unlike them, his vital functions have not been reduced to minimal activity. Just the contrary: as indicated by the vigorous self-caused vibration of his face, the self-generated energies of his hot "interior"—quite plainly evident in the shots of the exploding stars and expanding gases subsequently in Part III—his vital functions are maximally active. When he perceives the centralized space of the active, expanding galaxy, exploding star, and expanding gases, Dave ignores the questions of cause and age that arose from the speculative deductions of rational man at Clavius to behold the self-generated play of expansive energy. Then the light is not only active about him; it is openly active within him. The central man through perceiving things in and of themselves as centers of active energy has become centered and simultaneously moves out of his own center. When Dave so moves, there can be no doubt that in the transition from Part II to Part III the visual powers and the generative life inherent in images leap free of the thinking powers to devote themselves unobstructed to their inherent intentions. But it is also clear that when Dave's eye replaces HAL's intellect as the vehicle of the odyssey and ventures forth into the visual dimension beyond reason's ken, a new kind of man issues from the Discovery. The imagination incarnate, that man has new dimensions of vital power operative in him and is launched upon a new kind of odyssey.

II

That the visual and imaginative powers active in Dave have been the presiding agencies of the odyssey from its inception is evident from the plot of *2001*, with Part III providing the decisive revelations regarding the structure of its action as well as of Dave's visual powers. The opening shot of three heavenly bodies in conjunction and the division of the movie into three explicit parts blatantly designated by titles and Roman numerals announce in no uncertain terms that a trinary system informs and impels what happens in the movie. The subtlety and completeness with which that trinary system pervades *2001* is suggested by the way the plot doesn't simply break down into three numbered and labeled parts linearly but also consists of three acts exfoliating out of one another, only the most obvious being the act of conscious intellectual designation manifested in the movie's title and the abstract classifications of its three pasts.

Reason never really controls what happens in *2001*. The movie's visual title—the sequence of images before the verbal title, *2001: a Space Odyssey*—that begins with the camera already in motion immediately relegates reason to an ancillary function. And reason remains limited to that function even during its heyday in the talkie section of the movie. The first words of spoken dialogue, one-half hour into the movie: "Here you are, sir," establish, as the visual title does, that rational man enters an already existing here where an action is already in progress. Heywood Floyd awakens to find himself *in media res*, literally in mid-transit between the earth and the moon. Even then he has to be aroused by words, which along with the pen that floats in the air beside him, reminiscent of the bone flung in the air by the ape and the shot of the space vehicle it is replaced by, as well as being a citing instrument, identifies Dr. Floyd as rational man. But the words draw his attention only to the here, to the static space of his physical location, not to the action he is caught up in. His failure to be entertained by the images of two young lovers emerging from an automobile and then wordlessly conversing in a close-up—of developing individuality—on the TV screen before him further signify that he is not into the real action, only sitting on the periphery of it. Owing to his remoteness from moving images, rational man knows only the shell of things; his existence exteriorized, he moves only on the outside, as it were, and so only when prodded into action by an external stimulant acting upon him, such as occurs when the stewardess awakens Heywood Floyd and when he is sent on an assignment to investigate Clavius. Because rational man's motion is the product of an external relation, not self-generated, it consists of objects merely changing their spatial and temporal relations to one another, interacting, not intra-acting. Appropriately, he seems hardly to move at all, both in his personal movements and the changing relationships between the space ships. His moving slowly, minimally, and with difficulty frequently, his never getting much of anything done, and his coming to a dead end (which literally happens when the Discovery has stopped still the last time it is seen at the very beginning of Part III) follow inevitably from rational man's obliviousness to the images before him. At best he can lend his rational powers to enacting the intentions of other powers emanating from closer to the vital center than themselves. As a consequence, the intellectual act of *2001* amounts to no more than the veneer of the plot.

Neither Dr. Floyd nor anyone else in the talkie section of the movie other than Dave take the trouble to look and so never get into the all important dimension of *2001* where, in Kubrick's words, everything "is translated in terms of action." But even if they were inclined in the least to look, none of the people of the talkie section, including Dave, could get the whole picture. Confined inside the space ships, rational man cannot behold the forms and especially the extra-rational relationships of the vehicles they are transported in. They don't and can't see that while people are separated by walls and words, in the over-all images on the screen the space ships engage in sexually suggestive relations. To the music of "The Blue Danube," the rhythm for waltzing couples rotating around a dance floor, giant machinery revolves, positions itself for docking, and enters flaming red passageways of larger mechanical wombs. The Discovery ship bound for Jupiter, simultaneously resembling a long fossil-shaped spinal column having a head at one end with narrow black slits for eyesockets and a giant sperm, serves in both capacities as the rudimentary skeletal and sexual foundation of an organism. From the original docking of the space ship phallus results a pregnancy and then out of the skeletal and sexual basis of living form is born a pod. In this way, while the words of the talkie section generate antagonism, result in death, and abort the mission, the over-all images flow gracefully in an undertow of continuous activity, maintaining their potency despite the impotency of words. They link up, connect while disconnection occurs within HAL, the control center, and through that connection carry out to completion the reproductive act. All the while talk goes on in *2001*, it is caught up in a field of organic activity and encompassed by a cinematic irony whereby sexual energy, nor the past-oriented, backward-directed words of HAL, actually provide the means whereby the events of the talkie section of *2001* move forward.

Like the rational act, the organic act occurs in three linear parts, but not quite the same ones of the rational act. Its three linear parts are the opening silent section of the movie, the talkie section, and the closing silent section. The organic act has in common with the rational act Part III, but whereas the latter breaks the action where the conscious intellectual act begins, with the deliberately planned and controlled Discovery mission, the organic act breaks the action in the middle of Part I, ending its first part where the apes evolve into rational man when the organic bone thrown into the air instantaneously realizes its potential by extending itself technologically into a space ship. This asymmetrical, off-center division, in contrast to the balanced order of the rational divisions, emphasizes the tensions inherent in life's perpetual urge to go on living at the same time that it maintains organic continuity between man's physical and intellectual powers below the level of rational deliberation. Since in the action of *2001* the first organic division occurs before the first rational division, again the rational act takes place within the context of the organic one, as the middle man in the reproduction. (And sex is no more than that, part of the machinery of life as the skeleton of the body and the space ships are, and so it appropriately appears among the other machines, including reason, in the second part of the organic act.) But the birth of the embryo at the end of the movie out of Dave through the center of a circle of light is not, and cannot be, the offspring of sexual or organic activity. Dave does not mate with a woman, and he decidedly lacks the necessary organs of bisexual reproduction. Nor is that embryo begotten by the machinery of the space ships. It is literally born of light by parthenogenesis. For that birth not to be a *deus ex machina*, yet another kind of power, a third wave, in addition to the rational and organic ones, has to be active in the odyssey. The powers that nimbly encompass and sweep through the words of reason and the sexual machinery of reproduction, using both the brain and organism as it subsidiary vehicles, are engaged in a creative act.

Though more complicated, the linear parts of this third act are as explicitly designated as those of the other two acts. This act shares with the organic act its part one, the opening silent section of the movie, and also its part two, the talkie section up to Part III. But in Part III it diverges radically from the third parts that the other two acts have in common. Instead of its third part ending at the end of the movie, it ends, instead, at infinity in the light trip. Then, reversing the order of its parts, it proceeds through three more parts from infinity to the birth beyond infinity at the end of the movie—first, the section of the molten stars, the cooling planets and blinking eye; second, the room in which Dave metamorphoses; and, third, the birth of the new creature—for a total of six parts altogether, three for the trip out and three for the trip back. This nimbler act, moving through the same three batteries of pow-ers the other acts do, the sensory, intellectual, and imaginative, first passes through a destructive phase, completed at the vanishing point of infinity, then traverses the same three stages in a reconstructive phase. Proceeding slowly and arduously at first then accelerating to the speed of light, during which the physical body and rational categories are annihilated by light, the destructive phase of the act culminates in the total eclipse of the rational power at infinity. The reconstructive phase then reverses the process and pro-ceeds rapidly and facilely toward a reincarnation. Its progress involves Dave's coat, the room he metamorphoses in, and the formerly black slab assuming a fertile greenish hue; the grounded and static slab becoming autonomously free floating and outwardly active as well as vibrantly excited in itself; and the further stripping down of the body from the ape fur and clothing of the earlier stages to the streamlined, hairless nudity of the embryo. By these means, among others, a death-and-rebirth spiral is traversed in which old mortal coils are shed and new ones evolve.

The irregularities of Part III result from the imaginative powers having broken out of the rational framework of Part II to direct the odyssey through its crucial culminating phase. On their own, the imaginative powers not only increase the acceleration of the overt rhythms of the odyssey but also leap through a series of disjointed events. When openly and directly active, they disclose the creative act to have been the inciting and informing power of the over-all action of *2001* from its opening shot where the camera was already moving of its own inclination, out of ifs own center, in relation to three spherical heavenly bodies in conjunction and accompanied by the three chords of *Thus Spake Zarathustra*, music acclaiming the birth of Nietzsche's "artist-metaphysician." But, what is more important, they devote themselves to their particular specialty of creating, an activity in which life doesn't reproduce in kind but qualitatively alters organic structure, and go about their enterprise in their own special way.

The explicit creative act of the imaginative powers in the reconstructive trip back from infinity begins immediately after the final vestige of rational-ity, perspective space, dissolves into light. The orbital conjunction of the nine moons of Jupiter, the model in structure and number not only of com-plex atomistic unity but also of the three-times-three parts of *2001*, leads into a montage of circular shaped, wheeling galaxies, exploding stars, ex-panding fluid masses, a brilliantly red fish-like fetus, and primeval landscapes that decelerate while growing steadily larger and occupying a greater portion of the visual field. In this series of images Dave Bowman and the odyssey have been stripped to their active center. But, in addition, the active circular forms, while developing out of self-generated impulsions, progress from the largest kind of entity, a galaxy, to the more and more compactly individualized. In this individuation process, a huge eye occupying the entire screen issues from the heavenly bodies, blinks, and disappears into a landscape corresponding in color to the eye's changing colors. By the time of the eye's first appearance the twilight duskiness of Jupiter and its moons, the elementary black-and-white of the galaxy shot, and the primary red and yellow of the exploding star have developed into the secondary and tertiary greens, oranges, and fuchsias of the huge eye. With each appearance the blinking eye further cleanses itself, unites with the objects of its perception, and manifests another of the infinitely diverse possibilities inherent in light by mixing the primary colors into blended hues. This synthesis of the white light, that had been fractured first into black-and-white and then the primary colors, into individualized worlds of blended color, achieved the congealing of light into a definite form already begun in the landscape's advances through seven crystals that appear on the horizon—reflective of Christianity's seven days of creation—as well as literally imaging a crystallizing of the rudimentary skeletal or rational dimension of the new individual in the making. The imaginative part of the reconstructive phase then concludes with a shot of a fully formed, naturally colored light-brown eye. The initial period of the creative act has begotten a fetus, and that fetus issues into an integrated natural organ —radically distinct from the brain of Classicism and the heart of Romanticism—that functions as the central agency for the second part of the reconstructive trip back in the creative act.

The vibrating of Dave's face early in Part III reveals the image to be active in itself in the initial reconstructive period, not externally in relation to images as it is in rational motion. This quite explicit internal activity in and its leaps from wheeling galaxy to exploding star to fluid gaseous masses, etc., are probably a more starling phenomenon in the second or intellectual part of the reconstructive trip back where the images are of readily identifiable objects. What passes as natural on the cosmic scale appears fantastic in the ordinary human realm. However, the processes of the creative act operative in the first part continue their work in the second part. But because it is performing a more complicated reconstruction in the latter, the creative act proceeds with an increased degree of subtlety.

In the second part of the constructive trip back, after the eye blinks its way into and moves through the center of white light, the pod materializes again, sitting at rest in a room done up in an elegant style reminiscent of

18th century decor and comparable functionally in the trip back to the long second part of the organic act and destructive trip out extending from the shot of the space ship replacing the bone to the disconnection of HAL. An angularly geometrical box, this room in its main spatial characteristics possesses rational properties antedating those of the Discovery and the other spaceships. These spatial characteristics make it appear to be a throw-back to an earlier period of time, the age of reason. And it is—to the moment in Western history of rational enlightenment. But it is the formal properties of the room that are important, not any ideology they might suggest. In the context of the movie, the room's angularity relates to the angularity of the cobalt slab, and also to the rectangular frame of the picture that appears within the cineramic arc of the theatre screen. Like the rectangular screen and cobalt slab, the room serves as an intermediary for bearing energies that originate from circles. Along with words, the right angles they have in common, by setting integrated energies at all stages in man's growth in opposing vertical and horizontal tension, are necessary forces of abstraction and division within the organic and creative processes. But whereas the cobalt slab gives dominance to the vertical over the horizontal (except for the one occasion at the beginning of Part III where, dimly visible—its usual stark contrast to other natural entities minimized—it leads Dave into the light trip), the 18th century room emphasizes the tranquilizing horizontal line, thereby minimizing external tensions and keeping the rational powers coolly at rest.

The room's decor leaves no doubt about this role in the creative act suggested by its general architectural properties. While outwardly a more advanced mechanical structure than the 18th century room, the Discovery is exclusively rational, as is evident from its being devoid of sensory and imaginary elements both of the immediately physical and artistic kinds. Its ascetic functionalism even applies to the meager sensory activity of Frank Poole's exercising and eating and the equally meager imaginary activity of Dave's drawing. Within this austerely rational setting, and despite the basic circularity of the Discovery's interior, sensory and imaginative elements get pushed into the background and their activity held to a minimum. Along these same lines, the interior of the Discovery is lit by specific man-controlled lights. In contrast, the 18th century room includes vaguely seen landscapes and sculptures, imaginative vestiges of the sensory stage of human history and individual development, and a basic green and white color scheme that unites the elementary hue of natural, sensory life with the integrated light of the imagination. All that it houses is artifice, works of the imagination, but it incorporates the full range of sensory, intellectual, and imaginative art in the landscapes and sculptures, the architecture, and Dave's metamorphosis. Thus its basic rectangularity and intellectual properties actually are enclosed by sensory and imaginative qualities in a trinary aesthetic structure. Appropriately, within that trinary setting the dramatic action consists of a lone man, in more or less static poses, looking—at himself in a mirror, at stages in his metamorphosis, and at the cobalt slab. Rather than getting caught up in the binary polarizations and their resulting disputation that reigns in the Discovery, he relies upon his senses and flagrantly indulges his imagination. Moreover, in addition to a spaciousness appropriate for a large transaction, a clean, bright plastic floor lends a general translucency to the room, allowing its intellectual properties to be bathed in a light that has no discernable source and softly diffuses throughout the room. This soft white light of the 18th century room, unlike the harsh white light in the hallway of the Hilton Space Station that dissolves away the edges of the voluptuous red chairs and couches, reconstitutes the outlines and solidity of "material" objects.

In sum, light and the imagination create the 18th century room, not reason, and that makes it a wholly different affair than the interior of the Discovery. The 18th century room is enlightened reason, the head modified to serve as a bearer rather than censor of the visual and imaginative powers and as a delivery room for the creative feat occurring within it. True, it is a recognizable old form, as Dave Bowman is, but both have been inhabited by the light. In the second period of the creative act the furthest evolved rational and organic forms are infiltrated by the light and used as launching bases for a new evolutionary venture. Only with these structures as its media can the creative act complete its creation beyond them. But when the machinery and organism necessary to the reincarnation that is happening beyond infinity are no longer useful, the creative powers transform the rectangularity of the room into a new circularity and Dave's ordinary mortality into an extraordinary new creature.

The room is a necessary component in the creative act during the second stage of the reconstructive trip back, but the creative feat is transacted quite overtly in it when Dave metamorphoses into the embryo. The essential feature about this very evident chain of creative events in the room, not just the birth itself, is how creative motion differs from the ape's physical change of location and rational man's change of cause and effect. Like the cosmic events of the preceding reconstructive phase, the creative feats in the room transpire imaginatively in quantum jumps happening too fast for the conceptual and logical processes of reason to keep apace of them. Standing benumbed in a bathroom, Dave, appropriately for a visual man, cleanses himself by looking at his image in a mirror rather than by washing with water in the bath tub or wash bowl. Cleansed, his eye blinks through a series of life-perceptions. From his reflection Dave turns to see himself as an old man at a table through a doorway. As the old man turns to face the space-suited astronaut, Dave becomes the other, older man, who partakes of a last supper. Dave's visual powers, transcending organic continuity, see maturity and age as separate stages but nevertheless interconnected and engage in a holistic transition from one condition to the other that includes and eclipses the first. With the breaking of a crystalline wine glass that consummates the solidification of light begun in the landscapes and developed in the seven crystals, the inner motions of labored breathing heard from the bed precedes a cut to the image of Dave as an ancient withered figure. The heavy breathing of the old man, recalling the previous breathing of the thirsty apes and the space-suited mechanical astronauts who labored before him, testifies to the stirring of creative energy at the organism's center and the coming of new life. Both in this chain of creative events and the cosmic events before them a solitary, unbounded, expansive image leaps forward, when it is sufficiently integrated at its own center, to another such completely formed, solitary, unbounded, expansive image. The creative act moves in, through, and by individuals.

The arrival of the new life and the events immediately preceding it obviously transpiring by supra-logical connections, then, if not before, a different kind of consciousness has to be operative in Dave during the reconstructive phase of the trip back rather than the rational consciousness exemplified by HAL. Free of HAL's anxiety to control and of rational man's passion to explain things by their past, as well as of self-consciousness, Dave perceives through a creative consciousness. As a man of imagination, his attention is focused upon the center from whence the forward thrusting energy of creations issues, not upon what divides them against themselves and immobilizes them. His sensitivity to the unifying, dynamic inclinations at the matrix of the creative powers lets the processes operative on the grandest cosmic scale work in the ordinary human realm. But even beyond that and above all else his alertness to the active impulses of the creative powers allow him to see that the creative act is devoted to realizing the greatest possible specific integration of the cosmic and mundane—that the creative powers love the concrete particular. Seeing this, Dave's creative consciousness openly receives the creative powers active within it and lends itself to looking out ahead with them.

Clearly Part III is not a chaotic light show embellished with random surrealistic imagery but a process. In it, a very specific kind of structural system infuses the visual and imaginative powers of Dave Bowman with a very definite method. By means of that trinary system, every event in Part III, and also throughout *2001*, works as a creative agent in the creative act being accomplished during the odyssey, not simply as an organ within an organism. Organic structure might suffice for a painting, where the components have a fixed temporal relation to one another, or for an analysis of how an animate creature or community maintains its equilibrium. But organic structure cannot conduct or account for creative motion. The trinary system solves the elemental problem of creative motion, in life as well as in movie narration, by integrating Dave's powers of life into a finer coherence, efficiency, and effectiveness than they possess in either rational or organic structures. Under its direction each event in the odyssey not only contributes its distinctive virtues at the precise instant they are required functionally but is itself a creative matrix, a solitary phenomenon that keeps the creative process moving toward the birth of the embryo by transforming received packets of energy into more complexly active packets of energy. Obviously, anything but inert, such supremely charged phenomena of the trinary system do nor waste themselves in a riot of degeneration that, from the rational point of view, supposedly results when rational restraints are lifted.

The movie's three formal parts leave no doubt that the trinary system is the very explicit method in *2001* whereby the visual powers that move over the earth and the moon to center upon the sun in the visual title of the movie arrive at the destination they posit for themselves there, the source of light. At the same time that it is the means for the visual powers locating the center and making their way to this source, the trinary system is the method whereby light, rhythmically contracting and expanding about a center, emanates from its source, whether the source be the sun or the movie screen. The only actual movement between the two fixed points of Dave's catatonic face and infinity during his passage through the star gate is the pulsing of light. But in addition to directing the movement of the visual powers to the light source and the play of light from its source at infinity upon Dave's face, the trinary system negotiates the exchange that occurs in these goings and comings between the source and its agent. Since it corresponds identically in its manner of movement to, for example, the respiration cycle and the heart beat, the light Dave receives is not an imitation of life or life-like but literally alive. This common structural system shared by light and life enables light actually, not just fictionally, to by-pass Dave's physical and intellectual power and induce, first in his face, then at his viral center, the profoundest resonance of which life is capable, responsive vibrations in the infra-red portion of his energy spectrum, if you will. At the same time that it touches him to the quick, the light added to Dave's life, as happens when an electron fuses with an atom, generates in him a new set of properties and powers. It is in this way and at this moment that the trinary system conceives the new creature in Dave. Thereafter his adventure is taken up with giving body to the light of his new life.

In other words, the trinary system performs three functions simultaneously—in conducting to the source, it generalizes; in negotiating the transaction of energy between the source and its agent, it communicates in the sense of permitting things to share what they most profoundly have in common; and in releasing energy from the source; it particularizes. It can perform all these feats simultaneously, and also emphasize each at the appropriate moment in the creative act, because it concentrates on the third component in the existence of anything, the energy that flows between bodies, whether it be gravity, magnetism, electricity, light, or life. By specializing in what happens in the space in between things, the trinary system positions itself to be extra sensitive to what is going on and to enhance interaction between bodies. But to be in such a position it initially unites things structurally and operatively into a common single field of force. Its virtues and versatility arise from the fact that the trinary system is the method present in the begetting, perpetuation, and evolution of the individual. Since nothing can exist outside a relation, or an exchange of energy, and only individuals exist, individuality is inseparable from activity. And it follows that the greater the activity, the greater the individuality.

The genius of the trinary system at work in Dave is its capacity to get all his vital powers, the sensory, intellectual, and imaginative, into motion simultaneously and keep them moving while coordinating their mutual amplification of each other into a total creative activity and the pure motion of the embryo in the last shot of the movie. The trinary system becomes operative whenever the circuit of individuality is joined and it functions at the juncture of individuality. In the universe of individuals in *2001* and the movies as a medium it is the means for delivering individuals from individuals via individuals. For the activity of the trinary system in *2001* to culminate in the completed particularizing of a specific creature, the embryo, it had from the beginning of the movie to give priority to individuality and to the individualizing powers. In the exchange of individuality between individuals, the individual Dave Bowman is, of course, expendable. But as an agent of individuality, he transfers the powers of individuation along to the embryo born from him, where they not only live on in a new individual but with an enhanced potential for activity. Dave's specific role in the transformation of gravity and electromagnetism at the sun's center into radiant energy, that into light, then light into life, and finally life into creativity is to bring human consciousness out of the darkness of rational modes into awareness of the manner of working active at the heart of the creative powers it issues from, and to thereby equip the new creature to enter into the creative act and move in consonance with the creative universe.

III

The trinary system insures that when the fecund life of images first casts off the physical abstractions the apes suffered from and then bolts free after the disconnection of HAL, it not only has something of its own to accomplish but a way of going about it. It sees to it in conducting the liberation of the visual and imaginative powers that the rational, organic, and creative acts are not just superimposed upon one another accidentally or dogmatically but contribute to a common enterprise. It also sees to it that all that happens in and between the images in the purely visual Part III is directed toward a positive realization of possibilities inherent in Dave's visual and imaginative powers. That realization in the form of the embryo affirms the passion of Dave's eye to behold and be active in a universe made to be its image. But not just of Dave's eye; the eye of man as well.

From its opening shot *2001* is the eye's story. Only the eye, not even Dave, passes through all three parts of the odyssey. But the crucial fact is that only the eye grows. It literally expands from the timid, downcast, cowed eyes of the apes to the immense, brilliantly colored eye that completely occupies the screen in Part III. Since *2001* is the story of the eye, everything that happens during the odyssey figures in the eye's expansion. That expansion gets succinctly imaged, however, in the changes that the image of the eye itself undergoes. In its first distinctive image after the obscure ape eyes, the eye appears as a gleaming solid yellow agate, an incarnation of the sunlight that both brings about the literal dawn at the beginning of the movie and inspires the dawn of man when the apes turn their eyes upward along the vertical line of the cobalt slab. That concentrated eye of fierce light, via the emergence of the "bi-visual" perception of the apes—their ability to see up as well as before them and thereby to see bones in perspective, as having a use for ends beyond themselves—develops into HAL's deeply set, compound eye, which, appropriate for an analytical instrument, breaks the yellow eye down into three colors, a yellow pupil, red iris, and black eyeball. This eye of reason

introduces blood and death into the leopard's feral energy and then transforms into Dave's simple, depthless blue eye. Once the eye has transmuted
into blue, it no longer suffers from restrictive ape skins and space suits, and
moves without the awkward stumbling and formal posing of the earlier creatures. It sees without the peripheral confinement even of a helmet or face,
immediately perceiving and sharing the potency of the creation. Then the
odyssey just happens out there, in the outer space of the screen. The liberated
eye, unlike the stereoscopic, depth-perceiving eye of reason, no longer sets
things apart by kind or time and space, nor is it interested in making a sentimental journey into the past to discover the first cause or great authority.
Instead, like the sky, it assimilates unanalyzed all that it surveys. This vora-
cious ingestion of the entire visible creation empowers the eye to reach its full
size and maximum capability in the huge brilliantly colored eye.

Turned loose on its own, the eye is not propelled by one idea or ideal, by
thought or will. It is just naturally on the go, as it was in the opening shot of
the movie, and with no restrictions placed upon its activity, its inherent salient qualities of thrust, mobility, and agility boldly declare themselves. It
never becomes free of itself in Part III, however. The eye's special talent for
perceiving images, the form of things that distinguishes them from all other
things and endows them with a life of their own, makes it the indispensable
vessel for the odyssey of creation in *2001*. And the eye's story is preoccupied
with developing forms pleasing to the eye and consistent with its indigenous
values, so that *2001* is self-centered art, art about art, visual art spun out of
the visual medium of light and images for its own sake, the visual imagination at play. But the eye is not what is born. It is the central organ in light's
odyssey, capable of growing in the way organisms do, through which the
birth occurs.

During Part III, although it is also true from the first shot of the movie,
there can be no doubt that the eye thrives on and delights in form. That's all
there is in the imaginative parts of the odyssey: purely visual images in motion. But the eye not only perceives and participates in the creative act going
on in the reconstructive phase of Part III; it performs a synthesis there, an
auto-synthesis, which, since the eye has nothing else to work with, is a synthesis of forms. This synthesis is carried out, as it necessarily must be, in the
most concrete and at the same time least narratively specific features of the
movie—in the manner of the camera eye's telling of the story. Its achievement includes alterations in the photographic style, or modes of vision, over
the course of the eye's growth in which the fixed shots and abrupt cuts of the
ape section and the fluid, multiple points of view of the space flight section

yield to the single perspective of the moving eye in Part III. It also includes an alteration in background-foreground relations in the frame from a pronouncedly out of focus background in the ape section to a shallower space in the space travel section to an aperspectivity during the light trip and in the concluding images of the embryo—where everything to be seen, no matter how vastly different in size or far apart from a realistic point of view, is in sharp focus and given equal attention in and for itself. As that alteration occurs, the eye alters its relation to the objects of its perception from the remote detachment of the ape section to the analytical scrutinizing, including close-ups of Frank and Dave by HAL, of the space travel, to the identity of the eye and its object in Part III. That alteration is accompanied by the replacement of the haziness during the ape episode and the brightly lit but cultivated obfuscation in the space travel episode with a brightness that illuminates everything, in which nothing is hidden, in Part III. The over-all synthesis attained by means of these various alternations entails the naturalistic mode of the ape section being blended with the rationalistic mode of the space travel section, including the surrealism of the light trip and the symbolism of the 18th century room, into a new literal mode. (Incidentally, this synthesis parallels the development in the history of the movies from the flat, two-dimensional space of the silent movie to the three-dimensional space of black-and-white talkies to the centralized space of color movies. And both parallel what happens in visual perception as an object moves from the periphery of the visual field, where it is unidentifiable motion, into the range of recognition, and then to the center of the visual field where it can be looked at by itself straight on and perhaps close up.)

This fusion of the fixed box space the apes are confined to with the fluid conceptualized perspective space of rational man into the creative space of free images can be specifically observed in the varying relations to the cobalt slab during its different stages of the odyssey. The entire tribe of apes tactilely touch the slab. Owing to such a restricted relationship, they can only know it physically and be moved by pressure of its mass. Its impact, however, is to single one ape out from the tribe and equip him to act through the mediating agency of a bone. His predicament and enhanced strength carries over into the select group of men who approach the cobalt slab at Clavius, make contact with it through a glove—and only one man touches it—and then the effect, instead of its being visual and tangible as it had been for the apes, is aural and intellectual: the heads of the men are stunned by a high-pitched tone. When Dave Bowman subsequently follows the cobalt slab in the pod, he does so strictly out of visual stimulation. Nothing mediates between his eyes and the slab—no skin or gloves, no verbal questions or curiosity. Not even air. On that occasion and when on the bed as a withered ancient figure he raises his hand to point at the slab, a much greater distance separates visual man from the cobalt slab's force field than separated rational man from it.

This progression from a physical through an intellectual to a purely visual relation with the cobalt slab doesn't constitute a developing estrangement or alienation. It is the prerequisite of vision and the transfer of creative energy. The three relations illustrate that as man relates, so he sees. But in their progression it is evident that the increased separation provides the larger room necessary for greater activity. By keeping an appropriate visual distance—not getting up so close to the slab that his vision is limited to knowing but a part of it or getting so far back that it blends indistinguishably into the background—Dave allows the slab to maintain its autonomy and integrity as an individual entity. Since the eye sees only individuals, it is not a question of Dave's perceiving an individual but of the particular individual he singles out to focus upon, in this case a powerfully charged rectangular gateway, a rational abstraction, that equips his creative energy with the supplementary capacity for fission and transcendence. His gesture of pointing at the slab—the closest he comes to it—leaves room for these events to happen in the space between them. Dave thereby welds physical and rational objectivity into an imaginative objectivity that relates his eye as a field of force to the cobalt slab's field of force that combines, as his eye does, his vital powers, all the powers of which the slab consists. His visual distance facilitates his receiving the entire energy transmitted by the cobalt slab rather than a fragment of it. And this kind of perception is a prerequisite to the eye accelerating its rhythm over the three parts of the odyssey—of getting its timing right through a deft synthesis of the apes' change of location and rational man's cause and effect into the creative space-time of the eye's generative change.

This transfer of the individual entity's total force intact across a distance not only leaves Dave room to grow in but is chosen by, not forced upon him. By rising toward the slab he elects to focus upon and move in its direction, and in so doing he acts out of his own center while centering upon it. The result is that two active centers link up in a mutual intra-action. Instead of interacting as an aggressive and passive element at one point of contact, the individualized energy of the slab fuels the perceiving individual Dave for his development into greater individuation.

With that feat accomplished the eye is ready to perform its final—and also its simplest and most startling—synthesis of form. It occurs when Dave's ancient dessicated head is flooded with light and in a three-step process re-placed by the complete body of a hairless, streamlined, open-eyed embryo. No more adroit and significant use of the cut can be found in cinematic art than this amply prepared for transformation. All the potential for existence within the image bounds across the darkness of that cut, but as that happens the eye fully integrates itself by transforming the linear alignment of the three heavenly bodies of its opening shot into a concentric arrangement of the embryo's active eye within its moving head within the embryonic sac that at first moves in relation to Jupiter and the earth and then occupies the entire screen by itself, an autonomous entity equal as a creation to all other indi-viduals in the creation, including planets. In successfully begetting a con-crete new individual, the eye, cleansing itself beyond Blake's perception of the infinite in everything, realizes in a true marriage of heaven and hell the possibility of an enlightened finite individual. Its most crucial accomplish-ment when it travels through the cobalt slab as a doorway beyond infinity to spring the living form of the embryo free from the dessicated skull of Dave's head to perform this marriage is to transfer the energy of motion that acted from the outside over the three heavenly bodies in the opening shot to the centermost of the concentric circles. No embryo has ever before had its eyes open during its prenatal development, but this one not only has open eyes: they are active! The eye and the light have assumed the central role in the new form.

The eye's voracity does not lead to a gluttonous death but to a meta-physical feast whereby the physical and intellectual forms of the already ex-isting creation are transcended, not by escaping "reality," but by expanding those forms within an open universe into freer life. That means that the eye's feat of centralizing itself isn't a vain projection of its form of pupil within iris within eyeball upon the universe, but a selfless amplification of light. When it passes through infinity, the eye literally consummates man's perennial meta-physical quest for light. When enlightened, it doesn't know the light as a theoretical concept; it assumes the form of light. In the star gate then at infinity, where it is completely open, the eye sees nothing but light, which is all that any eye ever sees anyway. The reflected portion of the light of the star gate that strikes Dave's eye, like the radiant energy that pervades the black space of the solar system when it strikes the earth's atmosphere, synthesizes center and periphery, for there is no light strictly speaking, or phenomenally, until the radiant energy emanating from the center of the sun is intercepted by the skin of a body. Even then the light is not a soul added to a body in the manner of the long string of fuel tanks attached to the Discovery but a marriage of two kinds of energy, light with a more inert form of energy, into a unity as subtle as that of the radiant energy of light itself, which, it will be remembered, is a quantum simultaneously particle and wave. What happens on the skin of the eye also happens, but with profounder consequences, at the center of the eye. A photosynthesis of sorts occurs. While on its most rudimentary level photosynthesis transforms inorganic materials into organic life through the energy supplied by photons, in the star gate it entails the incorporation of light energy into Dave's life, or, more accurately, into the central organ of his life, the eye. More than illumination occurs; an organic form capable of perpetuating itself evolves into a wholly new form capable of "revising" itself. In this union of light and eye, the light not only annihilates itself in the eye as a body but passes its powers of synthesis over to the eye.

But as a form of light housing the form of light, the eye not only is charged with the light's power of synthesis bur also its passion for originating. Originating—the creation of freer life—entails violence, as all motion does since it cannot occur without energy being expended aggressively or exploded, no matter how small and innocuous the discharge may seem in relation to human proportions. And violence occurs in *2001* repeatedly— with the leopard, among the apes, in HAL's killing of Frank Poole, Dave's labotomizing of HAL, and the explosion of energy enacted by the cobalt slab every time it appears, making it the guiltiest of all. But while violence is done in *2001* even by the light, both to the eye in the star gate and in it during the cosmic eruptions and abrupt transformations of Dave beyond infinity, the eye that directly admits it also reaches the goal the visual powers arrived at in the opening shot of the movie, not just the center of the sun but the source of light. This synthesis of the eye with its source orients it in the way of light and empowers it to act as light does. That means specifically that as sunlight overflows from a spontaneous self-generated fusion of hydrogen atoms, so the eye in its photosynthesis is not only, because of its increased heat, more active within itself and under a pressure to expand, but also, owing to a fine excess, given to spontaneous generation. Accordingly, when the eye is filled with light, which it is at infinity, its pure vision perceives images as events, specifically as births. In its sufficiency each image in the cosmic phase of the reconstruction for it is a freshly born world seen for the first time and pregnant with the yet newer world ready to be born from it.

All through the reconstructive phase of the odyssey while it looks at the various cosmic events, Dave's eye emulates the light, but on the bed in the 18th century room it becomes readily apparent that Dave has taken the light into and undergoes its violence within himself. At that moment, not only full of light but with the light fully active in him, he transforms into a ball of white light slightly darkened at its center, which serves as the pregnant womb for the development, first, of a fetus, and finally, of the embryo. He emulates the light in this metamorphosis. As the light had annihilated itself in his eye and impregnated him, so he, following up on his self-annihilation in his one-to-one perception of the cosmic events, sacrifices himself to the metamorphosis that begins with the appearance of the ball of white light in place of the ancient dissicated head. Like the light, he adds nothing but himself to the process. And so with the eye. When it looks at the cosmic events, then through Dave at himself and at the slab at the foot of the bed, it participates in the transformation of "physical reality" by containing the explosive force of energy within itself and transmitting it into creative activity. Its synthesis of the destructive and creative powers within itself permits the creative powers, the light of life, to pass through the eye unimpeded and in fact strengthened by the addition of its own energy. Completely synthesizing their organic life with the light, both the eye and Dave spend themselves indiscriminately, as light does, without thought of their giving or to whom they give in the creative venture. And in their infinite generosity both originate a new living form that confirms and celebrates their source. Anything but vain, Dave, at the same time that he is the most active and far-ranging of men, is along with the eye the gentlest of protagonists in the gentlest of arts. They take only what is freely given, neither robbing nor diminishing, and freely spend themselves in their turn for the commonweal.

Occupant of a fertile, fecund universe made to the measure of his created and creative existence, the embryo glides smoothly in a richly endowed environment without fear or distaste and on its own power. Yet, despite his being composed of and charged with the visual, imaginative, creative, and synthesizing powers discussed in this essay as going into his making, the new creature is not actually born. It is only on the verge of being born. Its birth, the birth of imaginative man as the successor to intellectual man, depends upon the spectator of *2001*. For the viewer of *2001* sits in the same relation to the movie that Dave does to infinity. In a showing of the movie—any movie, for that matter—the primary event is not the illusion of linear movement upon the plane of the screen or into and out of the background of the picture on it, but the continuous stream of light radiating from a constant source, in effect, the center of the screen. There is no difference between what is happening to Dave in the narrative on the screen and in the theatre to the movie viewer. One is not a fiction, the other reality. Both Dave and his audience participate in precisely the same adventure. The fact that the movie viewer sees reflected instead of direct light doesn't matter; he experiences the light as originating from the screen. Even if he analyzes the light, all he can do is trace it back in an infinite regress to light bulb or carbon arc, dynamo, oil or coal, vegetation, carbon, the sun. Whenever he looks, the light will be streaming forward from a central source just as it does from the screen. Dave and the eye sustain and perpetuate the integrity of the light, exactly emulating its model of synthesis in passing it on not only intact but enhanced to the viewer and involving him directly in the odyssey of *2001*. This immediate interlinking of narrator, narrative, and audience, the eye's supreme synthesis, perfectly blends art and life, in a medium that is in fact the liveliest art, into an impeccable art of life. Thus when Dave sheds all his rational connections, including his name, and acts solely through his visual powers, he is the common vital center of all humans and his eye the eye of all life and the universe. Only if the viewer includes himself imaginatively and completes the entire creative odyssey of *2001*, trusting his eye to carry him through the distinctive and constructive phases of the purely visual trip out and back in Part III, can the embryo on the verge of birth actually be born. For only when he openly receives the creative power transmitted immediately by the light and images to his imagination and adds his life to them can the eye's final synthesis be achieved, that of the art becoming life. Not to make the purely visual trip of Part III is to remain unborn. To have made it is to follow Kubrick not only to "the threshold of a revolutionary new era in film" but into the new era of the greater individuality of creative man.

II.

Essays on Movies, Visions, and Values, in the Spirit of W. R. Robinson

Total Eclipse

ANNIE DILLARD

IT HAD BEEN LIKE DYING, that sliding down the mountain pass. It had been like the death of someone, irrational, that sliding down the mountain pass and into the region of dread. It was like slipping into fever, or falling down that hole in sleep from which you wake yourself whimpering. We had crossed the mountains that day, and now we were in a strange place—a hotel in central Washington, in a town near Yakima. The eclipse we had traveled here to see would occur early the next morning.

I lay in bed. My husband, Gary, was reading beside me. I lay in bed and looked at the painting on the hotel-room wall. It was a print of a detailed and lifelike painting of a smiling clown's head, made out of vegetables. It was a painting of the sort that you do not intend to look at and that, alas, you never forget. Some tasteless fate presses it upon you; it becomes part of the complex interior junk you carry with you wherever you go. Two years have passed since the total eclipse of which I write. During those years I have forgotten, I assume, a great many things I wanted to remember—but I have not forgotten that clown painting or its lunatic setting in the old hotel.

The clown was bald. Actually, he wore a clown's tight rubber wig, painted white; this stretched over the top of his skull, which was a cabbage. His hair was bunches of baby carrots. Inset in his white clown makeup, and in his cabbage skull, were his small and laughing human eyes. The clown's glance was like the glance of Rembrandt in some of the self-portraits: lively, knowing, deep, and loving. The crinkled shadows around his eyes were string beans. His eyebrows were parsley. Each of his ears was a broad bean. His thin, joyful lips were red chili peppers; between his lips were wet rows of human teeth and a suggestion of a real tongue. The clown print was framed in gilt and glassed.

To put ourselves in the path of the total eclipse, that day we had driven five hours inland from the Washington coast, where we lived. When we tried to cross the Cascades range, an avalanche had blocked the pass.

A slope's worth of snow blocked the road; traffic backed up. Had the avalanche buried any cars that morning? We could not learn. This highway was the only winter road over the mountains. We waited as highway crews bulldozed a passage through the avalanche. With two-by-fours and walls of plyboard, they erected a one-way, roofed tunnel through the avalanche. We drove through the avalanche tunnel, crossed the pass, and descended several thousand feet into central Washington and the broad Yakima valley, about which we knew only that it was orchard country. As we lost altitude, the snows disappeared; our ears popped; the trees changed, and in the trees were strange birds. I watched the landscape innocently, like a fool, like a diver in the rapture of the deep who plays on the bottom while his air runs out.

The hotel lobby was a dark, derelict room, narrow as a corridor, and seemingly without air. We waited on a couch while the manager vanished upstairs to do something unknown to our room. Beside us, on an overstuffed chair, absolutely motionless, was a platinum-blond woman in her forties, wearing a black silk dress and a strand of pearls. Her long legs were crossed; she supported her head on her fist. At the dim far end of the room, their backs toward us, sat six bald old men in their shirtsleeves, around a loud television. Two of them seemed asleep. They were drunks. "Number six!" cried the man on television, "Number six!"

On the broad lobby desk was a ten-gallon aquarium, lighted and bubbling, that contained one large fish; the fish tilted up and down in its water. Against the long opposite wall sang a live canary in its cage. Beneath the cage, among spilled millet seeds on the carpet, were a decorated child's sand bucket and matching sand shovel.

Now the alarm was set for six. I lay awake remembering an article I had read downstairs in the lobby, in an engineering magazine. The article was about gold mining.

In South Africa, in India, and in South Dakota, the gold mines extend so deeply into the earth's crust that they are hot. The rock walls burn the miners' hands. The companies have to air-condition the mines; if the air conditioners break, the miners die. The elevators in the mind shafts run very slowly, down, and up, so the miners' ears will not pop in their skulls When the miners return to the surface, their faces are deathly pale.

Early the next morning we checked out. It was February 26, 1979, a Monday morning. We would drive out of town, find a hilltop, watch the eclipse, and then drive back over the mountains and home to the coast. How familiar things are here; how adept we are; how smoothly and professionally we check out! I had forgotten the clown's smiling head and the hotel lobby as if they had never existed. Gary put the car in gear and off we went, as off we have gone to a hundred other adventures.

It was before dawn when we found a highway out of town and drove into the unfamiliar countryside. By the growing light we could see a band of cirrostratus clouds in the sky. Later the rising sun would clear these clouds before the eclipse began. We drove at random until we came to a range of unfenced hills. We pulled off the highway, bundled up, and climbed one of these hills.

II

The hill was five hundred feet high. Long winter-killed grass covered it, as high as our knees. We climbed and rested, sweating in the cold; we passed clumps of bundled people on the hillside who were setting up telescopes and fiddling with cameras. The top of the hill stuck up in the middle of the sky We tightened our scarves and looked around.

East of us rose another hill like ours. Between the hills, far below, was the highway that threaded south into the valley. This was the Yakima valley; I had never seen it before. It is justly famous for its beauty, like every planted valley. It extended south into the horizon, a distant dream of a valley, a Shangri-la. All its hundreds of low, golden slopes bore orchards. Among the orchards were towns, and roads, and plowed and fallow fields. Through the valley wandered a thin, shining river; from the river extended fine, frozen irrigation ditches. Distance blurred and blued the sight, so that the whole valley looked like a thickness or sediment at the bottom of the sky. Directly behind us was more sky, and empty lowlands blued by distance, and Mount Adams. Mount Adams was an enormous, snow-covered volcanic cone rising flat, like so much scenery.

Now the sun was up. We could not see it; but the sky behind the band of clouds was yellow, and, far down the valley, some hillside orchards had lighted up. More people were parking near the highway and climbing the hills. It was the West. All of us rugged individualists were wearing knit caps and blue nylon parkas. People were climbing the nearby hills and setting up shop in clumps among the dead grasses. It looked as though we had all gathered on hilltops to pray for the world on its last day. It looked as though we had all crawled out of spaceships and were preparing to assault the valley below. It looked as though we were scattered on hilltops at dawn to sacrifice virgins, make rain, set stone stelae in a ring. There was no place out of the wind. The straw grasses banged our legs.

Up in the sky where we stood, the air was lusterless yellow. To the west the sky was blue. Now the sun cleared the clouds. We cast rough shadows on the blowing grass; freezing, we waved our arms. Near the sun, the sky was bright and colorless. There was nothing to see.

It began with no ado. It was odd that such a well-advertised public event should have no starting gun, no overture, no introductory speaker. I should have known right then that I was out of my depth. Without pause or pre-amble, silent as orbits, a piece of the sun went away. We looked at it through welders' goggles. A piece of the sun was missing; in its place we saw empty sky.

I had seen a partial eclipse in 1970. A partial eclipse is very interesting. It bears almost no relation to a total eclipse. Seeing a partial eclipse bears the same relation to seeing a total eclipse as kissing a man does to marrying him, or as flying in an airplane does to falling out of an airplane. Although the one experience precedes the other, it in no way prepares you for it. During a partial eclipse the sky does not darken—not even when 94 percent of the sun is hidden. Nor does the sun, seen colorless through protective devices, seem terribly strange. We have all seen a sliver of light in the sky; we have all seen the crescent moon by day. However, during a partial eclipse the air does indeed get cold, precisely as if someone were standing between you and the fire. And blackbirds do fly back to their roosts. I had seen a partial eclipse before, and here was another.

What you see in an eclipse is entirely different from what you know. It is especially different for those of us whose grasp of astronomy is so frail that, given a flashlight, a grapefruit, two oranges, and fifteen years, we still could not figure out which way to set the clocks for daylight saving time. Usually it is a bit of a trick to keep your knowledge from blinding you. But during an eclipse it is easy. What you see is much more convincing than any wild-eyed theory you may know.

You may read that the moon has something to do with eclipses. I have never seen the moon yet. You do not see the moon. So near the sun, it is as completely invisible as the stars are by day. What you see before your eyes is the sun going through phases. It gets narrower and narrower, as the waning moon does, and, like the ordinary moon, it travels alone in the simple sky. The sky is of course background. It does not appear to eat the sun; it is far behind the sun. The sun simply shaves away; gradually, you see less sun and more sky.

The sky's blue was deepening, but there was no darkness. The sun was a wide crescent, like a segment of tangerine. The wind freshened and blew steadily over the hill. The eastern hill across the highway grew dusky and sharp. The towns and orchards in the valley to the south were dissolving into the blue light. Only the thin river held a trickle of sun.

Now the sky to the west deepened to indigo, a color never seen. A dark sky usually loses color. This was a saturated, deep indigo, up in the air. Stuck up into that unworldly sky was the cone of Mount Adams, and the alpenglow was upon it. The alpenglow is that red light of sunset which holds out on snowy mountaintops long after the valleys and tablelands are dimmed. "Look at Mount Adams," I said, and that was the last sane moment I remember.

I turned back to the sun. It was going. The sun was going, and the world was wrong. The grasses were wrong; they were platinum. Their every detail of stem, head, and blade shone lightless and artificially distinct as an art photographer's platinum print. This color has never been seen on earth. The hues were metallic; their finish was matte. The hillside was a nineteenth-century tinted photograph from which the tints had faded. All the people you see in the photograph, distinct and detailed as their faces look, are now dead. The sky was navy blue. My hands were silver. All the distant hills' grasses were finespun metal that the wind laid down. I was watching a faded color print of a movie filmed in the Middle Ages; I was standing in it, by some mistake. I was standing in a movie of hillside grasses filmed in the Middle Ages. I missed my own century, the people I knew, and the real light of day.

I looked at Gary. He was in the film. Everything was lost. He was a platinum print, a dead artist's version of life. I saw on his skull the darkness of night mixed with the colors of day. My mind was going out; my eyes were receding the way galaxies recede to the rim of space. Gary was light-years

away, gesturing inside a circle of darkness, down the wrong end of a telescope. He smiled as if he saw me; the stringy crinkles around his eyes moved.
The sight of him, familiar and wrong, was something I was remembering
from centuries hence, from the other side of death: yes, *that* is the way he
used to look, when we were living. When it was our generation's turn to be
alive. I could not hear him; the wind was too loud. Behind him the sun was
going. We had all started down a chute of time. At first it was pleasant; now
there was no stopping it. Gary was chuting away across space, moving and
talking and catching my eye, chuting down the long corridor of separation.
The skin on his face moved like thin bronze plating that would peel.

The grass at our feet was wild barley. It was the wild einkorn wheat that
grew on the hilly flanks of the Zagros Mountains, above the Euphrates valley,
above the valley of the river we called *River*. We harvested the grass with
stone sickles, I remember. We found the grasses on the hillsides; we built our
shelter beside them and cut them down. That is how he used to look then,
that one, moving and living and catching my eye, with the sky so dark behind him, and the wind blowing. God save our life.

From all the hills came screams. A piece of sky beside the crescent sun
was detaching. It was a loosened circle of evening sky, suddenly lighted from
the back. It was an abrupt black body out of nowhere; it was a flat disk; it was
almost over the sun. That is when there were screams. At once this disk of sky
slid over the sun like a lid. The sky snapped over the sun like a lens cover. The
hatch in the brain slammed. Abruptly it was dark night, on the land and in
the sky. In the night sky was a tiny ring of light. The hole where the sun
belongs is very small. A thin ring of light marked its place. There was no
sound. The eyes dried, the arteries drained, the lungs hushed. There was no
world. We were the world's dead people rotating and orbiting around and
around, embedded in the planet's crust, while the earth rolled down. Our
minds were light-years distant, forgetful of almost everything. Only an extraordinary act of will could recall to us our former, living selves and our
contexts in matter and time. We had, it seems, loved the planet and loved our
lives, but could no longer remember the way of them. We got the light wrong.
In the sky was something that should not be there. In the black sky was a ring
of light. It was a thin ring, an old, thin silver wedding band, an old, worn
ring. It was an old wedding band in the sky, or a morsel of bone. There were
stars. It was all over.

III

It is now that the temptation is strongest to leave these regions. We have seen enough; let's go. Why burn our hands any more than we have to? But two years have passed; the price of gold has risen. I return to the same buried alluvial beds and pick through the strata again.

I saw, early in the morning, the sun diminish against a backdrop of sky. I saw a circular piece of that sky appear, suddenly detached, blackened, and backlighted; from nowhere it came and overlapped the sun. It did not look like the moon. It was enormous and black. If I had not read that it was the moon, I could have seen the sight a hundred times and never thought of the moon once. (If, however, I had not read that it was the moon—if, like most of the world's people throughout time, I had simply glanced up and seen this thing—then I doubtless would not have speculated much, but would have, like Emperor Louis of Bavaria in 840, simply died of fright on the spot.) It did not look like a dragon, although it looked more like a dragon than the moon. It looked like a lens cover, or the lid of a pot. It materialized out of thin air—black, and flat, and sliding, outlined in flame.

Seeing this black body was like seeing a mushroom cloud. The heart screeched. The meaning of the sight overwhelmed its fascination. It obliterated meaning itself. If you were to glance out one day and see a row of mushroom clouds rising on the horizon, you would know at once that what you were seeing, remarkable as it was, was intrinsically not worth remarking. No use running to tell anyone. Significant as it was, it did not matter a whit. For what is significance? It is significance for people. No people, no significance. This is all I have to tell you.

In the deeps are the violence and terror of which psychology has warned us. But if you ride these monsters deeper down, if you drop with them farther over the world's rim, you find what our sciences cannot locate or name, the substrate, the ocean or matrix or ether that buoys the rest, that gives goodness its power for good, and evil its power for evil, the unified field: our complex and inexplicable caring for each other, and for our life together here. This is given. It is not learned.

The world that lay under darkness and stillness following the closing of the lid was not the world we know. The event was over. Its devastation lay round about us. The clamoring mind and heart stilled, almost indifferent, certainly disembodied, frail, and exhausted. The hills were hushed, obliterated. Up in the sky, like a crater from some distant cataclysm, was a hollow ring.

You have seen photographs of the sun taken during a total eclipse. The corona fills the print. All of those photographs were taken through telescopes. The lenses of telescopes and cameras can no more cover the breadth and scale of the visual array than language can cover the breadth and simultaneity of internal experience. Lenses enlarge the sight, omit its context, and make of it a pretty and sensible picture, like something on a Christmas card. I assure you, if you send any shepherds a Christmas card on which is printed a three-by-three photograph of the angel of the Lord, the glory of the Lord, and a multitude of the heavenly host, they will not be sore afraid. More fearsome things can come in envelopes. More moving photographs than those of the sun's corona can appear in magazines. But I pray you will never see anything more awful in the sky.

You see the wide world swaddled in darkness; you see a vast breadth of hilly land, and an enormous, distant, blackened valley; you see towns' lights, a river's path, and blurred portions of your hat and scarf; you see your husband's face looking like an early black-and-white film; and you see a sprawl of black sky and blue sky together, with unfamiliar stars in it, some barely visible bands of cloud, and, over there, a small white ring. The ring is as small as one goose in a flock of migrating geese—if you happen to notice a flock of migrating geese. It is one 360th part of the visible sky. The sun we see is less than half the diameter of a dime held at arm's length.

The Ring Nebula, in the constellation Lyra, looks, through binoculars, like a smoke ring. It is a star in the process of exploding. Light from its explosion first reached the earth in 1054; it was a supernova then, and so bright it shone in the daytime. Now it is not so bright, but it is still exploding. It expands at the rate of seventy million miles a day. It is interesting to look through binoculars at something expanding seventy million miles a day. It does not budge. Its apparent size does not increase. Photographs of the Ring Nebula taken fifteen years ago seem identical to photographs of it taken yesterday. Some lichens are similar. Botanists have measured some ordinary lichens twice, at fifty-year intervals, without detecting any growth at all. And yet their cells divide; they live.

The small ring of light was like these things—like a ridiculous lichen up in the sky, like a perfectly still explosion 5,000 light-years away: it was interesting, and lovely, and in witless motion, and it had nothing to do with anything.

It had nothing to do with anything. The sun was too small, and too cold, and too far away, to keep the world alive. The white ring was not enough. It was feeble and worthless. It was as useless as a memory; it was as off kilter and hollow and wretched as a memory.

When you try your hardest to recall someone's face, or the look of a place, you see in your mind's eye some vague and terrible sight such as this. It is dark; it is insubstantial; it is all wrong.

The white ring and the saturated darkness made the earth and the sky look as they must look in the memories of the careless dead. What I saw, what I seemed to be standing in, was all the wrecked light that the memories of the dead could shed upon the living world. We had all died in our boots on the hilltops of Yakima and were alone in eternity. Empty space stoppered our eyes and mouths; we cared for nothing. We remembered our living days wrong. With great effort we had remembered some sort of circular light in the sky—but only the outline. Oh, and then the orchard trees withered, the ground froze, the glaciers slid down the valleys and overlapped the towns. If there had ever been people on earth, nobody knew it. The dead had forgotten those they had loved. The dead were parted one from the other and could no longer remember the faces and lands they had loved in the light. They seemed to stand on darkened hilltops, looking down.

IV

We teach our children one thing only, as we were taught: to wake up. We teach our children to look alive there, to join by words and activities the life of human culture on the planet's crust. As adults we are almost all adept at waking up. We have so mastered the transition, we have forgotten we ever learned it. Yet it is a transition we make a hundred times a day, as, like so many will-less dolphins, we plunge and surface, lapse and emerge. We live half our waking lives and all of our sleeping lives in some private, useless, and insensible waters we never mention or recall. Useless, I say. Valueless, I might add—until someone hauls the wealth up to the surface and into the wide-awake city, in a form that people can use.

I do not know how we got to the restaurant. Like Roethke, "I take my waking slow." Gradually I seemed more or less alive, and already forgetful. It was now almost nine in the morning. It was the day of a solar eclipse in central Washington, and a fine adventure for everyone. The sky was clear; there was a fresh breeze out of the north.

The restaurant was a roadside place with tables and booths. The other eclipse-watchers were there. From our booth we could see their cars' California license plates, their University of Washington parking stickers. Inside the restaurant we were all eating eggs or waffles; people were fairly shouting and exchanging enthusiasms, like fans after a World Series game. Did you see...? Did you see… ? Then somebody said something that knocked me for a loop.

A college student, a boy in a blue parka who carried a Hasselblad, said to us, "Did you see that little white ring? It looked like a Life Saver. It looked like a Life Saver up in the sky."

And so it did. The boy spoke well. He was a walking alarm clock. I myself had at that time no access to such a term. He could write a sentence, and I could not. I grabbed that Life Saver and rode it to the surface. And I had to laugh. I had been dumbstruck on the Euphrates River, I had been dead and gone and grieving, all over the sight of something that, if you could claw your way up to that level, you would grant looked very much like a Life Saver. It was good to be back among people so clever; it was good to have all the world's words at the mind's disposal, so the mind could begin its task. All those things for which we have no words are lost. The mind—the culture— has two little tools, grammar and lexicon: a decorated sand bucket and a matching shovel. With these we bluster about the continents and do all the world's work. With these we try to save our very lives.

There are a few more things to tell from this level, the level of the restaurant. One is the old joke about breakfast. "It can never be satisfied, the mind, never." Wallace Stevens wrote that, and in the long run he was right. The mind wants to live forever, or to learn a very good reason why not. The mind wants the world to return its love, or its awareness; the mind wants to know all the world, and all eternity, and God. The mind's sidekick, however, will settle for two eggs over easy.

The dear, stupid body is as easily satisfied as a spaniel. And, incredibly, the simple spaniel can lure the brawling mind to its dish. It is everlastingly funny that the proud, metaphysically ambitious, clamoring mind will hush if you give it an egg.

Further: while the mind reels in deep space, while the mind grieves or fears or exults, the workaday sense, in ignorance or idiocy, like so many computer terminals printing out market prices while the world blows up, still transcribe their little data and transmit them to the warehouse in the skull. Later, under the tranquilizing influence of fried eggs, the mind can sort through these data. The restaurant was a halfway house, a decompression chamber. There I remembered a few things more.

The deepest, and most terrifying, was this: I have said that I heard screams. (I have since read that screaming, with hysteria, is a common reaction even to expected total eclipses.) People on all the hillsides, including, I think, myself, screamed when the black body of the moon detached from the sky and rolled over the sum. But something else was happening at that same instant, and it was this, I believe, that made us scream.

The second before the sun went out, we saw a wall of dark shadow come speeding at us. We no sooner saw it than it was upon us, like thunder. It roared up the valley. It slammed our hill and knocked us out. It was the monstrous swift shadow cone of the moon. I have since read that this wave of shadow moves 1,800 miles an hour. Language can give no sense of this sort of speed—1,800 miles an hour. It was 195 miles wide. No end was in sight— you saw only the edge. It rolled at you across the land at 1,800 miles an hour, hauling darkness like plague behind it. Seeing it, and knowing it was coming straight for you, was like feeling a slug of anesthetic shoot up your arm. If you think very fast, you may have time to think: Soon it will hit my brain. You can feel the deadness race up your arm; you can feel the appalling, inhuman speed of your own blood. We saw the wall of shadow coming, and screamed before it hit.

This was the universe about which we have read so much and never before felt: the universe as a clockwork of loose spheres flung at stupefying, unauthorized speeds. How could anything moving so fast not crash, not veer from its orbit amok like a car out of control on a turn?

Less than two minutes later, when the sun emerged, the trailing edge of the shadow cone sped away. It coursed down our hill and raced eastward over the plain, faster than the eye could believe; it swept over the plain and dropped over the planet's rim in a twinkling. It had clobbered us, and now it roared away. We blinked in the light. It was as though an enormous, loping god in the sky had reached down and slapped the earth's face.

Something else, something more ordinary, came back to me along about the third cup of coffee. During the moments of totality, it was so dark that drivers on the highway below turned on their cars' headlights. We could see the highway's route as a strand of lights. It was bumper-to-bumper down there. It was eight-fifteen in the morning, Monday morning, and people were driving into Yakima to work. That it was as dark as night, and eerie as hell, an hour after dawn apparently meant that in order to *see* to drive to work, people had to use their headlights. Four or five cars pulled off the road. The rest, in a line at least five miles long, drove to town. The highway ran between hills; the people could not have seen any of the eclipsed sun at all. Yakima will have another total eclipse in 2019. Perhaps, in 2019, businesses will give their employees an hour off.

From the restaurant we drove back to the coast. The highway crossing the Cascades range was open. We drove over the mountain like old pros. We joined our places on the planet's thin crust; it held. For the time being, we were home free.

Early that morning at six, when we had checked out, the six bald men were sitting on folding chairs in the dim hotel lobby. The television was on. Most of them were awake. You might drown in your own spittle, God knows, at any time; you might wake up dead in a small hotel, a cabbage head watching TV while snows pile up in the passes, watching TV while the chili peppers smile and the moon passes over the sun and nothing changes and nothing is learned because you have lost your bucket and shovel and no longer care. What if you regain the surface and open your sack and find, instead of treasure, a beast, which jumps at you? Or you may not come back at all. The winches may jam, the scaffolding buckle, the air-conditioning collapse. You may glance up one day and see by your headlamp the canary keeled over in its cage. You may reach into a cranny for pearls and touch a moray eel. You yank on your rope; it is too late.

Apparently people share a sense of these hazards, for when the total eclipse ended, an odd thing happened.

When the sun appeared as a blinding bead on the ring's side, the eclipse was over. The black lens cover appeared again, backlighted, and slid away. At once the yellow light made the sky blue again; the black lid dissolved and vanished. The real world began there. I remember now: we all hurried away. We were born and bored at a stroke. We rushed down the hill. We found our car; we saw the other people streaming down the hillsides; we joined the highway traffic and drove away.

We never looked back. It was a general vamoose, and an odd one, for when we left the hill, the sun was still partially eclipsed—a sight rare enough, and one that, in itself, we would probably have driven five hours to see. But enough is enough. One turns at last even from glory itself with a sigh of relief. From the depths of mystery, and even from the heights of splendor, we bounce back and hurry for the latitudes of home.

Fellini: Changing the Subject

FRANK BURKE

> We should suspend the typical questions: how does a free subject
> penetrate the density of things and endow them with meaning .
> ...Rather we should ask: under what conditions and through
> what forms can an entity like the subject appear in the order of
> discourse; what position does it occupy; what functions does it
> exhibit...? In short, the subject (and its substitutes) must be
> stripped of its creative role and analysed as a complex and vari-
> able function of discourse.
>
> —Michel Foucault (118)

> The Author, when believed in, is always conceived of as the past
> of his book . . . in the same relation of antecedence as a father to
> his child. In complete contrast, the modern scriptor is born si-
> multaneously with the text, is in no way equipped with a being
> preceding or exceeding the writing, is not subject with the book
> as predicate....
>
> —Roland Barthes (145)

PREFACE

The career of Federico Fellini offers remarkable parallels to the recent
history of individualism and the subject, especially in the domain of film
theory. Particularly evident is the concurrence of Fellini's reputation and the
fate of *auteurism*. 1954 was the year of *La Strada* and of Truffaut's promulga-
tion of a *politique des auteurs*. 1959 saw the shooting of *La Dolce Vita* and the

emergence of the French New Wave. 1962-63 brought *8½* and Andrew Sarris's influential "Notes on the Auteur Theory."

Without question, Fellini's reputation benefited by an *auteurist* moment which valorized the film director as artist, gave strong impetus to the European art film movement, and, in so doing, aligned itself with the tradition of high modernism in the arts: privileging the uniqueness of artistic self-expression as an oppositional force in the face of industrialized society.

To some extent, that reputation was sustained through the sixties by proliferating *auteurism* (Sarris's book *American Film Directors* appeared in 1968), high modernism, and perhaps most important, the romantic individualism of the decade, which dovetailed with the media image of Fellini as maverick and genius.

However, despite Fellini's continued visibility, his critical reputation peaked with *8½*, especially among academic theorists. From the mid-sixties on, that reputation has suffered virtually uninterrupted decline. Robert Phillip Kolker is representative when he writes in the early 1980s that "*8½*...marks the end of [Fellini's] creative period.... In his following works, Fellini moved into the artifice of spectacle, the fantasies of memory, which became more insular and repetitive as he proceeded" (87). More telling than critique is neglect. In the 600-plus pages of *Movies and Methods* I, Fellini receives one paragraph of discussion. His name does not appear once in *Movies and Methods* II nor (as far as I can tell) in *Narrative, Apparatus, Ideology: A Film Theory Reader*.[1] These three anthologies delineate with great accuracy the critical and theoretical terrain of film studies for the past two decades.

Just as Fellini's international recognition corresponded with the rise of *auteurism* and the European art film movement, his decline has paralleled theirs. The sixties was marked by the structuralist and poststructuralist de-centering of the subject, the politicization of film theory and practice following May 1968, and an assault on the high art/mass culture hierarchy of modernism. By the early seventies, as the result of *auteur*-structuralism (Nowell-Smith, Eckert, Wollen) and post-*auteurism* (*Cahiers du cinéma*, Heath) the *auteur* was killed off as creative artist and resurrected as merely one system of codes among many or as the radically dispersed effect of ideological gaps and contradictions. Dead along the way was the European art cinema of the "great directors."

This is hardly to say that Fellini has been ignored only because the *auteurism* of the fifties and sixties has dissolved. Some directors, such as Hitchcock and Ford, have been reappropriated by post-*auteurism* because of the psychoanalytic and ideological richness of their work. Others, such as

Ozu and Oshima, have been privileged because of their non-Western signifying practices. And, ironically, Godard has acquired greater *auteur* status than ever because his politics have been so consistent with those of anti- and post-*auteurism*. Fellini's decline has occurred largely because, in a post-modernist, post-romantic, and post-*auteur* climate, he is seen as the embodiment of the purely reactionary. As Kolker puts it:

> Fellini slipped back to a melodramatic mode…an autobiographical expressionism…with history relegated to a backdrop and nostalgia elevated above analysis. He returns to a romanticism that insists that the productions of the artist's life and imagination must be of interest simply because they are the productions of the artist…. [T]he neo-realist urge to reveal and question has disappeared beneath an irrelevant…subjectivity. (87-89)

For Nöel Carroll: "Fellini's reflexivity only subserves the propagation of his world view…. Indeed, one suspects that Fellini's intrusiveness in [*The Clowns* and *Roma*]…enables him to get away with his shameless exploitation of shopworn, universalist (clown as man; city as life) imagery" (105).

These critiques are surprisingly subject-centered—attacking Fellini for, among other things, autobiography, nostalgia, subjectivity, world view, and insidious motive. Focusing on the reviled *auteur* they say little about the films themselves. In conjunction with the widespread neglect of Fellini's work, they reflect a failure to acknowledge that, just as Fellini's early films formed part of the discourse of a prestructuralist era, his more recent films are part of poststructuralist discourse. In fact, from *8½* on, Fellini's films have lent themselves to sustained critiques of romantic individuality and to a thoroughgoing revaluation of subjectivity. His "autobiographical" films, moreover, have posited Fellini himself as subject only to dissolve him into other texts, subject positions, and intersecting discourses. Nowhere is Fellini the *auteur* more dead than in his own work.

I.

Fellini's earliest films focus principally on the exploits of well defined main characters—whether they be comic (Checco in *Variety Lights* [1950], Ivan and Wanda in *The White Sheik* [1952]), tragic (Zampanò in *La Strada* [1954], Augusto, in *Il Bidone* [1955]), or somewhere in between (Moraldo in *I Vitelloni* [1953], Marcello in *La Dolce Vita* [1959]). Fellini's emphasis on character is consistent with his oft-expressed concern with individuality—especially in contrast to what he sees as the collectivity of conventionalized existence:

self-acceptance can occur only when you've grasped one fundamental fact of life: that the only thing which exists is yourself, your true individual self in depth, which wants to grow spontaneously, but which is fettered by inoperative lies, myths and fantasies proposing an unattainable morality or sanctity or perfection....

(Fellini, *Playboy* 60)

Individuality attains its fullest expression in the early films with *The Nights of Cabiria* (1956). Cabiria's film-long struggle for "self-acceptance" culminates with an extreme closeup which individuates her from all else in her world and appears to offer striking testimony to Fellini's conviction that "every human being has [her] own irrevocable truth, which is authentic and precious and unique ..." (Fellini, *Playboy* 63).[2]

While Fellini's early films are decidedly individualist in emphasis, his comments about individualism are most intense not during the early period but during the making of *8½* (1963) and *Juliet of the Spirits* (1965).[3] This creates an interesting paradox because it is precisely with *8½* that I feel we can detect a radical change in the nature of characterization in Fellini's films— a process I might term "postindividualization." This process characterizes all Fellini's work from *8½* through *Roma* (1972) but can best be examined in light of the death of the author/subject in more recent Fellini films: *Amarcord* (1974) through *Intervista* (1987).

II.

Through reproductive technology postmodernist art dispenses with the aura. The fiction of the creating subject gives way to the frank confiscation, quotation, excerptation, accumulation and repetition of already existing images. Notions of originality, authenticity and presence...are undermined.

—Douglas Crimp (53)

In contrast to nearly all Fellini's preceding films, *Amarcord* has only an intermittent main character, Titta, who does not serve as a center of consciousness. He is absent from several episodes, some of them quite lengthy. He narrates only one (and that for only a moment). And he is supplemented by several narrators who vary radically in articulateness, storytelling motivation, and credibility. There is, in short, no unified voice, and despite the fact that "amarcord" means "I remember,"[4] there *is* no I who remembers.

Fellini's Casanova (1976) may seem to offer such an "I": Casanova is both protagonist and presumed author of his tale. However, his function as narrator is intermittent to the point of virtual irrelevance, he is portrayed as a posturer and sycophant rather than a creative artist, and the world he inhabits is one of blatant simulation rather than originality.

Both *Amarcord* and *Fellini's Casanova*, though in different ways, fulfil Linda Hutcheon's description of point of view in postmodern fiction: "Narrators in fiction become either disconcertingly multiple and hard to locate…or resolutely provisional and limited—often undermining their own seeming omniscience" (11).

The Orchestra Rehearsal (1979) lacks even *Casanova's* simulation of individuality, as the orchestra becomes a dominant metaphor for collectivity. Not only is there no main character, *all* the characters end up defined entirely in terms of their musical instruments and, even more restrictively, in terms of a piece of music composed by an absent ("dead") author. The conductor, who assumes the role of author-ity by film's end, is no less constructed and determined in his actions than anyone else. He is there because every orchestra needs its leader.

City of Women (1980), like *Fellini's Casanova*, initially seems to offer authorizing human agency: Snaporaz as main character, and even more important, Marcello as dreamer of the dream. However, in a crucial reversal, Marcello is established not as source of the dream but as its product. We begin *in medium somnium*, and Marcello only exists as a waking individual (briefly) at the very end. (In fact there is an implicit distinction drawn between "Snaporaz," the character in the dream, and "Marcello"—the "real" character—to whom Snaporaz, in effect, gives birth.) Moreover, the dream, like the orchestra, is a determining device, fixing Snaporaz/Marcello within the mechanisms of the unconscious, fuelled by culturally generated projections and distortions of "Women." The culminating symbol of the feminine within the dream—an absurd Madonna/Soubrette balloon, complete with a womblike basket into which Snaporaz crawls—is a grotesque conflation of cultural symbology which violently undermines any notion of integral imagination on the part of its fabricator. (The film's title further underscores the fact that the women represented in the dream are not the unique creation of a free imagination. They are "always already citified"—manmade, socially constructed.)

And the Ship Sails On (1984) recalls *The Orchestra Rehearsal* in its use of a musical community (this time operatic) to construct individuals in roles. (The ship's hierarchy also serves as a determining social structure.) As in *The Orchestra Rehearsal*, characters are determined by dead author-ity—in this case Edmea Tetua, whose death they are mourning with varying degrees of fervour. Moreover, the authority and identity of Tetua (her ashes) exist only to be *scattered* (the goal of the opera troupe's sea voyage). Authority is further undermined within the film's narrative structure by the arbitrary, sporadic, and quite absurd role of the film's narrator/journalist, Orlando. He himself is "scattered" or fragmented, becoming most important as *narrator* when he loses all capacity to *report*. (His narrative voice dominates the last few minutes of the film but only in the form of pure speculation, as he is forced to compensate with mere hypotheses for his absence from all the final crucial events aboard the ship.) The split within Orlando highlights the interplay between fiction and history throughout *And the Ship Sails On*, as the film blatantly fictionalizes the sinking of the Lusitania and the outbreak of World War I. This interplay undercuts the authority of artist (Fellini) as well as historian (journalist/narrator), for the fictionality of the film cannot escape the discourse of history, and the historically "real" cannot escape the discourse of fiction. Put another way, the film's fictionality reflects the journalist's "pure speculation" at the end: both are conditioned by actual events, without deriving any authority from them. In addition, there is no position outside the ceaseless play and mutual determination of fact and fiction from which a text, artist, or commentator can be author-ized.

Ginger and Fred (1986)—both the title and the film—promise then withhold individuality. While the title offers us two personal names which imply differentiated figures, those figures are named after other figures who themselves adopted stage names.[5] Moreover, Ginger and Fred have been virtually reinvented by television to come to Rome and imitate their past imitations of Astaire and Rogers. The world of *Ginger and Fred* is one of endless replication, of copies without originals, in which "lookalikes" become the stars of the day. Within this context, even Marcello Mastroianni and Giulietta Masina become "lookalikes"—allusions to their prior roles in Fellini films. The remark which a woman presumably addresses to Fellini at the beginning of *City of Women* would, with the addition of Giulietta's name, well apply here: "Marcello yet again? Please maestro."

"Fellini yet again?" could be the epigraph for *Intervista*, as Fellini functions not as a "real person" or even an "auteur" so much as a reproduction. He appears as the recycled product of his own films of forty years, of "memories" which exist only as cinematic representations, of the history of cinema, of the music of Nino Rota, of Cinecittà. Living in a world of reproduction, Fellini can be replaced as director. Mastroianni, dressed as Mandrake the Magician "creates" the Trevi fountain scene in *La Dolce Vita*, making it appear on a makeshift screen in Anita Ekberg's house. As this sequence suggests, Fellini's relationship to his recreated memories and (other) staged fantasies is hardly simple or consistent. Not only is he not always positioned as their author, but often (as with Marcello and his dream in *City of Women*) he appears generated out of them. Despite the seeming centrality of Fellini, his subjectivity is, for the most part, a series of momentary configurations forming and dissolving across a grid of cinematic quotations from Fellini's and Cinecittà's cinematic history.[6]

III.

Turning to *8½*, we initially seem to have a story of individuation along the lines of *The Nights of Cabiria*.[7] The film begins with Guido's literal and figurative awakening and with his acquisition of identity: his body and face gradually emerge from beneath bedclothes and robe, and he moves to the bathroom to discover himself in the mirror. Much of the remainder of the film traces the expansion of Guido's identity, awareness, control, and inventiveness as he moves from dreams (unconscious hence uncontrolled by Guido as conscious subject) to memories (conscious but merely recollective) to visions (conscious and creative). He also becomes more responsible, more accountable to himself and to others. The final scene, in which his lifetime companions join him in the circus arena, can be seen as a moment of integration.

However, *8½* centers Guido only in order to disperse him. The more aware Guido becomes, the more he must face his own confusion and instability. Moreover, though he appears to develop the capacity to create his own reality—as in the harem sequence and the screentests—his visions turn against him, revealing that his desire to control reality is a fundamental limitation. He is, in fact, stripped of his authorship. By the end of the harem sequence, he is positioned as spectator not creator, and he is severely troubled by the image and voice of Luisa which comprise the spectacle. At the screentests he is confronted by his directorial follies, reduced again to a spectator, and helpless to make any decisions about his film.

Not only does Guido acquire a certain measure of authority only to lose it, he undergoes a multiplication of identities that radically de-centers him. At the screentests there are at least four Guidos: the director who created the test footage, the director-actor whom we see on screen, and the spectator who himself is divided in two: the "ideal" Guido who whispers "I love you" to Luisa, and the "real" Guido who "lies with every breath" (the words of an actress playing Luisa onscreen which appropriately describe Guido-as-unfaithful-husband).

The de-authorization and splitting of Guido leads to a crucial loss of subjectivity in the press conference vision which follows upon the screentests. He has just renounced his film to Claudia Cardinale when the vision suddenly erupts. It is not, however, attributed to Guido. In fact, the point-of-view coding (closeup of Guido, memory or fantasy, return to Guido) which has characterized earlier imaginative sequences is pointedly sabotaged. The vision is preceded with a closeup not of Guido but of Cardinale (first in darkness, then suddenly illuminated by the headlights of a car). This not only eliminates Guido as source, it eliminates subjective origin altogether by offering the impossible: Claudia as author. The film then cuts to a relatively long shot of Guido (with Claudia), turning and shielding himself with his hat. Guido is presented only as the target, not as the creator, of this eruption. And, of course, the lengthy vision does not conclude with any (re)establishing closeup of Guido.

Guido does not just passively suffer loss of author-ity and subject-hood. In renouncing his film, he begins contributing actively to the process. He effectively kills off his film's "hero" who has become a surrogate self. (His hero in effect fails him, creating a complex mirroring effect: Fellini has trouble making a film about a character who has trouble making a film about a character who cannot sustain the role of hero.)[8] Then, at the press conference, Guido kills himself off more directly (though still symbolically): climbing under a table, putting a gun to his head, and pulling the trigger. Then, in the final vision/sequence, he dies by immersion or absorption. In so doing, he recapitulates the loss of subjectivity that is so crucial to the film as a whole. Though Guido is placed at the origin of the final vision through a medium close-up, he quickly moves from subject to object as he enters the circus ring and becomes a character ("the director"). He then surrenders his role as director, joining Luisa and the circle of lifetime companions in a dance of death as well as reunion. Finally, he disappears—as does the child-in-white (another surrogate Guido) who briefly replaces him in the circus arena. By the end of this vision—which is also the end of the film—there is no Guido for the camera to return to. In fact, there is no subjective source of anything.

This reading is strongly at odds with prevailing critical opinion of subjectivity in *8½*. In *Reflexivity in Film and Literature* Robert Stam maintains: "The most striking feature of *8½*…is the absolute centrality of Guido…. There is virtually no sequence…which Guido does not dominate" (104). And, in *Point of View in the Cinema*, Edward Branigan insists that "Fellini's *8½*…despite a startling, even virtuoso mixture of fantasy and reality, remains committed to the assumptions of traditional subjective narration" because it "finds its center in a single character or, more exactly, the consciousness of a character" (143, 144). While Stam's discussion of *8½* is brief, Branigan's is carefully argued and merits a response.

Branigan bases much of his reading on scenes early in the film when Guido is, indeed, developing consciousness and point of view (146-47, 151-52). He chooses as his quintessential example of *8½*'s "activity of narration" a moment that occurs less than half way through the film (163-64). In overdetermining the early scenes, Branigan fails to account for narrative progression—especially Guido's loss of authority towards the film's end. For this reason, he merely dismisses the increasing fragmentation and multiplication of identities: "It is important…not to overstate the plurality achieved in *8½*" (152). Moreover, he fails to note the rupture of point-of-view coding in the press conference sequence—a fact which is quite surprising given his scrupulous attention to such coding when Guido fantasizes the hanging of Daumier a few minutes earlier in the film.

Branigan also fails to attend to the construction and dissolution of subjectivity in the final sequence. In fact, he abandons his close reading of cinematic technique altogether. Instead, he posits an elaborate "semantic square" to argue that *8½* ends in a "*positive* transcendence" which "presents Art as the ultimate mediation between reality and fantasy" and a "resolution on a 'higher' plane of reality." Art "is offered as that term which is not limited by time, history or social condition. Through Art the text asserts its immortality." Through this transcendence "the confusion of reality is reconciled with the private meaning of Guido's fantasies…. Thus the film becomes, crucially, a working out of the precise status of the author with respect to reality, imagination, text, subject (consciousness), and the other terms" (161).[9]

Branigan's discussion is not only mystifying (especially in terms of his earlier treatment of the film), it entails a telling contradiction. Given his own insistence that Art becomes the encompassing term under which all else is subsumed, Branigan cannot logically claim that the film is equally "a working out of the precise status of the author…." Capital A Art and an individual artist are two quite different things, with the latter clearly subordinate to the former. What Branigan appears to be doing is seeking a term (Art) which enables him to resurrect the artist (Guido) despite the artist's obvious demise. Branigan's strategy actually confirms the fact that, by the end, Guido (the subject/author) is gone—and something (or perhaps nothing) else has taken his place.

Finally, in failing to trace the crucial shifts that occur in the final sequences of the film, Branigan remains tied to the assumption of a stable ground for Guido's subjectivity:

> the text never stops making sense with respect to a 'reality.' We know, for instance, that Guido is having trouble with his wife, that he has a mistress, that he is attempting to make a film, and so forth. The origin of the unreal is always located in Guido and referenced to a privileged, non-subjective level of narration which is, exactly, *reality* for the text…. (152)

This assumption refuses to acknowledge, among other things, that Guido's mistress never appears as a "real" person once the harem sequence begins (45 minutes before the film concludes), the real Luisa never reappears after telling Guido to go to hell at the screentests, and the film is abandoned. Also ignored is the fact that the press conference and the concluding sequence function precisely to strip away both the "privileged…*reality*" Branigan insists upon and any equally privileged subjectivity which both grounds and is grounded by such reality. In short, though Branigan does an excellent job detailing the individuating and grounding aspects of *8½*, he is unable to account for its postindividuating aspects.

In terms of jettisoning the individual, Fellini's next film, *Juliet of the Spirits*, is both an advance and a retreat. On the one hand, Juliet is fragmented into far more pieces than Guido. As the film's title suggests, she is a product of the many (all her spirits) rather than the one. Her subjectivity is, in short, fundamentally decentered. However, as in *The Nights of Cabiria*, the thrust of the film is to integrate the many into the one. (This is reflected in Fellini's claim that Juliet is forced "to find herself, to seek her free identity as an individual. And this gives her the insight to realize that all the fears—the phantoms that lived around her—were monsters of her own creation, bred of misshapen education and misread religion"—Fellini, *Playboy* 62).

It is a relatively simple task to deconstruct this attempted reintegration. First of all, Juliet's "oneness" could never exist without her multiplicity—a fact suggested even at film's end when her spirits assert their ever presence.[10] Second, she has become one or "self-identical" through a series of negations—rejecting (among other things) Bhisma, Suzy, Jose, the Godson, the image of her mother, and in fact her tormenting spirits. Based on a series of denials, her identity or self-presence is thus constructed out of absences, non-identities. Third, Juliet exists only because she is seen, and in effect made visible, by her principal "spirits": the camera eye, and, by extension, us-the-audience. (We and the camera waft in through the trees, spirit-like, at the beginning of the film, and she looks us directly in the eye, acknowledging our presence as "spirits," at the end.) Finally, the Juliet who walks off into the forest at the end is "contaminated" by cultural significations. She is, among other things, a princess in a fairy tale and a virgin/child. Her "individuality" is hardly indivisible. It is multiply intersected by socially produced and determined meanings.

However, while the subject can be deconstructed, we must do the work—in effect against the will of the film. For that reason, *Juliet of the Spirits* functions more as an anomaly at this point in Fellini's career—and as a throwback to earlier films.

Fellini's next film, "Toby Dammit" (1968)[11] takes an issue, death, that was principally subtextual and metaphoric in *8½* and makes it the (missing) center of its story. (Fellini had suffered a serious illness prior to the making of the film and had also been involved in an unsuccessful project—"The Voyage of G. Mastorna"—which focused on death.) In fact "Toby Dammit" is a film par excellence of the "dead subject" and dead author. Toby's past-tense voiceover at the beginning, plus his "death" at the end, make clear that he speaks from beyond the grave. That makes his signature at the beginning, written against the sky, the signature of a ghost or missing person. Identity becomes merely the citing/site-ing/sighting of its absence.[12]

More concretely, the film makes clear that Toby must renounce identity and subjectivity, since both are entirely constituted by society. As an actor (the film's most pervasive metaphor), Toby is "identified" only in roles created by other people—and only by speaking other people's words.

Toby's existence solely as a culturally inscribed actor is implicit in the fact that he originates in fiction—a short story by Edgar Allan Poe ("Never Bet the Devil Your Head"). It is reinforced by his resemblance—sartorial and facial—to Poe himself. (Fellini deliberately had Terence Stamp made up to look like Poe.) It is exemplified in his impersonation of Macbeth—not only reciting Macbeth's lines but losing his head. It is present even in the fact that his name is not personal but metaphoric, naming not an individual but a set of culturally coded meanings. Finally, it pervades Toby's very psychology: socially constructed oppositions (dark vs. light, salvation vs. damnation, head vs. body, private vs. professional) in which the most "personal" of Toby's weapons—the Devil—is, though tailored to Toby's bizarre tastes, a consummate cultural cliche.

Toby's paradoxical fate—to be by not being—informs his end and that of the film. Driving his Ferrari, Toby makes an impossible leap across an abyss—but we hear and see no crash. There is no corpse. Instead, there are metonymic substitutes for his death: a bloody rope (quite dissociated from the scene of the supposed accident), a waxen replica of his head. Toby, in short, dies and does *not* die, a fact underscored by his beyond-the-grave narration. Indeed Toby remains, but now only as the film that bears his name. He is gone as subject and as author. With this final displacement identity is again undermined as anything individual, indivisible, and unique. It is dispersed throughout a text that is consummately reproducible—via new prints, new screenings, re-viewings, etc. Moreover, as a text within a photographic medium, it is properly reproducible only through its negative. Medium, character, and story all come together to assert identity and selfhood only under erasure.

The erasure of character/actor/subject recurs in *Fellini-Satyricon* (1969), partly as a result of Fellini's continued emphasis on gaps and absences: "I reread Petronius and was fascinated by an element I had not noticed before: the missing parts; that is, the blanks between one episode and the next.... that business of fragments really fascinated me" (Grazzini 171-72).[13] The effacement of the subject recurs also as the result of Fellini's repudiation of character and acting in *Fellini: A Director's Notebook* (1968), a short film made between "Toby Dammit" and *Fellini-Satyricon*. The motivating force of *Director's Notebook* is the evasiveness, the nonmaterialization, of a hero or main character. The film begins with Fellini discussing his abandonment of a project, "The Voyage of G. Mastorna," because Mastorna "has not arrived yet."[14] This in turn leads to an examination of the inadequacy of Marcello Mastroianni, and to some extent Giulietta Masina, as stimuli to Fellini, because of their history as well-defined actor/characters within Fellini's films (see Foreman, "Poor Player"; Prats and Pieters). Acting itself is clearly critiqued in the appearance of Caterina Baratto and her dreadful attempts to portray a bloodthirsty Roman matron. The problem of character/acting then leads Fellini to a new strategy, a new kind of filmmaking, important not only for *Director's Notebook* but for all his films through *Amarcord*: he seeks out unprofessional actors with intriguing and appropriate faces in place of the familiar personae and skills of trained actors. He chooses, in short, a cinema of image or surface over one of character and depth. This leads directly to *Fellini-Satyricon*, not only with its cast of unknowns, but with its use of the fresco as its principal visual "unit."

(Fellini's search for unique and fresh faces is, of course, at odds with the self-reflexive use and re-use of Mastroianni, Masina, Ekberg, and himself in his most recent films. The former suggests a lingering romantic/modernist quest for novelty and originality as the wellsprings of inspiration—hence a lingering faith in the integrity of artistic creation. The latter reflects a postmodernist acknowledgement of repetition, reproduction, citation—the "always already"—as the inescapable condition of de/creation. Thus Fellini's rejection of actor/character/predefined subject contributes to the erasure of unified subjectivity while at the same time remaining invested in it.)

Fellini's new conception of casting and (de)characterization is immediately reflected in *Satyricon*'s Encolpio. In my experience, most people who have seen *Fellini-Satyricon* for the first time have remained unaware that the film has a protagonist of any sort. Encolpio is hardly a central character in the way that Guido, Juliet, and Toby were. Like the cracked frescoes and broken statues that litter *Satyricon*'s landscape, Encolpio is a fragment, relating to other events and characters, as well as the audience, only at the jagged edge of (dis)connection. The narrative itself is a series of fragments (dis)joined at *their* rough edges—narrative, in short, in absentia: "the potsherds, crumbs, and dust of a vanished world" (Fellini, *Satyricon* 46). Encolpio's capacity to narrate (and even articulate) comes and goes, reflecting the fracturing of individual intelligence. He even disappears at times, remaining absent from crucial events such as the suicide of the patricians.

Encolpio, like Toby, is a fictional reproduction (originating in Petronius as Toby originated in Poe). In reproducing him, Fellini jettisons his conventional underpinnings of character: depth or "growth" psychology, Christian symbolism, humanist ethics and values, and the teleology of motive and goal. Far more than Toby, Encolpio is pure fictional cipher, adrift in a flow of arbitrary narrative which itself is adrift in the arbitrary flow of historical, political, and social change.

At film's end, though Encolpio seems momentarily to emerge as a unifying voice, he is confirmed and preserved in a state of fragmentation. He begins to narrate his itinerary upon setting sail, only to have his words broken off in mid-sentence. His image turns into a cracked fresco which itself is separated by cracks from other figures on the same fresco. Then, as the camera draws back, the fresco is revealed to be only one fragment among several. The solid wall which opened the film has been fissured and, with it, unity and wholeness on every level—from the narrative to the historical to the individual.

The Clowns (1970) seems initially to reinstate character and subjectivity with a vengeance by situating Fellini himself as first-person narrator and protagonist. Yet, like *8½* and "Toby Dammit" (and unlike *Director's Notebook*, to which it is partially indebted) *The Clowns* ends up being far more about the death of the author/subject than about his(her) predominance. In killing Fellini off as auteur, *The Clowns* radically repositions Fellini in relation to his work—putting him at least in quotation marks and at most under erasure.

The Clowns reinstitutes a kind of autobiographical problematic that marks much of Fellini's earlier work. Though films such as *I Vitelloni, La Dolce Vita, 8½*, and *Amarcord* are superficially autobiographical, they open broad gaps between Fellini and his past. *I Vitelloni* is set in a town reminiscent of Fellini's own Rimini and features one character, Moraldo, who gets out at the end. However, the differences between the world of the film and Fellini's past are far greater than the similarities. The *vitelloni* are products of a specific economic and cultural moment (postwar provincial Italy of the 1950s) which has little in common with Fellini's youth. More important, Moraldo, as his name suggests, represents the morality or mores of the provinces—something with which Fellini himself would hardly identify.[15] And his alienated escape at the end has little in common with Fellini's move from the provinces to Rome. (See Alpert 30ff.) Marcello of *La Dolce Vita* is, like Fellini, a provincial who made it to the city (hence Moraldo's presumed fictional heir). He is, however, a jaded yellow journalist who is even further distanced from Fellini than was Moraldo. He mirrors the latter both in paralysed detachment and ultimate disillusionment, and his story represents an exhaustive study in character fragmentation. In short, he proves highly unsuitable for any kind of Fellinian working through of genuinely autobiographical issues.[16]

8½ and *Amarcord* seem initially to be much more promising in terms of autobiography, the former because of its protagonist, the latter because of its historical setting. However, the effacement of the Fellini surrogate in the first and the pointed absence of one in the second serve to eliminate the kind of grounding upon which genuine autobiography depends.

Such grounding is not lacking in two strongly autobiographical Fellini scripts that have recently been published: "Moraldo in the City" and "Journey with Anita" (Stubbs; Alpert 36-40, 118-21). However, the fact that Fellini never realized these projects seems to confirm an unwillingness or incapacity on his part to use autobiography in anything other than distanciating and deconstructive ways. This conjoining of autobiography and (self)deconstruction is precisely the kind of autobiographical problematic that informs *The Clowns*.

The opening segment introduces character and subjectivity as far more the product than the producer of experience. Fellini as a child enters a circus arena and is, in effect, refashioned—turned into a clown. (The film's title clearly includes Fellini, along with everyone else in the movie.) More specifically, Fellini-the-child's initial fear of clowns, especially the rowdy "Augustes," turns him into a "White Clown" (the authoritarian figure in the White Clown-Auguste relationship), who seeks to contemplate, understand, hence control his circus experience (Burke, "*Clowns*"). It is Fellini-the-White Clown who, as an adult, seeks to document the clown.

The subject is not only constructed (rather than pristine, autonomous) in *The Clowns*, it is culturally coded—since what refashions the young Fellini is an art form with a long tradition and a well-defined logic or ideational apparatus (i.e., the White Clown-Auguste dialectic). This emphasis on the pre-coded confirms a shift in Fellini's films from "original" stories to the reproduction of other stories, other art (Poe/Shakespeare in "Toby Dammit," Petronius in *Fellini-Satyricon*, now the art of the clown). Fellini's increasing acknowledgement of *re*production (vs. creation) becomes, in turn, the basis (as I have already suggested) for his deconstruction of subjectivity and authority in his most recent work.

The problem of author/subject in *The Clowns* is defined principally in terms of Fellini's attempts to make a documentary—i.e., to appropriate (as unified and autonomous subject) the clowns (as object and "other"). However, Fellini is no more successful in imposing his directorial will than was Guido. The documentary fails, and a different kind of filmic process takes its place. Even moreso than with Guido, creative experience happens to and around Fellini rather than originating within him. And just as Fellini-the-child was constructed by the clown/circus discourse (rather than vice versa), Fellini the adult becomes constructed within fictional/narrative discourse rather than standing outside it (Burke, *Clowns*; Prats).

Like *8½*, *The Clowns* concludes with a series of authorial deaths and effacements. First of all, Fellini must abandon his role as documentary film-maker—his principal role in the film. Then, as he directs a different kind of film (an extravagant "resurrection" of the clown Fischietto), he gets a bucket over his head. Moreover, the resurrection attempt is mechanical and laboured—and is followed by a hollow sense of anticlimax. Most important, Fellini, like Guido, ultimately disappears. In the final moments, an old clown (Fumigalli) assumes Fellini's narrative authority, resurrects the clown much more successfully, and brings *The Clowns* to a close.

Storytelling in *The Clowns* thus ends up occurring through erasure and substitution, making narrative fortuitous and fragmentary. At the same time, the grand controlling author is eliminated—not just in the surrogate guise of a Guido—but in the person of Fellini, the "grand romantic artist," himself.

Though *The Clowns* ultimately does in the author-as-subject, Fellini's presence as director is dominant until the very last moments. Also, through voiceover, Fellini-as-adult is made clearly continuous with Fellini-as-child in terms not only of identity but motivation. (Fellini-the-adult's desire to document clowns is clearly rooted in Fellini-the-child's experiences.) In this sense, characterization in *The Clowns* is more stable than in "Toby Dammit" or *Satyricon*. *Roma*, on the other hand, consistently undermines continuity and stability. In its original conception, *Roma* had virtually no voiceover: the screenplay includes only one brief instance of Fellini addressing the viewer (Fellini, Roma 272), and a theatrical print I saw in Rome (spring 1983) was true to the screenplay. (Some narration appears to have been added to prints shown on Italian television circa 1983.) Furthermore, neither the screenplay nor the Italian-language versions I have seen make any positive identification of either the child at the beginning or the young adult in Rome of the 1930s as Fellini. No narrative voice or character ever designates the child or the young adult as Fellini. (The screenplay is insistent on referring to the young adult only as "il ragazzo"—the boy or young man—even when it would be much simpler for purposes of both simple reference and clarity to refer to him as young Fellini.)

Even in the English-language version, which contains voiceover material requested by United Artists,[17] *Roma* cannot help but undermine the consistency of Fellini's presence. The narrative voice is not Fellini's. There is still no designation of the child or young adult as Fellini. (The closest we get is the narrator's statement, following the young adult's first day in Rome: "thirty years or more have passed since that fabulous evening"—which still keeps the connection oblique.) Both child and young adult are missing from many scenes which, in a conventional flashback-narrative, would have been justified narratively only by their presence or point of view. (*Roma* again differs sharply from *The Clowns*.) And the young adult is played by a Spanish American actor (Peter Gonzalez) whose origins, native tongue, look, and American mannerisms enhance the distance between Fellini as an adult and any possible earlier manifestation. (Incidentally, the circumstances of this figure's arrival in Rome are markedly different from Fellini's own—Alpert, 29ff.)

In short, though we may be inclined to assume a link between contemporary and younger Fellinis, the film itself refuses to forge one. Fellini refuses to materialize as a coherent and continuous persona, and as a result, "he" is at best an inference, scattered among a number of subject positions.

In addition, even the Fellini of the 1970s is barely in evidence. There is no establishing scene to define his documentary motives and purpose, as there was in *The Clowns*. After Fellini is shown directing the film crew's entry into Rome (a sequence which, tellingly, ends in chaos), he is absent for most of the film's remaining sequences. Even when he reappears at the Festa di Noantri, he is barely noticeable among the crowds, and Gore Vidal's interview is initiated not by Fellini but by one of his crew. The only time he becomes insistent in this final scene (with Anna Magnani), he is dismissed ("Go to sleep. . . . I don't trust you. . . . Good night.").

As in *The Clowns*, documentary filmmaking, as a centering, author-ized, project fails; even the documentary camera is stolen. And, again, Fellini is effaced at the end. Once Magnani dismisses him, a gang of motorcyclists rides into the frame, Fellini vanishes, and the cyclists bring the film to a close.

Even more than in *The Clowns*, Fellini exists as someone constructed entirely within cultural coding. For one thing, there is no Fellini figure who initially stands outside the "arena" of cultural conditioning (the child in *The Clowns* watched the erection of the circus tent from his window the night before he entered it). From the outset, Fellini is entirely positioned within and produced by the multiple discourses that are "Roma." This is true even if we infer a link between present-day Fellini and the child of the opening sequences, who first appears in uniform, amidst a crowd of students, getting a history lecture on Caesar. It is even truer if we refuse to infer this link—and see Fellini produced well into the narrative by discourse itself.

Unlike "the clowns," "Roma" does not constitute a highly specific personal experience such as Fellini's childhood encounter with the circus. Rome encompasses history, culture, ethnicity, religion, art, movies, government, geography, and so on ad infinitum. Consequently, individuality and subjectivity are situated at the intersection of an enormous aggregate of discourses.

Equally important, Rome is anything but a centering phenomenon, capable of fixing identity. It is ever shifting, unencompassable, indefinable. It comes to represent not a place or even site of discourses, but always what is *not there*. (This is true from the opening image of the rock, signifying "elsewhere," through the closing images of the cyclists, whose exodus again makes Rome "elsewhere.") Ultimately Rome is the force of change or difference, making history or meaning possible but also riddling it with instability. It is the surge of the present in the subway sequence that obliterates the underground frescoes—but at the same time, creates a tabula rasa on which anything can be painted. Rome is also the inexplicable materialization of the cyclists: impersonal, empowered, irresistible—configuring and dispersing, centering and decentering—origin and destination unknown. Ultimately Rome "names" that which is unnameable, all that escapes identification, hence identity.[18]

Roma's deconstruction of the subject/author culminates a process initiated in *8½*. It also points to the films that will follow (*Amarcord* to *Intervista*). It takes up a notion implied in "Toby Dammit" and *Fellini-Satyricon*—the self as mere *re*production—and paradoxically "personalizes" it by applying it to Fellini himself. (By applying it to himself rather than merely fictional figures, Fellini of course makes the issue all the more compelling.) Whereas *The Clowns* initially offers the possibility of a narrative "I" in charge of (re)creation and discourse, *Roma*—by completely absenting that "I"—turns Fellini into pure product. Not only is he reproduced by the multiple discourses that are "Roma," he is entirely a product of cinema. He is always and only the discourse(s) of his film. Unable to stand outside and create the text, he, like Toby, is dispersed through and by it. In an age and medium of mechanical reproduction, Fellini, the "original," ends up generated by the copy.

CONCLUSION

The dismantling of the subject, and Fellini himself-as-subject, does not automatically absolve Fellini's work from the charges of self-indulgence so often levied against it. To a large extent, his films must center the subject in order to decenter it. Moreover, their self-reflexivity can be seen as attempted recuperation of self-hood in the face of its acknowledged demise. Nonetheless, the issue of subjectivity in his work is far more complex than has generally been recognized. Much less about Fellini than his severest critics would claim, his films are insistently about the way the self is constructed and dissolved amidst the positioning of discourse and the play of signification. As such, Fellini's films not only reflect but help constitute the vibrant contemporary theorization of the subject under erasure.

NOTES

1. I am relying on recollection, the index, and a recent check of *Movies and Methods* I and II. *Narrative, Apparatus, Ideology* lacks an index, so I am relying here on recollection plus a check.

2. For a more detailed analysis of this "narrative of individuation," see Burke, *Federico Fellini,* especially chapters eight and ten.
   I employ qualifying terms such as "apparently" and "seems" in my remarks about *The Nights of Cabiria* because of the convincing poststructuralist critique of such notions as individuation, enlightenment, and self-integration (a critique which, I might add, is missing from my own study of Fellini cited in this

note). It is not my goal in this essay to undertake such a critique with regard to *The Nights of Cabiria*, especially since my discussion of Fellini's later films implicitly does the job for me.

3. The quotations about individuality are from an interview which focused equally on *8½* and *Juliet of the Spirits*. Perhaps Fellini's most frequently quoted statement on the subject was uttered in 1962, the year Fellini was making *8½*:

> …what I care about most is the freedom of man, the liberation of the individual man from the network of moral and social convention in which he believes, or rather in which he thinks he believes, and which encloses him and limits him…. (Fellini, *Fellini* 157)

It is interesting to note the utter lack of emphasis on individuality in Fellini's 1980s book-length interview (Grazzini).

4. Consistent with his problematizing of the subject in *Amarcord*, Fellini has both maintained that "amarcord" means "I remember" and, on other occasions, denied it.

5. Fred Astaire was born Frederick Austerlitz; Ginger Rogers, Virginia Catherine McMath.

6. Appropriately, there is no author implied in the film's title: *Intervista* is a noun, not a verb with a subject.

7. For a more extensive discussion of the consolidation and dissolution of Guido's identity in *8½*, see Burke, "Modes."

   Interestingly, as we examine Fellini's comments about preparing for this film, we find an immediate problem with the identity of the main character:

> I had not yet decided what type of man we would try to portray, what his profession would be: a lawyer? an engineer? a journalist?… One day I decided to put my dream hero in a spa…. But then the plot began to unravel altogether. It didn't have a central core from which to develop, nor a beginning, nor could I imagine how it might end. Every morning Pinelli asked me what our hero's profession was. I still didn't know…. I…couldn't manage to find my film again…. I admitted that maybe it had never existed. (Grazzini 160, 161)

We might say, then, that Fellini's attempts to make *8½* mark the search for a *missing* identity.

8. Christian Metz has, of course, analysed the mirroring aspects of *8½* in great detail in his well known essay "Mirror Construction in Fellini's *8½*."

9. I have somewhat rearranged the order of Branigan's statements to provide a concise summary of his logic.

10. In English-language prints, Juliet tells her spirits "I don't need you any more"—an act of dismissal that is *not* part of the original film.

11. For those unfamiliar with this short Fellini work, "Toby Dammit" was part of film anthology entitled *Spirits of the Dead* (*Tre passi nel delirio* in Italian), released in 1969. All the films were based on short stories by Edgar Allan Poe. The other directors involved were Roger Vadim ("Metzengerstein") and Louis Malle ("William Wilson").

    Though not as well known as other Fellini films from this period, "Toby Dammit" is crucial in highlighting shifts in Fellini's signifying practice.

12. For a penetrating analysis of "Toby Dammit"—and one quite consistent with the argument in my essay—see Foreman, "Poor Player."

13. Fellini also talks of making the fragments whole through dream, but as I will try to suggest, the effect of *Fellini Satyricon* is to privilege the fragment, not the whole.

14. Mastorna's role as inspiration for Fellini throughout the late sixties and seventies is further testimony to the importance of the "missing subject" in Fellini's work. ("I am certain that without *Mastorna* I would not have imagined *Satyricon* …nor *Casanova* nor the *City of Women*…. Even *And the Ship Sails On* and *The Orchestra Rehearsal* owe a small debt to *Mastorna*"—Grazzini 169.)

15. See Burke, *Federico Fellini*, pp. 21-28 for a more detailed analysis of *I Vitelloni* and Moraldo.

16. *La Dolce Vita* initially seems interesting in terms of the dismantling of the subject that occurs in later Fellini films. However, as the final shots of the film make clear, that dismantling takes place in light of a strong romantic yearning for purity and wholeness. Such yearning is strongly diminished even by the making of *8½*.

17. So Fellini informed me in a conversation in Rome in June of 1983.

18. For a fine analysis of *Roma* which makes some of the points made here, see Foreman, "Cinematic City."

REFERENCES

Alpert, Hollis. *Fellini: A Life*. New York: Atheneum, 1986.

Barthes, Roland. "The Death of the Author." *Image Music Text*. Ed. and Trans. Stephen Heath. London: Fontana, 1977. 142-48.

Bazin, André. "*La Strada*." *Esprit*. 5 (1955).

Branigan, Edward. *Point of View in the Cinema: A Theory of Narration and Subjectivity in Classical Film*. New York: Mouton, 1984.

Burke, Frank. *Federico Fellini:* Variety Lights *to* La Dolce Vita. Boston: G.K. Hall, 1984.

—. "Modes of Narration and Spiritual Development in Fellini's 8½." *Literature/ Film Quarterly*. 14.3 (1986): 164-70.

—. "The Three-Phase Process and the White Clown-Auguste Relationship in Fellini's *The Clowns*." Lawton. 124-42.

Cahiers du cinéma. "John Ford's *Young Mr. Lincoln*." 223 (1970): 29-47.

Carroll, David. *The Subject in Question: The Languages of Theory and the Strategies of Fiction*. Chicago: U. of Chicago P, 1982.

Carroll, Nöel. *Mystifying Movies: Fads and Fallacies in Contemporary Film Theory*. New York: Columbia UP, 1988.

Crimp. Douglas. "On the Museum's Ruins." Hal Foster, ed. *The Anti-Aesthetic: Essays on Postmodern Culture*. Port Townsend, WA: Bay Press, 1983. 43-56.

Eckert, Charles. "The English Cine-structuralists." *Film Comment*. 9.3 (1973): 46-51.

Fellini, Federico. *Fellini On Fellini*. Trans. Isabel Quigley. New York: Delacorte/ Lawrence, 1976.

—. *Fellini's Satyricon*. Ed. Dario Zanelli. Trans. Eugene Walter and John Matthews. New York: Ballantine, 1970.

—. "*Playboy* Interview: Federico Fellini." XIII (February 1966): 55-66.

—. Roma *di Federico Fellini*. A cura di Bernardino Zapponi. Bologna: Capelli, 1972.

Foreman, Walter C., Jr. "Fellini's Cinematic City: *Roma* and Myths of Foundation." *Forum Italicum*. 14.2 (1980): 78-98.

—. "The Poor Player Struts Again: Fellini's 'Toby Dammit' and the Death of the Actor." Lawton. 111-23.

Foucault, Michel. "What Is an Author?" *Language, Counter-Memory, Practice*. Trans. Donald F. Bouchard and Sherry Simon. Ed. Donald F. Bouchard. Ithaca: Cornell UP, 1977. 121-38. Rpt. in *The Foucault Reader*. Ed. Paul Rabinow. New York: Pantheon, 1984. 101-20.

Grazzini, Giovanni. *Federico Fellini: Comments on Film*. Trans. Joseph Henry. Fresno: California State UP, 1988.

Heath, Stephen. "Comment on `The Idea of Authorship.'" *Screen*. 14.3 (1973): 86-91.

Hutcheon, Linda. *A Poetics of Postmodernism: History, Theory, Fiction*. New York and London: Routledge, 1988.

Huyssen, Andreas. *After the Great Divide: Modernism, Mass Culture, Postmodernism*. Bloomington: Indiana UP, 1986.

Kolker, Robert Phillip. *The Altering Eye: Contemporary International Cinema*. New York: Oxford UP, 1983.

Lawton, Ben, ed. *1977 Film Studies Annual: Part I, Explorations in National Cinemas*. Pleasantville, N.Y.: Redgrave, 1977.

Metz, Christian. *Film Language*. New York: Oxford UP, 1974.

Movies and Methods: An Anthology. Ed. Bill Nichols. 2 Vols. Berkeley: U of California P. 1978, 1985.

Narrative, Apparatus, Ideology: A Film Theory Reader. Ed. Philip Rosen. New York: Columbia UP, 1987.

Nowell-Smith, Geoffrey. *Visconti*. London: Secker and Warburg. 1967, 1973.

Prats., A.J. "An Art of Joy, An Art of Life: The Plasticity and Narrative Methods of *The Clowns*." Lawton. 143-60. Rev. as "Plasticity and Narrative Methods: *The Clowns*" and rpt. in A.J. Prats. *The Autonomous Image: Cinematic Narration and Humanism*. Lexington, Ky.: U of Kentucky P, 1981. 122-157.

— and John Pieters. "The Narratives of Decharacterization in Fellini's Color Movies." *South Atlantic Bulletin*. 45.2 (1980): 31-41.

Sarris, Andrew. *The American Cinema: Directors and Directions: 1929-1968*. New York: Dutton, 1968.

—. "Notes on the Auteur Theory in 1962." *Film Culture*. 27 (1962-63).

Stam, Robert. *Reflexivity in Film and Literature From* Don Quixote *to Jean-Luc* Godard. Ann Arbor: UMI Research Press, 1985.

Stubbs, John. Ed. and Trans. Moraldo in the City *and* A Jurney With Anita. Urbana: U of Illinois P, 1983.

Truffaut, François. "Un certaine tendance du cinéma françois." *Cahiers du cinéma*. 31 (1954).

Federico Fellini:
Bifocal Views

R.H.W. DILLARD

I HAVE BEEN WATCHING the films of Federico Fellini for over forty years, and I have been teaching them and writing about them for nearly thirty of those years. My approach to these films and to cinema in general (as will soon be quite obvious) has been greatly influenced by the mind and work of Bill Robinson, my old office mate at the University of Virginia, my dear friend and guru. His essays, "The Movies, Too, Will Make You Free" in *Man and the Movies* (1967) and "If You Don't See, You're Dead: The Immediate Encounter with the Image in *Hiroshima Mon Amour* and *Juliet of the Spirits*" (1972-73) are, to my mind, two of the most deeply thoughtful and revelatory essays ever written on cinema.

I offer here two essays of my own which are in no way comparable to Robinson's own work but show the force of his influence in every line. I hum and whistle my own tunes over the great rolling bass line of his work while hoping all the time that I don't do that work too much discredit. The first, an essay on *Fellini Satyricon* as horror film was written in 1971 and revised in 1976. Today I would approach that film (and horror films in general, for that matter) quite differently, if for no other reason than that the availability of video prints of this film and so many of the other films mentioned in the essay would allow me to face the films themselves more directly without the mediation of inadequate notes and screenplays. I have resisted the impulse to re-write the entire essay, however, and have left its reading of the film intact while correcting only errors of detail and fact. The second was written in 1994 from another angle after the death of Fellini and in response to a particularly mindless response to his work by a well-known film "critic" on NPR. It is, as its title suggests, more clownish than its predecessor, but that does not mean that it is any less serious.

I wish to thank again the editors of *Contempora* and *Chronicles: A Magazine of American Culture* for the opportunity to write the two essays. Those essays will, however, now have to stand up and speak for themselves. I wish only to add that both of them are dedicated—with a gratitude beyond the power of mere words (without the help of moving images in light) to express—to W.R. Robinson, A.S.C.

I. "IF WE WERE ALL DEVILS":
FELLINI SATYRICON AS HORROR FILM (1971, 1976)

If George Romero's *Night of the Living Dead* (1969) is a film which gains its power by the negation of human values and the emasculation of belief, Federico Fellini's *Fellini Satyricon* (1970) would at first glance seem to be its twin. Exotic where Romero's film is ordinary, garishly colorful rather than dully black and white, fragmented structurally instead of organically unified, *Fellini Satyricon* does, however, lay open human failure with an intensity that asserts its kinship with *Night of the Living Dead* despite those differences. But, of course, Fellini's film, for all its immediate similarity to Romero's nihilistic "symphony," does and is a great deal more than that similarity might suggest.

According to Bernardino Zapponi, co-author of the screenplay of *Fellini Satyricon,* the film is "a psychedelic movie, historical science-fiction, a journey into time, a planetary world, away from our everyday logic and rhythm." Fellini has described it as "a 'science-fiction' in the sense that it is a journey into the unknown—a planet like Mercury or Mars, but in this case a pagan planet." And certainly it is. The film shatters all of our normal ways of seeing and understanding; it thrusts us into a world so alien that, at first, we do not have any of the right concepts necessary to perceive what is happening before our eyes. John Simon, for example, found *Fellini Satyricon* to be a series of "undigested dreams, the raw material of the subconscious, [that] do not make telling works of art." He could not make the film into the narrative whole that we have come to expect a movie (or any work of art) to be. But his expectations and the failure of the fulfillment of those expectations is part of the meaning of *Fellini Satyricon.* The film is fragmented precisely so that we will see and feel that fragmentation and know it for what it is. And by that knowing, we may come to an understanding of ourselves and of the world in which we live far richer than that which a less radical artistic form could have given us. By seeing the fragmentation of Fellini's alien world, we come to know both the dangers of fragmentation in and the wholeness of our own world with a fullness which most modern art and modern thought has denied us. *Fellini Satyricon* works on us by reversals, or as Zapponi would have it, "counterimages, counterdialogue."

But all of this is very abstract, a set of assertions. If the film is examined with some care, however, I believe that those assertions will hold true and that we will be able to see *Fellini Satyricon* as a Christian *comedie noire,* a rendering in terror of the awful truth of life which enables us to "walk as children of the light."

There are as many possible approaches to a film of this complexity as there are images in it, but we must begin somewhere, and I propose to start with the figure of Fortunata, the wealthy "poet" Trimalcione's wife. She struck me as a familiar figure the first time she appeared, her hair stacked up and back in an inverted pyramid, a gaudy parody of a Roman matron. But I only recognized her when she and Scintilla pecked away at each other's lips, "like lizards, like doves." Then her awkwardness in the dance and all of her quick, birdlike motions came together to form an echo, an allusion to the image of Elsa Lanchester as the intended bride of the monster in James Whale's *Bride of Frankenstein* (1935). And the allusion is an appropriate one, for Fortunata is as alien to us as Doctor Frankenstein's second creature with her body sewn together from those of dead women and with a synthetic brain, a child of murder and mad science. Both move like lizards and birds, both are parodies of women, and both are beyond any rational analysis. Think of Fortunata's image, soon to be spattered with sauce thrown in her face by her husband, dancing grotesquely and gracelessly; she is, as Doctor Pretorius describes Frankenstein's initial creature, "a monstrous lampoon of the living."

From this likeness, we can go on to understand *Fellini Satyricon* as a horror film, more kin to Whale's *Frankenstein* (1931) and *Bride of Franken-stein* than to Mervyn LeRoy's *Quo Vadis?* (1951) or Anthony Mann's *The Fall of the Roman Empire* (1964). The traditional historical film has approached the Romans as if they were modern men in costume; the approach has been rational, and the resulting films have had the formal wholeness which John Simon could not find in Fellini's film. But Fellini, knowing that "Our vision of the Roman world has been distorted by textbooks," set out to imagine a world so alien that it could as well be inhabited by "Martians." His Romans do not inhabit a world that is "archeological, or historical, or nostalgic." They inhabit a world without Christ, the Land of Unlikeness without the possibility of the values inherent in salvation, a pagan and fallen world not reconstructed rationally by a modern thinker but imagined by a modern Christian artist, a world which is "a species of nebula…nourished by nothing."

But if the film is, as Fellini says, "a fantasy," can it also be science fiction or even Zapponi's "historical science-fiction"? If we accept the usual understanding of the nature of science fiction, I think not, for science fiction is concerned more with rational rather than imaginative extrapolation from fact, and it fails most often from a lack of imaginative vision. A character in Fred Hoyle's novel, *October the First Is Too Late* (1966) states clearly the limitation of science fiction which is most appropriate to this discussion:

> Science-fiction is a medium that concerns, above all else, life forms other than ourselves. The real life forms of our own planet belong of course to natural history, to zoology, so science-fiction purports to deal with life forms of the imagination. Yet what do we find when we read science-fiction? Nothing really but human beings. The brains of a creature of science-fiction are essentially human. You put such a brain inside a big lizard, and bangwallop, you have a science-fiction story.

Fellini has gone much further toward creating "life forms of the imagination" than have Hoyle's science-fiction writers, for his human characters seem to have the brains of lizards or, even more accurately, synthetic brains like that of the bride of Frankenstein, brains thinking thoughts so alien to ours that we cannot understand or even see anything beyond the most superficial of resemblances.

But *Fellini Satyricon* is more than a fulfillment of science fiction's possibilities, for its purposes are much closer to that of the horror film. The horror film, for all its concern with "life forms other than ourselves," is really concerned only with ourselves and with an accommodation of ourselves with the mysterious and awful world of sin and death in which we live. It is, in its classic form, primarily concerned with making us feel the mystery and wonder of life and with helping us accept death as the natural ending of life, an ending to be desired. When Frankenstein's monster realizes in *Bride of Frankenstein* that he and his bride and the evil Doctor Pretorius all "belong dead," he is merely restating his creator's earlier fear that "Perhaps death is sacred, and I've profaned it." But if death is sacred, then life is sacred, too, and a film that accommodates us to the thought and the fact of death is also affirming the value of life with all of its perplexities and suffering.

When Fellini shows us pagans living without hope or meaning in a world as he put it, "before Christ, before the invention of the conscience, of guilt," he is showing us the value of life as we know it by giving us a vision of the world without guilt and conscience, and without love which is the source of them both. If the sight of immortal creatures in horror films—vampires, werewolves, and Frankenstein's monsters—accommodate us by awful example to our mortality, then Fellini's guiltless pagans offer us a similar awful example which should accommodate us to ourselves and all of the necessary pain of a life of guilt and conscience and love. It is as if *Fellini Satyricon* were an answer to a remark of Doctor Pretorius in *Bride of Frankenstein* when he says to Henry Frankenstein, "Sometimes I wonder if life wouldn't be much more amusing if we were all devils—with no nonsense about being angels and about being good." Perhaps Doctor Pretorius would find the nightmare world of *Fellini Satvricon* amusing, but it is just as deadly as the world of his own grotesque imaginings, a world of murder and death and a laughter that is only of the grave.

The world in which "we were all devils" is Fellini's ancient Rome, the land of his ancestors and of Italian glory, as alien to him as it is to us. It is the land of the living dead, people who are physically alive but spiritually dead, people who "belong dead" but do not have the Frankenstein monster's insight and self-knowledge. Trimalcione, the richest man in the film's world, the successful poet, is a figure from a horror film, one of the living dead. Fellini describes him as "a sort of gloomy, stolid Onassis, with a glazed look in his eye: a mummy," and he wanted Boris Karloff, the original mummy in Karl Freund's *The Mummy* (1932), to take the part. He also wanted Lica, the grotesque, walleyed imperial emissary to be played by "a Christopher Lee type." And how appropriate it would have been to have had two of Frankenstein's monsters in this grandest and most perfect of horror films.

There is no need to attempt a catalogue of the Roman horrors in the film; they fill it to overflowing. Fellini wishes the audience to "have the sensation of being surrounded by mysterious masks, ghosts and shadows the likes of which they have never seen before." The atmosphere of most of the first half of the film is itself horrible: the air is smoky or steamy, lit only by firelight and that often reflected from water; everything is dirty and dim; the elements themselves have no integrity, and fire, water, air and earth mingle obscenely in plastic confusion. Just before the collapse of the Insula Felices, the vast beehive building where Encolpio and Ascilto live, Encolpio looks up and sees, far above, the night sky and its cold stars ("lidless stars" like those which look down on the "stricken" world at the end of Faulkner's "Dry September"). They are the same changeless stars he sees much later through the roof of the villa of the suicides. His world bursts and falls away beneath his feet or goes up in flames, but the stars remain overhead, distant and immutable, an indication of a larger harmony and wholeness that he seldom sees and never attempts to comprehend. His world is unstable, fragmented and pointless—a world without belief or meaning. The horror is completed by the presence of the stars. Dante, upon emerging from his trip through hell, sees the stars again ("*e quinidi uscimmo a riveder le stelle*"), and even the monster in *Frankenstein* yearns for the light that flows down to him through the skylight and stretches his arms vainly to hold it, but Encolpio merely looks up at the sky, and we never know whether he really sees the stars or not.

If the world is unstable and disordered in *Fellini Satyricon,* human life is even more so. The film opens with Encolpio's lament for the loss of his slave, Gitone. He speaks of himself as in exile, having escaped being swallowed by the earth and the sea, "left out in the cold, alone" by his friend Ascilto who has stolen away Gitone:

> I loved you, Gitone, I love you still…I can't share you with the others,, because you are part of me, you are myself, you are my soul, and my soul belongs to me. You're the sun, you're the sea, you're all the gods at once. I must find you, no matter what, or I am no longer a man.

From this perverse expression of love, totally erotic and distorting Encolpio's perception of his world, the film moves on through a world without real love, a world of cruelty and excess. The theatre in which Encolpio finds Gitone offers us a first glimpse of the larger world it mimes. It is a theatre of gross humor and cruelty. The music is percussive; the clown Vernacchio plays a flat tune of farts. Vernacchio is assisted by an assortment of grotesques, and the center of his act is a "miracle" to be performed by divine Caesar. A man's hand is lopped off on stage, but when Caesar commands it, the hand is restored. The new hand is, however, of bronze, hastily tied on with scarves offstage, and the "cured" man is in shock, his jaws chattering while his blood drains. And for all this, the audience cheers wildly; they have finally been entertained and are as grotesque themselves as anything on the stage. Justice does intervene when Encolpio demands the return of Gitone. A magistrate forces Vernacchio to return the boy, but only because Vernacchio's "conduct has become unbearable" and his "arrogance is becoming tiresome." The world seen in small on Vernacchio's stage is cold and humorless despite all the jokes; its violence is cruel and pointless, and its justice is whimsical at best.

When Encolpio leaves with Gitone, he simply enters the larger world which is no different from the smaller. There are no distinctions between art and reality in this world, none between fantasy and fact, because there is no "reality." The world is bestial, each moment as real as each other, dream and reality both unreal, a world without a past and with no future. The past has been forgotten or remembered only as something to be misused or to be looted, and its values have been corrupted; the future will simply be the same as the present. Throughout the film, poetry seems to represent the highest striving and achievement of the ancient world, but at Trimalcione's feast, Homer's poetry has become just another diversion on a par with the stuffed pig or Fortunata's grotesque dance. Trimalcione, the successful poet, either writes doggerel or steals from Lucretius, and Eumolpo, who reveres the great poetry of the past and is a real poet himself, has food flung at him when he tries to recite and is almost thrown into Trimalcione's cooking fires when he protests his plagiarism. There are moments of beauty in the film, echoes of that classical beauty which our Renaissance forebears taught us to revere, but they are few and scattered, and they have no real potency in their surroundings of corruption. Even one of the statues in the art gallery where Encolpio meets Eumolpo has its head bandaged.

And the film moves on and on, to the street of whores, filled with grotesquerie and perversion, to Trimalcione's banquet where even the laughter seems organized and mirthless, to Trimalcione's tomb where a parody of death, grief and resurrection unfolds, to the ship of Lica, the villa of suicides, the hermaphrodite's cave, the labyrinth of the magic city, the garden of delights, Enotea's house, the murder of Ascilto, and finally to the death of Eumolpo by the sea. Everywhere the world constantly reverses itself. The manly and brutal Lica becomes Encolpio's simpering bride. The young Caesar (played by a woman) is slain, and a new political order arises no different from the one before. Gitone disappears and Encolpio does not seem even to remember him. The only calm, loving and traditionally "classical" man and woman in the film send their children away to safety and commit suicide. Apparent dangers (the minotaur in the labyrinth) turn out to be jokes, and apparently innocent pleasures (Trimalcione's banquet) prove to be deadly serious. The world is turned upside down and inside out.

The people themselves seem scarcely human. Fortunata moves like a bird or a lizard, and throughout the film people exhibit characteristics of other animals. The inhabitants of the Insula Felices cry out "like the buzzing of maddened bees." Characters scuttle around like insects and rats. The boatman who kills Ascilto looks like a fish. The film is peopled by dwarves and hunchbacks and huge fat men and women, so large as almost to be inhuman. And people speak in unknown tongues and with indecipherable gestures.

The beautiful oriental slave girl at the villa of the suicides speaks a musical and primitive (and indecipherable) language, and she moves "like a cat." Gitone moves his hands in a curious semaphore that we cannot interpret. These are all people who, in Fellini's words, are "so distant from us, who eat and drink different things, who love in other ways, who have different habits, thoughts, even different nervous systems." But always they are recognizably human; they are our ancestors as well as Fellini's. There is the source of the horror.

The atmosphere, the corruption, and the animal actions add up to a human world—one closer to the animal than ours, a world without hope, but a human world. And the absence of love, of simple human caring beyond the erotic, makes that love as tangible and real as any work of art ever has. By our response to the horror, we find the knowledge of good in ourselves. We cannot identify with the central characters of *Fellini Satyricon* any more than we can with Count Dracula or the bride of Frankenstein, but we can see enough of ourselves in those characters to discover what we are that they are not. By the distancing of art, we come closer to what we are and what we value.

As in *Night of the Living Dead,* in the midst of the horrors, the "bad," we do find moments of genuine good, of unselfish love. Those moments here, too, are small and fruitless. The kindly patrician who frees his slaves and loves his family dies by his own hand. The lovely oriental slave is alone and sad; when the two young men are asleep after their orgy, she "sings, pensive, absorbed, almost with tears in her eyes." Eumolpo offers Encolpio the melancholic gift of poetry, which is as well the gift of the natural world:

> I'll leave you my poetry…. I leave you life itself. I leave you the seasons, especially spring and summer. I leave you the wind, and the sun. I leave you the sea. The sea is good, and the earth, too, is good. I leave you the color of ripe grain; and the torrents and streams; the great clouds which fly solemnly and light…you'll look at them and perhaps you'll remember our brief friendship. And I leave you the trees and their busy inhabitants. Love, tears, happiness. The stars, Encolpio, I leave you those, too. I leave you sounds, songs, noises: the voice of man, which is the most harmonious of music…leave you….

But Encolpio, drunk and full of Trimalcione's wine and food, is asleep. In the midst of a nightmare landscape, lit as if by the fires of hell, Encolpio sleeps and does not receive the gift of love and poetry, the gift of the world and the stars, not even the gift of self implied by the last fragmentary sentence.

There is one tale at the center of the larger tale which does contain a victory of love and life. It is the story of the Widow of Ephesus which Hermeros, an enriched freed slave, tells in Trimalcione's tomb after the hideous parody of Trimalcione's burial has been enacted. The story transcends the circumstances of its telling and becomes a beautiful fable of life in the very face of death. In the story, the Widow remains weeping in the tomb of her husband after the funeral party has departed. A young soldier, detailed to guard the corpse of a thief, hears her sobs and enters the tomb. "Don't you want to come back to life?" he asks her as he offers her food. They make love in the tomb, but when the soldier returns to his post, the thief's relatives have stolen his body away. The soldier returns to the tomb and offers to kill himself in his fear and despair, but the Widow stops him, saying, "No, my dear. To lose the two men in my life, one after the other, would be too much." She suggests that they substitute the corpse of her husband for the missing thief, and she adds, "I'd rather hang a dead husband than lose a living lover!"

The tale is a simple one, and Fellini presents it simply. The Widow's face is pale and deathly when she is mourning. After the lovemaking, it is warm and freshly colored. The body of the husband is as dry and stiff as a matchstick as they carry it out. The lesson is simple and clear. The physical self is nothing without life, and life is nothing without love. Christ commanded that we "let the dead bury their dead," and the Widow of Ephesus knows that truth in her heart without ever hearing it. She acts out of her love, and her story is a true comedy in the center of a black comedy of grotesques.

If we are able to read the story of the Widow of Ephesus as a prefiguring of Christian truth, we have found another way of seeing *Fellini Satyricon,* a way of understanding how it is different from *Night of the Living Dead.* The Widow's story shifts the emphasis of her understanding away from death to the living present and the possibilities of the future, precisely as Christ brings the life of the spirit back into the stricken world after the fall. Fellini's film is, although he says that its subject is "the pagan attitude to life before the coming of the Christian conscience," a web of Christian symbols, none of them quite clear or complete. It is as if the world were moving toward Christ, shaping itself to his coming. Think of these symbols, only a few of those in the film: the miracle of Caesar in Trimalcione's theatre which prefigures those of Christ, the white horse of death in the falling Insula Felices, the "resurrection" of Trimalcione in his tomb, the story of the Widow of Ephesus, Lica's ship which is shaped like a cross, Lica's appearing once like a Judas by Masaccio, the huge misshapen "fish," the mass crucifixions ordered by the new Caesar with their clustered vultures, the hermaphrodite visited by sheep and the crippled shepherds and attended by men who are dressed almost like modern priests, Enotea's giving back fire to the world through her loins, Eumolpo's forcing those who would inherit his wealth to eat of his flesh, the uses throughout of fire and water. All of these are grotesque distortions of Christian emblems, just as the hideous wading bird in the house of Enotea might be seen as a version of a stork (symbolic of the Annunciation) or of the pelican (which was thought to feed its young with its own blood, and therefore symbolizing Christ's sacrifice on the cross).

But none of the prefigurings is whole or undistorted, and none of the characters in the film can see any of these symbols forming, just as they cannot see the coming of Christ or even the spiritual nature of being. They are trapped in the flesh without spirit; they are forever in the darkness of pagan understanding. Alberto Moravia described what he understood to be Fellini's vision of the pagan world in its hellish aspects during an interview with Fellini in 1969:

> All these monsters, whether hideous or beautiful, that you've crammed into your film, all these albino hermaphrodites, these hairy dwarfs, these elephantine prostitutes, these lascivious Gitones, these paralytic, maimed, dropsical, truncated, blind, halt, and lame etcetera people, reveal, besides your own baroque temperament with its inclination to wildly unrestrained imagination, the idea that antiquity signified nature without soul, sunk in the depths of irremediable corruption…. In fact the monster exemplifies corruption not of the spirit but of the body; not moral, but physical, putrefaction. Antiquity for you is nature once limpid, pure and young, then degenerate and fallen into decay. It is no mere chance that the dark, subterranean, sordid, mysterious surroundings of your film suggest the idea of the Inferno. An inferno that is in no wise moral but wholly physical, like that of certain primitive painters before Dante. An inferno without purgatory and without paradise.

Moravia correctly sees that Fellini's pagan Rome is an inferno, but he overlooks the prefigurings of Christ's coming throughout the film. Moravia accuses Fellini of seeing the pagan world like an early and primitive Christian, and certainly Eumolpo's value in the film does seem to rest in his anticipating Christian truths without the aid of Revelation. But Fellini is no medieval Christian; he is simply a Christian, unorthodox and often anti-clerical, but a Christian, shaping his artistic and moral perception to Christian belief and making his fictive worlds to conform to the truth of his Christian vision.

Fellini has always been a Christian artist, as his European critics have usually seen when his American critics have not. *La Dolce Vita* (1959) is an "Inferno," and *8½* (1963) is as much a "Purgatorio." The love which frees Giulietta in *Juliet of the Spirits* (1965) may in fact render it more a "Paradiso" than is at first apparent. And *Fellini Satyricon* has deep roots in Fellini's belief and strong bonds to his other work. Like *La Dolce Vita* it is an "Inferno," sharing with that film the image of a monstrous fish which appears to the meandering central characters of both films as an emblem of earthly corruption rather than Christian hope. Perhaps Paola's smile at the end of *La Dolce Vita* and the sunrise at the end of *Satyricon* indicate the future of love and hope that is available to those who have eyes to see, to the viewer of the films, even if the central characters in those films can only walk or sail away into hopelessness,

There is, however, an ambiguity in the ending of *Satyricon* which is intriguing and appropriate to the film. In the treatment, the film was to have ended with a scene in which the Roman gods appear to Encolpio but are dispersed back into nature "Whence they sprung" by the rising sun. Encolpio, like Marcello Rubini in *La Dolce Vita*, "walks on," godless and without even the illusion of soul. But in the film itself, Encolpio rejects the dead flesh of Eumolpo and sails away with the crew of cheerful young men. He tells us that "On an island covered by high sweet-scented grasses a young Greek introduced himself and told me that in the year…." But he does not go on; the colors of the sea fade away, and we are left only with a broken wall on which the faces of the characters in the film appear in an ancient fresco, all of them "with ambiguous smiles." Perhaps the young Greek told Encolpio the story of Christ, but we cannot know. A pagan book, even when translated into film by a Christian artist, must remain forever short of the truth. Like Virgil in Dante's *Divine Comedy,* Petronius may take us only to the gates of Paradise, but he may never enter. The Christian vision of the film is Fellini's and we may share it with grace and joy, but the world of pagan Rome must remain true to Petronius, a fragmented world which can be made whole only by later Christian understanding.

Fellini Satyricon is finally a film about seeing. Think of the eyes which are appropriate to its texture: Lica's bad eye, Trimalcione's eyes in the wall mozaic, Enotea's startling blue eyes. One of the earliest images in the film is of a giant stone head being drawn by horses down a narrow Roman street, its eyes dominating the screen, open, empty, forever blind. None of the characters in the film is able to escape that blindness. How appropriate that we know the

Romans by their statues, for, as we learn in the film, they were as blind and as alien as statues to our way of seeing and understanding. And our rational, intellectual understanding of the Romans is just as blind (we should always remember the suicide of the intellectual Steiner in *La Dolce Vita,* for his dependence on reason is as futile as the pagans' spiritual blindness in *Fellini Satyricon*). But Fellini gives us a visual understanding of that alien world which transcends fragmentation and blindness. By an art of light and motion, he gives us the opportunity to see the growing truth of the world through the empty motions of his alien and pagan characters.

W.R. Robinson's description of the power of the cinema as an art of light is especially appropriate to an understanding of *Fellini Satyricon:*

> In a world of light and a light world—unanalyzable, uninterpretable, without substance or essence, meaning or direction—being and non-being magically breed existence. Out of the darkness and chaos of the theater beams a light; out of the nothingness is generated brilliant form, existence suspended somewhere between the extremes of total darkness and total light. Performing its rhythmic dance to energy's tune, the movie of the imagination proves, should there be any doubt, that cinema, an art of light, contributes more than any other art today to fleshing out the possibilities for good within an imaginative universe.

Fellini's images formed in light give us a living Roman world in full color, but the colors are hot and garish and the living world is without spirit, a world of the living dead. And these imaginary characters—first imagined by Petronius, reimagined by Fellini, then reimagined by each of us in creative communion with them both—are all dead at the end of the film, are all figures on a crumbling wall. The film is a Christian horror film, but it is also a parable of art much like *8½.* None of the characters of the narrative are alive; they are all unreal, all dead, but by caring and by imagining we give them life, and the truth of their borrowed lives stays alive in us and in our lives after they have returned to the death and unreality of the painted wall, the closed book, the dark room, and the reel of film in the can. So, Fellini would have us know, do we all live by the grace of God, and we shall continue to live by the love of Christ which is the love of God. By seeing, we know; by imagining, we love; by knowing and loving, we live.

I have not even begun to exhaust the possibilities for learning available to us in *Fellini Satyricon,* for I have mentioned only a few approaches to the film among very, very many. I could have discussed Fellini's use of color in the film: how its brightness and garishness contrasts to the muted and harmonious colors in Antonioni's humanistic *Red Desert* (1964) or *Blowup* (1966) or Fellini's own *Amarcord* (1974), or how the tone of the colors change as the film progresses toward the coming of Christ and the natural light of the dawn (finally revealing the bright, false colors of the broken pagan wall in full sunlight at the very end). Or, I could have discussed Fellini's fidelity (or infidelity) to Petronius. The possibilities, as I said, are very many. But I shall conclude by returning directly to the idea of *Fellini Satyricon* as a horror film.

Since the decline of the horror film as a pure form after the great films of the 1930s and 1940s, there have been few genuinely fine horror films. Hitchcock's *Psycho* (1960) and Polanski's *Repulsion* (1965) come to mind, but they are both closer to psychological realism than they are to parabolic films like Carl Theodor Dreyer's *Vampyr* (1932), Whale's two Frankenstein pictures, Tod Browning's *Freaks* (1932), Karl Freund's *Mad Love* (1935), or Edgar G. Ulmer's *The Black Cat* (1935). And few of them have even begun to approach the poetry of Val Lewton's films of the 1940's. One of the difficulties, I suspect, is the advent of color. The great horror films were fashioned of black and white, just as their moral structure juxtaposed within them good and evil, life and death. When the English filmmakers at Hammer and other studios attempted to remake the black and white films in color, they succeeded in making some handsome films, but few in which color was able to function as a meaningful part of the parable. To my mind, they failed, although David Pirie does make strong arguments to the contrary in *A Heritage of Horror* (1973). Roger Corman's films are so lushly colorful that no one could take even their nights and shadows seriously, so they have appropriately been transformed into comedies. *The Exorcist* (1973) and its occult imitators share that lushness and that failure. The richness of Vadim's *Blood and Roses* (1961) and Nicolas Roeg's *Don't Look Now* (1973) is appropriate to their air of decadence, and Roman Polanski used the color in *Dance of the Vampires* (1967) and *Rosemary's Baby* (1968) brilliantly as did Ken Russell in *The Devils* (1971), but for the most part color has hindered more than helped the job of creating artistically valid horror films. Fellini's *Satyricon* is the brilliant exception; it is a film that cannot be conceived of in black and white. It has the parabolic richness of the earlier horror films, because Fellini was able to use color with the same skill with which Whale used black and white.

Aside from the problem of color, another reason the horror film has lost validity as a pure form is that postwar existential thought and its countless ugly offspring have questioned the validity of metaphor and parable in all art forms. The present high esteem, however, with which Nabokov and Borges and García Márquez are held is evidence that existential realism is burning itself out in fiction, and the success of filmmakers like Bergman and Fellini, Russell and Roeg, is evidence that the same thing is happening in serious films. Both Bergman and Fellini have been Christian filmmakers all along. Despite the darkness which is often such an important part of their vision, both of them have questioned the existential despair which has been fragmenting our understanding and draining our creative vitality. Bergman returned directly to the medieval vision in films like *The Seventh Seal* (1957) and *The Virgin Spring* (1959) from which he gained a sense of wholeness and a strength of belief which enabled him to make his later trilogy and films like *Persona* (1966) and *Shame* (1968) which test directly the lack of center and fragmentation of modern despair. And Fellini's *8½*, *Juliet of the Spirits*, and *Amarcord* are fulfillments of his ambition "to restore fantasy to the cinema" and are certainly testaments to his faith in the ability of the imagination to create a whole out of the shards and orts of contemporary disbelief.

It is only natural, then, for these two filmmakers to have made the finest horror films since the thirties—Bergman's *Hour of the Wolf* (1968) and *Fellini Satyricon*—both of which are not formally pure horror films, but both of which allude directly to the horror films of the thirties and both of which strive for that fantasy which is no substitute for reality but which is able to make reality truer and somehow more real by renewing the clarity of our perception. At least by seeing them as horror films, we are able to see both those richly enigmatic and perplexing films with a beginning of proper understanding.

At the Film Institute in Hollywood in early 1969, Fellini said that "My *Satyricon* is even more autobiographical than my *8½*," and *Fellini Satyricon* is autobiographical in the way *Hour of the Wolf* is or *Bride of Frankenstein*. Made almost entirely in the controlled world of the studio, it imaginatively recounts a portion of the autobiography of the inner life, of the life of the spirit, a life which we all share and know. It is autobiographical, but it is impersonal, in the way that C. Day Lewis said that a lyric poem is impersonal, "not because the poet has deliberately screened personal feelings or memories out of it, but because he has broken through them to the ground of their being, a ground which is the fruitful compost made by the numberless human experiences of like nature." Fellini said, after the completion of *Fellini Satyricon,* that it destroyed the need in him "to identify myself sentimentally and ideologically with the subject," and that he had made the film with "complete detachment." That detachment comes from his having "broken through" to the ground of our shared being, beyond the personal, the sentimental and the ideological to the true.

At the end of his preface to the treatment of the film, Fellini says that he wished to embody "the eternal myth; man standing alone before the fascinating mystery of life, all its terror, its beauty and its passion." To my mind, he has done just that and a great deal more, for you are not alone in the darkness and chaos of the movie theater in which you see *Fellini Satyricon*. You are actually creating a world in imaginative communion with Federico Fellini, a world mysterious, terrifying, beautiful, and passionate. And that world of your imagining, alien and awful as it may be, opens to you, because of that communal act of imagination, the mystery and beauty of the living world, our own.

II. FEDERICO FELLINI AND THE WHITE CLOWNS (1994)

Near the beginning of Federico Fellini's *Intervista* (1988), a very large camera crane is being prepared to rise, wreathed in smoke and artificial moonlight, high above the soundstages of Cinecittà.

One of the camera operators calls down to his director (Fellini being played by Fellini), "Aren't you coming up?"

"No," Fellini immediately replies, "I can imagine it from here."

The cameraman shrugs, turns to his colleague on the crane, and says, "What did I tell you?"

That brief exchange about sums it up: both the distinctive personal, imaginative, and visionary quality of Fellini's cinema and, at the same time, the response of his detractors, who have for years claimed that his work is composed of predictable and repetitive fantasies, without experiential, intellectual, or ideological content. But, in fact, the only truly predictable thing about Fellini's films over the years was the response of those critics, repeating in chorus, "What did I tell you?" or perhaps a Reaganesque, "There you go again."

Ideologues and social (as well as socialist) realists have always been uncomfortable with Fellini, so it came as no great surprise when National Public Radio's "All Things Considered" on the day of Fellini's death trotted out an insignificant critic named Stefan Scheiss (or something very like that) to denounce him, to declare that he was without artistic or social importance, to aver that his work had no influence on the history and development of film art, and generally to "disrespect" him. After all, Shorty Shrift (or whoever) was just joining a long line of attackers from the right and the left who have accused Fellini of not being politically correct. He was subjected throughout his career to Church interference and censorship on the one hand, and, on the other, to attacks in the press from Marxist intellectuals, which even led on occasion to actual brawls such as the one which followed Franco Zeffirelli's blowing a noisy whistle to disrupt the ceremonies awarding *La Strada* a Silver Lion at the Venice Film Festival in 1954.

Fellini, however, discovered the best way of dealing with his pompous critics: he simply wrote them into his films, made them a part of that cinematic world they despised so much. Think of the sterile intellectuals in his films, the infanticidal Steiner in *La Dolce Vita* (1959) or the French intellectual Daumier in *8½* (1963) who urges the director Guido Anselmi to achieve that purest of artistic expressions—silence. (Both of them, by the way, in look and behavior, are clearly allusions to Hjalmar Poelzig, played by Boris Karloff in Edgar G. Ulmer's *The Black Cat* (1935), the intellectual architect who lives in a cold, bare, modernist mansion built on the ruins of the fortress he betrayed in the First World War and who murders his beautiful young wives and preserves them in glass cases to be perfect forever.) Or, in a lighter vein, think of the gloating reporter in *8½* who gleefully says of Guido, "He's lost! He has nothing to say!" Or the woman who says offscreen during the credits of *City of Women* (1980), "With Marcello, again? Please, Maestro!" Or in *The Clowns* (1970), Fellini himself, over whose head a glue-filled bucket suddenly drops, just as he is about to tell an inquiring journalist what the "message" of his film is. So it doesn't really matter what Swinger Shift (or whoever) said on NPR; Fellini had already put him into the right place on the great screen of his imagining.

But what does matter is the great difference between the response of Fellini's detractors and that of his enormous and enthusiastic audience— perhaps most clearly stated recently by another visionary filmmaker, David Lynch. "He's just the greatest filmmaker in history in my book," Lynch said in the January, 1994 issue of *Interview*. "He really understood cinema and all the magical things it can do."

Fellini has always had a large international audience. His films have won four Oscars for Best Foreign Language Film (more than any other director), and he was given an Oscar for his life's work just last year. His influence on other filmmakers is large and international, ranging from Akira Kurosawa to Juzo Itami to Lina Wertmüller to Ken Russell to Bill Forsyth to David Lynch. Ingmar Bergman's *Hour of the Wolf* (1968) and *Face to Face* (1976) were both strongly influenced by Fellini's *Juliet of the Spirits* (1965). *8½* has essentially been remade (without credit) at least three times: by Paul Mazursky as *Alex in Wonderland* (1970), by Bob Fosse as *All That Jazz* (1979), and by Woody

Allen as *Stardust Memories* (1980). And could Robert Altman ever have made *The Player* (1992) without Fellini's having shown the way?

What, then, is there about Fellini's films that causes the Stepin Shiftits among the intellectually and ideologically correct so much trouble?

First, Fellini was an artist who depended upon individual and particular vision and expression rather than politically codified generalities and stereotypes. There is nothing by today's intellectual standards more offensive (to use a favorite word of the politically correct) than a belief in and commitment to the individual. We are informed by post-structuralists that the individual does not even exist, that it is the culture as a whole that speaks through the individual who is merely a conduit for the culture's expression. (Substitute the word 'state' for the word 'culture' in their writings, and you'll quickly discover why they seem so hauntingly familiar.) We are also informed by deconstructionists that expression itself does not exist, that every decoding is a new encoding, and that the very idea of artistic expression is just another illusion. And so on and so on, each intellectual or ideological coterie imposing its position upon the others and, alas, upon us all.

As Fellini's films progressed from the relatively realistic forms of *Variety Lights* (1950) and the other early films to the radical forms of the films following *8½* — especially those imaginary documentaries like *The Clowns* (1970), *Roma* (1972), and *Intervista*, his commitment to an exploration of his own way of seeing remained constant. Not since the later Dietrich films of Josef von Sternberg—*The Scarlet Empress* (1934) and *The Devil Is a Woman* (1935)—has a director transformed the interior of a soundstage into such a completely personal reality. Fellini was an artist determined to reveal his full vision as vividly and completely as possible, to discover the universal in the particular. "I don't want to demonstrate anything, " he said, "I want to show it." He would agree with William James that the individual consciousness is "the workshop of being where we catch fact in the making," and certainly James's description of Wordsworth is applicable to Fellini: "…that inner life of his carried the burden of a significance that has fed souls of others, and fills them to this day with inner joy."

Second, Fellini was a Christian—an unorthodox one, granted, in trouble with Catholic dogmatists off and on throughout his career, but a genuine Christian believer. He did not believe in the perfectibility of humankind by social, psychological, medical, political, or any other strictly human means. Rather, he believed that all humans are sinners, that all are capable of redemption, and that Providence moves in the world to provide the means of that redemption. His films are filled with angels in unlikely human forms:

clowns and tightrope walkers, whores on the beach and lovely blonde young actresses who can play the saxophone, smiling young women who have come to the city to be typists and sexy, smiling feminist terrorists who shoot holes in the ballooning sexist fantasies of bumbling Don Juans. Even a life-size mechanical doll brings a glimmer of salvation to a thoroughly despicable Giacomo Casanova in *Casanova* (1976). "Good luck to Guido," the neurotic young intellectual played by Barbara Steele says in *8½*, and even the Mafioso in *Ginger and Fred* (1985) has his moment of grace when he wishes good luck to Pippo and Amelia in the darkened television studio. *Ginger and Fred* and *Intervista* both take place at Christmas with Christmas greetings managing to transcend the ugliness and loss of values in the world in which they are uttered.

His films are, therefore, comic, even at their darkest. "Remember that this is a comic film," read the note attached to the camera during the filming of *8½*, and Dante, the divine comedian, is a presence in so many of the films from *La Dolce Vita* (1959) on. Even those among his characters who seem to reject redemption—Marcello Rubini in *La Dolce Vita* and the title characters in *Toby Dammit* and *Casanova*—are treated by Fellini with a gentleness that can only be a product of his genuinely forgiving and loving nature. His attitude toward his characters and their sinful natures is not, then, available or congenial to those who self-righteously proclaim their own virtue while eagerly condemning the failings of others.

Third, Fellini's films are politically and socially honest, rather than correct. His films have always been anti-fascist while at the same time admitting the deep Italian involvement in (or indifference to) fascism. Unlike Bernardo Bertolucci's films in which the fascists are psychotics, like Marcello in *The Conformist* (1971), or almost seem to have come from another planet, like Attila in *1900* (1977), Fellini's fascists are the people next door or even yourself. Titta, the semi-autobiographical central character in *Amarcord* (1973) wears his fascist youth uniform proudly if not very seriously, and Sergio Rubini, the actor hired to play the young Fellini in *Intervista*, snaps into the fascist salute as easily as everyone around him. *Orchestra Rehearsal* (1979) and *And the Ship Sails On* (1983) don't so much condemn any one side as they reveal the tragic absurdity of having to take sides. No wonder that politically committed critics disapprove so strongly of his films. Being without sin, they are always willing to cast the first stone, apparently not knowing, as Fellini does, that stones can hurt.

Socially, his films are just as honest. "Why do you always have prostitutes in your films?" a reporter asks Guido in *8½*. Fellini, perhaps in imitation of

Christ and certainly to the consternation of ideologues of both the left and the right, did concern himself with the lives of prostitutes and others who live the low (as opposed to the sweet) life, and almost all of his films concern the near impossibility of honest and equal relationships between men and women. No director has (with the possible exception of Ingmar Bergman) shown more consistently the intensity of the anger and fear that men and women are capable of generating in each other. *Juliet of the Spirits* is perhaps the finest film concerned with a woman's being abandoned by her husband, only to find that the experience is actually a liberation. And *City of Women* is, to my knowledge, the only film which so far has really explored the confusion of lust and fear that defines contemporary male responses to liberated women. What separates these films from their ideological counterparts (in which women discover that they have no need for or interest in the company of men, or men discover their primitive masculine identity by pounding drums around the fire far from women like comic versions of Edgar Rice Burroughs' apes performing the Dum-Dum) is that Fellini really loved women. Dreaming of a time "when men and women feel so naturally emancipated that they can meet each other in a naturally relaxed state," he nevertheless honestly knew that such a time is a long way off and that love, betrayal, and forgiveness must remain natural allies in all caring relationships between the sexes.

Fourth, Fellini the artist sprang from popular culture and used it in the creation of his art, while recognizing its essential barbarism and its real dangers. When asked to name films that he admired or which influenced him, he was more likely to mention the American films of his childhood—*Frankenstein* (1931) or *King Kong* (1933) or the comedies of Chaplin, Keaton, and the Marx Brothers—than the highly regarded films of his European contemporaries. His films were regularly peopled by circus performers and vaudevillians, street performers and bit players. When the stars did show up, the poets and actors in *Fellini Satyricon* (1969), the celebrities and beautiful people in *La Dolce Vita* and *Toby Dammit* (1968), the opera singers in *And the Ship Sails On*, they were shown to be clowns, too—only sadder and more pathetic than the real clowns because they were blinded by self-regard and fame.

But he also recognized the pernicious levelling of values in the modern world caused by advertising and television. From *La Dolce Vita* on, he showed the omnipresence of tabloid journalism and television to be the first signs of the return of the barbarians to the gates of Rome. Giulietta's husband in *Juliet of the Spirits* bids good evening to the face on the television with far more feeling and warmth than he shows to any living person in the film— especially to Giulietta. At the end of *Intervista*, the film crew are attacked by

Indians (more European barbarian than American), whose spears are television antennae. In *Amarcord*, Gradisca wastes the actual possibilities of her youth while looking for a perfect and unattainable Gary Cooper, and, during the funeral procession for Titta's mother, the cortege passes large posters featuring Norma Shearer and Laurel and Hardy. Fellini knew that already in the 1930's the reality of the tangible moment was being infected by the intangible imagery of modern technology, and that Mussolini and Hitler were very real and dangerous products of that infection. Even Dante was not immune; his head, with the top sheared off and filled with soup, appears on a large advertising poster in the tobacco shop where Titta's sexual dreams are fulfilled in overwhelming ways he is unable to deal with.

In *Ginger and Fred*, Fellini makes the point most fully. Not only does a puppet Dante in a television commercial find his way out of the dark wood using a compass (and thereby also missing his trip to revelation as well), but the modern cult of celebrity with its absurd blurring of values and meaning is at the center of the comedy. "Why is a convicted mafioso appearing on a television show with artists?" Amelia asks, to be answered by a Queen Elizabeth look-alike, who is also scheduled to appear on the show, "He's a star, too." The Bobbitts would be on that show, also, if it were being broadcast today. Fellini, a child of popular culture, knew its limitations in a way that his intellectually snobbish detractors like Signor Squazzi Scitti on NPR do not, for they are sure that they, too, are stars!

Federico Fellini, for all those reasons, then, despite the astonishing beauty of his images and the depth of his feeling for humankind, must remain forever beyond the comprehension or appreciation of those who, bound by ideological or intellectual abstractions, have neither ears to hear nor eyes to see. And what they are missing is what all those people miss who claim that he never made a love story: the simple truth that all of Fellini's films were and are love stories, are acts of love. They must be understood with a lover's comprehension, and, if they are, they will feed your soul and fill you with inner joy.

(Oh, by the way, for those of you who take offense at my vulgar and insensitive jokes at the expense of the noted critic Steven Shiftless, I advise you to read Fellini's brilliant essay "Why Clowns?" in *Fellini on Fellini* (1976) in which he explains that when a slovenly Auguste clown (the fool) is confronted with the purity and idealism and authoritarianism of an elegant White Clown, he has no choice but "to dirty his pants, get drunk, roll about on the floor, and put up endless resistance." I confess to being such a fool, and I assure you that Mr. Shaft is an archetypal White Clown. With all the wisdom of the fools, Stephen, here's a big honker for you from Federico!)

Two Movie Poems
for Bill Robinson

GEORGE GARRETT

GOODBYE, OLD PAINT, I'M LEAVING CHEYENNE

From my television set come shots and cries,
the hollow drum of hooves and then,
emerging from the snow of chaos, the tall riders
plunging in a tumultuous surf of dust.
The Stage, it seems, is overdue.
My children, armed to the teeth, enchanted,
are, for the moment at least, quiet.
I see the Badmen riding for the Gulch,
all grins, not knowing as we do
("The rest of you guys follow me.")
the Hero's going to get there first.
And as the plot, like a lariat, spins out
its tricky noose, I shrink to become
a boy with a sweaty nickel in his palm
 waiting to see two features and a serial
at the Rialto on Saturday morning:
Buck Jones, the taciturn, Tom Mix
of spinning silver guns and a splendid horse,
and somebody left face to face with a buzz saw,
to writhe until next Saturday morning

But how you have changed, my chevaliers,
how much we have all grown up!

No Hero now is anything but cautious.
(We know the hole a .45 can make.)
No Badman's born that way.
("My mother loved me but she died.")
No buzz saw frightens like the whine
of a mind awry. No writhing's like
the spirit's on its bed of nails.
I clench my nickel tighter in my fist.
 Children, this plot is new to me.
I watch the Hero take the wrong road
at the Fork and gallop away, grim-faced,
weary from the exercise of choice.
I see the Badmen safely reach the Gulch,
then fight among themselves and die
to prove good luck is worse than any wound.
My spellbound children smile and couldn't care
less about my fit of pure nostalgia
or all the shabby ghosts I loved and lost.

LITTLE MOVIE WITHOUT A MIDDLE

The big bad abstractions are back in town again.
Tall, slope-bellied, shaded by wide-brimmed hats,
dragging their huge shadows by the heels, they swagger
down the empty street. A hound dog rises from his snooze
near the swinging doors of the Red Eye Saloon and slinks away
without even pausing to stretch, boneless as poured water.
Chink-a-chinka-chink, bright spurs warn a dusty world.
Beneath an enormous sombrero, a Mexican crosses himself,
and then continues to snore more loudly than before.
Acting more on inspiration than logic,
the Sheriff pins his tin star on the Town Drunk
and runs to catch the last stagecoach for California.

Meanwhile into a sunny plaza ghostly with fountains
here come the generalizations in full dress uniforms,
all lavish in polished leather and brass buttons, tilting,
nearly topheavy with medals, these brilliant officers
of the old regime. Oompah-oompah-oompah blares a band
while the crowds wolf down bananas and chocolate bars,
buy every balloon and pound palms raw with sweaty applause.

Now cut directly to the inevitable moment
when the smoke is finally clearing away and there they are,
heels up and spurs down, those generalizations,
hanging conventionally from the streetlamps and phone poles.
Their rows of medals make a tinkly music.
See also, flat as oriental rugs along the street,
those are abstractions who once were fast on the draw.
While buzzards circle like homesick punctuation marks,
the simple and specific common nouns come forth again
to clean up the mess and mark the spot for scholars
        (Oh oompah-oompah, chinka-chink)
with a row of gravestones grinning like false teeth.

A New Geography of Paradise: George Stevens's *Shane* as Trans-Edenic Vision
A Meditation in the Spirit of and Dedicated to W. R. Robinson

ARMANDO JOSÉ PRATS

"And a new growth is rising all around, preparing another aspect for new infant eyes."
—Thoreau, Walden

FENCES AND THE AGRARIAN ETHIC IN SHANE

In the beginning this one, too, no less than the First Place itself, insists on its demarcations, heralds its forbidden zones. Eden will have its fences—in *Genesis* as in Jefferson, and no less so in the agrarian dream of Joe Starrett's cramped and myopic hopes. Joe labors hard at forging a common bond with the bounded land—the free yeoman farmer, lord of the land held in fee-simple, yet enslaved by the notion of cleared tracts and fenced-in spaces. When we first see him, Joe is bringing the ax down for one more futile bite of a huge tree stump—a massive, dead, and mutilated thing that embodies the agrarian war against the wilderness even before it comes to represent the entrenched and stubborn powers against which Joe, alone, shall prove nearly helpless. (It will be Shane's vitality that in turn energizes Joe to dislodge the stump at last, just as, in a parallel scene later, it shall be Shane's courage that inspires Joe to join him in the fistfight against the ranchers at Grafton's.) In our first view of Joe, the agrarian vision comes to be defined, perhaps appropriately, by its downward cast, by the gaze that at once curses and reveres the plot at the yeoman's feet. The fences that, though unfinished, surround him to overwhelming; the log house and shed in the background; the crater around the stubborn stump—all attest to his prowess, even perhaps to his genius, with the ax. Already fences make the man, yet a man not so much self-reliant as self-restricting.

For all the evidence of Joe's devotion to the agrarian life, all that we see growing within his domain is a meager garden (one, moreover, planted and tended by his wife Marian and his son Joey) and a cow and calf. Yet, to judge by the quantity of logs and boards that surround him, it seems as if Joe would fence the very globe itself, perhaps excluding an insignificant and remote plot only so that he may justify fencing in all the rest. And good fences make Joe neighborless, at once expressing and enforcing his instinctive xenophobia. For when his son Joey announces that someone is coming, Joe can only respond with a defiant, "Well, let him come," incapable as he is of conceiving that anyone who comes from beyond his fences can bode anything but ill. He looks beyond his fences only to identify his potential enemies. Later in the sequence, his blind isolationism will keep him from telling the difference between Shane and the evil, cattle-ranching Rykers.

Lee Clark Mitchell has noted the overabundance of fences in *Shane*, and something of their function and significance:

> Granted that doors, windows, fences, and other frames have been essential to cinematic composition from the beginning; granted even that experiments with narrative sequence and temporal suspension have been essayed more inventively than in most Westerns: still, the frequency with which liminal structures and moments appear in '50s Westerns suggests a strong ideological purpose at work.
>
> *Shane* is filmed with nearly every camera frame arranged this way, particularly those of the domestic interiors at Grafton's store and Starrett's farm.

[The last sentence of the quoted passage could be read in two ways. to suggest that the Starrett farm exhibits the concern with "liminal structures" or that the "domestic interiors" of the farm suggest the same structures. The latter possibility would hardly stand as a better example of "liminality" than the actual shots of the farm would—though certainly these shots of Joe's labyrinthine world create what could be called, if only figuratively, a domestic interior.] I have taken the passage out of its immediate context. Mitchell

attributes the "ideology" of "liminal structures" in *Shane* to a national concern, during the 1950s, with parental responsibility and its attendant anxieties (the same chapter devotes a section to the influence of Dr. Spock on
anxious post-War parents of baby boomers), whereas I would attribute the
concern with such structures to the historical forces that produced the ethical sites—the national "geography"—wherein Americans were most likely to
enjoy their institutionally guaranteed liberties. That place, from the time of
Jefferson to that of Wendell Berry, has been the individually owned farm.
Still, despite what seems to me its slightly misplaced emphasis, Mitchell's
insight confirms not only the excess of fences in *Shane* but also their restrictive function. I differ from Mitchell, then, not in my assessment of the role
that fences play in *Shane*, but of the context that they provide for the action.
Fences function not only as physical demarcations of property but also metaphorically, to identify Joe Starrett's moment in "history." In these two ways
they combine to produce an index of the agrarian ethic. The selfsame fences,
physically as well as metaphorically, confine the boy Joey. Yet from the first
sequence the limitation expresses itself not as a contemporaneous manifestation of postwar parental consternations but as the confinement to which
Joey would be doomed but for Shane. Shane's mission in the world is to
deliver Joey from such controls. That deliverance—its method no less than
the very hope of it—constitutes the "plot" of *Shane*.

Against the sublime expanse of Wyoming's Grand Tetons, where *Shane*
was filmed, Joe Starrett' s downward gaze—this line of sight that takes neither inspiration nor hope from the mountains or the big sky—functions as
index of an especially meager ideology, of the severe parsimony that hoards
so much of such little value. In this way, then, abstemious and prudent in the
midst of such glory, the agrarian ethic anticipates its need for a hero from
beyond the fences. Later in the first sequence, Joe shall admit before Shane
(in response to a sensible question from Marian: "Joe, why don't you hitch
up a team?") that he has been going at that stump "off and on" for almost
two years. The avowal suggests just how cruelly his world can exhaust the
very energies that it requires in such extravagant and wasteful plenty. Later
still, yet still within the long opening sequence, after he learns that Shane is
not his enemy and after the rapacious Rykers leave his place, Joe dogmatizes
over meat and potatoes about the virtues inherent in a judiciously enclosed
place. Shane listens politely; Marian has heard it all before; and Joey rocks
ceaselessly in his chair, dazzled by the holstered yet deadly six-gun slung from
the back of Shane's chair. Cattle ranching (such as the Rykers practice), Joe
contends,

takes too much space for too little results. Those herds aren't any good. They're all skin and bone. Now cattle that is bred for meat and fenced in and fed right—that's the thing. You've got to pick your spot; get your land, your own land. Now a homesteader, he can't run but a few beef, but he can sure grow grain and cut hay, and what with his garden and the hogs and milk—well, he'll make out all right. We make out, don't we Marian?

She supplies the perfunctory "Of course," but just then a noise outside interrupts the agrarian disquisition. Shane instinctively reaches for his gun, and the motion, so swift and unrehearsed, stuns Joey into the realization that he is now in the presence of a being much different from his father. But Joe, master of the realm, knows the local disturbances: "It's that calf again. Joey," he orders, "go 'round and chase her out of there." The calf, itself new life, has violated its assigned place. Still the boy stands awestruck, as if witness already to the heroic deed that this moment only foreshadows. "Joey!" the father shouts, "Run along, son. Don't forget to shut that gate."

Once Joey obeys, Joe returns to his obsession: "I wouldn't ask you where you're bound," he says to Shane. The question seeks to identify Shane—to assess his moral worth—by determining his attachment to place: identity obeys teleology. But the hero's reply baffles the yeoman: "One place, another," Shane muses, "some place I've never been." In response to such enigmatic candor, Joe produces nothing better than a grunt; but that inarticulateness itself, no less than Joey's amazement only moments earlier, acknowledges Shane's extraordinary nature. "I'll tell you one thing," Joe resumes, "the only way they're going to get me out of here is in a pine box." "What do you mean, Pa?" asks Joey, who has now returned to the cabin. "Well, I mean, son, they'll have to shoot me and carry me out." The agrarian passion spins its own irony: at the end of the struggle for the land, of the dream realized, the yeoman farmer has conquered only the meager plot allotted to all of us alike, farmers or not. How else could Joe Starrett, willing not only to live for place but to die for it as well, have been more appropriately introduced than as a man focused to obsession on the point at his feet? Though Joe may not yet know it, he is already at work on his grave. The apportioned plot, with its coffin below and its headstone above, marks the ironic consummation of the agrarian faith. This predicament of the agrarian passion, as we will see much later, reaches its dearest expression during the funeral of "Stonewall" Torrey, a farmer viciously gunned down by Ryker's hired gunfighter, Jack Wilson.

The distinction between Shane and Joe Starrett mirrors a basic difference between the two Wests, a difference that, according to Henry Nash Smith, was current at the time of Francis Parkman's sojourn in the Great Plains, in 1846:

> there were two quite distinct Wests: the commonplace domesticated area within the agricultural frontier, and the Wild West beyond it. The agricultural West was tedious; its inhabitants belonged to a despised social class. The Wild West was by contrast an exhilarating region of adventure and comradeship in the open air. Its heroes bore none of the marks of degraded status. They were in reality not members of society at all, but noble anarchs owning no master, free denizens of a limitless wilderness.

By such a stern calculus, Shane embodies the American romance of the wilderness, while Joe represents the class devoted to the soil, devoted to it yet held by it in abiding thralldom, the plaything of its indifference, an ephemera to its cruel whimsies. Yet the "inhabitants" of the "agricultural frontier," however despised by adventurers, could well claim an ideological privilege that predated (and claimed right of precedence over) the romantic contempt for the farmer. In her magnificent book on Puritan rage and righteousness, *The Name of War*, Jill Lepore tells us of the urgent need of third-generation Puritans to define themselves lest they become indistinguishable from the Indians among whom they lived. The concept of property answered to such a need. Lepore articulates the Puritan logic of individually owned place as follows: "If building a house on a piece of land makes that land your own, and if the land you own defines who you are, then losing that house becomes a very troubling prospect indeed." (Hence Marian to Shane in the Schaefer novel: "'It would just about kill Joe to lose this place.'") Losing the house is losing one's identity. One may as well be dead. Thus, spaces required boundaries—fences, walls, palisades—and these were the comforting tokens of one's cultural difference from those presumed to range and roam free. Hence the extension of the logic of place, according to the Puritans: "If doors marked liminal spaces between inside and outside, order and chaos, and houses represented the English body, those same houses also represented the English family—a house destroyed was a family destroyed."

More directly, perhaps, Joe Starrett's obsession answers obediently to the notion, so dear to the early days of the Republic, that a man's social identity—his trustworthiness, his civic fitness, so to say—depends crucially on (and is mirrored by) his ability to secure the boundaries of his land. Men who recognize no fences, as Crèvecoeur held to be true of hunters and backwoodsmen (or in the case of *Shane*, the Rykers, who demand the open range), trust to the natural fecundity of the earth, and therefore do little; carelessness in fencing often exposes what little they sow to destruction; they are not at home to watch; in order therefore to make the deficiency, they go oftener to the woods. That new mode of life brings along with it a new set of manners, which I cannot easily describe.

We will know the barbarians by their contempt of fences. Faulkner, though hardly a disciple of Crèvecoeur, gave us this barbaric type for all time in Ab Snopes—Ab, who refuses to fence in his hog even after his neighbor provides him with the coil of wire to do so, and who helps himself to whole planks from others' fences, even when he means to keep his fires "niggard" and "shrewd"—fires such as only deserters (or once and future barn burners) build during perilous times.

Yet one feels that Joe Starrett would also have kept out Whitman or Thoreau or Hemingway or Peckinpah, and Bill Robinson himself—and of course Shane—souls all that love "the wild not less than the good"—even as he would fence out the Snopeses or the Rykers. And he would keep his own boy within for the same reason that he would keep all these others out. For Joe will be no such near-savage. He knows, again with Crèvecoeur, that "If manners are not refined, at least they are rendered simple and inoffensive by tilling the earth." Better simple and inoffensive than unrestrained or passionate. Or if he must dream, let his be but dreams of limits, dreams of *completion*, hopes therefore whose fulfillment begets nothing but the one thing that they might most appropriately beget, closure. So readily does the rustic rapture become the tragic illusion of the ahistorical: fences should keep space within, time—its passage and its possibilities—without.

As if to give factual sanction to Joe Starrett's obsession, Billington and Ridge, in their monumental *Westward Expansion*, tell us that the first requirement of the pioneer farmer of the Great Plains was "efficient fencing material." Then, as if to mock Joe's vision of agrarian self-sufficiency, they offer the following incongruity:

> A Department of Agriculture report in 1871 estimated a 160-acre homestead which cost its owner $20 in land-office fees would require $1,000 worth of wooden fence "for protection against a single stock-grower, rich in cattle, and becoming richer by feeding them without cost on the unpurchased prairie."

And Eric Sloane, in his book *A Reverence for Wood*, gives an even more startling account of the agrarian mania for fences:

> After the Civil War, the U.S. Army made inventory of the nation's

seven million miles of wood fences, because they were considered to be of importance in the field of battle. This might sound strange, yet the word *fence* was originally short for *defense*, and the use of a fence to hold in cattle was something quite American and recent. General James Brisbin, who took over the job, estimated there was "over two *billion* [a word seldom used in those days] dollars worth of wood fencing in America," and the cost of repairing it came to about one hundred million dollars a year. At the then current average of three hundred dollars a mile, our wood fences had added up to something like the national debt.

When Joe, in response to Joey's announcement of an approaching stranger, says, "Well, let him come," we note the functional meaning of this old derivation of the term "fence": he is not only safeguarding his meager property but *defending* it, protecting the ideal of a personal identity so thoroughly based on place that he may as well be fencing himself in. Although they fail miserably at the task, Joe's fences mean to keep the barbaric Rykers out. But beyond their merely utilitarian function, his fences become the very source of his status, of his exalted identity not only as yeoman farmer but as embodiment of a distinctly American civilization, himself as blameless as he is self-sufficient, the living proof of an Adamic restoration. History pointed to him as the perfection of a type that had been in the making from the moment of the Fall. He now presides unchallenged over the ahistorical land, and serpents and cattle ranchers are to be kept out. Why else would Joe so vehemently correct Ryker, who calls him a "squatter," by insisting instead on the honorific "homesteader"? And why would he, much later (and on no less auspicious a day than the Fourth of July itself), give to Ryker a dialectical account of his vision, a vision in which he, Joe, is the synthesis and terminus of all moral evolution? "I'm not belittling what you and the others did," he tells Rufe Ryker, who claims the land by right of priority. "At the same time, you didn't find this country. There was trappers here, and Indian traders, long before you showed up. And they tamed this country more than you did." Ryker, greedy and old, childless and womanless—Ryker, above all else, *placeless* for wanting the whole place (we never see him but in Joe's place or at Grafton's saloon)—would thwart the moral advance of the yeoman farmer toward preeminence among the nation's classes, and so would retard the advent of the American *novus ordo seculorum*. Not surprisingly, then, fences become an end in themselves, so much so that we are hard-pressed to recall when Joe works at anything other than fences; so much so, indeed, that Shane's brief stint as Joe's only farm hand shows him at work only at one task, stringing barbed wire. Fences grow nothing; they set off and set apart. They institutionalize: the land itself is nothing until its wealth and fund of possibility have been so impoverished as to turn it into riches—into material riches, no doubt, but also into that other kind of "wealth" that the nation so continually frets over—social respectability. Fences function as the social blazon of men who, like Joe Starrett or Lije Evans, the agrarian dreamer of A. B. Guthrie's *The Way West*, "looked ahead to farms and schools and government, to an ordered round of living."

And yet, does history—not now the history of the Homestead Act of 1862 or of the fencing of the Great Plains or of the wars, so dear to the Western, between rancher and farmer, or even the history of independent yeomanry—but the history of a lost Eden, does it not drive and dominate Joe's compulsion, however ignorant he may be of his identity as Adamic avatar? Does it not seem appropriate that he should base his *ethic* on an *êthos* (literally, on "an accustomed place: hence…seats, haunts, abodes…. II. custom, usage, habit: in pl., like Lat. *mores*, the disposition, temper, character")? Does it not seem fitting, therefore, that his fences be meant to demarcate a regained Garden, and that he should aspire, accordingly, to contain and control all that would change therein? Has not place, so conceived, always opposed change, and has its ethic not always been the antagonist of a moral, which is to say a *creative*, vision? What would such an ethic have to do with growth and possibility? What would it do but emplace new life and, by emplacing it, render it no longer new?

Yet the eighteenth-century ideal of a static agrarian paradise, impervious to the forces of change, had nonetheless a long, even an illustrious history. In its eighteenth-century version, the Edenic ideal was only the latest manifestation of age-old impulses, predating even Socrates himself, to value permanence at the expense of change. Thus, the Great Unalterable was to be known by a devastating double paradox: it was itself the product of a history (and thus of the very processes that it repudiated) and could be known only by processes that, however implicitly, superseded it. Hence Leo Marx's apt comment on the evolution, in America, of the European pastoral ideal:

> With the appearance of Crèvecoeur's *Letters* in 1782 the assimilation of the ancient European fantasy to conditions in the New World was virtually complete. None of the obvious devices of the old pastoral could be detected in the farmer' s plausible argument for an American rural scheme. And yet, essentially the same impulse was at work beneath the surface: it manifested itself in the static, antihistorical quality of the whole conception, and by 1785 Jefferson said as much.

The nation has from its earliest days invested the agrarian dispensation with highest righteousness, compelling a deistic Jefferson to produce the pithy piety: "those who labor in the earth are the chosen people of God." It would be easy enough to view the Rykers and even Shane himself as the barbaric invaders of Joe Starrett's inchoate paradise: one recalls the close-up of horses' hooves trampling over Marian's little garden as the Rykers and their minions ride away, oblivious and callous, after warning Joe that he must leave the land. Nor does Shane, as we have seen, hold place in so reverent a light as Joe does. But if Eden is under siege at the beginning of *Shane*, it is the farmer who beleaguers it. Joe's ethic constitutes not only an imposition on the land but a perversion of the boy's natural urge to grow free.

None of which is to debase Joe's dream, only to appraise it for what it can beget. If Joe would tame the land, would forge civilization out of a single-bladed ax, so be it. That is no mean dream. Certainly Shane sees it as a noble dream: when Marian ask him if he is off to shoot it out with Jack Wilson and the Rykers "just for me," Shane responds most generously—that is, without bruising the vanity that compels the question: "For you, Marian, for Joe, for little Joe." But Joe would make *his* dream *his son's own*, and the dream comes to be defined not by what grows out of place but by what place contains and by that which it *confers* upon him who surrenders to its constraints. As if the boy could not dream his own dreams. For Joe, who would first look upon Shane as an enemy from without, would fence his boy's imagination even as he would fence the lovely land itself.

Let fences bind our pasts, then, that we may move on, free of such failures and regrets as yet fester therein. For fences, which *close* and conclude, also memorialize things only half finished or indifferently begun. And if they would be but emblems of our humanity—which is to say of our limitations— then let them delimit the possibilities that lie without rather than those that lie, already exhausted, within. For why should our humanity, our mortality itself, be known by nothing more noble than restrictions and boundaries? Why is it that our limitations themselves cannot be starting points, sources of adventure, even in the teeth and claws of *memento mori*? And let us take care, especially, that fences not choke the dreams of young lives entrusted to us. Let it then be with Joey as with the exuberant Thoreau:

> No yard! but unfenced Nature reaching up to your very sills. A young forest growing up under your windows, and wild sumacs and black- berry vines breaking through into your cellar; sturdy pitch-pines rub- bing and creaking against the shingles for want of room, their roots reaching quite under the house. …Instead of no path to the front-

yard gate in the Great Snow,—no gate,—no front yard,—and no path to the civilized world!

SHANE AND THE GENRE / SHANE AND THE CRITICS

"In *Shane*," Gilberto Perez writes in his beautiful book, *The Material Ghost*, "as in a Ford Western like *Stagecoach*, *My Darling Clementine*, or the unassuming, magnificent *Wagon Master*, the winners are good but what they win is only a start, a hope for the future." Perez implicitly questions the old commonplace that the hero of the Western labors on behalf of middle class values and aspirations—of civilization. The farm in *Shane* would be not a place from which one might win a "start" but an old and tired ideal—the ideal of the *civitas*. I have already suggested that Joe Starrett's agrarian dream is ultimately a dream that empowers institutions. Historically, the ideal of the city-to-be requires a looking back at the city that was—Troy, Thebes, Athens, Jerusalem, Rome: the dream of the possible becomes, paradoxically, nostalgia—literally the pain for the return home—a looking *back* for the sake of that which may yet be. Where then is the self-respecting Western that honors such a dream? Who shall seriously argue that the hero of the Western, let alone so indispensable a Western as *Shane*, sacrifices for an institution? Is this what Will Kane accomplishes at the end of *High Noon* (when he leaves the town of Hadleyville behind); or what the martyrdom of Pike Bishop and his bunch accomplishes at the end of *The Wild Bunch*? When, at the end of *Stagecoach*, Ringo and Dallas ride away from Lordsburg "saved," as Doc Boone puts it, "from the blessings of civilization," do we continue to hold that the hero performs no nobler deed than to bring about the consummation of the civic dream?

It is true that the Western, broadly considered, exhibits a marked ambivalence toward the hero's presence in the post-shootout community. Howard Hawk's *Red River* guaranteed the presence of its old hero, Tom Dunson, in just such a community, but only by fudging the direct deadliness of a climactic shootout. Hawk's *Rio Bravo* places the hero John T. Chance squarely within the town. Before the crisis begins, Chance is already in the town, fully in control of all possible contingencies, however formidable the opposition of the Burdette gang. And when the bad guys are all disposed of, Chance still pounds his nightly beat, at least until a potentially domesticating piece of lingerie, thrown playfully from above, lures him to entanglements more pleasant, if no less dangerous, than those with Burdette's men in the local saloon. Hawks of course could not stop making *Rio Bravo*, and, in a way, the later *Eldorado* and *Rio Lobo* came both to influence and mirror the tendency of the TV Western to find its home not on the range but in the increasingly civil and unbearably claustrophobic town, such as *Gunsmoke's* Dodge City. Indeed, series whose very premise celebrated the open spaces—*Bonanza, The Big Valley, The High Chaparral*—came to rely on massive, elaborate—dare I say ponderous—interiors, the tokens of a dynastic order, as if these were themselves the very source and origin of American civilization.

No heroes so consistently end up as participants in the blessings of civilization than those of Anthony Mann's endlessly under-appreciated Westerns. *The Tin Star, Winchester 73, Bend of the River, The Far Country, The Naked Spur*, and *The Man From Laramie*—all premise their heroes' initial fury, a barely constrained obsession manifested either as a festering rancor, or as an all-consuming need for revenge, or as a rapacious egotism. In time this rage dissipates and at last gives way to the hero's innate tenderness, to love and the longing to settle down (with the right woman, of course) in a community. And in *Man of the West*, (Mann's last Western but for his remake of *Cimarron*) the hero, a former outlaw who has become a respectable citizen, travels east, entrusted by his fellow citizens with no less civilized a task than that of hiring a school teacher. But he never makes it to Fort Worth. His train is held up by his old gang and, in defense of a saloon singer who falls helplessly in love with him—a defense that doubles as exorcism of the demons from his outlaw past—he ends up gunning them all down. In the last shot, as he and the singer ride in the wagon, we never doubt that he will return to the town with a schoolmarm, though we have no right to hope that the singer might render such civilizing services to the community. What (or perhaps I should say "who") the hero discovers along the way devalues (or at least recontextualizes) his original intent, and, at the end, he is ready for a new life. Yet amid all this blessedness accorded to the white hero in Mann Westerns, it seems proper to recall his first western, *Devil's Doorway*. This readiness to begin anew had been present here as well, and yet never again would it carry such ironic force: a Shoshone Indian returns from distinguished duty in the Civil War to his ranch in Wyoming, but he discovers the town awash in racism. He dies embattled, a victim not only of bigotry but of the American Dream itself, killed by soldiers of the very army that he had so honorably served. Thus Mann, before he would explore its other possibilities, would give his overriding theme a deadly racial spin, and so already expose the limitations of the Western's egalitarian vision. Mann's heroes, then, wear their humanity—their passions, their frailties—in far greater relief than those of Ford. This quality is perhaps best illustrated by the recurrent casting of James Stewart—perhaps the greatest cinematic Everyman in the talkies—as the protagonist (*The Tin Star* casts Henry Fonda and *Man of the West* Gary Cooper for their protagonists). Stewart is less sure of himself than Wayne, more passionate than Ladd or Peck or Cooper about household issues—and so we gladly accord him the right to enjoy domestic bliss, once his ghosts and demons are safely tucked away. Thus the Mann hero tends to lack, or perhaps he only renounces, *mythic* stature. And it is this lack that allows him a place in civil society—but only, of course, if he is not an Indian.

Toward the end of Sam Peckinpah's *Ride the High Country*, when Steve Judd and Oil Westrum deliver Heck Longtree and Elsa Knudsen from the coarse and depraved Hammond clan, are we to think that fate holds nothing better for the young couple than a return to the Knudsen farm, to that place whose own perversions and cruel abuses drove the young Elsa to the arms of the Hammonds? And do we locate the *high country* in a city such as we saw in the opening scene, a town in which progress takes the form of rigged races and belly dancers and—most depressingly—bankers, as much as of cars and gas lamps—a town with its uniformed cops and its sham hero (Gil Westrum as "The Oregon Kid") whose children and adults alike so shamefully fail to recognize the real hero when he rides through Main Street? In *The Man Who Shot Liberty Valance*, do we take Tom Doniphon's sacrifice—the sacrifice not only of the woman he loves and the place he builds for her but the supreme sacrifice, namely, his surrender to oblivion—do we take this to be inspired by an idea of progress such as we see fulfilled in the opening images of Shinbone—the railroad, the telephone, the modern newspaper? Why then is it that, in *The Shootist*, when the selfsame images (only in nauseating profusion) greet John Bernard Books's entrance to Virginia City, the heroic work is still all before the hero? Do I mean to imply that *Shane* has more in common with the so-called "revisionist" Western than with the so-called "classic" version? Classification is the least of what we can do for Shane; but if the revisionist Western compels the hero to see that he can never participate in the realized dreams of progress and prosperity, then Shane, more so even than Henry King's earlier *The Gunfighter*, may well be the classic of revisionism.

Does it not make sense, then, that Eastwood, too, should have shown such contempt for the city? Why not paint the whole town red, as the nameless hero does to the corrupt town of Lago in *High Plains Drifter*? It was in *High Plains Drifter* that the townspeople, infected with greed, showed their true mettle by hiring desperadoes to kill their own sheriff, so that money, as it so often does, triumphed over the very law that it as often invokes for its protection. Where else would cowboys (so consistently a symbol of American manhood) slash the face of a prostitute; and where else might we find a sheriff corrupted by power and by the history of the West, but in the aptly-named Big Whiskey? And in Eastwood's own tribute to *Shane*, the allegorically heavy handed yet earnest *Pale Rider*, where else would the aptly-named LaHood come from but Sacramento, where he has been bribing government officials to let him continue hydraulic mining? The hero of the Western, whether or not he wears a badge, is always in some profound sense an outlaw: he operates outside the law, outside the institutions that define "civilization" and its benefits. Even when he is sympathetic to the cause of civilization, he labors for wages far nobler than its meager blessings.

Yet, accomplished though they are—or should I say precisely because they are so accomplished—most of these Westerns disturbed (or would have disturbed) the great André Bazin, who found fault with most Westerns after *Stagecoach* (1939). Almost everything thereafter was but a "baroque embellishment" of *Stagecoach*, which exemplified "the maturity of a style brought to classic perfection" (of all things it was Nicholas Ray's garish and outré *Johnny Guitar* that Bazin exempted from such condemnation!). He dubbed the post-*Stagecoach* Western the "superwestern," and defined it as "a western that would be ashamed to be just itself, and looks for some additional interest to justify its existence— … some quality extrinsic to the genre and which is supposed to enrich it." Less generously still, he postulated the following devolution: "If the western was about to disappear, the superwestern would be the perfect expression of its decadence, of its final collapse." How else but by a misreading as colossally inept as Bazin's own colossal status among film theorists could one see rampant "decadence" and imminent collapse in the story of growth and possibility? In his ambivalent assessment of *Shane*, Robert Warshow referred (one suspects pejoratively) to its "aestheticizing tendency," thus seeming to suggest, with Bazin, that some other interests—social, ethical, aesthetic—had invaded and infected the genre. These are the Joe Starretts of film criticism, accounting the geography of genre settled and impervious: variation is violation, and possibilities are only and always generic. Perhaps like-minded critics should learn to look at the ending of Peckinpah's *Pat Garrett and Billy the Kid* and to see there not only a conscious inversion of the ending of *Shane* but a commentary on just such an inversion. Pat has shot Billy dead and, now that he rides away, a boy, about the same age as Joey, runs after him. But unlike Joey, this boy does not call after the hero. Instead he throws stones at him. By shooting Billy, Pat cheats the boy of his dream. Pat rides on, remorseful perhaps for the murder, but certainly insensible of any ruin he may have wrought in the boy's life. And did the boy pelt Pat in anger, or was he trying to get his attention? Could he have been trying to let him know of hopes that Pat himself might have fulfilled if only he would have acknowledged, as Shane and *Shane* do, the irrepressible yearnings of new life for that vast and open country that lies, as idea no less than as fact, both beyond the agrarian ethic and the institution of film criticism?

"CUTTING THROUGH…PLACE":
THE METHODOLOGY OF FREEDOM IN SHANE

"The agrarian imagination," writes Gilberto Perez, "envisions the pastoral, the land fruitful and contained; the imagination of the frontier contemplates the sublime, the uncontainable fields of possibilities, the unrealized that lies ahead." Let us now turn at last from the fences to the uncontainable. Let us, at last, look beyond the fences to Joey and Shane.

Even before we saw Joe we saw Joey, well beyond his father's fences, stalking a deer with his toy rifle. Sighting past his prey, far into the distance, he notices, briefly framed by the buck's antlers (emerging, then, out of an image of wildness), a stranger riding toward him. The boy's presence in the open spaces affirms his independence from his father's constructs and constructions. He is free, even if his freedom yet lacks the moral direction that Shane will provide. Moreover, we first see Joey where we see Shane, so that the open spaces bring together both his elemental freedom and the source of its nourishment. Though Joe may have sired him, Shane shall anoint him; though the agrarian vision may claim him, he is a scion of the wilderness. It is not fear but excitement that drives the boy to the father's maze of fences to announce the stranger's approach.

Shane comes not to secure the agrarian vision of the father but to liberate the son from it—not to consecrate the American Dream but to empower its transcendence. The movie, as Michael Cleary (echoing Fred Erisman and others) has well said of the novel, has for its "major theme…individual growth—more precisely, the determination of what it means to be a man." In the very first shot, we see Shane already in descent: larger than life, his back to the camera, he swoops down upon the vastness of the valley below, his heaven (to adapt Thoreau) as much under his horse's feet as above his head. The cut from this opening shot shows him in long shot, an almost indistinguishable image now become one with the open spaces, yet also an image on the move. The boy and the hero become kindred spirits in the act of seeing each other; and for all that *Shane* alludes to the general sweep of

American history, to Westward Expansion and Manifest Destiny, and for all that, as the authorities assure us, it is based on the so-called Johnson County War (or Invasion) of 1892, it is not history but the story of the hero and the boy that drives the action. Closer to the boy only moments later—the hero on his horse, the boy sitting on a fence rail—Shane says to him, "Hello, boy. You were watching me down the trail quite a spell, weren't you?" "Yes, I was," Joey admits. "You know," Shane reassures him, "I like a man who watches things going around. It means he'll make his mark some day." Shane sees him first as a "boy" but almost immediately sees in the boy the promise of noble manhood. So to behold new life is to revel in the devotion to that form of growth that, as John Dewey once put it, "is the only moral 'end.'" The hero's agency in the liberation of the boy traces the direction of growth in *Shane*—the deliverance of the boy from the plots and plats that his father so responsibly erects to keep him bound to the farm.

Certainly Joe suspects Shane from the moment that Joey announced his coming. Indeed, he *should* suspect him, not because it is so easy to assume, at a mere glance, that Shane is a hired gun, but because at the end Shane shall have so thoroughly disrupted Joe's dreams. Doubtless, then, Shane's first words are bound to sharpen Joe's distrust: "I hope you don't mind my cutting through your place." "No, I guess not," Joe responds, all too wary of the stranger. We shall come to know Shane not only by his mythic six-shooter and easy elegance but also by this gift of crossing into forbidden spaces, of trespassing upon borders meant to function as institutional proscriptions. Three times he ventures into town, two of them alone. In the first, he would have his crossing be inconspicuous; yet that first crossing from farm to town begets another—from Grafton's general store to the adjacent saloon, which the Ryker cowboys dominate. (Except for Joe Starrett, the only farmer to cross into the saloon is the hothead "Stonewall" Torrey. The second time he tries to go into the saloon, Jack Wilson shoots him dead. Fred Lewis, a sneaky idler of a farmer, has Will the bartender deliver the coveted pint of whiskey to the general store side of Grafton's.) And that first crossing, as we shall see in greater detail below, ends in a double humiliation, first at the hands of Chris Callaway and later at the hands of the farmers. In the second foray into town, Shane merely accompanies the rest of the farming community, for these will dare go only as a group, women and children included. Yet here, too, he crosses again, and again alone, from the store to the saloon, there now to pick a fight with Chris while Joe, safe for now in the store, flips through the hat section of the Sears, Roebuck catalog (there is not one Stetson in the bunch) and Marian marvels at mason jars ("What will they think of next?").

To be sure, Joe at last crosses into the saloon side of Grafton's to help Shane against the gang of ranchers. Yet, even when it does not seem certain that Shane will beat back his assailants, Joe has dawdled outside Grafton's, and Joey must announce that the cowboys "are killing Shane." The third and last time, Shane ventures out alone and armed; yet more important, Joey now follows him, and Shane's last crossing into the saloon suggests the resolution of the central conflict, and the climactic shootout, rather than ratifying the generic strategy of closure, confirms the dissolution of Joe's fences.

Yet Shane dares even more subtle, and more dangerous, crossings: for he entertains the hope of marrying Marian and of being a father to Joey. Virtually every scene with Shane and the Starretts insinuates, sometimes betrays, Shane's attraction to the woman and the boy. At Shipstead's farm, where the farmers celebrate Independence Day and Joe and Marian celebrate their tenth wedding anniversary, two boys place a makeshift arbor over Joe and Marian; but behind them, and framed so that they, too, appear within the arch, Shane has his arm protectively over Joey. Man and woman wed, but so do hero and child; nor are we to miss, in the same scene, the look of Shane's that mingles envy and regret, or the moment when Marian, heedless of Shipstead's rude epithalamium, turns around to look at Shane as much as at Joey. No moment in the scene reveals this conflict more than Shane and Marian's dance to "Old Paint." (Marian, it is worth recalling, wears her wedding dress to the Fourth of July celebration at Shipstead's.) Joe has been standing on the lower rail of Shipstead's post-and-rail gate, and as one of the farmers swings the gate shut, Joe finds himself suddenly fenced out. At first, he jokingly explains to Marian, "they fenced me out," but as the scene unfolds, a look of concern slowly clouds his face, and this look of Joe's confirms more about Shane's—and Marian's—desires than all the subtle hints and sly flirtations have before. Thus later, as Joe prepares to ride out to town to confront Ryker and while Marian pleads in vain for him not to go, Shane is teaching Joey how to knot and throw a lasso, as if oblivious of the danger at hand, clearly hopeful, in fact, that Joe will get killed at Grafton's. Moments after he wins the fistfight with Joe and earns the right to shoot it out with Wilson and the Rykers, he will have restrained the crossing instinct that draws him to Marian and Joey, only to redirect it as he leaves the farm and rides toward town and saloon.

When we first see Joey, he has already ventured beyond his father's fences. His very first image therefore attests to his impulse to cross. Moreover, he continually appears at the threshold—of his father's farm gates, of the swinging doors that separate Grafton's general store from Grafton's saloon, and then at the end, as he calls out to his hero, beyond the town, facing the lofty mountains themselves.

The spiritual kinship between Joey and Shane makes obvious the boy's own desire to "cut through place." At last, then, the long opening sequence is about to yield to a new one. Now that Shane has agreed to stay with and work for the Starretts, Joe asks him to take the wagon to town and pick up a load of barbed wire. Shane complies, and though he is still dressed in buckskin, he leaves the six-shooter behind—much to Joey's puzzlement, incidentally. Shane rode into the Starrett place alone and armed, and now he rides out of it alone and unarmed, though we already suspect that, contrary to his reassuring words to Joey, there is indeed "wild game in town." As Joey smiles, confident in Shane's own confidence, a quick dissolve shows Shane driving the horse-drawn wagon, emerging from behind the laundry that Marian has set out to dry in the splendid and clear day—the man of the wilderness and the open spaces, his own agrarian commitment, however tentative, at once underscored and belied by the rush of horses and wagon from behind the clothesline. In the next shot, the camera has moved outside to see Shane himself driving the rushing wagon past the open gate of the Starrett place. Joey appears in the background of this shot, but unlike Shane, he is still within his father's enclosure. Drawn as he is to Shane, he runs after him. Yet one senses that Shane—his presence, his allure, his genius—*draws* the boy after him, as if this rush out of place binds the two each to the other even more intimately than before. A cut to a high-angle long shot shows the Starrett place in the foreground, enclosures within enclosures, the presumptuous imposition of angle (and of *agon* and anguish) on and against the irregular tree line in the middle-ground, the intrusion of (en)closure and limit even upon the mountains, glorious and indifferent in the background. In the foreground of the place we see Joe, again bending over a log. Just this side of the gate stands Marian, laboring contentedly at her domestic duties. At the very threshold is Joey, still running after Shane, about to burst the boundaries of his father's place. But he has not gone more than ten strides past the gate when Marian runs after him and shouts, "Joey, get back here!" Joey stands transfixed, his exuberant motion and his boundless enthusiasm held in check by the agrarian ethic of containment and control. Aware, then, that I may be making a claim more extravagant than I can effectively support in the rest of this essay, I will nonetheless say that virtually everything that happens in Shane after this moment serves at once to *suspend* and *complicate* Joey's eventual release from his father's fences. Here, however, we must honor Marian, if only through a brief though necessary digression.

We first see Marian Starrett as she walks across a window of the cabin.

Unassertive flowers grow out of a rusted metal can on a corner of the window sill, and she sings contentedly as she goes about her daily chores. Such oblivious felicity suggests compliant domestication, her own acquiescence in Joe Starrett's reveries of easeful confinement. Also, she is quick to join her husband and boy outside the cabin when the Rykers first arrive. Steadfast and true, she will cast her fate with her man's own. Much later, however, before the savage and near-epic fistfight between Joe and Shane (just before the shootout), when she at last grasps the full extent of Joe's commitment to place as well as Shane's willingness to sacrifice his life for the Starretts, she rebels, instinctively if ineffectually denouncing her husband's tendency to equate place with life itself: "You're both out of your senses," she rebukes. "This isn't worth a life, anybody's life. What are you fighting for, this shack, this little piece of ground that's nothing but work, work, work? I'm sick of it! I'm sick of trouble!" Thus Marian's renunciation of her husband's hopes functions as a prerequisite of Joey's eventual liberation from place. Joey, embittered because Shane hit Joe unconscious with his six-gun, shouts, "I hate you!" But even as Shane rides away, Marian convinces the boy that he does not hate Shane, and that he should apologize to him. When she tells Joey that Shane did not hear him say he is sorry (so subtly urging the boy to follow the hero out and bid him farewell), she is in effect surrendering her claim on the boy, acknowledging that his inchoate manhood can no longer be contained within her husband's fenced-in dreams. We see her last as she ministers to the barely-conscious Joe, holding tenderly in her arms both the beaten man and the defeated vision, looking away to Joey, anxious, no doubt, yet also confident that his own passions, now set free, shall bring forth fine and noble versions of that which Whitehead so endearingly called "the adventures of hope."

But with the ethic of containment still holding such sway, Joey's adventures seem nearly impossible. For now, no fate seems more likely for Joey than that which we see in the scene immediately following his aborted foray beyond the fences. In this scene, Joe uses him as a counterweight: Joey sits at one end of a long piece of timber that his father intends to cut. Without ever looking at the boy, Joe works at the other end, his gaze once again on the point at his feet, while Joey, hardly content with being more than just dead weight, aims a stick "rifle" at the "Rykers" and asks his father, in dead earnest, whether he could "whip" Shane. Though the father would use the son himself for a mass as lifeless as the new-cut stump, the boy will affirm his freedom; though he may now lack the power and the wisdom to enact it, yet he shall at last cut through place on his own. Though the father would fix his gaze on the ground below, the boy will cast his own past the fences. He shall follow his hero's example and cut through place. If his father looks beyond fences to identify his enemies, Joey looks beyond them to the possible. In time, the action will insist on the release of the boy from the moment that Marian, by calling the boy back, suspended at the very threshold of possibility: Joey, drawn again by Shane, shall map a new geography of paradise, claiming for his own not the bounded place, or even the open range, but the full extent and terrain of the unfettered soul. And this time Marian will bless his adventure.

SHANE'S PAST: CONJECTURE AND REFUTATION

"I'm heading north," Shane explains to Joe after he apologizes for cutting through the place. "I didn't expect to find any fences around here." The declaration hints at a past, at a hope that this far in his journey he may have at last left behind (even if reluctantly) those things that at once limit and identify Joe. No less than some of the characters in movie and novel alike, critics too have speculated on Shane's misty (shady?) past; and some find it sufficiently telling of a postlapsarian tragedy that in this early encounter Shane waxes nostalgic about Joe's Jersey cow ("It's been a long time since I've seen a Jersey cow."). This, they surmise, binds him to an agrarian idyll that he has somehow been forced to relinquish, almost certainly in a violent way. And since only moments later Shane whirls around defensively, hand to the six-gun, when Joey cocks his tiny but real lever-action rifle, the critics have also surmised that a bloody deed so haunts Shane's exile from his paradisal home that he expects to come to terms with it at any moment. We took note above of Shane's explosive reaction at the noise of the calf that bolted from its assigned place. And only moments later, when Joey wonders at Shane's sudden absence from the dinner table (Shane is cutting down the stump) and asks where "Mr. Shane" is going and why he left without saying good-bye, Joe reassures him: "No, he's not going, Joey. He wouldn't go without taking that." Cut to a shot of the six-gun and gunbelt slung from the back of the chair.

Shane will not explain to Joey why he did not fight Chris Callaway that first time, when (already in Joe's employ) he entered Grafton's saloon and asked for "sody pop" to bring back to Joey. When Callaway mocks him (mistaking him for just another "sodbuster") and deliberately spills whiskey on his new denim shirt (so that Shane may smell more "like a man"), Shane backs away and makes his exit, amid the derision of the Rykers and the other cowboys at the poker table. Later that day, when the farmers assemble at Joe Starrett's to consider their strategy against the Rykers, one of them, Fred Lewis, reports on Shane's failure to stand up to Callaway: "He let this Chris buffalo him at Grafton's saloon." Throughout this scene, the action consists of crosscuts from the rustic dining room, where the men meet, to Joey's adjacent bedroom, where Marian tries in vain to finish reading him a bed-time story. Joey, whose interest in Shane is by now all-consuming, perks up when he hears his hero's name mentioned. As Lewis's account of Shane's encounter with Callaway drags on, the action cuts back to Joey, still eaves-dropping, incredulous: "He didn't! Shane wouldn't let him do that." Shane, explaining that the men will speak freely if he is not in the room, leaves the meeting and stands outside in the driving rain. Joey frets that Shane will go away. Marian sees Shane through the window and opens it, calling to him, as does the boy, who says, "I know you ain't afraid." Shane only says, "It's a long story, Joey." And Marian, reassuringly, perhaps oracularly, responds, "I think we know, Shane." *We*, too, know, as certainly as any eyewitness, that he has a past, and that in that past he engaged in a violent act, almost certainly killed a man, maybe many men. Why else, but to avoid repeating such a past, would he have allowed Callaway to humiliate him? Besides, does he not him-self admit to Joey—and this in the last scene—that he tried to overcome the past and could not? "There's no living with a killing. There's no going back for me. Right or wrong, it's a brand, and the brand sticks. There' s no going back." And he is, of course, right. In fact, we can take this wisdom to mean that here again, just fresh from killing Wilson and the Rykers, Shane has (re)enacted his past. Of what possible use can it then be to speculate about Shane's past *before* the action if we have just had it for all intents and pur-poses displayed in the climactic shootout at Grafton's? Yet, though "there's no going back," Joey shall not lose *his* paradise. Young as he is, Joey does not go back home. In the Schaefer novel, Bob, the Joey counterpart that doubles as first-person narrator, tells of hitching a ride back home with Mr. Weir. In the movie, Joey looks on as Shane rides away, an ending that marks a begin-ning as surely as does the new day.

The Schaefer novel produces its own tantalizing glimpses of Shane's past, for example, when Marian and Joe take Shane's use of the term "flannel cakes" as an indication that he is a Tennessean (he gently corrects them—it is Ar-kansas by way of Mississippi, but he "was fiddlefooted and left home at fif-teen"). It is, of course, significant that the Starrett couple would try to link the man to the past by way of a place. Nonetheless, the reference to Shane's past in the novel comes in the form of a revealing trope that Bob persistently deploys: he tells us that Shane's "past was fenced as tightly as our pasture." He means, of course, that Shane's history is a mystery, but the metaphor inevitably compels the connection between fences and the past, a connection that describes Shane even as it identifies a relation between time, space, and the human spirit: if time past should be no more than a continual recrudescence of rancor and remorse, it is best that it should be consigned to the space whence it can never again obtrude upon the longings of the soul. Shane's past is no less "tightly fenced" in the movie than it is in the novel, and both novel and movie leave little doubt of just how heavily it weighs on him.

Yet whose story does *Shane* narrate? Although both the movie and the novel bear the hero's name, is it his story alone? As the novel opens by marking the appearance of Shane—"He rode into our valley in the summer of '89"—so analogously does the movie, if not in its first shot then almost immediately after the opening credits, produce the image of Joey noticing Shane as he rides into the valley. Yet where the novel gives us, at the end, mostly the narrator's insistence that only he and his family remember Shane as he truly was, the movie gives us Joey—alone—moments earlier the sole witness to the climactic shootout at Grafton's, now watching as Shane rides out of the valley. If Shane tells, by turns both tragic and elegiac, the tale of a hero at once anointed and accursed by unavoidable violence, it also, and as clearly, enacts a release from that past. *Shane*, then, is no *Oresteia*, no *Oedipus Cycle*. I do not mean the distinction to stand for an aesthetic judgment but for a discernment about the sources of narrative action. Shane delivers Joey, true enough; and more: the deliverance itself disqualifies Shane for participation in a post-Ryker world, even as the selfsame sacrifice wipes out any chance that he may have had to consummate his love for Marian. All true enough. But Joey *validates* Shane, and thus performs his own act of deliverance on behalf of the hero: he confirms Shane's heroic righteousness, thereby releasing his past from unavoidable tragedy and fruitless regret, ennobling his sacrifice on behalf of the new life. *Shane* narrates the story of *both* Shane *and* Joey, then, their relation each to the other, the tale *of their reciprocal release*. In this way, the past ceases to be but a repository of remorse and becomes creatively implicated in the story of growth, in the narration that exchanges memory for possibility and that allows even deepest loss to nurture new dreams. The only freedom worth having is the freedom worth sharing.

After his last words with Shane, Joey comes around the corner of Grafton's building shouting for Shane to "come back," but he only looks on as the hero rides without acknowledging the boy's plea. Then, letting him go at last, Joey shouts, "'Bye, Shane!" The moment, so candidly suffused with sentimental value, often keeps us from realizing that, as Joey watches Shane leave, he stands witness to the completion of the action that began when he saw him arrive. Thus a more complete elucidation of the last scene awaits, in the last section of this essay. For now, however, it stands repeating that the boy is alone as the hero rides away, the camera alternately on a close-up of him and reversing to the eyeline match of Shane, his back alike to the camera as to the boy. Here, then, we also remember that Joey saw Shane *coming into* his world: the eyeline match on Joey, in close-up (sighting along the rifle's barrel and framed by the buck's antlers) cut to a frontal shot of Shane in the distance. In some ways, of course, the action of seeing the hero ride in and ride away parallels the first-person narration of the novel. But these opening and clos-ing sets of shots produce much more than a literary framing device. The relation between the two sets of shots—and particularly with the intervening "cutting through place" performed by both Shane and Joey—describes a 180° turn at the end of which the boy stands released from his father's enclosing structures and the hero rides away, delivered from his own past, even from such a past as the boy has just now meant to recall him to. Yet the boy's line of vision (confirmed by his good-bye to Shane) and Shane's own ride into the mountains, continue to extend the territory of the liberated spirit. Both Shane and Joey generate a revolutionary geography, the new *topos* of the American paradise. The whole of a new Eden lies before the boy, and Shane's past, justified and transformed in and by the sight of the boy, becomes itself a beginning—genesis of Joey's manhood, commencement of Shane's own de-liverance from his tragic past, origin of yet greater deeds in the prospects of free souls.

New Life: Torrey's Funeral and the End of the Institutional Ethic

"Stonewall" Torrey's burial draws all the farmers: the funeral marks the third and last time that all (or nearly all) of the farmers—men, women, chil-dren, dogs, mares and their foals—gather together: they did so first at Grafton's to purchase goods; then they celebrated the Fourth at Shipstead's; now they meet to mourn Torrey, who has been brutally gunned down in the muddy street in front of Grafton's. As a social entity, the farmers' presence on cem-etery hill tends to recapitulate the first image of Joe Starrett, the individual yeoman farmer preoccupied with the ground at his feet: we never saw any-thing that Joe himself grew on his farm, nor anything that any of the other farmers grew on theirs (though we do hear of crops that the Rykers burn).

But the one thing that we do see of this community's relation with the soil is the deep and nicely squared hole into which they lower Torrey's coffin. In this way, the funeral scene renders oracular Joe's earlier vow that he would leave the land only "in a pine box," a vow that Torrey recast as a foolish boast when the men met at Joe's: "There's nobody pushing me off my claim, and that's for certain."

Though all the farmers gather on cemetery hill, they are hardly united. Some, like the irresolute Fred Lewis (who at the same meeting had said that he'd stay "at least until the shooting starts") have come only to pay their respects, but only because the cemetery is on the way out of the valley. They are "pulling up stakes." Already before the funeral, Shipstead, who rode by Joe's place leading the horse with Torrey's body, predicted: "The other homesteaders, I think they run. I think they get out of here." And in the very next scene (still before the funeral) Joe appears at Lewis's, if not to talk him into staying then to shame him into attending Torrey's funeral and hoping that this will convince him to stay. Now that the coffin has been lowered into the ground, Lewis says his hasty good-byes, and another farmer, Howells, says that he will follow Lewis out of the valley. Here, Joe Starrett makes his last desperate plea, a plea for the institutional ethic, for the civilization that might emerge out of fences and enclosures. In the exchange below, the bracketed descriptions establish tone:

Joe: Now wait a minute, let's not be in a hurry. There's one more thing: Torrey was a pretty brave man, and I figure we'd be doing wrong if we wasn't the same.

Lewis: Joe, last time you argued us into staying, Torrey was alive.

Howells: Yeah, what do you want us to stay for, more of this?

Joe: [With evident lack of conviction] Because we can have a regular settlement here, we can have a town and churches and a school.

Lewis: Graveyards.

Joe: [Defeated and crestfallen, slumping down in one of the chairs in front of the open grave, out of arguments] I don't know, but you …you just got to, that's all.

What may appear to be cruel cynicism on Lewis's part is in reality a fitting articulation of an irony foreshadowed as early as the first time that we saw Joe Starrett, when he swung his ax down at the dead stump at his feet. If Joe failed to imagine his place as the locus of growth and possibility and envisioned it instead as source of personal identity and origin of institutions, then his failure is now as manifest in Lewis's ironic insight as in Joe's own despondency: the passion for an identity wrought of a commitment to fenced-in spaces exhausts itself in that most personal of institutions, the graveyard.

As Joe slumps in the chair, Marian enters the frame and stands behind him. Joey and Shane are already standing behind Joe and to the side, so that the shot recapitulates the earlier moment when Shane came up behind the Starretts to stand with them against the Rykers. (In this shot we also see that Joey has appropriated Torrey's dog.) As Shane came to Joe's rescue that earlier moment, so too does he now, only not by offering his skill with a gun but his vision of growth and possibility. No sooner has Joe stopped talking than Shane begins, addressing not only Lewis and Howells but the whole congregation as well:

> "You know what he wants you to stay for—something that means more to you than anything else—your families—your wives and kids. Like you, Lewis—your girls, and Shipstead with his boys. They've got a right to stay here and grow up and be happy. But it's up to you people to have nerve enough to not give it up."

Hence Shane's speech functions as a transvaluation of Joe Starrett's values. Place, as Shane envisions it, grows people, families. It is defined not by fences, nor by what grows within its limits but by that which grows from it, out of it, beyond it. Lewis has as many as five girls, and Shipstead as many boys, so that these references suggest a future where procreation itself is implicated in the reverence for place. Place promotes not "family"—not, that is, the institutional abstraction so often invoked as the basis of all institutions and which all institutions are in turn supposed to safeguard—but families, plural yet individual, different each from the other, each finite and discrete, yet acting together in the generation of boundless possibilities for the adventures of freedom. It is this that makes place worth fighting for.

Now Joe joins in, pursuing the same theme, elaborating the vision, with which Shane has rescued the failed agrarian ethic. As he did when Shane took to the stump and then later, when Shane took on the ranchers at Grafton's, so now that Shane speaks of growth Joe chimes in (even if, as the speech below suggests, he cannot quite give up the confrontational attitude, or the theologizing of the farmer's vision, or the idea that place precedes, and is the only possible source of, growth). Joe stands up, emerging from his hebetude:

> "That's right. We can't give up this valley and we ain't gonna do it. This is farming country—a place where people can come and bring up their families. Who is Rufe Ryker or anyone else to run us away from our own homes? He only wants to grow his beef, and what we want to grow up is families—to grow 'em good and grown 'em up

strong [here cut to a shot of Howells, his wife and two boys], the way they was meant to be grown. God didn't make all this country just for one man, like Ryker…"

Once again Lewis interrupts: "He's got it, though, and that's what counts." But here someone notices Lewis's house burning in the distance, and soon Joe rallies all the farmers, encouraging them to stay and help Lewis rebuild.

But the funeral scene, crucial as it is, owes its power not to Joe's or even Shane's words, but to the images that, of themselves, enact what the words, for all their elevated sentiment, can only confirm. For the images that dominate the scene are images of new life. The scene, which begins with a long shot of the farmers and their families singing "Abide with Me" and follows with Shipstead, flanked by his boys, leading a halting recitation of the Lord's Prayer, soon turns to the images of the young, who know little of grief or of the aggrieved ideology that has brought them there. Indeed, shortly after Shipstead begins to lead the farmers in the Lord's Prayer, the camera, with so little to see, cuts away and pans over the horses, one of which becomes refreshingly unruly when a tumbleweed blows under its legs. But almost immediately the camera returns to the solemn mourners—the men and the boys with their bare heads bowed, some of the women consoling Mrs. Torrey, most of the girls holding hands with each other, Torrey's mutt whining piteously and sniffing at the coffin, which rests on planks over the grave. As the mourners finish the Lord's Prayer, the camera settles on Mrs. Torrey, who sits on one of the grave-side chairs and is flanked by two other women, one of them Marian. Behind them stand Shane and Joey. As Mrs. Torrey lets out a wail, Joey walks away, careful not to disturb the woman's grief (or to be seen by his mother). While the men lower the coffin into the grave and "Yank" Potts plays 'Taps' on his harmonica, a shot of Shane shows him looking off at Joey, who now joins children already gathered apart from the adults, admiring a foal that nurses its mother. Joey pets the foal, and a tight close-up of a little girl shows her saying to him, "He's gonna bite you," and displaying mock fear when the foal nips at the boy. When the foal returns to the teat, the action creates its most stark contrast yet between new life and old: while the children create a world of their own, the farmers, including one of Shipstead's boys, stand around the grave, all of them looking down at the deep hole below—a collective participation in the earthbound gaze that characterized Joe from the beginning. From this shot the camera produces a slow pan right of all the mourners, some two dozen of them, each as motionless as a broken clock, in silhouette against the late afternoon sky. Yet even in this shadowy stillness, the pan right reveals an interesting contrast: the faces of most of the children are clearly turned in the direction of the foal and mare, which is to say, in the direction opposite the grave and the mourners. (The pan ends up looking at Grafton's. The ranchers and the gunman Wilson have gathered just outside to look in amusement at the mourners. The sole exception to this response is Chris Callaway who, contrite over his own treatment of the farmers, shall tell Shane that Ryker intends to kill Joe.)

Joe's feeble exhortation, followed by Shane's speech and Joe's own reenergized vision, come *after* the images that I have described above. It is then more precise to say that Shane's speech is based on what he sees going on around him. Shane speaks up, then, not to help Joe articulate an idea but in gracious and magnanimous celebration of this abundance of new life even in the midst of so much grief. If Shane's transvaluative speech—Michael T. Marsden calls it a "sermon on the mount"—rallies the farmers, it also reaffirms our assessment, above, that the source of growth in *Shane* is the reciprocal nature of Shane's relation with Joey. Specifically, the speech and the moments immediately preceding it evoke the first encounter between Shane and Joey, when Shane, still mounted and still outside the Starrett fences, said to the boy: "You were watching me down the trail quite a spell, weren't you? …I like a man who watches things going around. It means he'll make his mark some day." It is Shane who now watches Joey. In the young life's own attraction to new life, he sees the promise of an individual free from the commitments to conflict and grief that define the farmers' presence on cemetery hill. Only by some such turn from grief as that which Joey naturally enacts can he become the man who will make his mark, *his own mark*, some day. This, too, Shane sees; and it is this vision that begets the speech, the articulation of a new geography of paradise: 'They've got a right to stay here and grow up and be happy."

Days that are Over and Guns in the Valley: Endings as Beginnings

As it is in most great Westerns, so too in *Shane*: the climactic shootout, considered merely as a contest of fast draws, does not so much resolve as confirm, by which I mean that the shootout satisfies the expectations raised by the genre about justice and honor and right. The iconography of the Western is clear—clearer, certainly, than the egalitarian ideology that it is supposed to mirror: from the moment Jack Wilson rides into the valley— alone, somehow too big for his horse, black hat and neckerchief and vest, wearing not one but two guns, heartlessness itself stamped indelibly on his twisted smile—we know him for the bad guy, and thus know that he will lose in the decisive contest with the hero. So the shootout in *Shane* holds no suspense, not even when we remember to throw the two Rykers in on Wilson's side, and perhaps not even when we recall that but for Joey, who first sees Morgan Ryker up in the balcony with a rifle and warns Shane just in time, Shane might be dead. Yet when taken not by itself but rather as the central event in an extended sequence, the shootout in *Shane* transcends its common generic function.

This sequence, as I wish to treat it here, begins when Shane rides out of the Starrett place for the last time. He has just "cheated" in his fistfight with Joe, hitting him over the head with his revolver, and has for this sin enraged Joey, who now shouts, "I hate you!" As he rides out—once again he wears his six-gun—a cut gives us a last glimpse of the Starrett family: Joe, glassy-eyed, lies barely conscious in the arms of Marian who, along with Joey, looks on as Shane rides away. On his own, Joey says to Shane that he is sorry, but Shane does not hear him. Now Marian, whose command ("Joey, get back here!") earlier kept the boy from following after Shane, tells him that she does not think Shane heard the apology. Thus she effectively sends the boy into the very world from which she kept him back before. That world is no less dangerous now than it was before. If anything, indeed, it is more so, since on the earlier occasion Wilson had not yet arrived in the valley. Perhaps Joe's stupor reflects the exhaustion of the ethic of fences, so that the boy can now get away by virtue of a tacit breakdown of authority. Yet it seems more just to believe that Marian now acknowledges—though not without the mixture of apprehension and reverence, of regret and approbation, that forms the common emotional destiny of parents the world over—the inexorable demands of new life for experience and adventure. New life will have its way: she sends Joey out not to apologize but to live.

Without even acknowledging his mother's gentle and subtle counsel, Joey breaks from this picture of a family at once exhausted and hopeful. He scoots between the fence rails (in an instant undoing all his father's work of fencing) and takes off running after Shane. (Torrey's dog, as if revived by the boy's explosive energies, breaks his rope and follows.) Empowered now to let himself be drawn outward by Shane, Joey keeps up with his hero, following him through rivers and plains and over cemetery hill to Grafton's. Here he shall again be sole witness, present to confirm the heroic deed that he has so far only dreamed of. And yet, as we shall see, this deed itself will conform perfectly with Joey's intuition: in its full range of possibilities—formal cultural, moral—the shootout in *Shane* issues as much from the boy's imagination as from the hero's six-gun. Who can say, then, that in the bond between Joey and Shane it is not Shane who acts in accordance with Joey's dreams? Is the involvement of the witness not evident already in the very nature and form of the genre, with its implied acquiescence in *our* demand for a particular sort of hero and heroic deed? What law holds that the hero acts independently of those who imagine him? But Joey has not yet imagined Shane so completely that he can fathom the full extent of his humanity. If Joey witnesses the triumph of the hero, he also witnesses his humanity—that attribute which, precisely because it is so common, always appears in the hero as a great and singular virtue. He sensed it first only as recently as when he saw Shane hit Joe with the six-gun; and the very idea of it caused him to voice his deep disappointment: "Shane, you hit him with your gun! I hate you!"

Now positioned again at the threshold of the saloon, he listens to the terse and tense exchange between Shane (standing, with his back to the bar) and Rufe Ryker (seated, in the shadows, concealing a six-gun)—this preliminary bout to the gunfight:

Shane: I came to get your offer, Ryker.
Ryker: I'm not dealing with you. Where's Starrett?
        ......

Shane: What's your offer, Ryker?
Ryker: To you, not a thing.
Shane: That's too bad.
Ryker: Too bad?
Shane: Yeah, you've lived too long. Your kind of days are over.
Ryker: My days? What about you, gunfighter?
Shane: The difference is I know it.

Humanity—mortality, frailty, and self-deception no less than hope, adventure, and devotion—however familiar, is more difficult by far to imagine than heroism. The imagination of the heroic almost always betrays an obstinate innocence, a sort of unacknowledged refusal (at once salutary and dangerous) to adulterate nobility. At the moment of the exchange above, Joey still does not know that Shane has foresworn the agrarian life and intends to ride on. But he does learn that Shane confronts Wilson and the Rykers without expectation of reward. He learns, in other words, the power whereby the heroic transmutes mortality into disinterest: in full knowledge that his "kind of days are over," Shane will still fight for the Starretts—not because *he* has nothing to lose but because they have so much to gain. Nor does his continual remembrance of life *in extremis* yield to the illusion that he will have a place in the community that his heroic deed will make possible. Thus his humanity places on Joey the obligation not quite to remember Shane (as Bob does in the novel) but to fully integrate his spirit with his—to *become* Shane not, as has been foolishly suggested, by taking to the gun but by incorporating all that Shane is and yet do so without surrendering the individuality that alone validates such a feat of becoming. Shane is already mounted to go, and has actually finished his apology for leaving the valley ("A man has to be what he is, Joey. You can't break the mold. I tried it and it didn't work for me. …Joey, there's no living with a killing. There's no going back for me. Right or wrong, it's a brand, and the brand sticks. There's no going back.") when Joey, having reached for Shane's arm, realizes that Shane has been shot. We never see a spot of blood. No doubt Hollywood in 1953 retained some of its artificial squeamishness about showing a spot of blood bigger than a dime. But the moment warrants no concern with this sort of realism. Surprised by Shane's blood, the boy realizes that he has imagined him bloodless—lifeless, then, only an extension of the gun rather than a man with his own share of anxieties and his bag-full of faults. If Shane is a hero, now Joey sees, it is not because he does not bleed but because he does; not because he can set aside his humanity but because he can make it so necessary a part of his being that it is this deed itself, and not the fast and deadly draw, that renders him heroic.

"Now you run on home to your mother and tell her everything's all right, and there aren't any more guns in the valley." So says Shane to Joey just after he tells him that "There's no going back." I would like to consider the last part of the statement first. In *Shane*, as I have already suggested, the hero's gun—its image (especially as an object of Joey's worship), the iconography that consigns it to a specific moral function, even its generically determined role in the climax—decides the outcome well before the final shootout. What is crucial about the gun in *Shane* is not whose gun will win but whether or not the gun—deadly force—will bring about a social order in which the gun will no longer be crucial. When Shane declares that there are "no more guns in the valley," he is alluding to an earlier scene that announced this specific concern with guns. Shane had at last agreed to give Joey a shooting lesson: he adjusts Joey's toy gun and holster, shows him how the gun must be between the elbow and the wrist, convinces him that one gun is enough (Wilson carries two), and assures him that this is "as good a way as any and better than most." Already Marian, in her wedding dress, ready for the Fourth of July party, has come up behind them and listens—and witnesses. But more than learning how to shoot, Joey wants to see Shane shoot. And shoot Shane does, at a little white rock out in the distance. He draws the nickel-plated Colt's

.45 with the filed-off front sight and empties it on the rock. Shane's face registers an intensity of focus to frighten even the most hardened antagonist; and Joey's shows a wide-eyed astonishment even greater than it did on those earlier occasions when Shane, startled, reached for his gun. Yet all these details are heavily generic. The shooting lesson and the shooting exhibition constitute a ritual: "the scene," Edward Buscombe writes, "in which the hero passes on his knowledge of the gun is perhaps that which most obviously binds the genre into a system of patriarchal authority."

What makes the scene different, however, is Marian's intervention. She sends Joey away and tells Shane: "Guns aren't going to be my boy's life." Shane's reply articulates an axiom of the Western: "A gun is a tool, Marian, no better and no worse than any other tool—an ax, a shovel, or anything. A gun is as good or as bad as the man using it. Remember that." But Marian is not convinced: "We'd all be better off if there wasn't a single gun left in this valley, including yours." By the moral logic with which Shane justifies recourse to the gun, Marian should allow this one gun to remain in the valley. He is, after all, clearly the good man. Yet Marian makes certain that Shane's own gun is included in her paradisal vision. Why so? Could it be that Marian's declared fear of the gun expresses a fear of her attraction to Shane? In other words, is Shane so thoroughly identified with the gun that Marian can reject him by denouncing guns? Or is the moment a bit more subtle? Does the shooting lesson give her an excuse to hint at her attraction to him and, at the same time, to declare the impossibility of its consummation? And why, after all, if Marian so dreads guns, does she willingly send Joey after Shane, knowing that there would be a shootout? Is it because she now *remembers*, as he asked her to—remembers, despite her declared aversion to guns or her quick dismissal of Shane's moral discernments—that Shane is the indefeasibly good man? Does she not learn, then, to love the wild *and* the good—to reverence the wild *as* the good?

Especially where the woman is involved, discussions of the gun in the Western quickly degenerate into desultory conjectures on sublimated desires. We might avoid such reductionism by expanding the context of the shooting lesson scene slightly: Joe now rides in to interrupt the exchange between Marian and Shane. He is looking forward to the Fourth of July party, and he makes much of Marian's beauty, dressed as she is in her frontier finery. After telling Shane to hitch up the team to go to Shipstead's, he walks off with Marian, the two of them laughing, while Shane stands alone and somber, as if struck by an unavoidable recognition, holding the holstered gun wrapped in the gunbelt. The moment, however we interpret the function of the gun, succeeds unequivocally in identifying Shane and Shane alone with the gun. Joe himself, of course, had already done so, as early as when he assured Joey that Shane would not go away without his gun. But at this moment the action rushes headlong to its crisis: Wilson has ridden into town only moments before, and Torrey will ride in shortly after, this scene. As critical perhaps, Shane will have to decide whether he fights Wilson or lets Joe do it. This moment, then, when we see the hero holding his holstered gun after such a dazzling display of shooting, and see him, moreover, looking at once longingly and hopelessly at the woman of his desires (and at the couple that his nobility compels him to honor), determines Shane's course of action. Nowhere else in *Shane* is the hero more intimately identified with the gun, here echoing the famous passage from the Schaefer novel:

> Belt and holster and gun… These were not things he was wearing or carrying. They were part of him, part of the man, of the full sum of the integrate force that was Shane. You could see now that for the first time this man who had been living with us, who was one of us, was complete, was himself in the final effect of his being.

Yet in the image of Shane standing alone with the belt and holster and gun, we glimpse an ambivalence, an irony, that the passage above does not quite capture. For it is here that the gun foretokens his destiny, here that its moral function (his alone to enact) discloses the irrevocable denial of his dreams.

So now, when he tells Joey to tell Marian that "there are no more guns in the valley," Shane includes his own gun in the count; he excludes himself from the valley—from the new civic order that his gun has in part made possible. Yet perhaps more important, he also eliminates himself as a threat to the unity of the Starrett family. Whether or not Shane is reducible to the gun, then, the gun has become a synecdoche for Shane. This is his "mark," as no one else understands so clearly, the "mold" that cannot be broken, the token of irreversible fate that so often doubles as index of the heroic. Yet this is also—and this, too, he realizes better than anyone—his limitation, his own way of being fenced in. When Shane says that there are "no more guns in the valley," he is aware of the dual meaning that this declaration might hold for Marian, but he is also aware of this other tragic aspect of it: the hero always disenfranchises himself; indeed, he becomes, as possessor of the last gun, the last threat to civilization. He rides away to complete his "cutting through…place," and perhaps it is no coincidence that, from Joey's perspective, we see him last as he rides through cemetery hill.

Had Shane not been so intent on the proper farewell, however, he might have noticed that there is one more gun in the valley: Joey has worn his toy six-gun and gunbelt all throughout the scene. Not a real gun, to be sure, yet perhaps real enough as the source of the boy's imagination, which has never been so completely integrated with our own as it is at this moment. For our own spectatorship implies compliance with the "mystique," as John Cawelti would say, of the sixgun—our acquiescence in its power for fantasy, for freedom, for the mythic origins of American culture. If Joey wears his gun still it is not because it is needed in the founding of a civil society: by the millennialist lights of the Western, the new order of the ages has comes to pass as soon as Shane shoots the last Ryker. The real gun—and what gun in what Western is ever real?—has been itself the lure to imagine our hero, our sense of the good, our forms of freedom. There *must* be one gun in the valley; one only, for two would imply a continuing conflict. And it must be real enough to make possible new visions of the heroic—real, then, which is not to say deadly. Such is Joey's gun, the last one in the valley. What fine scruple of Marian's might cause her to object?

If Shane articulates his limitations he also, implicitly, illuminates the possibilities for Joey. He sends Joey home, yet somehow home is no longer defined by the fences that Joe put up. Indeed, in some important sense, the fences no longer exist. There are no Rykers to keep out, and Joey has already burst through them on his own. Home, then, is for one thing, where Joey is to go that he may herald the coming of a new day, the gospel of a new American geography. More important, home is the center out of which the boy may yet grow to greater manhood, to adventures yet undreamed, visions only dimly beheld. Already mounted and ready to ride, Shane, his hand affectionately on Joey's head, speaks his last words. But the visual moment, the last in which they share the screen, invokes its affinity with the first time they met, even as it revises it. For there is now no fence separating Shane from Joey, as there was that first time. And more important, the boy is well on his way to becoming the man that Shane had envisioned when he said: "I like a man who watches things going around. It means he'll make his mark some day." Now, however, before he speaks his last, Shane does not confirm Joey's attainment to manhood but counsels greater growth still, exhorts him to make of growth itself his life's enduring aim. "You go home to your mother and your father and grow up to be *strong* and *straight*. And Joey, take care of them, both of them." The child is indeed father to the man, yet not because the essential man is ever present in the tranquil recollections of times past, but because the energies of new life shall reinvigorate alike the exhausted

(Joe) and the merely hopeful (Marian). Strength becomes not might (not even the might of the will to power) but the force of the man's devotion to all life, the power to reverence it not by remembering merely but by investing it continually with novelty and possibility. To grow straight answers not to the obedience of old laws and precepts but to the creation of an integral oneness with life, that "integrity" whereby the soul celebrates its unfolding emergence into a world made more generous, more varied, more beneficent, by its immersion in life and living. Surely such a wish for new life attains to the status of the noblest prayer—prayer that *praises*, as Bill Robinson used to teach, rather than pleads.

If the man Joey now calls after is his hero, what blame to him? This business of growing can be most intimidating—and not just at first. As Shane rides away, Joey falls back upon the lore of the young hero-worshipper. He runs after him, shouting: "He'd [Morgan Ryker] never had been able to shoot you if you had seen him." And then, after Shane's "Bye, Little Joe," with tears running down his cheeks: "He'd [Jack Wilson] never even have cleared the holster, would he Shane?" Now coming around to look at Shane, who already has his back to him, riding toward the Grand Tetons, he resorts to another tactic: "Pa's got things for you to do. And mother wants you. I know she does." Then the plea becomes desperate; straining his eyes after him, perhaps realizing that he is not returning, his words echoing throughout the valley: "Shane! Shane! Come back!" But immediately after a dissolve from a tight close-up, as Shane rides up the mountain and disappears screen left, just where he appeared in the first shot, when he rode down into the valley, Joey shouts: "'Bye, Shane!" He answers Shane's farewell in kind, and thus acknowledges his individuality in the very moment he lets go of the hero. Shane never leaves him, however, no matter the many sunsets that he may yet ride into. For Joey has become Shane, not the gunfighter but the man cutting through place, tearing down fences. But also more than Shane: for it is vouchsafed to him to expand the terrain of the moral imagination beyond the expanse of it deeded him by Shane. He has seen Shane ride in and through and out, and has completed with him the 180° revolution that renders paradise not place but action, not boundaries but possibilities. He thus becomes more than the cartographer of a new Eden, for he is also its first denizen, at once inventor and discoverer. Yet what Adam shall grow in this garden of adventures is not as important as is the deed of vision that becomes ours through him—ours not to copy or preserve but rather ours as a lure to action, propelling us onward to the confident pursuit of dreams beyond, where place becomes a journey, where art transforms life.

After Words: The Western Movies of John Ford and Sam Peckinpah

A. Carl Bredahl, Jr.

THE WESTERN STORY plays a particularly important role within the context of the American imagination, for the western story explores and communicates the strengths and responsibilities of human life within social and physical ecosystems. Consciousness of surfaces leads to consciousness of rhythms common to the individual and to his environment, opening the way for new relationships and a new story.

Readers of canonical contemporary American literature are all too aware of its tormented voices, voices that reflect a loss of the sense of place. Because distrusting place leads to overweening ego, a sense of superiority within an ecosystem, and isolation, opening the canon to western as well as ethnic and feminist perspectives offers a significant corrective to the perspective of modern alienation.

Throughout my discussion I have focused on prose fiction, arguing that works accepted into the traditional literary canon have in common a preoccupation with enclosure based upon discomfort with the openness of space. This imagination finds the energy of the physical environment stimulating, but it is convinced that without the human commitment to enclosing and reshaping the natural, stimulation too often produces anarchy. This imagination therefore works within physical (houses, forts) or social (class structure) or cultural (myth) enclosures. In contrast, another aspect of the American imagination seeks to realign itself with the openness of space.

Narrative, of course, is not limited to prose fiction. The implications of my argument extend beyond the literary to the visual and practical arts and even to politics and foreign policy, where enclosed image has long had a troubling centrality. I will focus here on the visual arts, in particular on the western movies of two of America's most prominent directors, John Ford and Sam Peckinpah, whose work evidences the contrasting responses to the demands of space. Ford, an easterner by familial and cultural background, is attracted to but strongly distrusts space; his movies argue for the advantages of enclosure despite the unfortunate loss of energy it causes. Peckinpah, a westerner who is an outsider when judged by establishment values, loves to work with the challenges of open land. Each man narrates a particular story of change; together, their work demonstrates the diversity of the American imagination.

John Ford's vision of the West is quintessentially traditional.[1] He sees the West as simultaneously harsh and magnificent. The Monument Valley setting used in so many of his westerns is undeniably beautiful, but its beauty is most appreciated from a distance. Up close, the landscape threatens to swallow or violate the individual or group. Consequently, the setting of a Ford movie makes humanity and civilization appear highly vulnerable.[2] The beauty of the West must therefore always be placed within frameworks that offer protection to the white man and his values—I emphasize "the white man" because Ford's movies see the Indian as an element of the threatening land. When Indian vulnerability appears, it results from eastern interference. Ford's primary concern is civilization as the white man knows it.[3]

Consequent upon the concern for civilized values is the fact that Ford's western movies are highly protective of young white women— Dallas *(Stagecoach)*, Clementine Carter *(My Darling Clementine)*, Philadelphia Thursday *(Fort Apache)*, Olivia *(She Wore a Yellow Ribbon)*, and Debbie Edwards *(The Searchers)*, to mention a few. The casting of these roles emphasizes female vulnerability. Cathy Downs, Shirley Temple, and Natalie Wood all have delicate features that image fragility. Even when more visually aggressive women are cast—Joanne Dru and Maureen O'Hara, for example—their carriage and costumes indicate that they, like Cathy Downs and Shirley Temple, embody the refinements of civilization.

A Ford western therefore has much in common with James Fenimore Cooper's *The Last of the Mohicans* in that both feature the movement of young women into the interior of the wilderness. Their presence necessitates army troops and sheltering forts, but Cooper explodes his shelters, casting individual family members into the wilderness. Ford never portrays that kind of story—the struggles of the one female forced to live in the wilderness, Debbie Edwards in *The Searchers,* are not part of the movie. In Ford, threatening wilderness is held in check by representatives of society and by communities that strengthen as they pull together. Though Ford's doubts about the complete goodness of civilization are suggested in several places—for example, in *The Man Who Shot Liberty Valance* (1962)—such doubts are always subordinated to maintaining traditional values.

Stagecoach (1939) began John Ford's love affair with a carefully constructed image of the West. If we keep in mind the dusty, crumbling stagecoach that figures prominently in *Liberty Valance,* the earlier movie begins a story that concludes in *Liberty Valance* with Hallie Stoddard noting that the wilderness has finally been turned into a garden. However, there is no visual garden in 1939 or, for that matter, in 1962. The title of *Stagecoach* points to what the movie is all about, focusing our attention on the tiny, fragile enclosure carrying individuals of distinct social classes through a barren, threatening landscape. Even worse, the Indian inhabitants of that landscape have broken loose and begun to destroy. Appropriate to Ford's values, the one image of Indian destruction is a burning enclosure and a dead, very young, and very pretty woman.

The enclosure that is the stagecoach is pulled (it has no power to move itself) through the threatening landscape by numerous teams of horses guided by the capable but exceedingly nervous hands of Buck. Andy Devine plays Buck, and Devine will reappear in *Liberty Valance* as the town marshal of Shinbone, where he is incapable of maintaining law and order. The casting of the bumbling Devine as the driver in *Stagecoach* reinforces the image of vulnerability as the coach tries to work its way to the suggestively named town of Lordsburg. *Stagecoach* carries viewer and passenger from one physical construct to another, and most of its story takes place in a town or stage stop or the stagecoach itself. A relatively small amount of emphasis is given to the camera looking at the surroundings. Wilderness, in other words, is more a brooding concern than a reality in this movie, a technique that increases the terror associated with the physical world.

Ultimately, of course, neither Buck nor the stagecoach can protect the individuals inside. In an important and highly effective scene late in the movie, the camera pulls back to show the tiny stage racing across flats so barren that they might have been filmed on the moon. Savages chase behind, and clearly it is only a matter of moments before they will catch the fleeing stage. When all the little society's ammunition has been used on the Indians, destruction seems inevitable. But out of nowhere appears the cavalry, civilization's official protective arm on the frontier. The Indians are routed and the stage brought safely to Lordsburg, where the second concern of the movie, cruelty among men, is reconciled. Dallas and Ringo depart in the final scene to marry and settle down on Ringo's ranch.

Stagecoach presents us with a political as well as a social statement about the need of individual members of society to work together and draw upon the forces of law and order to defeat natural savagery inherent in any wilderness condition. After all, 1939 was the year savagery was threatening what Europe and America stood for, and it is not surprising that Ford was then concerned with the relationship of enclosure and wilderness. That he sets his concern in the ominous landscape of Monument Valley says a great deal about his perception of the West as a place to test and hone the values of civilization.

The implications established in *Stagecoach* are carried forward and explored in Ford's later westerns, all of which appear after World War II.[4] The title of *My Darling Clementine* (1946) and the music that accompanies the opening credits once again emphasize the vulnerability of the woman, a figure who, as the song says, is lost and gone forever. In several of his movies, Ford relies heavily on opening music to establish an upbeat tone that will prove dominant in spite of wilderness threats; the particular songs played, "My Darling Clementine," "Jeanie with the Light Brown Hair," and "She Wore a Yellow Ribbon," all praise the joys (and loss) of young womanhood.

Even though she will not appear until almost halfway through the movie, Clementine Carter is central to *My Darling Clementine* because of the values she brings to Tombstone, Arizona. Shortly after Wyatt Earp enters the town in the movie's opening minutes, he asks a question that is often repeated: "What kind of a town is this?" That question, and Clementine Carter, are what the movie is all about. *Stagecoach* visualized the dangers inherent in trusting oneself outside of the town construct. Once Ringo kills Hank Plummer, the town of Lordsburg is presumably safe for families. *My Darling Clementine* brings us out of the wilderness (as the movie opens) and into the town of Tombstone, where families are not safe; it then confronts the nature of civilized societies. At the end, when the town has been made safe for young people such as Clementine, Wyatt Earp rides on.

Given the centrality of Clementine Carter, the threat posed by the Clantons (a family without women) is not possible confrontation with the Earps but harm to the traditional values of family and culture. The movie's setting emphasizes the fragile nature of the town within the enormity of surrounding wilderness, but physical wilderness is of minor concern. Earp's question—"What kind of a town is this?"— asks about human wilderness and the need for culture (Shakespeare), women (Clementine), churches, and effective law enforcement. Against those forces, the Clantons are doomed, and we know all along that they are doomed—given the fact that the story of the Clanton/Earp shoot-out at the OK Corral is so great a part of western mythology. The Clantons are largely a brooding off-camera presence. The tone of the opening "My Darling Clementine," the seriousness with which Granville Thorndyke delivers Hamlet's soliloquy, and the placing of church and communal celebration at the center of the movie combine to make us believe in these values rather than worry about the Clantons. Having no fears about Wyatt and his brothers emerging victorious, we can enjoy the focus on the civilizing process.

After *My Darling Clementine,* Ford's story moves back into the wilderness, and the cavalry becomes the center of attention rather than the *deus ex machina* it was in *Stagecoach.* Though towns and presumably western civilization after World War II have been made safer, moving the subject of the movies to the communal life within wilderness forts suggests that western society continues to need vigilance and protection. Even the figures of Hank Plummer, Old Man Clanton, and Doc Holliday from the earlier movies indicated that the internal problems of white society itself are ultimately greater threats than the external savages. With *Fort Apache* (1948), *She Wore a Yellow Ribbon* (1949), and *Rio Grande* (1950), the same holds true. The movies again value women and family, as evidenced by such songs as "There's No Place like Home" and "I'll Take You Home Again, Kathleen."

The cavalry in *Stagecoach* arrived at the last moment to destroy savagery and to protect women and a newborn baby. *Fort Apache* opens with another stagecoach, which brings the new cavalry commander, Lieutenant Colonel Owen Thursday, and his daughter into the wilderness. Thursday curses the land, while his daughter (Shirley Temple) plays with his frustration and clearly enjoys the prospects of their new life. We do not open, in other words, with an externally threatened stagecoach and a timid female protected by soldiers. The appropriately named young lady from the East, Philadelphia, is in fact so in command of herself and the young men who surround her that she never seems threatened. Moreover, though the Indians commit terrible acts, the movie asks us to share their shame and outrage when Thursday humiliates them and treats them as a people without honor. We continue, therefore, to see society as a vulnerable construct set within a threatening environment, but the fort is much more protected than the earlier stagecoach. The commander of the fort and his strengths and weaknesses are the objects of focus; the threat to Fort Apache is primarily internal.

As the cavalry trilogy develops, the internal problem intensifies through two new elements in the Ford story. *She Wore a Yellow Ribbon* spends a great deal of time outside the fort, and Ford filmed the movie not just in color but in spectacular postcard color. The commander of the cavalry, Captain Nathan Brittles (played by John Wayne), is aging, and possible future commanders, such as Lieutenant Flint Cohill, seem too young for the task. The two new elements in the Ford story are therefore the almost unreal visual beauty of the physical wilderness and the image of loss prominent in the human story. When Captain Brittles saves both Indian and white from battle by driving away the Indians' horses, no one is hurt. We are left at the movie's end to worry more about the abilities of young Olivia and Flint Cohill than about a wilderness that has been visually highlighted more for its beauty than for its danger.

In 1956, loss becomes the entire subject of the appropriately entitled *The Searchers*. *Stagecoach* and *My Darling Clementine* asserted the need to build defensive personal and social structures in order to protect vulnerable values. In the cavalry trilogy, that theme was maintained but overshadowed by a sense of internal loss. The title of the 1956 movie makes it clear that loss is now real and search the central concern. The object of the search is embodied in the figure of the young girl, Debbie Edwards. Ethan Edwards, her uncle (played by John Wayne), searches for her accompanied by a young man of mixed blood, Martin Pawley. Ethan is retired from the southern army, a man who does not believe in surrender and who has lost to his brother the woman he loved, Mary Edwards. Throughout the movie, Ethan's driving passion is hatred, particularly hatred for savages.

Like *Yellow Ribbon*, *The Searchers* is filmed in almost extravagant color. When combined with Ethan's hatred of Indians, the intense color suggests something self-destructive working within the movie, for we are presented simultaneously with extremes of the land's beauty and with the central figure's hatred of the people who inhabit that land. The conflict thus established parallels that in Ethan, who remains so intensely loyal to the defeated South that he will not accept the authority of Samuel Clayton, captain of the Texas Rangers. Ethan is the ultimate loner, not, as with Cooper's Natty Bumppo, because of a love for the land but because of a strong sense of loss—loss of Mary to his brother, loss of the South, and loss of the beauty once found in the West.

Ethan searches for those things he has lost, a search that appropriately finds its object in a young girl. A defender of virginity. Ethan cannot deal with either the actual fact or the metaphorical implications of Debbie's having become the squaw of Chief Scarface; his response to loss of virginity is to destroy both the individual violated and the source of violation. The title and the plot of the movie finally force us to ask what is the object of Ethan's search—youth? family? daughter?—and why that search is undertaken. Ethan is part of the past, an intense and bitter man who becomes like the savages he hunts.

Set against Ethan's bitterness is the rollicking relationship of Martin Pawley and Laurie Jorgensen. Vera Miles plays Laurie and, in the 1962 *Liberty Valance,* Hallie Stoddard, imaging the appearance in Ford's later work of a woman no longer completely dependent upon male protection. Both Laurie and Hallie pursue and win men considerably different from the now obviously aging John Wayne figure so central throughout Ford's westerns. Martin Pawley and Ransom Stoddard are easterners and young men capable in their own right. For example, in the opening of *The Searchers,* Martin spots a problem with the Indian trail before Ethan does, for the latter is at that moment busily caught up in denouncing Martin for calling him "Uncle." Martin and Ransom are young men characterized as less traditionally masculine than the rugged John Wayne, so the Edenic, beautiful world of the embittered Ethan Edwards is being replaced by that of a new breed of male (talented but somewhat comic) and female.

When Nora Ericson, in *The Man Who Shot Liberty Valance,* tells her husband to go put his pants on, we find ourselves at the end of the John Ford western. In fact, *Liberty Valance* is a movie about the death of the western, as Ford imagined that story. The movie is therefore appropriately shot in black and white, a fact that in 1962 and after the spectacular color of *Yellow Ribbon* and *The Searchers* certainly calls attention to itself. The color has quite literally gone out of the Ford story. Reinforcing that death, the natural magnificence of Monument Valley is replaced by a setting that forces us to be conscious of its artificiality—even the makeup used for Pompey, Ranse, and Hallie during the opening and closing sequences calls attention to itself. As Robert Ray has discussed, the reverse camera shot of Liberty's death makes it clear that we cannot assume anything about the reliability of what the camera shows.[5] Finally, the major story line is told in flashback, a technique that keeps before us the black-and-white modern world of Senator Ranse Stoddard while pushing the West of Tom Doniphon far into the past. The cruel Liberty Valance is killed, but much continues to trouble the imagination of John Ford. Tom Doniphon (John Wayne), the color and energy of Ford's West, is dead; his coffin occupies center stage.

Ford's movies have significant titles, and *The Man Who Shot Liberty Valance* is no exception. On the surface, the title is ironic, seeming to refer to

Ranse Stoddard, though we eventually learn that it was Tom Doniphon who shot Liberty Valance. Both title and movie, while appearing to focus on Ranse and his rise to political power, in reality focus on the demise of Tom and his once colorful world. Equally prominent in the title and the movie is the man Tom shoots, the curiously named Liberty Valance. In spite of the confrontation between them, Doniphon and Valance are part of the same world that has yielded its energy to the law books of Ransom Stoddard. Tom and Liberty, for example, both use their guns to humble Stoddard by spilling a bucket of liquid on him; both expect Ranse to use a gun in self-defense or to get out of town. Ranse, in the restaurant scene, even yells that Tom is no different from Liberty. Thus, when Tom kills Liberty, he kills a central part of his own world, hastening the death that the movie makes the subject of its interest.

And surely we are invited to play with the various implications of the fact that the vicious Valance should be named Liberty.[6] We cheer his death and that of the repression he embodied, but the movie is also concerned about the "liberty" that replaces him. When Pompey, Tom's black companion, forgets the words "that all men are created equal" in his effort to describe Jefferson's document, Ranse notes that "a lot of people forget that line." Further, Maxwell Scott, editor of the *Shinbone Star,* tells Senator Stoddard that he cannot accept the senator's privacy—"purely personal is not good enough for my readers"—and that in fact he has a right to know the story of Tom Doniphon. Finally, when Custis Buck Langhorn is nominated to go to Washington, his supporters celebrate using a horse and cowboy rider to the music of "Home on the Range," but the scene is shot in a narrow hall which emphasizes restriction and confinement. Moments such as these raise questions about the nature of "liberty" in Ranse's world.

In the movie's final moments, Hallie Stoddard speaks of the fact that the wilderness is now a garden and asks her husband 'Aren't you proud?" The tone of her voice is absolutely neutral, and we are not surprised. We are not surprised because the line can be uttered in different ways, can underscore achievement or express sorrow. And that ambiguity is a fitting statement for the final effect of *The Man Who Shot Liberty Valance.*

Collectively, these movies, which span the years from 1939 to 1962, describe the imagination of John Ford in its preoccupation with enclosure. Though his imagination is attracted to the color, freedom, and energy of the West, it is committed to enclosing and reshaping wilderness in order to make it safe for young women, families, and Shakespeare. Like Crevecoeur, Parkman, Brown, Hawthorne, Adams, James, and Faulkner, John Ford finds wilderness stimulating to individual possibility but threatening to civilized values.

With *The Searchers* and *The Man Who Shot Liberty Valance,* possibility and threat are integrated in the figure of Ethan Edwards and in the relationship between Doniphon and Valance. Though we feel a loss as color goes out of the West, the movies indicate that without white man's laws and order, the line between individual and savage is indeed very fine.

A sense of loss for a myth of great beauty is the dominant impression created by the western movies of John Ford. With the energy gone, we are left with necessary but troubling questions about the future. Ford's story is thus part of the dominant eastern tradition of Owen Wister and Zane Grey. In contrast, the movies of Sam Peckinpah produce a very different final impression. Peckinpah carries forward that story begun by Lewis Garrard and Mary Austin and developed by Ernest Hemingway and Wright Morris.

1962 was the year of release for both Ford's *Liberty Valance* and Peckinpah's *Ride the High Country,* movies that seem to invite comparison as statements of loss. I have already discussed Ford's movie as one that focuses on the coffin of a man whose image had for two decades been made to represent the West. John Kitses says that "the elegiac tone [in *Ride the High Country*] of an autumnal world marks the passing of the old order."[7] And Paul Seydor finds in the movie's final shot "the effect of loss made visually poignant by the absence of Gil in the frame as Steve is left alone to look for one last time at the western horizon before turning slowly and lowering himself to the ground and to death."[8] Such comments urge a similarity between Ford and Peckinpah's concern with loss, but I do not find them accurate statements of what happens in this early expression of Peckinpah's imagination.[9]

In the introduction to the second chapter of this study, I indicate that what characterizes the noncanonical imagination is a rejection of eastern enclosures, both physical and mental, and a struggle to narrate the fascination with space and to thereby accept and draw upon the possibilities of wilderness. The effort to narrate exploration of, rather than taming of, the frontier marks the work of this imagination. Western "frontier" is an area of continual opening rather than a receding point between civilization and wilderness. I began with landscape because it is the land that initially draws the eye out into its act of exploration. In Mary Austin and Ernest Hemingway, land and the rhythms of the land are primary; in Guthrie and Fergusson, an individual struggles to relate his life to the physical environment; and Clark's *The Ox-Bow Incident* explores human relationships in the new high country. Exploration of a continually opening frontier is not synonymous with mapping out and taming the land. In these terms Sam Peckinpah's imagination is a crucial part of spatial exploration. Beginning with the land, Peckinpah emphasizes a visual world, using primarily images rather than ideas. He moves from one moment of possibility to another, less interested in past or future than in the multiple directions of an ever-changing present. And given Peckinpah's western heritage, it would indeed be surprising if he and the eastern John Ford told the same story.

What discussions of *Ride the High Country* fail to see in the movie is the centrality of Heck Longtree. If we focus on the story of the old-timers Gil Westrum and Steve Judd, making the romance of Heck and Elsa Knudson a conventional subplot, then the dying of Steve in the final frame does indeed conclude a story of loss.[10] However, when we look at the movie, we see that it involves the four characters, particularly the three men, equally. The story that emerges, then, transfers power from one generation to another. Peckinpah has been quoted in several places saying that "I have never made a 'Western.' I have made a lot of films about men on horseback."[11] The distinction is important, for it indicates that Peckinpah's movies are more about people within a physical world than about celebrating any particular region. The distinction is also useful in interpreting *Ride the High Country,* which is not a conventional western but a movie about men on horseback. It is not a story of the lost wonder that was the West; it is, rather, one of young people taking the reins of power from an aging generation, discovering the land, and beginning to explore their "place" within it.

Both *She Wore a Yellow Ribbon* and *The Searchers* set the image of the aging John Wayne against that of a young man who would be the future. Taking Martin Pawley *(Searchers)* as an example and comparing him with Heck Longtree, we find a considerable difference between Ford's and Peckinpah's visions of the future. Martin Pawley is likable and talented, but he is not John Wayne—few men are. Martin is a somewhat comic figure, easily manipulated by women—the Indian Look and Laurie Jorgensen. No one need feel depressed about a future of people like Martin and Laurie, but the movie makes clear that the world of Ethan Edwards is over. Heck Longtree is also likable and talented, but he is going to be able to build upon the values of Steve Judd. More than anyone else in *High Country,* Heck grows during the course of the movie. In many ways, the movie is his story and is therefore a story of growth that compensates for the necessary loss through death that occurs at the end. When Heck is first introduced to Steve Judd, the camera does everything it can to show that Heck has no interest in looking at Steve; Heck's eyes follow a shapely young waitress. Verbally he returns the matter-of-fact introduction, but visually his eyes demonstrate an interest in sex.

During the course of the movie, Heck's eyes focus more and more on Steve, finally seeing the values embodied in that aging man. Judd's encounter with the Samsons, the father and son who run the bank and hire Judd, emphasizes that Steve's eyes are getting old and that eyesight is crucial to survival. Consequently, to have Heck's eyes finally see both the excitement of a woman's body and the strengths of Steve Judd indicates that his rising up from the death of Judd in no way constitutes loss.

Steve Judd frequently refers to Heck as "Son": "No use tormenting yourself, Son," he says when Elsa is being married to Billy Hammond. And Heck is a son capable of learning; returning his gun to Judd, Heck says, "Sorry, Mr. Judd. I guess I was showing off." With that father-son relationship in contrast to the stultifying relationships of the Samsons or of Joshua Knudson and Elsa, the dying of Judd finally opens the future for Heck.[12] And Heck has always shown himself anxious to take advantage of openings: the camel race, Gil Westrum's proposal of robbery, Elsa's apparent willingness to intimacy. The first visit to Elsa's house contains a scene shot with Elsa inside (her father's world is one of the enclosing structures) washing dishes beside an open window. Suddenly Heck's head and shoulders appear through the window, and he invites Elsa to meet him outside. His willingness to take advantage of openings together with his growing willingness to see the strengths of Steve Judd establish Heck as the figure through whom this movie moves toward a beginning.

The camera has been active from the opening frame. The camera does not just give us an angle from which we can watch the action; it actively searches out, explores the world around it. This quality is particularly evident in the opening exploration of the high country's green land, in the early street scenes, in the crowd shots at Kate's Place in Coarsegold, and in the discovery of Knudson's dead body. And, when death pulls Steve Judd to the ground in the final frame, the camera does not freeze on a dead body; it moves up, back to the green of the high country. The lowering body thus implies that we are on the verge of seeing something rise. That something need not necessarily be Heck, but the sexual juices stirring in the characters, the activity of the camera, and the impressive growth of both Heck and Elsa suggest that *Ride the High Country* is a story of the integral bond between death and new life.

Major Dundee (1964) is a story of union, in every sense of the word.[13] In fact, what carries through between *High Country* and *Major Dundee* is Peckinpah's vision of union. The movie opens with a series of divisions that dominate much of the story's surface: verbal/visual; soldier/Indian; Union/

Confederate; Dundee/Tyreen. The list could be extended—white/black; Scottish/Irish; male/female; European/American; United States/Mexico—but the striking characteristic of the movie is that it is not a story of confrontation and division. In spite of seemingly endless individual confrontations, overriding everything is the impulse to union. Consequently, setting the story in 1864–65, when the Civil War was drawing to its close, emphasizes both the problem attacked and the effort being made during the movie. The story ends April 19, 1865, four days after the death of Lincoln, a time in America of needed healing.

The initial shot in *Major Dundee* has Corporal Ryan's *Journal* being opened and words spread out before us. We do not move from words to image; rather, the visual burns through the page, flames consuming words and leaving us with events. The effort to burn away divisive intellectual constructs is the imaginative thrust propelling the movie. Thus, after the opening scenes of destruction, the Apache Sierra Charriba asks defiantly, "Who will you send against me now?" and the movie itself answers with the words of the title and the background song, "Fall in Behind the Major." Words, music, and images-an integrated effort—respond to Charriba's defiance and destruction. As the song concludes, falling in behind the major is essential for the individuals to get home again.

Probably the line repeated most frequently throughout the movie is given initially as the Confederate Ben Tyreen's condition for working with the Yankee Amos Dundee: "Until the Apache is taken or destroyed." Literally, of course, the line has only one meaning, but as the movie progresses and the line is repeated, who or what "Apache" signifies begins to seem less certain. This is, after all, a border story, a story about thieves, deserters, renegades, blacks, and gentlemen of the South who leave the territory of the United States and cross the border into Mexico, chasing the Apache. The initial reason for the chase, to rescue captured children, is quickly disposed of as the children return and are sent north. Thus we have to ask about the concerns that really motivate the movie, Major Dundee, and his troops as they cross the border to take or destroy the Apache.

Movement into Mexico strips away external authority, so the chaotic band and the individuals within it are on their own. Unity can no longer be imposed; conditions now lay bare the dangerously divisive nature of their enterprise. North of the border, Dundee's authority is supported by rank and the superior Union force within his fort. South of the border, authority and rank crumble. When Lieutenant Graham tries to get the men together to march, chaos and confusion surround his assertion of authority by rank, and he is ineffectual, if humorous. No external authority is in place to keep Captain Tyreen and his Confederates from fleeing to join other Confederate troops, but they do not desert because Tyreen has given Dundee his word. Once the men are over the border, the destructive implications of their division become immediately evident when racial conflict erupts. "Until the Apache is taken or destroyed" begins to sound as though it were directed at a savagery at the core of the men, individually and collectively, that must be confronted before union can become a possibility.

Confronting savagery is central to the movies of John Ford as well as Sam Peckinpah, but the differences between the two are important. In Ford, savage wilderness is a direct threat to civilized values, and the threat must be met by the forces of law and order. The Cathy Downs/Shirley Temple/Natalie Wood figures must be protected from something external to them. In Peckinpah, savagery is not an evil to be held outside the walls of civilization but a distortion of internal energy. That energy therefore needs to be transformed from its destructive to its constructive possibilities. Women play a role in Peckinpah's movies unlike that in Ford's. The image of a woman like Senta Berger (Teresa Santiago in *Major Dundee*) contrasts sharply with the image of Cathy Downs or Shirley Temple. Berger's body is lush, and despite her declaration that the soldiers will not find what they want in the village, her gesture of opening her shawl indicates that they will find at least what she has to give. Berger's standing beside the village's ruined columns nicely images the vitality, the life existing within her that will replace impermanent efforts to build structures or violent efforts to destroy. In Ford's *Fort Apache*, Tombstone, Arizona, offers law and order and a church to counter the surrounding barren wasteland; in *Major Dundee,* the Mexican village offers flesh-and-blood people-their joys and their love. A different kind of energy exists in the latter—a natural energy referred to by Teresa when she says that she is with Major Dundee because she has seen too much dying, that she wants them both to "feel alive."

Major Dundee concludes with the remnant of the army uniting under Dundee's command and under the colors of the Union to battle European forces in Mexico before moving back into Texas. The movie ends as they slowly ride away from us, their faces weary—in particular that of Sergeant Chillum (Ben Johnson). Only one song is played, whereas earlier, Union and Confederate singing had fought for center stage. Four years later, Peckinpah's next movie, *The Wild Bunch* (1969), opens with a group of men riding toward the camera. Ben Johnson's face (now Tector Gorch) effects the carryover between the two bunches of men. After *The Wild Bunch, The Ballad of Cable*

Hogue (1970) will move us from the group to the single individual; but before the individual is allowed to emerge, our attention is focused on the wildness of the group.

Like *Major Dundee, The Wild Bunch* opens with a shot that indicates the movie is going to be concerned with the tension between and the transformation of an old form to a new one. In *Major Dundee,* the words of Ryan's *Journal* were burned through by images that carried the movie until the final shot, when the *Journal* is closed. The opening of *The Wild Bunch* unites the active camera of *Ride the High Country* and the transformed medium of *Major Dundee.* Now the opening shots establish a defined and frozen world in conflict with movement. We first see a black-and-white still image of the bunch. The still then breaks into color and movement. The camera then immediately moves off center, the image freezes once again into black and white, and the words *The Wild Bunch* appear. As though searching for the activity of the individuals in the bunch, the camera moves back to center on the frozen image, and once again color and activity appear. This interchange continues between the verbal black-and-white freezing and the effort of the camera to find faces. The extent of the freezing is most apparent when the bunch finally enters the town of Starbuck and the voice of the revival preacher rings out in the background; even the preacher's voice is stilled when the freezing occurs ("Now, folks…"), and it picks up exactly where it left off when action returns ("…that's from the good book"). The centering action of the camera is evident when children playing with a scorpion and ants become the focus of its interest—even their faces are searched by the moving camera. The opening of *The Wild Bunch* therefore values activity, color, and the individual, and that valuing is going to be the concern of the entire movie. Not until the next movie will our attention be entirely on an individual, although during *The Wild Bunch* we do search for individuals within the bunch. That kind of exploration constitutes the primary western element in the imagination of Sam Peckinpah.

We also search for the source of the bunch's wildness, a search made more interesting with John Ford and Mary Austin in mind. The imagination of Ford would never value the bunch; towns and forts are central to the stability of Ford's world. In Peckinpah, however, towns are sterile, and the forces of law and order are cruel and despotic. Austin said in *The Land of Little Rain* that "lawlessness" was a favorite topic of the eastern imagination in depicting the West, but the West had laws of its own. In the movies of Peckinpah, the lawlessness of civilized stability presents a center of attention. In *The Wild Bunch,* Harrigan of the railroad and Mapache of the Federales are the representatives of law and order, but they are vicious and corrupt. In this context, the wildness of the bunch seems more an expression of frustrated internal energies than a destructive principle harmful to civilization. The wildness of the bunch connects most closely with the lush bodies of the Mexican women, suggesting that in these two forces-energy and flesh—lie the dynamics of life. The bunch thus seems wild only to someone like Harrigan, for example, who must destroy it if his railroad empire can exist without threat. Neither in their home base nor in Angel's village is the bunch truly wild.

Many readers may feel that I am downplaying the violence in Peckinpah's work. This response, with which I do not agree, is not surprising: readers of canonical American literature, who have been trained in certain expectations and assumptions, are going to be made uncomfortable by many products of the western imagination. To them, *The Land of Little Rain* lacks form; *Green Hills of Africa* is self-indulgent posturing; *The Home Place* spreads itself too thin between text and photos; *This House of Sky* offers little more than pleasant biography; and the movies of Sam Peckinpah are politically irresponsible in their celebration of violence. I noted earlier that readers of *Main-Travelled Roads* have consistently failed to respond to the work's optimistic elements, and viewers who come away from Peckinpah's movies concerned about the violence they portray have similarly overlooked the laughter and the joy that equally characterize his work.

The common denominator running through many eastern responses to western narrative is the sense that something in the work does not come up to the expectations or standards of canonical narrative. However, given that the enclosed stance of canonical work develops from the conviction that the demands of the physical world run counter to the best possibilities of contemporary civilization, I would argue that western literature's "failure" is that it is not as negative as is traditional literature about the physical world. To the contrary, the westerner seems to be moving in the direction of sharing with the Indian and the Chicano an appreciation of the relationships among members of an environment. Instead of building "a world elsewhere" designed to preserve egos and a fixed set of values, as is amply demonstrated in Francis Parkman's *The Oregon Trail,* the western imagination asks about individual "place" within ecosystems. Because the ecosystems themselves contain violence, violence in Cooper or Austin or Fergusson or Hemingway or Morris or Peckinpah should be neither surprising nor troubling.

Building "a world elsewhere" is not a violent act; if anything, it seeks to avoid those activities of the physical world that appear unseemly to civilized tastes. There is not much that one might speak of as violent in Hawthorne or James; there is, of course, much personal and social cruelty, but not much physical violence. One must argue for the opposite in western work—violence occurs, but without any corresponding cruelty. Life is by nature a violent process; life can only take place if individual units of energy are consumed and transformed. In *Walden* the narrator speaks of chastity as the "flowering" of man—a conception that eliminates sexual intercourse or other forms of gross feeding and slights the physical and violent aspects of human life. In contrast, violence appears in western art as the necessary outcome of either of two processes: the natural activity of the physical world (as in *The Land of Little Rain, Green Hills of Africa,* and *Mountain Man)* or the suppression of natural impulses by an enclosing set of structures (as in *The Last of the Mohicans, In Our Time,* and *In Orbit).*

The movies of Sam Peckinpah portray both violent processes. In John Ford's work, violence occurs when white society goes out to tame the physical world, *tame* being a code word for *destroy.* When the cavalry arrives to save the day in *Stagecoach,* for example, it does so by obliterating the Indians—they completely vanish from the screen. In Ford's movies, the desire to wipe out resistance to the onrushing, enclosing civilization justifies violence. It seems to me rather curious that our society understands and applauds such acts. In a world comprehended in terms of right/wrong, good/evil, we support the effort of good to destroy evil using any means at hand—and evil is usually understood to be anything that is not what we define as good. This kind of violence, though unfortunate, we argue, is essential to protect the fragile flower of civilization. From this perspective, which accepts and perhaps appreciates violence in Ford, violent acts in Peckinpah seem at best extraneous, at worst celebrated.

In Peckinpah's movies, violence explodes out of situations that require violent reaction. The explosion is usually the result of cruelty that seems bent on destroying the natural world. In this, violence in Peckinpah's films is similar to the violence at the center of *The Last of the Mohicans:* one can rape and pillage only so long before the victims begin to take action. The cruelty imposed on the young couple in Peckinpah's *Straw Dogs* is another case in point: sooner or later, the gentle mathematics professor will explode in anger. The opening of *The Wild Bunch* concentrates on a group of children delighting in their torture of insects. Moments later, Harrigan's forces open fire on the bunch, and the act leads to the violence that explodes in the town of Starbuck. The bunch is out of date in the modern world (the movie is a border story), and, like the tortured scorpion, they will be crushed by the larger forces of society, in their case the railroad and the Federales. Peckinpah's stories frequently portray an older order being sloughed off, stories in which neither the representatives of the old nor the representatives of the new can really be termed "good guys." It is simply the sloughing that merits the attention of the movie, and the sloughing has violence built into its core. We watch worlds transit from old to new in everything from *One-Eyed Jacks* to *Convoy,* and the changes always involve resistance, force, and violence.

The violence that change involves is especially well portrayed in Peckinpah's *The Wild Bunch,* in which wildness provides a countering force to the repression imposed by so many groups in the movie, from a group promoting temperance to a group promoting Nazism. Whatever energies potentially unite them, the wild bunch is appropriately named, for they, like Amos Dundee's army, continually threaten to come apart. And like Dundee, their leader, Pike Bishop, struggles to keep them together. Ultimately, that internal wildness is more of a threat to their existence than the external pressure exerted by Harrigan or Mapache. In spite of the chaos that comes early in the movie when they discover that they have been tricked, the bunch gradually unites around the values of Pike Bishop. Like Steve Judd in *Ride the High Country,* Pike is aging in body but not in spirit; even the Gorch brothers can see in him the qualities that hold them all together, as is particularly evident in the scene that concludes the chaos of tumbling horses and men after lines became tangled. After Pike tells them that if they can't stick together, they're finished, the bunch watches him painfully mount his horse and ride away. They follow that image.[14] And also like Steve Judd, Pike Bishop dies, and his comrades die. The bunch is obliterated at the end of the movie in a scene of uncontrolled violence. Not loss, however, but transformation from old to new is Peckinpah's story. In *The Wild Bunch* that transformation is evidenced in the several scenes of laughter, a bursting forth of an internal joy that goes beyond the immediate individual, becomes contagious, and pulls in others. When Mapache or the body robbers who follow Deke Thornton laugh, the laughter is cruel and self-centered. Instead of uniting others, it separates them. But not so the laughter of the bunch: Freddie Sikes, the old-timer in the Bunch, begins the laughter after Harrigan's trick of substituting washers for gold has threatened Pike's authority, and it is laughter directed at themselves rather than at someone else. Laughter and childish playing recur frequently. And laughter is the image we are left with at the end after Freddie suggests to Deke that they reunite because they "got some work to do."

The laughter and that final reunion indicate that the transformation, visualized in the opening effort of the camera to seek out faces and turn still photographs into moving images, has worked and is continuing to work. For all the violence, perhaps because of the violence, laughter explodes out of this movie; in spite of the deaths of Pike and his men, a new bunch has work to do.

Peckinpah's imagination also has work to do, more territory to explore, carrying us forward to *The Ballad of Cable Hogue* (1970). The title of *Cable Hogue* indicates that earlier efforts of the camera to find the individual have been completed and that the laughter that rose out of previous violence will be an underlying force in *Cable Hogue*.[15] This movie is the narrative song of a particular individual thrust out of an initial three-man "bunch" who stumbles onto a source of nourishment after yielding up his ego; his final rejection of the desire for revenge makes possible the movement outward from Cable Springs that concludes the movie.

Cable's name indicates that he is a figure who unites. Cable pulls himself together; he establishes an important tie with Hildy; and he connects the efforts in earlier movies to find the individual and in the later movies to ask what that individual might be capable of. This is a movie, therefore, that culminates previous actions in Peckinpah and establishes the possibility of throwing those actions forward.

As one might expect in Peckinpah, the opening shots point the direction of the movie. Instead of burning away or transforming one medium into another, *Cable Hogue* opens with the individual directly confronting the natural world: Cable—and the camera—eyeing a Gila monster. Mary Austin's distinction between westerners' and easterners' view of the land is again useful because Cable is an individual who uses his eyes. He sees the lizard as a needed source of food, in contrast to his partners, who blast it into useless pieces; Cable then discovers that the desert is not ten million gallons of sand, as Bowen and Taggart say; and after discovering water, he looks in both directions along the stage route and "sees" the future transit along that highway and the future need for his water. He also sees Hildy, first with his eyes locked on her breasts and later as the person that she is—"Lady, nobody ever seen you before."

There is a great deal, of course, that Cable does not see or understand. He accidentally stumbles onto the desert water, does not think about filing a claim, cannot read, and has never before seen a car. He is therefore not unlike Pike Bishop, who stumbles into a woman carrying packages as the bunch prepares to rob Starbuck, but both Pike and Cable are able to adjust to opportunity within a given set of circumstances. As a consequence, the narratives of both the bunch and Cable Hogue do not have the linear plot usually employed by Ford and rejected by such midwesterners as Anderson, Hemingway, and Morris. In *Stagecoach,* for example, we know that the effort will be to get a certain number of people by stagecoach to Lordsburg; in *The Searchers,* it will be to find Debbie Edwards; and in *The Man Who Shot Liberty Valance,* it will be to find out what really happened to Tom Doniphon. However, something quite different is working in *The Wild Bunch* and *The Ballad of Cable Hogue.* Though both movies establish early an external plot—Deke Thornton hunting the bunch, Cable seeking revenge—in neither case is that external plot particularly relevant to later events. Instead, events spring internally from previous events. Both Pike and Cable are particularly talented at looking into the moment and seizing upon possibility. The bunch, for example, is not running from Deke; instead, they pick up on Angel's problem with Teresa and his village's problem with the Federales and begin a new adventure. Then, when the opportunity presents itself, they take to the idea of robbing the train. In this, Pike contrasts with Angel, who is so controlled by his desire for revenge that he allows externals to destroy him.

Similarly, Cable Hogue seizes upon a series of accidents to build a flourishing business. Events—such as both appearances of Hildy at Cable Springs—seem to happen fortuitously. We watch Cable's reaction to events; we do not give thought to an overarching plan and are therefore momentarily puzzled by Cable's statement about midway through the movie that he cannot leave with Hildy until "they" return. "They" are Taggart and Bowen, the partners who earlier deserted Cable, but most viewers would feel that Cable has long forgotten them—he has not mentioned them, nor has he been hunting them. In fact, the absence of plot and the presence of the fortuitous are in large part responsible for the lack of public interest in the movie, but to fault the movie for these two characteristics is to miss the importance in Peckinpah of the ability to see possibility inherent in each moment, each individual. Cable's initial concentration on Hildy's breasts, for example, is neither extraneous nor casual plotting; his developing ability to see her as a person is the essence of Cable's story.

As a consequence of being committed to the possibilities of the moment, Cable is not locked into Cable Springs. He gives up not only his desire for revenge against Taggart and Bowen but also Cable Springs. When Hildy returns, Cable is ready to move on, to move with her into new opportunity. That he does not understand the mechanics of the automobile leads to his death and indicates his limitations in the modern world, but his death is not important, and we do not even see him die; he is just gone. Early in the movie, the banker, Cushing, asks about Cable's collateral, and Cable responds, "I'm worth something, ain't I?" At the end, the Reverend Joshua Sloan talks about Cable's worth, and one can argue that Cable's developing worth as a source of value to others has been the focus of the entire movie. The final words are given to his worth; the final images are of machines and people moving out of Cable Springs in several directions as a coyote draws near to drink of the water. The song of Cable Hogue is thus the song of an individual who could find water where others could not, whose joy in life's possibilities is passed on to others. Appropriately, therefore, the concluding song ends with the line, "I'll see what tomorrow will bring."

As my concern has been to contrast two different imaginations rather than detail the complete work of Ford or Peckinpah, I need only briefly mention Peckinpah's films that follow *The Ballad of Cable Hogue*. *Straw Dogs* (1971), *Junior Bonner* (1972), and *The Getaway* (1972) pick up the image of the car, which concludes *Cable Hogue*. And the figure of Kris Kristofferson in both *Pat Garrett and Billy the Kid* (1973) and *Convoy* (1978) integrates the image of the dying horse outlaw and that of the emerging vehicle outlaw. The movies, in other words, continue Peckinpah's interest in exploring the continually opening frontier, in seeing "what tomorrow will bring."

Through the movies of Ford and Peckinpah, I have tried to indicate that in these two men who focus on the common image of the West we have radically different imaginations at work. The resulting stories reflect those characteristics of enclosure and space that I have detailed throughout this book. What is important is not the valuing of one perception over another but the recognizing what necessarily happens when we assume that in America only one imagination has a story to tell. To prefer the movies of John Ford, as traditionalists do, or to regard the work of Sam Peckinpah as politically irresponsible is to see one imagination only through another's eyes and to miss a dynamic, "lawless" story that has been developing in America for almost two centuries. Eastern perceptions such as those of Parkman, James, Faulkner and Ford are greatly troubled by wilderness and turn to the politically and culturally "responsible" values that created civilization as the East knows it, but other imaginations are also at work, fascinated with both the risks and the possibilities of "what tomorrow will bring."

NOTES

1.   To Ford, as to Francis Parkman and most eastern imaginations, the West is less important in itself than in its purpose of reminding how much wilderness needs shaping along traditional civilizing lines. John Baxter, in *The Cinema of John Ford,* says of Ford's cavalry films that "the subject of all these films is seldom the cavalry but rather the order of community life placed in conflict with an opposing destructive force" (p. 79). Andrew Sinclair describes Ford's vision of American history as being shown in the opening sequences of Abraham Lincoln in *The Iron Horse:* "With the father of the nation supporting Manifest Destiny, the building of the railroad to link the United States can be presented as a mission of strong men and iron machines against the resistance of the wilderness and the Indian tribes standing in their way" *(John Ford,* p. 35). Jim Kitses's brief statement in *Horizons West* indicates the inevitable problem created when a viewer is less interested in the object itself than in what it can be made to represent: "The peak comes in the forties when Ford's works are bright monuments to his vision of the trek of the faithful to the Promised Land, the populist hope of an ideal community. …But as the years slip by…we find a regret for the past, a bitterness at the larger role of Washington, and a desolation over the neglect of older values" (p. 13).

2.   Discussing the setting in *Stagecoach,* John Baxter describes Ford's handling of scene: "Ford's style is perfectly mirrored in this landscape, the measured flow of his theme in the flat plain, its dramatic peaks in the sudden eruptions of stone around which he always sets his major battles and dramatic confrontations, while his concept of society, in which man, orderly and respectful of rules, maintains the natural order in the shadow of unassailable principles, seems emblematised in his films of the cavalry fighting and dying among the valley's stones while overhead the omnipresent clouds suggest a higher reality of mind and of the spirit to which all are subservient" *(The Cinema of John Ford,* p. 71).

3.   In Ford, says Andrew Sinclair, "the Apache typify the wild forces of nature and nemesis"; against "the outer chaos of dying and war and wilderness" stand ritual, law, and the Catholic Church, which "guarded the soul as the American navy guarded the shores" *(John Ford,* pp. 81, 133, 135).

4.   The west was his peacetime nostalgia," according to Andrew Sinclair, who sees the postwar *My Darling Clementine* as "a western about the adjustment of natural outsiders to the rule of law and church and family" *(John Ford,* p. 129). This adjustment is enforced by the protective arm of the cavalry in the movies of the late 1940s.

5.   Robert Ray has a fine discussion of this technique in *A Certain Tendency of the Hollywood Cinema, 1930–1980,* pp. 229–37.

6.   "'What a name for a heavy!" [Lee] Marvin said of Liberty Valance. 'I never got over it! Liberty is a dangerous dangerous thing. It requires more discipline than anything else'" (Sinclair, *John Ford,* p. 195).

7. Kitses, *Horizons West*, p. 159.

8. Seydor, *Peckinpah*, p. 40.

9. A fine study of *Ride the High Country, The Ballad of Cable Hogue,* and *Convoy* is Marshall, "Within the Moral Eye—Peckinpah's Art of Visual Narration."

10. Jim Kitses, for example, sums up the movie by focusing on Gil Westrum and Steve Judd: "Discussion of this great work has often erred in relegating the Scott figure [Gil Westrum] to a secondary role. ... But these two heroes, like Dundee and Tyreen, are masks for the same face, expressions of the same spirit, the spirit of the American West. Judd and Westrum, judge and cowboy, vision and violence, Peckinpah insists that both were necessary in a savage land" *(Horizons West,* pp. 159–60). According to Paul Seydor, "The theme is diminishment, disillusion, and compromise" *(Peckinpah,* p. 33).

11. Seydor, *Peckinpah*, p. **32**.

12. Sinclair has noted that father figures and the authority associated with them are central in Ford's movies *(John Ford,* p. 35).* In contrast, father figures inevitably die or are absent in Peckinpah's movies. Peckinpah's are stories of young people transforming their fathers' values and discovering their own way.

13. Both Seydor and Kitses concentrate on the problems of making *Major Dundee;* in spite of those problems, Peckinpah's imagination dominates the movie, and it becomes "the story of a company divided against itself" (Seydor, *Peckinpah,* p. 55). For McKinney, "The problem is in determining who the enemy is" (Sam Peckinpah, p. 64).

14. Peckinpah's interest in images contrasts sharply with Ford's. As several scholars have noted, Ford's movies deny individuality. Because he is primarily concerned with the truth, as he understands it, about country and law, Ford's genius lies in taking stereotypes and creating archetypes (Sinclair, *John Ford,* p. 22). "Characters in Ford's films work under a strong disadvantage; deprived of individuality in favour of embodying the virtues of a society, they are types rather than people, and as they cannot alter without casting doubt on the virtues they represent, their personalities remain frozen in time" (Baxter, *The Cinema of John Ford,* p. 19). The continuing use of John Wayne, for example, creates what is recognized worldwide as the archetypal westerner. Peckinpah, however, finds within each new image its special qualities. When John Wayne rides on camera, the audience knows (rather than sees) what to expect from his character. Not so with William Holden in *The Wild Bunch* or Jason Robards in *Cable Hogue*: we have to focus on the event that is each character to see the story being told.

15. The centrality of the individual is made clear in Cable's early speech: "It's Cable Hogue talkin...Hogue...me...Cable Hogue...Hogue...me...me...I did it ...Cable Hogue...I found it...me." In the course of the movie, Cable will find other individuals and begin to relate to them.

Busby Berkeley and the Tradition of Emersonian Vision

STEVE SNYDER

"The eye is the first circle"
(Emerson, *Experience*)

THE SEPTEMBER 1936 COVER of *The Body Beautiful*, a popular magazine in which Hollywood stars like Marlene Dietrich extol their putative beauty secrets, features a painting of a nude woman (draped only in a diaphanous scarf) floating against a background of glossy black. As I study this remarkable cover, I am reminded of several things at once: first that the composition strongly resembles a William Blake engraving (and, as such, a John Singer Sergeant painting) and second that the cover also looks to be closely derived from the look of one of Busby Berkeley's famous dance routines, many of which would have been contemporary with the magazine. This concept, a luminescent human form buoyed upward from an ebony sea, is a trademark image of several Berkeley dance numbers, for example the "Lullaby of Broadway" number from *Gold Diggers of 1935*, which begins with Winnie Shaw's stylized face floating toward us (or alternately with the camera falling into it). The concept, of course, a milky secretion of light looming upward from the creative dark, would fit the romanticism of William Blake (or Sergeant) as much as it does the romanticism of Busby Berkeley; either reference is merely a debarkation point for reflection. Understanding the magazine cover as a lucky convergence of the two styles, Blake and Berkeley, we can find, I think, a credible and productive point of departure for thinking about Berkeley's cinema, Berkeley's cinema style. Berkeley's style, however, is a multiple style.

If there is a bit of Blake in Berkeley, there is also a resplendent Americanism, a sort of extraverted embrace of gum chewing crudities and public low-brow artifact (see Rubin, 5-35).

Harold Bloom, in various contexts, has suggested that the most distinct quality of American Romanticism, a quality minimized or absent in its European counterparts, is its *rage for vision*, for "seeing" as a moral end (Bloom. 25-45). If European romantics peer inward toward a symbolic landscape, their American counterparts peer outward toward a resistant, foreign challenging world. For Bloom European Romantics are distinguished by an orientation toward inner, or interiorized vision (Blake), while American Romantics, such as Emerson and Thoreau, are characterized by the stress they lay on literal seeing. I find, as a teacher of 19-century American literature, that the "American" portion of Bloom's thesis withstands some degree of scrutiny—Thoreau certainly, as Alfred Kazin and others have documented, narrated his life as a history of vision (Kazin, 63-81); Emerson in his most essential moments imagines himself a prism through which light of the world is refracted in its circulation through a hyaline cosmos (Emerson, 24); Whitman promises to peel the coins from our dead eyes; and Melville, in the midst of penumbral depressions, imagines his whalers sailing through a gigantic eye; Hawthorne's *Blithedale Romance* (as well as Anderson's *Winesburg Ohio*) could be positioned as a prelude to Hitchcock's *Rear Window*; and Henry James, in *The American* or *The Real Thing*, settles the role of protagonist upon the faculty of vision. My interest in this continuum of "spectation" settles upon the manner by which American film assumes a chair at the family table; how as a medium of light, American cinema exploits its very medium in terms of its narrative inheritance, how it modifies, resists or emerges as an individuated child of the American tradition of ocular supremacy.

Emerson, it seems to me, is the originary genius of the American "rage," the one who most fluently distils into language what can said about seeing. Indeed, Emerson's rendition of the Fall of man is a fable of fractured vision, and, as such, supplies a compelling nucleus of insights around which to orbit a discussion of American film. Emerson's first published essay, *Nature*, delineates his version of the "Fall of Man" by crystalizing the circumstance of human alienation from the world in a striking series of tropes of occlusion and transparency:

> The ruin or the blank that we see when we look at nature is in our own eye. The axis of vision is not coincident with the axis of things, and so they appear not transparent but opaque. The reason why the world lacks unity, and lies broken in heaps, is because man is dis-

united with himself… The invariable mark of wisdom is to see the miraculous in the common… To the wise, therefore, a fact is true poetry, and the most beautiful of fables. So shall we come to look at the world with new eyes. It shall answer the endless inquiry of the intellect,—What is truth? and of the affections,—What is good?

(Emerson, 55-56)

In regard to this distinction between the axis of vision and the axis of things, I interpret Emerson to mean, particularly in light of his qualifications within the same paragraph, that our powers of imagination and our powers of direct apprehension are not always aligned. We can imagine the miraculous, while remaining unable see it; we can imagine a reality and we can see, with dulled rapport, a world, but we fail to re-imagine that world in such a way as to experience ourselves as part of its creative continuum. Emerson prompts us to realize that imagination is not a splintered spectre of mind, but, rather, the animating origin of our very power of perception, the agent through which we complete reality. When a French post-structuralist may proclaim that "perception" as such does not exist (Derrida, Lacan, et al), what she or he means by perception is, in fact, identification. My eye slides across the form of a chair and the form registers in my mind as "chair." My mind, at a pre-conscious level, says "this is a chair." This sort of activity implies, of course, cultural-linguistic conditioning. Indeed, I might not see the chair as such (says Lacan somewhere) if I had not been taught to do so. For the post-structuralist the problem ends here. *There is no perception.* For Emerson the problem only begins here, for what the post-structuralist describes as vision is not what Emerson means by seeing at all. Perception, as Emerson fathoms it, begins with the diffusion of those calcified gargoyles of identification which the post-structuralists confuse with sight. Perception begins where the forms of familiar identifiable objects lose their verbally imposed identities and become like shapes in a nonrepresentational painting, elements *sans* external reference in an active field of energy where perceiver joins with the perceived— where the viewer joins the painting so to speak, as an element of the composition, relinquishing his own induced identity in that magnified and decisive moment when content disappears into form…a release not *from* the world, but *into* the world. "I do not," says Matisse somewhere, "paint people, I paint paintings."

And this deep power in which we exist, and whose beatitude is accessible to us, is not only self-sufficing and perfect in every hour, but the act of seeing and the thing seen, the seer and the spectacle, the subject and the object, are one. We see the world piece by piece, as the

> sun, the moon, the animal the tree; but the whole, of which these are the shining parts, is the soul... the soul is not a faculty but a light.., a light shines through us upon things and makes us aware that we are nothing, but the light is all.
>
> (Emerson, *The Over-Soul*)

One sees the bodies of Althusser, Lacan, Derrida and others piled like a cord of wood on a funeral pyre, post-structuralist smoke rising in the azure sky, and all around the children are singing, "we're free, we're free, we're free."

> *The Dance is the highest symbol of life itself.*
>
> – Joseph Campbell in *Reflections On the Art of Living*

Aided by Emerson's blueprint of moral vision, I wish to suggest that Berkeley's gargantuan spectacles have an innate moral dimension to them and that this dimension ought to be thought of in Emersonian terms as a stylistic enterprise, either in the completion of our perception of reality, or in the liberation of perception from the chains of identification. Of course, in this regard one might argue, what makes Berkeley's films any different from any other films? Are not most films, by nature of their medium, attempts at re-visioning our world? And aren't Berkeley's more alienated from a familiar reality than most? I respond by noting that most films may attempt a visual recuperation, but, lamentably, few succeed. Berkeley's do succeed, I believe, by virtue of their almost evangelical celebration of light, their extraordinary savouring of the moving image, their apotheosis of the human form and courage to translate that form into a nonrepresentational element of a composition. Berkeley's films not only jolt our sensibility, they lead that sensibility to a sense of fulfilment in modes which are not only unexpected, but uncharted, and they do so precisely because they can, at any given point, cease to function in terms of the principle of perception as identification. Berkeley's liquid imagery expands the map of the imagination itself. Further, this visionary completion insinuates itself so effectively into our dormant sense of sight specifically because it is conveyed to us as a series of compelling representations of the creative act. The films are moving images of creation just as they are perpetual dissolutions of content into form.

Emerson, also in *Nature*, proposes the existence of a moral nature to vision which is independent of interpretable content:

> There I feel that nothing can befall me in life,—no disgrace, no calamity (leaving me my eyes), which nature cannot repair. Standing

on the bare ground,—my head bathed by the blithe air and uplifted into infinite space,—all mean egotism vanishes. I become a transparent eyeball; I am nothing; I see all; the currents of the Universal Being circulate through me; I am part or parcel of God.

(Emerson, 24)

In this metaphor ego consciousness itself ("I") disappears in the action of intense "seeing." That act of seeing, however, integrates the individual centre of consciousness with the so called actual world, that nature out of which we emerge. Seeing is the aquifer by which we are re-united with our cosmos and with our original imaginal power of vision (our ability to imagine more than the given).

Still, one might accept the notion of redemptive vision as a facet of cinema while doubting the applicability of the concept to the vast, jocular spectacles of Busby Berkeley. Surely, it might be argued, within Berkeley's supererogatory cinema, one's moral imagination is not disclosed to itself as a bride of the universe. My feeling is that all Berkeley's routines and films are thaumaturgic medications for dystrophic vision; they are new as impressionist painting was (and is) in its discovery of light as the true subject of painting—enemies of conventional "content" perception. Berkeley's best numbers are allegories of marriage, whose flower is the release of form from identification: indeed enactments of marriage of the eye to the imagination which sustains and informs it. All Berkeley numbers are, in essence, re-discoveries of the grounds of vision. As such, they must to some degree re-invent us, as well, in so far as they challenge our habituated deformation of light into shadow, awakening our eyes, so to speak, no less than Picasso did, provoking astonishment at the possibilities of the human form as image, surprising us with the repeated transformation of the mundane into the miraculous (like Picasso turning a bike into a Bull, Berkeley will convert a fire-hydrant into an edenic fountain). Indeed, as we witness those endless "rhymed" permutations of human form shape themselves into rough abstract flowers or industrial forms not unlike those of Fernand Leger, we may wonder if Berkeley's "style" is a form of cinematic cubism. If the trajectory of Cubism is the transformation of the human image into volumetric geometry, then Berkeley's work has an occasional affinity with the cubist project. One need only recall those sinuous lines of slightly raffish, sudsy women and sallow faced men, converted into resplendent geometric patterns. Like the cubists, Berkeley paints with an eye toward designs in which the individual human hovers between two modes of reality, matter and light. But enrolling Berkeley in the school of cubism is not my goal, only a way of suggesting an analogy.

I concede that Berkeley's work often detours issues of human loss or suffering, but the films negotiate this deflection by turning back upon themselves in such a way that they become "about" (in terms of traditional notions of content) the construction of that spectacle which they present. The films are, in short, not character studies; but they are valuable, nevertheless, as vehicles of thaumaturgy and as ceremonies of the marriage of Emerson's two poles of vision, the literal and the imaginative. Berkeley's films are temporary victories over gravity in all senses of the word. His moving camera, the most active of its day (Tomlinson, 42) functions as a floating bridegroom of his illuminated scenes. For Berkeley the genre platitude of marriage is turned into an embodiment of the larger marriage of vision; and the sexual core of the physical marriage serves as model of the sinuous additive procedures of a processive imagination.

Now, specifically, it *might* be said that there are two Berkeley visions: one which by its emphasis upon "interiority," seems European rather than American, and another which by its pronounced stress upon the relationship of an outer to an inner world is entirely American, a version of re-imagining quotidian objects, culminating in an Emerson-like fusion of the eye with the imagination. The Berkeley/Bacon collaboration *Wonder Bar* frames for us a version of imagination whose nature, by Bloom's definition, is distinctly European. Interestingly enough, this film is one of the few Berkeley film I know of actually set in Europe (*Roman Scandals, Gold Diggers in Paris* would be two others). The presentation of imaginative act in this film is, I suggest, atypical Berkeley, but, nevertheless, well worth looking at. The "Wonder Bar" is a nightclub hosted by Al Jolson in the middle of Paris. One might say, in fact, the bar is an act of wonder occupying an imaginative space in a fictive city. The "wonder" in this film begins with the credit sequence which features the images of the central actors engendered in the spinning glass door which propels them into the lavish world of the Wonder Bar. This door is a marvellous churning womb, for the characters materialize directly within its centre and not from some vague space behind it—as though there were no outside. They emanate from the glass screen-like door into our spectatorial gaze and into the club itself. It would seem that the club holds a patent of sorts on visibility; one assumes visible form (or one's best visible form) within the space of the club—the space of a club which is the space of the human imagination. The gestation of the visible is made to assume from the "get-go" a decisive moral dimension (as though from a Coleridge or Blake poem) as the home of the self-generated image, that is, of the wonder and inexplicability of creative process, a vision of the act of imagining, itself. The club is a force field in which people achieve *incarnation in light,* a phrase W.R. Robinson used to describe his sense of the metaphysical nature of cinema. Berkeley's work, here, like that of his philosophical namesake, Bishop Berkeley, is a system of proofs against the existence of matter: victories of light over gravity and matter, over suffering and weight. These precipitant faces, therefore, testify to the originary power of imagination in seeing, and the film does much the same. The story confirms the reality of the space defined by Al Wonder's night club, minimizing all that happens outside as being a lesser form of existence.

This opening to *Wonder Bar* points to recurring process, a thematic dimension of the film, creation *ex-nihilio,* which is germane to most of Berkeley's films. I am not concerned with the scientific verifiability of the idea, so much as I am with its existence as an informing agent of Berkeley's work, or of the Berkeley\Bacon collaboration. And with nothing more to fuel our speculations, we might conclude that Berkeley qualifies as an artist who lives predominantly along one axis of Emerson's model of vision: that of a powerful imagination somewhat disjointed from a familiar world. Indeed, Excursions through Berkeley biographies do little to dispel this notion of a one dimensional imagination. He identified his studio space as his own imaginative space and seems to have lived within it for prolonged periods of time. Indeed one biographer (Thomas) relates the story of a Berkeley nuptial which was annulled because the director, so obsessed with his work, hurried from the wedding hall to his studio, never consummating the marriage. The episode suggests that Berkeley's erotic dance profusions are impelled as much by their life as embodiments of creative energy as they are by an agenda of commercial exploitation of sexual desire. Sexuality forms the perfect model for creative act. Emerson's metaphor of the transparent eye finds an almost nonmetaphoric epiphany in Berkeley's works (whose structures repeatedly approach the contours of the eye), and in the man Busby Berkeley, as well, for whom living was nothing less than the persistent merger of his transparent imaginings with the physical tools which produce light and motion. The Berkeley spectacle is a vast transparent eyeball whose subject matters are first, creative vision, second, sexuality within the fabric of social vulcanisation, and finally the integrative synthesizing nature of "imagining"— of seeing in the extended Emersonian way—which telescopes these different lenses together.

The mirror scene in *Wonder Bar* strikes me as a perfect metaphor of a "Transparent eye" kind of imagination. The scene is constructed on a stage manufactured by a girdle of mirrors whose contours define an "interior" imaginative arena while at the same time pointing, by way of infinite reflection, to the difficulty in setting limits on the imaginative space. Space is defined implicitly as that which the hands of imagination create. Here, the space of the dance is generated and multiplied upon itself, out of itself, like a complex cell replicating and growing through RNA exchanges. The dancers generate a kaleidoscopic image, but the reflection of the dancers, taken cumulatively, seem to have a life of their own. The effect, I think, is like that Astair achieves in his Bill Bojangles number in *Swingtime* in which the Astair shadows, near the end of the dance, begin a terpsichore of their own. I would say the Astair number in concept and meaning owes something to Berkeley. The image conveys my sense of one aspect of Berkeley's creative process. *Wonder Bar* projects a world in which almost everything happens within the luminescent imaginative arena which constitutes the nightclub. To enter, or materialize in light there, is to have life, to leave is to die. The film solves its plot problems by excluding those characters from the world of the club who lack a capacity for life; specifically the film prompts them to exit the club in a car which shortly plunges over a cliff. To leave is to die.

This particular Berkeley/Bacon collaboration, it seems to me, falls somewhat short of Emerson's idea of redemptive vision by virtue of the stress it lays upon imagination as a power largely alienated from a material external world. Here vision erupts like luminous volcanic magma from the mystery of light. It refers to little outside itself, and, indeed, virtually feeds only upon itself. What we think of as synthesizing proclivities, the transformation of resistant materials, are minimized. The film is atypical.

> *In song and dance man expresses himself as a member of a higher community…he is on the way toward flying…he no longer exists as an artist, he has become a work of art.*
>
> (Nietzsche, *Birth of Tragedy*)

In Berkeley's work the act of creation is not always self-referential, and the eye intends a world as often as it generates one. Imagination often invokes the axis of *literal* seeing, as well as *imaginative*, and in so doing directs Berkeley toward an integration of "things" outside with things inside. In one version of this unification of axis, Berkeley syphons fragments of his own life (he digests himself) into the "more real" interior force field that constitutes his private imagination, his transparent eyeball. Berkeley's life in an offstage world becomes the subject of a film. But that life consists of his onstage, behind the scenes, work. Thus, *Footlight Parade* is especially fascinating by virtue of the fact that the story has been derived from Berkeley's own working methods. This Berkeley/Bacon collaboration is a bit of an *8½* in which James Cagney is to Berkeley about what Marcello Mastroianni was to Fellini, a surrogate. The film sounds a challenge to itself in its opening shot of a movie marque which serves to locate Berkeley's narrative at the beginning of the "talking picture" film era. In essence the challenge issued by the film is twofold, that of entering and reclaiming the motion picture space for the project of spectacle, and that of realigning the relationship of word to image. Faced with the sudden destructive flood of words into the medium of the image, Chester plans to counter that invasion with a series of dance numbers whose spectacle will overwhelm the appeal of words. Chester's "preludes," incredibly complex dance routines, supply a thinly concealed metaphor of the Berkeley film—of the Berkeley film dilemma.

The most engaging of these pirouettes of creative process occurs when Chester leaves his studio in a rage. Intent on effacing a billboard which bears his name, Chester allows his eye to alight upon a clutch of small black children playing in the spray of a fire-hydrant. Inspired by the quotidian display, Chester's imagination explodes with its own spate of aqueous dance possibilities. He rushes back to his "interior" studio space, quickly flooding it in an utterly impossible way with the dual waters of inspiration and oceanic fountains. Water is the metaphor, yet water is the physical material. We have a perfect fusion of the axis of literal sight (seeing the water) with that of imaginative seeing (imagining the fountain as spectacle\imagining the fountain as image of creation). The image serves not only as a vehicle for the dance number, saturated with audacious sexual innuendo (both monumental male orgasm & female sex fantasy), but as a direct image of the inspired imagination.

In its course *Footlight Parade* becomes manically inclusive in its quest to embrace, digest and recreate the external literal world within its vast everturning inner eye. In the final number, the ultimate inner eye of the prince of light, Chester, Berkeley, unfolds both a self-referential metaphor of vision and a socially integrated vision of reality. Chester places himself at the center of the deluxe Shanghai Lil extravaganza, using himself "up" as Berkeley has used himself, digesting his life; and as the camera follows him, we are allowed to see a catalogue of integrations: integration of races, (as the camera trolls along the bar, it reveals a world club of Blacks, Arabs, Chinese, Israelis, and a smorgasbord of other cultures or ways of being in the world); and of sexuality (drugged degenerate lesbians and gay men lounge about in the same world where soldiers and sailors march in a celebration of order and chastity). This variegated panoply of odd individuals are dragooned into a unified spectacular dance which no sooner achieves a virtual militaristic order than it wavers, focusing on Ruby Keeler in male drag, a sailor uniform, flashing us a coy wink as she sneaks off with Chester Kent. One feels this number might, at any instant, shed its skin and turn into something else. Kent, by the way, has entered this number as a way of salvaging it. When the original cast member "chickens out," Chester is forced to enter the very world he has created. He stands inside his creation as its center; he enters to "use himself up" in the performance. The number itself is his quest for the one ultimate woman, "Lil," and, thus, embodies Kent's quest in the film plot (he is blind to that woman until film's end), and Berkeley's recurring quest from film to film. When Lil finally appears, (after a vast chaotic fight, a tour of an opium den, and a detailed cataloguing of world cultures) she pops out of a basket in the form of Ruby Keeler in a bizarre oriental disguise whose total effect is peculiar in the way Woody Allen's plastic face is peculiar in *Zelig*—almost a side-show circus effect. She doesn't look specifically "Chinese" so much as she does universally mongrel. The *Zelig* allusion is not un-apt, for part of the effect of this number is that of giant watercolour strokes bleeding into each other, somewhat like the way that Zelig himself bleeds into his environment. In Berkeley this cultural mingling is a creative concatenation. The "Lil" number emphasizes, I think, the capacity of one form of art to give birth to another. One complex organism takes shape, then surpasses itself, flowering into a series of gestations and deliveries. The Berkeley dance number is like a living cell; it achieves a stage of clockwork precision only momentarily; the moment the dance discovers itself as a representation of the mechanical, it tends to leapfrog itself into a new configuration. While Berkeley's overhead camera shots salute a ragged sort of mechanical order, the mechanism shots are, in fact, nearly always displaced by those which disclose a more organic life-like development in the images. Life, in the form of endlessly extended transformations of dance, emerges out of life. The conclusion of the entire transformation process is astonishingly perfect; Berkeley's camera comes to rest upon a set of "zoo-otrope" cards whose simulated motion image of a ship sailing calls to mind the origination of the concept of motion in the motion pictures. Chester's quest, thusly, in this expanding moment of sudden fruition, is disclosed to be what it always was, a repossession of the source of origination, a Frost-like cleaning of the spring, the completion of the quest set forth at the film's beginning. Therefore, the narrative arc traced by the film arrives at no end, but instead, a beginning. There are no periods in Berkeley's work, only articulate "commencements." The camera's isolation of the zoo-o-trope cards is a marriage, then, of the eye with the imagination that sustains it: not a reminder that one is looking at a movie, but a revelation of a re-imagined world. If the military number which concludes the film (and contains the zoo-o-trope cards) bothers one by virtue of the shadow of fascism it might cast, I can only point to the fragility of the dance's regimented order, and especially to the visual fragility, for here, indeed, once again we can witness how, as the number swells to its Behemoth-like proportions, it empties content into form. The uniforms vanish into the vast nonrepresentational canvas. The militarism is, of course, another facet of Berkeley using himself in this film, for his choreography career was born from his task of marshalling cadets in military drills.

Astair has his great Bojangles number in *Swingtime*, in which his multiplied shadows take on a life of their own. Berkeley's large scale routines convey a similar sense. *Footlight Parade* features three giant numbers, Honeymoon Hotel, By a Waterfall, and Shanghai Lil which have an organic relationship to each other. One seems to grow out of the other. The Honeymoon Hotel number arises naturally enough from Kent's preoccupation with marriage and divorce. This narrative is a male fantasy more than female and has a very public kind of presence: a group of young men going through a wedding night, some for real, some as frauds. The number celebrates a collective marriage, following the common activities of the men. By a Waterfall, in contrast, is all female (Dick Powell has gone to sleep) and seems rather an aesthetic presentation of women discovering the springs of their sexuality ("discovering concealed imaginings"). The stress is placed upon the private grotto-like atmosphere. Shanghai Lil can be seen as emerging out of the union of the two former numbers: a vast public arena, but one galvanized by the private quest of Kent. The number celebrates the marriage of Lil and Kent while celebrating their marriage to an oceanic world. In the final little zoo-o-trope card, the imaginative eye marries the literal eye. The beating heart of the movie space—that from which Chester was barred at film's beginning—has been regained, as the zoo-o-trope cards suggest, and widened, symbolically, to include the world, the movie being an art form which can include the world. The end embodies a double bow to the inner heart and social exterior of the movie form.

Footlight Parade contains a few actual exterior shots of Los Angeles, a few moments of "realist" photography. For the most part, however, Berkeley is forced to acknowledge an exterior world (one not a product of his personal fantasy) as other Hollywood films do, by set reconstructions. *Gold Diggers of 1933* (1933, co-directed by Mervyn Leroy) posits a particulary interesting spin on the internal/external issue. This is the film which begins with the large We're in the Money number in rehearsal. Bailiff's men, representing the "Depression" itself, as well as a rude outside world, come crashing into the private fantasy space, hauling away the scenery and stripping the girls of glitz and glitter. At this point, the film seems to argue the mutual exclusion of the "wonderbar" interior space of imagination and the brittle social world of economic hunger. Actually, we should note that hunger—physical, romantic, and imaginative is a constant theme in the movie. *Gold Diggers of 1933*, however, gradually discloses the wide social world to consist of a conglomeration of small imaginative bubbles. The bankers who back the show are only small private men (they do not want Dick Powell to be a public figure) who, like the girls in the opening number, hide behind large fantasy dollars. If the outside world can hurt you, it can also, as a flotilla of alternate imaginative bubbles, help you. Thus, when Ned Sparks needs some new material for his show, he need only look into the window of the adjacent apartment to find Dick Powell crooning away happily with a batch of new songs. The "outside" people who impinge upon you may also embody solutions to your problems. So, the concluding Berkeley number, My Forgotten Man, reclaims the depression, which initially ruined the rehearsal, making it the centerpiece theme of the spectacle. No more dollar fantasies divorced from reality; fantasy will "take on" the depression, turning it into art and social statement. J. Hoberman in his excellent book, *42nd Street*, remarks that these large numbers are implicit celebrations of American assembly line technology and "industrial opulence," spirit-raising challenges to the depression (Hoberman, 10-20). There is something to this view; at least in this film the audience at film's end feels as though it has become part of the on-screen army marching against universal hunger. Hunger and depression have been converted to dance material without entirely losing their critical, "realist" edge.

However, for sheer concentration upon the permutations of seeing, no number quite matches the I Only Have Eyes for You number from *Dames*. This number, like the opening scene of *Footlight Parade* initially positions the viewer outside a movie theatre, but, here, the film's quest will take an ingenious turn. Powell doesn't need to get inside the movie theatre for he already has one running in his head. Thus, one axis of Emersonian vision is supplied by the camera as it takes us for a lovely walk (moving camera) down a quotidian street (studio replication) in a work-a-day city world, following

Powell and Keeler in their quotidian boyfriend-girlfriend stroll past newspaper dealers, cops, and "regular" people. This portion of the scene is Berkeley's evocation of the axis of literal vision: everyday objects, average people in the business of doing average things. The other axis is Powell's imagination which insists on deliquescing this everyday world into an image of Ruby Keeler. The two modes of vision operate side by side, Powell tracking in to his personal extra-ordinary vision, Berkeley's camera pulling back to insist on the quotidian. At one point, while Powell croons "I only have eyes for you," the camera tracks further and further into Ruby's eye, until that eye opens like a camera aperture, allowing a full-sized living Ruby to rise through the opening. The eye gives birth to the image; one sees with the imagination. Powell's form of seeing is able to function with a minimal level of commerce with his "real" world. Thousands of Keelers, fluctuating between real and photograph images, swim into his gaze, revolving with a mercurial, riddled grace on a ferris wheel which stands for the eye of the imagination. Although the number seems more and more dedicated to a "wonderbar" world, Berkeley, for a few fragile seconds, fuses the two axis of vision. As Powell starts to carry Keeler across the unromantic trolley yards, the camera pulls back until it frames Powell in the upper right corner of the frame and converts the lines of trolley tracks into one of his lovely semi-abstract images. Powell sings "I must be in a garden," and here we have an Emersonian moment in which the two axes of vision are married, as Powell and Keeler are married, as the camera and the scene are married.

The complaint against Emerson, whether rightly or wrongly made, has always been that his "myth" of vision does not account for, or see, enough "evil." The criticism is probably not well taken, but it serves to highlight Berkeley's own occasional flirtation with mortality as a theme. Berkeley's very odd Lullaby of Broadway number from *Gold Diggers of 1935* (no collaborator here) embodies a kind of imagination of disaster in which we can find another variant upon the inside/outside relationship. Stage curtains part and the camera begins tracking slowly toward a small light in the upper middle portion of the screen. The effect of the track is as more that of going into the dark than into the light. Eventually we realize that the spot of light is the suspended face of a singer crooning Lullaby of Broadway. The singer is Winnifred Shaw and the closer we come to her face, the more we find it to look like something on a mortuary slab. The face turns on its back, emphasizing the death affectation. Now, as the camera tracks into the face it discovers not a hyper-interior fantasy like Jolson's pork-chop dream in *Wonderbar*, but a slice of the familiar work-a-day world (a representation of it). We penetrate an interior to find ourselves thrust back into an exterior space. Berkeley shows us a variety of girls, including Miss Shaw, awakening, dressing, going to work. Then he shows us Miss Shaw coming home and finally going out for a night on the town with Dick Powell. They witness a gigantic dance number in a jumbo-sized ballroom; then Miss Shaw in some sort of coy move rushes to the balcony and kisses Powell through the closed glass balcony door. For some reason all the dancers and spectators rush toward her, accidentally spilling her over the edge. The camera spins from her point of view as she falls to her death, then alights in her apartment where a kitten waits for the milk that will never come, then retreats the way it came, out of Shaw's face into the theatre. The effect of this number (which is partly a reprise of the 42nd Street number from *42nd Street*) is disturbing. While it documents death as the eternal wound in the side of life, it includes death as part of that imaginative space out of which vision emerges. The whole number is a track into the dark for the purpose of employing death in the ends of life.

"The sexual motifs that often appear in Berkeley production numbers are equally inventive, visually astounding, and yes, perhaps vulgar... the sexual presentations are not provocative but radiate a remarkable degree of innocence" (Solomon, 82). Rubin discusses this issue variously as well; but I think one aspect of the innocence in these numbers is their odd ragged edged roughness. Film-maker Guy Maddin has an interesting take on this aspect of Berkeley's work.

> His ethos remained primitive. His huge collections of sloppily dancing women could never be coaxed into moving into perfect synchronization; the failure individualizes every chorine and creates a sense of endless variety in his on-screen seraglios. The women often seem tired-out by something, bursting at the seams, and slightly out of focus. They jiggle in a rough world of jump-cuts and bad continuity. At certain points, Berkeley's films seem to other directors slovenly, a phrase which suggests promiscuity.
>
> (Maddin in conversation)

There is something to this sloppy view of Berkeley, as well, for it really does convey both innocence and raffishness at the same time. This double sided Berkeley garland settles naturally upon the head of Billy Barty, the odd leering baby figure in both *Gold Diggers* movies, who is, in fact, an adult in disguise. One of the more peculiar themes in Berkeley's work is that of infantilism. We have the Billy Barty figure from both *Gold Diggers* films, but we also have the Hugh Herbert figure in *Dames* and *Gold Diggers of 1935*, and usually one such infant figure in each film (Frank McHugh in *Footlight Parade*). Conventional comedy employs a *senex* figure as an impediment to the youthful torch bearers of imaginative energy. Youth overcomes *senex* and life goes on. Berkeley often makes his *senex* figures emotional infants. Thus Hugh Herbert is a childish and sexually unaware impediment to the show in *Dames* who is eventually won over to spectacle and a more "mature"(?) sexual life. In *Gold Diggers of 1935* he develops from collecting tobacco tins to collecting a sexually active girlfriend. These infant figures, while occasionally impeding the show, usually end up helping it, and they bear, clearly, part of the spirit of innocence and newness with them. I suppose we must see them, to some degree, as audience surrogates, figures who displace audience criticism and provide a sympathetic index for the manipulation of audience feeling. Barty's presence is especially intriguing. In *Gold Diggers of 1933* part of his function is to expose a quadrangle of seminude women. In the companion film he leads the police on a merry chase on roller skates through a snowstorm, throws a call at the camera which causes a seasonal change to Spring, and follows the ball till he finds himself staring up the leg of a beautiful woman: innocent as a babe of Spring, lusty as most of the equally frustrated male audience. The Barty figure embodies that old/new doubleness of Busby's numbers, nubile innocence coupled with a ragged, even sluttish, adult sexuality. Barty conveys, in a markedly peculiar way, an image of the ever new born creation—he is a baby in one sense—but an ebodiment of birth who is perpetually ringing in the eternal themes of romance and desire, and even loss. "Art," says Walter Kaufmann, "is a moving image of the eternal" (Kaufmann, 28). If we appended the word imagination to the end of that sentence we would have a fair description of Berkeley's spectacle. Berkeley's sex saturated extravaganzas revitalize our perception of the world as much as impressionism or cubism do, eventually transforming their sexual voyeurism into images of imaginative seeing, vehicles of the unification of literal and imaginative vision. One might say that they do not imitate reality so much as they illuminate the process by which we create and apprehend that reality.

REFERENCES

Bloom, Harold, *The Ringers in the Tower*, University of Chicago Press, 1971, 25-45.

Emerson, Ralph Waldo in *Selections from Ralph Waldo Emerson*, edited by Stephen Whicher, Riverside edition, Houghton Muffin Company, 1960.

Hoberman, J. *42ND STREET*, British Film Institute, 1993.

Kazin, Alfred. *An American Procession*. Random House/Vintage, 1984.

Kaufmann, Walter, "Art, Tradition and Truth," *Partisan Review*, (Winter, 1955), 9-28.

Pike, Bob and Dave Martin, *The Genius of Busby Berkeley*. Creative Film Society, 1973.

Rubin, Martin. *Busby Berkeley and the Tradition of Spectacle*. Columbia University Press, 1993.

Solomon, Stanley. *Beyond Formula, American Film Genres*. Harcourt, Brace, Jovanovitch, 1976.

Thomas, Tony and Jim Terry with Busby Berkeley, *The Busby Berkeley Book*. A & W Visual Library, 1973.

Tomlinson, Doug. "Berkeley, Busby," in *The St. James Film Directors Encyclopedia*, edited by Andrew Sarris. N.Y.: Visible Ink Press, 1998.

William R. Robinson's Philosophy of Image-Freedom and Robert Altman's *The Player* and *Short Cuts*

RICHARD P. SUGG

THE THEORETICAL CENTERPIECE of Bill Robinson's influential book *Man and the Movies* is his essay "The Movies, Too, Will Make You Free," reprinted on pages 1-19 of this book. It is an *apologia* from the late sixties for the movies as art (and not just the "cinema" or "film," but *all* the movies). The defense was aimed against several enemies of that early period in university film studies. In the English departments then, New Critical literature professors actively sought to exclude the movies from the English major's curriculum, on the grounds that movies weren't art, hence couldn't fulfill art's traditional promise to liberate the human spirit; and they actively worked to deny tenure and promotion to assistant professors who taught movies and published articles about their chosen subject. The second enemy were those professors and critics who liked movies for the wrong reasons, who used "the theorizing faculty to defend personal causes or taste." With his background in philosophy, Bill believed that film theory ought to be established on what might be termed an ontological/moral foundation, rather than New Critical "aestheticism" (which he attacks roundly in his essay "*Fellini-Satyricon's* Moral Process," pp. 153-160); and so the keystone of his theory of film was the basic element of the medium of film—which he posited as also the basic difference between film and literature—the moving image.

For Robinson the image has always been more than a mere picture of reality; it is a dynamic agent of change powering the movie's narration (in a recent conversation he affirmed again that "the notion of narration is my central notion"). Robinson links the process of narration with the image clearly in his essay "If You Don't See, You're Dead: The Immediate Encounter with the Image in *Hiroshima Mon Amour* and *Juliet of the Spirits*, Part II" when he parallels the narrative process of Fellini's heroine Juliet in the story, the dynamic operative in any image, and the vital principle in the whole universe: "Living by her eyes, [Juliet] becomes the image of man, a new kind of individual that fearlessly opens herself to the image, ingests the creation it embodies, and then, after the example of the image, transmits the creative thrust of the creative universe on through her enhanced into a new creation" (151). For Robinson, then, a movie's narrative process, whatever its surface story might be, is at another level also a meaningful version of the medium's story of the successful or failed quest for image-freedom, for seeing well enough to imagine further evoution, further seeing beyond.

The collection of essays in *Man and the Movies*, but especially Robinson's introductory essay, was taken as a rallying cry by the Sixties generation of movie and literature teachers in America, both for its argument and for the spirit in which it was delivered. Blurbs from some of the reviews used in the advertising for the book are revealing:

> "A 21-gun salute for this editor and his splendid book!...The mood is highly contemporary." – *TV-Radio Mirror*

> "One of the best books ever about motion pictures...the book is formidable in its variety as well as its excellence." –*Los Angeles Times*

> "Full of vitality, rich reflection, and genuine love for the film." – *Cinema Journal*

> "These writers are assertive, knowledgeable, very articulate." – *N.Y. Times*

There were reasons for the book's appeal to a new generation of movie watchers and teachers, besides the obvious one of welcoming influential support in defense of one's passion and turf; Robinson put forward a theory that fit perfectly with the most ambitious movies of the time. As he pointed out, Resnais, Antonioni, Kubrick, Bergman, and above all Fellini produced work that challenged the conventions of classical Hollywood narration that had guided earlier film makers, championing instead the free camera, the socio-economically emancipated and sometimes self-consciously fictional character, and the substanceless image, in movies set free from being limited to slavishly representing material reality. Not only their creative use of the film medium, but also their plots told the same story, about the promise of "getting free." Further, the historical moment and the film medium had come together. The *Zeitgeist* gave us Existentialism's dictum that humans were "condemned to be free" of absolutes, as well as Marshal McLuhan's mantra that "the medium is the message" (in his essay "2001 and the Literary Sensibility" Robinson criticizes McLuhan's superficial sense of the visual world, but he cannot deny that McLuhan the literary historian did introduce a mass audience to a new consciousness of the purely visual world in the Sixties), not to mention the slogans of the numerous anti-establishment social and political movements in America and elsewhere in that contentious decade.

The promise of the then-emerging image mediums, but especially the movies and the new movie artists, was integral to the sense of new possibilities that permeated the culture. Thirty years later a youthful critic writing in *Sight and Sound* (December, 1995) made what seems to me to be the still-valid point that the great films of the generation of Kubrick, Antonioni and Fellini still seemed new in 1995 because the promise which they offered has not been fulfilled, let alone superseded, by the work of the succeeding generations of film-makers who could have learned from them.

However economics still drives the overall image medium in America, and has made it nearly exclusively conservative in its exploitation of the image and other possibilities inherent in the medium, and of course in its demands upon the audience. Think of it: cable TV is a plus, but hasn't it led to making more movies for a video audience very much less sophisticated than the art-house audience it killed off in the 1970's and 80's? Further the proliferation of cable has threatened even big commercial movie chains, and has driven the independent theaters out of business, by making it so easy to stay home and see movies. But of course the single biggest cause of the lack of originality and experimentation in movies is still the cost of making movies; if a person could make a film as cheaply as he could write a novel, the mainstream movie business would have to compete seriously with the most creative and original minds of the time, because big audiences and big distribution wouldn't be necessary to pay for the cost of production. Then it wouldn't matter if "only" ten thousand people saw a film, just like a novel is still an economic success if it sells ten thousand copies, which explains why there are many more novels to choose from each year than there are movies. As the Tim Robbins' character explains it in *The Player*, each year a producer reads 50, 000 scripts but can choose only twelve to produce— and of course he has to chose twelve that make big money or else the studio will fire him and hire another producer.

But even if we saved the movies from economics, we'd still have to free academic movie criticism from its tendency to idolize the theoretical and undervalue the individual—what William Blake called the "minute particulars," whether of one film, one diretor, or one viewer. Here is where I believe Bill Robinson's theory of the image, as expounded upon in his essays in this book, can extend movie criticism to the next stage of its development: understanding the movie image not only as a guide to seeing what's happening in movies, but also as a model of freedom and self-creation useful for re-visioning—or re-imagining—yourself in your own life, whether with a psychotherapist or alone in the dark with a movie.

It might be useful to review Robinson's ideas that excited so many people, including his advocacy of the image as today superior to the word, in his seminal essay. In its last seven pages he delineates the salient differences between the verbal and the visual modes, between literature and the movies, especially in terms of their differing relationships to reality (and realism has been identified earlier as the prevailing bias of our time) and to the mind-set they create in a person.

First, according to Robinson, literature is inherently deductive, evoking visual images from words, which are arbitrary, abstract signs. Drama, poetry, and fiction evince some interesting differences, but their overriding commonality is that they are word-based, a medium in which the sign is forever chained and subordinated to the reality it signifies; whereas movies are based on literal images, not abstract signs evoking images of something other than themselves. Thus change in the movies is a change of appearances only (not of a hidden, underlying essence). Thus too movies evoke an emotional, rather than an intellectual, analytical response—in one of Robinson's memorable aphorisms, "literature testifies, while movies witness." One of the dangers of using literary sources, and of adaptations, in movies is that they tend to trigger in the audience a word-based mind set, thus subliminally encouraging the viewers to translate the image-based movie back into a word-based literature.

But finally, says Robinson, movies too "are an image-word medium, as is literature, and all for the better," because the tension between word and image, and our own ambivalent response to their interaction, today "reflects the human predicament." In earlier periods, like the Elizabethan, images were used merely to decorate a rational framework built of words; but in our time "the word has been superseded by sensation," and "in the movies, reason rides on the tiger back of images in motion." The two mediums and their differences are seen as both reflecting and causing the observed differences between the Modern and Elizabethan historical periods.

A schematic presentation of the contrasts Robinson's essay draws between Word and Image, fundamental elements of the verbal and visual modes, within different categories might line up like this:

VERBAL MODE	versus	*VISUAL MODE*
The Word	versus	The Light
Literature	versus	Movies
A Transcendent God	versus	An Immanent God
Creation of World by Fiat	versus	Creation by Emanation
Western Civilization	versus	Eastern Cultures
Old Testament	versus	New Testament: St. John's Gospel (Light mixed with the Word)
Greek Logos & Rationalistic Idealism	versus	Judaic Existential, Secular Vision
Religion	versus	Science

After identifying and explaining the two modes in their causes and effects, Robinson judges their relative power in the post-rationalistic world into which we have entered: "The movies derive their aesthetic stature, obviously, from being a closer analogue to reality than is literature….Thus the director's medium is inherently closer than any other to life, and he is the most advantageously equipped artist for adventuring in moral reality." For Robinson the primary Good, the moral reality of this new world, is freedom, and "today the movie is explicitly and confidently committed to freedom as the supreme value and truth, and the moral dialogue it is now participating in is probing the career of man's good in that direction—whether in great, good, bad, or indifferent films, in parts of films or in their entirety."

Robinson concludes his essay by tying his theoretical defense of movies' freedom-making power to insightful critical comments on three aspects of the medium itself, as it "has contributed to today's moral dialogue over freedom" in the movies of the previous decade (he cites *Tom Jones*, *Breathless*, *Zorba the Greek*, *A Hard Day's Night*, *The Easy Life*, *Viva Maria*, and generally the work of Bergman and Fellini). The three aspects are camera-work, the representation of character, and most importantly the image.

As regards the first, Robinson notes that "the free camera supports the free character" presented in these new stories, by enabling the viewers to see the world through "a projection of an individual's sensibility, not a mechanical eye" that only records but does not imagine. The camera, like the airplane, is a machine no longer regarded as yet another example of technology's antagonism toward the imagination; rather, it is now seen to be "a technological vehicle by which the human spirit can escape material limitations once thought to be narrowly restrictive."

Similarly, the movies' representation of characters has changed. Movies no longer have to be an illusion of "the real," but "are at liberty to be artifice and even to call attention to their fictional character." In this was they proclaim "the dominion of the imagination over substance," and over a substance/Word based vision of human nature and the world.

But Robinson believes it is the "emancipation of the image" from its enslavement by realism to the physical world that is the most important contribution to the Sixties dialogue on freedom. A movie image is immortal, living on for the viewers even after the person it represents (Marilyn Monroe is his example) has died, and in fact even if the person represented had never even been born, except as a celluloid image. The movies thus "liberated form from the physical world." Although it was modern physics which destroyed the traditional idea of substance, the mass medium of movies has done far more to spread the message, and therefore "to set the imagination free to dream upon human moral possibilities within a substanceless universe." By showing us that "an image does not necessarily signify substance, they have destroyed the last vestige of our materialistic mental habits"; no longer do we always have to subordinate the image to a separate, more authoritative substance, nor search outside the image for meaning, nor in fact labor under the traditional human burden of "the hunger for and anxiety about meaning." Invoking the spirit of the Sixties through its best known philosophical formulations, Robinson identifies what we may learn from the movies' free image: "to be is enough; existence needs no justification." Instead of humanity's age-old search for meaning, we may turn confidently to a new search, for an enhanced appreciation of our being.

There are several principles we might take from Robinson's essay that have application today, especially to the 1990's movies of one of the last active auteurs of the Sixties generation, Robert Altman. First, Robinson's idea that a movie seen as art "confronts its viewer with moral fact and engages him in a moral dialogue," either through the story or the style/medium, or both. As we have seen, in the Sixties the subject of the dialogue was getting free of the twin determinisms of realism in representation and materialism in philosophy. But times change, as Robinson's essay insists, and today it may be that new issues, even new ontological issues, have arisen. Is "getting free" from realism, and all that entails, still a compelling passion? (The recent "reality" TV shows, such as "Survivor," have been wildly successful by pretending to give us more reality.) But do we see this issue importantly in our art today, either in the new movie-makers or in proven auteurs such as Robert Altman? If not, what has taken its place?

A second principle of Robinson's essay is that critics should learn from the masters of imagination, the artists themselves. We are in an age when criticism, not to mention other intellectualisms, aspire to the premier role art formerly held, as deserving of our first attention and most enduring allegiance. But Robinson's essay advances the traditional argument that critics should learn from artists; indeed, the best critics often have been the practicing artists of the day. They, not the professional critics, are the "antennae of the race," and it is to them we must look for the earliest identification of the issues of the time's moral dialogue. But are there auteurs of imagination among us today? And has the medium of the movies lived up to its promise of offering the best venue for leading edge artistic insights into the contemporary condition, or have economics and ideology—to identify just two of the current antagonists of the imagination—stilled them? Basically, we ask the perennial question: does Altman or any other movie-maker today have anything to reveal to us?

Finally, what of the image? Is its role in the moral dialogue of movie-makers today as central as Robinson claimed it was for directors in the Sixties? If so, does it manifest itself in the same ways Robinson described it: the free camera supporting the free character, the movie-maker's imagination declaring its own freedom through its creation and affirmation of the substanceless image? Only today's movies can answer these questions. And so we turn to Robert Altman's *The Player* (1992) and *Short Cuts* (1994) to see how the image figures in one auteur's moral dialogue in the 1990's.

The Player is a movie about movies, as well as about the movie industry. It is about the powerful worlds movies create for the viewers—in each individual movie and in the media-touted "world of the movies." The central value of Altman's moral dialogue in this film about movie worlds is identified in the title: playing. Altman floods completely the world of his satire with examples, and metamorphoses thereof, showing the actions and the spirit of play, playing, players, "the play's the thing," *ad ridiculosum*. Altman's satirical goal is to undercut the pious claim of movies to represent reality faithfully to the viewer. To put the point baldly, the movie industry says, and most viewers conventionally believe, that one can accept movies at face value (assuming just a little exaggeration of reality—a cheap poetic license, say); but, says Altman, once the viewer knows how movies are produced she realizes those claims—explicitly made by movie executives, implicitly made by a Hollywood style of moviemaking—are lies. The power of the image is of course central to the movies' claim on the viewers' power of belief. While Altman's movie certainly does show us slime-ball bankers and producers, hack directors willing to change endings, and the artifices of movie-making, the most powerful attack of this *auteur* on bad movies in his own great one is his intentionally satiric use of the image's color, the soundtrack, and the happy-ending story convention in *The Player's* final scene. Such a combination exposes most completely the audience-manipulation values that the movie's plot has shown us to be typical of Hollywood. Altman's attack on *The Player's* ending is emphasized by his use of a near-subliminal sound track of children's voices jeering "ya, ya-ya, ya ya" at the phony happy ending the movie story presents in the too-perfect technicolor images.

The ending is well prepared for by the many ways in which the film embodies and invites the viewer to join in a moral dialogue on the subject of play—both bad and good—in the image-medium world that dominates today's culture in America. Structurally, the underlying story of Altman's sensibility as satirical auteur (and, for those viewers who know it, Altman's actual history as Hollywood outsider) ultimately subsumes and resolves the dilemma of the plot, where Tim Robbins' character Griffin (an allusive mythical name)—the Player himself—seems to be getting away with murdering the scripwriter Kahane and marrying his widow. In terms of camera-work, and of in-story discussion of how to use the camera—the movie presents an on-going debate of the antagonism between the longer shots of earlier Hollywood movies and the "cut, cut, cut" style of today's Hollywood movies. Also, Hollywood's antagonism towards foreign films with their "free camera" and unhappy endings, is emphasized on several occasions (e.g., the murderer Griffin, his victim Kahane, and the woman "eyewitness" all attend an art theatre for a showing of *The Bicycle Thief*).

Storywise, Griffin is a successful player in a world where play is a necessity (as he says, only 12 of 50, 000 scripts are actually produced as films each year), and he uses play as a value to override the plot's bearers of competing values: the moralist scriptwriter and Griffin's own writer-friendly, non-player sidekick Bonnie; the materialist producer-player Levy who wants to fire all writers and get stories from newspapers; the inept player, studio boss Joel, who gets conned by Griffin into buying Levy's "down" ending for the film-within-a-film, *Habeas Corpus* (translated as "produce the corpse" by the agent

Dean Stockwell plays); the detectives Lyle Lovett and Whoopi Goldberg, whose job description limits them to empirical reality, using the "eye-as-witness" only, in their pursuit of the player-as-murderer. Further, Griffin the Player marries the Icelandic girlfriend of the murdered writer Kahane, June Gottmansdottir (another allusive name, added to the original novel by Altman). June is the story's only pure artist, whose art is mixing words and images and purposefully designifying words—which recalls Robinson's comment from "*2001* and the Literary Sensibility" that a film director's success "in telling the new story and creating the new man resides...in how he connects words with images, thought with seeing." Even the viewers are encouraged to appreciate the seemingly amoral values of Griffin after his speech about having to choose only 12 scripts to produce each year, and after the viewer witnesses the failure of their surrogate, the movie-going murder witness, to recognize what she has seen with her own eyes. Thus Altman presents a movie-world inherently moving and unfixed, inherently uncertain, rewarding people with fluid skills rather than rigidly absolutistic moral judgements.

Presenting Griffin the Player as embodying some affirmative aspects of the central value of play for the movie's world is the major change Altman makes to the story he adapted from Michael Tolkin's novel. But Altman's movie also affirms the superiority of the independent artist-movie Director as generator of the most successful images and therefore values in *The Player's* world of the movies, and he does this by showing the Director to be the greatest master of the movies' most powerful tool, the image itself.

The prime example of this depends upon a conception of the image as potentially both friend and foe of contemporary humans, yet even in this duality (perhaps because of its harnessing and transcending the dualism in "a third thing," itself) possessing real power to bring even hidden or vague qualities out into the open, as Robinson says it should. In this movie, the quality exposed for the viewer's rejection of it in *The Player* is Griffin's overly controlling use of the image—the very basis of Robinson's philosophy of image-freedom. Griffin ignores the call to creativity emanating from the ordinarily multi-faceted, life-giving visual image, whether found in the movies he produces or in his own life (remember Griffin not only gets away with murder, but he gets to calls the shots in *The Player* as to how his character's story-line will end, and on his cell phone he makes a deal that of course guarantees himself a "happy ending"). Instead Griffin values the image as nothing more than a limited, dualistic means to a preconceived end, what in ordinary language we refer to accurately as being "two-faced," limiting your image to only two well-controlled sides.

The movie's final scene, viewed passively, makes the casual viewer think that the murderer Griffin has gotten away with his crime, that crime does pay, that being the type of two-faced player Griffin is in this story proves one can be master of the image. But when we view this final scene critically, as an almost iconic image of the happy-ending Hollywood family melodrama image, though here subtly undercut by the too perfect color and the nearly subliminal sound of voices jeering "ya, ya-ya, ya ya" at the image we realize that Altman has delivered to the alert viewer (and listener) a message opposite to what the image seems to convey according to our ingrained genre expectations (and genres, like words, are embodied experiences from the past, hence potential impediments to seeing the truly new). Thus movies can via genre be made to appear to conventionally "say" one thing yet signify via the image (to the active viewer) the opposite. Or, put another way, images can be free and forwarding looking images or conventional, pale shadows of the past, and looking backward.

Thus we see that rather than seeing Griffin as the story's winner, we are led to see him finally as entrapped in what is visually a non-playing, entirely predictable genre ending—one the viewer recognizes as a deeply satirical statement about the main character by the film's true player, the Director-auteur Altman himself. More to the point, Altman's satirizing of the audience-manipulating, happy, "up"-ending plot (which Griffin earlier has said is the *sine qua non* of the successful Hollywood movie), by signifying the movie's deepest meaning through the final image played against the story's final ending, wakes up the viewer and thus liberates her or him from being controlled by Hollywood conventions once again.

In *Short Cuts* the enemy is the acceptance of cuts as the dominant organizing principle, both in the movie and in the fragmented lives of the Raymond Carver inspired denizens of Los Angeles's suburban landscape, where people are presented as perpetually under siege, whether from the medfly-spraying helicopters of the *Mash*-like opening sequence or the sudden earthquake at the movie's end. Altman shows the disorder hidden by our cut-ordered and cut-represented busy urban lives, then suggests how the movie might better unify it. Further, the short cuts of the movie medium support its representation of the compartmentalized, fragmented lifestyle fostered by the city's many-named suburban sprawl; it is a style of intense but superficial excitement, masking its underlying instability, its failure of unity, as its unnoticed shadow side. But the structure of the film is that of a mosaic of short cuts pieced together by the film maker; and the "eye in the sky" camera-helicopter at the opening and closing shows how film is the medium capable of linking and integrating into some sort of order the typically fragmented, separate lives of today.

The movie generates an on-going dialogue regarding the effects of many different kinds of media, but especially the different imaging techniques, in our media-bound and media-based society. Most important is the implicit comparison and contrast between film images and TV images. This theme runs throughout the movie, because short cuts and sound bites are associated with TV's style of image presentation, especially newscasts. TV is even more controlled than Hollywood studio films; and Altman himself has a TV background and knows the medium well. Further, an important influence on current Hollywood movies is the TV and video market for movies; Altman in this movie is critiquing, as he did in *The Player*, a subspecies of movie that has altered the terms of the dialogue about the nature of freedom and creativity in an image-media dominated culture. Examples of this in the movie include the story of the eye-in-the-sky traffic reporter and medfly killer Stormy Weathers, who first sprays for medflies and then reports on it, and who floats like God in his heaven looking down and describing the entity known as LA. Another interesting case is the TV anchorman Howard, whose son—hit by a car—lies in a coma at the hospital until finally Howard, and the viewer too, "see" him die by observing the jagged line of life on the hospital monitor suddenly go flatline.

An interesting, supporting image-related theme involves the moving image of film versus the expressive images of painting or the private and personal images of snapshots, or the body-painting imagery of the make-up artist or the self-painted clown. Taken *in toto*, the movie's many examples of images in private as well as public, daily life strikingly remind the viewer of how prevalent, how diverse, are the manifestations of this human image-making and image-obeying impulse. In this regard they prepare the ground for what I feel is Altman's main thrust in the movie, and that is a critique of TV and TV-culture in both style and subject matter, of TV the culture-altering image-medium devoted to an audience-manipulating, "cut-cut-cut" style and the emotionally exploitative material typical of TV's commercialistic melodrama.

In a world where there is no time for the long sequence, and where lives are too fragmented for the "free camera" following a character's or even the director's sensibility, because even when free it reflects a fragmentation that exists there, Altman's movie can succeed in revealing more about the character's personal lives by using cross-cutting between sequences between lives. This technique, like the musical themes (primarily the blues) that bind the different stories, can expose and redeem the short cuts which both on TV and in the megalopolis seem to be the structural principle of our lives today, a fragmentation which destroys reality's coherence and in terms of the TV medium controls the audience's reactions. The second thing Altman's building up of a short-cuts film out of cross-cuts does is to let the audience see and feel their lives over time, to recognize how compartmentalizing a life actually covers up its fundamental lack of stability—thus the Earthquake at the end and the long shots of reactions of people running back to their families and loved ones remind us of our bonds to what endures.

Finally, by breaking up each individual character's narrative for the sake of the whole, Altman forces us to re-imagine the characters, via their images, over and over, and thus he encourages us to use upon ourselves the image-metamorphosing process the movie itself uses on its characters, to re-vision and re-feel ourselves in the same way the movie is imaginatively re-visioning our image of the characters in this movie. For me, this is the next step to take in developing Robinson's philosophy of image-freedom, using movies to help ourslves and others act in new ways. Robinson offers support for this line of development at the conclusion of his essay on *Juliet of the Spirits*, when he writes about the ultimate intention of the movie's images:

> Their intention is decidedly not to denominate but to unseat authority and make room for the angelic particular. So their impact ultimately addds up to a religious revolution that revives the classical and mythic modes of worship described by C. Kerenyi in *The Religion of the Greeks and Romans* when he wrote, "for the Greeks the divine was a self- evident fact of the given world, in respect to which one raised not the question of existence...but the question of behavior worthy of a human being." Like the divine for the Greeks, images, in Juliet's final view of them, challenge her not to believe but to behave. And her response to their self-evident virtue is worthy of a human being. It is that self-evident virtue that begins to flow in *Hiroshima Mon Amour* and reaches fullness in *Juliet of the Spirits*, a movie, like its protagonist, full of life, full of the life of images. (151)

Thus, after learning to see critically and appreciate images—as in *The Player*—then *Short Cuts* calls us to an image-based behavior via a visual and psychological re-visioning of ourselves. This is the Robert Altman's "new movies for the new man" answer to the recurring, if implicit, question posed by William R. Robinson's film theory: what is needed at present from the art of the movies to free us to act out of our truest selves in the world today?

Personal Retrospective on Theory

Vincent B. Leitch

I. Changing Paradigms from the 1960s Through the 1990s

Lately I have been wondering how I got here. I mean that I have been trying to map the stages of my profession's development during the past three decades—the time of my involvement in academic literary studies, particularly criticism and theory, my specialty. In retrospect, I see that it is a story, in large part, about U.S. university culture in the late twentieth century being Europeanized one more time, becoming self-consciously multicultural, and undergoing postmodernization. When I committed myself to literary studies as an undergraduate in the mid-1960s, New Criticism was the ruling paradigm, which had been in place, not without various telling challenges, for several decades. It was not until the mid-1970s that this oppressive formalism gave way to "poststructuralism" (as it was oddly called), a peculiar North American set of literary philosophical methods and frames of reference largely derived from Nietzsche but filtered through Derrida, de Man, and Foucault among others. Itself dominant for more than a decade—though not without significant challenges—U.S. poststructuralism mutated from its French roots in response to more local problems and challenges, particularly those surfaced in the late 70s and early 80s by feminists, ethnic autonomy groups, and postcolonial thinkers. I shall have more to say later about the branches of poststructuralism in the U.S. By the mid or late 1980s, various united fronts of literary social critics, feminists, postcolonial theorists, historians of culture, scholars of popular culture, rhetoricians, and left poststructuralists like myself began promoting cultural studies, many extending models developed during the 1970s in England's celebrated Centre for Contemporary Cultural Studies at the University of Birmingham. So what you had in North American university departments of literary studies through the late 1980s and throughout the 1990s was an ascendant cultural studies, increasingly capacious and broadly defined, simultaneously incorporating and displacing a once-dominant literary poststructuralism, both of which movements were held at arm's length by certain feminists, postcolonial theorists, ethnic critics, queer theorists, and leftists reluctant to join coalitions for fear of invisibility or cooptation. I hasten to add that New Criticism, to which many literary intellectuals trained in the 1940s and 1950s remained faithful, survived into the 1990s both as a besieged residual paradigm of "normative" literary education and a resurrected charter adopted by a small number of a young generation of new belletrists often associated with creative writing programs. To summarize using more emotional terms, in my experience U.S. academic critics and criticism can be characterized as comparatively complacent through most of the 1960s; frantic and expansive in the 1970s; embattled in the 1980s; and surprisingly ambitious yet generally glum in the 1990s. A detailed chronicle of everyday life during these years would enrich and complicate matters, needless to say.

To simplify matters even further, I came into literary studies at a moment of extreme critical contraction and purification, and I have lived through an era of staggering expansion and hybridization. Let me elaborate. At the point at which in the 1980s cultural studies first grappled with the question of postmodernity, that is, when it started to map the emergent global culture of the "new world order," academic literary horizons entered into a phase of extreme expansion, a time, still today, when popular music like West Coast Afrocentric rap is scrutinized beside Shakespeare's Italianate sonnets; when contemporary global corporate practices like downsizing and Renaissance patterns of aristocratic patronage both help explain publication practices as well as poetic themes and forms.(1)

Permit me to preview briefly the trajectory of this article. First, I shall offer a personal retrospective on the tumultuous period in U.S. literary studies from the 1960s through the 1990s, the time of my involvement as university student, professor, and scholar specializing in the history of literary and cultural criticism and theory. Second, I will compare and contrast the three dominant critical paradigms of this period, namely New Criticism, poststructuralism, and cultural studies, as a way to portray and assess the intellectual and cultural struggles of the times. I shall conclude with some personal reflections on theory now and in the future.

If I were to press a single overarching historical thesis, it would be that the peculiar coexistence within U.S. literature departments of different generational projects and critical paradigms reflects, in miniature, the wider disorganization characteristic of Western societies in recent decades—a form of disaggregation that renders pastiche arguably our dominant organizational mode—a mode resembling imploded geological formations with historical strata in kaleidoscopic disarray. Not incidentally, the contemporary university itself does not escape this form.(2)

II. WRITING SCHOLARLY BOOKS: INTERSECTIONS OF THE PERSONAL AND THE PROFESSIONAL

One way or another, I have been entangled in all these historical developments I have been enumerating, as have virtually all members of university departments of English and, to a lesser extent, departments of comparative and national literatures. My book publications offer four case studies of my various involvements over the years, providing a retrospective on what has happened in the profession. When I published *Deconstructive Criticism* in 1982 (which was six years in the making), it was, objectively speaking, a comparative historical account of first-generation French and American poststructuralist criticism, but, speaking personally, it represented an anxious effort on my part to master certain innovative contemporary Continental philosophical modes of criticism as a way to get free of the enervated Anglo-American criticism into which I had been indoctrinated as an undergraduate and then graduate student, and which I had been trying more or less unsuccessfully to modify and eventually jettison for almost a decade. Under the cover of an advanced introduction, this book facilitated an expansive practice of poststructuralist textual analysis. What it did not do was promote the shift of textual analysis to cultural critique, a project that younger French feminists and second-generation U.S. poststructuralists, intellectuals like Gayatri Spivak, were undertaking at that time and that, as I noted before, culminated some five to ten years later with the emergence of cultural studies. Shortly, I will have a word to say about cultural critique, which entails the explicit turn of poststructuralist styles of criticism to ethics and politics.

In the U.S., departments of literary study were especially embattled sites during the 1980s as different paradigms of interpretation and of the curriculum were pitted against one another. The paradigm wars of those times are still with us, though usually in less disruptive forms. When in 1988 I published *American Literary Criticism from the 1930s to 1980s*, I sought to retell a complex segment of the history of criticism from the perspective of a left cultural historiography sympathetic to all manner of contemporary antinomian groups and forces, ranging from Marxism and poststructuralism to the new social movements (notably feminism, the black power movement, and the New Left). U.S. cultural history had a different look from this point of view, of course, but what preoccupied me personally was the effort to help change literature departments by telling to graduate students and new professors, my main audiences, a story of their history culminating in the (momentary) triumphs of feminism, ethnic aesthetics, and cultural studies. This was my way of galvanizing myself and others toward transforming the institution of criticism and theory from its still powerful, yet too narrowly focused, formalist heritage to its expansive cultural studies future. To do this, I had to put myself step by step through an extensive education in the history of American criticism and theory, which willy-nilly helped me accrue a great deal of knowledge and become an authority, an unlooked for outcome.

It is one thing to write a partisan history and another to change the order of things through direct argumentation. I found in publishing *Cultural Criticism, Literary Theory, Poststructuralism* in 1992 that the effort to shape the emerging cultural studies project so that it took certain key techniques and solutions from poststructuralism on its way beyond poststructuralism offered narrow rewards. On the one hand, I personally worked up effective solutions to a number of key problems such as how to conceptualize "authorship," "genre," "discourse," and "institution" from the vantage of poststructuralist cultural theory and criticism. On the other hand, I experienced an obvious truth: an emerging paradigm or vanguard movement is not necessarily interested in learning lessons from its immediate predecessors, nor in resolving its debts to more distant and less threatening progenitors. To the considerable extent that one writes books not just for audiences, such as fellow critics, scholars, and students, but for oneself (oneself always being at a certain crucial stage of development), this particular book has been for me the most important, even though it was poorly targeted and not well-timed. It forced me to move from understanding and promoting poststructuralism and cultural studies, through writing comparative histories, to theorizing poststructuralist solutions to cultural studies problems via scholarly polemics. It is a matter of doing—not simply advocating—cultural critique, which entails investigating and criticizing contending positions and explanations with an eye toward not simply faulty logic, but questionable values, practices, and representations, requiring subtle yet frank ethical and political as well as aesthetic judgments. Robert Scholes nicely dubbed this "textual power" in a book with that title.

By the time I published *Postmodernism—Local Effects, Global Flows* in 1996, which offered a set of essays on different facets of post-1950s culture, cultural studies had triumphed, but only in the limited way that most theoretical movements and paradigms succeed in university literature departments.

Here let me diverge to say a word about universities and educational innovation before I return to cultural studies. While contemporary university presses, scholarly journals, and academic conferences often welcome the latest developments, the curricula of both the literature major and the liberal arts core remain largely unaffected, accommodating change at a snail's pace by adding on yet one more option to a large number of pre-existing options.(3) In my experience, curriculum innovation comes slowly and grudgingly—and long after the fact. Universities are strikingly conservative when it comes to undergraduate curriculum. None of this stops individual instructors or like-minded colleagues and students from making de facto changes, at first discreetly and then more boldly, often engendering in the process hostile enclaves and factions. During recent decades departments or frequently segments of departments refused or failed to change—with the result that at any given moment departments can be in very different stages of development, which is one site of the disaggregation characteristic of postmodern times.

All this explains why I included for the first time arguments about curriculum theory in the book on postmodern culture. Not incidentally, this text also offered expected chapters on contemporary criticism, poetry, philosophy, and feminism, plus new material on recent painting, theology, historiography, and economics, especially finance economics, today the leading edge of globalization along with media and advertising. In our postmodern condition, culture is in the last successful stages of incorporating nature, including nature's wildest zones. Media constitute the vanguard. Capital the engine.(4)

I want to circle back and comment on four important issues that I glossed over when discussing cultural studies. First, I prefer to think not that literary studies (or university education) was tragically politicized in recent decades, say since the 1960s, but that it was peculiarly depoliticized in the 1940s and 1950s as part of the "end of ideology" campaign waged during the early years of the cold war—a period now noted in U.S. history for its reactionary cultural politics symbolized by McCarthyism. In this scenario, cultural studies represents something like a return to normal after an aberrant period of reaction that tended to fetishize disembodied great works along with pure science and unending progress. Second, U.S. literary and cultural critics throughout the twentieth century have engaged in historical analysis and criticism, though historicism was largely out of favor during the mid-century hegemony of New Criticism. The return to historicisms in recent decades—if one can actually say "return"—strikes me as a healthy turn of events, especially for criticism and theory. (I will avoid discussing here today's contending modes of historiography.) Third, the triumph of cultural studies is, to be sure, a complicated matter. At best such a "triumph" is limited insofar as university programs often bear skimpy evidence of such success. To the extent that cultural studies has mutated into a broad academic front under which almost any research goes, it serves as an example of innovation as mixed blessing. This is what I intimated when I suggested that a point of maximum expansion had been reached. Not surprisingly, cultural studies is in the process of segmentation, involving an as yet indistinct (re)constellation of the field around relatively autonomous new problems and hybrid subfields. The maturation of visual cultural studies in the mid-1990s provides an example: here fashion, art history, design, architecture, film and television studies have been reconfigured so as to focus on "the look"—that is, the historically constructed visual styling and modes of perception—characteristic of periods and cultures (or, more commonly, subcultures). Fourth, there is a tragedy unfolding in that many current graduate students are at once dedicated to cultural studies and effectively cut out of the profession because there are virtually no departments of cultural studies to hire them. Once in a while a literature department hires a token person. When the remnants of this new generation get into power a decade or two from now, departments of cultural studies will, no doubt, belatedly spring up across the land. The glumness characteristic of literature departments throughout the 1990s had a great deal to do with both the depressed job market for new Ph.D.s and the institutional bottlenecking of cultural studies.

Let me conclude these comments on the changing historical situations surrounding my own research and publication by observing that, for good or ill, the professional conditions and shapes the personal and vice versa. One does not simply look into one's heart and write. To be heard and received at all requires submission to a period of training, credentialing, and professionalization. If in this case the personal is a much diminished thing, undergirded and determined (as it demonstrably is) by institutional and professional requirements, so be it: we might as well face the facts of our postmodernity, which seems at every turn to be closing in on the spaces of "individualism" so lauded during more Romantic periods. I for one refuse to be maudlin about this, since I find Romantic individualism to be an inadequate account of subject formation and dynamics. We are all post-Romantic, whether we admit it or not. None of this means that personal transformation or professional change have come to an end, but that their dynamics operate differently than traditional accounts allow.

III. ASSESSING READING PRACTICES: FROM NEW CRITICISM TO POSTSTRUCTURALISM TO CULTURAL STUDIES

It would be remiss of me in this retrospective not to spell out and assess the protocols and procedures involved in the different theories of interpretation advocated by New Criticism, poststructuralism, and cultural studies, respectively. This is the heart of the matter—the scene of instruction for several generations—and I like other literary intellectuals have had much to argue about regarding the formations and transformations of advanced reading practices in the closing decades of the twentieth century.(5) As I portray and evaluate each of the three modes of interpretation, I am working from my experience of these professional paradigms. Critical methods are recipes for personal performance that tend toward ritualization, which is what I shall mainly expound upon here, although I do not mean to discount the innumerable singularities, innovations, and inspired eccentricities characteristic of much exegesis. The breakdown of method provides its own rewards. When it tends toward heuristics rather than dogmatism, method attains its best form.

To interpret as a New Critic—to revisit this primal scene one more time—is to demonstrate by means of multiple rereadings and retrospective analyses of short individual canonical poetic texts the intricacy of highly wrought artistic forms, whose meanings consist not in extractable propositions or paraphrasable contents, but in exquisitely orchestrated textual connotations, tones, images, and symbols, intrinsic to the literary work itself preconceived as an autonomous and unified, dramatic artifact separate from the lives of the author and reader as well as from the work's sociohistorical milieu and its everyday language. In order to display the complex equilibrium, special economy, and internal purposiveness of the well-wrought verbal icon (i.e., the ideal literary work), the New Critic invariably takes recourse in paradox, ambiguity, and irony, which are pragmatic rhetorical instruments used to harmonize any and all textual incongruities so as to ensure unity.

There is, of course, a lot to criticize in this dense and powerful mid-century reading formation still referred to honorifically as both "practical criticism" and "close reading." This type of textual explication remains for many critics not only a valuable norm, but, even for its professed enemies, a main method of classroom teaching and professional demonstration. For the record, it dogmatically rules out or just plain ignores so much, including most notably personal response, social and historical context, ethical and political critique, institutional analysis, and "meaning." It devalues the experience of reading—that is, the special unfolding and risky temporal flow—by calling for multiple retrospective analyses in the search for mandatory textual unity and spatial form through which means literature gets turned into impersonal sculpture, icon or urn, freestanding and monumentalized, meriting thereby critical adulation and special treatment. Let me recall, however, that the mid-century threats of ascendant academic science and social science, in part, prompted this severe sacralization of literature into a distinctive and miraculous discourse worthy of its own special department of study.

It was and was not easy to call into question the widely successful reading practices and enabling presuppositions of New Critical formalism, which molded several loyal generations of readers, yet poststructuralists developed new points of departure and procedures that successfully impacted large numbers of university literary intellectuals, though not many undergraduate students. To read as a literary poststructuralist is to construct patterns out of the diffuse materials in a text and to impose meaning. Insofar as texts allow a wide range of possible meanings, they are, to recite the jargon yet again, "unreadable," that is, they are not by nature explicable through a single masterful or totalizing interpretation. Allow me to continue this rehearsal a bit longer, if only to set up my critique. Given the considerable extent to which elements in a text are subject to free play, there can never be for poststructuralists a single correct reading, nor an interpretation that uncovers the original meaning of a text, nor an account that contains all the potential readings. As a result, all reading is misreading, though one misreading is stronger than another to the degree that it itself prompts subsequent counter-readings. Characteristically, poststructuralists of this kind focus on and privilege textual loose ends, contradictions, incompatibilities, discontinuities, gaps, and elusive rhetorical tropes. In addition, they observe that an interpretation of a text is itself not the text, but rather an other separate later text, an assemblage, a paraphrase, a belated allegory. This deconstructive-style reading is for poststructuralists not, as is often thought, a case of undermining the stability, unity, or referential meaning of a text, but of demonstrating the inherent instability, heterogeneity, and referential aberration characteristic of language itself as well as its historical system of concepts. Poststructuralists, especially those influenced by Derrida, are particularly dedicated to demonstrating disorders and reversals in conceptual systems, putting on display the dependence of classical systems of concepts upon intertexts composed of prior linguistic conventions and cultural codes, which when aggregated overflow the much more strategically limiting traditional idea of context. An obvious anarchistic temper characterizes such poststructuralist reading, especially noticeable in its celebrations of randomness, unreadability, infinite abysses, and undecidable concepts.

The poststructuralist reading I have been talking about stemmed, of course, from the members of the Yale school (unquestionably the dominant poststructuralist group in the U.S.), who followed Derrida, but who were eventually challenged successfully by more politically-oriented followers of Foucault and of French feminists (Kristeva, Irigaray, Cixous). My point is the various branches of poststructuralism went different ways relatively early in their development.(6) And while the Derridean-Yale line was and is highly influential among literary critics, the feminist and Foucaultian lines function as seminal elements for cultural studies groups in the U.S.

The influential poststructuralist reading practices I have described merit, and have received, much criticism, which I shall recount here briefly. To its discredit, the Yale-style of deconstruction shares much with earlier New Criticism. It favors canonical literary texts, keeping alive the habit of worshipping great books and especially dense modern texts to the exclusion of most other discourse. It prefers to focus on the text itself, discounting the author, reader, and milieu. It furthers the New Critical attenuations of literary "meaning" and linguistic reference in stressing textual free play, randomness, and undecidability. Reminiscent of its forebear, it privileges exacting explication, multiple retrospective reading, and rhetorical analysis of figurative language. It systematically avoids social and political subject matter, skirting institutional, ideological, or cultural critique. These compatibilities account in part for how it happened that poststructuralism was so quickly accommodated by U.S. literary critics. And yet it differs dramatically and decisively from New Criticism in its preoccupations not with unity but with heterogeneity and distortion, that is, with discontinuity, difference, incompatibility, and contradiction. In addition, poststructuralism proudly affiliates itself with such hostile critics of the Western humanist tradition as Nietzsche, Heidegger, and Freud, all of whom were ignored, if not deplored, by New Critics. The poststructuralists's various emphases on misreading, on criticism as itself narrative text, and on the deconstructive transformation of once stable conceptual systems provoke widespread angry responses. This is also the case with the poststructuralist conception of the intertext as simultaneously 1) an inescapable and determining archive of historical materials and forces, and 2) an unlimited hodgepodge of sources, conscious and unconscious, infiltrating and disrupting all stable discourse. This radical formulation of the intertext ruins the cherished idea of the artist as a supremely conscious artificer, and it undermines the received notion of context, thereby disabling normative historical criticism.

To read as a practitioner of cultural studies, to complete this triangular account, is to employ a wide array of methods (often inspired by current literary studies and especially by sociology), including surveys, interviews, background inquiries, ethnographic descriptions, case studies, discourse analyses, close readings, and institutional and ideological critiques. With each of its objects of inquiry, such cultural studies typically attend to the fundamental circuits of production, distribution, and consumption through which means it sets all objects inside cultural flows where occur formative processes of commodification, routinization, cooption, and hegemony as well as countervailing forces of resistance and subversion. By design, the analyst is located within, not outside or above, the circuits of culture, enmeshed in everyday life—and also positioned to assist coalitions involved in counterhegemonic activity. Opposed specifically to the aestheticism, formalism, and quietism of much contemporary literary criticism, cultural studies generally opposes reigning establishments, reflecting its roots in left social criticism. In particular, it castigates the isolation, monumentalization, and sacralization of the arts, propounded by the arts and humanities disciplines, seeking instead to scrutinize and assess social foundations, institutional parameters, and ideological effects. It tends to examine not elite genres and canonical works, but common culture and popular forms. Among the many objects it finds valuable to study are rock music; youth subcultures; fashion; shopping malls; popular dance; movies; advertising; gossip; race, class, and gender codes; magazines; television; working-class, minority, and postcolonial literatures; and popular literary genres (i.e., romances, thrillers, westerns, and gothic and science fiction). Potentially, the whole spectrum of cultural objects, practices, and discourses of a society provide materials for cultural studies. In its more self-reflexive moments, cultural studies also concerns itself with the social and political responsibilities of intellectuals; the political uses of education and literacy; the functions of institutions, especially the state and the media as well as the schools; the status of low and mass culture in the context of globalization; and the nexus of knowledge-interest-power.

There is much to question in the reading practices of cultural studies, which a considerable body of negative criticism makes clear. One major complaint singles out its politicization of method and subject matter: cultural studies makes ideological analysis mandatory, and it gravitates toward only certain kinds of discourse based on oppositional status and class affinities. Many of its materials and methods belong to sociology, having little to do with textual analysis or literary study. It is generally hostile to capitalism and market societies, siding with critics and opponents and celebrating resistance, subversion, and counterhegemonic activity. It renounces scholarly objectivity in favor of engaged activism. It largely ignores the great traditions and books of Western culture. It seems captive to social trends and fashions, attending to the latest television shows, ads, rock tunes, women's magazines, or romance novels. It is overly ambitious, even imperialistic, in the range and scope of its objects of inquiry. In its choice of educational materials and methods, it politicizes classroom teaching, engaging in indoctrination. While it seeks a place in the university, it is critical of disciplinarity, departmentalization, and professionalization, making it antagonistic to the institution.

I have my own complaints about cultural studies. Its obsession with cooptation betrays a merely rebellious sensibility much too prepared to despair. A richer and more modulated account of cultural resistance is needed to accommodate innumerable types of life-enhancing activity. I am against academic loyalty oaths and mandatory political programs, believing the business of criticism is ultimately incompatible with party lines.(7) (I hasten to add that I have never complained about "political correctness.") However much aesthetics gets entangled with political economy and ethics, there is a demonstrable aesthetic dimension to cultural artifacts, which cultural studies risks ignoring. While cultural studies helpfully demystifies etherealized culture by insisting on underlying processes of commodification and hegemony, it frequently mystifies subcultural, countercultural, and minority resistance by exaggerating both their real impact and their compensatory symbolic significance. Elsewhere I have criticized the all-important Birmingham model of cultural circuits, arguing that production itself partakes of consumption and distribution—the result being that there is no justification for automatically assigning methodological priority to production, ironically a move characteristic of capitalist societies, which, furthermore, is out of step with capitalism in its consumer stage.(8) I shall end this critique of cultural studies with three admonitions for departmental colleagues everywhere that bear on the future of cultural studies: first, not everything is cultural studies; second, cultural studies's willingness now to incorporate all manner of historical scholarship is short-sightedly generous; and third, to appear paradoxical, the success of cultural studies should not require its too hasty and limited enclosure.

In its defense, I would observe that cultural studies, even when viewed from the dominant liberal perspective, offers life-enhancing balance to the rigidified and lopsided status quo operating in many places. For instance, it adds to the study of accredited aristocratic and middle-class literatures discourses of other classes and groups, which tend to be either ignored or denigrated. In doing so, it usefully highlights the different values, interests, and self-representations characteristic of these contending texts. (Incidentally, there is nothing in the tenets of cultural studies that excludes close reading of language or deconstructive analysis of conceptual systems—quite the contrary.) Its self-conscious promotion of critiques of capitalist societies is more than matched by the ubiquitous, largely unconscious affirmations of commodity culture, which is widely presumed to be an innocent eternal form of nature rather than a historical formation of recent centuries. If the job of criticism is criticism and not just silent approval of the status quo, then cultural studies is doing the job, however uncomfortable that may sometimes be. Admittedly, one tires of hearing about resistance, subversion, and counterhegemonic strategies, but then one grows weary also of being astonished at literary language, types of irony, and textual unity or heterogeneity. The claim that cultural studies engages in classroom indoctrination does not hold up, if only because a moment's thought shows that there is no undoctrinaire teaching. In my judgment, the scholarly focus of cultural studies on contemporary popular culture predictably and poignantly reflects the changing dynamics of late modern mass society with its symptomatic new types of art and entertainment that antiquate older forms. To close off this brief defense, the university has an obligation not just to study contemporary cultural discourse, according it as much support and prestige as the study of historical documents, but also to encourage the creation of new disciplines and departments, something that has not happened on a wide scale in decades.

IV. THEORY CONSOLIDATED: WORK IN PROGRESS

When in 1995 I signed on as general editor of *The Norton Anthology of Theory and Criticism* (2001), I did so primarily in order to consolidate in a durable way and with maximum impact the many changes in the field of criticism and theory during the closing decades of the twentieth century. Let me explain. I confess to being an advocate of theory, and I admit to succumbing in this case to the impulse to canonize, which, it may interest you to know, I personally experience as a defensive move to conserve vital recent gains so as to increase the certainty of the ongoing transformation of literature departments under the influence of "theory," a phenomenon that has yet to reach fully into undergraduate education.(9) I cannot recite here the contents of this comprehensive anthology, but briefly it covers the field from the pre-Socratics to the present with significant improvements over similar texts, notably in medieval theory, the history of women's criticism, and contemporary theory. I envision this anthology as something like a rainbow coalition, a patchwork of pieces in a polycultural mosaic and, as such, an example of postmodern disaggregation at the level of the university textbook. What this work does not do, however, is go global. I mean that the teaching of theory has yet to incorporate fully materials from around the world, characteristically excluding contributions from Africa, Asia, the Middle East, and South America. In the future this will have to change.

It is worth recalling that until the late 1970s and mid-1980s, depending on where you were located, U.S. graduate students could not specialize in criticism and theory. Only in a few select departments of comparative literature was it a recognized area of specialization. Before, say, 1975, there were almost no programs in this field. It would have been considered both odd as well as highly risky to study theory as a primary area, which is a view that lives on today in fewer and fewer places. Parenthetically, this explains the special importance for my generation, the postwar "boomers," of such key institutions as the School of Criticism and Theory, opened in 1976; the Society for Critical Exchange, established that same year; the International Summer Institute for Semiotic and Structural Studies, started in 1980; and numerous NEH Summer Seminars on theory between the mid-70s and mid-80s (the years before the advent of the right wing culture wars during the Reagan era and the resulting increased political surveillance of the NEH). These were recognized and respected meeting and training grounds for theorists, who at that time frequently had little or no formal training in the field. They were life savers for many theorists—I can testify to that. I summon up this background information from several decades ago in order to illuminate a large part of my motivation (and perhaps that of the other five baby-boomer editors involved in the Norton anthology project): although theory has lately "triumphed," it is more certain to be here to stay with a substantial anthology and the accompanying imprimatur from W.W. Norton, the granddaddy of university textbook publishers.

I wish to end by underscoring various limitations of this retrospective. I have not considered a whole array of important historical factors impinging on the university in the *fin de siecle*, ranging from recent mutations in departments of language and literature to the broader set of changing sociopolitical and economic forces. Nor, closer to home, have I cast poststructuralism and cultural studies as local examples, respectively, of the wider global virtualization and pastiching—the postmodernizing—of innumerable institutions of culture. It may happen, given the ongoing disorganization and recombination of the disciplines, that cultural studies will turn out to be the postmodern discipline par excellence. In any event, my ruminations here have not pretended to be rigorous historical analysis, but rather testimony to some of what I have learned during three decades inside academic literary life in the U.S.

NOTES

1. Let me note for the record that in recent years "restructuring" has impacted university departments of literary study in devastating economic ways: faculty lines have been reduced; older faculty members have been enticed to retire; many retirees have not been replaced; tenure-accruing positions have dried up; the percentage of low-paid adjuncts and part-timers (who usually receive no benefits) has increased dramatically; and Ph.D. study has lengthened, causing students to go into debt while waiting out a job market that offers to many candidates unemployment, part-time work, and visiting appointments.

2. I have elaborated the thesis about disaggregation being characteristic of postmodern culture in my *Postmodernism—Local Effects, Global Flows* (Albany: SUNY P, 1996), esp. chap. 12, where I follow the lead of, among others, Scott Lash and John Urry, *The End of Organized Capitalism* (Madison: U of Wisconsin P, 1987).

3. On this topic, see Gerald Graff, *Professing Literature: An Institutional History* (Chicago: U of Chicago P, 1987).

4. Here I am summarizing observations made by both Fredric Jameson, *Postmodernism, or, the Cultural Logic of Late Capitalism* (Durham: Duke UP, 1991), and David Harvey, *The Condition of Postmodernity* (Cambridge: Blackwell, 1990).

5. I detail segments of the complex modern history of shifting reading practices and theories in my *American Literary Criticism from the 1930s to the 1980s* (New York: Columbia UP, 1988).

6. On the different branches of early U.S. poststructuralism, see my *Deconstructive Criticism* (New York: Columbia UP, 1983 [1982]), which also underscores significant differences among first-generation members of the Yale school of deconstruction. (This book was published in early autumn of 1982, but the book's editor decided to date it 1983 in order "to extend its shelf life," a common practice.)

7. I am echoing an argument often made by Edward Said—see, for example, "Secular Criticism," *The World, the Text, and the Critic* (Cambridge: Harvard UP, 1983).

8. On the problematic of "production," see my *Cultural Criticism, Literary Theory, Poststructuralism* (New York: Columbia UP, 1992), chap. 8 and pp. 165-67; and also Jean Baudrillard, *The Mirror of Production*, trans. Mark Poster (St. Louis: Telos, 1975).

9. "Theory," I hasten to add, has expanded in recent decades to include not just poetics, aesthetics, and interpretation theory, but also rhetoric, semiotics, media and discourse theory, gender theory, and visual and popular culture theory. On the changing definitions of "theory," see the Preface, *The Norton Anthology of Theory and Criticism*, gen. ed. Vincent B. Leitch, eds. William Cain, Laurie Finke, Barbara Johnson, John McGowan, and Jeffrey Williams (New York: W. W. Norton, 2001).

"Like Light": The Movie Theory of W. R. Robinson

DAVID LAVERY

> The acute intelligence of the imagination, the illimitable resources of its memory, its power to possess the moment it perceives—if we were speaking of light itself, and thinking of the relationship between objects and light, no further demonstration would be necessary. Like light, it adds nothing, except itself.
>
> –Wallace Stevens, *The Necessary Angel*

> The movies are the supreme imaginative act.
>
> –W. R. Robinson

THE YEAR IS 1978. The scene: a lecture hall on the campus of the University of Florida. The occasion: a forum on film studies, hosted by Florida's English Department. Three UF faculty were to speak. The first was a professor of philosophy who began his remarks by insisting that he was hardly an expert on film theory, and then went on to lay out some prolegomena to the future of the discipline, speaking in a jargon which would become only too commonplace in the decades since. Next was a junior faculty member in English who would in the '80s make a name for himself as paracritic *par excellence*; he prefaced his talk by explaining that he, too, was an amateur. The third speaker was William R. Robinson. Walking slowly to the podium, he paused dramatically to take out his reading glasses, surveyed slowly the two hundred or so in attendance, and then announced with a wicked smile that "amateur night" was over.

It was not over, of course; the amateurs would have their night and their day. The very American, very 1960s movie theory of W. R. Robinson would become passé as we went on to decode signifiers, demarcate the diegesis, deconstruct the gaze, dismember the suture, foreground the enunciation, track the syntagmatic. But, etymologically speaking, I have, in playing off of Robinson's joke, mixed my metaphors: for it was, in fact, W. R. Robinson who was the "amateur": the lover, unrequited, of the movies. His movie theory was a product of that love.

Twenty years ago, during the Fall Quarter of 1974, I enrolled in a graduate seminar on the films of Federico Fellini at the University of Florida. Though I was not, at the time, terribly interested in film, and my prior experience of Fellini was limited to a freshman-year-in-college late-night-screening of *La Dolce Vita* (which my then still vivid memory of its Legion of Decency rating led me to suspect, deliciously, might guarantee my eternal damnation) and a required-for-class junior year screening of an incomprehensible, boring, and pretentious (or so it seemed at the time) *8½*, the professor's reputation among the TA's with whom I shared an office was so high that I took the risk. His name was Dr. W. R. Robinson.

The seminar was a watershed, the *metanoia* of my own intellectual life. My rationality, under the influence of Carlos Castaneda and *Zen and the Art of Motorcycle Maintenance* and Wallace Stevens, was rapidly dissolving: I had developed an intense dislike for some of my earlier heroes. I found Alexander Pope nasty, brutish, and short. I no longer believed that criticism was, as Eliot thought, "the correction of taste." I was becoming an adherent of the imagination, and I would remain one, always.

W. R. Robinson, "Bill," was unlike any teacher I had ever had. He was, indeed, the teacher I had always been looking for. I was in the mood for a guru, and though, as he later explained, nothing scared him as much as people who took him seriously, he nevertheless taught in a style guaranteed to acquire disciples. That semester he gained a dozen. We listened worshipfully in class, staying one night (if memory serves correct—for it seems incredible now) an hour and a half after the class was supposed to be over, so involved in the discussion that we did not even notice the time. After class, we went to the Red Lion bar on South 13th to listen to our visionary hold forth over beers. I remember discussions of the genius of Mickey Mouse, of Robinson's earlier, pre-college career as a truck driver, his love of handball, his dislike for the designation "film" (a "film" covers and obscures things; movies reveal). I remember his vaunting insistence that if he had not come to Florida (whose heat sapped his energy) he might have been "the Aristotle of the 20th Century." I remember his admonition, in response to a personal question I asked about my continued obsession with an old girl friend, that "light doesn't go backwards" and thinking it was the most profound thing I had ever heard.

We explored, too, in greater detail, the ideas we were hearing about in class. We mastered the Robinsonian vernacular, easier to pronounce than the semiotic/Lacanian/post-structuralist discourse that was to come, but in its own very American way, Gnostic to the core. I learned to distinguish character and genius, educated myself to differentiate between the Old Story and the New, verified the proper way to "get right with the light," trained myself to distrust the binary and love the trinary. I took pride that I was in the know, part of the inner circle.

It was in the Red Lion that I became a disciple. I am not one now. I fell away from the flock within a few years. By the time I wrote my dissertation, *To Discover That There is Nothing to Discover: Imagination, the Open, and the Movies of Federico Fellini*, a phenomenological approach which owed as much to the Geneva school and Merleau-Ponty as it did to Robinson, I was already considered a heretic. I was finding many of the pronouncements from on high difficult if not impossible to swallow. I recall the exchange where I mentioned to the master my interest in seeing the new Woody Allen film *Interiors,* only to be told that such a title was antithetical to the very nature of the movies (movies being superficial, concerned with the surface of things). I remember his dismissal of a new book on phenomenology which I excitedly shared with him because it was divided into two parts and must, therefore have been mired in binary thinking. I remember Robinson's loving description (in a class I was auditing) of the shotgun blast that kills the gangster in *Bullitt*—his insistence that such supreme violence had to be seen in purely formal term as "an eruption of vital powers," because movies do not refer. It is a characteristic of the modern, Karl Stern has observed, that "methods become mentalities." Inevitably, I grew weary (and wary) of the Robinsonian mentality.

Half way though the Big D, I explained to the master with a trembling voice that "I must create a system or be enslaved by another man's," and his only response was his characteristic Olympian laugh. At the defense, as he coordinated the questions of my committee seated around a round conference table, he quipped with good natured sarcasm, "We'll proceed counterclockwise as Lavery goes backwards." (But light doesn't go backwards...) The final falling, my excommunication, out came later that year, not at the hands of Robinson himself but his disciples, when I refused to acknowledge to other Robinsonians the imaginative genius of Sam Peckinpah's *Convoy.* The break was fairly clean. I did not even need de-programming.

For a time, though, W. R. Robinson's theory of film was, quite literally, enthralling. I was under its spell, a True Believer in its powerful, liberating vision of the medium. So, too, were the many other students who became his disciples in the 1970s, many of whom have written essays for this volume. The very titles of his essays promised so much: "The Movies, Too, Will Make You Free," "The Movies as a Revolutionary Moral Force." And the theory promulgated in these and other essays—on "Making Sense of the Movies," on *2001: A Space Odyssey* and Fellini's *Juliet of the Spirits* and Resnais' *Hiroshima Mon Amour*, on the "movies as strip tease"—confirmed the promise. In their pages we learned to understand "the special assignment" of the movies as an art, these "products of the age of the image…":

> to urge us to espouse as man's good the will to go on going on, to remain eternally young and continually grow, to expand, create, and realize, to open up and move out in adventure and joy on the frontier of life. (58)

We accepted the faith that

> the imagination's method [is] a closer imitation of nature than reason's. And among the arts, obviously the movies, an art of light, emanate from greater depths within the living center than any other art in a universe of light. The essence of words, the mass of sculpture, the harmonies of tones—these modes, for example, are aesthetic epigones in such a universe. The advantage of the movies places them on the frontier of moral history, and so to them we must go if we are to know ourselves and exist in our time. (38)

W. R. ROBINSON WAS BORN IN 1927 IN STEUBENVILLE, OHIO. After a stint in the U. S. Navy, he received his BA (1952), MA (1956), and Ph.D. (1962) at Ohio State University, where he worked under Roy Harvey Pearce. He went on to teach at the University of Virginia (1962-67), and since 1967 at the University of Florida, where he recently retired. His *Edwin Arlington Robinson: A Poetry of the Act* was published by Case Western Reserve Press in 1967. That same year, an anthology of essays on film by various hands, *Man and the Movies*, edited by Robinson, was published by Louisiana State University Press. (It was later reissued by Penguin.) His own essay in the volume, "The Movies, Too, Will Make You Free" remains perhaps the best single statement of his ideas on the movies. In subsequent years he published a series of essays on the movies in journals like *Georgia Review* and the now defunct *Contempora* and was a regular attendee and participant at SAMLA. During the 1970s and 1980s he was, as I have already described, an influential professor of literature and film at the University of Florida, teaching

SEEING BEYOND

courses on Movies as a Narrative Art, The Metaphysics of Modern Literature, and seminars on Ernest Hemingway, the western and the detective movie,
Antonioni, Fellini, and Sam Peckinpah.

"Bad artists borrow, and great artists steal," Stravinsky once admitted. W.
R. Robinson was a great artist. He seldom cited his critical sources, infre-
quently acknowledged his philosophical influences. He had, he would admit, been much affected by the precepts of John Crowe Ransom, and not
surprisingly his formalistic movie theory remained at its core New Critical.
In his book on Robinson he had insisted that

> poetry in a poem resides primarily in the form, the tone, the style,
> those tangible elements that encompass and permeate the specific
> words and hold them in suspension, thereby allowing poetry to tell
> us what cannot be said. (62)

and

> a poem does not mean but simply is; it does not represent but pre-
> sents; it is not a symbol remotely standing for something beyond
> itself; nor is it a self-contained structure of words or a fiction. (123)

Replace the word "poem" with "movie" in both these passages and you have
the germ of Robinson's movie theory. Thus "the movie maker," as he would
later insist, "does not imitate, refer to, or symbolically represent a value but
gives body to it there in the movie" (8), and "body" here is Ransom's "world's
body."

Robinson on Robinson reveals many other early influences as well: the
Romantic theory of organicism, the heuristics of Lancelot Law Whyte, the
pragmatism of William James and John Dewey, the aesthetics of George
Santayana, the existentialism of Nicolai Berdyaev and Miguel de Unamuno,
Wallace Stevens' theory of the imagination, the philosophy of Alfred North
Whitehead. Of these, the latter was of central importance to a man who once
taught a graduate seminar on the medium using five of Whitehead's books as
the only texts. In the late sixties and seventies, the discoveries of 20th century
physics began to inform his metaphors in a powerful way. The movie theory
of W. R. Robinson, was the product of a collision between New Critical
sensibility, process philosophy, and the new physics. It had nothing whatso-
ever to say about the site of production, nothing about what happens "when
the woman looks," nothing about the mirror stage, nothing about the post
structuralist agenda.

Robinson was passionate about theorizing. He lamented that "most of
what passes for film theory is not, strictly speaking film theory at all; or,

350

rather, it is applied, not pure, theory, for in it the theorizing faculty is made to defend personal causes or taste" (1). [1] He castigated the tendency in theorists for "one aspect of the movies" to be "singled out as definitive and assigned ontological dominance" (2). He criticized the "naturalistic fallacy"—the tendency to judge as valuable that which makes film "real." While noting that "most theorizing stems from a hunger for substance or weightiness" and "serves to anchor an airy moral entity to solid intellectual earth" (2) and observing that most critics "don't look closely at movies because they distrust them" (29), his own theory, the method he developed, and the criticism he undertook based on the principles he sought to lay down originated in a love for the medium in all its superficiality. [2]

At the heart of W. R. Robinson's movie theory is a virtual mysticism concerning "the light." In his book on Edwin Arlington Robinson, Robinson had quoted, as epigraph to a chapter on "The Light of Poetry," the following vatic utterance from Ralph Waldo Emerson:

> Time and space are but physiological colors the eye makes, but the soul is light. (27)

Emerson's verbal medium, however, could do no more than testify to this visionary truth. The movies, however, have become a primary means—the primary artistic means—of "getting right with the light," of "aligning man's *vital powers* with their source and the medium of human life." "The ultimate motion in our universe," Robinson, amateur student of 20th Century physics, insists "is light, which is the source of vision. All narration today seeks to tell the story of the light, but the movies, a medium of light, are best equipped to do so" ("Propositions"[3]).

In Robinson's system, "light" is the paradigm: "the source and model of *unity*, simultaneously particle, wave, and quantum; an excess or overflow that breaks out in energy *exchanges*; has zero mass, no electrical charge, and an infinite life time; [it] is the offspring of interactions." "Art," the electronic composer Edgard Varèse once noted, "mean keeping up with the speed of light." Only the movies—"the most powerful visionary instrument at man's disposal today" (49)—keep up.

Hence the extreme importance Robinson places on sight, on physical vision. In "*2001* and the Literary Sensibility" he quotes with emphatic approval Teilhard de Chardin's evolutionary dictum

> Union can only increase through an increase in consciousness, that is to say, in vision. And that, doubtless, is why the history of the living world can be summarized as the elaboration of ever more perfect eyes

within a cosmos in which there is always something more to be seen....
To see or perish is the very condition laid upon everything that makes
up the universe. (79)[4]

"We have reached the stage in the development of our culture," Robinson
writes in an essay characteristically entitled "If You Don't See You're Dead:
The Immediate Encounter with the Image in *Hiroshima Mon Amour* and
Juliet of the Spirits," "where the eyes and images are in a position to overthrow
the rule of reason" (117-118). Robinson remained the strongest possible advocate for that revolution.

As an art of light, the movies make possible the narration of the "New
Story." The Old Story had been, simply, "a narrative in which the old defeats
the new, keeping it from breaking on through in a completely successful
creation." The New Story, on the other hand, is "a narrative in which the
new frees itself from the old." When, many years ago, we stayed long after
the Fellini seminar was over, the evening's film had been *Nights of Cabiria*
(1955), the third movie in three years (following *La Strada* [1954] and *Il
Bidone* [1955]), the third movie in three weeks, in which Fellini's narrative
imagination had taken his characters to the same dead end, the third, stuck-
record story in which the main character had ended up prostrate on the
earth, defeated, a failure. But Cabiria the unlikely prostitute had, after a cut
which Robinson had convinced us was miraculous, arisen; Cabiria had returned to the road, to "*la strada*," to be joined by a band of revelers who
restore her to life's procession, who bring to her angelic face, seen in extreme
close-up in the movie's final shot, the slightest smile, Fellini's greatest affirmation. Zampano, wailing in grief on the beach in *La Strada*, Augusto, dying by the road at the end of *Il Bidone*—their stories were the Old Story, the
story of defeat, of the impossibility of growth. *Nights of Cabiria* told the New
Story.

Zampano, Augusto were, in Robinsonian terms, "characters." Cabiria,
however, was a "genius." Like Bakhtin, who argues in *Rabelais and His* World
that a whole new, rigid conception of human being has arisen since the Renaissance under the reign of the "bodily canon," Robinson insisted that "character" as we ordinarily use the term in the discussion of narrative art is time-
bound and reactionary: "a 19th century idea of what a man should be." Character, he writes in "The Movies as a Revolutionary Moral Force,"

specifies exactly what the term means etymologically, "an engraved
mark or brand." It designates the rigid properties that a man bears
indelibly, like the mark of cain, throughout his existence. That means

that character is that part of him that has an enduring identifiability, a reliable stability, and predictability. For this reason, character is that part of him that can be named. And since it can be named, it dwells in names—in titles or functions and roles—and thrives on words—in belief and ideologies, or intellectual stances and philosophical positions. (61)

Since "character is an abstraction, an inorganic fixation resulting from the conceptualizing powers of man's intelligence…" (62), it becomes a kind of exo-skeleton, curtailing and restricting motion and growth.

Characters in a movie thus "serve as the metaphorical vehicles by which the word is manifest." They carry the values of the word:

This three-dimensional man of perspective, depth, substance, and contrary forces uses his intelligence, like a navigator uses geometrical coordinates, to locate himself at a fixed point in existence. He intends to know at all times who he is and where he is. That knowledge allows him to feel that he is rational master over the forces of change. Character, as the intellectual exemplifies, provides just such an absolute in man. (62)

Products of words and rationality, characters, Robinson concludes, "have no existence in the world of the movie, as we have no existence in the world of movement, apart from appearances" (74).

The genius, however, is, literally, another story. "An organic individual," "disposed, not to remember, but to do as life does, to let go and go on, to be open and ready for growth, expansion, life now, the new" (136)[5], the genius "saves and is saved by the inherent powers of light and life" ("Propositions"). In sharp etymological contrast to "character," "a genius" is, in keeping with the root meaning of the word, "a spirit of generation and birth" (69).

Robinson waxes eloquent when he tries to describe genius' nature. Genius "repudiates the old humanistic claim that…humanity resides in suffering…" and "rejects the tragic sense of life and, beyond that, the notion that a valid human identity must be rooted in sin or guilt…" (69-70). "An agent of light" ("Propositions"), not an agent of words, the genius possesses "the capability…to abstract vital energy from its encumbering circumstances, enabling it to let go and go on" (70); it "seeks to grow continuously, to ever expand and enhance life" (70). Capable of "coordinat[ing] all…faculties, including…intelligence, toward performing life's quintessential task of creating greater life" (70), the genius "know[s] that evil is a place and that to do good they must elude being placed. Life is bad from the genius' point of view when it is at a standstill, when it has nothing going for it." Willing to surrender "to seizure by a power greater than ego or character that momentarily depersonalizes," the genius is "an artist of life" (72).

The genius "thrives on images" (74). Like them, the genius "is superficial, shallow, changeable, ephemeral" (74). Not restricted by names and words, the genius "antecedes and perpetually eludes the bondage of family, society, and culture, and without a past—no father and no institutional and ideological connections—…travels light" (74).

A genius, Robinson hastens to remind, is "not inhuman or a freak."

> For rather than being a weakness, his depthlessness is, instead, his strength. It is the condition of his radiance, versatility, plasticity, resiliency, and mobility, and makes it possible for him, since he doesn't have to keep looking back while dragging his historical tale behind him, to expand his energy in thrusting forward. (74)

"Upsetting to the personal security of others and social order because he can't be stood in his niche and made to stay there,…[a]lways threatening to metamorphose into a strange new creature, to succumb to the temptation of any novel possibility that excites new dimensions of…existence" (74), the genius takes as motto Thom Gunn's pronouncement (oft quoted by Robinson) from "On the Move":

> At worst, one is in motion, and at best
> Reaching no absolute in which to rest,
> One is always nearer by not keeping still.
>
> (58)

Needless to say, the movie theory of W. R. Robinson had convinced all of us who fell under its sway that we were geniuses.

For W. R. Robinson, the movies are an arena—*the* arena—for the final showdown of the word and the image. If the Old Story is the story of character, and the New Story the story of genius, it also follows that the Old Story narrates the story implicit in words, while the New Story represents the genetic narrative form of images: the story of the light. "The tension generated between images and words in an impure movie and our ambivalent response to their interaction," Robinson cautioned us to remember in "The Movies, Too, Will Make You Free," "begat a truth that would otherwise be lost. As literature is enriched by the tension between word and image, so too are the movies" (16).

The art of the word, literature, "testifies," according to the Robinsonian system, but *the* art of the image, the movies, "witness" (15). Movies are "empirical revelations lighting the thing itself and revealing change as nothing more than it appears to be. In their world there is no becoming, only being, or pointless change, no innate potential to be realized in time, no essence to be released from original darkness, no law to be learned and obeyed" (14). "Whereas the word is mysterious, the image is evident; everything it has is showing" (15).

The genius lives in the world of the image, "dwells in the present, in a world all surface,…without complexity—without irony, meaning, or necessity," in a world of "process, activity, energy." In the Robinsonian system, the image indeed possesses almost magical, talismanic powers, when seen through the eyes of a genius. The image, when seen correctly, "is alive, active, plastic, and one…." Seen by the eyes of Juliet after she frees her childhood self from its crucifixion and escapes the grand guignol of her dark night of the soul, seen by the about-to-give birth ancient-of-days David Bowman as he rises from his deathbed in recognition of the monolith at the end of *2001*, seen by genius, an image, indeed any aspect of the visible world, "passes the creation, including its creative potency, through it intact" (151).

There is, of course, so much more to Robinson's movie theory than I am able to touch on here: his fascinating approach to color, his understanding of narration as both an art and a science of action, his emphasis on value and morality, "the study and rendering of change"; his views on technology, violence, method, his theory of the binary and trinary.

"THE ACUTE INTELLIGENCE OF THE IMAGINATION, the illimitable resources of its memory, its power to possess the moment it perceives—if we were speaking of light itself, and thinking of the relationship between objects and light, no further demonstration would be necessary. Like light, it adds nothing, except itself." These words from Wallace Stevens' "The Figure of the Youth as Virile Poet" W. R. Robinson quoted with proper veneration. But my excerption of Stevens' essay leaves out, of course, the words which immediately precede this passage, Stevens' epithet: "Poetry is the scholar's art." Movie theory was W. R. Robinson's "scholar's art." Its acute intelligence, its illimitable resources, its power to possess, its imagination seemed at one time "like light." As a teacher and as a lover of the movies, W. R. Robinson sought to add nothing, except himself, and in so doing he was and still remains for many of us who were, to use a word of which he was very fond, "moved" by him, the most liberating, most imaginative force in our life of the mind.

WORKS CITED

Seeing Beyond (SB) Pagination Added by Editor

Gunn, Thom. *Selected Poems: 1950-1975*. New York: Farrar, Straus, Giroux, 1979.

Robinson, W. R. "The Birth of Imaginative Man in Part III of *2001: A Space Odyssey.* SB, 161-187.

___. *Edwin Arlington Robinson: A Poetry of the Act*. Cleveland: Case Western, 1967.

___. "If You Don't See You're Dead: The Immediate Encounter with the Image in *Hiroshima Mon Amour* and *Juliet of the Spirits*, Part I." *SB*, 114-134.

___. "If You Don't See You're Dead: The Immediate Encounter with the Image in *Hiroshima Mon Amour* and *Juliet of the Spirits*, Part II." *SB*, 135-152.

___. "The Imagination of Skin: Some Observations on the Movies as Striptease," *SB*, 92-113.

___. "Juliet's Love of Life" (unpublished essay).

___. "Making Sense of the Movies." *SB*, 20-29.

___. "The Movies as a Revolutionary Moral Force, Part I." *SB*, 47-59.

___. "The Movies as a Revolutionary Moral Force, Part II." *SB*, 60-76.

___. "The Movies, Too, Will Make You Free." *SB*, 1-19.

___. "The Narrative Feats of Plato and Aristotle" (unpublished essay).

___ and Mary McDermott. "*2001* and the Literary Sensibility." *SB*, 77-91.

___, ed. *Man and the Movies*. 1967; rpt. Baltimore: Penguin, 1971.

Stevens, Wallace. *The Necessary Angel: Essays in Reality and the Imagination*. New York: Knopf, 1951.

Teilhard de Chardin, Pierre. *The Phenomenon of Man*. Trans. Bernard Wall. New York: Harper and Row, 1955.

A W. R. ROBINSON LEXICON[6]

Abstraction: A factor that is operative in transcendence, in dying to be reborn again.

Act, an: What is done in a unit of *passion*.

Action, an: The *process* of what is done in a unit of *passion*.

Actuality: An *action* realized, brought off.

Aperspectivity: Without depth, flat.

Art: A solution to the problem of *unity*; is what it does and can do; its history the evidence and what it has done; what it can do, its potential, can only be known by working with it; it begets *art*.

Center, the: The source that is everywhere and nowhere in a field of force from which the energy of the field of force flows; or the total forces in a field of force coordinated in a single *act*.

Change: Any alteration that makes a difference; there are three kinds: **a)** of place; **b)** by cause and effect; and **c)** creative.

Character: A person's mark; the public identity that establishes him as a known and predictable figure.

Communication: To make common; a mutual *exchange* of *value*s: *image*s communicate *image*s.

Composition: To unite by linking together in place; spatial organization..

Concrete: Growing together.

Concrete thinking: A discipline in which the reflective powers concentrate on the individual rather than generalizations.

Concretion: Growing together, coalescing.

Conflict: A complication or friction in the *plot*; there are three kinds: **a)** of man with the physical conditions of life; **b)** of man with himself—his head and his heart, his *conscience* with his *passion*; **c)** of man with the medium of his creative effort.

Conjunctive powers: The forces that move toward *unity*.

Conscience: To know together with; the science of relations.

Consecution: To be united by linking sequentially; "temporal" organization.

Convergence: Inclined to come together; the pre-condition of any *plot* and the major direction of the *action* of any *plot* up to the climax.

Correspondence: An eye-to-eye alignment; a *one-on-one* relation.

Creation: A radical *change* in *form*; the supreme instance of *growth*.

Cut, a: The space in between movie *image*s (since it is dark, it raises the question of whether the dark and death should be feared, of what happens in the dark; it is the key to what is carried across from one *image* to another; whereas with words, inventions of man's reflective powers, artifice is carried across; with *image*s. entities within the visible *creation*, it is creative power that carries across the *cut*).

Disjunctive powers: The forces that move toward dis*unity* or differentiation.

Emotion: The faculty of reacting to threatening or friendly forces.

Energy transformation: An *exchange* of *value* that has qualitative consequences.

Evaluation: Getting the *value* out of; building upon the strength of.

Evolution: In contrast to *revolution*, which is a 180 degree reversal, it is progression by refinement in the relations of the *vital powers*.

Exchange: A transfer of *value* or energy. as when electrical energy turns into *light*.

Feeling: The faculty of sensing the ebb and flow in the interaction of the *vital powers*.

Form: The key to the perception of concrete individuals.

Getting right with the light: Aligning man's *vital powers* with their source and the medium of human life.

Growth: An increase in the total energy of a system and therefore of its power to *act* (the opposite of entropy).

Ideographics: The *method* for describing the peculiar or unique, the concrete individual.

Image: A sensory, not a mental *image*; a visual event, specifically a birth.

Imagination: The *image* inventing capabilities whereby the potentialities of an *image* are given birth in a new *image*.

Individuation: The *objec*tive of the *growth process*.

Judgment: Opposite of *evaluation*; assessing the worth of an individual in relation to a general principle or universal standard, thus emphasizing deficiency or looking for imperfections and weakness.

Juxtaposition: The *method* of composition and *consecution* (it means "to put together").

Light: The source and model of *unity*, simultaneously particle, wave, and quantum; an excess or overflow that breaks out in energy *exchange*s; has zero mass, no electrical charge, and an infinite life time; is the offspring of interactions.

Media: The surrounding, enveloping, pervading conductor, the source of the power for and means of *change*, not a vehicle for carrying a message or an intervening substance or device.

Method: A disciplined, systematic way of going after, pursuing, or seeking out.

Moral: Pertaining to the behavior of things or to systems of *action*.

Narration: The study and rendering of *change*, or of relating to and relating *change*; simultaneously an *art form* and a science.

New Story, The: A narrative in which the new frees itself from the old.

Object: Throws itself in the way of or forward; an active, alive entity.

Old Story, The: A narrative in which the old defeats the new, keeping it from breaking on through in a completely successful *creation*.

One-on-one: An interaction between concrete individuals.

Organic: A functional integration that includes all of the powers and all of the *form*s of *growth*.

Particularization: The discipline devoted to creating concrete individuals.

Passion: The power of *action*.

Plasticity: Renewability, not just moldability; readiness to undergo qualitative alteration.

Plot: The structure of an *action* (as opposed to just changing places); there are two kinds: **a)** that which moves toward dis*unity* or disintegration. and **b)** that which moves toward *unity* or integration.

Point of view: Perception limited to a relation between one facet of perceiver and perceived.

Pragmatics: Knowledge of *value*, of know-how; ability to work with, to make something of or actualize.

Process: A systematic activity that is capable of going forward.

Realization: *Method* by which the potential is made into an *actuality*.

Relativity: Recognizing that relations are all that is "real"; that there is nothing out there but interactions.

Space-in-between: Where relations occur, interactions transpire.

Technology: Extensions of man's physical powers that amplify and accelerate his capacity for *action*, his mobility; all *art* is *technology*.

Transaction: An *exchange* in which the powers of *action* are transferred or communicated from one individual to another.

Trinary system: Opposite of binary structure; means by which *change* occurs, of the dynamic *process*; its three aspects are **a)** the senses: the powers that conduct *exchange*s with the *creation* and the body of the system; **b)** the intellect: the powers that analyze or polarize and section the energy of the system; **c)** the *imagination*: the powers that integrate and coordinate the system as an on-going enterprise.

Unity: A *juxtaposition* of powers that allows and enables them to work together in a common enterprise.

Value: Strength; appears only in concrete instances; a field of energy at work, or of work in progress in which potential is being actualized.

Violence: An eruption of *vital powers*, as when the embryo breaks the egg shell.

Vital powers: All the activities life is capable of.

White out, the: Complete infusion of the eye and an *action* with *light*.

PROPOSITIONS FOR REFLECTION, INVESTIGATION, AND PAPERS

1. Narration is the science of action; a narrative is a solution, or attempted solution, to the problem of action.

2. The first fact of life in the 20th century is that change rules supreme.

3. The first thing the eyes behold is color in motion or moving color.

4. Western man's primary occupation since Galileo has been the study of motion, the realm of the eyes.

5. The first fact of life in the 20th century is that change rules supreme.

6. Western man…has been dedicated to narrating the truth about his world and himself for 500 years. Thus narrative has been his presiding interest, instrument, and discipline in the development of his culture and the individual's growth over the course of this period of time. In effect, Western man in his modern phase is a narrator caught up in the adventure of getting the story of motion right so that he can act out his life to its proper completeness.

7. The ultimate motion in our universe is light, which is the source of vision. All narration today seeks to tell the story of the light, but the movies, a medium of light, are best equipped to do so.

8. The light
   • seeks to shine through
   • wants to be light and alive
   • wants to be born
   • loves to exist
   • intends to break out of whatever would it in

9. Narration today, and especially in the movies, continues the Romantic traditions, attempts to tell the story of life; it bears, therefore, our drive, borne by anthropology, etc., to cast off the chains of rational civilization and become supremely mobile.

10. The light exerts a pressure to expand or grow. It wants to generalize itself, but organically, not by conceptual abstractions.

11. To move, to act, to grow, as a creature of the light, man must 'put it all together,' as athletes say.

12. The story of the light enters the dynamic inner and resultant outer action of the living process. Its subjectivity or internalization, like science's attempt to uncover the secrets of nature, equips it to look into the secrets of human action.

13. For we now live, the new narrative insists, in the culture of the imagination.

14. The movies are the supreme imaginative act.

15. The essential act the light seeks to perform is that of stripping down, sloughing it off, taking it off.

16. The light loves skin—new, fresh, shiny skin.

17. The image is nothing but surface; it is only what it appears to be; it is depthless, without substance, pure form.

18. The image distinguishes the individual.

19. The image
    - lives out of its own
    - is a model of form
    - is radiant, not linear
    - Full of light, it throws itself forward.
    - is an energy pellet, packaged light
    - is self-contained and autonomous, the paradigm, in fact, of autonomy

20. Only the concrete can be seen and photographed.

21. The human face is the ultimate image, the most individuated thing in creation.

22. Only the concrete can be seen and photographed.

23. The human face is the ultimate image, the most individuated thing in creation.

24. If one thing drops from sight, another will immediately replace it; the eyes are never without wonders to behold; there is no deficiency in the eye or what it sees as long as it remains open.

25. Character is a 19th century idea of what a man should be.

26. [Character exhibits] three-dimensionality, a surface plane and a depth plane at right angles and so at odds or in tension with each other.

27. Character suffers and it is irremedial.

28. The new imaginative man is not a character but a genius.

29. Genius
    - lives for creation and joy
    - transcends self by making something better than self
    - saves and is saved by the inherent powers of light and life
    - is the agent of light
    - replaces debilitating intellectual self-consciousness with imaginative self-consciousness

30. The movies are a machine art, but then so is literature, whether it's made with pen, pencil, or typewriter.

31. There is no action, movement, or creation without, or apart from, machine.

32. The body serves as the light's, or the human spirit's, initial machine; the 'soul' cannot exist or act except in and through the body.

33. Movement is objectification in and through a machine; thus objectivity is not the death but the life of the spirit.

34. The machine, instead of diminishing or destroying the spirit, extends its power and range; the more machine the more soul.

35. [the more machine] the more 'humanity,' for affirmation of the machine eliminates expectations that owing to romantic excess are false to creation and creates greater living space for the individual.

36. An anti-machine movie is a contradiction, a moral lie.

37. The new narrative delights in the body.

38. The story of the light continues, extends, and refines the strip tease; it is a voyeur adventure in peeling off the obscuring and obstructing garments and immediately behold the naked flesh.

39. Nothing is more natural to the movies than the skin flick.

40. You can't get values from fact. To get value, you have to start with value.

41. Either everything has value or nothing does.

42. If the former is true, then everything that exists, everything that the light shines upon, is good.

43. Every image or form, as value, is simultaneously engine and fuel, and energy system.

44. The new narrative shows us a world that is nothing but value.

45. The basic narrative problem in the story of the light is to relate vitally or functionally the light and the image, motion and the concrete, energy and form; each tends toward the other.

NOTES

[1] With James Agee, Pauline Kael, Stanley Kaufman, and Susan Sontag in mind, Robinson scolded "all [those] 'sophisticated' reviewers" as "essentially doctors of society; using the movie as a symptom, their passion is to diagnose moral sickness in man, the culture, the times, a class, the artist. Whatever they attack they do so doctrinairely, praising or condemning in the name of a faction or ideal. Their criticism, correspondingly, is elitist and conservative; it discriminates against the present, viewed as 'fallen,' and against the movies, the living art of the present, as a medium" (30-31).

[2] "Nothing," Robinson insisted, "is more natural to the movies than the skin flick" (quoted from a course handout Robinson often distributed in class, hereafter referred to as "Propositions"). "Peel away layer after layer, still all is skin, the empirically witnessed exterior that happens to be charged with energy. Actually, like the electrons in an atom, the outer rings are energy charges and all human interactions…result from discharging them" (73-74).

[3] Taken from a University of Florida handout Robinson distributed to classes in the 1970s. A selection from this handout can be found at the end of this essay.

[4] In the same essay Robinson also quotes admiringly the 19th Century American novelist William Gilmore Simms concerning how fortunate it is that "the mouth and not the eyes, had been endowed with the faculty of eating. Had the eyes and not the mouth been employed for this purpose, there would soon be a famine in the land, for of all gluttons, the eyes are the greatest" (80).

[5] The words quoted here describe Juliet in Fellini's *Juliet of the Spirits*.

[6] This lexicon (like the selection of "Propositions" which follows it) is taken from a handout Robinson distributed to classes in the 1970s.

Preparing to See "The Birth of Imaginative Man..."

ELAINE MARSHALL

...but I
Forgot the rest, and was all Sight, or Eye
      –Thomas Traherne, "The Preparative"

WITH THE MILLENNIUM APPROACHING, "The Birth of Imaginative Man in Part III of *2001: A Space Odyssey*," an unpublished essay by W. R. Robinson, kept coming to mind. How, I wondered, could what I felt to be the best essay written on one of the 20th century's most important movies continue to go unseen, unread, especially when the year 2001 was upon us and would likely bring with it a revival of Kubrick's great film and, even more likely, a meteor shower of retrospective essays, none of which, in my view, would come close to what Robinson had seen and written in the 1970s.

Offering a complex and compelling view of the movie, Robinson's essay is also intriguing in itself. It doesn't conform to a conventional pattern of film theory or criticism. It doesn't assert a thesis about the movie, doesn't use the movie to prove a thematic claim or to defend an ideological point of view. It doesn't construct a theoretical paradigm that it uses the movie to illustrate. It doesn't comment reflexively on its own activity. Anyone desiring these characteristics (or wishing to deconstuct something) could extract them as an invisible subtext, but that would ignore what the essay, on its surface, is doing.

To focus on the surface of Robinson's essay is not to underrate it or to imply it is superficial, but to see in it a closer relation to the movie it views than that which most film theory and criticism achieves. Although theoretical types often dismiss or distrust the visible surfaces of things, looking for some deeper "meaning" hidden "behind" them, those who want to learn from a movie like *2001* dismiss its images, its visible surfaces, at their peril. Robinson does not make this mistake. He attends entirely to the "surface" of the movie, trusting that in its images "everything it has is showing." The same can be said of his essay: everything it has is showing. There is no theoretical agenda hidden behind an illusory verbal surface. He "theorizes" perhaps in a more fundamental way, that suggested in the original sense of "theory," whose root means "to see."

To better see how Robinson's way of theorizing with *2001* differs from what film theory typically is thought to be, it might be useful to view his approach in relation to philosophy, the most theoretical of all disciplines. Alfred North Whitehead wrote that "philosophy is the endeavor to frame a coherent, logical, necessary system of general ideas" (*Process and Reality* 3) and that it "is explanatory of abstraction...not of concreteness" (20). Reading only a page or two into Robinson's *2001* essay, one finds not a "system of general ideas" applied to or extracted from the movie, but an intense focus upon its concrete, especially visual, details. His method would appear to be what literary criticism (originating with the New Criticism) calls a "close reading"—what film criticism might call a "close viewing"—that is, an analysis that attends exclusively to the movie as it appears on the screen. But a closer look shows that while an analytically capable mind is at work in the essay, the essay's method is not analytical. Its approach would better be called "narrative": it "narrates" the story it sees proceeding up on the screen. Nor is it simply plot summary; the story of the movie it narrates extends far beyond "what happens" *in* the movie to reveal what the movie *as movie* is doing.

Should one want a philosophical context for Robinson's essay, Whitehead could provide it. More than once, he wrote of the major pitfall of philosophy—what he called "the fallacy of misplaced concreteness." In *Process and Reality*, he said that this fallacy

> consists in neglecting the degree of abstraction involved when an actual entity is considered merely so far as it exemplifies certain categories of thought. (7-8)

In *Science and the Modern World*, he explained the fallacy more simply as "the accidental error of mistaking the abstract for the concrete" (51). A philosopher himself, Whitehead knew that "an abstraction is nothing else than the omission of part of the truth" (*Modes of Thought* 138), that it is "only one variable" in the larger totality he termed "life" (166). If a central philosophical notion informs Robinson's aim in the *2001* essay, the effort to avoid the fallacy of misplaced concreteness could well be the one. The essay does not mistake the abstract for the concrete. It passionately values the concrete acts of the movie—most especially its moving images—exhibiting in this method a Whitehead-like awareness that any conceptualizations about the movie can have their source only in its vital visual details, and can have value for it only insofar as they are returned into its larger cinematic life.

Narration, an inherently concrete discipline, is no stranger to philosophy. For all the abstract idealism of Platonic philosophy, for instance, Plato himself "narrated," employing literary devices like dialog and character (features of both Homeric narrative and Greek drama) as his method of doing philosophy. One could even say that his idea of "plot" was the syllogism. Some contemporary philosophers and film/literary critics (as well as practitioners of other non-literary disciplines like history and theology) also use narrative as an aspect of their method. But despite these ventures into the narrative domain, the tendency remains for philosophy and criticism to assert the primacy of analytical generality over narrative concreteness, by using the "actual entity" of a narrative to exemplify a "category of thought." Robinson's *2001* essay turns this approach on its head, giving narration priority in its method of focusing on what is concretely, visibly "there" in the movie.

In "The Movies, Too, Will Make You Free," an earlier, more conventionally theoretical article, Robinson sounds a lot more like a philosopher, in particular like Whitehead. Not only does he link up the movies as an art with the traditional philosophical categories of The Good, The Beautiful, and the True, he demonstrates a further alliance with Whitehead that also elucidates his method in the *2001* essay. Asserting that "a movie as art...confronts its viewer with a moral fact" ("The Movies, Too" 6) and that "the movies...open our eyes to values" (12), Robinson goes on to elaborate the special value for our time of movies as an art of visual narration:

> The movies..., a visual art, are immersed in the sensory, physical world, viewing it from within as a passing parade ceaselessly coming and going. They have no way, except for words [i.e., words as they enter into a movie via dialog, titles, etc.], to gain a vantage point outside it. In this respect, they are the archetype for the contemporary intellectual predicament characterized by the twilight of absolutes— they have no revealed word or a priori ideas, nor any criterion within experience itself, by which to ascertain reality or value; they are face to face with "what is" in its full multiplicity and glory....

> On the face of things appear process, activity, energy, and behind this
> mask is nothingness. Whereas the word is mysterious, the image [i.e..
> the cinematic image, a movie, "the" movies] is evident; everything it
> has is showing. (15)

This description of movies as self-evident appearings of value recalls
Whitehead's definition of "actual entities" as

> ...the final real things of which the world is made up. There is no
> going behind actual entities to find anything more real. (*Process and
> Reality* 18)

The *2001* essay treats this movie as just such an "actual entity," one whose
visible surface cannot be "gone behind" for some "more real" abstraction that
its images merely illustrate or represent. By opening his eyes to *2001*'s value
through and only through the images that narrate it, Robinson frees the
movie from a critical scheme or ideology "outside" it, and frees his own perception to see and "do" narration. In effect, he does what Nietzsche implied
that the critical intelligence cannot do. If "rational thought [read here "film
theory/criticism" or "philosophy"] is interpretation according to a scheme we
cannot escape" (Nietzsche 455), then by assimilating his critical intelligence
into the service of an explicitly narrative approach, Robinson has "escaped
the scheme" of his earlier article on the movies and given moral priority in
the *2001* essay to a more completely visual method that allows a more complete vision of the movie's life.

Robinson shows that the movie viewer who would enter into *2001*'s moral
and narrative life, the one who would be "born" through it to become "imaginative man," must, like Dave Bowman, slough off the old analytical forms of
his critical enterprise, open his eyes to the movie's evident values, and narrate
his view of the movie from that new moral perspective. Once his eyes and
mind are opened by and to the creative vision of *2001*, he cannot go back to
what he was, cannot return to the formalities of a rationally detached theorizing that sets itself above or against the movie. It is not that he becomes
"irrational"; rather, he becomes creative. His mind, visually involved in and
evolved by the movie's narrative advance, works in a new way, the new way of
the movie itself. The movie's narrative discipline becomes his discipline. His
aim, then becomes not to "convince" his reader of what he believes or thinks
about the movie, but to show the reader, in the most clarified way his abilities allow, what he sees.

And just as Robinson's narration in the *2001* essay is not an abstract
theorizing about the movie, neither is it a narrative of the kind currently

appearing in academic disciplines, the first-person "voiced" story of a socially constructed "self." It is instead a self-effacing narration in the fullest sense, one that does not interpose "self" or the critic's autobiography between the movie and its viewing, but that opens the mind to and through what the eye sees, a forward-looking narration whose outcome is not a thesis about the movie, but a coherent and complete vision of it. The story the essay narrates is that of a mind giving itself to see the movie and making of that experience all it can in relation to all the movie offers. To borrow Emerson's phrase, the essay narrates "man thinking" about the movies, or more appropriately, a man doing "visual thinking" in relation to a particular movie, giving the full power of his mind to seeing and relating the value of what and how he sees.

The full story of Robinson's vision of and beyond *2001* appears in his essay, but, as with movies, a preview might help the first-time reader anticipate the story. As Robinson sees it, *2001* narrates a vision of "late technological man," which is to say of the human enterprise poised at the limit of its rational intelligence, as this individual human life ventures forth in and through an odyssey that moves him beyond that threshold. The third phase of the movie, "Part III," assumes central importance because that is where we see what the odyssey is coming to, what is being born—in the movie, in the "the movies," and in the evolution of human vision and narration.

That third phase is also where, as Robinson points out, most viewers of the movie give up on it: "they can't recognize what is there before their eyes, and what's more, allow that something really is there." He doesn't waste time citing these viewers since, for him, it's more interesting and important to get on with illuminating the "something [that] really is there." But I will cite one to show the problem his essay offers a solution to. In a thorough and impressive discussion of *2001*, Thomas Allen Nelson finally views Part III, Dave's journey through the Star-Gate, as "both the most 'cinematic' (visual) and least enduring part of the film" (128). He goes on to say that

> In a gesture of creative fallibility, [Kubrick] all but announces through the film's conclusion that the Mystery Beyond eludes his grasp... (129) [and that] While the experience of seeing represents the meaning of the Star-Gate, understanding what is seen defines the ambiguity of the film's last sequence. (131)

In a gesture of his own "creative fallibility," Nelson admits that he can really do nothing with the "most 'cinematic' (visual)" part of the film, with "the experience of seeing." At best he surmises that this visual experience "represents" some "meaning" that neither he, nor Kubrick, can verbally articulate.

Those very aspects of the movie that elude Nelson's grasp Robinson's vision makes the most of. In a way, the contrast between Nelson's attitude toward Part III and Robinson's demonstrates the difference between a mind that prefers the rational, supposedly "enduring" abstractions of words (again, the fallacy of misplaced concreteness) and a mind open to vision and the visible as "moral facts," one that sees "evident" in images and in "the experience of seeing"; the "full multiplicity and glory" of "process, activity, energy." While Nelson keeps looking for rational answers to what he sees on the screen in the science fiction novel that Arthur C. Clarke wrote in conjunction with the making of the movie, Robinson jettisons the literary version, just as the movie itself does. *2001* the movie does not fall back upon the conventional sci-fi plot that discovers the "first cause" of the odyssey in a rational or verbal intelligence "higher" than the one that has reached its limit. Instead, as Robinson shows, Kubrick narrates the odyssey so that the source of the birth in process cannot be traced back to some prior cause, but appears as a vital, fecund, energizing potency within the images themselves, within vision itself. It's no accident, in other words, that Part III of the odyssey is a completely visual trip into and through the most generous and fecund energy of all, light, and that it gives birth to a new creature of light and vision, the star-child with eyes wide open.

In focusing on the birth the movie performs, Robinson sees *2001* as a creation story, not only in its vision of the emergence of a morally new, creative human individual, but also in its self-evolving narrative discipline. That discipline, a complex "trinary method" which Robinson discerns in the movie, and employs in his essay, serves as the means by which the narrative's creative advance brings itself into complete appearance through the images of the movie. Robinson's method, moreover, is perfectly suited to *2001*'s creation story—a story in which there is no external "creator" operating from outside the system, and which must create from the potencies inherent within it. For Robinson's narration of the movie's creative feat to be morally accurate and true to its cinematic source, he, too, like Kubrick and Dave Bowman, must narrate out of what he sees, "trusting his eye to carry him through."

What ultimately becomes so interesting, so exciting. about Robinson's *2001* essay is not so much what he says at any given moment about the movie (though that is interesting, too), but his way of seeing and what it allows him to do with the movie. His way values the fact that, in viewing *2001*, he is foremost in the presence of a complex, creative event, and he refuses to reduce that event to illustrating a theme or ideology. He engages the movie on its own terms. Further, in opening himself to the creative feat of *2001*, he attends to the discipline of creation itself, showing that a creative event has a discipline and demonstrating in his own narrating how that discipline can be seen, learned from, and passed on. He views the movie's narrative feat, moreover, as bringing into appearance a new era in the evolution of human imagination and vision. "Creation," Robinson is fond of saying, "happens one cell at a time." He sees *2001* as a "cell" in the creation of the new individual he calls "imaginative man"; and in working out that view, his essay becomes something commensurate with the movie, another "cell" in that creative venture.

"No philosopher," wrote Whitehead, "is satisfied with the concurrence of sensible people, whether they be his colleagues, or even his own previous self. He is always assaulting the boundaries of finitude" *(Modes of Thought* 172). The odyssey of metaphysics to assault and escape the boundaries of the finite has led the human mind, and continues to lead it, on some of its most profound adventures. Yet there is another odyssey, a further adventure, a third story, the one undertaken "Beyond Infinity" in the "purely visual" third phase of *2001* when Dave Bowman, or more precisely Dave Bowman's eye— and the movie's—leaps free of the limits of physical matter and rational thought and enters openly and completely into a new, creatively moral universe of vision. This is the story that Robinson's essay alerts us to in the movie and gives itself to clarify for us. It is nothing short of a vision for our time. No one, philosopher or otherwise, should be satisfied to miss the trip.

WORKS CITED

Nelson, Thomas Allen. *Kubrick: Inside a Film Artist's Maze.* Bloomington: Indiana University Press, 1982.

Nietzsche, Friedrich. "Notes (1887)." *The Portable Nietzsche*, Ed. Walter Kaufmann. New York: The Viking Press, 1974

Robinson, W. R. "The Birth of Imaginative Man in Part III of *2001: A Space Odyssey.*" *Seeing Beyond*, 161-187.

——"The Movies, Too, Will Make You Free." *Seeing Beyond*, 1-19.

Whitehead, Alfred North. *Modes of Thought.* 1938. New York: The Free Press, 1968.

——*Process and Reality.* 1929. Eds. David Ray Griffin and Donald W. Sherburne. New York: The Free Press, 1979.

——*Science and the Modern World.* 1925. New York: The Free Press, 1967.

Rounding Up *The Usual Suspects*: The Comforts of Character and Neo-Noir

J. P. Telotte

Character is an abstraction, an inorganic fixation resulting from the conceptualizing powers of man's intelligence; it is a man's idea of himself. As such it is his base of intellectually comforting certainty in the flux of all that changes in and between man.

— W. R. Robinson ("The Movies II" 62)

They've got my whole life in here.   —Fenster, *The Usual Suspects*

Just because you *are* a character doesn't mean you *have* character.

— Wolf, *Pulp Fiction*

IN THIS PIECE I want to examine the generally "comforting" nature of movie characters in order to bring into sharper focus some of the changes being wrought in the new wave of films noir, or "neo-noir" as they are being termed. More specifically, my concern here is with the emergence of a type of characterization that marks the recent resurgence of this form, a use of character that we find foregrounded in a film like *The Usual Suspects* (1995). It is a film whose narrative turns on a dynamic tension between different conceptions of character, and one that pointedly denies us that sense of comfort Robinson identifies in many classical narratives. To effect this examination, I want to draw upon two complementary assessments of film character, one the "historical poetics" of David Bordwell, and the other the process-oriented phenomenology of W. R. Robinson, for, taken together, these two vantages can help us situate this key element of the neo-noir.

I want to begin with Bordwell not just because his work represents one of the most influential currents in mainstream film criticism, but because, in his ongoing effort at crafting a historical poetics of the cinema, he has offered the most rigorous description of the various strategies that together comprise the practice of classical narrative. That approach has led him to a rather conservative view of the film noir. While he describes this film type in its peak period of 1940-1957 as a "deeply problematic" form, he also finds, upon close examination, that it "no more subverts the classical film than crime fiction undercuts the orthodox novel" (75, 77). For all of its admitted "psychological ambiguity and abnormal mental states," despite its many treacherous black widows, shell-shocked war veterans, and "gun crazy" killers, the form's characters, he argues, were still "strongly motivated," fully in line with "current conceptions of realism" (77).

That assessment largely follows from his efforts to sketch a normative view of the various elements of classical narrative practice, among them character and what Robinson identifies as its "comforting" effects. That element is one Bordwell wants especially to frame as homogeneous, since he sees character as the key to narrative logic; as he puts it, "character-centered—i.e., personal or psychological—causality is the armature of the classical story" (13). Since a single central character typically functions as the narrative's "prime causal agent," "he or she must be defined as a bundle of qualities or traits" (13), which are then constantly reaffirmed by a pattern of externalized effects, such as speech, mannerisms, and physical actions—the marks of character. These effects in turn sketch a pattern of desire or goal directedness that drives the narrative, that gives it motivation and coherence, and that conveys our conventional sense of the "rounded" character. While he admits that at times this practice produces types who seem somewhat ambiguous or unpredictable—as in the case of noir—Bordwell views them as "anomalies," as inconsistencies that, in the Hollywood tradition of "concealed artistry," individually serve to support the "transparent" reality of the world the film materializes—and by implication, the cultural patterns classical practice mirrors (32, 24). This systematic, formalistic—and ultimately monolithic—view thus allows him to submerge any "patterns of nonconformity" in a surface of "realistic and generic motivation" (Classical 77), as difference becomes less important than the pattern of sameness that points toward the dominant ideology supported by classical practice.

I turn to Robinson's work here as a complement to this non-differentiating view, as a way of addressing seeming anomalies, for as part of what Dudley Andrew has termed "the neglected tradition of phenomenology in film" (44), it focuses precisely on a differentiating confrontation with specific visual texts. While Robinson is concerned with a dominant practice, it is less as a determining force, ruling cinematic narrative, than as one of the ways in which film often goes "wrong," fails to achieve its potential as what he terms "a revolutionary moral force" ("The Movies I" 47), a conveyor of value, a site of difference. He consistently emphasizes the effects of such practices, our experience of movie narrative, how the movies confront—or fail to confront—their viewers with stories that might reveal what he describes as "the scope, complexity, and subtlety of life" ("The Movies II" 73). Difference, then, is precisely Robinson's central concern: the difference between the visual emphasis of movie narrative and older, word-based forms[1]; the difference in the ways movies work to achieve their potential; and the difference they might make, as they literally "open our eyes to value" (*Man* 12) by helping us to see our world and ourselves.

All these senses of difference are bound up in his conception of character. In the classical novel, character is typically conceived of in much the way Bordwell describes it, as rounded, as fully fleshed out, as seemingly having a life of its own. That "life" is, of course, measured in terms of the status quo, in the context of a kind of conventionalized, word-bound realism. In practice, Robinson suggests, such figures are actually just a set of specific marks, an illustrated pattern of abstract "character"-istics, a site of predictability that draws on cultural—and narrative—expectations. The movie character, on the other hand, because it is based in the visual image with its immediate sensory impact, because it so immediately evokes life itself and thus instantly argues for its own existence, or as Vivian Sobchack, paraphrasing Maurice Merleau-Ponty, argues, because it seems to be "life expressing life…experience expressing experience" (5), appears more as an event, an enactment of human possibility, and thus as a source of value that speaks directly to us. What Robinson finds important is the extent to which movies enact this possibility, forcing us to look beyond the status quo and releasing a kind of natural subversive power that, he would offer, is potential in even their most conventional forms, including the practices of classical narrative. The movie character should, in effect, literally "make" a difference, denying us the comfort of projection into a rational, psychologically-driven, goal-oriented figure that Bordwell finds to be the norm in American narrative film in favor of confronting us with a figure who embodies "the flux of all that changes in and between man" ("The Movies II" 62). In that way the movie figure carries a subversive message, the possibility that we might see ourselves differently, less as abstract beings inhabiting an abstract world than as humans *living in* our world.

If we take these different approaches to character as an access point to the film noir, especially as it has in recent years been resuscitated as neo-noir, we might make better sense of those anomalous instances Bordwell notes and establish a key line of development from those instances to current noir. Certainly, film noir has always provided us with a host of characters who seem to challenge our expectations, whose motivations are far from transparent, whose desires seem to cut across the grain of the status quo—hence the many figures who are haunted by nightmare or trauma (e.g., *Nightmare* [1956] or *The Dark Past* [1948]), who cannot contain their desires (e.g., *Double Indemnity* [1944] or *The Postman Always Rings Twice* [1946]), or who, when measured by the yardstick of a rational norm, simply seem crazy (e.g., *Possessed* [1947] or *Gun Crazy* [1950]). Bordwell's perspective suggests, though, that such characters still largely function within a broad classical pattern, their anomalous characters predictably producing anomalous actions which ultimately sketch the boundaries of the status quo and even reinforce those boundaries. They are simply warnings, not carriers of value.

While this nondifferentiating view requires considerable stretching to account for some of the most troubling characters in the noir pantheon and overlooks the extent to which noir itself was symptomatic of a turn from classical narrative restrictions, it does provide us with a useful background against which to see such recent films as *Reservoir Dogs* (1989), *Romeo is Bleeding* (1993), *The Last Seduction* (1993), *Pulp Fiction* (1995), and especially *The Usual Suspects*. For here are films in which characters are anything but comforting, and for the most part anything but knowable, films, in fact, wherein the *nature of character* becomes a key issue. In *Reservoir Dogs*, for instance, the central figures are supposed to remain unknown to each other, and hence are identified only by the colors they adopt as aliases—colors that become simply mocking points of reference in light of the similar black and white outfits they all wear. *Romeo is Bleeding* is a first-person flashback narrative, told by a character who misidentifies himself from the start, as he apparently now stands at some distance from his real self and tries to better understand how he has come to his current pass, how he has, in effect, lost his identity and become simply a generic "Romeo." Bridget of *The Last Seduction* seems to so embody desire ("seduction") that the film's protagonist finds he can never quite locate anything in her that he, in his conventional, small-town way, can recognize as "character." And in *Pulp Fiction* we watch two hitmen, Vincent and Jules, who have to "get in character" before each job. As part of that character, Jules repeatedly spouts a Biblical passage whose meaning, he finally admits, was never as important as the impression of him it gave to his victims. In every instance, the narrative foregrounds our traditional, comforting sense of character, draws upon what we expect, but then mocks that notion with figures who, disconcertingly, simply "are," who underscore their sense of difference, and who, in their ability to move beyond the boundaries of roundedness—as Jules abandons his well-rehearsed, linguistically-defined character at the end of *Pulp Fiction*—add a new dimension to the cultural challenge that has always marked the film noir.

With the recent *The Usual Suspects*, character, as well as the ways in which we approach or think of character, clearly becomes a central issue. Of course, the very title points in this direction, as it suggests figures who, we might expect, would prove more or less undifferentiated— "usual" types, manifesting only the sort of minor differences an eyewitness might pick out. Yet the five central figures—Keaton, Kint, Hockney, Fenster, and McManus—are pointedly quite different in size, dress, speech, and manner, not the similar types we expect to find in a line-up. And the film repeatedly underscores that oddity. While four of them have apparently been involved in hijackings such as the one they are being questioned about, Kint notes that "It didn't make sense that I'd be there," and sums up the others' common feeling that the line-up was suspicious, did not "figure," that "This whole thing was a shakedown."

That note of "making sense" reminds us of the larger narrative pattern of *The Usual Suspects*, while it also eventually resounds in relation to several key figures who schematize the narrative's exploration of character, most notably Keaton, Kint, and U.S. Customs Special Agent David Kujan. Much of the narrative is a flashback by "Verbal" Kint who, with the others, six weeks before had been drawn into a caper, a jewel heist that promised to bring them each a large payoff, while also embarrassing a police department they knew to be corrupt. With his four accomplices apparently dead, Verbal, under the interrogation of Agent Kujan, tells how the group was then lured into another heist that went wrong and eventually into a nearly suicidal attack on a freighter supposedly bearing $91 million dollars in cocaine. Kint's narrative, seemingly drawn out under much pressure, piece by piece by Kujan, represents an apparent effort to make sense of these events, to find the coherent pattern here; as Kujan hammers home, "I want to know why 27 men died on that pier for what looks to be $91 million worth of drugs that wasn't there."

However, Kujan already has a theory, one tied precisely to his—and indeed a very classical—view of character, a view that binds everything up neatly, puts it, as it were, all in one envelope. He believes that, ultimately, "there's no mystery," only a series of complications that lead back to one of those thieves, Dean Keaton. As he conceives it, he simply has to straighten out the twisted tale of one crook, Verbal, that has been made further crooked by a master crook Keaton. Keaton, after all, has accomplished this feat before, as Kujan, in one of a number of embedded narratives here, tells how Keaton once beat a rap by faking his own death and reappearing after the charges were dropped and all the witnesses had mysteriously died. That story obviously speaks to the larger mystery plot which is *The Usual Suspects*, and which links Kujan's conception of how these events might "make sense" with our own desire for a more "comfortable" narrative, one in which, despite the opening images of a wounded Keaton, a gun pointed at him, and the gun firing, despite a sort of Eisensteinian "montage of attractions" with all its attendant narrative logic, Keaton might have survived and might even have orchestrated all of these terrible events simply to escape at last from the constant pursuit of good cops like Kujan. Such a scenario, at least, would locate us in the sort of clever, character-driven, and goal-directed action we have come to expect from classical narratives. Moreover, it would frame Kujan's repeated assertion, "I know Dean Keaton. I've been investigating him for the past 15 years," as a telling sign of predictability and reliability, an account of character as sameness. In this way even the transgressive figure becomes ultimately a knowable character of the sort that Bordwell and others see as common to the film noir. Kujan's attitude affirms the knowability of these mysterious characters, assures us of his own central position in the narrative as the resolver of this enigma, and enthrones a kind of rational hegemony in this seemingly mysterious world; as he tells Verbal, he will find out what he wants to find out "because I'm smarter than you."[2]

The key issue, though, as Robinson might suggest, is what that rationality cannot account for, the potential for change and unpredictability that seems central to Kujan's antagonist and, as a former cop, alter ego Keaton. At least as portrayed in Verbal's flashback, Keaton seems very different from his accomplices—in dress, in attitude, and especially in his aims. Unlike these other career criminals, he has apparently tried to put his past behind him and begin a new life, with the help of his lawyer fiancee Edie Finneran, as a restaurateur. Thus we see him initially resisting McManus' seductive offer of a "sweet deal" to hijack the New York's Finest Taxi service, later adding to the hijacking a twist that exposes the widespread corruption in the police force—thereby, we assume, underscoring the unjust way he seems singled out for police harassment and kept from changing—-and eventually acceding to the deal with Keyser Soze's representative, not because Soze has his whole life neatly packaged in an envelope that might be turned over to the police, but in order to protect Edie. Regardless of Verbal's purpose, throughout this narrative Keaton seems a sympathetic, caring, and even principled character, one who challenges Kujan's stereotyped reading of him as a corrupt ex-cop, one who belies his theory that "a man can't change what he is," and one who tries in his own ways to "make a difference" here.

And as this film reminds us with its narrative about New York's Finest Taxi service, not all cops are good—or predictable—and not all are so adept at putting the pieces of a mystery together. As Verbal mockingly offers, "To a cop, the explanation is always simple." But the characters here, as the visual clues immediately begin to assert, are far from easy or even possible to read. As the film opens, for instance, we see not only Keaton wounded, slumped on the deck of the freighter he is preparing to blow up, but also a shadowy figure who quite literally pisses on his plans, putting out a stream of burning gasoline by which he planned to blow up that freighter, to demonstrate in a most immediate way what Robinson might term "the explosive potency of individuality" (*From Myth* 24). The close-up of Keaton's face, however, gives way to a series of medium and close-up shots that repeatedly frame only parts of this shadow figure's body—torso, legs, hand holding a gun—effectively contrasting Keaton's individuality with this ambiguous physical presence, his face and its glance of knowledge with that elusive, fragmented, impersonal body. While these tightly framed shots frustrate our desire to come face to face with and identify this figure who apparently shoots Keaton, a series of cross cuts between the trail of gasoline set burning again and a tangled coil of rope at dockside, behind which we see Verbal hiding, point up the key issue here. Right from the start, the film is introducing a character who is unknowable, at least in the manner of classical narrative: as a figure who is marked by easily observable traits, whose motivations are readily understood, and who sets the plot in motion along a straight line. While, as we eventually learn, there is indeed a "prime causal agent" here, the mysterious and unphotographed Keyser Soze, he remains little more than an enigma, a figure whose very existence is only conjectured for most of the narrative: his traits pointedly unknown, his motivation simply to maintain power, the plot he sets in motion a Borgesian "garden of forking paths," or in keeping with that one recurring image, a tangled coil of rope.

What Kujan gleans from Verbal's account, in fact, is that all of these events are actually *about character*, or rather the obliteration of character in a classical sense with all of its attendant marks. For Verbal claims that everything was orchestrated by the Turkish master criminal Soze who, in the fashion of Orson Welles' Mr. Arkadin, had employed these "usual suspects" to eliminate some troublesome traces of his existence, especially a government informant who could identify him. To the skeptical Kujan, who has trouble even believing in Soze's existence, Verbal insists that this complex plotting is simply the ultimate mark of this mysterious figure's power; as he offers, "The greatest trick the devil ever pulled was convincing the world he didn't exist." The mark of his power—and evil—then, is his ability to disguise or eliminate character, or simply reduce it to an abstraction.

That reference to "the devil" is significant in a number of ways here. For one, it reminds us that the narrative Verbal recounts is designed to have a kind of frightening effect, that it is meant to offer a glimpse of an evil that the conventional world, as exemplified by the skeptical Kujan, hardly recognizes and is loath to acknowledge. Yet it is an evil—and a challenge to the status quo—that Bordwell might assure us is pointedly contained by the narrative's bounds, by Kint's words that have simply served up the essential "trick" of this film, the surprise ending in which we realize that Kint is himself Soze, whose account has worked to distract the authorities, disguise his true character, and give him a chance to escape. The shift from Verbal's first-person, flashback account to the third-person vantage that finally lets us "in on" the trick is, of course, motivated by our need to know and by the narrative's own desire to spring its suprise—after the fashion of Hitchcock's *Stage Fright* (1950)—the revelation that its narrator is a trickster, the point of view narration in which we have been immersed simply a twisted fabrication, his gimpy, timid, compulsively talking identity nothing more than an elaborate fiction of character—as may be, for all we know, even the portrayal he offers of Dean Keaton.

Of course, that is precisely how he describes Keyser Soze—himself—anyway, as "a spook story that criminals tell their kids at night." And indeed, the tale of Soze is certainly frightening too, as Verbal tells how this figure, confronted by a group of Hungarian gangsters, shot his own wife and children in order to demonstrate his will to do whatever was necessary to succeed, and then allowed one Hungarian to escape so that he might relate these terrible events, testify to his power, describe the things that mark his character. Thereafter, he becomes for the rest of the world nothing more than these marks, just an abstraction, or as he is variously styled, "a shield," "a myth," "a spook story." In effect, Soze—and Verbal in the recounting—has simply generated a narrative driven by a goal-directed character who is just a collection of horrific marks or exaggerated impressions, in the process demonstrating how easily the components of such narratives—dramatic speech, compulsive action, distinctive features—are generated and hold us in their thrall, or stall us in our movements, as they do Kujan who lets him escape.

But as we eventually see, Soze is quite real, a figure whose strength lies precisely in his ability to change, to adapt, to adopt whatever marks or traits—such as the stutter, crippled walk, and nervous chatter of a Verbal—he needs to survive. In effect, his power lies in his ability to play at *being* a character in a world that seems inclined to see people in static ways, in terms of what Robinson calls "an enduring identifiability, a reliable stability" ("The Movies II" 27), even while taunting those around him with tales of change and unpredictability, as with Keaton. As the name "Verbal" implies, he relies on our rational predilection, the obeissance we pay to language, as he offers a torrent of words—and playfully notes, "people say I talk too much"—and draws upon whatever his confining world presents him with—in this case, the random elements found in the San Piedro police station—to conjure up just the sort of character the police are looking for and the type of narrative in which they want to situate him.

Of course, that ability does not render him into a figure of value, one of any heroic status—a rather irrelevant notion, in any case, in the context of both this style of character and neo-noir. Rather, Kint/Soze becomes a figure of difference, as he mediates between Kujan, who insists to the last that his view of character as constant is reliable, and Keaton, who, even as a product of Kint's narration, represents a challenge to that notion, as a sign of possible change and moral value. As he plays at the very margins of difference, as simultaneously a prisoner and someone who, as one policeman puts it, "is protected from up on high," as a frightened, manipulated man and the ulti-mate manipulator and purveyor of fear, Kint/Soze interrogates the system—psychological, cultural, narrative—in which we seem so "comfortable." To a world that denies change, he is thus the ultimate outlaw, truly the devil, a changeling who moves in and out of character at will, in and out of plots, within and beyond the laws this world employs to maintain its illusory order. In the process he reveals just how contingent this world and its sense of order are. Ultimately, he embodies a kind of destructive power inherent in a world that insists change and difference are impossible, and thereby indicts that world's values.

In letting Verbal/Soze go, in setting him loose to continue his manipula-tions, Agent Kujan demonstrates the danger of hearing but not seeing, espe-cially of not looking at the stuff that crowds all around us, that clutters our existence. His dogged insistence that Keaton was ultimately behind this crime

that made no sense evokes a tradition of problematic noir investigators, such
as the insurance company detective Riordan of *The Killers* (1946), the private detective Brad Galt of *The Dark Corner* (1946), or the poisoned accoun-
tant Frank Bigelow of *D.O.A.* (1950), all of whom claim that they only want
to uncover a reason or logic behind events, to turn what Mike Hammer of
Kiss Me Deadly (1955) terms "the Great Whatsit" into an answered question,
even if it means, as in the last film, unleashing an atomic calamity, or, in *The
Killers*, producing a nearly pointless result: "the basic rate of the Atlantic
Casualty Company…will probably drop one-tenth of a cent."

That mocking trivialization of Riordan's "splendid efforts" reverberates
in *The Usual Suspects*'s unsettling conclusion, as Kujan receives, too late, a
sketch of Soze/Kint, a portrait of the face that has been staring back at him
and, via a number of subjective shots, us, for much of this narrative, the face
that completes those various fragmentary shots of the figure who pisses on all
plans at the film's start. In this case that rationalizing of events with an almost
ludicrous payoff becomes a warning about all such single-minded pursuits:
all that subordinate seeing to language, knowledge of another to the marks
that stand-in for—and effectively become—character. Yet it is a warning that
resounds throughout the recent crop of neo-noirs, populated as they are with
elusive, enigmatic, role-playing figures who seem to function in much the
same way, that is, mainly to bring us face to face with our expectations of
character. For repeatedly films like *The Last Seduction*, *Romeo is Bleeding*, and
Pulp Fiction play at trying to pin characters down, to put them in an envelope, as Soze does with all five of the "suspects" in this film, to reduce them to
a series of simple marks, or like Wolf in *Pulp Fiction*, to clean up the "mess"
of character and render our narrative world comfortable again. Yet a disturbing difference always remains, and the difference that marks the figures in
such films is what now propels their narratives—and often seems to send
them spinning not in the easy, goal-directed, goal-attaining direction of classical narrative, but seemingly out of control, or at least out of the "usual,"
suspected trajectory. But along that path there also lies the potential for a
new subversive development, for projecting a rather different sense of character, of individuality, one that might even challenge our usual values.

I recognize that those who tend to see classical narrative in that monolithic, non-differentiated way described above might anticipate this sort of
development. It would simply illustrate how, over long periods of time and
changing cultural dynamics, Hollywood "has selectively borrowed from the
international art cinema," as Bordwell explains, through a process of "stylistic assimilation" (373). He sees "psychologically ambivalent or confused char-

acters" as a key structure in the larger semiotic of "art" or modernist narrative. While that structural approach has provided us with a rather neat, even
"comfortable" way of conceptualizing the development of cinematic narrative, it does draw upon a sense of the cinema as a kind of monological voice,
addressing an ideal and passive spectator. While Robinson's value approach
never sought to schematize the nature of that spectatorship, it did approach
the cinema as a vital visual encounter, in the phenomenological tradition of
Maurice Merleau-Ponty and Gaston Bachelard. We might note that in an
early overview of such approaches, Dudley Andrew warned that "the classification of general formal codes" which typified structural film theory threatened "to retard the…tasks of describing the peculiar way meaning is experienced in cinema and the unique quality" of the cinematic experience(46). By
returning to this tradition, as more recently Vivian Sobchack and several
others have tried to do[3], and in the way that Robinson's analysis of character
suggests, perhaps we can better situate the seeming anomalies of movie narrative; by incorporating an emphasis on the filmic experience itself into that
useful but monolithic conception of narrative development—one that divides narrative into classical and art forms—we might better understand specific films which challenge classical norms and, in their subtle ways, point up
the nature and potential of the movies.

The Usual Suspects offers an especially telling illustration in this regard,
particularly of the impact of character in the neo-noir. It is a film that begins
with a mystery and almost literally invites its viewers to play at guessing that
mystery, at ferreting out the clues to its narrative and anticipating its twist
ending. Moreover, that mystery depends totally on the film's conception—
and our own orchestrated and convention-driven misconception—of character, a set of reactions that pointedly flies in the face of our anticipation of
narrative conservatism and undercuts one sort of pleasure or comfort we
have come to expect from our films. In its place it offers us a different take on
character, one that underscores the very real—changing, self-creating, even
unfathomable—nature of character that truly characterizes our era's noir and
that, as Robinson pointed out, has always stood as an energizing potential in
our movies.

NOTES

[1] For more particular elaboration on the literary narrative/film narrative contrast, I would recommend Robinson's co-authored article, "*2001* and the Literary Sensibility," as well as my application of this approach in an all-too-obviously derivative essay, "The Organic Narrative: Word and Image in *Barry Lyndon*."

[2] That boast carries significant weight because it also identifies our idealized place within the film, as spectators who typically know more than the diegetic characters. Our alignment—if not quite identification—with Kujan in this regard thus becomes not only part of the narrative's strategy of surprise, but also part of its examination of character, as it ultimately challenges us to question the position of superiority that attaches to his person and that derives from those notions of predictability, rationality, and sameness he espouses.

[3] In her ambitious text, *The Address of the Eye*, Vivian Sobchack has made a more systematic move in the direction Robinson staked out in the 1960s and 1970s. Grounded specifically in the European tradition of phenomenology, as exemplified by Merleau-Ponty, she describes how film holds the potential for confronting us with "the perceptual correlations that are the film's activity," a potential for the "production of vision as visible" (226), even if that capacity usually "remains *implicit* in its materiality," disguised in the material bodies that classical narrative thrusts to the foreground (226). See too Dudley Andrew's article, "The Neglected Tradition of Phenomenology in Film Theory," wherein he describes how "phenomenology seeks to put reason and language at the service of life or at least of human experience" (49), as well as Kevin Sweeney's review of recent developments in this regard, "The Persistence of Vision: The Re-Emergence of Phenomenological Theories of Film."

WORKS CITED

Seeing Beyond (SB) Pagination Added by Editor

Andrew, Dudley. "The Neglected Tradition of Phenomenology in Film Theory." *Wide Angle* 2.2 (1978): 44-49.

Bordwell, David, Janet Staiger, and Kristin Thompson. *The Classical Hollywood Cinema: Film Style and Mode of Production to 1960*. New York: Columbia UP, 1985.

Robinson, W. R. *From Myth to Monism: The Narrative Feats of Plato and Aristotle*. Unpublished manuscript.

___. "The Movies as a Revolutionary Moral Force, Part I." *SB*: 47-59. "Part II." *SB*: 60-76.

___. "The Movies, Too, Will Make You Free." *SB*: 1-19.

___, and Mary McDermott. "*2001* and the Literary Sensibility." *SB*: 77-91.

Sobchack, Vivian. *The Address of the Eye: A Phenomenology of Film Experience.* Princeton: Princeton UP, 1992.

Sweeney, Kevin W. "The Persistence of Vision: The Re-Emergence of Phenomenological Theories of Film." *Film and Philosophy* 1 (1994): 29-38.

Telotte, J. P. *Voices in the Dark: The Narrative Patterns of Film Noir.* Urbana: U of Illinois Press, 1989.

___. "The Organic Narrative: Word and Image in *Barry Lyndon*." *Film Criticism* 3.2 (1979): 18-31.

Meriwether Lewis in Imagination's Hell: The Journals and Robinsonian Aesthetics[1]

Walter C. Foreman, Jr.

I FIRST ENCOUNTERED W. R. Robinson's ideas about movies and narrative in the early 70s when, with no particular training, I began to teach film courses. What I learned in this encounter, above all, was to pay attention to what is actually there, in the images of a movie, in the sequence of changes in a movie. It really did feel like a liberation ("the movies, too, will make you free"), not from the claims of other film critics, for at that point I had never read them, but from a state of passivity, which, in Robinsonian terms, amounts to a confinement in an older story. I began to think about stories, about a sequence of images *as* a story, about people both in and out of movies living by stories or making stories to live, or both; about the fact that not only is the story not the same as the plot or the dialogue, but that in the sequence of images the movie may tell a story that reveals the limits of the verbal story, or even contradicts it; about the fact that it makes a big difference whether the story is old (shaped, for instance, by guilt or genre or habit) or new (shaped by curiosity or imagination).

In the early 90s I began to think about the 1803-1806 expedition of Lewis and Clark and their Corps of Discovery across the American continent and about what they, especially Lewis, missed, as well as what they saw. I realized that in important ways I was making sense of the expedition—in both its successes and its failures—in what I, at least, take to be Robinsonian terms, with a text that is neither a movie nor, formally, literature (though frequently called an "epic" or an "odyssey").[2] In particular I found myself focusing on the habits of eye and mind of Meriwether Lewis.

Lewis and Clark never shaped their notes—the Journals—into a more formal story. Lewis was supposed to write the book of the trip and in April 1807 advertised a three-volume traversal, but he died, apparently by suicide, on October 11, 1809, before he could do so. Clark didn't feel equal to the task, so it fell to a young Philadelphian named Nicholas Biddle, later the target of Jacksonian economics, to produce a coherent narrative, the authorized version. Fortunately, the Journals themselves have survived, so that we can draw all sorts of stories out of them, or see all sorts of stories that went into them, stories of Jeffersonian imagination and ambition, both political and scientific; stories of imperialism and Manifest Destiny, of diplomacy and paternalism, of the struggle for political and economic domination of the Mississippi-Missouri drainage and if possible of the Columbia drainage as well, all the way to the Pacific; stories of map-making, about discovering where they were, and we are; stories of curiosity and scientific investigation— the discovery and description of "new" species, often by talking to people for whom they were not new; stories of ethnographic investigation and linguistics; stories of naming—putting words, often English words and names, on the species and places of the West—claiming by naming; stories of cultural exchange, the trading with strangers of knowledge about each other, becoming a brief community, dancing and feasting together. We find the story of the daily problem of moving forward, of finding a way, of surviving, and the great adventure stories, in legendary versions like the one of two men crossing the never-before-seen wilderness, perhaps with a single Indian woman as a guide, or in a more authentic version in which the party numbered as many as 42 and the woman brought her husband and baby along and they got information most of the way across from people—white or Indian—who had been there before. With hindsight, we can recognize the story of the first encounter between the US Army and the Sioux. In modern terms, we can identify a story of classic "male bonding" against a difficult and hostile landscape; or of the manly force, penetrating "the Virgin Land," or, in more Fellinian (and accurate) terms, the cross-country trip of two white clowns unable to control a band of horny augustos who spread European seed among the women of various tribes, perhaps bestowing "powerful medicine,"[3] certainly giving and taking the pox (and thus *needing* medicine). All these stories come back to the words and occasional images of the Journals, a verbal record of moving and seeing, whose characteristic phrase, its refrain, is "we proceeded on."

Let's look at the story of Meriwether Lewis seeing a brave new world. Put Lewis in the present moment, he's magnificent—alert, resourceful, knowledgeable, intrepid, observant, tough, agile, cool in a crisis, intelligent, resilient, open, honest, even sociable. (I'd like to say: a genius.) Or keep him thinking about material problems, present or future, and he remains clear sighted and capable. But let him step out of time and think himself into stories of the past or the future, putting the past or the future between himself and what he sees at the moment, using his imagination to recall a "legendary" past or project a wish-fulfilling future, and he grows depressed, fearful, alienated, racist, and blind.

Consider the Corps of Discovery at Ft. Clatsop, near the coast of what is now Oregon, in the winter of 1805-06. The triumph of having made it all the way across was tempered by the knowledge that they had the whole damn thing to cross again. They felt the weight of the continent behind them, or now, come spring, again in front of them, keeping them from home. Linguistically and culturally as well as geographically isolated, they had no language in common with any of the local Indians. Frequently ill, short of supplies, short of the coveted blue beads to trade with, they worried about food as they killed off many of the region's elk and caused the rest to move away. The daily refrain "we proceeded on" was replaced by "again today it rained." The coastal winter was too cold to be comfortable but not cold enough to keep things from rotting, whether the elk they shot in the woods, their clothes, their own bodies, or their souls.

I still have trouble believing that Lewis, once they moved to the Oregon side of the Columbia and built Ft. Clatsop on the Netul River, never crossed the few miles to the ocean.[4] Clark went, and at least three quarters of the men, and even Sacagawea and her 11-month old son went, to see a whale on the beach. But not Lewis. He held the fort and wrote in his journal, fixing himself in the details, haunted by the big picture.

Someone—often Indians—would bring him a plant or animal he'd never seen before. For instance, on February 24, 1806, the eulachon, or candlefish, a kind of smelt. Lewis is enthralled:

> This evening we were visited by Comowooll the Clatsop Chief and 12 men women & children of his nation…. The chief and his party had brought for sail a Sea Otter skin some hats, stergeon and a species of small fish which now begin to run, and are taken in great quantities in the Columbia R. about 40 miles above us by means of skiming or scooping nets. on this page I have drawn the likeness of them as large as life; it as perfect as I can make it with my pen and will serve to give a general idea of the fish. the rays of the fins are boney but not sharp tho' somewhat pointed, the small fin on the

back next to the tail has no rays of bone being a thin membranous pellicle. the fins next to the gills have eleven rays each. those of the abdomen have eight each, those of the pinna-ani are 20 and 2 half formed in front. that of the back has eleven rays. all the fins are of a white colour. the back is of a bluish duskey colour and that of the lower part of the sides and belley is of a silvery white. no spots on any part. the first bone of the gills next behind the eye is of a bluis cast, and the second of a light goald colour nearly white. the puple of the eye is black and the iris of a silver white. the underjaw exceeds the uper; and the mouth opens to great extent, folding like that of the herring.it has no teeth. the abdomen is obtuse and smooth; in this differing from the herring, shad anchovey &c of the Malacopterygious Order & Class Clupea, to which however I think it more nearly allyed than to any other altho' it has not their accute and serrate abdomen and the under jaw exceeding the upper. the scales of this little fish are so small and thin that without minute inspection you would suppose they had none. they are filled with roes of a pure white colour and cooked in Indian stile, which is by roasting a number of them together on a wooden spit without any previous preperation whatever. they are so fat they require no additional sauce, and I think them superior to any fish I ever tasted, even more delicate and lussious than the white fish of the lakes which have heretofore formed my standart of excellence among the fishes. I have heard the fresh anchovey much extolled but I hope I shall be pardoned for beleiving this quite as good. the bones are so soft and fine that they form no obstruction in eating this fish. [Monday, February 24, 1806; M6:342-44[5]; Lewis's text is arranged around a delicate drawing of the fish which extends diagonally from corner to corner of the journal page]

This is in part simply the Linnaean program, carried out in the wilderness by the emissary of the European Enlightenment, working from a motionless specimen, a corpse. But Lewis's descriptions of what he sees show a sensitivity to differences as much as to classification by likenesses, an intense encounter with novel details, and a sense of wonder and joy that goes beyond the need to name and classify. It's the difference, the newness, that excite Lewis and Clark. To some extent, they showed a similar receptivity to *human* difference, particularly when they were seeing material culture. But behind their interest in the new could lie a classification of human "kinds" marked by a violent suppression of the novel and particular in order to live by the old and the general:

This forenoon we were visited by *Tah-cum* a principal Chief of the

Chinnooks and 25 men of his nation. we had never seen this cheif before he is a good looking man of about 50 years of age reather larger in statue than most of his nation; as he came on a friendly visit we gave himself and party some thing to eat and plyed them plentifully with smoke. we gave this cheif a small medal with which he seemed much gratifyed. in the evening at sunset we desired them to depart as is our custom and closed our gates. we never suffer parties of such number to remain within the fort all night; for notwithstanding their apparent friendly disposition, their great averice and hope of plunder might induce them to be treacherous. at all events we determined allways to be on our guard as much as the nature of our situation will permit us, and never place our selves at the mercy of any savages. we well know, that the treachery of the aborigenes of America and the too great confidence of our countrymen in their sincerity and friendship, has caused the distruction of many hundreds of us. so long have our men been accustomed to a friendly intercourse with the natives, that we find it difficult to impress on their minds the necessity of always being on their guard with rispect to them. this confidence on our part, we know to be the effect of a series of uninterupted friendly intercouse, but the well known treachery of the natives by no means entitle them to such confidence, and we must check it's growth in ourselves, and repeating to our men, that our preservation depends on never loosing sight of this trait in their character, and being always prepared to meet it in whatever shape it may present itself. [Thursday, February 20, 1806; M6 :330-31]

The Indians are marked by a certain *character*, and it's this character—"well known treachery"—that colors this episode, not the present (and by Lewis's own account, genuine) openness and friendliness of *Tah-cum* and his company, not what's actually in front of him at that moment. Lewis as movie critic sees a story that isn't there, a traditional plot, one he has brought with him. He sees below the surface, to an absent treachery.

I don't mean to deny the need for "being always prepared." About five months later, on July 27, 1806, a slight lapse of vigilance led to the Expedition's only fatal encounter with Indians, along the Marias River, back east of the continental divide, high in what is now Montana: "This morning at day light the indians got up and crouded around the fire, J. Fields who was on post had carelessly laid his gun down behind him near where his brother was sleeping…." What ensued was a fight that left two Blackfeet dead and Lewis and his three men racing cross-country for their lives. But back in Ft. Clatsop on February 20, vigilance doesn't mean being alive to the next moment; it seems rather to mean expecting the next moment to repeat an absent and at least partly fanciful past.[6]

Lewis did not look out of time only toward the Indians. Writing about himself, on his 31st birthday, August 18, 1805, right after one of his great successes—the encounter with the Shoshone that promised the Corps an escape from freezing and starving high in the Rockies and allowed them to reach the Pacific—he looks to past and future and becomes depressed:

> This day I completed my thirty first year, and conceived that I had in all human probability now existed about half the period which I am to remain in this Sublunary world. I reflected that I had as yet done but little, very little indeed, to further the hapiness of the human race, or to advance the information of the succeeding generation. I viewed with regret the many hours I have spent in indolence, and now soarly feel the want of that information which those hours would have given me had they been judiciously expended. but since they are past and cannot be recalled, I dash from me the gloomy thought and resolved in future, to redouble my exertions and at least indeavour to promote those two primary objects of human existence, by giving them the aid of that portion of talents which nature and fortune have bestoed on me; or in future, to live for *mankind*, as I have heretofore lived for *myself*. [Sunday, August 18, 1805; M5:118; Lewis's emphasis]

This shows a self-lacerating nobility, I suppose, like Hamlet. Tragically, Lewis had already lived far more than "half the period which [he was] to remain in this Sublunary world." He died, apparently by suicide, only three years and two weeks after the return of the expedition to St. Louis on September 23, 1806.[7]

If one were searching in the Journals—unfairly, since the depression itself was more than punishment enough—for an appropriate punishment of Meriwether Lewis for looking, in Taoist terms, at "that" instead of "this," one could choose the episode near the end, on August 11, 1806, in what is now western North Dakota, when Lewis goes hunting with the Expedition's half-Indian, half-French master boatman and principal violinist, one-eyed, near-sighted Peter Cruzatte. Now if you were wearing elkskin clothes, would you go elk hunting with a man who was one-eyed *and* nearsighted? When Lewis felt the bullet, he thought at first there were Indians around, and afterwards Cruzatte maintained he *had* shot at an elk. In any case, Lewis couldn't sit down comfortably for quite a while and ceased his journalizing, leaving Clark to finish the story of the float back to civilization.

Since in a *festschrift* for Bill Robinson I should say *something* about the movies, I will consider *The Far Horizons*, an amusing little film, if you've read the Journals. (I use the word "film" advisedly.) This 1955 movie, directed by Rudolph Maté, has very little to do with the Journals or most of their stories.[8] It's not what I would think of as a Robinsonian movie, but he'd likely see something I haven't. Besides, one of the things I've learned from Bill is that there's no movie that won't yield things of value to thoughtful attention. That *The Far Horizons* doesn't follow the Journals is not itself a problem, just an observation, and if I take the movie seriously, I may learn something.

In *The Far Horizons* there is more or less constant tension between Lewis (played by Fred MacMurray) and Clark (Charlton Heston), in contrast to the remarkably uniform harmony between them as it appears in all the surviving documents, including the journals of the enlisted men. At the center of the story are love triangles: Lewis and Clark and Julia Hancock, Lewis and Clark and Sacajawea, Clark and Charbonneau and Sacajawea, Clark and Wild Eagle and Sacajawea, all of which include Clark.[9] The movie begins with Clark unwittingly stealing Lewis's intended, Julia Hancock (played by Barbara Hale), to whom Lewis has been too slow to propose (he is interrupted by Clark's arrival and Jefferson's invitation to lead an expedition to the west). Out on the trail, Clark gradually takes up with Sacajawea (Donna Reed, looking well tanned), much to Lewis's disgust and anger, and when Clark insists on bringing Sacajawea back to Washington, Lewis declares his intention to court martial him. These are the Lewis and Clark of Gary Larson's cartoons, of *The Far Side*, not of history.[10]

The primness of MacMurray's Lewis was perhaps a characteristic of the historical Lewis as well. Certainly the control of their men's sexuality became a major medical (if not moral) problem for the two captains during the two winters spent among Indians. On Saturday, March 15, 1806, Lewis and Clark made their men promise to have no intercourse with a particular group of women who had been "brought for market" to Ft. Clatsop by a Chinook chief and "the old baud his wife...the same party that had communicated the venerial to so many of our party in November last, and of which they have finally recovered" [M6:416]; on Monday the 17th the captains recorded their belief that "the men have preserved their constancy to the vow of celibacy which they made on this occasion" [M6:425-26].[11] Two days later, on Wednesday, March 19, Lewis concludes a detailed description of the woven cedar-bark skirts of Clatsop women by noting that the garment is "of sufficient thickness when the female stands erect to conceal those parts usually covered from formiliar view, but when she stoops or places herself in many other attitudes, this battery of Venus is not altogether impervious to the inquisitive and penetrating eye of the amorite" [M6:435]. The eye penetrates to the skin, but Lewis's coy burst of Latinisms suggests that perhaps he thinks it shouldn't. Here, in contrast to the record of his frank visual exploration of the candlefish, language puts a buffer between Lewis's eye and the world, in this case between his eye and the human being beneath the artifact. I am reminded of Prof. Robinson's complaints about skin flicks:

> Though the clothes [in this case the cedar-bark skirts] are absent, something else, some artifice, unnatural and invisible, overlays the skin, acting as a transparent protective shield that prohibits the naked eye from negotiating a direct exchange with the natural skin, and the imagination, as a consequence, from contacting its creative source.[12]

In movies that, on the contrary, accept their capacity to be an art of the senses, "Indulgence of the eye in the visible creation acts as a corrective to dogma; it leads to conforming the mind to life rather than life to the mind." And despite lapses into prejudice or wishful thinking (as in Lewis's response to the visit of *Tah-cum*), indulging their eyes in the visible creation is what the historical Lewis and Clark, and their men too, did often on their long journey, for more than two years seeing new lands and new waters, new plants and animals, new people. And if these people were new to the Corps of Discovery, so the men of the Corps of Discovery were new to them. Some episodes in the story of Lewis and Clark tell a story of a relation between travellers and natives in the West much different from the one that eventually prevailed. In many pages of the Journals, the Corps and the Indians find mutual delight in novelty and difference.

But not in *The Far Horizons*, whose sense of "skin" appears in Donna Reed's clearly cosmetic dark face, not really skin at all. Nor do the film's Lewis and Clark "indulge" their eyes in "the visible creation." In *The Far Horizons*, we do not see Lewis and Clark doing any investigation of either natural history or ethnography. We do see a good deal of geographical measurement. Clark tells Sacajawea the records and maps are more important than he is. The expedition is important here for political reasons, to *possess* the land, and the mapmaking serves that end, as indeed it did in history. But there is little or no sense of curiosity involved. As for the "otherness" of the Indians, they might as well be from *F-Troop*.

There is far more interhuman violence in this movie's 108 minutes than there was in the three years of the actual trip. In history, the Corps killed two Indians, in a single fight less than two months from the end, and lost only one of their members, much earlier, to appendicitis, not warfare. In the movie, there are two major battles, in which a number of Indians and at least three Corpsmen are killed. *The Far Horizons* shows the generic story of the American Western with Indians—but also the story of a later stage in the relation between whites and Indians in the West, a stage only latent in the Journals, featuring systematic violence, treachery, dispossession, containment, and elimination.

Virtually all of the movie's outdoor scenes appear to have been shot in Jackson Hole, near the Tetons, so that anyone who has actually been across the western United States may get the uncanny sensation that the Corps of Discovery is going around in circles, which is appropriate to the movie's telling of what are clearly old stories, love triangles and patriotic celebrations in which possession of women and possession of land are metaphorically linked. "Possession" was clearly a motive on the part of Jefferson, the public justification for spending the money. But Lewis and Clark's Journals tell the story of moving and seeing and telling about where they went and what they saw, a story of relentless curiosity about the people and plants and animals and land that lie around the next bend in the river or over the next hill. As for "relentless curiosity," I noted earlier that after he was wounded by one of his own men, Lewis stopped keeping his journal for the last six weeks of the journey. But feverish and suffering as he was, he couldn't stop easily: "as wrighting in my present situation is extreemly painfull to me I shall desist untill I recover and leave to my frind Capt. C. the continuation of our journal, however I must notice a singular Cherry which is found on the Missouri in the bottom lands about the beaverbends...the stem is compound erect and subdivided or branching without any regular order...," and so on in Lewis's usual meticulous manner, until he concludes with "I have never seen it in blume," his last words in the Journals [M8:158]. Lewis, his eye at once the scientist's and the artist's, ends with these words of both caution—he cannot describe what he has not seen—and regret—for beauty he has not seen, perhaps never would, probably never did: "I have never seen it in blume."

But the story in *The Far Horizons* is simply about possession.[13] The women—Julia and particularly Sacajawea—are metaphors for the land. At the end, Thomas Jefferson, the Great White Father, who never leaves the White House, may save the appearances by sending Sacajawea back "to her people," but visually, she who earlier in the story had moved over the land more vigorously and effectively than anyone else in the movie, by horse and on foot, or by swimming in rivers, ends as a verbal narrator riding in a fancy European coach on a paved road (again in Jackson Hole!), isolated and confined, curtains drawn. Motion over this now-familiar landscape may be easier than it was earlier in the movie, but it's contained, closed off, and there is less to see: the wilderness is paved, the Indian is trapped, and the camera "escapes" only to see a motionless postcard image of a land without people, over which "The End" appears. Not the same story as the Journals, certainly, but in its own way disturbingly realistic.

The sovereignty, paternalism, and control of Indian movement toward which *The Far Horizons* moves were certainly possibilities already in the aims of the Corps of Discovery. Jefferson as "father," taking care of the Indians as a demonstration of his sovereignty, appears as part of the plan, before the expedition, in some last-minute instructions the President sent to Lewis on January 22, 1804, in the light of the formal conclusion of the Louisiana Purchase, before the Corps crossed into what would have been French territory:

> Being now become sovereigns of the country, without however any diminution of the Indian rights of occupancy [but not ownership!] we are authorised to propose to them [the Indians] in direct terms the institution of commerce with them. It will now be proper you should inform those through whose country you will pass, or whom you may meet, that their late fathers the Spaniards have agreed to withdraw all their troops from all the waters & country of the Missisipi & Missouri, that they have surrendered to us all their subjects Spanish & French settled there, and all their posts & lands: that henceforward we become their fathers and friends, and that we shall endeavor that they shall have no cause to lament the change: …that we shall endeavor to become acquainted with them as soon as possible, and that they will find in us faithful friends and protectors.[14]

The Far Horizons itself emphasizes the success of the expedition in terms of United States sovereignty, not the happiness or community of individuals of any race or country. Except for Jefferson, the major characters all end rather unhappy, separate from each other, all the triangles broken into scattered points.

Cinematically, morally, aesthetically, *far* horizons are not to be seen in this movie, not glimpsed and fallen back from as in *Hiroshima Mon Amour* and certainly not crossed, as in *Juliet of the Spirits*.[15] But what about the Journals themselves? Might the Journals be a movie that crosses far horizons?

Might Meriwether Lewis after all be dancing out there in imagination's heaven? It would be eccentric, especially in a context of Robinsonian aesthetics, to claim that a huge collection of words, with some drawings and maps, is a "movie." And yet…

> As the camera, setting the example, points toward and beholds what light illuminates, so movie criticism must follow its lead by opening the mind through opening the eyes, and that can happen only via specifying, or pointing to, what is there in fact. The movie provides the model of how to study it and, indeed, study "reality," for as a moral phenomenon, as art, it exemplifies the true and the good. It persuades by the power of its being, not by precept; by attraction, not compulsion—as all art does.[16]

Hardly intended as art, the Journals, the record of a daily encounter with life as well as the daily pursuit of imagination across far horizons, have seemed to many to have the power of art, to be, for instance, the great epic poem of American culture, its very roughness suited to an unfinished country and an unfinished people. As art, the Journals have persuaded, by attraction, many people of quite various intellectual backgrounds to move across the land, following the Journals as their "model" for seeing what is there now, taught by the "dailyness" of the Journals, as well as for imagining the America of two hundred years ago, before highways and maps, motels and fast-food restaurants, dams and power lines, instant communication.[17] If the Journals are art, they are so by virtue of their record of Lewis and Clark following the light across the continent and back as men with (mostly) open eyes, looking (mostly) not out of time but at the moment, to what was there in fact.

NOTES

[1] This essay is a revision of a paper I delivered on 26 January 1996 in a section on Robinsonian aesthetics at the Florida State University Comparative Literature Circle's 21st Annual Conference on Literature and Film. My title alludes to a statement near the end of Prof. Robinson's essay "The Movies, Too, Will Make You Free," in *Seeing Beyond* (SB),pp. 1-19: "She [the example is Marilyn Monroe] has been released, as has the moviemaker and the viewer, and, indeed, man's mind everywhere, to dance in imagination's heaven" (18)

[2] See Albert Furtwangler, *Acts of Discovery: Visions of America in the Lewis and Clark Journals* (Urbana & Chicago: U of Illinois P, 1993) 192-207 ("Themes for a Wilderness Epic").

[3] See James P. Ronda, *Lewis and Clark among the Indians* (Lincoln & London: U of Nebraska P, 1984) 62-64.

[4] He had seen the ocean back in November, from what is now the Washington side of the Columbia.

[5] I quote Lewis and Clark from *The Journals of the Lewis & Clark Expedition*, 11 vols., ed. Gary E. Moulton (Lincoln & London: U of Nebraska P, 1986-97). "M6:342" means page 342 of Vol. 6 of this edition. The irregularities of spelling, punctuation, and usage follow the original journals.

[6] Ronda (212) says of the end of the passage quoted above from Lewis's February 20 entry that "With those words Lewis moved from common-sense vigilance of the sort required of every explorer to a dangerous flirtation with paranoia.... A long way from home, the expedition felt hemmed in by a strange environment and seemingly unpredictable people. Isolation, loneliness, and fear—all extract a high price from even the strongest and most moral."

[7] The question of whether Lewis committed suicide or was murdered remains of both scholarly and popular interest; it was recently the topic, for instance, of a program on the History Channel. Lewis seems, in any case, given to depression, and we might wonder whether finally among the causes of his depression, along with questions about his governorship of the Louisiana Territory and his fiscal management, was writer's block, his failure to shape the story of his accomplishments into publishable form.

[8] And in fact it does not claim to be based on the Journals, but on *Sacajawea of the Shoshones*, by Della Gould Emmons. It does, however, subtitle itself "The Story of the Lewis & Clark Expedition."

[9] Lewis is not in love with Sacajawea, but he deeply resents Clark's falling in love with Sacajawea as a betrayal of Julia which only compounds Clark's unknowing betrayal of Lewis himself.

[10] Lewis and Clark appear several times in Larson's cartoons. For example: the elkskin-clad explorers are sitting by a campfire in the wilderness; one of them—in Larson we can't always tell which is which—writes in his journal while the other cleans his rifle. We see the journalist's thoughts as he writes, "July 2, 1805. Well, the cur did it again today. While walking behind me he stepped on the heel of my shoe, causing my foot to come out. The frequency of this occurrence has made me begin to doubt its accidental nature...." The caption: "Tensions mount on the Lewis and Clark expedition."

[11] Venereal disease among the Chinooks originated in trade with men from the European and American ships that began visiting the area regularly from the 1790s. See Ronda, 208-09, for an account of the economics of sex between the Chinooks and the white visitors.

[12] "Stripping the Eye: Some Observations on the Movies as Striptease," *SB*, 92-113. My quotations are from pgs. 98 and 113.

[13] For an account of the modes of possession introduced on this continent by European settlers, including the importance of the land survey (the principal research activity of Clark in *The Far Horizons*), see James Howard Kunstler, *The Geography of Nowhere: The Rise and Decline of America's Man-Made Landscape* (New York: Simon and Schuster, 1993), chapters 2 and 3.

[14] *Letters of the Lewis and Clark Expedition with Related Documents, 1783-1854,* 2nd ed., ed. Donald Jackson (Urbana, Chicago, & London: U of Illinois P, 1978) 1: 165-66. The tangled web of French and Spanish claims to the Mississippi-Missouri drainage needn't concern us here.

[15] I allude, of course, to W. R. Robinson, "If You Don't See, You're Dead: The Immediate Encounter with the Image in *Hiroshima Mon Amour* and *Juliet of the Spirits*," *SB*, 114-152.

[16] W. R. Robinson, "Making Sense of the Movies," *SB*, 34.

[17] See, e.g., Dayton Duncan, *Out West: American Journey Along the Lewis and Clark Trail* (New York: Penguin, 1987).

Hemingway's *Green Hills of Africa* as Evolutionary Narrative:
Helix and Scimitar

SUSAN LYNN DRAKE AND A. CARL BREDAHL, JR.
(WITH THE ASSISTANCE OF WILLIAM R. ROBINSON)

FROM "THE NARRATIVE CONTEXT"

THE FOREWORD TO *Green Hills of Africa* (Charles Scribner's Sons, 1935) proposes the narrator's attempt to present "the shape of a country and the pattern of a month's action." Taking initiative from this direction, our discussion pursues a concern with "shape," "pattern," and action in Hemingway's 1935 narrative. Such scrutiny demonstrates that the narrative's opening images reveal twentieth-century Western man at a cultural moment of transition, presented with two views of the world. The first, the orthodox view from the cross, glorifies the urge to transcend the earth, to be above its processes. The alternative, the heterodox view from the hunting blind, acknowledges and accepts the creative earth. The Christian option being found bankrupt, the narrator chooses the secular perspective. From then on, his journey through Africa articulates the process by which he heals himself of the tradition of the cross and proceeds to create his own story.

The Foreward also states that the narrator wants to see how his narrative will compete with a work of the imagination, a statement that can create confusion if we assume only two kinds of writing: imaginative/fictional and rational/non-fictional. In the terms of this binary opposition, the narrator appears to propose a piece of autobiography to "compete" with a piece of fiction; not much is to be gained from that proposition because it does not make sense. We, however, offer a third alternative to the binary trap, that of creative energy. *Green Hills of Africa*, we suggest, competes with a work of the imagination in the sense that the act of imagining is itself part of the traditional intellectual activity. In the mental process, reason works with abstractions, and the image-making faculty visualizes those abstractions; it *makes* images and is, therefore, aligned with reason as part of overall mental processes which in every phase seek to distinguish the individual, set him apart from his natural environment by calling attention to what is unique about the human species.

But what if the individual wants to work with images of the eye rather than images of the mind? This is, for example, what a movie-maker like Federico Fellini does when his camera focuses on faces and places in Rome. It is also something each of us does every day as we look at the world around us; our bodies and minds respond to visual images as any natural organism does to its environment. The visual response necessarily involves us in the action of our world; it does not describe, therefore, a superior faculty but rather an additional capacity that the human being has to work with. What must be stressed is that this capacity is distinctly different from the rational and fiction-making acts of the mind. By definition, therefore, it is an element of potentiality, one which has not been valued by a western civilization which from the time of the Greeks has committed itself to the intellect and to the denial of vision as illusory, "fictional," and immoral.

We suggest, then, that *Green Hills of Africa* is a narrative which results from the effort to push beyond the strictly mental in order to ask about an individual's creative energy in relation to those same energies in its environment. *Green Hills* competes with a work of the imagination, creating its own genre in the process, because the story is neither fictional nor autobiographical as those terms are traditionally understood.

Asking about an individual's creative energies results in a new basis for action, thus the commitment made by Hemingway's narrator to pursuing "how far prose can be carried if any one is serious enough and has luck." Hemingway signals his effort to carry prose further than it has gone before through his use of existing literary forms—epic, drama, satire, novel, farce, and film. Traditional intellectual systems work on the assumption that movement is caused from the outside—by God, for example. In literature this assumption is evident in the perception that words carry a message that comes from outside the medium; the author has something to express and carefully chooses the medium that facilitates the expression. On the other hand, post-modernists focusing on intertextuality construct a different system in which texts play off against each other; external meaning is rejected in this view, but so is any evolutionary dynamic. In contrast, when Hemingway makes *Green Hills of Africa* out of previous literary forms, he looks at those forms genera- tively, as genres which enabled human beings at some earlier period to carry out certain mental actions by creating the needed forms. Now those forms become the means of new action. Actions are thus created out of actions; narratives become the source of narrative, not God or the author's mind or social realities. At the end of *Green Hills*, therefore, the narrator does not attempt to go beyond language or outside narrative to some external spiritual source. He cannot romantically repudiate man-made forms. Instead he turns to and recalls those forms, drawing on their power to generate the emerging form that is *Green Hills*.

Outwardly, the form of *Green Hills* is dramatic, the story beginning *in medias res* with Parts 1, 3, and 4 presenting the traditional structure of rising action, climax, and denouement. In fact, the serial publication of the narra- tive in *Scribner's* lists dramatic personae, including one "Mr. Hemingway, a braggart."[1] Individual sections (Parts) take the form of satire (the conversa- tions with Kandisky), novel (the struggle for dominance between the narra- tor and Karl), farce (the stumblings presented by M'Cola and the unclean gun), and film (the misdirected Chaplinesque effort to shoot the sable). Unifying all these internal forms is dependence on epic, the journey or quest, the going off to a new land, in this case an epic of vision. Chapter 1, for example, sets up the test for the narrator—does he have the passion to go beyond the limitations established by the figure of Kandisky; Part 2 estab- lishes his need to journey on the quest of healing his inner deficiencies. Part 4 carries him into the virgin land where the quest will be completed, allow- ing him to return to his world.

"The writer," says the Foreword, "has attempted to write an absolutely true book to see whether the shape of a country and the pattern of a month's action can, if truly presented, compete with a work of the imagination." What is the relationship, he asks, between the structure of an individual life and that of a literary work created by the rational mind? Can the structures benefit each other? As units of action, can the genres become means, sources of growth and used in such a way as to be gone beyond? These are different questions than using literary structures as norms to be imitated. Instead of breaking down structures, as does James Joyce in *Ulysses*, for example, Hemingway assimilates structures. In Joyce, epic serves as a moral model and ironic commentary on modern experience. According to Joyce, the modern world has devolved, degenerated; it is therefore necessary to look back to an ancient model for instruction Hemingway, however, evolves narrative out of the energy of former structures, looking forward rather than back. The fascist mind sees an inherited world coming apart and thus in need of imposed control; the post-modern mind argues that a world of inherited forms is the only world; but the mind fascinated by creative energy perceives growth emerging out of the process of assimilating and going beyond.

The relativity universe described by Einstein and Heisenberg cannot get energy from outside itself. A universe is a field of force and as such gets its energy from within. So also does narrative structure as it evolves in Hemingway. Consequently, the use of forms within the narrative of *Green Hills* and within the larger Hemingway canon is not a gimmick, not experimental playing with disintegration which consumes much of the energies of his contemporaries—e. e. cummings, for example—who concentrate on the collapse in experience. Hemingway uses form as part of the total action, the larger reintegrating vision that drives all his work.

We should stress, therefore, that *Green Hills* provides none of those rational markers such as "realistic" or "autobiographical" which allow the reader to give a piece a generic label. There is, for example, no factual background information on the organizing of the safari. And the reader is given little information on the past of the narrator—how he became sick or what his relationships were with P.O.M., Karl, or Pop before his narrative—nor on his future effort to write. There is no recounting of events, no history of safari. Dates or place names were removed from the holograph, resulting in few conventional grids by which a reader could logically locate himself in the narrative. Beginning *in media res*, the narrative quite literally springs out of itself rather than from any rational preparation for a trip. We focus entirely on the middle events of the narrator's experience, the exploration of shape and pattern as fuel for the creative enterprise.

Commitment to the process, the action, the going forward of life needs the quality of genius to sense where that action is, what its possibilities are, and how to make the best of those possibilities. It demands the ability to take forward the growth of writing rather than join the existing club of writers swept up in modern chaos. The title chosen for *Green Hills* indicates this commitment to going forward. After rejecting several other considerations, Hemingway chose *Green Hills of Africa,* an interesting decision which calls attention to the fact that there are remarkably few green hills in the narrative. The title makes little sense in terms of the narrative's apparent subject, but it makes considerable sense in terms of the action of assimilation and evolution. Lions as predators, the object of the opening hunt, do not constitute physical evolution; they transform meat to meat, providing for no change. Herbivores however, internally transform vegetation to meat. When the narrator of *Green Hills* goes into the virgin land, he consumes the internal organs of the kudu, purifying himself of his intellectual frustrations and carrying forward the evolution from herbivore to rational man and on to creative human being.

The resulting narrative springs from the consciousness of the safari as model for releasing the evolutionary capabilities of the human imagination. We watch the creator as part of creative processes, creating out of his own capacities rather than from the external surfaces of life that for example, the hero Achilles defines for another time as his alternatives. In other words, the life being committed to is not the flood of physical everyday events, the home and farm that Achilles rejects for glory, honor, and death. The life committed to in *Green Hills* is its evolutionary capacity, making the narrative both a pivotal story in twentieth-century experience and in the evolutionary continuum of the human experience.

In the following discussion, we seek to extend Carlos Baker's comments in *Hemingway: The Writer as Artist*, comments which point to patterns in the narrative but which fail to recognize the function of those patterns. Baker, for example, describes matters of "suspense," "conflict," "character," and "structure" to suggest that such elements do appear in a work otherwise concerned with verisimilitude. But such an approach really says little more than that *Green Hills* is a book about Africa written by the craftsman that was Ernest Hemingway. In contrast, we will stress that the shapes and patterns of the African safari supply the means by which the narrator's journey is consumed and put into motion. Seeing as event (as opposed to the physical mechanism of seeing) occurs "out there" as our eyes encounter an object. The image produced by the mating of eye and object is neither static and apart from viewer nor abstractly symbolic of something other than itself. The image is, rather, an event, an individual moment in which the action of creative evolution takes place. In these terms, we focus on the images of *Green Hills of Africa* which themselves evolved out of the images of the original experience. Both are acts of relating forward because the act of seeing is occurring "out there." "I looked back…then I looked ahead" (214). In the following discussion we look at the images, then, for their inherent power to throw the action forward. Three native guides, for example, conduct separate segments of the safari's travels, segments which correspond to distinct phases in the narrator's growth. The first guide schools his American pupil in the wisdom of the body, the second in the lessons of the mind, and the third in the powers of life. The combination of these three facets—the sensory, the intellectual, and the creative—produces a completeness of action which enables the narrator-as-artist to write the account of his moral journey: *Green Hills of Africa.*

The two American companions, the narrator's wife P.O.M. and his friend Karl, function as indicators of their husband and friend's progress under the guides. Each correlates with a different part of the narrator's moral capabilities. The companions emerge into the foreground of the story when the values clustered about them are active in the narrator, and are surpassed when those values lessen.

The native guides and the American companions move against the background of a landscape whose prevailing forms relate the narrator's story on an archetypal level. The most dominant topographical feature is the road the safari travels upon, which is equated with the inventive, forward-thrusting urge in mankind. The road takes the narrator's steps through a succession of archetypal matriarchal forms: the Rift Valley, the hunting blind, and the ground cloth tent. An overview reveals that these shapes constitute advances in man's relationship to the earth. From the primordial chasm, to the quantitatively-shaped hollow, to the qualitatively-transformed cotton shelter, the earth proves responsive to man-as-maker.

Just as the African earth dynamically structures the narrative with its shapes, so do the major animals of the safari with the patterns of their horns. For example, the narrator hunts the more elemental rhinoceros, whose "horn" is merely a fleshy extension of its nose, when he himself is embroiled in the functionings of the body. The series of antelope encountered in the course of the safari—the reedbuck, eland, oryx, water buck—play prologue to the most intricate of all the horned game, the kudu and the sable. In a closing examination, these two animals are considered as aesthetic phenomena. The pair together climax the narrator's creative vision. In the extraordinary shaping of their horns, the narrator sees the workings of the life process itself, the spiraling helix of the kudu evoking the evolutionary thrust of generation, the scimitar curve of the sable, the inevitable and necessary consequence of death. From the helix and the scimitar we take our title for this study, the images around which Hemingway organized his green narrative.

PART IV. "In The Eye Of The Imagination"

The advent of the rainy season entails a time of great transition for the land of Africa, from the smallest guinea to the largest elephant. The present of the narrative is lived on the crest of a mounting wave of change, which breaks over the landscape in the onslaught of rain. As depicted in these pivotal four days between the dry and rainy seasons, the world the narrator lives in is characterized above all by flux. The physical reaction of the earth to the inundating waters indicates the nature of such change. One immediate consequence is, of course, the rust that eats at the metal of the narrator's gun; another is the flooded saltlick. Both chemical decomposition and structural damage bear witness to the destructive facet of the process of change. But while the rain causes decay in the present, it simultaneously prepares the continent for renewal. These seasonal rains supply the forward-looking factor in the landscape of *Green Hills of Africa*, their waters insure for the coming year the very greenness of the hills. As evidenced in these multiple, coexistent perspectives, rain as the agent of change brings both corrosion and generation to the continent of Africa.

Nowhere is the pervasiveness of this change reflected more concisely than in the first scene in Part IV. On the last afternoon of the safari, natives have come to the narrator's camp bearing electrifying news: "'He says,' Pop began, 'They have found a country where there are kudu and sable.'" At this sudden release from what had been thought a doomed enterprise, the narrator catapults out of the doldrums of Chapter Eleven into the motion of Chapter Twelve as he heads out to the new, unhunted country with the natives. But the archetypal landscape so central to Part I has been washed by the rains of Part III. Now as the narrator moves through that landscape in the first scene of Part IV, three of its major components betray the effect of the change; the guide, the road, and the blind have been either destroyed or transformed.

Immediately evident is the change effected in the human component, the guide M'Cola. The figure of an African guide looms less large as the safari nears its end, declining from the heroic Droopy to the more fallible M'Cola. By the time of Part IV, when the narrator abandons the road and the blind, M'Cola has become only one among a handful of less commanding figures. The current status of his participation in the narrator's growth shows itself in the guide's reaction to the moment for which they've all waited, when the narrator and his party strike out for the kudu and the virgin land in the first scene of Chapter Twelve. From the front seat the narrator "looked around at the back of the car. M'Cola was asleep."

The sleeping guide has fulfilled the potential resident within him from his first appearance in the narrative. From the moment M'Cola raises his "bald black skull" and displays the "thin Chinese hairs at the corners of his mouth," his exterior is always cast in Oriental terms. The ethnic imagery, reinforced by his geographical duties as guide, serves as a constant visual reminder that above all this guide helps "orient" the narrator within the world. When in Part III the American pupil internalizes the accepting, appreciative viewpoint held toward the world by his African mentor, he is then provided with the means to relate to that world. The vision of the Oriental African furnishes an internal gyroscope for his pupil, permitting sure movement in a world increasingly fluid. The need for such ability becomes paramount when the hunting party separates from the rest of the safari and deserts the road, directing their car toward parts unknown. As the party ventures out, M'Cola takes a backseat and closes his eyes in sleep. In the blind and along the road, the black countenance has always acknowledged and valued the world passing before it, but now it closes itself to the world, its faculties in suspension. The new land the narrator travels generates demands beyond the elder guide's capabilities. Therefore, having equipped his pupil with a working legacy, M'Cola releases him to the vision of the Wanderobo seated in the front seat …and lapses into sleep. The narrator, now a more capable agent of life, must answer the demands of the virgin land.

The placement of the hunting company in the car reveals the shifting emphasis in the narrator as he begins to track kudu. M'Cola has previously commanded the strategic position by the narrator's side, first in the roadside blind and then in the makeshift tent. But now one of the natives who has brought news of the kudu and sable occupies that place. The native, a Wanderobo tribesman, flanks the narrator in the front seat. It is important to the development of the narrator, however, that one authority figure not merely replace another. Consequently, because neither his personal name nor a nickname is ever given in Part IV, the Wanderobo functions less as a personality and more as the qualities the name of his tribe suggests; when the narrator ventures into the virgin country, into the unknown, the qualities of the wanderer/wonderer come to the fore. This transposition of a Wanderobo for M'Cola indicates the active realignment going on in the narrator. An intellectual observer, M'Cola lives apart from the life observed. As the narrator grows into his full potential as an artist—incorporating Droopy's sensory health and M'Cola's mental tolerance—he must reach beyond the latter's innate passivity to become a participant in the creation before him. This emphasis on participation finds its representative in the Wanderobo. Unlike M'Cola, whose unblinking vision comprehends an eternal present of counterbalancing beginnings and endings, the new native—like the rains in Part III—turns to the future. He has seen the kudu and sable, the magnetic quarries that draw the narrator on. His forward-directed vision leads the hunters into Part IV.

The thrust of this vision becomes evident upon examination of the role of the Wanderobo as a group throughout the safari. From the sentence that initiates the narrative—"We were sitting in the blind that Wanderobo hunters had built of twigs and branches"—the Wanderobo functions as the narrator's predecessor in the journey of the road, the builder of forms the narrator still inhabits. They are the first artificers mentioned in the book and come to represent all the people on the road, the westward travelers who carry arrows and spears, pots and pans, in their hands. These implements mark the moment when the circumstances of their wanderings set these people to wondering; the artifacts are the answers of their invention to the challenge of the environment. The same urge to manipulate one's world that moved the travelers to shape weapons and containers, the anonymous Wanderobo hunters to construct the blind, now moves the narrator. He exhibits those values of mobility and curiosity that provoked another wanderer/wonderer to realize in twigs and branches the form in the landscape.

Just as M'Cola, the human component in the landscape, undergoes change, so do the manmade forms. *Green Hills* begins with the narrator crouching by a structure that winds its way through the geography of eleven chapters—the road. But the downpour of Part III renders that road impassable, and in the first scene of Part IV this trace of man's presence quickly dissipates. The narrator's car launches out on a "road that was only a track," "only a cattle track." The hunters then pursue "a faint trail the Wanderobo pointed out" until "there was no track, only general direction to follow." Soon, having broken free of the road and all outside points of reference, the party rely instead on inner references, "driving with intelligence and a sound feeling for the country." As a form, the road is a product of the past, its very existence the evidence of others who have gone before. But before the establishment of roadways, pioneers must walk the virgin lands. If the routes they ferret out are advantageous, others will follow and the subsequent communal effort create the road. But first must come the individual who dares to veer away from the past of the road into the future of the unknown. The road disappears from the landscape of Chapter Twelve when the narrator enters the virgin land, when the road's fixed, known direction renders it an instrument inadequate to the scope of his wanderings.

Rather than disintegrating like the road, the second manmade form in the landscape—the blind—undergoes a metamorphosis. Images of matrices mark the narrator's trek across Africa: the Rift Valley, the Wanderobo blind, the makeshift tent. The several permutations signify the narrator's intensifying involvement with the world: their construction shows man's advances in shaping his earth. A primordial matrix commands the vista at the outset of the safari, the awesome chasm of the Rift Valley, within whose rock walls the waters of Lake Manyara quench the dust of the plain. This first hollow is an entirely natural phenomenon, singular and ponderous in its domination of the countryside. The narrator and his companions feast on its abundant supplies of water and game. The next womb image, the blind built by the Wanderobos, exhibits in its making an advance beyond the geological formation; it requires the quantitative rearrangement of nature by man. Wanderobo hands dug the hollow beside the road and placed the twigs and branches above its sides in an effort to facilitate the exploitation of another natural resource, the saltlick. In the rift the range of the hunters is circumscribed to the fertile shore of Lake Manyara; but with blinds that can be built in any number and any place, the matrical form multiplies to answer the needs of the human hunter. The narrator, following in the footsteps of the Wanderobos, is heir to their ingenuity; he too hunts from the blind. But this construction never permits capture of the greater kudu for which he searches, and in the rain of Part III, both the saltlick and the nearby blind are washed away. The thus outmoded form is altogether absent from the opening of Part IV. However, its function does not vanish from the landscape; the blind metamorphoses into the makeshift tent.

Throughout the African countryside, green tents have dotted the path of the safari. For nine chapters the narrator has lived in enclosures that are both structured (house-like, with flaps for doors) and communal (such as the dining tent, the most frequently mentioned tent, and others large enough to accommodate couples). But a change transpires after the destruction of the blind by the rain. The tent that rises out of the flood in Part III differs from its predecessors. First of all, it is improvised from its very inception, beginning as a canvas ground cloth packed in the narrator's car along with other supplies. And secondly, it is uniquely suited to the individual: when the narrator is stranded on the road, the tent provides ideal housing for this transient with its immediate response to the environment ("My ground sheet tent was slung between a tree and one side of the chicken coop"). This adaptibility qualifies it for the exigencies of the kudu hunt, which is manifestly an individual, not a communal, enterprise. Just as the blind heralds an advance beyond the Rift Valley, so the makeshift tent supercedes the blind. The blind entails a quantitative reshaping of the earth; the processing of cotton into canvas necessitates a qualitative transformation of the material universe. The end product of this process, a canvas cocoon, reaffirms in its connotation of gestation the tent's identity as a matrical form. From a chasm that dwarfs the hunter to a shelter that answers his every demand, the matrix proves a viable form for the landscape of *Green Hills of Africa*. The plural attributes of its most refined version, the ground sheet tent, qualify the tent for the world of change. It is strong enough to withstand the country of rain, plastic enough to go into the virgin land. With the re-emergence of the tent in Part IV, the narrator comes into his own as a maker of forms. The narrator/artist carries this ability as maker with him just as the narrator/hunter carries the tent. In both capacities this individual commands the means to create a world.

The Foreword to *Green Hills of Africa* issues an intriguing invitation to the narrative's readers: "Any one not finding sufficient love interest is at liberty, while reading [this book], to insert whatever love interest he or she may have at the time." That a seeming "travelogue" should introduce the subject of love in its second sentence reveals an unusual concern with that subject on the part of the narrative; and in many ways, *Green Hills* is a love story. The "love interest" of the narrator is revealed straight away in Chapter One; he and his friends are sitting in the blind at the side of the road because they have seen "long, heart-shaped, fresh tracks of four greater kudu bulls that had been on the salt the night before." Beginning with this first sign and continuing throughout the narrative, the kudu is always described in terms of the heart—in fact, the story opens upon a most propitious day: when one examines the timing of the February journey, one discovers that *Green Hills* begins on Valentine's Day.[2] But the employment of heart imagery ranges beyond the sentimentality of the valentine to embrace the heart and circulatory system in a subtle actualization of the processes of life itself. The narrator tracks the elusive kudu to the "last hour of the last day" of the safari, for not until then does a greater Kudu bull appear before him. Thus the "love interest" first raised in the Foreward has to sustain the American hunter many, many African miles. Like the rains which promise the future fertility of the hills and the Wanderobo whose vision leads the hunting party to the virgin land, the narrator's "love interest" provides a major thrust in the narrative, as is so deftly indicated in the homonymic "Foreward." The varied wildlife the narrator meets in the course of the safari serves to prepare him for his encounter with the kudu in Part IV. The first animal killed under Droopy's eye, the reedbuck, is an antelope like the kudu and functions as an antecedent for the more significant member of its species. It initiates the heart imagery: "I felt for the heart behind the foreleg with my fingers and feeling it beating under the hide slipped the knife in but it was short and pushed the heart away" (53). Beginning with this initial contact, the narrator's effort is to get to the heart, to grasp the living center. The reedbuck is a beginner's clumsy try; at the elemental phase in Droopy's country the American hunter has much to learn. But he senses intuitively what is most important about the task before him and he learns. The proliferation of heart imagery in the African bush country reflects the life quickening within the narrator. His heart beats even more strongly in the virgin land of Chapter Twelve when, having absorbed M'Cola's contribution as well as Droopy's, he in effect hunts alone. The new country and the people who live there initially present to the narrator a living creature not to be killed but to be touched: "[I] could feel the thumping of his heart through the soft, warm, furry body, and as I stroked him the Masai patted my arm" (220). Skin-to-skin, the rhythms of the newcomer and his welcomers beat in time.

After meeting the magnificent Masai tribesmen, the narrator encounters natives, dressed in what look like "Roman togas," he had never seen before: "Their faces were a gray brown, the oldest looked to be about fifty, had thin lips, an almost Grecian nose, rather high cheekbones, and large, intelligent eyes" (224). These natives will serve as the guides for the kudu kill, the final act of purification, and their ancient characteristics (Greek nose and Roman toga) suggest their part in the long purification process. Like Part II, a narrative trip back in order to make possible the narrative movement forward, the presence of these natives suggests that the sources have been reached and that the complicating patterns of behavior and emotional turmoils have ended. Appropriately, therefore, when they leave camp the final time before shooting kudu, they leave behind Garrick, his theatrics and values.

The American hunter finally meets his elusive prey in the virgin country that opens up Chapter Twelve. On the last afternoon of the safari's last day, just when he has almost resigned himself to defeat, suddenly comes news of the spotting of the kudu. It is as if a hole opens suddenly in what had been a closed universe and the narrator shoots through in Part IV into the universe of change and chance. Initially the narrator brings with him the weight of preconceptions from Part III ("my exhiliration died with the stretching out of this plain, the typical poor game country"), but the land surprises him as he moves on into the veritable explosion of green that burgeons before him: "the grass was green and smooth, short as a meadow that has been mown and is newly grown, and the trees were big, high-trunked, and old with no undergrowth but only the smooth green of the turf like a deer park" (217). "Putting-green smoothness," "this green valley"—the virgin land is hallmarked by fertility, both vegetative and animal. In his first impression of this land, the narrator dubs it "a deer park." Indeed, he points in the text to his choice of words pondering "how to describe this deer park country and whether deer park was enough to call it" (281). On a simple level, the narrator's choice of words is appropriate, since the antelope of the virgin country is related to the deer family. But additionally, "deer" conjures up "dear," a heart word. In the case of the kudu, the pun on "dear" operates in both senses, something loved and something valued.

The most penetrating encounter of the narrator with the beloved and valued creatures of the deer park is, of course, his long-awaited rendezvous with the kudu. In the "last hour best hour" of the safari, the hunting party suddenly spots across a stream "a large, gray animal, white stripes showing on his flanks and huge horns curling back from his head as he stood, broadside to us, head up, seeming to be listening" (229). The narrator gets off two shots at the bolting game; then "none of us (were) breathing as we saw him standing in a clearing a hundred yards ahead,…looking back, wide ears spread, big, gray, white-striped, his horns a marvel, as he looked straight toward us over his shoulder" (230-231). After firing once again, the narrator stumbles over a carcass he discovers to be the first bull seen at the stream. Then several yards ahead he finds the second bull who had looked back. How prolific this green deer park! Not only does the narrator finally see a kudu after nearly exhausting his allotted time, but it is a prize specimen and there is not one, but two! It is as if in addition to the unexpected new space of the unhunted land, the animal life too begins to replicate.

The most extraordinary moment of the hunt occurs when the second kudu looks straight back over his shoulder at the hunting party; as M'Cola explains, the second bull, having run with the wounded first bull, turns to discover why that one no longer follows. The image the animal presents as he turns etches itself into the narrator's vision: framed in a clearing set off from the furor of the chase, the kudu stands pristinely alone in its uniqueness. This is the encounter to which the other antelope were prologue, and it is neither clumsy as with the reedbuck or surreptitious as with the water buck. The bull halts briefly in its forward plunge and for a moment two living creatures behold each other in a direct exchange. The moment does not linger—the kudu at the stream is already dead, and soon so is its fellow. But in that one, clear moment the hunter beholds his deer, the lover his beloved.

The narrator kills the two kudu cleanly, shooting just twice. "He was lying on the side where the bullet had gone in and there was not a mark on him and he smelled sweet and lovely like the breath of cattle and the odor of thyme after rain" (231). Much of the description early in the book is given to the dust and heat and famine of the country and to the stench of the animals, in particular the baboons and the hyenas who feed on death. With the kudu it is different, as though the narrator has truly moved as far into the clean new world as he can go and where the Romans and Masai now accept him as an equal. Before the kill he tried to use a dictionary to communicate; now there is no need for common verbal language: "We were all hunters except, possibly, Garrick, and the whole thing could be worked out, understood, and agreed to without using anything but a forefinger to signal and a hand to caution" (251).

The narrator's preference for the greater kudu as his "love interest" over trophies more traditionally associated with African safaris discloses his concern with private, not public, values. The structure of *Green Hills of Africa* mirrors this emphasis by relating only one of the obligatory big game kills. The relegation of the confrontation between the narrator and the lion to Chapter Two diffuses the impact of the incident early on. The hunt practically ignores the bigger game, three lion and two leopard being the only carnivores taken. The other meat-eaters, for the most part, are the hyenas and the humans themselves. Instead, the expedition centers more upon herbivores, not even African exotica like elephants (of which we see only tracks and dung)but mostly antelope, roan, reedbuck, water buck, oryx, impala eland, bushbuck, Grant's gazelle, kudu and sable. Indeed, as Pop says of the narrator's love interest, "[kudu are] the commonest big antelope in this bush country. It's just that when you want to see them you don't." Given the availability of the quarry, the "dearness" of the deer park creatures must lie not in their scarcity, but in their fulfillment of an inner need in the narrator, in an inward response they alone evoke in him.

The sign of the heart leads here, to the clearing in the wood where the kudu turns. These two factors, the place and the manner in which the narrator discovers the bull, illuminate what the narrator finds at the end of the heart-shaped path. Having gotten off two shots, he spots an animal he believes to be the first bull "standing in a clearing a hundred yards ahead." The gerund "clearing" indicates not only a place that has been cleared but also an act that clears. This verbal attribute of the word carries the kudu hunt passage. The hunter's first shot, for example, depends entirely upon his expertise in "clearing": "[I] commenced to crawl forward to be clear of the bush, sick afraid the bull would jump." As the narrator/hunter successfully clears his vision, so the narrator/artist clears his. His eye catches the bull in a clearing, free of interference from the terrain, free of human intrusion from the chase. It is as if that narrative eye blinks to wash the scene of all extraneous matter and opens, virgin, upon its long-awaited object of desire.

In that one moment, "looking back…his horns a marvel…[the kudu] looked straight toward us over his shoulder." In this direct exchange, the narrator discovers the bull in motion: in the momentary turn of its flight, and in the more enduring turnings of its life as captured in its spiralling horns. From the helix of the kudu to the arc of the sable, horns are the layered excrescences of life. Unlike antlers which are lost yearly, horns are lifetime tracings of the growth of their formative organism. They acquire their shape from constant contact with a vital center, the keratin beneficiaries of the pith that wells up from within. In addition to the origins, the multitudinous shapes of the horns also provide insight, the kudu horns in particular. The helical growths incorporate a distinctive element of thrust in their design; they grow not aimlessly, nor circle repetitively, but evolve. This evolution in their physical configuration also governs the appearance of the horns in the timespan of the narrative. The sequence in which certain horns are pursued at certain times in the narrative reveals a pattern; beginning with the simple hook of the rhinoceros, through the more intricate variations of the intervening water buffalo and lesser antelope, to the complex spiral of the kudu, the narrator pursues increasingly more developed horns at the same time he is adding new dimensions to his own experience. In the clearing when he finally sees before him the spiral in its full complement, it is because he has laid a proper foundation for it and can now be suitably receptive. This correlation between the hunting trophies and the narrator's existence is strengthened when he expresses the impulse of his own life in horn-like terms: "I've had a better time every year since I can remember." The kudu horns prove particularly apt with their distinguishing thrust; the comparative degree of "a better time every year" suggests not just an annual accumulation of experience but a qualitative advance.

The principle of advance operative in the kudu horns finds its linguistic equivalent in the part of speech most conducive to action, the verbal, which carries the kudu passage. The phrase "in the clearing" which initiates the passage, utilizes the gerund. The narrator's subsequent perception of the horns employs the attributes of another verbal, the participle. These verbals imbue their subject with activity; the magnificent kudu at the stream sports "huge horns curling back from his head," "great, curling, sweeping horns." The participles prepare the way for the triumphant image the narrator relates when the hunting party breaks camp in the virgin land. He stands alone before the prizes of his journey and takes in their full beauty: "From the white, cleanly picked skulls the horns rose in slow spirals that spreading made a turn, another turn, and then curved delicately in to those smooth, ivory-like points" (276). In the narrator's observation, the participles give way to the even more commanding vigor of active verbs. The horns shape themselves right before the narrator's eyes: "the horns rose in slow spirals that spreading made a turn, another turn, and then curved delicately in." The spirals embody the upward-struggling, ever-aspiring impulse forward and outward that has informed the story from its first word to the end of the heart-shaped path and beyond. These curling sweeping, spreading growths that rise, turn, and curve present a dynamic model of life—not of what life is, but how it works, its evolutionary possibilities.

When the narrator and his party finally enter the virgin land and set up camp in the oncoming darkness, they manage to sight the kudu in record time; "we had not been gone ten minutes" when the first bull appears. Soon after, the darkness that circumscribed their hunting to the last hour of the last day falls, yet brings with it a full night of feasting: "It was getting cold and the night was clear and there was the smell of the roasting meat, the smell of the smoke of the fire…. Each man had his own meat or collection of pieces of meat on sticks stuck around the fire, they turned them and tended them and there was much talking" (239). It is fitting that this hunt, more than any other, should climax in a festival of food. Like the reedbuck before it, the body of the kudu provides nourishment for the hunters who have brought down their prey. The kudu is the gift of the green hills. From the rains that fail yearly, the grass grows and turns the land to green; on that bounty the kudu feed, and they in turn nourish man. This transformation of energies, from the plant life of the green hills, to the grass-eating antelope, to the meat-eating man enacts more and more complex stages in the mighty chain of earth's regeneration of life with life. But the festival of the kudu does not end with sated senses. At the same time kidney and liver, the animal's purifying organs, satisfy the narrator/hunter's hunger, the horns of the kudu furnish aesthetic nourishment for the narrator/artist. This revitalizing property of the horns is stressed by their depiction as a visual feast; their colors are cast in terms of food imagery, "brown as walnut meats" and "the color of black walnut meats." Rather than satiation, the festival of the kudu invigorates the narrator. His eyes do not close at all in sleep that night.

The narrator's quest for kudu ends with darkness, as the hunters feed upon the takings of the day. The festival of the kudu brings to a close the fourth day of the present time of the narrative, the day designated in the first few pages as the end of the safari. But this original time limit of four days suddenly gives way in Part IV. The bounds of the narrator's world have already expanded to include the new space of the virgin land; now they yield an additional day, a new animal, and a bonus chapter. Significantly, the capture of the long-sought kudu does not climax the narrator's hunt. A "romantic and quite untrue" (216) story might end with the kudu kill, but *Green Hills* stresses process rather than trophy. The first twelve chapters narrate the story of the narrator's drive to unify his powers, a drive that carries him into new country and into relationships based upon internal skills rather than external desires. The final chapter is, quite literally, the trip back, back to Pop and P.O.M. and Karl, but with new perceptions and as a whole being. He will now seek to work well—write, for example, *Green Hills*—in a world of dust and heat and mosquitoes.

As part of this trip back, the sable hunt is crucial, for during this part of the safari the narrator becomes aware of his weaknesses and accepts responsibility for them as well as for his strengths. From the first—"they have found a country where there are kudu and sable"—the virgin land is identified as the home of the sable as well as the kudu. Implicit in the Wanderobo's founding vision, and borne out in the subsequent realization of that vision, is this coupling of the helix-bearing kudu with the other antelope. Neither species is even glimpsed by the narrator outside the virgin land, while within its grounds both flourish. The equal emphasis upon each one of the antelope determines the structure of the narrative as well: of the two chapters comprising Part IV, Chapter Twelve deals with the kudu on the afternoon of the fourth day, and Chapter Thirteen covers the sable on the fifth.

Chapter Twelve has established the first antelope, the grey-and-white kudu, as a carrier of life. In Chapter Thirteen its dark twin, the sable, becomes the champion of death. The narrator's first glimpse of the sable parallels his initial meeting with the kudu: "I saw the dark, heavy-built antelope with scimitar-like horns swung back staring at us." In the directness of the moment two features stand out that are unique to the dark antelope—its color and its horns. The striking blackness of the sable, the only antelope in *Green Hills* with this hue, immediately calls up connotations of death. The animal's very name is synonymous with black, and phrases such as "dead black" and "black as hell" in the narrator's description reinforce funereal associations. In addition to the color of the sable, its horns also confirm its identification with death. The "two great curves nearly touching the middle of [the sable's] back" duplicate the dark coloring of the coat. More profoundly, the function of the horns in the survival of the animal is recalled when the adjective "scimitar-like" compares their arc to a weapon. Dyed in the signature of mourning and armed with a death-dealing crest, the sable radiates the energy of death.

The thematic and structural ascendancy of the dark antelope brings into prominence the narrative's concern with death. One of the safari guides provides an insight along these lines in Chapter Five at the shooting of the water buffalo: "'Kufa!' M'Cola said, making the word for dead almost explosive in its force." This pronouncement carries implications crucial to the narrator's story; death in *Green Hills* is, as indicated by the verbal expression M'Cola gives it, an explosive phenomenon. The informing vision of the narrative conceives destruction to be as dynamic, necessary, and valid a part of experience as preservation or generation. The means with which this concern with death is most completely worked out is in the image of the modern day scimitar, the gun, the artifact which delivers this explosive force into the hands of the hunter. The access to the power that the gun offers faces each hunter with the question of how one exercises this power.

The attitude of each hunter toward the gun reveals his viewpoint toward the larger phenomenon of death in the world. Kandisky, the representative of European organization, does not fire a shot. As evidenced by his participation in the German war effort, he prefers the group exertion of this power and the concomitant organizational decisions that buffer him from facing death as an individual. When Kandisky meets the narrator on the road in Chapter One, the European chides the American's willingness to deal directly in death—while dining on Grant gazelle at the narrator's table and sporting conspicuous leather shorts. Kandisky's solution to the dilemma of death is to refuse to confront the question; the parasitic and obtuse image he presents in the narrator's camp refutes this solution outright. In contrast to the Austrian expatriate, the native Africans exhibit a much more empirical approach. For Droopy and M'Cola, the gun has functioned as the supreme test of their fitness to guide the narrator through the land of Africa. Their proficiency determines their span of influence: the former's failure to master the shotgun at the border of his country ends Droopy's domination of Part II; the latter's laxity in safeguarding the rifle from the rain marks M'Cola's decline in Part III. But both Droopy and M'Cola are limited to the role of gunbearer; they do not activate the arms they carry. The role of discharger of the gun's explosive power is reserved to the narrator.

The American has shot well throughout the safari, beginning with the reedbuck and rhino and culminating with the kudu. Within the deer park so

green that it verges on the idyllic, it seems there is nothing the narrator can't
do. Yet on the fifth day of the safari when the narrator and his party take up
the trail of the dark game, this success evaporates. The kudu has appeared
before the narrator in the clearing within ten minutes of his making camp in
the virgin land. But the sable must be tracked for hours, forcing the hunting
party to scramble through nearby hills. Worst of all is the shooting. The first
female animal in the entire safari is mistakenly killed, and the much-prized
sable bull is not killed but terribly wounded. The resultant chase after the
bull culminates in a peak of physical punishment and mental frustration for
the narrator; once lost, neither he nor any of his guides can regain the trail of
the wounded sable. Garrick is once again hunting with them, making the
narrator nervous, but ultimately he himself takes responsibility for the gut-
shot animal: "If I'd gone to bed last night I would not have done that. Or if
I'd wiped out the bore to get the oil out she would not have thrown high the
first time. Then I would not have pulled down and shot under the second
shot. Every damned thing is your own fault if you're any good" (281). Not
only is this an acceptance of his fault but also a statement of the fact that he
is good. He has become good, a healthy working individual, and that demands the awareness of his responsibility for what fails as well as what succeeds.

The unattainable sable bull, resplendent in dusky coat and horn, teaches
the man who follows its tortuous path a central lesson—when one fully enters into the possibilities of mortality, one eschews any promise of an after-
life; one cannot kill death. The narrator rejects such an escape in favor of
being a part of the present creation—and participation in that creation entails mortality, limits, faults. After the rapturous encounter with the kudu,
the sable hunt provides just such an exercise in limits; at its conclusion the
American hunter is momentarily overwhelmed with thoughts of escape,
musing morosely about the "decline" of America and his planned return to
"unspoiled" Africa. But by the time the hunting party has driven the fifty-
five miles from the deer park to where Pop and P.O.M. are camped, the
narrator has emptied himself of this nostalgic self-indulgence. Those illusions are abandoned, along with any desire to transcend the world, in the
country of the dark antelope.

Instead, the narrator finds his own answer to the question of death in the
final moments before the party abandons the deer park camp. His inner
resolution of this problem finds expression in the image that climaxes his
stay in the virgin land and that he carries with him as he leaves its uncharted
spaces for the givens of the road:

> From the white, cleanly picked skulls the horns rose in slow spirals
> that spreading made a turn, another turn, and then curved delicately
> into those smooth, ivory-like points. One pair was narrower and taller
> against the side of the hut. The other was almost as tall but wider in
> spread and heavier in beam. They were the color of black walnut
> meats and they were beautiful to see. I went over and stood the Spring-
> field against the hut between them and the tips reached past the muzzle
> of the rifle. (267)

The horns are, of course, the precious helixes from his two kudu, gifts of the
virgin land, their reaching and curving "beautiful to see." But to this element
of the image the narrator adds another, placing between the two kudu racks
the artifact that made possible their capture. In this juxtaposition of horns
and gun lies the narrator's solution. In one sense the weapon, the death-
dealing rifle, stands in place of the other, unattainable trophy and weapon,
the sable's scimitar horn. But in a more subtle and thorough-going sense
those sable horns are vividly present in the hutside composition after all.
Their distinctive dark color makes up the base of the spiralling kudu columns, and their geometric configuration of the arc comprises half a helical
evolution. Thus by color and by shape the kudu horn incorporates the sable
into itself.

The same act of integration occurs with the Springfield rifle. Save for a
ceremonial burst upon arrival at Pop's camp, the study the gun forms with
the kudu horns marks its last appearance in *Green Hills*. Placed side by side
with the pairs of horns, the line of the muzzle parallels the reach of the horns;
in similar manner the explosive power potential in the gun complements the
thrusting of the helix. As set out in this final image, the narrator comes to see
that life does not reject death nor separate itself from it; rather, just as the
longer kudu horns encompass the shorter gun in their upward progress, so
life incorporates death and goes on. Nowhere is this integration more complete than in the particular rifle that the narrator inserts between the horns.
Named for the season of rebirth, the "Springfield" captures the vital interplay between death and renewal.

When the narrator returns to Pop and P.O.M. to discover that once again
Karl has shot a more impressive trophy—using, as usual, four or five shots to
do it—the complicating emotions reappear only to be accepted and put aside:

> But I was bitter and I was bitter all night long. In the morning, though,
> it was gone. It was all gone and I have never had it again....
> "I'm really glad he has him," I said truly. "Mine'll hold me."

"We have very primitive emotions," Pop said. "It's impossible not to be competitive. Spoils everything, though."

"I'm all through with that," I said. "I'm all right again. I had quite a trip, you know." (293)

As the carnivore killing the herbivore and eating its purifying organs, the narrator does not intrude into but participates in the chain of life initiated in the energy of the sun. That process does not end with the killing of the kudu; consuming the kudu signals health and the possibility of growth, the stimulation of creative powers and the concern as expressed in the book's last sentence—"I can remember him," I said. "I'll write you a piece some time and put him in"—for creating *Green Hills of Africa*. That act is also one of consumption, of the experiences and lives of those beings who participated in the two-month safari in Africa. The book is, therefore, in a very real sense, not *about* life but the *product* of a living act: the writer has attempted to write an "absolutely true book to see whether the shape of a country and the pattern of a month's action can, if truly presented, compete with a work of the imagination" (Foreword). The narrator moves from sickness to health as a result of his ability to perceive the processes emerging out of shape and pattern and to consume the meat of his experience.

As the narrator stands before the kudu horns and the gun, his eye ascends the length of horn, moving from the darker blacks and browns to the "ivory-like points." The allusion to ivory furnishes, of course, a direct assessment of the value of the horn. From the very first night of the safari a major source of ivory, the African elephant, has crossed the expedition's trail, dotting the landscape with its leavings (10, 249-250). But the elusive mammoth never shows itself. This well-defined absence sheds light upon the operating values. In the beginning of the narrative when the American hunter tells Kandisky that he is in Africa "shooting," the European admonishes, "Not ivory, I hope." "No. For kudu," the narrator replies. But later in the same conversation he tells Kandisky that he would "kill a big enough [elephant].... A seventy pounder. Maybe smaller." This spell of braggadocio proves prophetic, for in the end the narrator does indeed shoot for ivory—though not for that of the elephant. The acclaim of the big game trophy and the monetary worth of the tusks may well lure other hunters on other safaris, but on the narrator's private quest through the hills of Africa those public considerations are deemed as insubstantial as the phantom elephant. Instead he ventures after, and wins, the real ivory of *Green Hills*. The narrator/hunter takes home the ivory pointed helix, although his pairs are bested by the horns—"the biggest, widest, darkest, longest-curling, heaviest, most unbelievable pair of kudu horns"—Karl has brought to Pop's camp. The superlative degree of Karl's success underscores once again that for the narrator/artist the value of his horns lies not in their signification of public success, but in their function as images in rendering his story of individual growth. And it is as an image in the service of the imagination's creative advance that the kudu horns climax the African adventure; beyond the text a line drawing of a triumphant kudu bull emblazons "The End" across the last page of the narrative. This flourish of the kudu at the end of the narrator's imaginative quest validates the achievement of that quest: the resultant work of his art is the narrator's true trophy, *Green Hills of Africa* his ivory.

In the final scene of the book, "P.O.M., Karl, and Karl's wife who had come out and joined us at Jaifa, were sitting in the sun against a stone wall by the Sea of Galilee eating some lunch and drinking a bottle of wine and watching the grebes out on the lake…. There were many grebes, making spreading wakes in the water as they swam, and I was counting them and wondering why they never were mentioned in the Bible. I decided that those people were not naturalists." In this moment, the narrator distinguishes himself from the narrators in the Bible who paid no attention to the natural world. During his month's safari he has become a naturalist, not in the nineteenth-century sense of one who abstracts laws but as someone who can look at his world and see particular grebes. The naturalism discovered during this experience, consequently, has no previous model, neither in the Bible nor in the work of his predecessors. As new, it creates new form and cannot be fit into an earlier category. *Green Hills of Africa* does not discuss or define the new; it does the new. The narrative is not a definition but an action, an event correlating life and the imagination. And that event demands something new of us. We cannot remain readers, trying to classify one more work into a set of previous expectations. We need to become viewers, seeing the value of *Green Hills* in itself, within Hemingway's own work, and within the ongoing enterprise of American narration.

Notes

[1] *Scribner's Magazine*, 97, #5 (May, 1935), p. 259.

[2] "We had only three days more because the rains were moving north each day from Rhodesia and unless we were prepared to stay where we were through the rains we must be out as far as Handeni before they came. We had set the seventeenth of February as the last safe date to leave" (11).

An Expedition to the Pole

ANNIE DILLARD

I

THERE IS A SINGING GROUP in this Catholic church today, a singing group that calls itself Wildflowers. The lead is a tall, square-jawed teenaged boy, buoyant and glad to be here. He carries a guitar; he plucks out a little bluesy riff and hits some chords. With him are the rest of the Wildflowers. There is an old woman, wonderfully determined; she has long orange hair and is dressed country-and-western style. A long embroidered strap around her neck slings a big western guitar low over her pelvis. Beside her stand a frail, withdrawn fourteen-year-old boy, and a large Chinese man in his twenties, who seems to want to enjoy himself but is not quite sure how to. He looks around wildly as he sings, and shuffles his feet. There is also a very tall teenaged girl, presumably the lead singer's girlfriend; she is delicate of feature, half serene and half petrified, a wispy soprano. They straggle out in front of the altar and teach us a brand-new hymn.

It all seems a pity at first, for I have overcome a fiercely anti-Catholic upbringing in order to attend Mass simply and solely to escape Protestant guitars. Why am I here? Who gave these nice Catholics guitars? Why are they not mumbling in Latin and performing superstitious rituals? What is the Pope thinking of?

But nobody said things were going to be easy. A taste for the sublime is a greed like any other, after all; why begrudge the churches their secularism now, when from the general table is rising a general song? Besides, in a way I do not pretend to understand, these people—all the people in all the ludicrous churches—have access to the land.

The Pole of Relative Inaccessibility is "that imaginary point on the Arctic Ocean farthest from land in any direction." It is a navigator's paper point, contrived to console Arctic explorers who, after Peary and Henson reached the North Pole in 1909, had nowhere special to go. There is a Pole of Relative Inaccessibility on the Antarctic continent, also; it is that point of land farthest from salt water in any direction.

The Absolute is the Pole of Relative Inaccessibility located in metaphysics. After all, one of the few things we know about the Absolute is that it is relatively inaccessible. It is that point of spirit farthest from every accessible point of spirit in all directions. Like the others, it is a Pole of the Most Trouble. It is also—I take this as given—the Pole of great price.

The People

It is the second Sunday in Advent. For a year I have been attending Mass at this Catholic church. Every Sunday for a year I have run away from home and joined the circus as a dancing bear. We dancing bears have dressed ourselves in buttoned clothes; we mince around the rings on two feet. Today we were restless; we kept dropping onto our forepaws.

No one, least of all the organist, could find the opening hymn. Then no one knew it. Then no one could sing anyway.

There was no sermon, only announcements.

The priest proudly introduced the rascally acolyte who was going to light the two Advent candles. As we all could plainly see, the rascally acolyte had already lighted them.

During the long intercessory prayer, the priest always reads "intentions" from the parishioners. These are slips of paper, dropped into a box before the service begins, on which people have written their private concerns, requesting our public prayers. The priest reads them, one by one, and we respond on cue. "For a baby safely delivered on November twentieth," the priest intoned, "we pray to the Lord." We all responded, "Lord, hear our prayer." Suddenly the priest broke in and confided to our bowed heads, "That's the baby we've been praying for the past two months! The woman just kept getting more and more pregnant!" How often, how shockingly often, have I exhausted myself in church from the effort to keep from laughing out loud? I often laugh all the way home. Then the priest read the next intention: "For my son, that he may forgive his father. We pray to the Lord." "Lord, hear our prayer," we responded, chastened.

A high school stage play is more polished than this service we have been rehearsing since the year one. In two thousand years, we have not worked out the kinks. We positively glorify them. Week after week we witness the same miracle: that God is so mighty he can stifle his own laughter. Week after week, we witness the same miracle: that God, for reasons unfathomable, refrains from blowing our dancing bear act to smithereens. Week after week Christ washes the disciples' dirty feet, handles their very toes, and repeats, It is all right—believe it or not—to be people.

Who can believe it?

During Communion, the priest handed me a wafer that proved to be stuck to five other wafers. I waited while he tore the clump into rags of wafer, resisting the impulse to help. Directly to my left, and all through Communion, a woman was banging out the theme from *The Sound of Music* on a piano.

The Land

Nineteenth-century explorers set the pattern for polar expeditions. Elaborately provisioned ships set out for high latitudes. Soon they encounter the pack ice and equinoctial storms. Ice coats the deck, spars, and rigging; the masts and hull shudder; the sea freezes around the rudder and then fastens on the ship. Early sailors try ramming, sawing, or blasting the ice ahead of the ship before they give up and settle in for the winter. In the nineteenth century, this being "beset" in the pack often killed polar crews; later explorers expected it and learned, finally, to put it to use. Sometimes officers and men move directly onto the pack ice for safety; they drive tent stakes into the ice and pile wooden boxes about for tables and chairs.

Sooner or later, the survivors of that winter or the next, or a select polar party, sets off over the pack ice on foot. Depending on circumstances, they are looking either for a Pole or, more likely, for help. They carry supplies, including boats, on sledges, which they "man-haul" on ropes fastened to shoulder harnesses. South Polar expeditions usually begin from a base camp established on shore. In either case, the terrain is so rough, and the men so weakened by scurvy, that the group makes only a few miles a day. Sometimes they find an island on which to live or starve the next winter; sometimes they turn back to safety, stumble onto some outpost of civilization, or are rescued by another expedition; very often, when warm weather comes and the pack ice splits into floes, they drift and tent on a floe, or hop from floe to floe, until the final floe lands, splits, or melts.

In 1847, according to Arctic historian L. P. Kirwan, the American ship *Polaris* "was struck by an enormous floe. And just as stores, records, clothing, equipment, were being flung from the reeling ship, she was swept away through the Arctic twilight, with most, but not all, of her crew on board. Those left behind drifted for thirteen hundred miles on an ice-floe until they were rescued, starving and dazed, off the coast of Labrador."

Polar explorers were chosen, as astronauts are today, from the clamoring, competitive ranks of the sturdy, skilled, and sane. Many of the British leaders, in particular, were men of astonishing personal dignity. Reading their accounts of life *in extremis*, one is struck by their unending formality toward each other. When Scott's Captain Oates sacrificed himself on the Antarctic peninsula because his ruined feet were slowing the march, he stepped outside the tent one night to freeze himself in a blizzard, saying to the others, "I am just going outside and may be some time."

Even in the privacy of their journals and diaries, polar explorers maintain a fine reserve. In his journal, Ernest Shackleton described his feelings upon seeing, for the first time in human history, the Antarctic continent beyond the mountains ringing the Ross Ice Shelf: "We watched the new mountains rise from the great unknown that lay ahead of us," he wrote, "with feelings of keen curiosity, not unmingled with awe." One wonders, after reading a great many such firsthand accounts, if polar explorers were not somehow chosen for the empty and solemn splendor of their prose styles—or even if some eminent Victorians, examining their own prose styles, realized, perhaps dismayed, that from the look of it, they would have to go in for polar exploration. Salomon Andrée, the doomed Swedish balloonist, was dying of starvation on an Arctic island when he confided in his diary, with almost his dying breath, "Our provisions must soon and richly be supplemented, if we are to have any prospect of being able to hold out for a time."

The People

The new Episcopalian and Catholic liturgies include a segment called "passing the peace." Many things can go wrong here. I know of one congregation in New York that fired its priest because he insisted on their passing the peace—which involves nothing more than shaking hands with your neighbors in the pew. The men and women of this small congregation had limits to their endurance; passing the peace was beyond their limits. They could not endure shaking hands with people against whom they bore lifelong grudges. They fired the priest and found a new one, sympathetic to their needs.

The rubric for passing the peace requires that one shake hands with whoever is handy and say, "Peace be with you." The other responds, "Peace be with you." Every rare once in a while, someone responds simply "Peace." Today I was sitting beside two teenaged lugs with small mustaches. When it came time to pass the peace, I shook hands with one of the lugs and said, "Peace be with you," and he said, "*Yeah.*"

The Technology: The Franklin Expedition

The Franklin expedition was the turning point in Arctic exploration. The expedition itself accomplished nothing, and all its members died. But the expedition's failure to return, and the mystery of its whereabouts, attracted so much publicity in Europe and the United States that thirty ships set out looking for traces of the ships and men; these search parties explored and mapped the Arctic for the first time, found the Northwest Passage that Franklin had sought, and developed a technology adapted to Arctic conditions, a technology capable of bringing explorers back alive. The technology of the Franklin expedition, by contrast, was adapted only to conditions in the Royal Navy officers' clubs in England. The Franklin expedition stood on its dignity.

In 1845, Sir John Franklin and 138 officers and men embarked from England to find the Northwest Passage across the high Canadian Arctic to the Pacific Ocean. They sailed in two three-masted barques. Each sailing vessel carried an auxiliary steam engine and a twelve-day supply of coal for the entire projected two or three years' voyage. Instead of additional coal, according to L. P. Kirwan, each ship made room for a 1,200-volume library, "a hand-organ, playing fifty tunes," china place settings for officers and men, cut-glass wine goblets, and sterling silver flatware. The officers' sterling silver knives, forks, and spoons were particularly interesting. The silver was of ornate Victorian design, very heavy at the handles and richly patterned. Engraved on the handles were the individual officers initials and family crests. The expedition carried no special clothing for the Arctic, only the uniforms of Her Majesty's Navy.

The ships set out in high style, amid enormous glory and fanfare. Franklin uttered his utterance: "The highest object of my desire is faithfully to perform my duty." Two months later a British whaling captain met the two barques in Lancaster Sound, near Baffin Island; he reported back to England on the high spirits of officers and men. He was the last European to see any of them alive.

Years later, civilization learned that many groups of Inuit— Eskimos— had hazarded across tableaux involving various still-living or dead members of the Franklin expedition. Some had glimpsed, for instance, men pushing and pulling a wooden boat across the ice. Some had found, at a place called Starvation Cove, this boat, or a similar one, and the remains of the thirty-five men who had been dragging it. At Terror Bay the Inuit found a tent on the ice, and in it, thirty bodies. At Simpson Strait some Inuit had seen a very odd sight: the pack ice pierced by the three protruding wooden masts of a barque.

For twenty years, search parties recovered skeletons from all over the frozen sea. Franklin himself—it was learned after twelve years—had died aboard ship. Franklin dead, the ships frozen into the pack winter after winter, their supplies exhausted, the remaining officers and men had decided to walk to help. They outfitted themselves from ships' stores for the journey; their bodies were found with those supplies they had chosen to carry. Accompanying one clump of frozen bodies, for instance, which incidentally showed evidence of cannibalism, were place settings of sterling silver flatware engraved with officers' initials and family crests. A search party found, on the ice far from the ships, a letter clip, and a piece of the very backgammon board that Lady Jane Franklin had given her husband as a parting gift.

Another search party found two skeletons in a boat on a sledge. They had hauled the boat sixty-five miles. With the two skeletons were some chocolate, some guns, some tea, and a great deal of table silver. Many miles south of these two was another skeleton, alone. This was a frozen officer. In his pocket he had, according to Kirwan, "a parody of a sea-shanty." The skeleton was in uniform: trousers and jacket "of fine blue cloth…edged with silk braid, with sleeves slashed and bearing five covered buttons each. Over this uniform the dead man had worn a blue greatcoat, with a black silk neckerchief." That was the Franklin expedition.

Sir Robert Falcon Scott, who died on the Antarctic peninsula, was never able to bring himself to use dogs, let alone feed them to each other or eat them. Instead he struggled with English ponies, for which he carried hay. Scott felt that eating dogs was inhumane; he also felt, as he himself wrote, that when men reach a Pole unaided, their journey has "a fine conception" and "the conquest is more nobly and splendidly won." It is this loftiness of sentiment, this purity, this dignity and self-control, that makes Scott's farewell letters—found under his body— such moving documents.

Less moving are documents from successful polar expeditions. Their leaders relied on native technology, which, as every book ever written about the
Inuit puts it, was "adapted to harsh conditions."

Roald Amundsen, who returned in triumph from the South Pole, traveled Inuit style; he made good speed using sleds and feeding dogs to dogs on
a schedule. Robert E. Peary and Matthew Henson reached the North Pole in
the company of four Inuit. Throughout the Peary expedition, the Inuit drove
the dog teams, built igloos, and supplied seal and walrus clothing.

There is no such thing as a solitary polar explorer, fine as the conception
is.

The People

I have been attending Catholic Mass for only a year. Before that, the handiest
church was Congregational. Week after week I climbed the long steps to that
little church, entered, and took a seat with some few of my neighbors. Week
after week I was moved by the pitiableness of the bare linoleum-floored sacristy, which no flowers could cheer or soften, by the terrible singing I so
loved, by the fatigued Bible readings, the lagging emptiness and dilution of
the liturgy, the horrifying vacuity of the sermon, and by the fog of dreary
senselessness pervading the whole, which existed alongside, and probably
caused, the wonder of the fact that we came; we returned; we showed up;
week after week, we went through with it.

Once while we were reciting the Gloria, a farmer's wife—whom I knew
slightly—and I exchanged a sudden, triumphant glance.

Recently I returned to that Congregational church for an ecumenical
service. A Catholic priest and the minister served grape juice Communion.

Both the priest and the minister were professionals, were old hands. They
bungled with dignity and aplomb. Both were at ease and awed; both were
half confident and controlled and half bewildered and whispering. I could
hear them: "Where is it?" "Haven't you got it?" "I thought you had it!"

The priest, new to me, was in his sixties. He was tall; he wore his weari-
ness loosely, standing upright and controlling his breath. When he knelt at
the altar, and when he rose from kneeling, his knees cracked. It was a fine
church music, this sound of his cracking knees.

The Land

Polar explorers—one gathers from their accounts—sought at the Poles something of the sublime. Simplicity and purity attracted them; they set out to perform clear tasks in uncontaminated lands. The land's austerity held them. They praised the land's spare beauty as if it were a moral or a spiritual quality: "icy halls of cold sublimity," "lofty peaks perfectly covered with eternal snow." Fridtjof Nansen referred to "the great adventure of the ice, deep and pure as infinity…the eternal round of the universe and its eternal death." Everywhere polar prose evokes these absolutes, these ideas of "eternity" and "perfection," as if they were some perfectly visible part of the landscape.

They went, I say, partly in search of the sublime, and they found it the only way it can be found, here or there—around the edges, tucked into the corners of the days. For they were people—all of them, even the British—and despite the purity of their conceptions, they man-hauled their humanity to the Poles.

They man-hauled their frail flesh to the Poles, and encountered conditions so difficult that, for instance, it commonly took members of Scott's South Polar party several hours each morning to put on their boots. Day and night they did miserable, niggling, and often fatal battle with frostbitten toes, diarrhea, bleeding gums, hunger, weakness, mental confusion, and despair.

They man-hauled their sweet human absurdity to the Poles. When Robert E. Peary and Matthew Henson reached the North Pole in 1909, Peary planted there in the frozen ocean, according to L. P. Kirwan, the flag of the Dekes: "the colours of the Delta Kappa Epsilon Fraternity at Bowdoin College, of which Peary was an alumnus."

Polar explorers must adapt to conditions. They must adapt, on the one hand, to severe physical limitations; they must adapt, on the other hand—like the rest of us—to ordinary emotional limitations. The hard part is in finding a workable compromise. If you are Peary and have planned your every move down to the last jot and tittle, you can perhaps get away with carrying a Deke flag to the North Pole, if it will make you feel good. After eighteen years' preparation, why not feel a little good? If you are an officer with the Franklin expedition and do not know what you are doing or where you are, but think you cannot eat food except from sterling silver tableware, you cannot get away with it. Wherever we go, there seems to be only one business at hand—that of finding workable compromises between the sublimity of our ideas and the absurdity of the fact of us.

They made allowances for their emotional needs. Overwintering expedition ships commonly carried, in addition to sufficient fuel, equipment for the publication of weekly newspapers. The brave polar men sat cooling their heels *in medias* nowhere, reading in cold type their own and their bunkmates' gossip, in such weeklies as Parry's *Winter Chronicle* and *North Georgia Gazette*, Nansen's *Framsjaa*, or Scott's *South Polar Times* and *The Blizzard*. Polar explorers also amused themselves with theatrical productions. If one had been frozen into the pack ice off Ross Island near Antarctica, aboard Scott's ship *Discovery*, one midwinter night in 1902, one could have seen the only performance of *Ticket of Leave, a screaming comedy in one act*. Similarly, if, in the dead of winter, 1819, one had been a member of young Edward Parry's expedition frozen into the pack ice in the high Arctic, one could have caught the first of a series of fortnightly plays, an uproarious success called *Miss in Her Teens*. According to Kirwan, "'This,' Parry dryly remarked, 'afforded to the men such a fund of amusement as fully to justify the expectations we had formed of the utility of theatrical entertainments.'"And you yourself, Royal Navy Commander Edward Parry, were you not yourself the least bit amused? Or at twenty-nine years old did you still try to stand on your dignity?

God does not demand that we give up our personal dignity, that we throw in our lot with random people, that we lose ourselves and turn from all that is not him. God needs nothing, asks nothing, and demands nothing, like the stars. It is a life with God that demands these things.

Experience has taught the race that if knowledge of God is the end, then these habits of life are not the means but the condition in which the means operates. You do not have to do these things; not at all. God does not, I regret to report, give a hoot. You do not have to do these things—unless you want to know God. They work on you, not on him.

You do not have to sit outside in the dark. If, however, you want to look at the stars, you will find that darkness is necessary. But the stars neither require nor demand it.

The Technology

It is a matter for computation: How far can one walk carrying how much silver? The computer balks at the problem; there are too many unknowns. The computer puts its own questions: Who is this "one"? What degree of stamina may we calculate for? Under what conditions does this one propose to walk, at what latitudes? With how many companions, how much aid?

The People

The Mass has been building to this point, to the solemn saying of those few hushed phrases known as the Sanctus. We have confessed, in a low, distinct murmur, our sins; we have become the people broken, and then the people made whole by our reluctant assent to the priest's proclamation of God's mercy. Now, as usual, we will, in the stillest voice, stunned, repeat the Sanctus, repeat why it is that we have come:

> Holy, holy, holy Lord,
> God of power and might,
> heaven and earth are full of your glory…

It is here, if ever, that one loses oneself at sea. Here one's eyes roll up, and the sun rolls overhead, and the floe rolls underfoot, and the scene of unrelieved ice and sea rolls over the planet's Pole and over the world's rim, wide and unseen.

Now, just as we are dissolved in our privacy and about to utter the words of the Sanctus, the lead singer of Wildflowers bursts onstage from the wings. I raise my head. He is taking enormous, enthusiastic strides and pumping his guitar's neck up and down. Drooping after him come the orange-haired country-and-western-style woman; the soprano, who, to shorten herself, carries her neck forward like a horse; the withdrawn boy; and the Chinese man, who is holding a tambourine as if it had stuck by some defect to his fingers and he has resolved to forget about it. These array themselves in a clump downstage right. The priest is nowhere in sight.

Alas, alack, oh brother, we are going to have to sing the Sanctus. There is, of course, nothing new about singing the Sanctus. The lead singer smiles disarmingly. There is a new arrangement. He hits a chord with the flat of his hand. The Chinese man with sudden vigor bangs the tambourine and looks at his hands, startled. They run us through the Sanctus three or four times. The words are altered a bit to fit the strong upbeat rhythm:

> Heaven and earth
> (Heaven and earth earth earth earth earth)
> Are full (full full full)
> Of your glory…

Must I join this song? May I keep only my silver? My backgammon board, I agree, is a frivolity. I relinquish it. I will leave it right here on the ice.

But my silver? My family crest? One knife, one fork, one spoon, to carry beneath the glance of heaven and back? I have lugged it around for years; I am, I say, superlatively strong. Don't laugh. I am superlatively strong! Don't laugh; you'll make me laugh. The answer is no. We are singing the Sanctus, it seems, and they are passing the plate. I would rather, I think, undergo the famous dark night of the soul than encounter in church the dread hootenanny—but these purely personal preferences are of no account, and maladaptive to boot. They are passing the plate and I toss in my schooling; I toss in my rank in the Royal Navy, my erroneous and incomplete charts, my pious refusal to eat sled dogs, my watch, my keys, and my shoes. I was looking for bigger game, not little moral lessons, but who can argue with conditions?

"Heaven and earth earth earth earth earth," we sing. The withdrawn boy turns his head toward a man in front of me, who must be his father. Unaccountably, the enormous teenaged soprano catches my eye, exultant. A low shudder or shock crosses our floe. We have split from the pack; we have crossed the Arctic Circle, and the current has us.

The Land

We are clumped on an ice floe drifting over the black polar sea. Heaven and earth are full of our terrible singing. Overhead we see a blurred, colorless brightness; at our feet we see the dulled, swift ice and recrystallized snow. The sea is black and green; a hundred thousand floes and bergs float in the water and spin and scatter in the current around us everywhere as far as we can see. The wind is cool, moist, and scented with salt.

I am wearing, I discover, the uniform of a Keystone Kop. I examine my hat: a black cardboard constable's hat with a white felt star stapled to the band above the brim. My dark Keystone Kop jacket is nicely belted, and there is a tin badge on my chest. A holster around my hips carries a popgun with a cork on a string, and a red roll of caps. My feet are bare, but I feel no cold. I am skating around on the ice, and singing, and bumping into people who, because the ice is slippery, bump into other people. "Excuse me!" I keep saying, "I beg your pardon— woops there!"

When a crack develops in our floe and opens at my feet, I jump across it—skillfully, I think—but my jump pushes my side of the floe away, and I wind up leaping full tilt into the water. The Chinese man extends a hand to pull me out, but alas, he slips and I drag him in. The Chinese man and I are treading water, singing, and collecting a bit of a crowd. It takes a troupe of circus clowns to get us both out. I check my uniform at once and learn that my rather flattering hat is intact, my trousers virtually unwrinkled, but my roll of caps is wet. The Chinese man is fine; we thank the clowns.

This troupe of circus clowns, I hear, is poorly paid. They are invested in bright, loose garments; they are a bunch of spontaneous, unskilled, oversized children; they joke and bump into people. At one end of the floe, ten of them—red, yellow, and blue—are trying to climb up on each other to make a human pyramid. It is a wonderfully funny sight, because they have put the four smallest clowns on the bottom, and the biggest, fattest clown is trying to climb to the top. The rest of the clowns are doing gymnastics; they tumble on the ice and flip cheerfully in midair. Their crucifixes fly from their ruffled necks as they flip, and hit them on their bald heads as they land. Our floe is smaller now, and we seem to have drifted into a faster bit of current. Repeatedly we ram little icebergs, which rock as we hit them. Some of them tilt clear over like punching bags; they bounce back with great splashes, and water streams down their blue sides as they rise. The country-and-western-style woman is fending off some of the larger bergs with a broom. The lugs with the mustaches have found, or brought, a Frisbee, and a game is developing down the middle of our floe. Near the Frisbee game, a bunch of people including myself and some clowns are running. We fling ourselves down on the ice, shoulders first, and skid long distances like pucks.

Now the music ceases and we take our seats in the pews. A baby is going to be baptized. Overhead the sky is brightening; I do not know if this means we have drifted farther north or all night.

The People

The baby's name is Oswaldo; he is a very thin baby, who looks to be about one. He never utters a peep; he looks grim, and stiff as a planked shad. His parents—his father carrying him—and his godparents, the priest, and two acolytes, are standing on the ice between the first row of pews and the linoleum-floored sacristy. I am resting my bare feet on the velvet prie-dieu—to keep those feet from playing on the ice during the ceremony.

Oswaldo is half Filipino. His mother is Filipino. She has a wide mouth with much lipstick, and wide eyes; she wears a tight black skirt and stiletto heels. The father looks like Ozzie Nelson. He has marcelled yellow hair, a bland, meek face, and a big, meek nose. He is wearing a brown leather flight jacket. The godparents are both Filipinos, one of whom, in a pastel denim jumpsuit, keeps mugging for the Instamatic camera that another family member is shooting from the aisle.

The baby has a little red scar below one eye. He is wearing a long white lace baptismal gown, blue tennis shoes with white rubber toes, and red socks.

The priest anoints the baby's head with oil. He addresses to the parents several articles of faith: "Do you believe in God, the Father Almighty, creator of Heaven and earth?" "Yes, we believe."

The priest repeats a gesture he says was Christ's, explaining that it symbolically opens the infant's five senses to the knowledge of God. Uttering a formal prayer, he lays his hand loosely over Oswaldo's face and touches in rapid succession his eyes, ears, nose, and mouth. The baby blinks. The priest, whose voice is sometimes lost in the ruff at his neck, or blown away by the wind, is formal and gentle in his bearing; he knows the kid is cute, but he is not going to sentimentalize the sacrament.

Since our floe spins, we in the pews see the broken floes and tilting bergs, the clogged, calm polar sea, and the variously lighted sky and water's rim, shift and revolve enormously behind the group standing around the baby. Once I think I see a yellowish polar bear spurting out of the water as smoothly as if climbing were falling. I see the bear splash and flow onto a distant floeberg, which tilts out of sight.

Now the acolytes bring a pitcher, a basin, and a linen towel. The father tilts the rigid baby over the basin; the priest pours water from the pitcher over the baby's scalp; the mother sops the baby with the linen towel and wraps it over his head, so that he looks, proudly, as though he has just been made a swami.

To conclude, the priest brings out a candle, for the purpose, I think, of pledging everybody to Christian fellowship with Oswaldo. Actually, I do not know what it is for; I am not listening. I am watching the hands at the candlestick. Each of the principals wraps a hand around the brass candlestick: the two acolytes with their small, pale hands at its base, the two families— Oswaldo's and his godparents'—with their varicolored hands in a row, and the priest at the top, as though he has just won the bat toss at baseball. The baby rides high in his father's arms, pointing his heels in his tennis shoes, silent, wanting down. His father holds him firmly with one hand and holds the candlestick beside his wife's hand with the other. The priest and the seated members of Wildflowers start clapping then—a round of applause for everybody here on the ice!—so we clap.

II

Months have passed; years have passed. Whatever ground we gained has slipped away. New obstacles arise, and faintness of heart, and dread.

The Land

Polar explorers commonly die of hypothermia, starvation, scurvy, or dysentery; less commonly they contract typhoid fever (as Stefansson did), vitamin A poisoning from polar bear liver, or carbon monoxide poisoning from incomplete combustion inside tents sealed by snow. Very commonly, as a prelude to these deaths, polar explorers lose the use of their feet; their frozen toes detach when they remove their socks.

Particularly vivid was the death of a certain Mr. Joseph Green, the astronomer on Sir James Cook's first voyage to high latitudes. He took sick aboard ship. One night, "in a fit of the phrensy," as a contemporary newspaper reported, he rose from his bunk and "put his legs out of the portholes, which was the occasion of his death."

Vitus Bering, shipwrecked in 1741 on Bering Island, was found years later preserved in snow. An autopsy showed he had had many lice, he had scurvy, and had died of a "rectal fistula which forced gas gangrene into his tissues."

The bodies of various members of the Sir John Franklin expedition of 1845 were found over the course of twenty years, by thirty search expeditions, in assorted bizarre postures scattered over the ice of Victoria Strait, Beechey Island, and King William Island.

Sir Robert Falcon Scott reached the South Pole on January 18, 1912, only to discover a flag that Roald Amundsen had planted there a month earlier. Scott's body, and the bodies of two of his companions, turned up on the Ross Ice Shelf, eleven miles south of one of their own supply depots. The bodies were in sleeping bags. His journals and farewell letters indicated that the other two had died first. Scott's torso was well out of his sleeping bag, and he had opened wide the collar of his parka, exposing his skin.

Never found were the bodies of Henry Hudson, his young son, and four men, whom mutineers in 1611 had lowered from their ship in a dinghy, in Hudson's Bay, without food or equipment. Never found were the bodies of Sir John Franklin himself, or of Amundsen and seventeen other men who set out for the Arctic in search of a disastrous Italian expedition, or the bodies of Scott's men Evans and Oates. Never found were most of the drowned crew of the United States ship *Polaris* or the body of her commander, who died sledging on the ice.

Of the United States Greely expedition to the North Pole, all men died but six. Greely himself, one of the six survivors, was found "on his hands and knees with long hair in pigtails." Of the United States De Long expedition to the North Pole in the *Jeannette*, all men died but two. Of the *Jeannette* herself and her equipment, nothing was found until three years after she sank, when, on a beach on the other side of the polar basin, a Greenlander discovered a pair of yellow oilskin breeches stamped *Jeannette*.

The People

Why do we people in churches seem like cheerful, brainless tourists on a packaged tour of the Absolute?

The tourists are having coffee and doughnuts on Deck C. Presumably, someone is minding the ship, correcting the course, avoiding icebergs and shoals, fueling the engines, watching the radar screen, noting weather reports radioed in from shore. No one would dream of asking the tourists to do these things. Alas, among the tourists on Deck C, drinking coffee and eating doughnuts, we find the captain, and all the ship's officers, and all the ship's crew. The officers chat; they swear; they wink a bit at slightly raw jokes, just like regular people. The crew members have funny accents. The wind seems to be picking up.

On the whole, I do not find Christians, outside of the catacombs, sufficiently sensible of conditions. Does anyone have the foggiest idea what sort of power we so blithely invoke? Or, as I suspect, does no one believe a word of it? The churches are children playing on the floor with their chemistry sets, mixing up a batch of TNT to kill a Sunday morning. It is madness to wear ladies' straw hats and velvet hats to church; we should all be wearing crash helmets. Ushers should issue life preservers and signal flares; they should lash us to our pews. For the sleeping god may wake someday and take offense, or the waking god may draw us out to where we can never return.

The eighteenth-century Hasidic Jews had more sense, and more belief. One Hasidic slaughterer, whose work required invoking the Lord, bade a tearful farewell to his wife and children every morning before he set out for the slaughterhouse. He felt, every morning, that he would never see any of them again. For every day, as he himself stood with his knife in his hand, the words of his prayer carried him into danger. After he called on God, God might notice and destroy him before he had time to utter the rest, "Have mercy."

Another Hasid, a rabbi, refused to promise a friend to visit him the next day: "How can you ask me to make such a promise? This evening I must pray and recite 'Hear, O Israel.' When I say these words, my soul goes out to the utmost rim of life…. Perhaps I shall not die this time either, but how can I now promise to do something at a time after the prayer?"

Assorted Wildlife

INSECTS

I like insects for their stupidity. A paper wasp—*Polistes*—is fumbling at the stained-glass window on my right. I saw the same sight in the same spot last Sunday: Pssst! Idiot! Sweetheart! Go around by the door! I hope we seem as endearingly stupid to God—bumbling down into lamps, running half-wit across the floor, banging for days at the hinge of an opened door. I hope so. It does not seem likely.

PENGUINS

According to visitors, Antarctic penguins are…adorable. They are tame! They are funny!

Tourists in Antarctica are mostly women of a certain age. They step from the cruise ship's rubber Zodiacs wearing bright ship's-issue parkas; they stalk around on the gravel and squint into the ice glare; they exclaim over the penguins, whom they find tame, funny, and adorable; they take snapshots of each other with the penguins, and look around cheerfully for something else to look around at.

The penguins are adorable, and the wasp at the stained-glass window is adorable, because in each case their impersonations of human dignity so evidently fail. What are the chances that God finds our failed impersonation of human dignity adorable? Or is he fooled? What odds do you give me?

III

The Land

Several years ago I visited the high Arctic and saw it: the Arctic Ocean, the Beaufort Sea. The place was Barter Island, inside the Arctic Circle, in the Alaskan Arctic north of the North Slope. I stood on the island's ocean shore and saw what there was to see: a pile of colorless stripes. Through binoculars I could see a bigger pile of colorless stripes.

It seemed reasonable to call the colorless stripe overhead "sky," and reasonable to call the colorless stripe at my feet "ice," for I could see where it began. I could distinguish, that is, my shoes, and the black gravel shore, and the nearby frozen ice the wind had smashed ashore. It was this mess of ice—ice breccia, pressure ridges, and standing floes, ice sheets upright, tilted, frozen together and jammed—that extended out to the horizon. No matter how hard I blinked, I could not put a name to any of the other stripes. Which was the horizon? Was I seeing land, or water, or their reflections in low clouds? Was I seeing the famous "water sky," the "frost smoke," or the "ice blink"?

In his old age, James McNeill Whistler used to walk down to the Atlantic shore carrying a few thin planks and his paints. On the planks he painted, day after day, in broad, blurred washes representing sky, water, and shore, three blurry light-filled stripes. These are late Whistlers; I like them very much. In the high Arctic I thought of them, for I seemed to be standing in one of them. If I loosed my eyes from my shoes, the gravel at my feet, or the chaos of ice at the shore, I saw what newborn babies must see: nothing but senseless variations of light on the retinas. The world was a color-field painting wrapped around me at an unknown distance; I hesitated to take a step.

There was, in short, no recognizable three-dimensional space in the Arctic. There was also no time. The sun never set, but neither did it appear. The dim round-the-clock light changed haphazardly when the lid of cloud thickened or thinned. Circumstances made the eating of meals random or impossible. I slept when I was tired. When I woke I walked out into the colorless stripes and the revolving winds, where atmosphere mingled with distance, and where land, ice, and light blurred into a dreamy, freezing vapor that, lacking anything else to do with the stuff, I breathed. Now and then a white bird materialized out of the vapor and screamed. It was, in short, what one might, searching for words, call a beautiful land; it was more beautiful still when the sky cleared and the ice shone in the dark water.

The Technology

It is for the Pole of Relative Inaccessibility I am searching, and have been searching, in the mountains and along the seacoasts for years. The aim of this expedition is, as Pope Gregory put it in his time, "To attain to somewhat of the unencompassed light, by stealth, and scantily." How often have I mounted this same expedition, has my absurd barque set out half-caulked for the Pole?

The Land

"These incidents are *true*," I read in an 1880 British history of Arctic exploration. "These incidents are true,—the storm, the drifting ice-raft, the falling berg, the sinking ship, the breaking up of the great frozen floe: these scenes are *real*,—the vast plains of ice, the ridged hummocks, the bird-thronged cliff, the far-stretching glacier."

Polar exploration is no longer the fashion it was during the time of the Franklin expedition, when beachgoers at Brighton thronged to panoramas of Arctic wastes painted in shopwindows, and when many thousands of Londoners jammed the Vauxhall pleasure gardens to see a diorama of polar seas. Our attention is elsewhere now, but the light-soaked land still exists; I have seen it.

The Technology

In the nineteenth century, a man deduced Antarctica.

During that time, no one on earth knew for certain whether there was any austral landmass at all, although the American Charles Wilkes claimed to have seen it. Some geographers and explorers speculated that there was no land, only a frozen Antarctic Ocean; others posited two large islands in the vicinity of the Pole. That there is one continent was not in fact settled until 1935.

In 1893, one John Murray presented to the Royal Geographic Society a deduction of the Antarctic continent. His expedition's ship, the *Challenger*, had never come within sight of any such continent. His deduction proceeded entirely from dredgings and soundings. In his presentation he posited a large, single continent, a speculative map of which he furnished. He described accurately the unknown continent's topology: its central plateau with its permanent high- pressure system, its enormous glacier facing the Southern Ocean, its volcanic ranges at one coast and, at another coast, its lowland ranges and hills. He was correct.

Deduction, then, is possible—though no longer fashionable. There are many possible techniques for the exploration of high latitudes. There is, for example, such a thing as a drift expedition.

When that pair of yellow oilskin breeches belonging to the lost crew of the *Jeannette* turned up after three years in Greenland, having been lost north of central Russia, Norwegian explorer Fridtjof Nansen was interested. On the basis of these breeches' travels he plotted the probable direction of the current in the polar basin. Then he mounted a drift expedition: in 1893 he drove his ship, the *Fram*, deliberately into the pack ice and settled in to wait while the current moved north and, he hoped, across the Pole. For almost two years, he and a crew of twelve lived aboard ship as frozen ocean carried them. Nansen wrote in his diary, "I long to return to life…the years are passing here… Oh! at times this inactivity crushes one's very soul; one's life seems as dark as the winter night outside; there is sunlight upon no other part of it except the past and the far, far distant future. I feel as if I *must* break through this deadness."

The current did not carry them over the Pole, so Nansen and one companion set out one spring with dog sledges and kayaks to reach the Pole on foot. Conditions were too rough on the ice, however, so after reaching a record northern latitude, the two turned south toward land, wintering together finally in a stone hut on Franz Josef Land and living on polar bear meat. The following spring they returned, after almost three years, to civilization.

Nansen's was the first of several drift expeditions. During World War I, members of a Canadian Arctic expedition camped on an ice floe seven miles by fifteen miles; they drifted for six months over four hundred miles in the Beaufort Sea. In 1937, an airplane deposited a Soviet drift expedition on an ice floe near the North Pole. These four Soviet scientists drifted for nine months while their floe, colliding with grounded ice, repeatedly split into ever smaller pieces.

The Land

I have, I say, set out again.

The days tumble with meanings. The corners heap up with poetry; whole unfilled systems litter the ice.

The Technology

A certain Lieutenant Maxwell, a member of Vitus Bering's second polar expedition, wrote: "You never feel safe when you have to navigate in waters which are completely blank."

Cartographers call blank spaces on a map "sleeping beauties."

On our charts I see the symbol for shoals and beside it the letters "PD." My neighbor in the pew, a lug with a mustache who has experience of navigational charts and who knows how to take a celestial fix, tells me that the initials stand for "Position Doubtful."

The Land

To learn the precise location of a Pole, choose a clear, dark night to begin. Locate by ordinary navigation the Pole's position within an area of several square yards. Then arrange on the ice in that area a series of loaded cameras. Aim the cameras at the sky's zenith; leave their shutters open. Develop the film. The film from that camera located precisely at the Pole will show the night's revolving stars as perfectly circular concentric rings.

The Technology

I have a taste for solitude, and silence, and for what Plotinus called "the flight of the alone to the Alone." I have a taste for solitude. Sir John Franklin had, apparently, a taste for backgammon. Is either of these appropriate to conditions?

You quit your house and country, quit your ship, and quit your companions in the tent, saying, "I am just going outside and may be some time." The light on the far side of the blizzard lures you. You walk, and one day you enter the spread heart of silence, where lands dissolve and seas become vapor and ices sublime under unknown stars. This is the end of the Via Negativa, the lightless edge where the slopes of knowledge dwindle, and love for its own sake, lacking an object, begins.

The Land

I have put on silence and waiting. I have quit my ship and set out on foot over the polar ice. I carry chronometer and sextant, tent, stove and fuel, meat and fat. For water I melt the pack ice in hatchet-hacked chips; frozen salt water is fresh. I sleep when I can walk no longer. I walk on a compass bearing toward geographical north.

I walk in emptiness; I hear my breath. I see my hand and compass, see the ice so wide it arcs, see the planet's peak curving and its low atmosphere held fast on the dive. The years are passing here. I am walking, light as any handful of aurora; I am light as sails, a pile of colorless stripes; I cry "heaven and earth indistinguishable!" and the current underfoot carries me and I walk.

The blizzard is like a curtain; I enter it. The blown snow heaps in my eyes. There is nothing to see or to know. I wait in the tent, myself adrift and emptied, for weeks while the storm unwinds. One day it is over, and I pick up my tent and walk. The storm has scoured the air; the clouds have lifted; the sun rolls round the sky like a fish in a round bowl, like a pebble rolled in a tub, like a swimmer, or a melody flung and repeating, repeating enormously overhead on all sides.

My name is Silence. Silence is my bivouac, and my supper sipped from bowls. I robe myself mornings in loose strings of stones. My eyes are stones; a chip from the pack ice fills my mouth. My skull is a polar basin; my brain pan grows glaciers, and icebergs, and grease ice, and floes. The years are passing here.

Far ahead is open water. I do not know what season it is, know how long I have walked into the silence like a tunnel widening before me, into the horizon's spread arms, which widen like water. I walk to the pack ice edge, to the rim that calves its floes into the black-and-green water; I stand at the edge and look ahead. A scurf of candle ice on the water's skin as far as I can see scratches the sea and crumbles whenever a lump of ice or snow bobs or floats through it. The floes are thick in the water, some of them large as lands. By my side is passing a flat pan of floe from which someone extends an oar. I hold the oar's blade and jump. I land on the long floe.

No one speaks. Here, at the bow of the floe, the bright clowns have staked themselves to the ice. With tent stakes and ropes they have lashed their wrists and ankles to the floe on which they lie stretched and silent, face up. Among the clowns, and similarly staked, are many boys and girls, some women, and a few men from various countries. One of the men is Nansen, the Norwegian explorer who drifted. One of the women repeatedly opens and closes her fists. One of the clowns has opened his neck ruffle, exposing his skin. For many hours I pass among these staked people, intending to return later and take my place.

Farther along I see that the tall priest is here, the priest who served grape juice Communion at an ecumenical service many years ago, in another country. He is very old. Alone on a wind-streaked patch of snow he kneels, stands, and kneels, and stands, and kneels. Not far from him, at the floe's side, sitting on a packing crate, is the deducer John Murray. He lowers a plumb bob overboard and pays out the line. He is wearing the antique fur hat of a Doctor of Reason, such as Erasmus wears in his portrait; it is understood that were he ever to return and present his findings, he would be ridiculed, for his hat. Scott's Captain Oates is here; he has no feet. It is he who stepped outside his tent, to save his friends. Now on his dignity he stands and mans the sheet of a square linen sail; he has stepped the wooden mast on a hillock amidships.

From the floe's stern I think I hear music; I set out, but it takes me several sleeps to get there. I am no longer using the tent. Each time I wake, I study the floe and the ocean horizon for signs—signs of the pack ice that we left behind, or of open water, or land, or any weather. Nothing changes; there is only the green sea and the floating ice, and the black sea in the distance speckled by bergs, and a steady wind astern, which smells of unknown mineral salts, some ocean floor.

At last I reach the floe's broad stern, its enormous trailing coast, its throngs, its many cooking fires. There are children carrying babies, and men and women painting their skins and trying to catch their reflections in the water to leeward. Near the water's edge there is a wooden upright piano, and a bench with a telephone book on it. A woman is sitting on the telephone book and banging out the Sanctus on the keys. The wind is picking up. I am singing at the top of my lungs, for a lark.

Many clowns are here; one of them is passing out Girl Scout cookies, all of which are stuck together. Recently, I learn, Sir John Franklin and crew have boarded this floe, and so have the crews of the lost *Polaris* and the *Jeannette*. The men, whose antique uniforms are causing envious glances, are hungry. Some of them start roughhousing with the rascally acolyte. One crewman carries the boy on his back along the edge to the piano, where he abandons him for a clump of cookies and a seat on the bench beside the short pianist, whose bare feet, perhaps on account of the telephone book, cannot reach the pedals. She starts playing "The Sound of Music." "You know any Bach?" I say to the lady at the piano, whose legs seem to be highly involved with those of the hungry crewman; "You know any Mozart? Or maybe 'How Great Thou Art'?" A skeletal officer wearing a black silk neckerchief has located Admiral Peary, recognizable from afar by the curious flag he holds. Peary and the officer together are planning a talent show and skits. When they approach me, I volunteer to sing "Antonio Spangonio, That Bum Toreador" and/or to read a piece of short fiction; they say they will let me know later.

Christ, under the illusion that we are all penguins, is crouched down, posing for snapshots. He crouches, in his robe, between the lead singer of Wildflowers, who is joyfully trying to determine the best angle at which to hold his guitar for the camera, and the farmer's wife, who keeps her eyes on her painted toenails until a naval officer with a silk scarf says "Cheese." The country-and-western woman, singing, succeeds in pressing a cookie upon the baby Oswaldo. The baby Oswaldo is standing in his lace gown and blue tennis shoes in the center of a circle of explorers, confounding them.

In my hand I discover a tambourine. Ahead as far as the brittle horizon, I see icebergs among the floes. I see tabular bergs and floebergs and dark cracks in the water between them. Low overhead on the underside of the thickening cloud cover are dark colorless stripes reflecting pools of open water in the distance. I am banging on the tambourine, and singing whatever the piano player plays; now it is "On Top of Old Smokey." I am banging the tambourine and belting the song so loudly that people are edging away. But how can any of us tone it down? For we are nearing the Pole.

Contributors' Biographies

WILLIAM R. ROBINSON, a member of what might be termed the Discoverer generation, the first generation of university movie theorist-critics, is author of the first eleven essays in this book, and in different ways the *eminence gris* behind the fifteen others. Bill taught at the University of Virginia and the University of Florida during his career. While at the University of Virginia, he taught and wrote about literature, while feeding his long interest in movies via the faculty/student film club and in other ways

Bill Robinson, facing the camera.

(during Bill's time there, U.VA. offered no courses in film), but his work on the writers Edwin Arlington Robinson, Carson McCullers, John Hawkes, Lawrence Durrell, and Ernest Hemingway has interesting parallels with his work on his major interest, movie theory and criticism. When he moved to the University of Florida, Bill created and taught the first film course, and over three decades there he directed many dissertations and master's theses on movie topics. Wherever he has been during his long career, Bill has influenced people as teacher, colleague, and friend—as readily can be seen by reading the contributors' biographical statements that follow.

Bill was a young paratrooper at the end of World War II, and was with the University of Kentucky football team as a red-shirted freshman when the team was coached by Bear Bryant—examples of his engagement with the life and wisdom of the body via physical activity, a theme that finds its place in Bill's movie theory as well as in his personal life. From 1950 to 1962 Bill attended Ohio State University, earning a degree in philosophy and then a Ph. D. in English, and writing a dissertation that became his first book (*Edwin Arlington Robinson: A Poetry of the Act*) under Roy Harvey Pearce.

Bill described the origin of his interest in the movies in this way: During the twelve years he was at Ohio State the Journalism School sponsored a free film series that offered a movie every Tuesday evening, and so for 12 years Bill had, in effect, an extended self-taught course in the then-classics of world cinema. He would attend each week, either with his wife Mina or by himself. At the same time, the art movie theater phenomenon—including coffee, cookies, and foreign subtitled films—was arising in American cities, including Columbus, Ohio, and there Bill would see contemporary European movies of note as they became available. Thus Bill was a constant moviegoer when Italian Neo-realism, French New Wave, Ingmar Bergman, Luis Bunuel, and then the second generation Italian directors like Fellini and Antonioni, etc., were first bursting into people's consciousness.

Bill remembers the general excitement of the times that surrounded attending art movies, a time when going to a classic or foreign movie was thought of as equivalent to going to a concert of classical music or a theatre performance of a serious drama. Bill had never had a course in movies, for the obvious reason that very few universities offered them at the time. Never having been trained in a college course, let alone a curriculum leading to a degree in film studies, on how to look at movies or how to critique them, Bill, like the other members of that Discoverer generation of university movie critics, was free to create his own approach to movies and to select his own set of movies to teach in his courses. This Discoverer generation of critics enjoyed the excitement of discovering movies as a source of new vision and novel possibilities, and in this enthusiasm they were reinforced by the excitement of the movies from Europe that they were being offered by the first post-war generation of European directors.

For Bill, the excitement his generation felt about movies has disappeared in our current era of post-modernism, and the second and third generation of university movie critics have all been processed through an academic curriculum that has taught them the academic habits of codification and survey of the tradition, rather than discovery and invention. So it is with the movies themselves. As each country around the globe passes through the first, exciting stage of movie-making, they then tend to move into a more organized, less individual phase that privileges the controlling values associated with the word, rather than the liberating values associated with the image. Hence today, Bill says, the great modernist classics have been supplanted by special-effect movies.

Bill's first movie book *Man and the Movies* received very strong praise when it appeared: "A 21-gun salute for this editor and his splendid book!...The mood is highly contemporary," wrote the reviewer in *TV-Radio Mirror*; *The New York Times* called it "assertive, knowledgeable, very articulate"; and from *The Los Angeles Times*, "One of the best books ever about motion pictures."

Bill's essay in that book, "The Movies, Too, Will Make You Free," had made a philosophical statement about the movies, but it was left to his later essays, published in various journals or in several instances unpublished but circulated in manuscript among his colleagues and students, to elucidate the specifics of his movie theory and demonstrate the fruitful movie criticism the

theory could produce. It is only in this book, *Seeing Beyond: Movies, Visions, and Values,* where all of Bill's essays on the movies can be read together for the first time, that the coherent vision which they form is fully evident. In these essays can be seen Bill's movement towards a complete moral view of the movies.

Bill Robinson at home in Charlottesville, 1964. (courtesy of A. Dillard)

ANNIE DILLARD, Pulitzer Prize winning author, has taught at a number of universities. She describes herself thusly:

Annie Dillard is a utility infielder, has written books of nonfiction, fiction, and poetry. She lives in North Carolina and idolizes Bill Robinson, who once said there was no use in writing anything, as Emerson had already said it all. This was true. He and Mina threw a big party when they left Charlottesville; we danced all night.

R. H. W. Dillard and Annie Doak [Dillard], 1964 or 1965.

Cheers — Annie

FRANK BURKE was born and raised in New York City. He graduated from Loyola High School, Holy Cross College, and in 1966 began graduate work at the University of Florida. He left for a job at U. of Kentucky in 1972, completed his doctorate in 1974, and in 1975 moved to the University of Manitoba (Winnipeg), and in 1987 to Queen's University (Kingston, Ontario), where he now lives with wife Annette Burfoot, Professor of Sociology. Frank has been a researcher into Italian, American, and Italian-American cinema for more than 25 years, specializing in Fellini, about whom he has written two books and co-edited a third. His approxi-

Frank Burke and wife, Annette, with Bill Robinson, 1997.

mately 45 other publications related to all three of his areas of interest include a special films edition for *Canadian Journal of Political and Social Theory.*

Frank writes: I talk quite a bit about my relation to Bill in my introduction to this volume. However, I can't help but use this opportunity to reminisce about first meeting him. I had written a brief analysis of Joyce Cary's *The Horse's Mouth* for another professor, and was toying with the idea of doing a dissertation on Cary. Dick Sugg was working with Bill, knew he was a Cary fan, and encouraged me to meet with him. (Dick had by this time talked me out of writing a dissertation on *Beavis the Boy Wonder*, an obscure Victorian novel by a happily forgotten Victorian novelist named Jeffries. My reasons for considering this were as absurd as the novel's title.)

On a Gainesville winter's day in 1968, I journeyed to the top floor of Anderson Hall and announced to Bill my interest in Cary. He asked me to elaborate, and without in any way being confrontational, gave me the clear impression that my ideas were hogwash. Nothing insulting or abrasive, just unmistakable disagreement with everything I had to say. My *Horse's Mouth* was turned into another anatomical part in a matter of minutes.

And the whole time, he was looking out the window, never at me. And maybe even smoking a cigar. (Probably not, but my memory insists on this detail because it plays up my sense of having been neglected and lends support to my grad school nickname for Bill: "Smokey" Robinson.)

Just a touch miffed, I tracked Dick down to ask him what manner of yo-yo he was working for. Dick just said "that's the way he is" and told me to

Bill Robinson, Frank Burke, and Mina Robinson in Gainesville, mid-1990s.

have patience, because Bill was also thoughtful and kind and took great care with his students.

I have to admit I was also a bit fascinated by my unsettling encounter, so when Bill offered to read my essay and talk with me again, I agreed. And I discovered that Dick was right. By the time I next saw him, Bill had written more than I had, in every free space he could find on the copy of the essay I had given him. Having graded many an annoying paper since, I now realize it was out of outrage and frustration as much as anything else. However, at the time I saw it only as enormous intellectual generosity, especially since I was not even a student in one of his courses. Which it also was, because he could have just chucked the paper in the basket. And though I understood probably not a word of his commentary, I did sense its originality and breadth. I realized that what I took as neglect had been shyness, and that he would indeed be someone quite special to work with. To make things brief, I began writing a dissertation with Bill on Cary. When the job market collapsed at the end of the Sixties, and inspired by Bill's interest in movies, I moved to film and, eventually, Fellini.

In reminiscing about Bill I cannot help but reminisce also about the entire Robinson family: Mina, Chris, Monica, Theresa, and Keenan. Their family became family for Val (my first wife) and me, after we had married and were living in Gainesville year round. Through the years, and most recently and sadly on the occasion of Mina's death, I have been able to maintain some (certainly not enough) contact with the "kids" as Mina always called them. They still feel very much like family to me. Mina was especially important to me. She was as outgoing as Bill is shy, as unrestrained as he is reserved. I remember vividly the lavish parties she and Bill threw (one in particular on the occasion of a visit by George Garrett), with the lavishness so clearly a reflection of Mina's exuberance. I still take enormous pleasure in the good fortune of having known her.

A Memory of Mina J. Robinson,
by Annette Burfoot

After Frank and I met in the early 1990s, we began visiting the Robinsons in Gainesville on a regular basis, so I became a friend of Mina. She was the enthusiastic homemaker in the Robinson household, and I use the term "homemaker" with utmost and feminist regard. She was generous with her time, insights (especially in terms of inter-personal relations), and with things that she knew would give others pleasure. She had begun asserting herself within a much larger social and natural world when she was diagnosed with brain cancer. Her 1999 Christmas card carried the exciting and excited news that she had planned a trip to India for the new millennium. I can only imagine how this would have stimulated her imagination and exuberant curiosity. And every time I look at her paintings in my home and my office, I see her sensitive and intelligent gaze upon the world around her as a form of prayer, a complete sensory connection of soul and other. Thanks, Mina.

R.H.W. DILLARD: First, let's get the biographical details out of the way. I was born and still reside in Virginia. After graduating from Roanoke College, I went to graduate school at the University of Virginia. I finished my doctoral work there in the summer of 1964 and moved to Hollins College (now Hollins University) where I am Professor of English and chair of the creative writing program, a position I have held since 1971. I have over the years between then and now published six collections of poetry, two novels, one collection of short fiction, two critical monographs, and two verse translations of classical drama. I should add that I have taught a film course entitled "Film as a Narrative Art" (a title "borrowed" from W.R. Robinson) every semester since the fall of 1970.

The photograph that accompanies this note was taken by my father, Benton O. Dillard, in my parents' house in (I think) the summer of 1963. It is a picture of the Robinson family (Bill, Mina, Monica, Chris, Teresa, and Keenan) as I think of them most often—young, bright, good looking, and full of beans. Chris has casts on both of his arms after a misadventure with a tree house, and the Modess box is one of those comic delights of snapshot photography that appear to be unavoidable (it was full of, I think, books and not blue polyethylene shields).

The fellow on the back row is me. Like Mr. Thornhill in *The Vicar of Wakefield*, I got into the family portrait, but with less dire consequences. I have told elsewhere ["George Garrett: An Appreciation," *Virginia Quarterly*

Review, LXXV (No. 3, Summer 1999), 459-472] how John Rodenbeck and I came to be officemates of Bill and George Garrett, but I have never told how I came to be an honorary member of the Robinson family. In my final years at Virginia, Bill and Mina basically adopted me; I was the fifth child, a

R.H.W. Dillard (back) with Bill and Mina Robinson and their four children, 1963.

large ungainly cuckoo in a nest of songbirds. They fed me, inspired me, goaded me through my dissertation (which Mina even typed for me), let me hang out and pester them endlessly, and never once treated me unkindly. They were, in short, as close and as fine friends as anyone could ever hope and few deserve. Bill was my guru in more ways than one, and, looking back, I realize how much of my thinking was shaped for the better by his ways of observing the world and thinking about it. The rest of the family meant and means as much to me. I have not even begun to pay them back, nor can I ever. The heart knows more than it can speak; I'll have to let E.A. Robinson finish this for me: "And I say now, as I shall say again, / I love the man this side idolatry."

GEORGE GARRETT is author of 30 books and editor or co-editor of 19 others. An itinerant academic, he has taught at many schools, among them Wesleyan, Rice, Princeton, Columbia, V.M.I., Florida International, Johns Hopkins, Bennington, Michigan, Hollins, and Virginia (twice), from which he retired recently. He has worked for CBS Television and Sam Goldwyn, Jr. Three of his feature film scripts have been produced and released. Together with R. H. W. Dillard and John Rodenbeck (friends of Bill Robinson), he wrote the script for cult favorite *Frankenstein Meets the Space Monster*, a.k.a. in Latin America as *Mars Invades Puerto Rico* and in Britain as *Duel of the Space Creatures*.

George submits the following anecdote about W.R. Robinson:

"BILL GOES TO A PARTY"

I could tell you a whole lot of stories about Bill during our mutual days of servitude at the University of Virginia. We had some good times together before the Bad Guys finally ran us out of town and in search of new places and people. I could go on and on. But I won't. Instead, on and for this occasion I'll go with a thematically appropriate anecdote—the Van Johnson story.

It was, must have been, the summer of 1962, give or take, when Bill and Mina and the children arrived in Charlottesville, coming from Columbus and Ohio State. They arrived and found their address in a faculty apartment and were busily (and loudly—the noise level is important) unpacking and uncrating and setting things up when the phone rang. Mina answered, talked awhile to whoever it was, then hung up and reported to Bill. Mina allowed as how an assistant to the Chairman, Fredson Bowers, who was out of town, had called to welcome them and to invite them to a dinner party. This seemed very kind and hospitable. A good omen.

"There's only one thing I don't understand," Mina said.

"What's that?"

"He said this is a Van Johnson Party. What is a Van Johnson Party?"

They decided, not without reason, it was some kind of jokey, campy Hollywood party with everyone dressing up like movie people. So they lined up a baby sitter and then dressed up to kill in a parodic West Coast style—a lot of bright color, dark glasses, funny shoes, the whole bit.

Arriving at the right address, they parked, walked to the front door, knocked and entered. Entered a candlelit room full of people in vaguely Elizabethan costumes. Lute music played on the hi-fi. They were welcomed, handed a drink, and introduced to a crowd of strangers, soon (alas) to be colleagues.

It turned out to be a <u>Ben</u> Jonson party. Bill and Mina never had a chance to explain their misapprehension and why they happened to be dressed the way they were. It was just assumed by one and all, on the basis of first impression, that this was the Robinson style.

You would think that anyone could shake off a first impression like that.

George Garrett in office he shared with Bill Robinson and Richard Dillard in Cabell Hall at the University of Virginia in 1963-64. George writes, "I am sitting at Richard Dillard's desk. The books in the bookcase (on the left) and the *Playboy* calendar belonged to Bill Robinson...You can see Bill's spiritual influence everywhere."

Especially when that was the one time anyone ever saw Bill and Mina in Hollywood regalia.

Not so.

A few years later, when Bill was up for promotion, up or out, at the Departmental meeting on that business, the assistant (flunky in residence) led the attack against Bill, arguing that in spite of his teaching, accomplishments, and service, he had a bad attitude, was "not one of us," citing the Ben Jonson party as a prime example of Robinson's shrugging and satirical indifference to Virginia mores and manners.

And so Virginia's loss became Florida's good fortune.

What else? For years and years, some of us, from among the thirteen or fourteen members of the Department of English who were set free that same year, have raised a toast from time to time in honor of Bill Robinson and Van Johnson. We used to scheme and plan how we would pool our resources and hire Van Johnson, himself, and have a real live Van Johnson party. To which we would invite the Bad Guys. Who would, of course, be under the misapprehension that they were coming to a Ben Jonson party.

We have never (so far) gotten to that. Even so, it's a pretty thing to think about.

Armando José Prats

ARMANDO JOSÉ PRATS wrote his dissertation under Bill Robinson's direction in the 1970s. He teaches at the University of Kentucky, and he has published widely on film.

A. CARL BREDAHL, JR. On a recent trip to Denmark, I came across a saying of Hans Christian Anderson: "*At reise er at leve*." Translated, that means "to travel is to live." One of the pleasures of spending time with Bill Robinson is the discovery of the need to travel, explore. Bill's imagination invites, insists that one travel; fortunately, I have been able to benefit from that invitation.

Equally central to the Robinson narrative is the need for the traveler to have his own potential which can respond to the invitation. These two motivations, the impulse and the invitation, have been significant factors in my

Carl Bredahl in a recent photo.

life while at the University of Florida. Of the thirty years I have taught at UF, 3 years, 10 percent, have been spent overseas. And in Gainesville, I have had the opportunity to travel beyond the work of my rather traditional dissertation. Encouraged and stimulated by Bill, like so many others who have known and worked with him, I have been able to explore multiple narratives which open continually new vistas.

Both personally and professionally, I have taken advantage of the opportunities to teach in India, Pakistan, and Holland. Using my experience in India as an example, what I discovered was a country as large as the United States with a rich variety of literatures; the art of Bengal differs significantly from that of Rajasthan. When I returned to Gainesville, I wanted to know about the variety of literatures in America, somewhere other than on the East Coast. Thus this past decade has been spent in part enjoying the writing of the American West, inclusive of Native American, Chicano/a, and Anglo. It has been a wonderful adventure, one that had its roots in the long conversations with Bill Robinson. I would never expect to be able to see the world through Bill's eyes, but even a "peep" is a rich and rewarding experience.

STEVE SNYDER. In the 1970's I became very intrigued with the films of Federico Fellini (and through Fellini in the works of Antonioni and De Sica). A friend at the University of Florida told me that Bill Robinson was also a Fellini fan and was going to offer a Fellini course. I was very much interested and enrolled. I had never met Bill at that time. For the first half of his lecture on opening night Bill did a convoluted space-walk which left ripples of confused faces in its wake and concluded with him falling off a chair

Steve Snyder in New York, 1992

Steve Snyder, 1995

upon which he had precariously perched himself. The fall, at least, seemed to prompt him to awaken a bit and he capped the lecture with some sweeping configurations of thought which located Fellini somewhere between Einstein and Emerson. The course was a superb eye-opener which served to generate my present career, a professor of film and literature at the University of Manitoba. Inspired by Bill, I began writing about Fellini, placed an essay in an anthology, and corralled an actual job (a rare occurrence in those days) and ended up where I am. A Thank-You to Bill for everything.

DICK SUGG: I teach movies, literature, and Humanities courses at Florida International University in Miami, and have since 1977. I have published four books on literature (*Hart Crane's "The Bridge," Robert Bly, Jungian Literary Criticism*, and *Appreciating Poetry*), as well as published and presented a number of essays on the movies, and recently have been working with the Miami Film Festival. Reading Bill's account of how he first came to the movies, I remembered my own origins. I can't determine its significance, but I'd like to note for the record a very early exposure to "art movies," in 1962 or so, when I was hired as a tuxedo-wearing usher at the Apollo theater in St. Louis, my hometown.

1968, looking beyond.

Dick Sugg, 1968, with Franny and Sam (the dog).

There, for example, I saw, between usher duties, parts of *Last Year at Marienbad* on thirty three consecutive nights. It played to small audiences after the first week, but the theater owner, Mrs. Piccione, loved it, and so it stayed. Also, I got my little sister Carolyn on the payroll as candy girl. Exotic movies, free candy, and steady paychecks for family members made for a lasting positive impression—the tuxedo notwithstanding.

I met Bill in 1967-68, when he first came from U. Va. to Florida; I was the first to write a dissertation under Bill's direction, and I remember well how our relationship grew from, first, our weekly meetings over coffee at the Crystal to discuss what I had written, to nights out at the Windjammer or Red Lion drinking beer and talking, often with his wife Mina in attendance. Soon other students writing for Bill—Frank Burke, Annie Fry, Franny Fevrier, Ellen Ashdown— began to get together and talk about Bill and his ideas on movies and literature. At that time it seemed to us that Bill was a fountain of new approaches to what interested us, and the advocate for a deeper theoretical, philosophical explanation than our other professors, who were by and large New Criti-

cism practitioners, and original thinkers only within New Critical parameters. And, of course, that was only the beginning of the Bill Boom in Gainesville, since I left in 1970; I do believe it is true that Bill must have directed more dissertations and theses than any of the other professors in the English department from the 1960s through the 1980s.

One thing that was interesting about Bill was that he was all the great things he was for his graduate students while still being a man with a dynamic family life—four kids, a dog, big house, sum-

1999, Pete Sugg and Dad at high school graduation.

mer vacations camping, a wife who came to the Red Lion and drank beer with him and his graduate students. No doubt other professors had passionate family lives, but they never shared them with us twenty-something students the way Bill did. Looking back, I think that was a powerful, if subconscious, positive model for his single-but-looking or living-together-but-uncertain graduate students. Somehow he made it seem that the life of the mind and life lived in real time weren't as far apart as they sometimes seemed at English department social events. Maybe that model was the best gift Bill gave us.

VINCENT B. LEITCH. I am currently the Paul and Carol Daube Sutton Chair in English at the University of Oklahoma. Before that I taught at Purdue University where I co-founded a Theory and Cultural Studies program and co-directed a doctoral program in Philosophy and Literature. Prior to Purdue, I worked at Mercer University. I have published *Deconstructive Criticism*

Vincent Leitch, 1999, at the University of Oklahoma.

(1983), *American Literary Criticism from the 1930s to the 1980s* (1988), *Cultural Criticism, Literary Theory, and Poststructuralism* (1992), *Postmodernism— Local Effects, Global Flows* (1996), and *The Norton Anthology of Theory and Criticism* (2001), on which I served as general editor along with a team of five editors.

Bill Robinson was the first and only university professor I had during the 1960s to lecture on contemporary theory, especially European currents like phenomenology and structuralism. He skillfully and seductively planted a theory seed in me which has bloomed in subsequent years.

DAVID LAVERY is a Professor of English at Middle Tennessee State University, where he teaches courses in popular culture, film studies, and science fiction. He is the author of *Late For the Sky: The Mentality of the Space Age* (1992), and editor/co-editor of *Full of Secrets: Critical Approaches to Twin Peaks* (1994), and *Deny All Knowledge: Reading the X-Files* (1996).

David Lavery

ELAINE MARSHALL: While pursuing graduate work at the University of Florida, Elaine first encountered Bill Robinson in a course on literary criticism. She continued study under him, enrolling in his courses on the movies and modes of narration while writing her doctoral dissertation on "the moral eye" of Sam Peckinpah. Elaine received her Ph. D. in 1984 and now teaches composition, literature, and the movies at Barton College in Wilson, NC.

Bill Robinson once praised a campfire that I had built that, having burnt itself out, was reduced completely to ash. "That was a good fire," he said; it's emitted every last photon." If a good fire is one that emits every last photon, then I suppose a good life is one that gives all the light it has to give. In my eyes, that is the life Bill is living, except that his light, unlike my campfire's, appears inexhaustible.

It's his light that drew me, and others, to him, expressed foremost in his brilliance and generosity of mind. As his graduate student, I learned from him to ask the question of a movie or a poem, "What are you in the presence of?" With him, I felt I was in the presence of genius. One should hesitate to use this word, but not with Bill, for certainly in the sense that we all have our own genius, Bill's is extraordinary. And nowhere is his genius more evident than in his vision of the movies "as a revolutionary moral force," and of "narration" as the moral and creative discipline of life.

I became Bill's student at the end of his academic career; I was his last doctoral student. The group that had drawn around him, many of whom are contributors to this book, had gone on to careers of their own. Although I missed out on the spirited camaraderie of that group, "the Robinson crowd," as he sometimes called it, I benefitted from a different spirit. I had him to myself, at a time when he was more excited about the discoveries he was making than he had ever been. His excitement was, to understate it, contagious—and whatever I have learned to see and know of movies, of Peckinpah, of narration, of visual thinking, of life as moral advance, of beginnings, I owe to Bill and to that time and to all the times since when he has so generously shared his light with me.

I have heard Bill say more than once that he likes to leave a place so there's no trace of his having been there. I'm afraid he hasn't entirely succeeded on that score. This collection is the trace of his having been here with each of us. I know his trace on me is indelible, and as

Elaine Marshall

Pike says to Dutch in *The Wild Bunch*, I wouldn't have it any other way. There is an image I have of him scrambling up the last few feet of a mountain trail, reaching the highest ground, standing to his full height with arms wide open as if to embrace the whole of creation. He does this, as he lives, not to be on top, but to find the place from which he can see farther beyond.

J. P. TELOTTE is a Professor of Literature, Communication, and Culture at Georgia Institute of Technology, where he teaches courses in film studies and serves as Director of Undergraduate Studies. He co-edits the journal *Post Script* and has authored *Dreams of Darkness: Fantasy and the Films of Val Lawton* (1985), *Voices in the Dark: The Narrative Patterns of Film Noir* (1989), *The Cult Film Experience* (1991), *Replications: A "Robotic" History of Science Fiction* (1995), and *A Distant Technology: Science Fiction Film and the Machine Age* (1999). Telotte received his Ph. D. in English from the University of Florida, where he first encountered Professor Robinson. Through his courses on Film Theory and The Western and Gangster Films and in informal discussions regarding the films of Fellini and Kubrick, Robinson had a formative influence on Telotte's subsequent work, and particularly on his writings about the *film noir*, as the contribution to this volume testifies.

Walt Foreman and daughter Abby

WALTER C. FOREMAN, JR. was born in Berkeley, CA, but since his family moved to Oregon about the same time he became aware of geographical extension, he considers himself a Northwesterner. He has an A.B. from Harvard College and a Ph.D. from the University of Washington, where he wrote a dissertation on Shakespeare under the direction of Roger Sale. He has taught in the English Department at the University of Kentucky for almost thirty years. Since the late 80s he has been involved with several interdisciplinary teaching programs and currently holds a joint appointment in the Honors Program. The focus of Mr. Foreman's research these days is revenge in English Renaissance drama. He lives in Lexington, KY, with his wife Nancy and his daughter Abigael.

Speaking of "seeing beyond," the theme of this collection, Mr. Foreman remembers an evening sometime in the mid-70s, probably 1976, probably in late August or September, when W. R. Robinson was visiting Lexington. A half-dozen or so people leaving a gathering one unusually clear night were standing by their cars on a street in a residential neighborhood, saying good night. "Look there," said Bill, guiding eyes along a pattern of stars to a fuzzy little spot in the sky. "That's the Andromeda galaxy, the most distant object the naked eye can see."

So far.

SUSAN LYNN DRAKE lives in Atlanta and teaches writing.

Index

A

Achilles, 401
Adler, Renata, 33
aesthetics, 3-5; 20, 24, 29, 323
aestheticism, 153-155, 340, 341
Alain Resnais: Or The Theme of Time, 20
Alex in Wonderland, 240
Alfie, 16, 29, 52-53
Allen, Woody, 240-241, 312, 348
Althusser, Thomas, 306
Altman, Robert, 241, 324-333
Agee, James, 30, 31,
Agrarian ethic, 249-257
All That Jazz, 240
Amarcord, 206, 207, 214, 216, 220, 237, 238, 242, 243
American Dream, 254-256, 261
American Romanticism, 304
American story, the, 43-44
Amundson, Roald, 425
And The Ship Sails On, 207-208, 242, 243
Anderson, Sherwood, 304
Andrew, Dudley, 372, 381, 382
Antonioni, 2, 31, 36, 37, 64, 65-76, 87, 92, 93, 94-95, 320, 321
Apache, 292
Aristotle, 24, 42, 45, 383
Arnheim, Rudolph, 116, 118, 128, 152

Astaire, Fred, 208, 310, 313
Austin, Mary, 289, 294, 298
auteurism, 203-204
auteur-structuralism, 204
author/subject, death of, 205, 206, 207, 208, 209-220
L'Avventura, 64, 65-76

B

Bachelard, Gaston, 381
Bacon, Francis, 108
Bacon, Roger, 117
Baker, Carlos, 401
Bakhtin, 352
The Ballad of Cable Hogue, 293, 298-300
Bardot, Brigitte, 18
Barrato, Caterina, 214
Barthes, Roland, 203
Baxter, John, 301
Bazin, André, 25-27, 260
Belazs, Bela, 110
Belmondo, Jean-Paul, 18
Benayoun, Robert, 27
Berdyaev, 5, 48, 350
Bergen, Candace, 101
Bergman, Ingmar, 3, 18, 43, 49-56, 66, 75, 110-111, 238, 243, 319
Bergson, Henri, 21

S

T

U

Easy Order Form

(Copy this form, complete, and send it to Golden String Press)

Visit Web Site: www.GoldenStringPress.com
for current postal order information and information on annual
SEEING BEYOND Essay Prize
E-mail orders: GoldenStringBook@cs.com
Telephone orders: Toll Free. 1-866-299-2338

❏ **I want to order:**
SEEING BEYOND: MOVIES, VISIONS, AND VALUES
26 Essays by William R. Robinson and Friends
Edited by Richard P. Sugg

I understand that I may return books within 30 days from date of invoice for a full refund.

Please send books to me at:

Name: _____

Address: _____

City: _____ State _____ Zip _____

Telephone: _____

E-mail Address: _____

Please send _____copies @ ....$ 29.95 per copy.
New York and Florida residents only, add sales tax (8%).

Postage and Handling: *U.S. and Canada orders*, add $3.50 for first copy, $.75 for each additional copy. *Foreign orders*, add $5 (U.S.) for first copy, $1 for each additional copy.

Payment: Total $_____. Make payable to **Golden String Press**
Orders from individuals must be prepaid by check or postal money order.
(Sorry, no credit cards).

Golden String Press • Cathedral Station X, P.O. Box 28, New York, NY 10025
www.GoldenStringPress.com